**SECOND EDITION 2015**

# DISTRIBUTION AND MARKETING OF DRUGS

A GLOBAL GUIDE FROM PRACTICAL LAW

**General Editors:**
Eric Stupp and Markus Schott
Bär & Karrer AG

Alison Dennis
Fieldfisher

**THOMSON REUTERS**

**General Editors**
Eric Stupp and Markus Schott, Bär & Karrer AG
Alison Dennis, Fieldfisher

**Commissioning Editor**
Emily Kyriacou
emily.kyriacou@thomsonreuters.com

**Commercial Director**
Katie Burrington
katie.burrington@thomsonreuters.com

**Publishing Editor**
Dawn McGovern
dawn.mcgovern@thomsonreuters.com

**Editors**
Aditi Mene
aditi.mene@thomsonreuters.com

Charlotte Wylie
charlotte.wylie@thomsonreuters.com

**Editorial Publishing Co-ordinator**
Nicola Pender
nicola.pender@thomsonreuters.com

Published in October 2015 by Thomson Reuters (Professional) UK Limited
Friars House, 160 Blackfriars Road, London, SE1 8EZ
(Registered in England & Wales, Company No 1679046.
Registered Office and address for service:
2nd floor, 1 Mark Square, Leonard Street, London EC2A 4EG)

A CIP catalogue record for this book is available from the British Library.

ISBN: 9780414051232

Thomson Reuters and the Thomson Reuters logo are trade marks of Thomson Reuters.
Crown copyright material is reproduced with the permission of the Controller of HMSO and the Queen's Printer for Scotland.

While all reasonable care has been taken to ensure the accuracy of the publication, the publishers cannot accept responsibility for any errors or omissions.
This publication is protected by international copyright law.
All rights reserved. No part of this publication may be reproduced or transmitted in any form or by any means, or stored in any retrieval system of any nature without prior written permission, except for permitted fair dealing under the Copyright, Designs and Patents Act 1988, or in accordance with the terms of a licence issued by the Copyright Licensing Agency in respect of photocopying and/or reprographic reproduction. Application for permission for other use of copyright material including permission to reproduce extracts in other published works shall be made to the publishers. Full acknowledgement of author, publisher and source must be given.

© 2015 Thomson Reuters (Professional) UK Limited

# CONTENTS

**PREFACE** Eric Stupp, Markus Schott, *BÄR & KARRER AG* and Alison Dennis, *FIELDFISHER*  v

**FOREWORD** Dr Oliver P Kronenberg, *GROUP GENERAL COUNSEL, GALENICA*  vii

**AUSTRALIA** Dr Simone Mitchell, Alexandra Chubb, Jessie Buchan and Matthew Evans, *DLA PIPER*  1

**AUSTRIA** Gabriela Staber and Egon Engin-Deniz, *CMS REICH-ROHRWIG HAINZ* Patricia Kaindl, *PUBLIC PROSECUTION OFFICE VIENNA*  21

**BELGIUM** Claudio Mereu, Maud Grunchard and Raf Callaerts, *FIELDFISHER*  39

**BRAZIL** Lívia Figueiredo and João Luis Vianna, *KASZNAR LEONARDOS*  53

**CANADA** Jeffrey S Graham, *BORDEN LADNER GERVAIS LLP*  67

**CHINA** Jianwen Huang, *KING & WOOD MALLESONS CHINA*  83

**DENMARK** Nicolaj Kleist, *BRUUN & HJEJLE*  105

**EUROPEAN UNION** Alison Dennis, *FIELDFISHER*  121

**FINLAND** Mikael Segercrantz, Johanna Lilja and Elina Saxlin-Hautamäki, *ROSCHIER*  135

**FRANCE** Olivier Lantrès, *FIELDFISHER*  151

**GERMANY** Dr Cord Willhöft, *FIELDFISHER*  165

**INDONESIA** Eri Raffaera Budiarti and Muhammad Iqsan Sirie, *ASSEGAF HAMZAH & PARTNERS*  181

**ITALY** Laura Opilio and Maria Letizia Patania, *CMS ITALY (CMS ADONNINO ASCOLI & CAVASOLA SCAMONI)*  193

**JAPAN** Shinya Tago, Atsushi Ueda, Landry Guesdon and Ryohei Kudo, *IWATA GODO LAW OFFICES*  209

**THE NETHERLANDS** Willem Hoorneman, Rogier de Vrey, Bart Essink and Anastasia Chistyakova, *CMS DERKS STAR BUSMANN*  229

**POLAND** Marcin Matczak, Tomasz Kaczyński and Krzysztof Kumala, *DOMAŃSKI ZAKRZEWSKI PALINKA SP. K.*  247

**PORTUGAL** Fernanda Matoso and Eduardo Maia Cadete, *MORAIS LEITÃO, GALVÃO TELES, SOARES DA SILVA & ASSOCIADOS, SOCIEDADE DE ADVOGADOS, R.L.*  265

**RUSSIAN FEDERATION** Vsevolod Tyupa, *CMS, RUSSIA*  287

**SOUTH AFRICA** Danie Dohmen, Alexis Apostolidis, Jenny Pienaar and Natasha Wright, *ADAMS & ADAMS*  301

## CONTENTS

| | |
|---|---|
| **SOUTH KOREA**  Hyeong Gun Lee and Jin Hwan Chung, *LEE & KO* | 319 |
| **SPAIN**  Teresa Paz-Ares and Beatriz Cocina, *URÍA MENÉNDEZ ABOGADOS S.L.P* | 331 |
| **SWEDEN**  Helén Waxberg and Maja Edlund, *MANNHEIMER SWARTLING ADVOKATBYRÅ* | 351 |
| **SWITZERLAND**  Markus Schott, *BÄR & KARRER AG* | 367 |
| **THAILAND**  Alan Adcock, Siraprapha Rungpry and Areeya Pornwiriyangkura, *TILLEKE & GIBBINS* | 383 |
| **TURKEY**  Özge Atılgan Karakulak and Tuğçe Avcısert Geçgil, *GÜN + PARTNERS* | 399 |
| **UK (ENGLAND AND WALES)**  Alison Dennis, *FIELDFISHER* | 417 |
| **UNITED STATES**  Jamie K Wolszon & Andrew J Hull, *HYMAN, PHELPS & MCNAMARA, PC* | 435 |
| **VIETNAM**  Tu Ngoc Trinh and Huong Lan Nguyen, *TILLEKE & GIBBINS* | 453 |
| **CONTACT DETAILS** | 469 |

# PREFACE

*Eric Stupp, Markus Schott, BÄR & KARRER AG and Alison Dennis, FIELDFISHER*

Given the recent developments in the field, two years after the successful launch of the first edition seemed to be a good time to follow up with a second edition of the handbook. We are delighted that so many of the authors of the first edition have been able to work over their contributions within a short timeframe. We are equally happy to have new, distinguished colleagues among the contributors who have agreed to participate in this book's second edition, adding some new jurisdictions such as Australia, Brazil, Canada, Indonesia, Russia, and South Korea. We also thank Emily Kyriacou and her fine editorial team at Thomson Reuters for all their efforts in bringing the project to fruition. Any errors or omissions are, however, ours alone and we welcome comments and ideas for the improvement of future editions from our readers.

*Eric Stupp, Markus Schott and Alison Dennis*

# FOREWORD

Dr Oliver P Kronenberg, Group General Counsel, GALENICA

Demand for effective medicines is rising. As the population ages and increases, new medical needs emerge and the disease burden of the developing world increasingly resembles that of the developed world. The main emerging countries (that is, Brazil, China, India, Indonesia, Mexico, Russia and Turkey) are also becoming increasingly prosperous, with projections suggesting that these countries could account for as much as one-fifth of global pharmaceutical sales by 2020.

At the same time, commercialisation of pharmaceutical products has become more complex as the competitive and regulatory environment has evolved. Today, regulatory regimes not only aim to protect public health and to ensure that there is robust data to support the safety and efficacy of pharmaceutical products, but also to limit expenditure on pharmaceutical products by countries (for example, market access, pricing and reimbursement and distribution channels, among others). One recent development is the implementation of transparency regulations in the US, Europe and some other countries. These regulations require manufacturers of medicines, medical devices and medical supplies to collect and track all financial relationships with healthcare professionals and healthcare organisations, and to report this information to either the local regulators or to publish it on their own website.

This book focuses on the legal environment surrounding the distribution and marketing of medicines. As explained above, the legal framework has been tightened and the standards for compliance have been raised by the regulators. This has led to an increasing need for legal support (whether in-house or external). Jurisdictions differ significantly around the world and, as a consequence, this book has become an important reference guide for the industry.

As in the first edition, the topics addressed in this book cover all relevant aspects of the sale, distribution and marketing of drugs for human use. These range from substantive issues such as the existence of compassionate use programs; admissibility of direct mailing; provision of free samples and discounts and the ability to communicate directly with consumers, to more procedural aspects such as identifying the competent authorities and legal remedies available to parties. As professional and other industry organisations have set up their own codes of conduct in many countries, individual chapters also refer to such codes and describe their implementation.

In conclusion, this book provides everything in-house or external counsel need to understand the distribution and marketing of medicines in the jurisdictions covered. This will assist readers in evaluating legal risks and in providing sound legal and compliance advice to the organisations which they support.

Dr Oliver P Kronenberg, Group General Counsel, Galenica

# AUSTRALIA

Dr Simone Mitchell, Alexandra Chubb, Jessie Buchan and Matthew Evans, DLA PIPER

## DISTRIBUTION

### PRE-CONDITIONS FOR DISTRIBUTION

**1. WHAT ARE THE LEGAL PRE-CONDITIONS FOR A DRUG TO BE DISTRIBUTED WITHIN THE JURISDICTION?**

**Authorisation**

Marketing applications for drugs must be made to and approved by the Therapeutic Goods Administration (TGA). Subject to some exceptions, a product cannot be marketed in Australia before it is listed on the Australian Register of Therapeutic Goods (ARTG).

**Authorisation conditions**

Before approving a medicine, the TGA must be satisfied that it complies with all legislative requirements in force in Australia. Statutory standards under the Therapeutic Goods Act 1989 (Cth) (TG Act) include the:

- Therapeutic Goods Orders (TGO).
- British Pharmacopoeia (BP).
- European Pharmacopoeia (Ph Eur).
- US Pharmacopoeia-National Formulary (USP).

Since 1 July 2009, the BP, Ph Eur and the USP are defined under the TG Act as default standards. Therefore, if no relevant standard is specified in a TGO, any of the pharmacopoeia applies.

An exemption can be sought from the requirements of the TG Act with the consent of the Secretary of the Department of Health and Ageing.

Offences and civil penalties apply if therapeutic goods that do not comply with the relevant standards are imported into, exported from, or supplied in Australia (*sections 14 and 14A, TG Act*).

**Exceptions**

Schedules 5, 5A and 7 of the Therapeutic Goods Regulations 1990 (Cth) (TG Regulations) provide a detailed list of exemptions to the requirement that drugs must be listed on the

ARTG. In addition, Schedule 8 sets out the persons that are exempt from the requirement to obtain ARTG listing.

## 2. DO ANY TYPES OF NAMED PATIENT AND/OR COMPASSIONATE USE PROGRAMMES OPERATE? IF SO, WHAT ARE THE REQUIREMENTS FOR PRE-LAUNCH ACCESS?

There are a number of ways that patients can gain access to drugs that have not been approved by the Therapeutic Goods Administration (TGA).

### Authorised prescribers

An authorised prescriber can prescribe a drug that has not been approved by the TGA to an individual patient in their care. Medical practitioners who have been granted authority by the TGA to become an authorised prescriber can prescribe specified unapproved drugs (or a class of unapproved drugs) to specified patients (or a class of recipients) with a particular medical condition.

To become an authorised prescriber, the medical practitioner must:

- Have the necessary training and expertise for the condition being treated and the proposed use of the product.
- Be able to best determine the needs of the patient.
- Have the ability to monitor the outcome of the therapy.

### Special access scheme

The special access scheme is a scheme that provides for the import and/or supply of an unapproved therapeutic good for a single patient, on a case by case basis. Applications for access to unapproved drugs under the special access scheme are made to the TGA by registered medical practitioners. For the purposes of administering the special access scheme, the TGA places patients into two categories depending on whether their condition is terminal or not. Terminally ill patients are given greater access to unapproved drugs.

### Clinical trials

Limited access is provided to unapproved drugs for the purposes of clinical trials in Australia that are conducted under either the:

- Clinical Trial Exemption Scheme (CTX Scheme).
- Clinical Trial Notification Scheme (CTN Scheme).

All CTN and CTX trials must have an Australian sponsor who is responsible for the conduct of the trial. In addition, before commencing a clinical trial, there must be legal and financial agreements in place between all relevant parties. This must include, in particular:

- Indemnities.
- The procedure for the compensation and treatment of trial participants.

The relevant insurances must be obtained and all documents required by the Guideline for Good Clinical Practice must be filed.

The Guideline for Good Clinical Practice also sets out the various procedural requirements for running a clinical trial. These are significant and include the maintenance of quality assurance and quality control systems with standard operating procedures for the conduct of the trial.

In addition, the trial must also be monitored and any adverse events reported. A number of documents are required to be filed both during and after the clinical trial.

**Personal import scheme**

Unapproved drugs can also be imported by an individual in circumstances where the drug:

- Is for use by the individual or their immediate family.
- Is not a controlled substance under any of the Commonwealth, State or Territory legislation.
- Complies with the relevant Commonwealth, State or Territory quarantine law.
- Quantity does not exceed three months' supply per importation and the total quantity per year does not exceed 15 months' supply at the manufacturer's recommended maximum dosage.
- Is a prescription medicine, and the importer has a prescription issued by an Australian registered medical practitioner.

## LICENSING

### 3. WHAT IS THE PROCEDURAL STRUCTURE REGARDING LICENSING A DRUG FOR DISTRIBUTION?

**Structure**

In general, a drug must be entered on the Australian Register of Therapeutic Goods (ARTG) prior to distributing it in Australia.

Australia has a two-tiered system for the regulation of drugs:

- Higher risk drugs (which include all prescription products, most over-the-counter (OTC) medicines and some complementary medicines) must be registered on the ARTG. This involves individually evaluating the quality, safety and effectiveness of the product.
- Lower risk drugs (which include some over-the-counter medicines and most complementary medicines) that contain pre-approved, low risk ingredients and make limited claims can be listed on the ARTG.

**Key stages and timing**

Prescription products and many OTC medicines are subject to registration requirements. The registration process involves a detailed review by the Therapeutic Goods Administration (TGA) of the quality, safety and efficacy of the medicinal products in question.

Registration requires a sponsor to apply to the TGA, providing data supporting the quality, safety and efficacy of the product for its intended use. The Australian Regulatory Guidelines for Prescription Medicines (2013) (ARGPM) assists sponsors in preparing applications to register new prescriptions or other high risk medicines for human use in Australia.

The timeline for processing an application for registration is set down by the Therapeutic Goods Regulations 1990 (Cth) (TG Regulations). The TGA must:

- Accept or reject an application for evaluation within 40 working days.
- Evaluate the application within a further 255 working days (if the application is accepted).

# AUSTRALIA

Some OTC products are subject to listing requirements. Listed goods are classified as low risk medicines and only contain ingredients that have been pre-approved by the TGA (that is, the TGA has assessed the safety and quality of the ingredients). The TGA does not assess the final product (as opposed to the ingredient), the label or the efficacy of the product for its intended use. However, the applicant must hold relevant evidence, including evidence that supports any claim they make about the product.

**Regulatory authority**

The Therapeutic Goods Act 1989 (Cth) is administered by a Commonwealth Federal agency called the Therapeutic Goods Administration, which is part of the Australian Government's Department of Health and Ageing.

The TGA administers compliance with the TG Act and TG Regulations and regulates the import and supply of drugs in Australia.

### 4. IS THERE A SIMPLIFIED LICENCE PROCEEDING, OR RELAXED LICENSING CONDITIONS, FOR DRUGS WHICH HAVE ALREADY BEEN LICENSED FOR DISTRIBUTION IN ANOTHER JURISIDICTION?

There is an expedited application process available for drugs that have been previously approved in two acceptable countries. The countries currently identified by the Minister as acceptable are Canada, Sweden, The Netherlands, the UK and the US. The application process is provided under subregulations 16C(3)(a) and 16D(3)(a) of the Therapeutic Goods Regulations 1990 (Cth) (TG Regulations).

For the applications, two independent evaluation reports from acceptable countries, (where the product is already approved) are required to be provided at the time of application. The evaluation reports must be independent (*subregulations 16C (4) and (5) and 16D (4) and (5), TG Regulations*) and the product proposed to be registered in Australia must be identical to that registered in the acceptable countries in relation to formulation, directions for use and indications.

### 5. IS VIRTUAL DRUG DISTRIBUTION POSSIBLE FROM YOUR JURISDICTION?

There is currently no Australian jurisprudence on virtual drug distribution.

The Therapeutic Goods Act 1989 (Cth) (TG Act) provides for a number of offences that is likely to make virtual drug distribution in Australia unlawful, but the limits of the provisions have not yet been tested in the context of virtual drug distribution networks.

In addition, both wholesalers and pharmacies are highly regulated in Australia and are required to hold relevant licences. This regulatory regime helps to maintain the integrity of the drug distribution system.

### 6. WHAT IS THE PROCEDURE TO APPEAL (LEGAL REMEDY) A LICENSING DECISION?

Under section 60 of the Therapeutic Goods Act 1989 (Cth) (TG Act) a person can seek a review of a licensing decision to the relevant minister. An appeal can be lodged by any person whose interests are affected by the decision. Appeals to the minister must be lodged within 90 days of the decision.

The process for appeal is by way of letter. The letter must contain all supportive information for the minister to consider as there is no opportunity for an aggrieved party to present additional information under this process. Supportive information must include the following as a minimum:

- The reason why part of the original decision is incorrect or objectionable.
- How the aggrieved parties interests are affected by the original decision.
- A copy of the original decision.

If an aggrieved party is not satisfied with the minister's review under a section 60 appeal, it can apply to the Administrative Appeals Tribunal (AAT) for a further review. The timeframe for lodging an application with the AAT is within 28 days of the minister's decision.

The AAT will review the merits of the case, that is, reconsider the application on its merits and not on a question of law. If an aggrieved party wishes to review the decision on legal grounds, it can seek judicial review in the federal courts on the grounds of the legality of the original decision.

## 7. WHAT ARE THE COSTS OF OBTAINING LICENSING?

The costs of obtaining licensing as at 1 July 2015 is as follows:

- For a new chemical entity classified as a prescription medicine there is an application fee of AUD$44,200 and an evaluation fee of AUD$177,200. In order to maintain registration of the product, an annual charge of between AUD$3,110 and AUD$6,725 (depending on whether the drug is biological and how long it has been registered for) will apply.
- For a new chemical entity classified as a non-prescription medicine there is an application fee of AUD$1,475 and an evaluation fee of between AUD$9,870 and AUD$69,000 (depending on the length of the clinical or toxicological data to be evaluated). In order to maintain registration of the product, an annual charge of AUD$1,380 will apply.

A summary of fees can be found at *www.tga.gov.au/sites/default/files/fees-140701-8.pdf*.

These fees can be waived if the drug is not commercially viable or intended to treat, prevent or diagnose a rare disease. To obtain a waiver, an application to have the drug designated as an "orphan drug" must be made to the Therapeutic Goods Administration before an application to register the drug on the Australian Register of Therapeutic Goods is made.

## DISTRIBUTION TO CONSUMERS

## 8. WHAT ARE THE DIFFERENT CATEGORIES OF DRUGS FOR DISTRIBUTION?

Australia has a national classification system that controls how drugs are made available to the public. Legally, the scheduling of drugs is a matter for the States and Territories, but all States and Territories adhere either closely or exactly to the national standard. Drugs are classified into different schedules of the Poison Standard 2015 according to the level of regulatory control required in the interests of public health and safety.

The categories are as follows:

- **Schedule 2 (pharmacy medicine).** These drugs are considered safe to use and made available to the public with minimal regulatory requirements.
- **Schedule 3 (pharmacist only medicine).** These drugs require the professional advice of a pharmacist for safe use but are available to the public without a prescription.

AUSTRALIA

- **Schedule 4 (prescription only medicine).** These drugs require a prescription from a registered health care practitioner or other authorised medical personnel.
- **Schedule 8 (controlled drugs).** These drugs have a high potential for addiction or abuse.

## 9. WHO IS AUTHORISED TO DISTRIBUTE PRESCRIPTION DRUGS AND OVER-THE-COUNTER DRUGS TO CONSUMERS?

Authorisation for distributing drugs to consumers will be granted depending on the schedule in which the drug is classified and the State or Territory in which the drug is being distributed.

**Over-the-counter drugs**

Pharmacy medicine (Schedule 2) does not require an authorised person to dispense the drugs. However, the drugs must be supplied to consumers at a pharmacy as they typically require advice from a pharmacist. However, in most States and Territories a person can obtain a licence to supply Schedule 2 drugs where they operate a country (remote) store that is located a prescribed distance away from a retail pharmacist.

Pharmacist only medicine (Schedule 3) can only be distributed by pharmacists.

In addition, some drugs (such as small packs of paracetamol) are unscheduled which means that as long as certain conditions are met, they are available from any retailer that wishes to stock them.

**Prescription drugs**

Prescription only medicine (Schedule 4) can only be distributed by pharmacists and if the buyer has a valid prescription for the drug.

Controlled drugs (Schedule 8) can only be distributed by pharmacists and if the buyer has a valid prescription. The regulations regarding who can write a valid prescription differ between States and Territories but in general are limited to specialists in the relevant field, or health care practitioners who have applied, and been granted, a licence to prescribe Schedule 8 drugs.

## 10. WHAT DRUGS CAN AN ATTENDING PHYSICIAN DISTRIBUTE AND UNDER WHAT CIRCUMSTANCES?

The distribution and prescription of drugs is regulated by each of the States and Territories. Each jurisdiction's laws are relatively consistent and generally allow health care practitioners to prescribe drugs (including controlled drugs with authorisation) in the course of their profession.

In addition, physicians are generally permitted to distribute drugs for emergency use with patients.

## 11. WHO IS AUTHORISED TO PRESCRIBE PRESCRIPTION DRUGS TO CONSUMERS?

Authorisation to prescribe prescription drugs is based on individual State and Territory legislation and therefore differs between each State and Territory.

## Prescription of a Schedule 4 (prescription only medicine)

The following professions are able to prescribe prescription drugs for the purpose of practicing in their respective professions (provided they have the valid State or Territory authorisation):

- Medical practitioners.
- Dentists.
- Veterinary surgeons.
- Optometrists.
- Podiatrists.
- Nurse practitioners.
- Midwife practitioners.

The requirements and extent of the authority to prescribe for each profession varies between States and Territories. For example, in New South Wales a person must be an authorised practitioner to issue a valid prescription. Authorised practitioners include medical practitioners, dentists, veterinary surgeons, optometrists and podiatrists. Nurse and midwife practitioners are also considered authorised practitioners provided they have obtained authorisation in writing by the Director-General. The authorisation to prescribe drugs is limited to the purpose of practicing their respective professions.

## Prescription for a Schedule 8 (controlled drug)

Individual State and Territory laws vary, but generally in order to prescribe controlled drugs, a medical practitioner must obtain authorisation. In addition, some Schedule 8 drugs are limited to use by specific specialists.

## 12. IS DIRECT MAILING/DISTANCE SELLING OF DRUGS PERMITTED IN YOUR JURISDICTION?

Distance selling via direct mailing or other means is generally legal within Australia. However, there may be conditions imposed depending on the classification of the drug being sold.

In practice, some of these conditions make it difficult or impossible to direct mail or distance sell some categories of drugs. These conditions differ depending on which State or Territory the drug is being sold from and to, as each of the States and Territories have their own set of conditions imposed through their regulations and laws.

Selling intrastate requires adherence to that State or Territories conditions only, whereas selling interstate can require adherence to both State and Territories conditions.

### Conditions

**Pharmacy Medicines (Schedule 2).** There is no specific regulation in any State or Territory that deals with direct mailing or distance selling of Schedule 2 drugs. The only conditions imposed are the relevant quarantine, drug and trade regulations.

**Pharmacist Only Medicines (Schedule 3), Prescription Only Medicines (Schedule 4) and Controlled Drug (Schedule 8).** Indirect sales, including distance selling, is effectively prohibited in all the States and Territories. Each have various requirements including that the pharmacist:

- Directly and personally sells to the person (Western Australia).

- Personally supervises the person (Victoria).
- Sells only at a dispensary to the person (Queensland).
- Personally hands the substance to the person (New South Wales (NSW) and Australian Capital Territory).

There is an exception in NSW to this prohibition if the buyer has a prescription for the drug being sold. The Victorian law on what constitutes personal supervision is also unclear, and it may be possible to discharge the duty by means of remote supervisions (such as Skype or a telephone conversation).

**Cross-border sales**

For commercial export of medicines, Australia requires that the drug:

- Is listed or registered in the Australian Register of Therapeutic Goods (ARTG) for supply in Australia or export.
- Has been granted an exemption by the Therapeutic Goods Administration from the need to register on the ARTG.

If the drug is not listed, a company wishing to export can either apply to become the sponsor of the drug or, if the drug is already listed, arrange to export the drug on behalf of the listed sponsor.

In addition, exporters must comply with the relevant State and Federal laws regarding the procurement and storage of medicines and other relevant legislation including quarantine, customs, wildlife protection, patents and trademarks.

Additional regulations exist on exporting certain drugs such as narcotics, psychotropic substances or their precursors as listed in the Customs (Prohibited Exports) Regulations 1958 (Cth).

### 13. WHAT REGULATORY AUTHORITY IS RESPONSIBLE FOR SUPERVISING DISTRIBUTION ACTIVITIES?

Dispensing over-the-counter and prescription drugs is controlled under State and Territory drugs and controlled substances legislation. The supervisory role is performed by each of the States' and Territories' relevant government agencies.

In addition, pharmacists are regulated at a national level by the Pharmacy Board of Australia (PBA). All pharmacists must comply with the PBA's Code of Conduct and Guidelines for Dispensing Medicine. Failure to comply can lead to a suspension or surrender of the pharmacist's registration, which is required in order to legally dispense drugs.

### 14. WHAT IS THE PROCEDURE TO APPEAL (LEGAL REMEDY) A DISTRIBUTION DECISION?

Any decision regarding a company or person breaching the relevant State or Territory legislation is subject to judicial appeal in the Australian courts.

The Australian Health Practitioner Regulation Agency (the entity responsible for enforcing the Pharmacy Board of Australia's codes) allows appeals for decisions that:

- Impose or change a condition on a person's registration.
- Refuse to change or remove a condition imposed on the person's registration.
- Refuse to change or revoke an undertaking given by the person to the board.

- Suspend the person's registration.

The decisions can be appealed to the following tribunal for each relevant State and Territory:

- Civil and Administrative Tribunal (New South Wales).
- Civil and Administrative Tribunal (Australian Capital Territory).
- Health Professional Review Tribunal (Northern Territory).
- Civil and Administrative Tribunal (Queensland).
- Health Practitioners Tribunal (South Australia).
- Health Practitioners Tribunal (Tasmania).
- Civil and Administrative Tribunal (Victoria).
- State Administrative Tribunal (Western Australia).

### 15. WHAT ARE THE LEGAL CONSEQUENCES OF NON-COMPLIANCE WITH CONSUMER DISTRIBUTION LAWS?

The States and Territories each have their own consumer distribution laws. The penalty for breach of these consumer laws differ between each State and Territory. The penalties range from small fines to lengthy imprisonment terms depending on the severity of the breach.

See *Question 12* for the penalties for breaching the Pharmacy Board of Australia's codes.

## WHOLESALE DISTRIBUTION

### 16. WHAT IS THE LEGAL REGIME REGARDING WHOLESALE DISTRIBUTION OF DRUGS?

Under the various State and Territories Poisons and Controlled Substances legislation, a person who supplies drugs by way of wholesale is required to hold a wholesaler's licence. A licence must be obtained from the relevant State or Territory department. In general, an applicant for a wholesale licence must meet certain requirements, including being able to demonstrate that they are a fit and proper person to hold the licence and that the premises are appropriate for the supply of the drugs.

In addition, the Therapeutic Goods Administration publishes the Australian code of good wholesaling practice for medicines in Schedules 2, 3, 4 and 8 (Wholesale Code) that is implemented through applicable State and Territory legislation and licensing arrangements, making the Wholesale Code mandatory.

The Wholesale Code is applicable to persons or organisations, including manufacturers, wholesalers, manufacturer's agents, importers and distributors who store and/or supply by wholesale substances and preparations included in Schedules 2, 3, 4 and 8 of the Poisons Standard.

The Wholesale Code is in addition to, and in no way diminishes, the wholesaler's other obligations under relevant state and federal legislation in relevant areas including:

- Occupational health and safety.
- Customs and excise.
- Poisons (including narcotics).
- Australian consumer law.
- Dangerous goods.

The Wholesale Code contains a number of obligations, including in relation to the following:

- **Building and grounds.** Properties that store medicine need to be safe and secure with good housekeeping and adequate protection.
- **Storage facilities.** Proper policies and procedures need to be in place regarding the storage conditions of the drug to ensure that the quality and safety of the drug is preserved.
- **Personnel.** Staff involved in the process must have the necessary skills and knowledge to ensure the safe handling and maintenance of drug quality.
- **Stock handling and stock control.** Policies and procedures must be in place to provide for stock handling and stock control.
- **Transport.** Transport of drugs must be safe, secure and provide for a timely delivery of all medicines to the destination.
- **Management of complaints, return of unused and/or damaged goods and product recalls.** A comprehensive complaints system must be in effect to provide for the receipt, handling, measuring, evaluating and resolution of complaints in order to prevent recurrence.
- **Policies and procedures.** Certain policies and procedures need to be in place to ensure that:
  - damaged medication that is unsuitable for sale is quarantined and accounted for;
  - all returned unused or damaged medicine is accounted for through the Return of Unwanted Medicines Program until disposal occurs;
  - appropriate actions are taken in the event of a recall of medicines held in stock;
  - appropriate actions are taken in the event of recalling medicines on behalf of a sponsor;
  - records are able to be generated of recalled medicines.
- **Management of records, documentation and standard operating procedures.** Records must be kept in accordance with legislative requirements and documentation must be adequate to achieve the requisite standard of recording and control, including documents relating to quarantined stock.
- **Cold chain medicines.** Special policies must be implemented to ensure that the integrity of cold chain medicines is maintained according to the sponsor's recommendations as set out in on the Therapeutic Goods Administration approved product packaging.
- **Security arrangements and procedures.** Policies and procedures must be in place for an appropriate level of protection of stored medicines to prevent theft, pilferage, diversion, misuse and illegal distribution. This includes the security and management of the facility and a reporting regime for missing or stolen drugs.

Additional security measures exist for the wholesale supply of a controlled drug or other drug with high illicit value.

## 17. WHAT REGULATORY AUTHORITY IS RESPONSIBLE FOR SUPERVISING WHOLESALE DISTRIBUTION ACTIVITIES?

**Regulatory authority**

The supervision of wholesale distribution activities lies with each of the relevant State and Territory departments as follows:

- Department of Health and Ageing (South Australia).
- New South Wales Ministry of Health (New South Wales).

- Queensland Health (Queensland).
- Department of Health of the Northern Territory Government (Northern Territory).
- Department of Health (Western Australia).
- ACT Health (Australian Capital Territory).
- Department of Health and Human Services of the Tasmanian Government (Tasmania).
- Department of Health of Victoria (Victoria).

**Rights of appeal**

The appeal rights in respect of decisions relating to wholesale distribution rights are subject to the applicable State and Territories' legislation. However, generally a decision by the relevant minister to suspend or revoke a licence can be appealed to the relevant State or Territories' administrative tribunal.

18. WHAT ARE THE LEGAL CONSEQUENCES OF NON-COMPLIANCE WITH WHOLESALE DISTRIBUTION LAWS?

The legal consequences of non-compliance with wholesale distribution laws are determined by the relevant legislation in each State and Territory. For example, in New South Wales the penalty for supplying without or not in accordance with a wholesale licence is AUD$1650 and/or imprisonment for six months.

# MARKETING

PROMOTION

19. WHAT IS THE GENERAL LEGAL REGIME FOR THE MARKETING OF DRUGS?

**Legal regime**

Marketing activities must comply with:

- Therapeutic Goods Administration.
- Therapeutic Goods Regulations 1990 (Cth).
- Competition and Consumer Act 2010 (Cth) (CC Act).
- Other relevant state and territory legislation.

In addition, the industry is self-regulated or co-regulated, with a number of bodies administering various codes relevant to the marketing of drugs, including:

- Therapeutic Goods Advertising Code.
- Medicines Australia's Code of Conduct.
- Generic Medicines Industry Association Code of Practice (GMiA Code).
- Australian Self Medication Industry Code of Practice (ASMI Code).
- Complementary Healthcare Council of Australia's Code of Practice for the Marketing of Complementary Healthcare and Healthfood Products (CH Code).

### Limits to marketing activities

Off-label marketing is prohibited. An advertisement for a drug can only refer to the indications that have been included in the Australian Register of Therapeutic Goods for that specific product.

In addition, advertising prescription products and certain over-the-counter products directly to consumers is prohibited.

The CC Act regulates all types of advertising in Australia. Under the CC Act, representations made in advertisements must be documented, genuine and not misleading.

The marketing of drugs to health care practitioners is largely carried out though a self-regulated scheme operated by industry bodies such as Medicines Australia (which is the peak industry body representing prescription only pharmaceutical companies).

**20. ARE THERE OTHER CODES OF CONDUCT FOR THE MARKETING OF DRUGS (FOR EXAMPLE, BY PROFESSIONAL OR INDUSTRIAL ORGANISATIONS)?**

The advertisement of prescription drugs is regulated through a self-regulatory arrangement described (*see Question 18*).

## MARKETING TO CONSUMERS

**21. WHAT IS THE LEGAL REGIME FOR MARKETING TO CONSUMERS?**

### Legal regime

Marketing activities directed at consumers must comply with:

- Therapeutic Goods Administration (TG Act).
- Therapeutic Goods Regulations 1990 (Cth) (TG Regulations).
- Competition and Consumer Act 2010 (Cth) (CC Act).
- Other relevant state and territory legislation.

### Products

The advertisement of prescription medicines to consumers is strictly prohibited. The TG Act defines promotion and advertising broadly to include any statement, pictorial representation or design, however made, that is intended, whether directly or indirectly, to promote the use or supply of the goods.

Generally, advertisements for over-the-counter (OTC) medicines can be directed to consumers. However, the TG Regulations prohibit the advertising of certain OTC medicines, including medicines that are included in Schedule 3 (pharmacist-only medicine).

Where direct to consumer advertising is permitted, prior approval is required for certain types of advertisements. Approval will be assessed based on whether the advertisement complies with the relevant legislation and codes.

## 22. WHAT KINDS OF MARKETING ACTIVITIES ARE PERMITTED IN RELATION TO CONSUMERS AND THE PRODUCTS WHICH MAY BE ADVERTISED TO THEM?

There is no exhaustive list of specific restrictions placed on marketing activities but the Therapeutic Goods Advertising Code (TGAC) provides that advertisements must not:

- Offer free samples.
- Offer any personal incentive to a pharmacy assistant, or other non-healthcare professional sales person, to recommend or supply the good.
- Be directed at minors.
- Encourage inappropriate or excessive use.
- Abuse the trust or exploit the lack of knowledge of consumers.
- Be likely to provoke unwarranted and unrealistic expectations of product effectiveness.

The promotion of prescription products to the general public is strictly prohibited. The only information that can be provided to the public is educational information. Educational messages must never be designed with the purpose of encouraging consumers to request a specific prescription product from their doctor.

## 23. IS IT PERMITTED TO PROVIDE CONSUMERS WITH FREE SAMPLES? ARE THERE PARTICULAR RESTRICTIONS ON SPECIAL OFFERS (FOR EXAMPLE, "BUY-ONE-GET-ONE-FREE")?

For prescription products, all advertising to the general public (including giving free samples) is prohibited. For over-the-counter products, the Therapeutic Goods Advertising Code provides that advertisements for therapeutic goods must not contain an offer of a sample.

## 24. ARE THERE PARTICULAR RULES OF PRACTICE ON THE USE OF THE INTERNET/SOCIAL MEDIA REGARDING DRUGS AND THEIR ADVERTISING?

In general, the relevant laws, regulations and codes do not distinguish between different types of media. Consequently, as there is a complete prohibition on the promotion of prescription drugs to consumers, advertisements for such products cannot appear on websites directed to Australian consumers.

The internet can be used to promote prescription pharmaceutical products to professionals, provided that the:

- Advertisement complies with the regulatory regime.
- Internet site can only be accessed through a secure system designed to prevent access by members of the general public.

Certain over-the-counter drugs can be promoted to consumers. If promotion direct to consumers is allowed, the promotion must comply with the Therapeutic Goods Advertising Code.

Social media can be a useful tool for the marketing of drugs and the provision of non-promotional information to consumers. However, companies can be held responsible for content posted by third parties on social media pages and therefore companies need to continuously monitor and moderate any social media content. A number of guidelines and codes require that any misleading or inappropriate content be taken down from social media sites within 24 hours.

## 25. WHAT REGULATORY AUTHORITY IS RESPONSIBLE FOR SUPERVISING MARKETING ACTIVITIES TO CONSUMERS?

**Regulatory authority**

The regulatory authorities responsible for supervising marketing activities to consumers are the:

- Therapeutic Goods Administration.
- Australian Competition and Consumer Commission.

In addition to the responsible government bodies, the industry is self-regulated or co-regulated, with the following bodies administering various codes relevant to the marketing of drugs to consumers:

- Therapeutic Goods Advertising Code Council.
- Medicines Australia.
- Generic Medicines Industry Association.
- Australian Self Medication Industry.
- Complementary Healthcare Council of Australia.

**Rights of appeal**

The various laws and codes provide for their own unique avenues of appeal. For example, any decision made by a court in relation to breaches of the Competition and Consumer Act 2010 (Cth) can be appealed judicially, through the typical court hierarchy.

## 26. WHAT ARE THE LEGAL CONSEQUENCES OF NON-COMPLIANCE WITH CONSUMER MARKETING LAWS?

**Therapeutic Goods Act 9TG Act**

Advertising offences under the TG Act including not complying with the Therapeutic Goods Advertising Code, carry a penalty of 60 units (AUD$10,200) per offence.

**Therapeutic Goods Advertising Code (TGAC)**

Breaches of the TGAC are assessed by the Complaints Resolution Panel (CRP). If the CRP determines that an advertisement has breached the Code, it can make a request of the advertiser/sponsor but has no power to impose any penalties. If the request is not complied with, the CRP can make recommendations to the Secretary who can order the withdrawal of the advertisement or the publication of a retraction or correction. The CRP can also recommend that the secretary order that an advertiser does not repeat misrepresentations. In extreme cases, regulatory action to remove the product from the market may be necessary.

**Self-regulated codes**

Sanctions for breaching the various codes vary depending on the code and the severity of the breach. For example, where breaches of the Medicines Australia's Code of Conduct have been found, sanctions can include:

- The cessation of conduct and withdrawal of the advertisement.

- Corrective action.
- Monetary fines of up to AUD$300,000.

**Australian Competition and Consumer Commission (ACCC)**

Contravention of the Competition and Consumer Act 2010 (Cth) is subject to remedies including injunctions, damages and compensatory orders. In addition, punitive fines of up to AUD$1.1 million for corporations and AUD$220,000 for individuals can also be ordered.

## MARKETING TO PROFESSIONALS

### 27. WHAT KINDS OF MARKETING ACTIVITIES ARE PERMITTED IN RELATION TO PROFESSIONALS?

The types of marketing activities that can be directed to health care professionals will largely depend on the type of product (that is, whether it is a prescription or over-the-counter medicine).

Despite the broad powers of the Therapeutic Goods Administration (TGA) in relation to advertising, in practice much of the regulation of the advertising of products, particularly advertising directed to professionals, is through self-regulatory schemes. The most prescriptive requirements are set out in Medicines Australia's Code of Conduct that prescribes standards for the advertising of prescription products to health care professionals.

The TGA, in its marketing approval, requires the promotion of all prescription products to comply with the Medicines Australia Code of Conduct. The current edition of the Medicines Code of Conduct is Edition 18 (Edition 18). Updates on the can be found at *https://medicinesaustralia.com.au/code-of-conduct/*.

Edition 18 contains new transparency reporting obligations that are expected to commence on 1 October 2015.

### 28. ARE THERE ANY RESTRICTIONS ON MARKETING TO PROFESSIONALS?

The types of marketing activities that can be directed to professionals will largely depend on the type of product (that is, whether it is a prescription or OTC drug). Most of the restrictions relating to marketing directed at professionals are contained within Medicines Australia's Code of Conduct (Code of Conduct), which regulates the marketing of prescription medicines.

The Code of Conduct requires that no financial or material benefit be conditional on any obligation by the healthcare professionals to recommend, prescribe, dispense or administer a company's prescription product(s).

In addition, the Code of Conduct expressly prohibits some form of marketing to professionals, including:

- The giving of items or offers to healthcare professionals, except educational items that do not bear the name of any medicine or product. Consequently, brand name reminders are prohibited.
- Hospitality offered to professionals must be simple, modest, secondary to the educational content and provided in an environment that enhances education and learning.
- The travel costs of professionals can be provided if it is justifiable in the context of the

educational content or origin of the delegates. If this includes air travel, tickets are restricted to economy class only. Travel arrangements cannot include any additional time over what is reasonable for the professional to attend the event and must be the most practical direct route.

- Reasonable levels of accommodation can be provided to a professional if it is justified by the arrangements of the meeting.
- Companies are forbidden from providing entertainment, remuneration for their attendance and subsidies to professionals' families or travel companion(s).

### 29. WHAT INFORMATION IS IT LEGALLY REQUIRED TO INCLUDE IN ADVERTISING TO PROFESSIONALS?

The information required to be included in an advertisement will depend on the type of product as well as the length of time it has been on the market. For example, for advertisements placed in print for a prescription medicine which has been entered Australian Register of Therapeutic Goods on the ARTG for less than 24 months, The Medicines Australia's Code of Conduct requires that the following information be included:

- The product's brand name.
- The Australian Approved Name of the active ingredient(s).
- All Pharmaceutical Benefit Scheme (PBS) listings, including any restrictions (the PBS is a government scheme which provides certain prescription drugs at a heavily-subsidised price).
- The product information or minimum product information.
- The name of the supplier and the city, town or locality of the registered office.
- A clear and unambiguous statement for prescribers to review the product Information before prescribing in a form prescribed by the Code of Conduct.

Each portion of mandatory information must meet the minimum size and/or formatting requirements as prescribed by the Code of Conduct.

### 30. ARE THERE RULES ON COMPARISONS WITH OTHER PRODUCTS THAT ARE PARTICULARLY APPLICABLE TO DRUGS?

The Medicines Australia's Code of Conduct, which applies to the promotion of prescription products, prescribes a number of rules with regard to the making of comparative claims, including that:

- Care must be taken to ensure that any comparison with another product properly reflects the body of evidence and does not mislead by distortion, by undue emphasis or in any other way. Comparisons of products must be factual, fair, capable of substantiation, referenced to its source, and must not be disparaging. "Hanging" comparatives (those that merely claim that a product is better, stronger, or more widely prescribed) must not be used.
- Claims of comparative efficacy or safety must not be based solely on a comparison of product information documents that does not reflect the general literature, as those documents are based on different databases and are not directly comparable. This applies to Australian as well as overseas product information documents.
- Comparative claims must be substantiated with respect to all aspects of efficacy or safety. Where a comparative claim relates to a specific parameter, any claims must be clearly identified as pertaining to that parameter. The accepted level of statistical significance is $p < 0.05$. If comparative data that is not statistically significant is used, the data must

comply with the following conditions:
- the lack of significance must be stated explicitly, it is insufficient to state the p value;
- the data must not be used to generalise or to indicate superiority or inferiority.
- If comparative data is used where the relevant study does not include a statement of the significance or lack of significance of the comparative data, the lack of a p value must be explicitly stated.
- A statement that the difference is not statistically significant or p value is not stated must be linked to the original claim by a readily identifiable symbol such as an asterisk or a similar device, and appear directly below or adjacent to the claim using a type size not less than 3 mm based on the font's lower case "e" for printed materials. Care must be taken to distinguish between mathematically determined statistical significance and clinical significance.

## 31. WHAT OTHER ITEMS, FUNDING OR SERVICES ARE PERMITTED TO BE PROVIDED TO PROFESSIONALS?

The Medicines Australia's Code of Conduct (Code of Conduct) requires that no financial or material benefit be conditional on any obligation by the healthcare professional to recommend, prescribe, dispense or administer a company's prescription product(s).

In addition, the Code of Conduct contains the following specific requirements:

- Starter packs can only be supplied on their request to authorised healthcare professionals, including medical practitioners, dentists, veterinarians, hospital pharmacists and nurse practitioners. They can only be supplied when required for any of the following reasons:
  - for immediate use in the surgery for relief of symptoms;
  - for the use of alternative treatments, prior to a prescription being written;
  - for after-hours use;
  - for gaining familiarisation with products.
- Sponsoring a healthcare professional's attendance at an educational event is permitted provided the event is directly related to their area of expertise. Sponsorship must have the purpose of enhancing the quality use of medicines and be able to withstand public and professional scrutiny.
- A company can temporarily loan a piece of equipment to a medical practice or health related organisation, provided it facilitates the quality use of medicines. If the equipment is provided as part of a loan arrangement, the company must have a mechanism for retrieval of the equipment.
- A company can provide a grant or financial support provided that the support is made only to a medical practice, hospital, institution or health related organisation:
  - for education, training or academic purposes;
  - for medical research;
  - for activities that improve the quality use of medicines;
  - to improve the outcome for patients.
- A company can sponsor "in-institution" educational events, such as journal clubs, grand rounds, multidisciplinary and in-service meetings held within the healthcare professional workplace. To qualify for sponsorship, the primary purpose of the event must be the provision of medical education.

# AUSTRALIA

## 32. WHAT REGULATORY AUTHORITY IS RESPONSIBLE FOR SUPERVISING MARKETING ACTIVITIES REGARDING PROFESSIONALS?

**Regulatory authority**

The regulatory authorities responsible for supervising marketing activities regarding professionals are the:

- Therapeutic Goods Administration.
- Australian Competition and Consumer Commission.

In addition to the responsible government bodies, the industry is self-regulated or co-regulated, with the following bodies administering various codes relevant to the marketing of drugs to consumers:

- Therapeutic Goods Advertising Code Council.
- Medicines Australia.
- Generic Medicines Industry Association.
- Australian Self Medication Industry.
- Complementary Healthcare Council of Australia.

**Supervision and rights of appeal**

The various laws and codes provide for their own unique avenues of appeal. For example, any decision made by a court in relation to breaches of the Competition and Consumer Act 2010 (Cth) can be appealed judicially, through the typical court hierarchy.

In addition, see *Question 25* for information regarding the Medicines Australia Complaints Resolution Board.

## 33. WHAT ARE THE LEGAL CONSEQUENCES IN CASE OF NON-COMPLIANCE WITH PROFESSIONAL MARKETING LAWS?

See *Question 25*.

---

# ENGAGEMENT WITH PATIENT ORGANISATIONS

## 34. WHAT KINDS OF ACTIVITIES ARE PERMITTED IN RELATION TO ENGAGEMENT WITH PATIENT ORGANISATIONS? WHAT ARE THE RESTRICTIONS THAT ARE IMPOSED ON RELATIONSHIP WITH PATIENT ORGANISATIONS?

The Medicines Australia's Code of Conduct (Code of Conduct) that applies to the promotion of prescription products, prescribes a number of obligations and prohibitions in relation to the engagement by companies of patient organisations.

The Code of Conduct encourages and supports positive and beneficial relationships between industry and patient organisations. In addition, Medicines Australia has produced a set of guidelines for relationships between patient organisations and pharmaceutical companies called "Working Together – A Guide to relationships between Health Consumer Organisations and Pharmaceutical Companies".

The guide is an informal document addressing how the relationship can be formed in an ethical and transparent manner and to comply with the Code of Conduct. Prohibited activities include:

- Requesting to be the sole funder.
- Interfering with the independence of the patient organisation.
- Using the patient organisation's logo or proprietary material without agreement.
- Exerting influence on the text of a patient organisation's material in a manner favourable to the commercial interests of a company.

## REFORM

**35. ARE THERE ANY PLANS TO REFORM THE LAW ON THE DISTRIBUTION AND PROMOTION OF DRUGS IN YOUR JURISDICTION?**

In December 2011, the Therapeutic Goods Administration (TGA) published *A blueprint for TGA's future* that contains plans that are currently underway to reform many aspects of the TGA so that it remains adaptable to community and industry expectations.

With regards to the promotion of products, the main reforms aim to achieve:

- Consistency of therapeutic sector industry codes.
- Accessibility to the industry codes.
- The educating of members and non-members about requirements of the relevant codes.
- A streamlined portal to channel complaints to the appropriate industry association.

The TGA are also reforming the advertising framework to develop a more effective approach to sanctions and penalties (including use of the infringement notice provisions of the Therapeutic Goods Act 1989 (Cth).

# AUSTRIA

Gabriela Staber and Egon Engin-Deniz, CMS REICH-ROHRWIG HAINZ
Patricia Kaindl, PUBLIC PROSECUTION OFFICE VIENNA

## DISTRIBUTION

### PRE-CONDITIONS FOR DISTRIBUTION

**1. WHAT ARE THE LEGAL PRE-CONDITIONS FOR A DRUG TO BE DISTRIBUTED WITHIN THE JURISDICTION?**

#### Authorisation

The distribution of drugs is governed by the Austrian Medicinal Products Act 1983 (AMG). Generally, a marketing authorisation that is effective in Austria is required to distribute drugs there. There are certain exceptions, for instance for compassionate use, herbal drugs, certain homeopathics, and parallel imports.

There are four procedures that can be used to obtain a marketing authorisation that is valid in Austria. These are the:

- Centralised procedure.
- Decentralised procedure.
- Mutual recognition procedure.
- Austrian national procedure.

A marketing authorisation under the centralised procedure is valid throughout the EU, while the decentralised procedure, the mutual recognition procedure and the national procedures enable the applicant to obtain national marketing authorisations.

#### Exceptions

The following drugs can be distributed without a marketing authorisation, provided they have been properly registered with the Austrian regulatory authority:

- Certain homeopathics.
- Herbal medicinal products.
- Drugs that are prepared in a pharmacy solely from compounds that are identified in the Austrian Pharmacopoeia, do not require a prescription and are distributed by the pharmacy that prepares them.

AUSTRIA

## 2. DO ANY TYPES OF NAMED PATIENT AND/OR COMPASSIONATE USE PROGRAMMES OPERATE? IF SO, WHAT ARE THE REQUIREMENTS FOR PRE-LAUNCH ACCESS?

Named patient use programmes are allowed if an authorised healthcare professional confirms that the drug is urgently needed to treat a life-threatening or serious condition, and the same result cannot be achieved with an authorised and available drug (*section 8, para 1, no 2, Austrian Medicinal Products Act (AMG), which transposes Article 5(1) of Directive 2001/83/EC*). Named patient use does not require notification or prior approval, and is the sole responsibility of the treating physician.

Compassionate use programmes are available in Austria. In contrast to named patient use programmes, which refer to treatment of a single individual, compassionate use programmes are implemented for groups of patients. Section 8a AMG and the Federal Office for Safety in Healthcare (BASG) Guidelines set out the following conditions for compassionate use programmes:

- The centralised procedure must be available for the drug in question.
- The patient group must suffer from a debilitating or life-threatening disease.
- The patient group cannot be treated satisfactorily with a drug that is authorised in Europe.
- The drug is either the subject of an application for a centralised marketing authorisation or undergoing clinical trials in the European Economic Area (EEA) or elsewhere.
- Data from a mature randomised phase III trial is available (in exceptional circumstances, data from phase II trials will be sufficient).
- The applicant must confirm that they will make the drug available to patients in the time between the approval of the marketing authorisation application and the introduction of the drug to the market.
- Compliance with pharmacovigilance requirements.

Compassionate use programmes are not available for drugs which have already been authorised under the centralised procedure, even if the symptoms and patient populations differ from those specific to the marketing authorisation. Conversely, the existence of a national authorisation in another member state of the EU does not prevent implementation of a compassionate use programme in Austria.

Compassionate use programmes are subject to approval by the BASG. The application for a compassionate use programme can either be submitted at the same time as an application for marketing authorisation, or earlier, provided that the applicant declares their intent to file an application for marketing authorisation in the near future.

## LICENSING

## 3. WHAT IS THE PROCEDURAL STRUCTURE REGARDING LICENSING A DRUG FOR DISTRIBUTION?

**Structure**

Only authorised manufacturers or wholesalers of the drug in question under the Austrian Trade Code, owners of Austrian public pharmacies, and pharmaceutical companies that are established within the EEA and authorised to distribute the drug in question can apply for a marketing authorisation. Generally, each type of drug, composition, strength, and use requires a separate application. The Austrian Medicinal Products Act (AMG) contains detailed provisions regarding the documents needed for an application. Application forms are available at *www.basg.gv.at/arzneimittel/formulare/nationale-zulassung/*.

During the authorisation procedure, the regulatory authority assesses the drug for compliance with the provisions of the AMG. In particular, it determines whether the benefits of the drug have been proven to outweigh the risks (efficacy-safety balance), and will only grant a marketing authorisation if this is the case. Sometimes, marketing authorisations are granted subject to further conditions to ensure the protection of human or animal health or drug safety. The regulatory authority can also require the drug to be distributed in certain package sizes, if this is necessary to ensure therapy-appropriate use.

The regulatory authority must either grant or refuse marketing authorisations within seven months from receipt of the completed application (within 45 days, for parallel import applications).

Marketing authorisations are initially valid for five years, and can be renewed. Renewed authorisations are usually granted for an unlimited period of time, although the regulatory authority can limit the validity to five years, for pharmacovigilance reasons. If the drug is not launched within three years from the grant of the marketing authorisation, or not marketed for a continuous period of three years after its launch, the marketing authorisation expires.

**Regulatory authority**

The regulatory authority in charge of the authorisation procedure is the Federal Office for Safety in Healthcare (BASG).

## 4. IS THERE A SIMPLIFIED LICENCE PROCEEDING, OR RELAXED LICENSING CONDITIONS, FOR DRUGS WHICH HAVE ALREADY BEEN LICENSED FOR DISTRIBUTION IN ANOTHER JURISDICTION?

The mutual recognition procedure and the decentralised procedure allow the applicant to obtain authorisations in multiple member states more rapidly, and with less administrative burden, by relying on the recognition of a first assessment performed in one member state. The mutual recognition procedure is available for drugs that have already been licensed in another European Economic Area (EEA) country, and essentially asks that other member states recognise an earlier authorisation, whereas the decentralised procedure can be used for drugs that have not yet been licensed anywhere in the EEA.

In addition, a simplified procedure is available for parallel imports. The applicant can obtain a parallel import licence, provided that:

- The drug corresponds to a drug that is licensed or registered in Austria.
- The drug is imported from a member state of the EEA.
- The drug's evaluation of safety and efficacy can be used without any risk to health.

Finally, there is a simplified procedure for generic drugs which allows the applicant to rely on a reference drug's documentation to obtain a marketing authorisation. The applicant can also use this procedure if the reference drug is not licensed in Austria but in another EEA country.

## 5. IS VIRTUAL DRUG DISTRIBUTION POSSIBLE FROM YOUR JURISDICTION?

An Austrian wholesale licence enables the holder to both obtain drugs from a marketing authorisation holder who is established outside of Austria, and to distribute the drugs outside of Austria. Therefore drugs can be distributed from Austria without physically entering Austria.

Even so, the wholesaler must maintain an office and have personnel in Austria to fulfil the obligations under the Austrian Medicinal Products Act (AMG) with respect to documentation, reporting of complaints, and so on.

## 6. WHAT IS THE PROCEDURE TO APPEAL (LEGAL REMEDY) A LICENSING DECISION?

The applicant can file an appeal against the Federal Office for Safety in Healthcare's (BASG) decision with the Federal Administrative Court. There is further recourse available to the Supreme Administrative Court or the Constitutional Court if the decision of the Federal Administrative Court touches on a material question of law or violates the constitutional rights of the applicant.

## 7. WHAT ARE THE COSTS OF OBTAINING LICENSING?

The official fees are determined by the Federal Office for Safety in Healthcare (BASG) in its fee regulation, which is available at *www.basg.gv.at/ueber-uns/tarife/*. This regulation is usually modified once a year. Fees currently range from EUR1,000 for a parallel import licence, to EUR50,000 for obtaining a marketing authorisation under the decentralised procedure where Austria is the reference member state. A marketing authorisation under the national procedure for a new active ingredient presently costs EUR10,700. Annual fees vary between EUR300 and EUR2,900, depending on the type of marketing authorisation.

## DISTRIBUTION TO CONSUMERS

## 8. WHAT ARE THE DIFFERENT CATEGORIES OF DRUGS FOR DISTRIBUTION?

Austrian law distinguishes between prescription and over-the-counter (OTC) drugs.

## 9. WHO IS AUTHORISED TO DISTRIBUTE PRESCRIPTION DRUGS AND OVER-THE-COUNTER DRUGS TO CONSUMERS?

**Prescription drugs**

Prescription drugs can only be distributed to consumers by public pharmacies. Operation of a public pharmacy requires a licence (*Austrian Pharmacy Act 1906*). In addition, some physicians are entitled to dispense prescription drugs if they have the appropriate licence under the Austrian Pharmacy Act (*see Question 10 below*).

**Over-the-counter drugs**

Most over-the-counter (OTC) drugs can only be distributed to consumers by public pharmacies or physicians that are entitled to dispense drugs. However, some OTC drugs can be distributed to consumers by drugstores or by other professionals (for instance contact lens fluids by opticians).

## 10. WHAT DRUGS CAN AN ATTENDING PHYSICIAN DISTRIBUTE AND UNDER WHAT CIRCUMSTANCES?

If there is no public pharmacy in a municipality and the nearest public pharmacy is more than six kilometres away, physicians can apply for a licence to dispense prescription and over-the-counter (OTC) drugs to consumers. In addition, hospitals with in-house pharmacies can dispense drugs to their patients.

## 11. WHO IS AUTHORISED TO PRESCRIBE PRESCRIPTION DRUGS TO CONSUMERS?

Drugs for human use can only be prescribed by physicians and dentists. Some prescriptions are required to be approved by a physician of the Austrian social security administration in order to receive reimbursement for the drug. In emergencies, pharmacies are permitted to distribute prescription drugs without a prescription, in the smallest available package.

## 12. IS DIRECT MAILING/DISTANCE SELLING OF DRUGS PERMITTED IN YOUR JURISDICTION?

While cross-border distance sales of over-the-counter (OTC) drugs to Austrian customers have been allowed for a couple of years, distance selling of drugs by Austrian pharmacies was prohibited until very recently. This changed on 25 June 2015, when a provision permitting distance sales of OTC drugs by Austrian pharmacies came into force.

**Conditions**

Austrian pharmacies that would like to engage in distance selling of drugs must register with the Federal Office for Safety in Healthcare (BASG) and fulfil the requirements set out in the implementing regulation. In particular, they must operate a physical point of sale and mail the drug from there to the customer, provide telephone consultation, maintain a quality management system, dispense the drugs without delay and only in quantities for personal use. Distance selling is only allowed for OTC drugs that are licensed in Austria. BASG administers a register of all pharmacies that are authorised for distance sales. The pharmacies must display a common logo on their website which functions as a link to the BASG register.

**Cross-border sales**

Only European Economic Area (EEA) pharmacies can offer distance sales to Austrian customers. Cross-border distance selling is only permitted for OTCs that are licensed in Austria. Distance selling of prescription drugs is not permitted in Austria. This includes distance sales by Austrian pharmacies to customers in countries that allow distance selling of prescription drugs.

## 13. WHAT REGULATORY AUTHORITY IS RESPONSIBLE FOR SUPERVISING DISTRIBUTION ACTIVITIES?

Distribution activities are supervised by the general administrative bodies and by the police.

## AUSTRIA

### 14. WHAT IS THE PROCEDURE TO APPEAL (LEGAL REMEDY) A DISTRIBUTION DECISION?

Non-compliance with the laws regarding distribution of drugs is an administrative offence. Decisions imposing a fine can be appealed to the Regional Administrative Court. There is further recourse available to the Supreme Administrative Court or the Constitutional Court if the decision of the Regional Administrative Court touches on a material question of law or violates constitutional rights.

### 15. WHAT ARE THE LEGAL CONSEQUENCES OF NON-COMPLIANCE WITH CONSUMER DISTRIBUTION LAWS?

The supply of prescription drugs without prescription, or by someone who is not authorised to sell prescription drugs, is subject to an administrative fine of up to EUR3,600. Drugs which are unlawfully kept for sale, offered or supplied, and any revenues from such sales, are subject to forfeiture.

The violation or attempted violation of the provisions of the Austrian Medicinal Products Act (AMG) regarding distribution of drugs to end users (for instance violation of the rules regarding distance selling or disposal of drugs to end users) is subject to an administrative fine of up to EUR7,500, or up to EUR14,000 for repeat violations.

Furthermore, violation of any of the above provision entitles competitors and certain organisations to file an unfair competition complaint in court, asking for an injunction (including interim relief), damages and publication of the judgment.

## WHOLESALE DISTRIBUTION

### 16. WHAT IS THE LEGAL REGIME REGARDING WHOLESALE DISTRIBUTION OF DRUGS?

Drug wholesalers must obtain a trade licence for the wholesale of drugs (*Austrian Trade Act 1859*), and a wholesale licence from the Federal Office for Safety in Healthcare (BASG), under the provisions of the Austrian Medicinal Products Act (AMG). An Austrian wholesale licence is not required if the wholesaler already has a wholesale licence in another member state of the European Economic Area (EEA).

In order to obtain (and to maintain) a permit, a wholesaler of pharmaceuticals must fulfill the requirements set out in the Austrian Pharmaceutical Products Regulation 2009 and the European Commission Guidelines on Good Distribution Practice of medicinal products for human use (GDP). In particular, wholesale distributors must maintain a quality system with competent personnel and on suitable premises. In addition, there must be adequate documentation available on site. The wholesale distributor must also implement a system that ensures that complaints are recorded and examined, and that products can be recalled without delay if necessary. The wholesale distributor must designate a responsible person with appropriate skills and education who is responsible for the compliance of the wholesale distributor with all applicable legal provisions, who should be immediately contactable.

The AMG contains a list of recipients to which drug wholesalers can dispense drugs. For example, they are permitted to sell drugs to:

- Pharmacies or hospitals with in-house pharmacies.
- Drugstores and professionals who are permitted to dispense drugs.
- Manufacturers for the sole purpose of manufacturing drugs or if they hold a trade permit that entitles them to sell drugs.

- Other drug wholesalers.

It is prohibited to dispense drugs to recipients that are not mentioned in the list. This includes hospitals without in-house pharmacies or physicians who are entitled to dispense drugs. They are both required to obtain their supplies from public pharmacies. In some cases, the regulatory authority will allow direct supply to hospitals without a hospital pharmacy, provided a public pharmacy is involved in the ordering process.

## 17. WHAT REGULATORY AUTHORITY IS RESPONSIBLE FOR SUPERVISING WHOLESALE DISTRIBUTION ACTIVITIES?

**Regulatory authority**

Wholesale licences are issued by the Federal Office for Safety in Healthcare (BASG). The wholesaler must file an application with the BASG, which then inspects the premises and makes a decision based on the results of the inspection. The decision must follow within 90 days from receipt of the application, unless the application is incomplete, in which case the applicant is ordered to submit additional information.

**Supervision**

The BASG must carry out routine inspections at least every five years. The persons carrying out the inspections are entitled to enter the premises, take samples and inspect the files. The BASG can revoke the licence or impose further conditions if necessary. It can shut down the premises where there is a serious danger to human health.

**Rights of appeal**

Decisions of the BASG can be appealed to the Federal Administrative Court. There is further recourse available to the Supreme Administrative Court or the Constitutional Court if the decision of the Federal Administrative Court touches on a material question of law or violates constitutional rights.

## 18. WHAT ARE THE LEGAL CONSEQUENCES OF NON-COMPLIANCE WITH WHOLESALE DISTRIBUTION LAWS?

Wholesale of drugs without, or in excess of, a wholesale licence, violating the condition of a wholesale licence, or any obstruction of the Federal Office for Safety in Healthcare's (BASG) inspection rights, are all subject to an administrative fine of up to EUR25,000, or up to EUR50,000 for repeat offences. In addition, the licence can be revoked if the violation has been repeated at least three times. Some less serious violations of the rules governing the wholesale distribution of drugs are subject to an administrative fine of up to EUR7,500, or up to EUR14,000 for repeat violations.

Violation of any of the above provisions entitles competitors and certain organisations to file an unfair competition complaint in court asking for an injunction (including interim relief), damages and publication of the judgment.

# AUSTRIA

# MARKETING

## PROMOTION

### 19. WHAT IS THE GENERAL LEGAL REGIME FOR THE MARKETING OF DRUGS?

**Legal regime**

The Austrian Medicinal Products Act (AMG) provides the legal regime for the marketing of drugs. The term "advertising" encompasses the provision of information, market research, market development and the creation of incentives intended to increase the prescription, supply, sale or use of drugs. It includes activities such as dispensing of samples to physicians, promotional events, sponsorship, hospitality and reimbursement of travel expenses. Different rules apply depending on whether the advertising is directed at consumers or professionals.

**Limits to marketing activities**

Generally, where advertising is allowed, it is only permitted for drugs that are:

- Authorised or registered in Austria.
- Approved for parallel import.
- Prepared by a pharmacy according to the instructions of a qualified physician or dentist.

Advertising for drugs that do not have a marketing authorisation in Austria is not permitted unless it is at a scientific event where the participants are mainly from outside Austria.

Any advertising must describe the properties of the drug objectively and without exaggeration, and cannot include information or illustrations which:

- Attach to the drug an effect exceeding its true effect.
- Give a false impression that success can usually be expected.
- Contradict the labelling, instructions for use or summary of the product characteristics (SPC).

### 20. ARE THERE OTHER CODES OF CONDUCT FOR THE MARKETING OF DRUGS (FOR EXAMPLE, BY PROFESSIONAL OR INDUSTRIAL ORGANISATIONS)?

The Association of the Austrian Pharmaceutical Industry (Pharmig) provides a Code of Conduct and implementing ordinances, which are available at *www.pharmig.at*. The Pharmig Code of Conduct contains rules governing the provision of information regarding drugs, advertising of drugs (including via the internet), events, co-operation with specialist circles, institutions and patient organisations, raffles, benefits, and transparency. In addition, any violation of the advertising rules of the Austrian Medicinal Products Act (AMG) is also regarded as violation of the Pharmig Code of Conduct.

The Pharmig Code of Conduct is only binding for members of Pharmig (which include all major pharmaceutical companies in Austria). Under the Pharmig Code of Procedure, anybody can file a complaint against a Pharmig member. However, non-members must conclude a written agreement with Pharmig on the relevant proceedings before the complaint will be dealt with by the Pharmig Committee of Experts. Complaints against non-members will be forwarded to the Association of the Austrian Chemical Industry, which is a division of the

Austrian Federal Economic Chamber. The members of Pharmig undertake not to bring the same matter before a court of law for the duration of Pharmig proceedings.

In addition, the Austrian Physicians Association and the Austrian Pharmacists Association have codes of conduct that apply to their members. There is also the Association of Austrian Manufacturers and Wholesalers of Medicinal Products (IGEPHA) Code of Conduct, which applies to the distribution of over-the-counter (OTC) drugs and is binding for the members of IGEPHA.

## MARKETING TO CONSUMERS

### 21. WHAT IS THE LEGAL REGIME FOR MARKETING TO CONSUMERS?

**Legal regime**

Marketing activities that are directed at consumers must be designed in such a way that they are recognised as advertising and that the product is clearly identified as a drug. Advertisements and editorials must be separate from each other.

Any advertising directed at consumers must contain the following information:

- The name of the drug and the active ingredient (provided the drug contains only one active ingredient).
- Any information that is necessary for the reasonable use of the drug.
- A clearly visible notice that the drug can have adverse effects and that the consumer must follow the instructions for use or consult a physician or pharmacist.
- Additionally, for traditional herbal drugs, the notice that it is a traditional herbal drug, for use for certain symptoms or certain indications due to long-standing use.

Exceptions apply to advertisements that solely consists of the drug's name (reminder advertisements).

**Products**

Advertising prescription drugs and registered homeopathic drugs to consumers is prohibited. Over-the-counter (OTC) drugs can be marketed to consumers, unless their name contains the same invented or scientific term as a prescription drug.

### 22. WHAT KINDS OF MARKETING ACTIVITIES ARE PERMITTED IN RELATION TO CONSUMERS AND THE PRODUCTS WHICH MAY BE ADVERTISED TO THEM?

Advertisements that are directed at consumers must not contain any information that exceeds the authorised summary of the product characteristics (SPC). They can refer to the marketing authorisation or registration, provided such a reference is unlikely to create an erroneous view of the drug's safety or efficacy. In addition, the following elements/activities are prohibited:

- Pictures of healthcare professionals or healthcare institutions.
- Creating the impression that a medical consultation or surgery is unnecessary, in particular by offering a diagnosis or suggesting treatment through correspondence.
- Suggesting that the effects of taking the drug are guaranteed, are unaccompanied by adverse reactions, or are better than, or equivalent to, those of another treatment or drug.

# AUSTRIA

- Suggesting that the health of the patient can be improved by taking the drug.
- Advertising that is directed exclusively or principally at children.
- References to a recommendation by scientists, health professionals or celebrities.
- Suggesting that the drug is a foodstuff, cosmetic product or other consumer product.
- Suggesting that the safety or efficacy of the drug is due to the fact that it is a "natural product".
- Detailed description or presentation of medical history which could lead to erroneous self-diagnosis.
- Inappropriate, alarming or misleading references to recovery reports.
- Inappropriate, alarming or misleading use of pictorial representations of changes in the human body caused by disease or injury or action of a drug on the human body or parts thereof.
- Encouraging mail-orders of prescription drugs.

### 23. IS IT PERMITTED TO PROVIDE CONSUMERS WITH FREE SAMPLES? ARE THERE PARTICULAR RESTRICTIONS ON SPECIAL OFFERS (FOR EXAMPLE, "BUY-ONE-GET-ONE-FREE")?

The supply of specimens or free samples of drugs or gift coupons to consumers is prohibited. Raffles or prize competitions in connection with the supply of drugs are also prohibited. There are no rules that specifically address "buy-one-get-one-free" promotions, but it would appear that these are similar to offering a free sample, and are therefore not permitted.

### 24. ARE THERE PARTICULAR RULES OF PRACTICE ON THE USE OF THE INTERNET/SOCIAL MEDIA REGARDING DRUGS AND THEIR ADVERTISING?

While the Austrian Medicinal Products Act (AMG) does not contain any additional rules for internet advertising, the Association of the Austrian Pharmaceutical Industry (Pharmig) Code of Conduct dedicates an entire section to this topic and sets out the following rules:

- The presentation on the internet must clearly name the pharmaceutical company that is running the website, or directly or indirectly supporting it, and which information on the website is addressed to specialist circles and/or to the general public.
- Websites must be updated on a regular basis and checked for accuracy, and should provide up-to-date information.
- Websites can contain non-promotional information on the medicinal products sold by the company for patients and the general public (including information regarding symptoms, side-effects, interactions with other substances, application, reports on clinical research, and so on). This information must be balanced, accurate and consistent with the summary of the product characteristics (SPC).
- The website can contain a link to the complete, unmodified evaluation report as published by the Committee for Human Medicinal Products (CHMP) or by a competent national authority.
- The website can contain links to other websites containing reliable information on medicinal products (websites of authorities, medical research institutions, patient organisations, and so on).
- As well as the brand name, the international non-proprietary name (INN) must also be mentioned.
- The website must always contain a reference to a physician or pharmacist for further information.

## 25. WHAT REGULATORY AUTHORITY IS RESPONSIBLE FOR SUPERVISING MARKETING ACTIVITIES TO CONSUMERS?

### Regulatory authority

The Federal Office for Safety in Health Care (BASG) is in charge of supervising and enforcing the advertising restrictions of the Austrian Medicinal Products Act (AMG).

The Committees of Experts of the Association of the Austrian Pharmaceutical Industry (Pharmig) will act under the Pharmig Code of Procedure in case of complaints against members of Pharmig about violations of the Pharmig Code of Conduct.

### Supervision

BASG is entitled to request the submission of documents and to enter premises and inspect any documents that it deems relevant and to make copies of these documents. BASG can order any measures that are required to ensure conformity with the rules of the AMG.

Pharmig does not carry out any supervision, and acts only on complaints by members or non-members.

### Rights of appeal

BASG decisions can be appealed to the Federal Administrative Court. Further recourse is available to the Supreme Administrative Court or the Constitutional Court if the decision of the Federal Administrative Court touches on a material question of law or violates constitutional rights.

Under the Pharmig Code of Procedure an appeal to the Committee of Experts of the second instance is available. The decisions of the Committee of Experts of the second instance are final.

## 26. WHAT ARE THE LEGAL CONSEQUENCES OF NON-COMPLIANCE WITH CONSUMER MARKETING LAWS?

The Federal Office for Safety in Health Care (BASG) can order any measures that are required to ensure conformity with the rules of the Austrian Medicinal Products Act (AMG). In addition, the violation or attempted violation of the advertising rules of the AMG is subject to an administrative fine of up to EUR25,000, or up to EUR50,000 for repeat violations. If such a violation is repeated three times or more, the marketing authorisation for the drug in question can be revoked. In addition, under the AMG some organisations can file for an injunction if the infringer has refused to sign an appropriate cease and desist declaration. Competitors and certain organisations can also file an unfair competition complaint asking for an injunction (including interim relief), damages and publication of the judgment.

Under the Association of the Austrian Pharmaceutical Industry (Pharmig) Code of Procedure, a decision establishing a violation of Pharmig's Code of Conduct must be accompanied by a warning and by an obligation for the company concerned to stop the behaviour that formed the basis of the complaint. In addition, the following sanctions can be imposed in combination:

- In the case of a serious violation, a penalty of not less than EUR5,000, up to a maximum of EUR100,000 (repeat violations and violation of the provisions regarding events and transparency are usually deemed serious).

- The penalty range is increased to EUR200,000 if the company concerned has committed three violations of the provisions regarding events and transparency within 24 months.
- The violation can be publicised and the company concerned named in a Pharmig publication.
- The parent company of the company concerned will be notified accordingly.
- The Secretary General of the European Federation of Pharmaceutical Industries and Associations (EFPIA) will be notified accordingly.
- Exclusion from Pharmig or termination of the Pharmig Code of Conduct Agreement, in which case the company will not be released from existing payment obligations or other imposed sanctions.

## MARKETING TO PROFESSIONALS

### 27. WHAT KINDS OF MARKETING ACTIVITIES ARE PERMITTED IN RELATION TO PROFESSIONALS?

Advertising directed at professionals can contain information that exceeds the summary of the product characteristics (SPC), but it must not contradict the SPC. Any documentation that is provided for advertising purposes must be accurate, up-to-date, verifiable and sufficiently complete to enable the recipient to form an opinion about the therapeutic value of the drug concerned. Quotations, tables and illustrations taken from medical journals or other scientific works have to be reproduced accurately, and must indicate the source. References to literature have to accurately report its essential content and indicate the source.

### 28. ARE THERE ANY RESTRICTIONS ON MARKETING TO PROFESSIONALS?

**Marketing activities**

No gifts, pecuniary advantages or material benefits can be supplied, offered or promised to healthcare professionals, unless they are inexpensive and are relevant to medical or pharmaceutical practice.

The Association of the Austrian Pharmaceutical Industry (Pharmig) Code of Conduct explicitly prohibits companies from granting, offering or promising premiums, financial or material benefits to healthcare professionals in return for prescribing, dispensing or using a drug or recommending a drug to a patient. Furthermore, the Code of Conduct prohibits pharmaceutical companies from advertising through raffles in which the prize is exclusively subject to a random draw. Prize competitions, in which participation is subject to scientific and technical performance and in which the prize awarded to the winner is a benefit that is admissible under the provisions of the Code of Conduct, are permitted. The provision of drugs in the course of prize competitions is not permitted.

Under the Pharmig Code of Conduct, a non-interventional study must be set up, verified and authorised under the supervision of a medical department of the pharmaceutical company or, if this is unavailable, under the supervision of an appropriate medically qualified person. For the required documentation in the course of a non-interventional study, a financial consideration that meets the local standard and appears appropriate for the service provided can be paid, but this cannot represent an incentive for the prescription of a drug.

## Frequency

Pursuant to the Pharmig Code of Conduct, visits to physicians and hospitals should not seem unduly persistent with regard to frequency and the manner in which they are conducted. Furthermore, employees who work as medical sales representatives must be compelled by their companies to observe the standard practices in the trade.

A physician or a third party must not be granted, offered or promised any remuneration or benefit in kind to ensure that the physician agrees to receive a medical sales representative or accept information from members of other companies.

## Provision of hospitality

The Austrian Medicinal Products Act (AMG) provides that hospitality must always be strictly restricted to the main objective of the event and must not be extended to persons other than health care professionals (for example, their family). Direct or indirect reimbursement of reasonable expenses for travel, accommodation and entry fees at solely business-related scientific events is permitted.

Under the Pharmig Code of Conduct, hospitality is only admissible in the course of events and business dinners for the purpose of an information exchange with members of specialist circles, and only to a reasonable degree, that is not lavish, and to the extent that is considered socially appropriate. The occasion for such hospitality must be documented. Under the Code, the following also applies to the organisation, implementation and/or support or assumption of costs for participants in symposia, scientific congresses, workshops, lectures and similar occasions:

- These events must exclusively serve to provide scientific information and/or further specialisation.
- Leisure-time activities and/or social programmes (for instance, theatre, concerts, sports events) must not be financed or organised for participants.
- The attendance of the participants, the programme and the scientific and/or technical content of the event implemented must be documented.
- The venue must be appropriate for the purpose of the event, located in the home country and be chosen based on objective factors rather than the recreational value of a conference venue.
- The organisation, implementation and/or support of or the assumption of costs for participation in international events is only admissible if the majority of participants come from a different country than that in which the member company of Pharmig is based, or the necessary resources or specialised knowledge are available at the event venue, and in view of this there are appropriate logistical reasons for choosing a venue in a different country.
- The invitation of persons as participants or speakers to events cannot be made dependent on the recommendation, prescription or distribution of specific drugs.
- In the case of services being provided by healthcare professionals within the framework of events, pharmaceutical companies must ensure that all potential conflicts of interest are disclosed to the organiser and the participants in a suitable manner prior to the event starting.
- If pharmaceutical companies distribute information regarding the content of an event, they must ensure that it is accurate.

Transfers of value granted in connection with events, such as admission and attendance fees, travel costs and costs for overnight accommodation, and fees for services rendered and consulting provided, must be disclosed according to the new transparency rules of the Pharmig Code of Conduct.

### 29. WHAT INFORMATION IS IT LEGALLY REQUIRED TO INCLUDE IN ADVERTISING TO PROFESSIONALS?

Advertising in printed matter, in electronic form or via means of telecommunication must contain the essential information about the drug in question in accordance with the summary of the product characteristics (SPC), provided an SPC was published for the drug. Any documentation that is provided for advertising purposes must indicate the date when the documentation was compiled or last modified.

### 30. ARE THERE RULES ON COMPARISONS WITH OTHER PRODUCTS THAT ARE PARTICULARLY APPLICABLE TO DRUGS?

The general rules of the Unfair Competition Act 1984 (UWG) apply to comparative advertising of drugs. Strict standards must be observed irrespective of whether the advertisement is directed to consumers or healthcare professionals.

The Austrian Medicinal Products Act (AMG) explicitly states that information which is incorrect or likely to be misleading cannot be given in connection with the distribution of drugs. The following is regarded as especially misleading:

- If it is suggested that the drug has effects which are not sufficiently confirmed by scientific findings or practical experience.
- If it is suggested that its effects are guaranteed, or that normal or prolonged use will not lead to any adverse reactions.
- If the name or design is likely to be confusing.

The Association of the Austrian Pharmaceutical Industry (Pharmig) Code of Conduct states that references to brands of competitors can be made if permission has been granted to do so, or if such reference is admissible according to the provisions of the Unfair Competition Act (UWG). It is prohibited to imitate typical advertising features of competitors, the presentation, packaging or labelling of competitor products, or to publish advertisements that are misleading or damaging to their reputation.

With respect to generic drugs, a comparison to the price of the original product is permitted. Advertisements can mention the equivalence of the generic and the original drug, provided that no unfair advantage is taken as to the original product's or its manufacturer's reputation.

### 31. WHAT OTHER ITEMS, FUNDING OR SERVICES ARE PERMITTED TO BE PROVIDED TO PROFESSIONALS?

**Discounts**

Discounts are generally allowed. Rebates in kind are allowed if they are granted to wholesalers or hospitals. Furthermore, rebates in kind that are granted to health care practitioners are allowed, provided they relate to drugs that are not included in the Reimbursement Code of the Federation of Austrian Social Insurance Institutions. Rebates in kind for drugs included in the Reimbursement Code that are granted to health care practitioners are prohibited.

**Free samples**

Authorisation holders can provide free-of-charge samples of authorised drugs to healthcare providers, if so requested in writing. Samples can only be supplied in a package that is no larger than the smallest presentation on the market, with a clearly legible and irremovable notice attached with the wording *unverkäufliches Ärztemuster* ("free medical sample – not for sale"). Samples of drugs containing psychotropic or narcotic substances are not permitted.

Samples can only be provided as follows:

- Within a period of one year following the launch of the product in Austria, only in a quantity sufficient to evaluate the treatment success in a maximum of ten patients and overall not more than 30 samples per drug per recipient.
- After expiry of this period, only two samples per request, and overall not more than five samples per drug per year and recipient.

The authorisation holder is obliged to keep records of the type, timing and amount of their sampling activities and to provide these records to the Federal Office for Safety in Health Care (BASG) on request.

**Sponsorship of professionals**

Both the Austrian Medicinal Products Act (AMG) and the Association of the Austrian Pharmaceutical Industry (Pharmig) Code of Conduct prohibit donations and subsidies to individual healthcare professionals. However, according to the Pharmig Code of Conduct, it is allowed to provide donations and subsidies to institutions, organisations or establishments which predominantly comprise healthcare professionals for the purpose of training/education, research or support of the healthcare system or within the framework of scientific or specialist activities. When making financial donations or providing subsidies, pharmaceutical companies are required to keep records and to disclose them on the internet under the new transparency rules of the Pharmig Code of Conduct. The provision of donations and subsidies by pharmaceutical companies must not be linked with conditions relating to the recommendation, prescription or administering of medicinal products.

**Other items, funding or services**

Remuneration can be provided to a healthcare professional for services rendered to a pharmaceutical company (for instance for lectures, consulting, clinical trials, non-interventional studies). Under the Pharmig Code of Conduct, any such service must serve the purpose of training/education, research, support of the healthcare system or be provided within the framework of scientific and specialist activities. A written contract must be concluded which clearly indicates the service and remuneration to be provided, as well as the scope, type and purpose of the service. Remuneration can only consist of money, and must be proportionate to the service provided. Hourly fees can be agreed to compensate for the time spent in providing the service. Any expenses incurred, including travel costs, can be additionally reimbursed to an appropriate degree. Any fees and expenses for services rendered and consulting provided must be disclosed on the internet, under the new transparency rules of the Pharmig Code of Conduct.

## AUSTRIA

### 32. WHAT REGULATORY AUTHORITY IS RESPONSIBLE FOR SUPERVISING MARKETING ACTIVITIES REGARDING PROFESSIONALS?

**Regulatory authority**

See *Question 25*.

**Supervision**

See *Question 25*.

**Rights of appeal**

See *Question 25*.

### 33. WHAT ARE THE LEGAL CONSEQUENCES IN CASE OF NON-COMPLIANCE WITH PROFESSIONAL MARKETING LAWS?

See *Question 26*.

The provision of financial or material benefits to health care providers or institutions to induce them to order or prescribe a certain drug can be considered as bribery, which is a criminal offence.

## ENGAGEMENT WITH PATIENT ORGANISATIONS

### 34. WHAT KINDS OF ACTIVITIES ARE PERMITTED IN RELATION TO ENGAGEMENT WITH PATIENT ORGANISATIONS? WHAT ARE THE RESTRICTIONS THAT ARE IMPOSED ON RELATIONSHIP WITH PATIENT ORGANISATIONS?

While the Austrian Medicinal Products Act (AMG) does not contain any rules regarding engagement with patient organisations, the Association of the Austrian Pharmaceutical Industry (Pharmig) Code of Conduct contains detailed rules for such engagement. Patient organisations are defined by the Code of Conduct as voluntary, non-profit-orientated associations which predominantly comprise patients and/or their families and/or patient organisations which solely represent the interests of patients and/or their families, and exist or were founded to protect their interests. Co-operation between patients' organisations and pharmaceutical companies is based on common interests, and has to take place in an ethical and transparent way.

Any support for patient organisations, other than inexpensive non-financial or indirect contributions, can only be provided under the conditions set out in the Pharmig Code of Conduct. In particular:

- The support must solely serve the interests of the patients and/or their families.
- The support can only be provided on the basis of a written agreement.
- Pharmaceutical companies cannot influence the editorial work of the publications of patient organisations supported by them, without a justifiable factual reason (for example, in order to correct inaccuracies in content or scientific aspects).

- Pharmaceutical companies must detail on their publicly accessible internet home page all the patient organisations they support, and must ensure contractually that patient organisations disclose to the public the relevant support transparently and clearly at all times from the outset.
- The exclusive support of patient organisations and/or their programmes must not be required by pharmaceutical companies and/or granted by patient organisations.

Regarding events for members of patient organisations, patients and/or their families and other invited participants, the following rules apply:

- The assumption of costs must be restricted to travel costs, room and board, as well as the original admission fee, and must be appropriate. Activities which have no factual and/or technical connection with the actual aim and purpose of the event must not be supported or organised by the pharmaceutical company.
- At events taking place outside the country in which the pharmaceutical company is based, the organisation, implementation and/or support as well as the assumption of costs are only admissible if the majority of the participants come from a different country than the country in which the pharmaceutical company is based, or necessary resources or specialised knowledge are available at the chosen event venue and, in view of this, there are logistical reasons for choosing a venue in a different country.

## REFORM

### 35. ARE THERE ANY PLANS TO REFORM THE LAW ON THE DISTRIBUTION AND PROMOTION OF DRUGS IN YOUR JURISDICTION?

We are not aware of any plans to reform the law on the distribution and promotion of drugs in Austria.

# BELGIUM

Claudio Mereu, Maud Grunchard and Raf Callaerts, FIELDFISHER

## DISTRIBUTION

### PRE-CONDITIONS FOR DISTRIBUTION

### 1. WHAT ARE THE LEGAL PRE-CONDITIONS FOR A DRUG TO BE DISTRIBUTED WITHIN THE JURISDICTION?

**Authorisation**

A medicinal product can in principle only be distributed or commercialised on the Belgian market if a marketing authorisation has been issued.

**Exceptions**

The legal framework in Belgium provides for exceptions and different categories. The main different categories are named patient, compassionate use and urgent medical need programmes.

As exceptions with regards to the authorisation, for example, a market authorisation is not required for drugs:

- Prepared for named patient programmes.
- Delivered for experimental purposes.
- Radio-pharmaceuticals in their finished form, which are made up exclusively from authorised kits, generators or precursor radiopharmaceuticals in healthcare establishments.

### 2. DO ANY TYPES OF NAMED PATIENT AND/OR COMPASSIONATE USE PROGRAMMES OPERATE? IF SO, WHAT ARE THE REQUIREMENTS FOR PRE-LAUNCH ACCESS?

"Named patient" programmes for magistral or officinal formulae, made available on prescription and prepared for each individual patient, and compassionate use programmes and programmes for drugs delivered in the framework of a "medical need" operate in Belgium.

A Guidance document on compassionate use and medical need programmes has been adopted by the Federal Agency for Medicines and Health Products (FAMHP), which can be found on its website (*www.fagg- afmps.be/en/human_use/medicines/medicines/ research_development/compassionate_use_medical_need/*).

A positive evaluation from both an ethical committee and the Commission for Medicines for Human Use, as established within the FAMHP, are needed for pre-launch access in case a compassionate use programme or a medical need programme are established.

In urgent situations, if a patient is in immediate risk of dying or that the risk of non-treatment is higher than the inherent risks of the treatment, a non-authorised drug can be used if certain strict conditions are met. The physician must provide a sworn statement that informed consent was obtained in accordance with the law of 22 August 2002 on patient rights and indicate that without appropriate treatment, it is expected that the patient's death would occur with a short delay, or that the risk of no treatment would be greater than the risk for the consequences of starting the treatment. A notification to the FAMPH and the ethics committee of the site concerned is strongly recommended, but is not required to start the treatment. Additionally:

- The medicinal product in question cannot be a drug used in a compassionate use programme, in a clinical trial or/and is not a drug for which a registration or a marketing authorisation is not required.
- The patient in question cannot be treated with a marketed medicinal product, a product under hospital exemption or with a magisterial preparation.
- It should not be possible to import a marketed medicinal product with the same qualitative and quantitative composition of active drug substance and the same pharmaceutical form.

## LICENSING

### 3. WHAT IS THE PROCEDURAL STRUCTURE REGARDING LICENSING A DRUG FOR DISTRIBUTION?

**Structure**

**First entry.** Drugs can be authorised at EU level (central procedure) or at national level, possibly linked with a mutual recognition procedure (decentralised procedure).

In the central procedure at the European Medicines Agency (EMA) in London, applications to license a drug for distribution are assessed by the Committee for Medicinal Products for Human Use (CHMP). A positive evaluation will result in a European authorisation with a European authorisation number allowing the product to be distributed within every member state of the EU. Products with this authorisation can therefore be legally distributed in Belgium. This central procedure is obligatory for certain medicinal products. An exhaustive list of the types of drugs that are to be authorised can be found in the Annex of Regulation (EC) 726/2004 on the authorisation and supervision of medicinal products and establishing a European Medicines Agency (EMA Regulation).

In a national or decentralised procedure, the Commission for Medicines for Human Use (or the Commission of Herbal Medicines for Human Use) established within the Federal Agency for Medicines and Health Products (FAMHP) will assess the application. A positive evaluation will result in a national authorisation and a national authorisation number granted by the Belgian Minister of Health in Belgium.

If an authorisation has already been issued by an EU member state following a national procedure, this authorisation can be recognised by another EU member state through the mutual recognition procedure. In this case, the concerned member state (CMS) can recognise the evaluation of the reference member state (RMS). If this evaluation is positive, this will result in a national authorisation and a national authorisation number granted by the minister in any CMS and RMS involved in the procedure. After a positive evaluation, the drug can be distributed within Belgium should Belgium be a CMS or RMS.

For generic and biosimilar products, simplified and abridged licence procedures exist in case the reference product is already registered within the European Community. In Belgium the reference product must be on the EU market for ten years before the distribution of a generic or biosimilar product can be authorised.

For orphan drugs, or drugs developed to treat rare medical conditions, a special procedure exists.

For some homeopathic or herbal substances, simplified and abridged licence procedures (registration) exist.

**Renewal.** The authorisation of a drug is valid for five years. This authorisation can be renewed. After a first renewal of the authorisation, a medicine authorisation has an indefinite period of validity, unless for justifiable reasons related to pharmacovigilance, it is decided to extend for only five years.

In Belgium, there is a backlog of five-year renewal dossiers of registrations and authorisations for medicinal products for human use granted under the national procedure. In order to remedy this backlog, the Directorate General of the FAMHP has taken further measures in order to introduce new filing elements.

**Regulatory authority**

The marketing authorisations are granted by the Belgian Minister of Health, based on the advice of the Commission for Medicines for Human Use (or the Commission of Herbal Medicines for Human Use) established within the FAMHP.

### 4. IS THERE A SIMPLIFIED LICENCE PROCEEDING, OR RELAXED LICENSING CONDITIONS, FOR DRUGS WHICH HAVE ALREADY BEEN LICENSED FOR DISTRIBUTION IN ANOTHER JURISDICTION?

A mutual recognition procedure exists in Europe between EU member states. If the jurisdiction in question is a member state of the European Union (such as Belgium), the mutual recognition procedure can be applied. Additionally, for generic and biosimilar products, simplified and abridged licence procedures exist in case the reference product is already registered within the European Community.

A specific licence procedure exists for parallel imports and parallel distribution of medicines for human use. Such parallel imports are in line with the European principle of free circulation of goods and are applicable in all member states. The European legislation does not require that the composition of the imported medicine must be identical to the medicine that is acting as the reference point. However, the qualitative and quantitative composition in terms of active substance must be the same and the imported medicine must have the same therapeutic effect as the reference medicine. The procedure is laid down in the Royal Decree of 19 April 2001.

### 5. IS VIRTUAL DRUG DISTRIBUTION POSSIBLE FROM YOUR JURISDICTION?

In principle virtual drug distribution is possible if:

- The other country accepts the evaluation of Belgium as a reference member state (RMS) in a mutual recognition programme.
- The procedural export requirements are met.
- The necessary certificates regarding the patient information leaflet (PIL) and summary of product characteristics (SPC) are obtained from the Federal Agency for Medicines and Health Products (FAMHP).

Virtual distribution would also be possible in the case of distance sales.

### 6. WHAT IS THE PROCEDURE TO APPEAL (LEGAL REMEDY) A LICENSING DECISION?

A Belgian licensing decision can be appealed, at Belgian level, to the Council of State or to a civil court.

### 7. WHAT ARE THE COSTS OF OBTAINING LICENSING?

The following fees (as of 2015) are applicable for the following types of applications for registration (whether through the national, mutual recognition or decentralised procedures):

- Complete application for a known active substance(s): EUR6,098.55 for a marketing authorisation document (MAD).
- Generic application and/or bibliographic application: EUR4,875.30 for a MAD.
- Complete application for a new active substance: EUR9,141.20 for a MAD.
- Traditional herbal medicinal products: EUR3,047.07 for a MAD.
- Allergens: EUR1,523.54 for a MAD.
- Orphan medicinal product: EUR4,570.59 for a MAD.

If Belgium is acting as the reference member state (RMS), all the fees above are doubled.

## DISTRIBUTION TO CONSUMERS

### 8. WHAT ARE THE DIFFERENT CATEGORIES OF DRUGS FOR DISTRIBUTION?

In terms of distribution, the main categories of drugs are prescription drugs and over-the-counter (OTC) drugs. These categories of drugs can be further divided in sub-categories.

Other more specific categories, such as orphan drugs, exist.

### 9. WHO IS AUTHORISED TO DISTRIBUTE PRESCRIPTION DRUGS AND OVER-THE-COUNTER DRUGS TO CONSUMERS?

**Prescription drugs and over-the-counter drugs.**

The distribution of prescription and OTC drugs to consumers is limited to pharmacists. However, a physician (or the dentist) can deliver a drug to his/her patients, in certain circumstances. For example, over-the-counter (OTC) drug samples can also be distributed by a doctor to his or her patients, but only free of charge. Specific provisions also exist for the distribution of medicines in hospitals.

A pharmacy open to the general public can only exist if it has been authorised by the Minister responsible for public health. The pharmacy is subject to regulations, which for example cover:

- The different conditions for keeping and delivering medicines for human use.
- The working of magistral and officinal preparations (especially narcotic and psychotropic drugs).
- The keeping of registers and relevant documentation.

A pharmacy must be managed by at least one registered pharmacist who meets all legal requirements.

## 10. WHAT DRUGS CAN AN ATTENDING PHYSICIAN DISTRIBUTE AND UNDER WHAT CIRCUMSTANCES?

A physician can only distribute drugs in specific circumstances (such as in emergencies, for compassionate use or for the treatment of venereal diseases) as set out by Royal Decree No.78 of 10 November 1967.

## 11. WHO IS AUTHORISED TO PRESCRIBE PRESCRIPTION DRUGS TO CONSUMERS?

Physicians and dentists are authorised to prescribe prescription drugs to consumers.

## 12. IS DIRECT MAILING/DISTANCE SELLING OF DRUGS PERMITTED IN YOUR JURISDICTION?

The Royal Decree of 21 January 2009 (concerning instructions for pharmacists) only allows public pharmacies in Belgium to sell online, under very strict conditions, medicinal products for human use which are not subject to medical prescription, and some medical devices.

Pharmacists who include on the website of their pharmacy a system for the online sale of medicinal products or medical devices have to notify the Federal Agency for Medicines and Health Products (FAMHP) and the College of Pharmacists of the existence of their website within one month of this system being provided for, whether or not this concurs with the launch of the website itself. Further modifications to the notified website or the deletion of it have to be notified as well. A standard form for this notification can be found on the website of the FAMHP.

Provisions are also included to ensure that the offer for sale, ordering, packaging and delivering are organised in accordance with the legislation for the protection of patient privacy. The website must also be designed to encourage the rational use of medicinal products and medical devices, and must therefore contain an adequate amount of information to ensure their proper use. This information must include the information contained in the package leaflet for all medicinal products for human use which are offered for sale on the site.

## 13. WHAT REGULATORY AUTHORITY IS RESPONSIBLE FOR SUPERVISING DISTRIBUTION ACTIVITIES?

The regulatory authorities responsible for supervising distribution activities are the Federal Agency for Medicines and Health Products (FAMHP) and the Order of Pharmacists (which has the legal obligation to supervise the pharmacists).

## 14. WHAT IS THE PROCEDURE TO APPEAL (LEGAL REMEDY) A DISTRIBUTION DECISION?

The decisions of the Federal Agency for Medicines and Health Products (FAMPH) or the Minister of Health can be appealed before the Council of State and/or the civil courts. The criminal procedure will be conducted in court, with all available criminal legal remedies.

## 15. WHAT ARE THE LEGAL CONSEQUENCES OF NON-COMPLIANCE WITH CONSUMER DISTRIBUTION LAWS?

Some general provisions of the Belgian penal code can be applicable in some cases, together with the specific non-compliance provisions as laid down in the Royal Decree No.78 of 10 November 1967.

Distribution of medicinal products to consumers by non-authorised persons is subject to criminal prosecution. Any interested person or civil servant who identifies an illegal distribution, in the framework of his or her activities, is entitled to disclose any infringement to the police or the prosecutor.

### WHOLESALE DISTRIBUTION

## 16. WHAT IS THE LEGAL REGIME REGARDING WHOLESALE DISTRIBUTION OF DRUGS?

Only authorised individuals or companies can distribute medicines for human use through wholesale.

The wholesale dealers' authorisation is granted by the Federal Agency for Medicines and Health Products (FAMHP) on request. This is only if the applicant meets some basic requirements, such as having appropriate premises and personnel to ensure safe storage and distribution of the products and ensuring adequate control of the distributed drugs.

If the wholesale dealer is also the manufacturer, additional requirements, such as having an authorised licensed pharmacist, also apply.

The wholesale of drugs can only be made to people who are authorised to distribute those products to other wholesalers, pharmacists or, in the few permitted instances, physicians authorised to keep and distribute some medicinal products.

## 17. WHAT REGULATORY AUTHORITY IS RESPONSIBLE FOR SUPERVISING WHOLESALE DISTRIBUTION ACTIVITIES?

The regulatory authority responsible for supervising wholesale distribution is the Federal Agency for Medicines and Health Products (FAMHP), under the supervision of the Federal Minister of Health. Recourse against decisions of the Minister or FAMHP is possible in civil and administrative courts (the Council of State).

## 18. WHAT ARE THE LEGAL CONSEQUENCES OF NON-COMPLIANCE WITH WHOLESALE DISTRIBUTION LAWS?

The authorisation can be suspended or withdrawn if there is non-compliance with wholesale distribution laws. Some general provisions of the Belgian penal code are also applicable in some cases.

# MARKETING

## PROMOTION

### 19. WHAT IS THE GENERAL LEGAL REGIME FOR THE MARKETING OF DRUGS?

The general legal regime for the marketing and advertising of drugs for human use is laid down in the Law of 25 March 1964 on medicinal products and in the Royal Decree of 7 April 1995.

Advertising and promotion of medicinal products is prohibited for any medicinal product for which a marketing authorisation has not been granted. Advertising for medicinal products for human use is, beside the general rules about advertising, also subject to specific legislation whose objective is the rational use of medicines, on the basis of accurate and complete information. Belgian courts have a wide interpretation of what might constitute advertising.

General provisions also regulate the content of advertising for medicinal products and limit the means of dissemination. Some provisions are specific for advertising to the public or for advertising to health professionals.

### 20. ARE THERE OTHER CODES OF CONDUCT FOR THE MARKETING OF DRUGS (FOR EXAMPLE, BY PROFESSIONAL OR INDUSTRIAL ORGANISATIONS)?

Industry associations have adopted codes of conduct, which are available on the websites of these associations (for example, the Pharma code of ethics, the FeBelGen code of ethics). A legal code of conduct has also been developed by Mdeon, which is a common ethical platform constituted of associations of physicians, pharmacists, veterinarians, dentists, nurses, paramedics, physiotherapists, hospital technicians and others from the pharmaceutical and medical devices industry.

Physicians, dentists and pharmacists are also bound by their codes of conduct. Those codes of conduct are not legally binding per se. However, they can result in disciplinary sanctions. Additionally, since those codes are inspired by the legal regime that is applicable to those professionals, infringement of those codes can also be an infringement of the legal requirements.

## MARKETING TO CONSUMERS

### 21. WHAT IS THE LEGAL REGIME FOR MARKETING TO CONSUMERS?

The legal regime for the marketing and advertising of drugs for human use is laid down in the Royal Decree of 7 April 1995, relating to information and advertising concerning medicines for human use.

Different rules apply for the advertising of medicinal products which require a prescription and/or which are reimbursed. Only medicinal products which have a valid marketing authorisation in Belgium can be the subject of advertising. Only those products which are available without prescription (OTC products) can be advertised to consumers.

The advertising must be consistent with information that has been given and approved of under the authorisation of the medicinal product on the market.

## BELGIUM

### 22. WHAT KINDS OF MARKETING ACTIVITIES ARE PERMITTED IN RELATION TO CONSUMERS AND THE PRODUCTS WHICH MAY BE ADVERTISED TO THEM?

The advertising must encourage the rational use of the medicinal product by presenting it objectively and without exaggerating its properties. It should also be clear that the product is a medicinal product. Any advertising of drugs to the general public must bear the notice "this is a medicinal product, not for prolonged use without a medical opinion". It cannot be misleading. Advertising must contain a number of mandatory elements essential for proper use of the medicinal product. These mandatory elements must be legible.

In addition, this advertising should not, for example:

- Present a medicinal or surgical intervention as useless.
- Suggest that the effect of the drug is certain and has no side effects.
- Suggest that the overall health of the consumer would be improved by the use of that product or could be affected if not using the product.
- Refer to the testimonies of scientists, professionals or other well-known people who could influence people to use the product.

Advertising broadcasts on radio or television must obtain prior approval granted by the Minister of Public Health, upon notice from the Commission for the control of medicinal product advertising. Advertising broadcasts on other media must be notified to the Federal Agency for Medicines and Health Products (FAMHP) at least 30 days before publication.

However, specific exceptions apply for nicotine-based medicines against dependence on smoking (for which advertising on public roads is authorised).

For traditional herbal medicinal products, the advertising must also mention the notice "traditional herbal medicinal product for use in specified indication(s) exclusively based upon long-standing use".

Some media cannot be used, such as signs on the motorway (except for nicotine-based medicines against dependence on smoking), telephone, direct mail, electronic mail, objects of any kind to be used, partially or totally, for any purpose other than to communicate information.

### 23. IS IT PERMITTED TO PROVIDE CONSUMERS WITH FREE SAMPLES? ARE THERE PARTICULAR RESTRICTIONS ON SPECIAL OFFERS (FOR EXAMPLE, "BUY-ONE-GET-ONE-FREE")?

A physician can provide his or her patient with free samples legally received from the industry.

No individual special offers can be made by pharmacists, although consumers can get rebates directly through the pharmacist on groups of products.

### 24. ARE THERE PARTICULAR RULES OF PRACTICE ON THE USE OF THE INTERNET/SOCIAL MEDIA REGARDING DRUGS AND THEIR ADVERTISING?

Except for nicotine-based medicines used for dependence on smoking, advertising through the internet, by e-mail or social media is prohibited in Belgium.

## 25. WHAT REGULATORY AUTHORITY IS RESPONSIBLE FOR SUPERVISING MARKETING ACTIVITIES TO CONSUMERS?

Marketing to consumers is supervised by the Federal Agency for Medicines and Health Products (FAMHP), the Federal Minister of Public Health and the commission for the control of medicinal product advertising.

A "contact point" has been created within the FAMHP to centralise and receive information about any possible infringement to the regulation on marketing for medicinal products. This contact point is a key player in the entire control activity of the FAMHP.

## 26. WHAT ARE THE LEGAL CONSEQUENCES OF NON-COMPLIANCE WITH CONSUMER MARKETING LAWS?

Non-compliant advertising can be withdrawn without prior notice. Moreover, infringement of the advertising regulation is subject to criminal prosecution. Disciplinary sanctions can also be applied if the advertiser is bound by a code of conduct specific to his or her profession.

The Federal Agency for Medicines and Health Products (FAMHP) can:

- Give warnings.
- Help the offender to fix delays to become compliant.
- Write reports leading to either administrative fines or to be passed on to the judicial authorities.

The Minister of Public Health, or his representative, can:

- Order the discontinuation of an illicit advertising or information campaign.
- Forbid the dissemination of the campaign.
- Require the publication of the decision banning the advertising information campaign or require the publication of a rectification.

If there are concerns about an advertising or information campaign spread on the television or the radio, the Minister or his representative takes these measures following the advice of the Commission of Control of Advertising of Medicinal Products. In case of an illicit advertising or information campaign on the television or radio, the Minister can withdraw his or her approval following the advice of the Commission of Control of Advertising of Medicinal Products. In the case of an emergency, the Minister can suspend the visa for three months without prior consultation with the Commission of Control of Advertising of Medicinal Products.

Any interested person can act in court in order to obtain an injunction to stop the prohibited advertising.

### MARKETING TO PROFESSIONALS

## 27. WHAT KINDS OF MARKETING ACTIVITIES ARE PERMITTED IN RELATION TO PROFESSIONALS?

The legal regime concerning the marketing and advertising of drugs for human use is laid down in the Royal Decree of 7 April 1995 relating to information and advertising concerning medicines for human use. The general provisions of this decree concerning any advertising for medicinal products are also applicable to the advertising intended for healthcare professionals.

In principle, marketing activities are permitted but must conform to the summary of product characteristics (SPC) and to the elements of the case accepted with the marketing authorisation.

If the advertising is written, it must include, on at least half of its surface area, some scientific information extracted from the SPC.

Guidelines on "Advertising intended for healthcare professionals" are available on the website of the Federal Agency for Medicines and Health Products (FAMHP).

Advertising intended for nurses must respect the provisions concerning the advertising intended for the general public, though the provisions regarding premiums and advantages in Article 10 of the Law of 25 March 1964 on medicinal products are applicable to them.

Medical delegates promoting the drugs must be properly trained so as to have sufficient scientific knowledge to give the correct and as full as possible information about the medicinal products that they promote.

## 28. ARE THERE ANY RESTRICTIONS ON MARKETING TO PROFESSIONALS?

**Marketing activities**

Advertising by fax, e-mail and mailing is authorised only if requested by the addressee. E-mail concerning patients' data cannot include advertising for medicinal products.

Advertising in software processing patient's medical files is forbidden. Scientific studies and information by audio-visual or electronic means, without the intention of promoting the sale or prescription of medicinal products, cannot include advertising for medicinal products. Advertising in prescription books, folders, publications and software is authorised. Quotations and tables from medical journals or books should be exactly reproduced and the source mentioned.

All sponsoring activities, including training or information meetings, will be subject to prior visas and specific rules, in order to prevent any kind of inducement or bribery.

Further information can be found on the website of Mdeon and in Mdeon brochures (Mdeon is an industry association comprising of associations of physicians, pharmacists, veterinarians, dentists, nurses, paramedics, physiotherapists, hospital technicians and others from the pharmaceutical and medical devices industry).

## 29. WHAT INFORMATION IS IT LEGALLY REQUIRED TO INCLUDE IN ADVERTISING TO PROFESSIONALS?

Apart from the form the advertising must take (written), the following information must be included:

- The status of delivery of the medicinal product.
- The public selling price of each package.
- The date of creation or of the last revision of the advertising.
- The details of the "essential information" that must appear:
  - the name of the medicinal product;
  - the qualitative and quantitative composition in active substances;
  - the pharmaceutical form;

- section indications of the summary of product characteristics (SPC);
- section posology of the SPC;
- section contraindications of the SPC;
- section undesirable effects of the SPC;
- the patient information leaflet (PIL)/labelling if it is a homeopathic medicinal product;
- the name of the marketing authorisation (MA) holder; and
- the MA/registration number.

If reference is made to elements of a study which are approved in the scope of the MA/registration, it either concerns a study which appears in the MA/registration file or it concerns a study which does not appear in the MA/registration file, but which has been realised in accordance with the data contained in the approved SPC, and confirms data already approved. In this case, the study has been published in a peer review magazine. The original text of the publication or study must be provided to the professional who has requested it.

## 30. ARE THERE RULES ON COMPARISONS WITH OTHER PRODUCTS THAT ARE PARTICULARLY APPLICABLE TO DRUGS?

There are no rules on comparisons with other products that are particularly applicable to drugs.

## 31. WHAT OTHER ITEMS, FUNDING OR SERVICES ARE PERMITTED TO BE PROVIDED TO PROFESSIONALS?

Any inducement to prescribers must be avoided as prohibited bribery. Article 10 of the Law of 25 March 1964 on Medicinal Products includes a general prohibition on offering or granting advantages or benefits of any kind or even of a pecuniary nature to healthcare professionals, either directly or indirectly, in the context of prescribing, issuing and supplying medicinal products.

**Discounts**

It is forbidden when prescribing, providing, supplying or administering medicinal products, to promise, offer or grant, directly or indirectly, premiums or monetary advantages or benefits in kind to persons qualified to prescribe, dispense or administer medicinal products and to the institutions in which the prescribing, dispensing or administering of medicinal products take place.

**Free samples**

The regulation of free samples is laid down in the Royal Decree of 11 January 1993 establishing the conditions under which the delivery of medicinal products for human use as samples can be performed.

The delivery of free medicinal product samples by pharmaceutical companies, which is also a form of advertising, is regulated. The person responsible for the marketing of a medicinal product can provide samples, exceptionally, only to persons authorised to prescribe medicinal products and on their demand.

The maximum number of samples that can be awarded is limited to eight per medicinal product, per calendar year and per person authorised to prescribe medicinal products.

The person responsible for placing the drugs on the market must have an adequate system for controlling the distribution of samples, under the responsibility of the person responsible for pharmaceutical information.

**Sponsorship of professionals**

Sponsorship of professionals is not allowed. Other than indirect incentives (*see Other direct incentives*), it is forbidden when prescribing, providing, supplying or administering medicinal products, to promise, offer or grant, directly or indirectly, premiums or monetary advantages or benefits in kind to persons qualified to prescribe, dispense or administer medicinal products and to the institutions in which the prescribing, dispensing or administering of medicinal products take place.

**Other items, funding or services**

Certain premiums and advantages are allowed, as long as a number of conditions, which are set out in the law are strictly adhered to. This is the case, for example, for compensation for legitimate services of a scientific nature or the invitation and support costs related to participation in certain events for purely scientific purposes. In this situation, the regulations provide that prior to any scientific event comprising at least one night, it is mandatory to obtain a visa from Mdeon (an industry association constituted of associations of physicians, pharmacists, veterinarians, dentists, nurses, paramedics, physiotherapists, hospital technicians and others from the pharmaceutical and medical devices industry).

## 32. WHAT REGULATORY AUTHORITY IS RESPONSIBLE FOR SUPERVISING MARKETING ACTIVITIES REGARDING PROFESSIONALS?

The Law on Medicinal products provides a penal co-responsibility between the companies which provide sponsorship and the (associations of) healthcare professionals who are the beneficiaries. Internal control inside the company by the person responsible for information concerning all advertising and information campaigns spread by the company and concerning the supply of sample usually exists.

The Federal Agency for Medicines and Health Products (FAMHP) is the only competent authority to do *a posteriori* controls as to the observance of the application procedure.

The industry association, Mdeon's, tasks are limited to investigating the dossiers for sponsorship, without examining the content and accuracy of the application. Mdeon provides prior authorisation for the sponsoring of both the attendees of scientific events and the organisers of those events. This organisation can also provide some advice on marketing tools and the organisation of events. Organising such events without that prior authorisation is forbidden under Article 10 of the Medicinal Products Act.

## 33. WHAT ARE THE LEGAL CONSEQUENCES IN CASE OF NON-COMPLIANCE WITH PROFESSIONAL MARKETING LAWS?

The Federal Agency for Medicines and Health Products (FAMHP) can give warnings, fix delays to the offender to be compliant, write reports leading to either administrative fines or to be passed on to the judicial authorities.

The Minister or his representative can:

- Order the discontinuation of an illicit advertising or information campaign;

- Forbid the campaign's dissemination.
- Require the publication of the decision banning the advertising information campaign or require the publication of a rectification.

If it is concerning an advertising or information campaign on the TV or radio, the Minister or his representative takes these measures following the advice of the Commission of Control of Advertising of Medicinal Products. In the case of an illegal advertising or information campaign on the TV or radio, the Minister can withdraw the visa following the advice of the Commission of Control of Advertising of Medicinal Products. In the case of an emergency, the Minister can suspend the visa for three months without prior consultation with the Commission of Control of Advertising of Medicinal Products.

In the case of sponsorship, the law provides sanctions (that is, fines and imprisonment of up to one year) for the sponsoring company as well as for the healthcare professional who receives the sponsorship.

## ENGAGEMENT WITH PATIENT ORGANISATIONS

**34. WHAT KINDS OF ACTIVITIES ARE PERMITTED IN RELATION TO ENGAGEMENT WITH PATIENT ORGANISATIONS? WHAT ARE THE RESTRICTIONS THAT ARE IMPOSED ON RELATIONSHIP WITH PATIENT ORGANISATIONS?**

No specific legal restriction exists in relation to engagement with patient organisations. However, codes of conduct adopted by the pharmaceutical industry usually include specific provisions in this regard.

## REFORM

**35. ARE THERE ANY PLANS TO REFORM THE LAW ON THE DISTRIBUTION AND PROMOTION OF DRUGS IN YOUR JURISDICTION?**

There are no plans for reform.

# BRAZIL

*Lívia Figueiredo and João Luis Vianna, KASZNAR LEONARDOS*

## DISTRIBUTION

### PRE-CONDITIONS FOR DISTRIBUTION

**1. WHAT ARE THE LEGAL PRE-CONDITIONS FOR A DRUG TO BE DISTRIBUTED WITHIN THE JURISDICTION?**

#### Authorisation

The distribution of medicinal products is regulated by the National Sanitary Surveillance Agency (ANVISA).

Pharmaceutical products can be marketed and distributed if the following requirements are met:

- They are registered with ANVISA.
- They are manufactured or imported by establishments duly authorised by the federal government.
- They are manufactured or imported by establishments duly licensed by the state government.

To receive approval to launch and distribute drugs on the market, the applicants must submit to ANVISA regulatory data of the potential candidate, such as details of the manufacturing process, clinical trial results, safety and efficacy data. If all data is in accordance with the requirements established by ANVISA, marketing authorisation is eventually granted, therefore formally allowing the medicinal products to enter the market.

#### Exceptions

Exceptions to the requirement for a marketing authorisation exist, for example, if the new drug is intended to be exclusively used in a clinical trial or if it is required to meet the prescription for a specific patient. In these cases, it can be supplied and imported in Brazil without being previously approved, if the importation is formally authorised by ANVISA.

**2. DO ANY TYPES OF NAMED PATIENT AND/OR COMPASSIONATE USE PROGRAMMES OPERATE? IF SO, WHAT ARE THE REQUIREMENTS FOR PRE-LAUNCH ACCESS?**

The National Sanitary Surveillance Agency's (ANVISA) RDC No. 38 of 13 August 2013 sets out several pathways through which patient access to new drugs is provided before these drugs are officially approved and available for purchase.

In the compassionate use programme, ANVISA provides authorisation, under a public welfare programme, by promising access to a new drug without agency registration for the treatment of patients with serious or rare diseases. These specific pathways comprehend the possibility of importing new, unregistered drugs, if needed.

According to ANVISA, the authorisation approval for the compassionate use is evaluated, depending on the severity of the illness. The absence of satisfactory treatment alternatives available for the patient's condition is assessed before issuing an authorisation. The patient's doctor must submit a formal request to obtain the drug from the entity funding the assistance programme and the entity places a corresponding request with ANVISA.

The entity funding the treatment provides for the complete treatment and medication at no cost for the patient under the expanded access, compassionate use or post-study programmes (*chapter VIII, section 18, RDC No. 38/2013*).

## LICENSING

### 3. WHAT IS THE PROCEDURAL STRUCTURE REGARDING LICENSING A DRUG FOR DISTRIBUTION?

**Structure**

Licensing of a drug is mandatory before its widespread use.

Licences are only granted if predefined standards of safety and quality are met, covering the whole development and manufacturing process of a drug.

To be granted a licence, the drug must be developed and tested.

**Regulatory authority**

The health surveillance over products and services is conducted by the National Sanitary Surveillance Agency (ANVISA), which covers the supervision of processes, used ingredients and applied technologies (*Law No. 9782, 26 January 1999*).

According to Law No. 9782/1999, ANVISA is the only authority responsible for granting licences for medicinal drugs and other health-related products.

### 4. IS THERE A SIMPLIFIED LICENCE PROCEEDING, OR RELAXED LICENSING CONDITIONS, FOR DRUGS WHICH HAVE ALREADY BEEN LICENSED FOR DISTRIBUTION IN ANOTHER JURISDICTION?

When dealing with a drug with a foreign licence, marketing authorisation from the National Sanitary Surveillance Agency (ANVISA) is still required.

With imported drugs and active pharmaceutical ingredients, in addition to the usual registration requirements, the applicant must also show evidence proving that the product is already registered in the country of origin (*Article 18, Law No. 6360, September 23, 1976*) and further complies with the good manufacturing practices (GMP) standards in that country.

Regarding parallel imports, a product manufactured in accordance with a process or a product patent that has not been placed on the internal market directly by the patentee or with his consent can represent a violation of the patent holder's exclusive rights, therefore allowing the patent holder to enforce its exclusive rights (*section 43, item IV, Brazilian Industrial Property Law*). Whether implicit consent can avoid the parallel importer's liability for patent infringement is always a hot topic before the courts, so all situations must be examined on a case-by-case basis and bear in mind their own particularities.

### 5. IS VIRTUAL DRUG DISTRIBUTION POSSIBLE FROM YOUR JURISDICTION?

The sale of drugs through the internet can only be undertaken by accessing websites from pharmacies and drugstores with fixed commercial establishments, which are open to the public.

The services provider must also provide for a direct and immediate method of communication between the patient and a pharmacist.

Drugs subject to special control (*Ordinance No. 344, 12 May 1998*) cannot be sold on the internet.

Brazil-based pharmacies can attend online orders with some restrictions. According to the law, only licensed Brazilian pharmacies can sell prescription drugs online. An internet pharmacy must post its National Sanitary Surveillance Agency's (ANVISA) authorisation number on its website. Personal importation of medicine is legal where the patient has a valid prescription and where the frequency and quantities are clearly limited in the prescription signed by the medical doctor.

### 6. WHAT IS THE PROCEDURE TO APPEAL (LEGAL REMEDY) A LICENSING DECISION?

It is possible to proceed with an administrative appeal from rejections on the granting of the licensing for a drug within ten days starting from the day immediately after the publication of the rejecting decision.

The appeal is filed before National Sanitary Surveillance Agency (ANVISA) and this authority does not have to provide its decision within a prescribed term.

It is not possible to appeal from the final decision, issued by ANVISA after analysis of the technical appeal.

### 7. WHAT ARE THE COSTS OF OBTAINING LICENSING?

There are fees to be paid to the National Sanitary Surveillance Agency (ANVISA) to obtain the marketing authorisations. These fees vary depending on the type of product and on the size of the applicant (*Annex I, Resolution No. 222, 28 December 2006*).

For example, considering a large company as the applicant, the costs can vary from R$6,000 (generic drug) to R$80,000 (new drug).

## DISTRIBUTION TO CONSUMERS

### 8. WHAT ARE THE DIFFERENT CATEGORIES OF DRUGS FOR DISTRIBUTION?

For distribution to consumers, medicinal drugs can be classified into the following categories:

- Drugs that can only be dispensed under a medical prescription (with retention).
- Drugs that can only be dispensed under a medical prescription (without retention).

- Drugs that can be sold without a prescription, known as "non-prescription products" or "over-the-counter drugs" (OTCs), which present a remote risk of causing side effects to patients.
- Drugs exclusively used in hospitals.
- Drugs subjected to special control, where the medical prescription must be notified to the health authority.

In considering whether a drug can be sold without the need for a prescription, the National Sanitary Surveillance Agency (ANVISA) takes into account, among other issues, whether the product is likely to, if incorrectly used:

- Present a substantial risk to the patient.
- Lead to addiction.
- Be used for illegal purposes.

## 9. WHO IS AUTHORISED TO DISTRIBUTE PRESCRIPTION DRUGS AND OVER-THE-COUNTER DRUGS TO CONSUMERS?

### Prescription drugs

Prescription drugs are sold in licensed pharmacies, under medical prescription. This licence is obtained from the National Sanitary Surveillance Agency (ANVISA).

Pharmacist technicians can perform activities that are not exclusive to pharmacists, including dispensing or selling prescription medicines (*ANVISA's Resolution No. 44, 17 August 2009*). However, the pharmacist technicians must be under direct supervision of the registered pharmacist technically responsible (or a substitute, also a pharmacist), whose presence is required during working hours of the commercial establishment. The sale of prescription medicines can only be made on the presentation of a prescription, issued by a registered physician.

### Over-the-counter drugs

Over-the-counter drugs are sold freely in licensed pharmacies, drugstores and some large supermarkets, without the need of a medical prescription.

## 10. WHAT DRUGS CAN AN ATTENDING PHYSICIAN DISTRIBUTE AND UNDER WHAT CIRCUMSTANCES?

Physicians can distribute free samples of marketed drugs to any patient, provided that it follows the medical prescription.

## 11. WHO IS AUTHORISED TO PRESCRIBE PRESCRIPTION DRUGS TO CONSUMERS?

Only physicians (medical doctors), dentists (for dental use only), veterinarians (for veterinary use only) and nurses (for medicines established by public health programmes and approved by the health institution) can prescribe drugs.

## 12. IS DIRECT MAILING/DISTANCE SELLING OF DRUGS PERMITTED IN YOUR JURISDICTION?

Resolution No. 96/2008, dealing with advertising and promotion of drugs, does not expressly mention the possibility of using e-mails as a way to buy or sell drugs.

There are also no particular rules referring to marketing medicinal products by mail order. However, provided all requirements for the acquisition of a particular drug on the internet are met, this may be a possibility (*see Question 5*).

## 13. WHAT REGULATORY AUTHORITY IS RESPONSIBLE FOR SUPERVISING DISTRIBUTION ACTIVITIES?

The regulation of the sector that distributes medicines is conducted on three levels:

- The federal government.
- The state governments.
- Municipalities.

The federal government enacts laws and regulations of general applicability, which are enforced and complemented by actions of the state governments and municipalities. At the federal level, the health and pharmaceuticals sectors are regulated and supervised by the Ministry of Health, through the National Sanitary Surveillance Agency (ANVISA).

## 14. WHAT IS THE PROCEDURE TO APPEAL (LEGAL REMEDY) A DISTRIBUTION DECISION?

The National Sanitary Surveillance Agency (ANVISA) can suspend the distribution, sale and use of a drug if the proprietor entity does not meet the requirements of the agency. In this case, eventually, a final decision is published in the *Official Gazette* and all the remaining lots have to be collected. The company can appeal from the initial ban (notification from ANVISA) within ten or 15 days, depending on the case. If the sentence is maintained, it can be appealed at the government level within 20 days counted from the date the decision was acknowledged or from the publication. All legal deadlines are set out in Law No. 6437/1977.

## 15. WHAT ARE THE LEGAL CONSEQUENCES OF NON-COMPLIANCE WITH CONSUMER DISTRIBUTION LAWS?

The consequences of non-compliance with consumer distribution laws include:

- Suspension of the authorisation to distribute.
- Suspension of the product registration licence.
- Fines.
- Imprisonment.

### WHOLESALE DISTRIBUTION

## 16. WHAT IS THE LEGAL REGIME REGARDING WHOLESALE DISTRIBUTION OF DRUGS?

Distributors of pharmaceuticals must comply with the regulations (Good Distribution Practices) and hold the appropriate licences. Such distributors must obtain a:

- Licence to operate.
- Authorisation to operate.
- Special authorisation for medicines under special control, if necessary.

It is necessary to pay to obtain these licences and to present a certificate of the technical responsibility of the responsible pharmacist. It is also necessary to undergo an inspection carried out by the local health authority. These distributors must obtain a document called "Certificate of Good Distribution Practices", which is issued by the National Sanitary Surveillance Agency (ANVISA) to operate legally. This certificate is a statement confirming that the distributor is in conformity with all the good practices established and allows the distributor to operate.

## 17. WHAT REGULATORY AUTHORITY IS RESPONSIBLE FOR SUPERVISING WHOLESALE DISTRIBUTION ACTIVITIES?

### Regulatory authority

The distribution and promotion of medicinal products by the wholesale distributors are subject to the legal regulation of the National Sanitary Surveillance Agency (ANVISA).

### Supervision

ANVISA can issue legal provisions on human health issues (*Article 24, section XII, Brazilian Constitution* and *Article 7, Law No. 9.782/1999*). These enable the ANVISA to:

- Proceed with the surveillance and regulation of medicines and medical goods.
- Supervise the corresponding entities that manufacture and distribute them.
- Provide the registration of medicinal products.

Companies that apply for permission to distribute drugs must comply with the requirements of Good Distribution Practice and Storage established by ANVISA. As per this regulation, the distributor must comply with certain procedures to control the quality and keep track of the medicinal products distributed.

### Rights of appeal

The same procedure of appealing a distribution decision applies for wholesale distribution activities (*see Question 14*).

## 18. WHAT ARE THE LEGAL CONSEQUENCES OF NON-COMPLIANCE WITH WHOLESALE DISTRIBUTION LAWS?

The consequences of non-compliance with wholesale distribution laws include penalties such as:

- Fines.
- Suspension of the Good Distribution Practices.
- Suspension of the authorisation to operate.

# MARKETING

## PROMOTION

### 19. WHAT IS THE GENERAL LEGAL REGIME FOR THE MARKETING OF DRUGS?

**Legal regime**

The main applicable legal instruments for marketing, advertising and promotion of medicinal products are:

- Law No. 6360 of 23 September 1976 (amended by Law No. 13,097 of 2015) that regulates the Sanitary Surveillance and describes general rules for the advertisement of drugs, medical products and other health-related products.
- Decree No. 79074 of 5 January 1977 (amended by Decree No. 8,077 of 2013), which regulates Law No. 6360/1976 that provides further provisions concerning the advertisement of medicinal products.
- Law No. 9294 of 15 July 1996 that regulates the advertisement of drugs.
- Decree No. 2018 of 1 October 1996, which regulates Law No. 9294/1996.
- Law No. 6437 of 20 August 1977 that defines violations of the federal health law and imposes the respective sanctions.
- Resolution RDC No. 96 of 17 December 2008 (amended by RDC 023/2009) that regulates the advertising and promotional practices of prescription drugs and OTCs.
- Normative Ruling No. 5, of 20 May 2009 that provides further clarifications concerning Resolution RDC No. 96/2008.
- Resolution RDC No. 60 of 26 November 2009 that regulates free samples.
- Ordinance No. 344 of 12 May 1998 that imposes specific restrictions on the advertising or promotion of medicinal products containing substances under special control such as anorexigenic drugs, immunosuppressant drugs and others.
- Law No. 8078 of 11 September 1990 (Consumer Protection Code) (CDC) that contains general provisions for the advertisement of products in general.

**Limits to marketing activities**

To market medicines, the entities must have been granted the necessary authorisations by the sanitary authorities.

Besides the general prohibition on direct marketing of medical products under prescription, the legislation aims to keep the relationship between industry and healthcare professionals or medical institutions, transparent and fully documented.

Another principle regarding the promotion of medicinal products is that the advertisement of drugs cannot differ or exceed the information provided in the dossier of register submitted to the National Sanitary Surveillance Agency (ANVISA).

## 20. ARE THERE OTHER CODES OF CONDUCT FOR THE MARKETING OF DRUGS (FOR EXAMPLE, BY PROFESSIONAL OR INDUSTRIAL ORGANISATIONS)?

The Advertising Self-Regulation Code, enforced by the Advertising Self-Regulation Council (CONAR) and adopted in 1978 regulates ethical rules related to advertisements as well as defining rules to over-the-counter drugs (OTCs). CONAR's objective is to eliminate misleading advertisements and campaigns that may be offensive or abusive in content, or could, among other things, distort competition.

There is also the Codes of Conduct of Class Associations such as the Association of Research Based Pharmaceutical Industries (INTERFARMA).

Finally there are the Resolutions of the Federal Council of Medicine:

- 1931/2009 that is the Medical Profession Code of Ethics.
- 1939/2010 that prohibits participation of doctors in medicinal products campaigns.
- 1974/2011 that sets out the criteria for the participation of members of the medical profession in promotion and advertising.

The National Sanitary Surveillance Agency's (ANVISA) regulation on advertising drugs is not related to any self-regulatory bodies like CONAR or INTERFARMA, whose decisions are not made public. ANVISA investigates only matters that cannot be compliant with the law and its regulations but can use the decisions of any such self-regulatory body to support their decision.

## MARKETING TO CONSUMERS

## 21. WHAT IS THE LEGAL REGIME FOR MARKETING TO CONSUMERS?

**Legal regime**

Generally, advertising is a non-regulated area, subject to the self-regulatory body, the Advertising Self-Regulation Council (CONAR). The limitations on advertisement to consumers are regulated by RDC No. 96/2008. Law No. 6360/1976 establishes that marketing of medicinal products is subject to authorisation by the Ministry of Health.

**Products**

Only over-the-counter drugs (OTCs) can be directly advertised to end consumers in all types of media (*Law No. 9294/1996*). This law limits advertising prescription drugs to healthcare professionals.

## 22. WHAT KINDS OF MARKETING ACTIVITIES ARE PERMITTED IN RELATION TO CONSUMERS AND THE PRODUCTS WHICH MAY BE ADVERTISED TO THEM?

Law No. 6360/1976 limits the advertising and marketing of prescribed medicines to medical professionals and prohibits such activities in relation to consumers.

To avoid self-medication and the indiscriminate use of drugs, there are several provisions regulating the advertisement of over-the-counter drugs (OTCs).

Although it is not possible to advertise prescription drugs to the public, disease awareness campaigns are allowed. However, it is prohibited to mention any medicinal product.

It is possible to issue press releases concerning prescription products in non-scientific journals. In this case, the release cannot be "advertising" in its nature.

It is also possible to describe products and research initiatives in corporate brochures or annual reports.

## 23. IS IT PERMITTED TO PROVIDE CONSUMERS WITH FREE SAMPLES? ARE THERE PARTICULAR RESTRICTIONS ON SPECIAL OFFERS (FOR EXAMPLE, "BUY-ONE-GET-ONE-FREE")?

Free samples can only be distributed by entities to prescribing professionals (doctors and dentists), exclusively in ambulatories, hospitals, clinics and medical offices.

The concession of discounts is not prohibited according to RDC No. 96/2008, however, the promotional material offering such discounts must abide by the regulation.

## 24. ARE THERE PARTICULAR RULES OF PRACTICE ON THE USE OF THE INTERNET/SOCIAL MEDIA REGARDING DRUGS AND THEIR ADVERTISING?

RDC No. 96/2008 has some specific regulations on internet advertising.

Entities are free to convey whichever information they wish to place on their websites, the exception being advertising or promotional materials related to prescription products, which are not permitted.

Online promotion of these medicines can only be accessible to professionals qualified to prescribe or distribute medicines. This is possible by means of an electronic registration system, and a liability statement setting out the legal restrictions on access must be provided.

The National Sanitary Surveillance Agency (ANVISA) often monitors sites of pharmaceutical companies, pharmacies, distributors, clinics and so on.

## 25. WHAT REGULATORY AUTHORITY IS RESPONSIBLE FOR SUPERVISING MARKETING ACTIVITIES TO CONSUMERS?

**Regulatory authority**

The National Sanitary Surveillance Agency (ANVISA) is the authority responsible for supervising advertising or promotional violations of marketing activities related to drugs.

**Supervision**

The supervision of these activities is done by the ANVISA's department called the General Management of Inspection, Quality Monitoring, Control and Supervision of Raw Materials, Medicines and Products, Advertising and Publicity (GGIMP).

According to Resolution RDC No. 96/2008, ANVISA can also demand the issuance of a corrective statement.

### Rights of appeal

Violators can appeal a decision of ANVISA that considered an advertisement or promotion as contravening the regulation or a decision to request the issuance of a corrective statement.

This appeal is decided by the ANVISA's board of directors and any final administrative decision can be subjected to a judicial procedure.

### 26. WHAT ARE THE LEGAL CONSEQUENCES OF NON-COMPLIANCE WITH CONSUMER MARKETING LAWS?

Law No. 6347/1977 establishes penalties for failing to comply with the rules governing the advertising of medicines. It is the National Sanitary Surveillance Agency's (ANVISA) responsibility to enforce these rules.

These penalties can vary from warnings to suspensions of sales, prohibition of advertising and corrective statements. They can be also accompanied by a fine, the value of which depends on whether the failure was considered by the authority as "light", "serious" or "very serious".

## MARKETING TO PROFESSIONALS

### 27. WHAT KINDS OF MARKETING ACTIVITIES ARE PERMITTED IN RELATION TO PROFESSIONALS?

Advertisements, visits by representatives, distribution of free drug samples or other gifts and sponsoring of meetings and seminars are all permitted provided that this interaction does not influence a physician's prescription decisions inappropriately.

### 28. ARE THERE ANY RESTRICTIONS ON MARKETING TO PROFESSIONALS?

#### Marketing activities

There are some restrictions related to marketing to professionals. For example, pharmaceutical companies cannot provide professionals with off-label information using the trademark of the product.

Additionally, advertising medicinal products that are not registered by the National Sanitary Surveillance Agency (ANVISA) is not permitted. A common practice used to overcome this prohibition is to promote campaigning with medical societies on the awareness and prevention of diseases, without specifically mentioning products.

#### Frequency

The frequency of sales representatives' visits to medical doctors is not regulated by RDC No. 96/2008. However, health institutions can elaborate specific regulations establishing criteria for receiving sales representatives, provided that other conditions set out in RDC No. 96/2008 are respected.

#### Provision of hospitality

There is not a direct mention of hospitality in RDC No. 96/2008.

BRAZIL

Any contribution, including travel expenses, meals and hospitality to support healthcare professionals' attendance at medical conferences and scientific events (national or international) is allowed. However, it is important that the relationship is clearly declared by the physician and the company, in the prospectus, brochure or leaflets of the seminar and in the application form.

The Association of Research Based Pharmaceutical Industries' (INTERFARMA) Code depicts some restrictive rules related to payments made to a professional whenever attending a scientific meeting.

### 29. WHAT INFORMATION IS IT LEGALLY REQUIRED TO INCLUDE IN ADVERTISING TO PROFESSIONALS?

The required information in advertising to healthcare professionals is regulated in RDC No. 96/2008. According to this resolution, the promotional material must contain the:

- Brand name of the medicine.
- Name of the active ingredient.
- Number of the register granted by the National Sanitary Surveillance Agency (ANVISA).
- Therapeutic indications, including the dosage.
- Side effects.
- Interactions and contraindications.
- Warnings and precautions.
- Proof of safety and efficacy by scientific sources.
- The date of printing.

### 30. ARE THERE RULES ON COMPARISONS WITH OTHER PRODUCTS THAT ARE PARTICULARLY APPLICABLE TO DRUGS?

RDC No. 096/2008 sets out the rules for comparative advertising of medicinal products. Generally, comparative advertising is regulated by different legislations, including the Code of Ethics and the Advertising Profession and the Advertising Self-Regulation Code.

Products that are not authorised by the National Sanitary Surveillance Agency (ANVISA) cannot be mentioned in advertising.

Price comparison is only allowed between interchangeable products. If the products are not interchangeable, the price comparison can only be made to professionals, under specific conditions.

### 31. WHAT OTHER ITEMS, FUNDING OR SERVICES ARE PERMITTED TO BE PROVIDED TO PROFESSIONALS?

**Discounts**

No incentives to prescribing professionals can be (or be understood as) an exchange for assuring the prescriptions of a particular product.

global.practicallaw.com/**drugsdistribution-guide**

### Free samples

The restrictions for free samples are regulated in RDC No. 60/2009.

It is possible to provide professionals with sample of products, except for:

- Non-prescription products.
- Biological products.
- Products prepared in compounding pharmacies.

They can be distributed only in ambulatories, hospitals, medical and dentist's offices. The prescribing professional must sign a document indicating the receipt of the samples.

Generally, the amount offered in a free sample package must be 50% of the original and must clearly include the term "free sample".

### Sponsorship of professionals

The scientist or physician must report to the conference organisation if they received financial support.

If a pharmaceutical company sponsors scientific events, this support must be made clear in all materials of communication.

RDC No. 096/2008 prohibits linking sponsorship of events (medical or health congresses, symposia, conferences and meetings) within assurance in prescribing or dispensing a medicine.

### Other items, funding or services

The advertisement and indirect sale or the granting, offer, promise or distribution of promotional gifts, benefits and advantages to professionals are prohibited.

Only institutional gifts that are not related to any specific product can be given to professionals.

## 32. WHAT REGULATORY AUTHORITY IS RESPONSIBLE FOR SUPERVISING MARKETING ACTIVITIES REGARDING PROFESSIONALS?

### Regulatory authority

The National Sanitary Surveillance Agency (ANVISA) is the authority responsible for supervising advertising and deciding on possible violations conducted on marketing activities related to drugs.

### Supervision

The supervision of these activities is done by ANVISA, as it is in marketing to consumers (*see Question 25*).

### Rights of appeal

The rights of appeal are the same ones related to marketing to consumers (*see Question 25*).

### 33. WHAT ARE THE LEGAL CONSEQUENCES IN CASE OF NON-COMPLIANCE WITH PROFESSIONAL MARKETING LAWS?

The consequences are the same of non-compliance with consumers marketing laws (*see Question 26*).

## ENGAGEMENT WITH PATIENT ORGANISATIONS

### 34. WHAT KINDS OF ACTIVITIES ARE PERMITTED IN RELATION TO ENGAGEMENT WITH PATIENT ORGANISATIONS? WHAT ARE THE RESTRICTIONS THAT ARE IMPOSED ON RELATIONSHIP WITH PATIENT ORGANISATIONS?

Generally, meetings with, and funding of, patient organisations are permitted and no specific requirements must be observed. Health authorities have been looking very closely at this issue.

RDC No. 096/2008 determines that the organisers of scientific events in which advertising and promotion of medicinal products are allowed must report to the National Sanitary Surveillance Agency (ANVISA) three months in advance of any such event indicating the date and place of the event and the professional categories that will participate in the event.

## REFORM

### 35. ARE THERE ANY PLANS TO REFORM THE LAW ON THE DISTRIBUTION AND PROMOTION OF DRUGS IN YOUR JURISDICTION?

With regard to advertisement and distribution of drugs in Brazil, no changes in the regulation are expected for 2015, however, a review of RDC No. 096/2008 is scheduled to occur.

# CANADA

*Jeffrey S Graham\*, BORDEN LADNER GERVAIS LLP*

## DISTRIBUTION

### PRE-CONDITIONS FOR DISTRIBUTION

**1. WHAT ARE THE LEGAL PRE-CONDITIONS FOR A DRUG TO BE DISTRIBUTED WITHIN THE JURISDICTION?**

**Authorisation**

Before a drug can be distributed in Canada, its manufacturer must receive a Notice of Compliance (NOC) from Health Canada, and the drug must be assigned a Drug Identification Number (DIN). The NOC represents the fact that the drug meets the required standards for use in humans and the DIN represents the fact that the drug has been evaluated and authorised for marketing and sale in Canada. A manufacturer can obtain a NOC by submitting a New Drug Submission (NDS) or an Abbreviated New Drug Submission (ANDS) for a generic drug. The ANDS scheme was implemented to make the approval process for generic drugs simpler and more cost effective with the hope that the cost of drugs for provincial governments and members of the public would in turn be reduced. To receive a NOC, under an ANDS, the manufacturer only has to prove that its product is pharmaceutically equivalent and bioequivalent with the innovator's drug. Because the decision on whether a medication will be listed on the Prescription Drug List is made during the review of the NDS, and therefore require a prescription before its distribution to a patient, both prescription, non-prescription and over-the-counter (OTC) medications must go through the NDS process.

**Exceptions**

A Notice of Compliance with Conditions (NOC/c) can be issued for drugs with promising but unverified clinical benefit. This designation is reserved for drugs that:

- Potentially provide treatment, prevention or diagnosis of a disease or condition for which no drug is presently marketed in Canada.
- Shows significantly improved efficacy or reduced risk compared to other available therapy.

A pre-condition to the grant of a NOC/c is that the safety of the drug must be reasonably established.

Another exception to the general drug approval and distribution process in Canada is the priority review process. Manufacturers can submit an application for priority review of their NDS if the drug provides therapy for a serious, life-threatening or severely debilitating disease or condition. If granted, priority review allows a drug submission to be fast-tracked through the approval process.

CANADA

### 2. DO ANY TYPES OF NAMED PATIENT AND/OR COMPASSIONATE USE PROGRAMMES OPERATE? IF SO, WHAT ARE THE REQUIREMENTS FOR PRE-LAUNCH ACCESS?

Under certain circumstances, Canadians can obtain access to unapproved drugs on a case-by-case basis through the Special Access Programme. The Special Access Programme provides for the emergency release of drugs that are not available in Canada and the non-emergency release of drugs that have not been approved in Canada but are used for the treatment of rare disorders. If access to a drug is granted via the Special Access Programme, the practitioner requesting access must follow specific reporting requirements, including the communication of the effect of the drug and any side effects, to the Director of the Therapeutic Products Directorate and the manufacturer.

There are also various provincial programmes that allow for access to drugs on a compassionate use basis, with requirements for approval determined on a province-by-province and case-by-case basis.

## LICENSING

### 3. WHAT IS THE PROCEDURAL STRUCTURE REGARDING LICENSING A DRUG FOR DISTRIBUTION?

**Regulatory authority**

Health Canada is the federal body that regulates the drug approval process (*see Question 1*). Health Canada is the department of the government responsible for national public health, including ensuring that Canadians have access to safe and effective medical products, including drugs. The Food and Drugs Act (FDA) applies to all medical products (that is drugs, medical devices and natural health products) sold in Canada, whether manufactured in Canada or imported. The FDA and the Food and Drug Regulations (FDA Regulations) seek to ensure the safety of medical products by governing their manufacture, sale and advertisement.

While Health Canada is responsible for determining whether a drug requires a prescription or not, the distribution of drugs to the public is otherwise largely governed by provincial regulatory bodies. As such, despite the classification of a drug by Health Canada, provinces can place further restrictions on its sale and distribution.

**Structure**

The licensing of drugs is regulated by the FDA, and the associated FDA Regulations. Specifically, Part C of the FDA Regulations outlines the procedure and requirements for the licensing of a drug. A drug must receive a Notice of Compliance (NOC) and Drug Identification Number (DIN) before it can be distributed to the public, subject to certain exceptions (*see Question 1*).

New drugs must go through extensive testing before being granted a NOC. During the pre-clinical phase, the efficacy and safety of drugs is examined before it is administered to patients. During the first three phases of clinical testing, the drug is given first to both healthy non-patient volunteers and then to patients suffering from the condition that the drug is intended to treat. The fourth phase of testing occurs after the drug has gone to market and consists of follow up studies designed to optimise the drug's use. The progression through the phases of pre-clinical and clinical trials is also governed by the FDA, and the results of the pre-clinical and clinical testing form a portion of the information that is required for a New Drug Submission (NDS).

The information supplied in a NDS must be detailed enough that the Minister for Health can make an assessment on the safety and effectiveness of the drug. A non-exhaustive list of required information includes:

- A list of ingredients.
- A description of manufacturing methods and equipment.
- Reports of tests made to establish the safety of the new drug.
- Evidence of the clinical efficacy of the new drug.
- A copy of all clinical case reports where a subject died or suffered a serious or unexpected adverse reaction.
- A statement of all the representations to be made for the promotion of the new drug.

If there is insufficient information contained in the NDS, the manufacturer is notified and a NOC is not granted. However, if an initial application is refused, the manufacturer can re-submit with additional data. Health Canada aims to have information submitted as part of a NDS screened for acceptability within:

- 45 days of receipt for a regular submission.
- 25 days of receipt after a request for priority review.

If the initial screening is deemed acceptable, a full review of the submitted information takes place. If the initial screening is deemed to be unacceptable, Health Canada issues a Notice of Deficiency (NOD), to which the manufacturer can respond. If the response is sufficient to meet the requirements, the review of the submission continues. If after the review process is complete the submission is found to be deficient or incomplete, Health Canada issues a Notice of Non-compliance (NON), to which the manufacturer can again respond. If the manufacturer responds, and the response is again deemed deficient, a NON-withdrawal letter is issued by Health Canada, and a NOC is not granted. However, the manufacturer can file a submission again in the future. If after review the information is found to be sufficient to establish the safety and effectiveness of the drug, a NOC and DIN is granted by Health Canada.

4. IS THERE A SIMPLIFIED LICENCE PROCEEDING, OR RELAXED LICENSING CONDITIONS, FOR DRUGS WHICH HAVE ALREADY BEEN LICENSED FOR DISTRIBUTION IN ANOTHER JURISDICTION?

Generally, there is no simplified licensing procedure for drugs that have already been licensed in another jurisdiction. The Special Access Programme (*see Question 2*) provides an exception to this general rule and there are further exceptions allowed for the importation of drugs for personal use. However, without one of these exceptions, Health Canada goes through the full drug review process before a drug is available for sale.

The Food and Drugs Act (FDA) and the Food and Drug Regulations (FDA Regulations) do not provide for parallel imports. Also, because the FDA Regulations require that both the inner and outer label of a drug display the Drug Identification Number (DIN) assigned by Health Canada, parallel importation is not legally possible.

## CANADA

### 5. IS VIRTUAL DRUG DISTRIBUTION POSSIBLE FROM YOUR JURISDICTION?

Neither the Food and Drugs Act nor the Food and Drug Regulations specifically contemplate the virtual distribution of drugs. Therefore, there is no prohibition against the practice. However, the distribution of these drugs is subject to the legislation of the importing country.

### 6. WHAT IS THE PROCEDURE TO APPEAL (LEGAL REMEDY) A LICENSING DECISION?

Manufacturers can formally appeal a drug licensing decision by going through the reconsideration process. Within 30 days of having a drug submission rejected, the manufacturer must submit a Letter of Intent to the Therapeutic Products Directorate outlining its intention to go through the reconsideration process. If the decision referred to in the letter of intent is eligible for reconsideration, the manufacturer receives an eligibility letter. Following receipt of the eligibility letter, the manufacturer has 45 calendar days to file a formal request for consideration. After reviewing the request, the Director General of Health Canada decides whether to uphold or reverse the previously made decision. Manufacturers also have the option of taking any issues with the review of its drug submission to court. However, if the manufacturer chooses to do so, any commenced reconsideration process is automatically terminated.

### 7. WHAT ARE THE COSTS OF OBTAINING LICENSING?

From 1 April 2015, the fee for the review of a New Drug Submission (NDS) is CAN$328,498. The fee for the review of an Abbreviated New Drug Submission (ANDS) ranges from CAN$11,096 to CAN$166,383 depending on the type of information being reviewed.

### DISTRIBUTION TO CONSUMERS

### 8. WHAT ARE THE DIFFERENT CATEGORIES OF DRUGS FOR DISTRIBUTION?

Drugs are categorised into one of three schedules defined by the National Association of Pharmacy Regulatory Authorities (NAPRA):

- Schedule I drugs require a prescription to be distributed. Some Schedule I drugs are subcategorised as controlled substances by the Controlled Drugs and Substances Act (CDSA), and have different restrictions on their distribution than other Schedule I drugs under provincial pharmacy legislation.
- Schedule II drugs, or behind-the-counter drugs, must be sold by a pharmacist from an area of a pharmacy that is not accessible to the general public.
- Schedule III drugs must be sold in a pharmacy, but they can be located in an area accessible to the general public.

Drugs that are not assigned to one of the three schedules are considered to be unscheduled, and their sale is not restricted to pharmacies.

## 9. WHO IS AUTHORISED TO DISTRIBUTE PRESCRIPTION DRUGS AND OVER-THE-COUNTER DRUGS TO CONSUMERS?

### Prescription drugs

The Food and Drugs Act states that a person cannot sell a prescription drug to a member of the general public unless they are licensed by a province to dispense prescription drugs. This means that the distribution of drugs to consumers is governed provincially in Canada. While each province has its own governing legislation, the dispensing and sale of drugs is generally considered to be a controlled act that is restricted to members of regulated healthcare professions. Regulated healthcare professionals must also be specifically authorised to sell and dispense drugs by the legislation that governs their profession. Most often prescription drugs are distributed to consumers from licensed pharmacies and by licensed pharmacists. However, other regulated healthcare professionals, such as physicians and dentists, are also authorised by their governing legislation to dispense drugs.

### Over-the-counter drugs

Authorisation to distribute over-the-counter drugs is dependent on the National Association of Pharmacy Regulatory Authorities (NAPRA) schedule assigned to the drug. Schedule II and Schedule III drugs must be sold under the supervision of a licensed pharmacist (*see Question 8*). However, unscheduled drugs can be sold from any retail outlet and therefore no specific authorisation is required for a person to be allowed to sell them.

## 10. WHAT DRUGS CAN AN ATTENDING PHYSICIAN DISTRIBUTE AND UNDER WHAT CIRCUMSTANCES?

Physicians can distribute drugs to their patients by the provincial legislation that governs the practice of medicine in the relevant province (*see Question 9*). The authorisation is a general one and is not subject to restrictions on the type of drug, unless the restrictions have been specifically applied to the terms of an individual physician's licence, for example, as a disciplinary measure.

## 11. WHO IS AUTHORISED TO PRESCRIBE PRESCRIPTION DRUGS TO CONSUMERS?

Similar to the sale and distribution of drugs, the prescribing of prescription drugs is also an act that is governed by provincial legislation in Canada. Again, it is an act that is generally restricted to members of certain regulated healthcare professions. Generally, drugs are prescribed by physicians and dentists, although other regulated healthcare professionals (for example, nurses, pharmacists and midwives) can also prescribe prescription drugs in certain circumstances.

## 12. IS DIRECT MAILING/DISTANCE SELLING OF DRUGS PERMITTED IN YOUR JURISDICTION?

### Conditions

The distribution of drugs in Canada is governed in each province by provincial legislation (*see Question 9*). Direct mailing of medications under a prescription is generally allowed.

## CANADA

**Cross-border sales**

Cross-border sales of drugs are also generally allowed by provincial legislation. However, the dispensing and sale of prescription drugs must be under a prescription authorised by a Canadian prescriber. Therefore, if a person attempts to obtain drugs under a prescription written in another country, the prescription must be either co-signed by a Canadian physician or rewritten by a Canadian prescriber before it can be dispensed.

### 13. WHAT REGULATORY AUTHORITY IS RESPONSIBLE FOR SUPERVISING DISTRIBUTION ACTIVITIES?

Distribution of drugs to consumers is largely regulated by provincial Colleges of Pharmacy or Pharmacy Boards (*see Question 9*), irrespective of the fact that drug scheduling and classification of narcotics and controlled substances occurs at the federal level. For regular prescription drugs, the rules for distribution to consumers are relatively uniform across the provinces with limited exceptions. One such exception is in the case of some vaccines, where some provinces require a prescription before they can be provided to consumers while other provinces do not. In the case of narcotic drugs and controlled substances, there is more inter-province variation in the requirements for distribution. The greatest differences are found in the requirements for prescriptions for narcotics and controlled drugs. For example, some provinces have a triplicate or duplicate prescription programme for narcotic drugs, whereas other provinces' prescribing requirements are similar to regular prescription drugs.

### 14. WHAT IS THE PROCEDURE TO APPEAL (LEGAL REMEDY) A DISTRIBUTION DECISION?

Distribution decisions and any associated discipline are governed by the provincial College or Board of the healthcare professional involved in the activity that led to the decision. With drug distribution, this will generally be pharmacists, although physicians, dentists or other healthcare professionals could be implicated as well. Generally, an initial decision is made by a discipline committee or review board of the College or Pharmacy Board. From that point, the procedure for appeal varies depending on the province. Some provinces have an appeal process within the College or Pharmacy Board and a privative clause in the governing legislation indicating that decisions are final. Other provinces have legislation that explicitly provides for a right to judicial review by a court if the registrant is not satisfied with the decision of the committee or board. Canadian administrative law principles allow for judicial review of a decision even in the presence of a privative clause in the legislation. However, courts often show significant deference to the initial decision of the committee or board under these circumstances.

### 15. WHAT ARE THE LEGAL CONSEQUENCES OF NON-COMPLIANCE WITH CONSUMER DISTRIBUTION LAWS?

The legal consequences of non-compliance with consumer distribution laws vary depending on the offence committed. Penalties associated with the contravention of the federal Controlled Drugs and Substances Act (CDSA) range from:

- Fines of up to CAN$5,000.
- Revocation or suspension of a registrant's licence.
- Imprisonment.

Financial penalties under provincial statutes can be significantly higher, with fines of up to CAN$100,000 being allowed. Provincial Colleges and Pharmacy Boards can also impose conditions on, suspend or revoke the licence of a registrant.

## WHOLESALE DISTRIBUTION

### 16. WHAT IS THE LEGAL REGIME REGARDING WHOLESALE DISTRIBUTION OF DRUGS?

The wholesale distribution of drugs is one of the activities that requires a Drug Establishment Licence (DEL) under the Food and Drug Regulations (FDA Regulations). A person wishing to sell drugs wholesale must apply to Health Canada for a DEL and provide a significant amount of information regarding, among other things:

- The drug(s) that will be sold.
- The establishment that they will be sold from.
- The establishment where records of the business will be kept.

Provincial drug legislation also provides for the distribution of drugs by wholesale. Generally, a wholesaler must meet the requirements of the province's College of Pharmacy or Pharmacy Board and must be registered. Generally, wholesalers are also only allowed to sell drugs by wholesale to individuals who are authorised to sell the drugs by retail. Generally, wholesalers of drugs must also be accessible to an inspector of the provincial regulatory body and must be able to account for their drug inventory.

### 17. WHAT REGULATORY AUTHORITY IS RESPONSIBLE FOR SUPERVISING WHOLESALE DISTRIBUTION ACTIVITIES?

**Regulatory authority**

Regulatory authority for the wholesale of drugs comes from two sources (*see Question 16*):

- Health Canada issues the Drug Establishment Licence (DEL) that is required to establish a drug wholesale operation.
- The provincial Colleges of Pharmacy or Pharmacy Boards regulate the activity of wholesaling drugs.

Therefore, drug wholesalers must hold a valid federal DEL and be registered with the appropriate provincial pharmacy regulatory authority to sell drugs by wholesale.

**Supervision**

Supervision of drug wholesalers is again conducted on two regulatory levels:

- The Minister of Health is responsible for supervising the DELs that Health Canada grants.
- The provincial pharmacy regulatory bodies are responsible for supervising the activity of wholesaling drugs.

DELs require annual renewal and each year the licensee must submit all of the information required in the initial application for a DEL to the Minister for review. Before granting a licence renewal, the Minister can request additional information and order an inspection of any premises listed on the renewal application. The Minister can suspend the DEL if the licensee contravenes any provisions of the FDA or makes false or misleading statements in the DEL application. The Minister can cancel a DEL if it has been suspended for more than 12 months or if the holder of the DEL does not submit an annual renewal.

The provincial pharmacy regulatory authorities have supervisory authority over the activity of wholesaling drugs. While the legislation differs from province to province, generally wholesalers must sell their drugs to a person that is licensed to sell them by retail. Drug wholesalers must be registered in the province that they supply drugs in, and must supply information pertinent to their operations such as the name of the wholesaler and the address of each place of business.

**Rights of appeal**

With a DEL, the Minister cannot suspend or refuse to issue a licence without giving the licensee or applicant an opportunity to be heard. An exception to this general rule occurs where the Minister believes it is necessary to suspend a licence to prevent injury to the health of the consumer. Where a licence is suspended without the licensee being given the opportunity to be heard, the licensee can request in writing to the Minister that the suspension be reconsidered. Following such a request, the Minister must provide the licensee an opportunity to be heard within 45 days.

The appeal process for decisions made by the provincial regulatory authorities differs by province. However, there is a general administrative right to judicial review of a decision made by a provincial College or Pharmacy Board, and some legislation explicitly allows for an appeal to a court in the province.

18. **WHAT ARE THE LEGAL CONSEQUENCES OF NON-COMPLIANCE WITH WHOLESALE DISTRIBUTION LAWS?**

Contravention of the Food and Drugs Act (FDA) or the Food and Drug Regulations on wholesale distribution of drugs can result in suspension or even cancellation of a Drug Establishment Licence (DEL), which effectively prohibits a person from distributing drugs by wholesale (*see Question 17*).

The legal consequences stemming from the contravention of provincial drug wholesale regulatory requirements differ by province. Irrespective of the fact that there is not always a penalty directly associated with contravention of drug wholesaling provisions of provincial legislation, governing legislation can contemplate penalties associated with contravention of the FDA generally. For example, in the province of Ontario, contravention of the applicable legislation can result in a fine of up to CAN$50,000 for a second or subsequent offence.

# MARKETING

## PROMOTION

### 19. WHAT IS THE GENERAL LEGAL REGIME FOR THE MARKETING OF DRUGS?

**Legal regime**

The Food and Drugs Act (FDA) prohibits medical product advertising that is false, misleading or deceptive or is likely to create an erroneous impression regarding its character, value, quantity, composition, merit or safety. Only drugs that have been authorised for sale in Canada by Health Canada can be advertised. The advertising must not exceed the terms of the market authorisation.

Any person that promotes the sale of a specific health product is subject to this legislation, including physicians, when they use their websites or other means for this purpose.

With the marketing of drugs, Health Canada, with the assistance of advertising pre-clearance agencies, administers and directs compliance with the FDA and Food and Drug Regulations (FDA Regulations). Advertising pre-clearance agencies will review and pre-clear advertising material to help industry ensure compliance with the applicable regulatory provisions, and the various Health Canada guidance documents and codes of advertising (for example, Pharmaceutical Advertising Advisory Board (PAAB) Code of Advertising Acceptance).

Advertising material for all health products directed to healthcare professionals, including prescription and non-prescription drugs, is reviewed and pre-cleared by the PAAB. The PAAB, as well as Advertising Standards Canada (ASC), provides advice on messages directed to consumers for prescription drugs and on educational material discussing a medical condition or disease to ensure they meet the regulatory requirements.

**Limits to marketing activities**

Advertisement includes any representation by any means whatever for the purpose of promoting directly or indirectly the sale or disposal of any food, drug, cosmetic or device. Health Canada has issued guidance documents that explain how Health Canada uses contextual factors to help determine whether a given message is information or advertising. Some messages, depending on the content and the context in which they are disseminated, can be considered non-promotional. These could include:

- Press releases.
- Consumer brochures.
- Help-seeking announcements.
- Scientific exhibits.
- Journal articles.

However, if the message is an advertisement, it must comply with the advertising provisions of the FDA and the FDA Regulations.

## 20. ARE THERE OTHER CODES OF CONDUCT FOR THE MARKETING OF DRUGS (FOR EXAMPLE, BY PROFESSIONAL OR INDUSTRIAL ORGANISATIONS)?

The Pharmaceutical Advertising Advisory Board (PAAB) publishes a Code of Advertising Acceptance that serves as guidance for drug advertisers. The Canadian Code of Advertising Standards of the Advertising Standards Canada (ASC) sets the criteria for acceptable advertising in Canada on advertising directed to consumers.

The Code of Ethical Practice of Canada's Research-Based Pharmaceutical Companies (Rx&D) applies to the activities of all member employees that interact with stakeholders for the purpose of commercialising prescription medicines. The Commercial Practice Standards of BioteCanada sets out standards to guide biopharmaceutical company members in their interactions with:

- Healthcare professionals.
- The scientific research community.
- Government officials.
- Public office holders.
- The general public.

## MARKETING TO CONSUMERS

## 21. WHAT IS THE LEGAL REGIME FOR MARKETING TO CONSUMERS?

**Legal regime**

Specific regulatory provisions exist to limit the type or extent of advertisements of prescription drugs to consumers. For example, prescription drugs cannot be advertised to the general public in relation to specific diseases. Advertising of narcotic and controlled drugs to consumers is prohibited.

The Food and Drug Regulations (FDA Regulations) prohibit consumer-directed prescription drug advertising beyond the drug's name, price and quantity. This means, for example, that when a prescription drug is advertised by name to consumers, no reference can be made to its therapeutic use or benefits. The FDA Regulations also prohibit the advertising of new drugs that have not been authorised for sale by Health Canada. The advertising of pharmaceutical manufacturers must either be non-promotional in nature or must comply with federal advertising requirements. Under the regulatory framework, Health Canada has permitted two types of prescription drug messages directed to consumers:

- Reminder ads, where the name of a prescription drug is mentioned but no reference to a disease state appears in the advertisement, are interpreted as not going beyond the name, price and quantity restrictions of the FDA Regulations.
- Help-seeking messages, where a disease state is discussed but no reference is made to a specific prescription drug product, are considered information and not advertising when they meet the criteria outlined in Health Canada policies.

The Food and Drug Act (FDA) and the FDA Regulations prohibit consumer-directed advertisements for medical products that make claims to treat, prevent or cure any of the serious diseases listed in Schedule A to the Act (for example, alcoholism, arthritis, cancer, congestive heart failure, diabetes and obesity) other than prevention claims for over-the-counter drugs and natural health products.

**Products**

See *Legal regime*.

**22. WHAT KINDS OF MARKETING ACTIVITIES ARE PERMITTED IN RELATION TO CONSUMERS AND THE PRODUCTS WHICH MAY BE ADVERTISED TO THEM?**

See *Question 19*.

**23. IS IT PERMITTED TO PROVIDE CONSUMERS WITH FREE SAMPLES? ARE THERE PARTICULAR RESTRICTIONS ON SPECIAL OFFERS (FOR EXAMPLE, "BUY-ONE-GET-ONE-FREE")?**

Free samples of drugs can only be provided to consumers by a person that is entitled to prescribe that drug. Therefore, samples cannot be provided to consumers directly from drug manufacturers. Under the Food and Drug Regulations, samples can be given to physicians, dentists, veterinary surgeons and pharmacists if:

- The packaging of the drug conforms to the general labelling requirements.
- The person ordering the sample has provided a written order to the person distributing it.

After receiving the samples, the physician, dentist, veterinary surgeon or pharmacist can distribute them to consumers provided that they would be entitled to prescribe the drug. The effect of this restriction is that samples of prescription drugs are generally given to consumers by physicians.

Given the limitations around providing drug samples to consumers, special offers on prescription drugs are not allowed. With non-prescription drugs, special offers, discounts and promotions at the point of sale to consumers are allowed.

**24. ARE THERE PARTICULAR RULES OF PRACTICE ON THE USE OF THE INTERNET/SOCIAL MEDIA REGARDING DRUGS AND THEIR ADVERTISING?**

There are no specific legislative requirements for the advertising of drugs via the internet or social media. The content restrictions on advertising as outlined in the Food and Drugs Act and the Food and Drug Regulations apply to advertising through these mediums as they do to print and other forms of advertising.

**25. WHAT REGULATORY AUTHORITY IS RESPONSIBLE FOR SUPERVISING MARKETING ACTIVITIES TO CONSUMERS?**

**Regulatory authority**

See *Question 21*.

**Supervision**

See *Question 21*.

**Rights of appeal**

The Health Products and Food Branch (Inspectorate) of Health Canada has an internal appeal process for regulated parties who are unsatisfied with decisions that have been made against them. Each of the private sector bodies noted above have their own appeal process:

- Pharmaceutical Advertising Advisory Board (PAAB).
- Advertising Standards Canada (ASC).
- Research-Based Pharmaceutical Companies (Rx&D).
- BiotecCanada.

### 26. WHAT ARE THE LEGAL CONSEQUENCES OF NON-COMPLIANCE WITH CONSUMER MARKETING LAWS?

The legal consequences of non-compliance with the Food and Drugs Act and the Food and Drug Regulation requirements for consumer marketing are assessed based on the health risk level of an advertisement. When a complaint is made, an assessment by Health Canada is conducted to determine the level of risk to human health associated with the exposure to the advertising. After the assessment is made, appropriate risk management actions are taken. These actions can range from the:

- Issuance of a warning letter.
- Request for the immediate cessation of the advertisement.
- Suspension or cancellation of marketing authorisation or even prosecution.

## MARKETING TO PROFESSIONALS

### 27. WHAT KINDS OF MARKETING ACTIVITIES ARE PERMITTED IN RELATION TO PROFESSIONALS?

Promotion of drugs to healthcare professionals is generally allowed. Physicians must follow their licensing body's code of ethics and the Canadian Medical Association policy when interacting with industry representatives, which means that they should not typically receive any sort of gift or significant monetary gain from their interactions with the drug industry.

### 28. ARE THERE ANY RESTRICTIONS ON MARKETING TO PROFESSIONALS?

**Marketing activities**

The restrictions around marketing to professionals relate more to the content of the material than to its form. Even when it is directed to professionals and not the general public, advertising:

- Must not be false, misleading or deceptive.
- Cannot be likely to create an erroneous impression regarding a drug's character value or safety.

## FREQUENCY

There are no explicit legislative requirements that address the allowable frequency of interaction with drug marketing representatives or what types of hospitality can be provided to healthcare professionals. Healthcare professionals are typically required by their respective provincial legislation, Colleges or Boards to avoid conflicts of interest. This serves as a guideline for healthcare professionals to judge what types of hospitality and what frequency of interaction are appropriate, but generally healthcare professionals must not receive personal benefit through interactions with drug industry representatives. With meals specifically, the provision of a meal to a healthcare provider and appropriate staff while a drug industry representative is informing them of a drug product is typically acceptable provided that the meal is not excessive in nature.

The Codes of Research-Based Pharmaceutical Companies (Rx&D) and BioteCanada also provide guidance to their members on what is considered to be acceptable for their respective members.

**Provision of hospitality**

See above.

### 29. WHAT INFORMATION IS IT LEGALLY REQUIRED TO INCLUDE IN ADVERTISING TO PROFESSIONALS?

Health Canada has delegated the judgment of whether prescription drug advertising to professionals is appropriate or not to the Pharmaceutical Advertising Advisory Board (PAAB). The PAAB has several general requirements relating to the information contained in Advertising or Promotion Systems (APS). APSs must be designed to promote credibility and must be accurate, complete and clear. They must be presented in a way that accurately interprets research findings, while at the same time reflecting an attitude of caution regarding drug use and emphasising rational drug therapy. An additional requirement that is reflective of this cautious approach is that an APS cannot state or imply in absolute terms that:

- Any product is safe.
- It has guaranteed efficacy.
- Its effects are totally predictable.

A general guideline is that an APS must provide the healthcare professional with sufficient information to allow them to properly assess the risks and benefits of use for their patients.

### 30. ARE THERE RULES ON COMPARISONS WITH OTHER PRODUCTS THAT ARE PARTICULARLY APPLICABLE TO DRUGS?

Under the Food and Drugs Act (FDA), drugs cannot be advertised to any person in a manner that is:

- False.
- Misleading.
- Deceptive.
- Is likely to create an erroneous impression regarding its character or safety.

The Pharmaceutical Advertising Advisory Board (PAAB) has incorporated these requirements into its advertising standards for making comparisons of drugs. This means that comparisons between drugs must be made on the basis of:

- The same indication for use.
- The same conditions for use (that is in a similar patient population).
- Must not conflict with any of the terms of market authorisation for any of the compared products.

The comparison must also be of clinical relevance to humans, and rely on evidence that is conclusive, complete and scientifically accurate. At a minimum, when comparing two or more drugs, the Advertising or Promotion Systems (APS) must:

- Identify the compared drugs.
- Identify the medical use related to the claim.
- Not obscure the therapeutic use.
- Not attack the compared drug in an unreasonable manner.
- Be expressed in terms that will be understood by the intended audience.

The PAAB also provides more specific guidelines around drug comparisons, over and above those that stem from the FDA requirements. The overarching theme is that:

- Comparisons are made in a fair and accurate manner.
- All relevant evidence is considered.
- It is of good quality.

## 31. WHAT OTHER ITEMS, FUNDING OR SERVICES ARE PERMITTED TO BE PROVIDED TO PROFESSIONALS?

**Discounts**

To prevent a real or apparent conflict of interest, healthcare professionals are generally not allowed to accept personal gifts or compensation of any kind from drug industry representatives in return for seeing them in a promotional capacity. Discounts from a drug company generally fall into this description in many cases, and therefore are not allowed. This framework for assessing things received from drug industry representatives is applicable to all other types of indirect benefits as well.

**Free samples**

Free samples can be accepted from drug industry representatives by certain healthcare professionals. However, these samples must be distributed to patients and not used by the healthcare professional or a member of his family. Distribution of free samples to healthcare professionals for personal use could be considered a gift or other form of compensation, which would not be appropriate.

**Sponsorship of professionals**

Sponsorship of professionals can occur in a variety of ways, such as sponsorship of an educational event or conference or sponsorship of research studies. While this type of sponsorship is not prohibited, any healthcare professionals that are involved are still expected to maintain professional autonomy and independently ensure the validity and accuracy of any information they are presenting. With research specifically, it is the responsibility of the healthcare professional to ensure that the research is conducted in an ethically and scientifically defencible manner and that it complies with all relevant guidelines, such as the Tri-Council Policy Statement on Ethical Conduct for Research Involving Humans (TCPS-2). An over-arching requirement of any kind of healthcare professional sponsorship is that the professional must disclose the nature of the relationship between himself and the sponsoring industry representative.

## 32. WHAT REGULATORY AUTHORITY IS RESPONSIBLE FOR SUPERVISING MARKETING ACTIVITIES REGARDING PROFESSIONALS?

### Regulatory authority

Health Canada and the Pharmaceutical Advertising Advisory Board (PAAB) are responsible for supervising the content of marketing and advertising material provided to healthcare professionals regarding prescription drugs (*see Question 29*). With the provision of gifts, sponsorship and other benefits, the provincial Colleges or Boards of the healthcare professionals have regulatory authority.

### Supervision

The supervision over the content of advertising provided to healthcare professionals is the responsibility of Health Canada, the PAAB and other independent agencies in the case of non-prescription drugs (see *Question 29*). The supervision of other interactions between healthcare professionals and drug industry representatives is the responsibility of the provincial Colleges or Boards that govern the profession. This supervisory role includes the assessment of real or apparent conflicts of interest described in the preceding sections.

### Rights of appeal

Any right of appeal is determined by the relevant supervisory body. Rights of appeal range from a reassessment of the decision by a committee of the provincial regulatory body to a right of appeal to a court in the province.

## 33. WHAT ARE THE LEGAL CONSEQUENCES IN CASE OF NON-COMPLIANCE WITH PROFESSIONAL MARKETING LAWS?

With drug marketers, non-compliance with Pharmaceutical Advertising Advisory Board (PAAB) standards can result in various types of penalties and remedial measures. Non-compliance with Health Canada or federal legislative requirements can result in fines or potentially loss of marketing authorisation.

With healthcare professionals, consequences of non-compliance vary depending on the offence committed and its severity. Potential consequences can include:

- Fines.
- A reprimand by the College or Board.
- Imposition of terms or conditions on a professional's licence.
- Suspension or revocation of a healthcare professional's licence.

Appropriate consequences are generally decided by a committee of the appropriate College or Board that is responsible for member discipline.

## ENGAGEMENT WITH PATIENT ORGANISATIONS

**34. WHAT KINDS OF ACTIVITIES ARE PERMITTED IN RELATION TO ENGAGEMENT WITH PATIENT ORGANISATIONS? WHAT ARE THE RESTRICTIONS THAT ARE IMPOSED ON RELATIONSHIP WITH PATIENT ORGANISATIONS?**

There are no specific rules governing interactions between drug advertising representatives and patient organisations. Allowable activities are determined using the same principles discussed above, such as whether activities are promotional in nature and whether they are directed to the general public or to a healthcare professional (*see Questions 19 to 33*).

The Codes of Research-Based Pharmaceutical Companies (Rx&D) and BioteCanada also provide guidance to their members on what is considered to be acceptable for their respective members.

## REFORM

**35. ARE THERE ANY PLANS TO REFORM THE LAW ON THE DISTRIBUTION AND PROMOTION OF DRUGS IN YOUR JURISDICTION?**

Canada has the second highest level of *per capita* spending on drugs after the US. Historically each Canadian jurisdiction has managed its public drug plans independently of other jurisdictions. The Canadian provinces and territories have recently taken collective action to bring drug prices more in line with the experience of other countries. A Pan-Canadian Pharmaceutical Alliance (pCPA) has been created to facilitate the creation of collective purchasing strategies for drugs.

*With assistance from Rocky Swanson, student lawyer.

# CHINA

*Jianwen Huang, KING & WOOD MALLESONS CHINA*

## DISTRIBUTION

### PRE-CONDITIONS FOR DISTRIBUTION

**1. WHAT ARE THE LEGAL PRE-CONDITIONS FOR A DRUG TO BE DISTRIBUTED WITHIN THE JURISDICTION?**

**Authorisation**

The term "drug" is defined in the Drug Administration Law of the People's Republic of China (PRC) (Drug Administration Law), as substances used in the prevention, treatment, and diagnosis of human diseases and intended to regulate the physiological functions of human beings, for which indications, usage, and dosage are established. This definition of drugs includes:

- Traditional Chinese drug materials.
- Prepared slices of traditional Chinese drugs.
- Traditional Chinese medicine preparations.
- Crude chemical drugs and their preparations.
- Antibiotics.
- Biochemical drugs.
- Radioactive pharmaceuticals.
- Serums.
- Vaccines.
- Blood products.
- Diagnostic agents.

Drugs must be licensed for distribution in China. Before a drug can be distributed legally, the following must apply:

- The drug must be registered and approved by the China Food and Drug Administration (CFDA).
- The distributor must receive a valid drug distribution licence.
- The distributor must have good supplying practice for pharmaceutical products certification (GSP certification).

GSP certification is a new requirement that must be met by 31 December 2015. For more details, see *Question 3*.

The drug approval and registration process for imported drugs is not the same as the drug approval and registration process for drugs produced domestically (domestic drugs). Drugs distributed wholesale are also subject to a different approval process than drugs that are distributed retail. Details of the drug approval process are outlined below. For details on obtaining a drug distribution licence and GSP certification in China, see *Question 3*.

**Imported drugs.** Imported drugs must first be registered with the CFDA and receive an imported drug registration certificate (import certificate) from the CFDA.

**Domestic drugs.** Domestic drugs can be classified as either new or generic. "New" drugs refer to drugs that have never been marketed in China before. "Generic" drugs refer to drugs that have already been approved for marketing by the CFDA. The application processes for new drugs and generic drugs are the following:

- **New drugs.** Before producing a new drug, domestic manufacturers must apply for a new drug certificate. Applications are first submitted to the provincial Food and Drug Administration (provincial FDA) in the jurisdiction where the manufacturer is located. The provincial FDA then organises an on-site inspection and takes samples for examination. The CFDA's drug review centre conducts a technology review and evaluates the application materials once the materials are submitted from the provincial FDA. If the application passes this evaluation, the CFDA's drug review centre will notify the applicant to apply for an on-site inspection and will also notify the CFDA's drug accreditation management centre. The results of the technology review and the examinations of the samples are then sent to the CFDA for a decision on whether to issue a new drug certificate and drug approval number or a clinical trial approval document, depending on which phase the drug is in.

- **Generic drugs produced in China.** Domestic drugs must receive a drug approval number (or clinical trial approval document) from the CFDA. Applications for generic drugs are submitted to the provincial FDA in the jurisdiction where the manufacturer is located. The provincial FDA then organises an on-site inspection and take samples for examination. The provincial FDA will send the results to the CFDA for a decision on whether to issue a drug approval number.

**Exceptions**

Categories such as compassionate use do not currently exist under PRC law.

However, drugs can be imported into China without an import certificate if either of the following applies:

- The CFDA considers the drug safe, effective, and urgently needed (this may be possible even if the drug is not approved in the country or region where it is being produced).
- Medical institutions apply to the CFDA for permission to import small amounts of drugs that are necessary and urgently needed and the CFDA grants such permission.

In certain circumstances, provinces may issue one-time import registrations which allow a drug to enter China without an import certificate. For example, in Guangdong province, the following may be approved for import by the CFDA without an import certificate:

- Drugs that are necessary in major disasters and epidemics.
- Drugs needed for special and urgent treatments.
- Donated drugs, for example donated drugs from overseas used in natural disaster relief.
- Sample drugs.

## 2. DO ANY TYPES OF NAMED PATIENT AND/OR COMPASSIONATE USE PROGRAMMES OPERATE? IF SO, WHAT ARE THE REQUIREMENTS FOR PRE-LAUNCH ACCESS?

Currently, there are no named patient and/or compassionate use programmes in place in China. There are also no rules governing named patient and/or compassionate use programmes under PRC law.

## LICENSING

## 3. WHAT IS THE PROCEDURAL STRUCTURE REGARDING LICENSING A DRUG FOR DISTRIBUTION?

**Structure**

Distribution licences are divided into two categories:

- **Wholesale.** Wholesalers sell drugs to manufacturers, other wholesalers, retailers, and medical institutions. For more information about wholesalers, see *Question 16*.
- **Retail.** Retailers sell drugs directly to consumers.

The application procedures for wholesale and retail licences vary slightly.

**Wholesale drug distribution licensing procedure**

An application to establish a wholesale drug distribution enterprise must be filed with the provincial Food and Drug Administration (provincial FDA) where the enterprise is to be established. The provincial FDA must, within 30 working days from accepting the application, make a decision on whether to permit initial preparations to establish the wholesale drug distribution enterprise and notify the applicant in writing. If the provincial FDA does not grant the applicant the right to complete the initial preparations, an explanation of why such right was denied and a notification of the applicant's right to apply for administrative reconsideration or institute an administrative hearing must be sent to the applicant.

If approved, the applicant can complete the initial preparations. After completing the initial preparations, the applicant must request the provincial FDA to confirm completion (known as the application for examination and acceptance). The provincial FDA must, within 30 working days from receipt of the application, accept and examine the application and decide whether or not to issue the drug distribution licence.

Enterprises that meet the requirements will then be issued the drug distribution licence. Those not meeting the requirements must be notified in writing with an explanation of why the provincial FDA issued a denial.

**Retail drug distribution licensing procedure**

The procedures are the same as those regarding the sale of drugs wholesale, apart from the following:

- The applicant must file an application with the municipal or county-level FDA where the enterprise is to be established rather than to the provincial FDA.
- The municipal or county-level FDA after receipt of the application must, within 15 working days, rather than 30 working days from the date of receipt of the application for

examination and acceptance, accept and examine the application and make a decision on whether or not to issue the drug distribution licence.

**Manufacturer's licence**

Domestic drug manufacturers must receive a drug manufacturing licence before producing drugs in China. Those with a drug manufacturing licence do not need an additional drug distribution licence to distribute the drugs that they have produced. However, they can only distribute the drugs that they have produced.

**Medical institutions**

Medical institutions can also sell drugs to patients in China. A medical institution is an institution that engages in the diagnosis and treatment of diseases (for example, hospitals and clinics). To form a medical institution, an organisation must apply for and receive a medical institution licence.

**The 2013 Good Supplying Practice (GSP) for Pharmaceutical Products**

All drug distributors must also attain GSP certification demonstrating compliance with the 2013 version of the GSP for pharmaceutical products (2013 GSP). The 2013 GSP (a revision of the 2000 GSP) was promulgated by the Ministry of Health (now the National Health and Family Planning Commission) and took effect on 1 June 2013. It sets higher standards for quality management systems including tracking mechanisms, computer hardware, drug storage, and transportation. All current distribution enterprises must meet the requirements of the 2013 GSP by 31 December 2015 or cease operations.

A GSP certification is attained after receiving the appropriate distribution and business licences. The CFDA's Notice on Implementing the Revised GSP for Pharmaceutical Products outlines a three-step timeline for complying with the 2013 GSP. The CFDA aims to gradually integrate the drug distribution licence and the GSP certification into one administrative licence. Several provinces, such as Fujian Province and Guizhou Province, have already begun reforming their administrative procedures to merge the two licences.

Drug manufacturers and medical institutions are not defined as drug distributors under PRC law, even though they may sell drugs under certain circumstances. As a result, they are not required to attain GSP accreditation. However, they may be subject to other rules and regulations. For example, drug manufacturers are required to comply with the good manufacturing practice standards.

**Regulatory authority**

See above, *Structure*.

**4. IS THERE A SIMPLIFIED LICENCE PROCEEDING, OR RELAXED LICENSING CONDITIONS, FOR DRUGS WHICH HAVE ALREADY BEEN LICENSED FOR DISTRIBUTION IN ANOTHER JURISDICTION?**

There are no simplified licensing procedures for drugs that have already been licensed for distribution in another jurisdiction. Those that are interested in importing drugs produced by foreign enterprises into China must apply for an import certificate from the China Food and

Drug Administration (CFDA) under the same registration procedures as any other imported drug.

The CFDA follows the Drug Registration Management Measures (Drug Registration Measures) when reviewing a drug application for an import certificate. Under the Drug Registration Measures, certain types of drugs (that is, chemical and biological), which are approved for licence in another jurisdiction, can substitute some clinical research required by the application. However, the licensing procedures themselves are not simplified.

There are no rules regulating the parallel imports of drugs under PRC law.

### 5. IS VIRTUAL DRUG DISTRIBUTION POSSIBLE FROM YOUR JURISDICTION?

Under PRC law, drug distribution licences obtained in China only allow drugs to be distributed within mainland China. Virtual drug distribution is not provided for under PRC law.

### 6. WHAT IS THE PROCEDURE TO APPEAL (LEGAL REMEDY) A LICENSING DECISION?

Applicants applying for drug registration certificates or drug distribution licences can apply for administrative reconsideration or file an administrative hearing against a licensing decision of the China Food and Drug Administration (CFDA).

### 7. WHAT ARE THE COSTS OF OBTAINING LICENSING?

Fees are charged for processing drug registration, approval, and distribution licence applications.

**Drug registration and approval costs**

On 27 May 2015, the CFDA published a new fee schedule for drug and medical device registrations. Previously, approval and registration fees generally ranged between RMB13,500 and RMB24,300 depending on the type of drug (that is, imported, produced domestically, new, and/or generic). Generic drugs generally cost less than new drugs. The relevant drug regulatory body may also charge fees for clinical trials for drugs produced domestically and for drug tests. In the past, the registration fees for importing drugs were RMB45,300.

After the publication of the new fee schedule in May 2015, drug registration fees dramatically increased. For example, the new drug registration fee for an imported drug is comprised of an RMB376,000 clinical trial fee and an RMB593,900 manufacturing and marketing fee. For imported generic drugs, the registration fee is divided into two categories depending on whether the drug needs clinical trials before they are manufactured and put into the market. The registration fee for an imported generic drug that does not need clinical trials is RMB367,600 and the registration fee for an imported generic drug that needs clinical trials is RMB502,000.

Drug manufacturers are also subject to registration fees for supplemental applications. An imported drug's supplemental application fee is RMB9,600 for regular items and RMB283,600 for items that require technical review. In addition, drug re-registration fees of imported drugs must be paid once every five years at a price of RMB227,200 per drug.

The above fees are calculated on the basis that one active pharmaceutical ingredient/preparation is classified as one type of drug specification. Adding another specification will incur an additional 20% charge in registration fees depending on whether the drug is a domestic drug or an imported drug.

These costs are mainly governmental fees directly associated with obtaining a licence for a drug. It is difficult to estimate other related expenses and costs, which in practice vary on a case by case basis.

**Drug distribution licensing costs**

Drug distribution licence fees differ depending on the locality. The application fee for a drug distribution licence is usually minimal (for example, RMB10 or less). As mentioned in *Question 3*, distributors now must also apply for GSP accreditation. Factors that may affect GSP accreditation fees include the:

- Turnover of the enterprise.
- Number of chain stores.
- Location of the distributor.

## DISTRIBUTION TO CONSUMERS

### 8. WHAT ARE THE DIFFERENT CATEGORIES OF DRUGS FOR DISTRIBUTION?

After approval and licensing, the distribution of drugs is primarily classified under two categories:

- Prescription drugs.
- Non-prescription drugs.

Non-prescription drugs are further divided into two subcategories: "Type A" and "Type B". Type A non-prescription drugs are considered more hazardous and are more strictly regulated than Type B non-prescription drugs which are generally considered safer. For more details, see *Question 9*.

### 9. WHO IS AUTHORISED TO DISTRIBUTE PRESCRIPTION DRUGS AND OVER-THE-COUNTER DRUGS TO CONSUMERS?

**Prescription drugs**

As discussed in *Question 3*, drug distribution licences are held by wholesalers and retailers. Each licence lists the types of drugs (prescription and non-prescription) that the distributor is able to sell.

A drug retailer can sell drugs directly to consumers, but can only sell prescription drugs to consumers if:

- The customer has a written prescription from a licensed physician.
- The drug falls within the category of prescription drugs permitted by the drug distribution licence.
- A pharmacist at the retailer reviews and signs the prescription before the drug is distributed to the consumer.

The prescription must be kept for two years at the retailer for inspection.

**Over-the-counter drugs**

As a general rule, only a drug retailer is entitled to distribute non-prescription (over-the-counter) drugs. A drug retailer can sell non-prescription drugs to consumers if it has obtained a drug distribution licence and the drugs fall within the category of non-prescription drugs permitted by the drug distribution licence.

Non-prescription drugs can be purchased and used by patients without prescriptions from a licensed physician or licensed physician's assistant. The types of enterprises permitted to sell non-prescription drugs directly to consumers include the following:

- **Retail pharmacies or enterprises.** The sale of Type A non-prescription drugs (which bears more restrictions than Type B non-prescription drugs) requires a drug distribution licence and must be sold by an in-store licensed pharmacist or pharmacy technician.
- **Regular business enterprises.** The sale of Type B non-prescription drugs requires that the enterprise have full-time employees who are well trained and authorised to sell these drugs.
- **Other businesses.** Other businesses include supermarkets, grocery stores, hotel shops, and shopping malls that have a separate stall or counter for the purpose of operating as a drug retailer. Other businesses can only sell Type B non-prescription drugs if authorised to do so.
- **Medical institutions.** Medical institutions can decide or recommend the use of non-prescription drugs in accordance with medical needs.

## 10. WHAT DRUGS CAN AN ATTENDING PHYSICIAN DISTRIBUTE AND UNDER WHAT CIRCUMSTANCES?

Under PRC law, physicians can prescribe drugs, but are prohibited from distributing prescription drugs to patients. The law does not provide for the distribution of drugs by an attending physician in case of emergency.

## 11. WHO IS AUTHORISED TO PRESCRIBE PRESCRIPTION DRUGS TO CONSUMERS?

Licensed physicians and licensed physician's assistants can prescribe prescription drugs to consumers. Prescription drugs must not be allocated, purchased, and used without a prescription.

## 12. IS DIRECT MAILING/DISTANCE SELLING OF DRUGS PERMITTED IN YOUR JURISDICTION?

**Conditions**

The direct sale of prescription drugs by a drug manufacturer or distributor to the public by mail or through the Internet is forbidden. Medical institutions are also prohibited from selling prescription drugs directly to the public by mail or through the Internet.

In May 2014, the China Food and Drug Administration (CFDA) published the Draft of the Measures for the Supervision and Administration of Internet Food and Drug Business Operations (Draft Measures) for public comment. The Draft Measures propose allowing drug manufacturers and distributors with valid qualification certificates for internet drug transactions to sell prescription drugs online when prescriptions are shown. No official version of the Draft Measures has been published yet. It is advisable to monitor developments related to the Draft Measures since they may be promulgated in the future.

Non-prescription drugs can be sold by direct mail/distance selling by currently licensed distributors if a copy of the drug distribution licence or the certificate issued by the local FDA is submitted to the post office that is mailing the drugs. In addition, a drug distributor can sell non-prescription drugs to consumers through the Internet by obtaining an Internet transaction of drug services certificate issued by the CFDA and its local branches.

With regard to narcotics and psychotropic drugs, the sender must, for each mailing, apply for and obtain a certificate for the mailing of narcotics and psychotropic drugs at the provincial FDA by submitting the relevant documents, which must then be presented to the post office when mailing the narcotics and psychotropic drugs.

**Cross-border sales**

There is no specific law regulating the sale of drugs beyond the borders of China. However, if the drug is imported from outside of China, then the relevant laws regarding the importation of drugs will apply.

### 13. WHAT REGULATORY AUTHORITY IS RESPONSIBLE FOR SUPERVISING DISTRIBUTION ACTIVITIES?

There are many agencies that are responsible for supervising distribution activities regarding consumers.

The China Food and Drug Administration (CFDA) and its local FDA branches are the primary agencies responsible for drug supervision. These are the agencies that issue drug registration certificates, distribution licences, and manufacturing licences and that conduct inspections to ensure that drugs meet quality standards. The CFDA is responsible for managing and supervising issues related to drugs at the national level while the local FDAs are responsible for the supervision and management of drugs in their respective geographic areas.

The State Council of the PRC (State Council) and provincial-level governmental departments also play a role in the overall supervision and promulgation of policy regarding drug distribution. The State Council is responsible for the overall supervision and management of drug-related work at the national level. Provincial-level governmental departments are responsible for the overall supervision and management of drug-related work in their respective geographic areas.

In addition, the Administration of Industry and Commerce (AIC), which supervises market operations in China, may also regulate drug distribution at various levels because drugs are considered commercial products.

### 14. WHAT IS THE PROCEDURE TO APPEAL (LEGAL REMEDY) A DISTRIBUTION DECISION?

The legal remedies against decisions made by the agencies in *Question 13* include filing for administrative reconsideration or initiating an administrative lawsuit.

## 15. WHAT ARE THE LEGAL CONSEQUENCES OF NON-COMPLIANCE WITH CONSUMER DISTRIBUTION LAWS?

Under PRC law, consequences for non-compliance can be criminal, administrative, or civil. Violators may be subject to the following penalties, among others:

- Warnings.
- Detention.
- Seizure of assets.
- Fines.
- Mandatory corrections within a specified period of time.
- Revocation of licences.
- Confiscation of illegal income.

**Criminal consequences**

Under PRC Criminal Law, whoever produces or sells counterfeit or substandard drugs will be sentenced and fined. If the production or sale of counterfeit drugs causes death or other severe consequences, the offender is subject to a fixed-term of imprisonment of no less than ten years, life imprisonment or the death penalty, and fines or confiscation of property.

In November 2014, the Supreme People's Court and the Supreme People's Procurator issued the Interpretation on Several Issues Concerning the Application of Law in Handling Criminal Cases Related to Endangering Drug Safety (Interpretation). The Interpretation provides for criminal penalties for counterfeiting and substandard processing. It provides harsher penalties for certain types of drugs (for example, narcotics, contraceptives, and vaccines). Harsher penalties are also provided for in cases where there are drug violations involving the sale of drugs to pregnant women, infants, and children and under certain circumstances (for example, drug violations involving responses to natural disasters, repeat offences, failure to secure a business licence, among others). Penalties also vary in accordance with the severity of the injury caused and the volume of profits attained from the sale.

**Administrative consequences**

The drug supervisory and regulatory department may impose different penalties depending on the circumstances, as described below:

- If drugs were distributed without a drug distribution licence, the distributor will be subject to regulations that require the confiscation of the illegal product and income, and either a fine will be imposed, or in serious cases, the distributor may be subject to criminal liability.
- If a medical institution sells prescription drugs directly to the public by mail or through the Internet, they will be instructed to rectify the error, given a warning, and given a fine.
- If the distribution of drugs involved secret kickbacks, or the drug distributor or its agents offered property or other items of interest to the staff, physicians, and other relevant personnel of the medical institution that purchased the drugs from the distributor, a fine will be imposed and any illegal gains will be confiscated. In cases of serious violations, the distributor's business licence and the drug distribution licence will be revoked. Criminal liability may also be imposed if these acts constitute a crime.
- If a medical institution unlawfully accepts public donations and sponsorships or accepts donations and sponsorships that may have an adverse effect on fair competition, such activities must be handled by the relevant authorities in accordance with the law.

## WHOLESALE DISTRIBUTION

### 16. WHAT IS THE LEGAL REGIME REGARDING WHOLESALE DISTRIBUTION OF DRUGS?

The legal regime regulating wholesale distribution of drugs is outlined in *Questions 1* and *2*. A drug wholesaler is a drug enterprise that purchases drugs and then sells them to drug manufacturing enterprises, drug distributors, and medical institutions.

Several requirements are necessary to receive and maintain a wholesale distribution licence, including:

- **Licensed pharmacists.** The applicant must have a certain number of licensed pharmacists that are commensurate with its business scale, that is, the larger the business, the more licensed pharmacists that are required. The person responsible for quality control must hold a bachelor's degree or above, and must be a licensed pharmacist.
- **Warehouse temperature.** The applicant for a wholesale distribution licence must have warehouses that maintain room temperature, and warehouses that maintain relatively colder temperatures or refrigerators to satisfy storage requirements commensurate with its drug varieties and business scale. The warehouses must be equipped with installations and equipment that qualify it as a modern logistics system for drugs.

A drug wholesaler is also subject to certain good supplying practice (GSP) requirements, including:

- **Quality management.** The drug wholesaler must establish a specialised quality management department that maintains quality management and upholds internal standards on drug quality within the corporation.
- **Drug inspection.** The drug wholesaler must set up drug inspection, acceptance and maintenance departments that correspond to the scale of its operations. The drug inspection and acceptance department must be closely linked to the quality management department.
- **Purchasing procedure.** For drug wholesalers, quality must be the primary factor when selecting drugs and suppliers. Procedures that govern the purchase of drugs must be established to ensure quality standards are met when purchasing drugs.

### 17. WHAT REGULATORY AUTHORITY IS RESPONSIBLE FOR SUPERVISING WHOLESALE DISTRIBUTION ACTIVITIES?

**Regulatory authority**

The government agencies supervising wholesale distribution activities are the same as the government agencies supervising retail activities (*see Question 13*).

**Supervision**

The government agencies supervising wholesale distribution activities are the same as the government agencies supervising retail activities (*see Question 13*).

**Rights of appeal**

The government agencies supervising wholesale distribution activities are the same as the government agencies supervising retail activities (*see Question 14*).

## 18. WHAT ARE THE LEGAL CONSEQUENCES OF NON-COMPLIANCE WITH WHOLESALE DISTRIBUTION LAWS?

See *Question 15* for more information about criminal consequences of non-compliance. In addition to criminal consequences, administrative consequences include warnings, fines, mandatory corrections under time limits, confiscation of drugs and income, and other administrative penalties.

# MARKETING

## PROMOTION

## 19. WHAT IS THE GENERAL LEGAL REGIME FOR THE MARKETING OF DRUGS?

**Legal regime**

In China, there is no specific legislation dedicated to the marketing of drugs. Instead, the controlling regulatory authority is referred to in many drug-related laws and regulations. These laws include the Drug Administration Law, the Law of the PRC on the Protection of Consumer Rights and Interests (Consumer Protection Law), the Advertising Law of the PRC (Advertising Law), the Criminal Law, the Provisions for the Supervision of Drug Distribution, and the Standards for the Examination and Publication of Drug Advertisements (Drug Advertising Standards).

Marketing of drugs can be divided into two categories:

- Marketing to consumers (*see Question 21*).
- Marketing to professionals (*see Question 27*).

**Limits to marketing activities**

Certain types of drugs are prohibited from advertising to the public (*see Question 22*). Additionally, bribery in marketing activities is strictly prohibited and violation may incur criminal liabilities.

## 20. ARE THERE OTHER CODES OF CONDUCT FOR THE MARKETING OF DRUGS (FOR EXAMPLE, BY PROFESSIONAL OR INDUSTRIAL ORGANISATIONS)?

The Research and Development-Based Pharmaceutical Association Committee (RDPAC) is a member-based, self-regulating industry association that regulates interactions between drug suppliers and healthcare professionals in China. RDPAC currently has 40 members, which are all major multinational, research-based drug companies with substantial investments in China. Members include:

- Bayer HealthCare.
- GE Healthcare Genzyme.
- Lundbeck.
- Novartis.

# CHINA

- Novo Nordisk Nycomed.
- Pfizer.
- Sanofi Aventis.

The most recent version of the RDPAC Code of Practice on the Promotion of Pharmaceutical Products (RDPAC Code) was published in 2012. The 2012 RDPAC Code is limited to prescription drug products, but regulates nearly all interactions with healthcare professionals. For more information on the RDPAC Code, see *Question 27*.

The RDPAC Code is voluntarily implemented by its members and not legally enforced or mandatory. Therefore, it is not a source of law.

## MARKETING TO CONSUMERS

### 21. WHAT IS THE LEGAL REGIME FOR MARKETING TO CONSUMERS?

**Legal regime**

In China, there is no specific legislation for the marketing of drugs. Instead, the relevant provisions are interspersed throughout various provisions of other drug-related laws and regulations.

**Products**

Since a drug is a product, it must comply with both safety and efficacy standards according to the Drug Administration Law. In addition, when a drug product is to be marketed to consumers, the drug manufacturer must ensure compliance with various laws including the Advertising Law and the Consumer Protection Law.

### 22. WHAT KINDS OF MARKETING ACTIVITIES ARE PERMITTED IN RELATION TO CONSUMERS AND THE PRODUCTS WHICH MAY BE ADVERTISED TO THEM?

Generally, activities not expressly prohibited by law are considered permissible. Under the Circulation and Supervision Regulations and the Interim Provisions, the following conduct is prohibited:

- A drug manufacturing or distribution enterprise must not sell drugs available on-hand at exhibitions, expositions, trade fairs, order placement meetings, or product advertisement meetings.
- Drug manufacturers or distribution enterprises must not give any prescription drug or any type a non-prescription drug to the public through tie-in sales, or through the provision of drugs to those who buy other drugs or other (non-drug) products.
- Prescription drugs must not be sold directly to the public by mail or through the internet.
- Drug wholesale enterprises must not directly recommend or sell prescription drugs to patients in any manner.
- Prescription drugs and non-prescription drugs must not be sold via the winning of prizes through drug purchases, or via the receipt of free drugs or gifts with purchases.
- Ordinary commercial enterprises (for example, supermarkets, grocery stores, hotel shops, shopping malls, that have a separate stall or counter for the purpose of operating as a drug retailer) must not:

- sell prescription drugs and Type A non-prescription drugs;
- sell Type B non-prescription drugs via the winning of prizes through purchases, or via the receipt of free drugs or gifts with purchases; and
- sell non-prescription drugs of Type B online (this may be subject to change in the future).

**Advertising**

Under the Drug Administration Law, the Advertising Law, and the Drug Advertising Standards, the general rule is that prescription drugs must not be directly advertised to consumers by any drug manufacturing or wholesale enterprise.

**Approval.** Advertisements of drugs must be approved by the provincial drug supervisory and regulatory department where the enterprise is located and must be issued an advertisement registration number. Without a registration number, the drug cannot be advertised. The content of the drug advertisement must be true, legitimate, and consistent with the drug label instructions (or the included manual).

The following drugs must not be advertised:

- Narcotics, psychotropic drugs, poisonous substances for medical use, radioactive drugs, chemicals in medications which are easily used to make drugs, medications, medical devices, and treatment for drug detoxification.
- Drugs prepared by medical institutions.
- Drugs needed by the military.
- Drugs whose production, distribution, and use have been suspended or prohibited as expressly ordered by the then State Food and Drug Administration (SFDA) (now the CFDA) according to the law.
- Drugs approved for trial production.

The following restrictions apply to drug advertisements:

- Drug advertisements must not directly or indirectly unduly induce people to purchase and use drugs below or in excess of its required dosage. PRC laws also expressly prohibit certain content in drug advertisements. For example, drug advertisements must not contain any baseless (non-scientifically tested) statements/assertions, that is, referring to a drug's effects, safety, awards won or rankings (such as, "best" and "number one") or referring to any institutions, experts or military entities.
- Content such as the general name of the drug, advice, drug advertisement licence numbers and drug production licence numbers must be stated in the drug advertisement. The drug advertisement must state the name of the manufacturing or distribution enterprise of the drug.
- Drugs must not be advertised in publications, radio or on television or on any programs targeting minors (that is, persons under 18 years old).
- Advertisements of substances that are not drugs must be separate from the advertisements of drugs. Additionally, non-drug advertisements must not make reference to drugs.

**Advertisements of prescription drugs.** The following restrictions apply specifically to the advertisements of prescription drugs:

- Prescription drugs can be advertised in professional medical science or drug publications jointly designated by the Health Administration under the State Council and the CFDA, but must not be advertised in any mass media or in any other form directed towards the general public.

CHINA

- Prescription drugs must not be advertised to the general public through the presentation of professional medical science and drug publications or in any other way.

**Advertisements of non-prescription drugs.** The following restrictions apply specifically to the advertisements of non-prescription drugs:

- Subject to approval, non-prescription drugs can be advertised through any mass media outlet to the general public.
- The advertisement of a non-prescription drug must include the special "OTC" drug symbol.
- If the chemical/generic name of a prescription drug is used as the title of an advertisement, only the chemical/generic name of the drug can be advertised.

### 23. IS IT PERMITTED TO PROVIDE CONSUMERS WITH FREE SAMPLES? ARE THERE PARTICULAR RESTRICTIONS ON SPECIAL OFFERS (FOR EXAMPLE, "BUY-ONE-GET-ONE-FREE")?

Currently, there are no regulations specifically regulating free samples for consumers. However, the general consensus among the food and drug administration officials at the local level is that drugs distributed to consumers must be registered and approved, and providing consumers with free samples is prohibited.

In relation to restrictions on special offers, according to the Circulation and Supervision Regulations and the Detailed Implementation Management Rules to Regulate the Quality of the Drug Trade, no drugs can be given as free gifts with respect to purchases. Accordingly, special offers such as "buy-one-get-one-free" offers are not permitted.

### 24. ARE THERE PARTICULAR RULES OF PRACTICE ON THE USE OF THE INTERNET/SOCIAL MEDIA REGARDING DRUGS AND THEIR ADVERTISING?

Several laws and regulations directly address or extend their scope to cover advertising on the Internet and social media. For example:

- Drugs cannot be advertised in publications, broadcasting or television channels or programmes targeted at minors (persons under 18 years old).
- Prescription drugs can be advertised in professional medical science or pharmaceutical publications jointly designated by the Ministry of Health and the China Food and Drug Administration (CFDA), but must not be advertised in any mass media or in any other form toward the general public.
- Prescription drugs must not be advertised to the general public by way of presenting professional medical science and pharmaceutical publications or in any other way.
- Non-prescription drugs can be advertised through any mass media medium directed towards the general public on approval.

Under the Research and Development-Based Pharmaceutical Association Committee (RDPAC) Code, the following applies to drug related websites:

- The identity of the drug company and of the intended audience must be readily apparent.
- The content must be appropriate for the intended audience.
- The presentation (content, links) must be appropriate and apparent to the intended audience.
- Country-specific information must comply with local laws and regulations.

The above rules may also apply to the use of the internet/social media with respect to drugs and their advertising.

## 25. WHAT REGULATORY AUTHORITY IS RESPONSIBLE FOR SUPERVISING MARKETING ACTIVITIES TO CONSUMERS?

**Regulatory authority**

The regulatory authorities for the oversight of marketing activities to consumers include the China Food and Drug Administration (CFDA), its local FDA branches, and the administration of industry and commerce.

**Supervision**

The CFDA and its local FDA branches are the primary regulatory institutions responsible for overseeing marketing activities to consumers. For drug advertising, local FDA branches review and approve drug advertisements for their respective jurisdictions. The administrations of industry and commerce above the county level supervise and manage such advertisements.

**Rights of appeal**

The legal remedies against decisions made by the agencies above include filing for administrative reconsideration or initiating an administrative lawsuit.

## 26. WHAT ARE THE LEGAL CONSEQUENCES OF NON-COMPLIANCE WITH CONSUMER MARKETING LAWS?

If drugs are sold at exhibitions, fairs, trade fairs or product promotion meetings, the illegally sold drugs and any illegal income will be confiscated, and a fine of two to five times the amount of the value of the illegally sold drugs will be imposed.

In cases involving the unlawful gifting of any prescription drugs or any Type A non-prescription drugs to the public through tie-in sales, or through gifting drugs to those who buy other drugs or other (non-drug) products, violators will be ordered to redress the situation within a specified period of time, and will be admonished. If the violator fails to make the requisite corrections within the time limit or if the circumstances are severe, a fine must be imposed.

## MARKETING TO PROFESSIONALS

## 27. WHAT KINDS OF MARKETING ACTIVITIES ARE PERMITTED IN RELATION TO PROFESSIONALS?

PRC law strictly prohibits distributors from offering money or things of value to professionals in the course of selling drugs. However, there is no law in China specifically regulating marketing to professionals. However, the Research and Development-Based Pharmaceutical Association Committee (RDPAC) extensively regulates interactions between drug suppliers and healthcare professionals (*see Question 20*).

Under the RDPAC Code, many marketing activities directed at professionals are permissible. However, permissible activities are regulated and include:

- Distribution of printed and electronic promotional materials.
- Events and meetings.

- Sponsoring medical professionals to attend events.
- Distribution of promotional aids.
- Distribution of medical utility items.
- Distribution of samples.
- Engaging in services such as consulting, advisory, speaking, the chairing of meetings, involvement in scientific studies, clinical trials, training services, and market research.

For RPDAC restrictions on the above activities see *Question 28*.

## 28. ARE THERE ANY RESTRICTIONS ON MARKETING TO PROFESSIONALS?

**Marketing activities**

Under PRC law, offering money or items of value to healthcare professionals in the course of selling drugs is strictly prohibited.

Under the Research and Development-Based Pharmaceutical Association Committee (RDPAC) Code, the provision of personal gifts, cash, entertainment and leisure events is strictly prohibited. The following restrictions also apply:

- Promotional materials must be consistent with approved labelling and uses, possess a non-misleading nature, and only contain claims that can be validated.
- Printed and electronic materials must:
  - be legible;
  - list the active ingredients of the drug;
  - include the name and address of the pharmaceutical company; and
  - include a statement of the drug's side effects.
- Promotional aids must be of minimal value.
- Medical utility items must be of modest value.
- Engaging a healthcare professional for consulting or advisory purposes requires a written contract specifying the nature of the services and a legitimate need for the services, among other requirements.
- For restrictions with respect to events and meetings, see below, *Provision of hospitality*.
- For restrictions with respect to samples and sponsoring, see *Question 31*.

**Frequency**

Regarding the sale of drugs, the term "sales representative" is not clearly defined under PRC law. In 2008, the then Ministry of Health published the Draft on Managing Medical Representatives (Draft), which has not yet been enacted. The Draft defines medical representatives as personnel employed by drug manufacturers and distributors for drug publicity and promotion, including personnel who go to medical institutions for business activities under the name of drug manufacturers and drug distributors. It requires that such personnel be formally employed by the drug manufacturer or distributor.

The Draft proposes that medical representatives be reviewed by and registered with each health institution before they can conduct business there. Permitted activities are limited to promoting pharmaceutical products and collecting information on the drugs sold by the representative (including adverse drug reaction information). Promotion methods are limited to:

- Seminars.
- Lectures.
- Distributing promotional materials.
- Other approaches agreed to by the medical affair management department of the health institution.

No healthcare professional or other personnel can meet with medical representatives in private and all meetings must be approved by the personnel in charge of the medical department. Medical representatives must report to the healthcare institution's medical affair management department for the business activities that they participated in within seven days after such activities are finished.

As the Draft has not yet been enacted, it can only be used for reference at this point.

**Provision of hospitality**

Apart from the Draft on Managing Medical Representatives, there are no express provisions under PRC law regulating meetings with professionals or hospitality.

The RDPAC Code (*see Questions 20 and 27*), restricts events, meetings, and hospitality in the following ways:

- The objective of events must be limited to providing scientific or educational information and/or informing healthcare professionals about product information.
- Events must avoid extravagant venues and can only provide meals and refreshments that are moderate, reasonable, and limited to the main purpose of the event.
- A company must not organise or sponsor an event taking place outside of their home country unless justified by logistical or security reasons. International scientific congresses and symposia with participants from many countries are therefore justified and permitted.
- No payments can be made to healthcare professionals for time spent attending events.
- Companies must not pay the costs of the guests of the invited healthcare professionals.
- No entertainment or other leisure or social activities should be provided or paid for by members.

## 29. WHAT INFORMATION IS IT LEGALLY REQUIRED TO INCLUDE IN ADVERTISING TO PROFESSIONALS?

According to the Advertising Law, the advertisement of a prescription drug must, in an obvious way, state that "this advertisement is only for medical and pharmaceutical professionals to read".

## 30. ARE THERE RULES ON COMPARISONS WITH OTHER PRODUCTS THAT ARE PARTICULARLY APPLICABLE TO DRUGS?

Drugs are generally treated as a distinct category of products under PRC law. However, they are also regulated as common products under the Product Quality Law, the Consumer Protection Law, the Advertising Law, and other relevant laws and regulations.

The Advertising Law provides that drugs must not be compared to other drugs in advertisements with respect to the function and safety of the drugs.

## 31. WHAT OTHER ITEMS, FUNDING OR SERVICES ARE PERMITTED TO BE PROVIDED TO PROFESSIONALS?

PRC law does not provide for indirect incentives. However, legal documents and the Research and Development-Based Pharmaceutical Association Committee (RDPAC) Code contain relevant regulations on discounts, samples, and sponsorships.

**Discounts**

Relatively strict regulations regarding drug pricing in China can be found in the Drug Administration Law. Discounts are permitted in the course of the purchase and sales of drugs only if they are explicit and recorded faithfully in the account book of both parties. Off-the-book kickbacks are considered bribery under PRC law.

**Free samples**

Apart from the Draft on Managing Medical Representatives (Draft) (*see Question 28*), PRC law does not specifically regulate the distribution of samples to healthcare professionals. Under the Draft, sample drugs provided to healthcare professionals must be clearly marked as "sample" or "not for sale" on the package. It also states that the drug supplied and the amount supplied must be commensurate with the relevant business activities.

Under the RDPAC Code, samples can be provided to enhance patient care if the samples are marked as samples. This is to ensure that they cannot be resold, or otherwise misused, and are limited in quantity. These samples can be used to promote familiarisation with the product. Additionally, companies that distribute samples must have adequate control of the samples provided to healthcare professionals, including monitoring of the samples while they are in the possession of healthcare professionals, and will be held accountable for the samples.

**Sponsorship of professionals**

Sponsoring of professionals is allowed under certain circumstances. According to the Interim Provisions on Medical Institutions Receiving Public Donations and Sponsorships (Donations and Sponsorships Provisions), the following applies:

- Medical institutions receiving public donations and sponsorship (for example, the provision of funds, supplies and other forms of assistance by natural persons, legal persons, and other organisations voluntarily and without compensation to medical institutions) must not harm the public interest and/or the lawful interests of citizens. Any donations and sponsorship with conditions attached that may affect fair competition and that connect donations and sponsorships with the purchase of products or services are prohibited.
- Public donations and sponsorship must be managed and used properly. Departments or individuals of medical institutions must not accept donations and sponsorship. If the donor and/or sponsor require a donation and/or sponsorship to be accepted in the name of an individual, it must be reported to and approved by the governing body of the medical institution in advance, and managed and administered solely by the finance department of the medical institution.
- Medical institutions must complete certain entry procedures under the relevant laws if they are receiving donations and sponsorships from abroad. Medical institutions must not accept donations and sponsorships from abroad which do not comply with the laws regarding quantity and environmental protection, among others.

The conditions for receiving donations and sponsorships are the following:

- If a medical institution accepts public donations and sponsorships, the donation and sponsorship plan of the donor and sponsor must be examined and verified by the medical institution. The institution will then decide whether to accept the donations and sponsorships.
- Medical institutions must enter into written agreements with donors and sponsors when accepting public donations and sponsorships. The donors and sponsors must perform their obligations under the relevant agreements lawfully and must deliver the donated and sponsored property to the medical institutions. Medical institutions must issue receipts to the donors and sponsors.

The use of the property from public donations and sponsorships is regulated in the following ways:

- Property from public donations and sponsorships received by medical institutions must be used primarily for:
  - the treatment of poor patients;
  - public health education;
  - training for health personnel;
  - medical communications;
  - scientific research;
  - construction of service facilities for medical institutions; and
  - other non-profit business activities.
- Medical institutions must not unilaterally change the restrictions set out in the agreement. The donated and sponsored funds must not be used for the payment of employee bonuses, allowances and other personal outlays, and no management expenses may be extracted.

Under the RDPAC Code, companies can sponsor healthcare professionals to attend events provided that:

- No payment is made for time spent attending events. Compensation must be limited to travel, meals, accommodation, and registration fees.
- Any sponsorship must not be conditional on an obligation to prescribe, recommend, purchase, supply, administer, or promote any pharmaceutical product.

**Other items, funding or service**

The RDPAC Code also provides that:

- Payments of fees and reimbursement of out-of-pocket expenses must be reasonable and based on fair market value and can be provided to healthcare professionals who are providing genuine services as speakers or presenters on the basis of a written contract.
- Members can offer or provide items of medical utility free of charge provided that the items are of modest value and are beneficial to the provision of medical services and for patient care, such as an anatomical model or medical textbooks.

## 32. WHAT REGULATORY AUTHORITY IS RESPONSIBLE FOR SUPERVISING MARKETING ACTIVITIES REGARDING PROFESSIONALS?

**Regulatory authority**

The regulatory authorities for the oversight of marketing activities regarding professionals include the China Food and Drug Administration (CFDA), its local FDA branches, and the administration of industry and commerce.

**Supervision**

The CFDA and its local FDA branches are mainly responsible for the oversight of marketing activities regarding professionals. For drug advertising, local FDA branches review and approve drug advertisements for their respective jurisdictions. The administrations of industry and commerce above the county level supervise and manage these advertisements.

**Rights of appeal**

The legal remedies against decisions made by the agencies above include filing for administrative reconsideration or initiating an administrative lawsuit.

## 33. WHAT ARE THE LEGAL CONSEQUENCES IN CASE OF NON-COMPLIANCE WITH PROFESSIONAL MARKETING LAWS?

For an overview of the legal consequences associated with non-compliance, see *Question 15*. Additionally, according to the Opinions Concerning the Application of Law in Criminal Commercial Bribery Cases published by the Supreme People's Court and the Supreme People's Procuratorate, the following applies:

- Public servants of medical institutions who, by abusing their positions in purchasing medicines, medical apparatuses, medical hygiene materials and other medical products, solicit property from sellers, or illegally accept any property from the sellers in consideration of acting in favour of such sellers will be convicted for accepting bribes and will be sentenced (*Article 385, Criminal Law*).
- Non-public servants of medical institutions who commit the offence specified in the previous paragraph will be convicted for accepting bribes as a non-public servant and will be sentenced if the value of the bribes in question is relatively high (*Article 163, Criminal Law*).
- Medical staff of medical institutions who, by abusing their power to give prescriptions, illegally accept any property of a relatively high value from the sellers of medicines, medical apparatuses, medical hygiene materials, and other medical products for any reason in consideration of acting in favour of the sellers will be convicted for accepting bribes as a non-public servant and will be sentenced (*Article 163, Criminal Law*).

# ENGAGEMENT WITH PATIENT ORGANISATIONS

### 34. WHAT KINDS OF ACTIVITIES ARE PERMITTED IN RELATION TO ENGAGEMENT WITH PATIENT ORGANISATIONS? WHAT ARE THE RESTRICTIONS THAT ARE IMPOSED ON RELATIONSHIP WITH PATIENT ORGANISATIONS?

There are currently no official national patients' associations in China. A small number of local or provincial associations are known to exist (for example, the Patient Right and Interest Protection Association in Gansu Province). However, there currently are no systematic regulations determining which activities are or are not permitted relating to engagement with these organisations.

There are no restrictions imposed on relationships with patient organisations.

# REFORM

### 35. ARE THERE ANY PLANS TO REFORM THE LAW ON THE DISTRIBUTION AND PROMOTION OF DRUGS IN YOUR JURISDICTION?

On 24 April 2015, the Standing Committee of the National People's Congress passed both the newly amended Drug Administration Law and the amended Advertising Law.

The highlights of the 2015 amendment are:

- Cancellation of the "drug licence before business licence" system for establishing drug manufacturing or distribution enterprises.
- Removal of the fixed pricing and guided pricing mechanisms.

After April 24, obtaining a drug manufacturer's licence or drug distribution licence is no longer a pre-condition for registration with the Administration of Industry and Commerce (AIC). Additionally, the new system for establishing drug manufacturing and distribution enterprises conforms to the procedures for establishing general enterprises. This has simplified the process.

Under the old regime, drugs were priced in three ways:

- The government fixed prices.
- The government guided prices.
- The market regulated prices.

The 2015 amendment has transformed the government planned pricing model to a market pricing model and allows medical institutions to autonomously negotiate purchase prices with drug enterprises. PRC regulators will check drug prices to ensure that their prices correspond to their quality and are determined in accordance with the principles of fairness, rationality, honesty, and good faith.

The amended Advertising Law will take effect on 1 September 2015. It enlarges the scope of prohibited advertisements to cover chemicals in medications which are easily used to make drugs, medications, medical devices, and treatments for drug detoxification. Additionally, it provides that advertisement of medication must be consistent with the drug's instructions and contraindications. It also states that adverse reactions must be prominently labelled. The use of endorsements in drug advertisements and publication of such advertisements in public media targeting minors are now prohibited. These provisions may affect the ability of drug manufacturers to reach out and market to consumers.

# DENMARK

*Nicolaj Kleist, BRUUN & HJEJLE*

## DISTRIBUTION

### PRE-CONDITIONS FOR DISTRIBUTION

**1. WHAT ARE THE LEGAL PRE-CONDITIONS FOR A DRUG TO BE DISTRIBUTED WITHIN THE JURISDICTION?**

**Authorisation**

Requirements for the authorisation and distribution of medicinal products are set out in Act No. 1180 of 12 December 2005 (as amended) (Medicines Act).

Marketing and distribution of a medicinal product requires a marketing authorisation issued by either Danish or European authorities. For pharmacy-restricted medicinal products (that is, products that can only be distributed through licensed pharmacies, including prescription drugs and some over-the-counter drugs), the price of the product on the Danish market must be notified to the Danish Health and Medicines Authority (DHMA) no later than 14 days before the product is placed on the Danish market. For some over-the-counter medicinal products the pack sizes must in some cases be reported to the DHMA at 14 days' prior notice.

**Exceptions**

Under the Medicines Act, the DHMA can permit the sale of a medicinal product without a marketing authorisation valid in Denmark (for example, for named patient supply or compassionate use).

**2. DO ANY TYPES OF NAMED PATIENT AND/OR COMPASSIONATE USE PROGRAMMES OPERATE? IF SO, WHAT ARE THE REQUIREMENTS FOR PRE-LAUNCH ACCESS?**

The Danish Health and Medicines Authority (DHMA) can permit the sale or dispensing in limited amounts of medicinal products that are not covered by a marketing authorisation or not marketed in Denmark (named patient supply). This option is available with regards to both medicinal products with no valid Danish or European marketing authorisation and medicinal products with a marketing authorisation, but which are not available on the Danish market.

Permission generally requires that the medicinal product cannot be replaced by an already authorised medicinal product available in Denmark and that the use of a medicinal product not marketed in Denmark is motivated by therapeutic reasons. Application for permission is made by the prescribing doctor.

## LICENSING

### 3. WHAT IS THE PROCEDURAL STRUCTURE REGARDING LICENSING A DRUG FOR DISTRIBUTION?

**Structure**

As in other EU member states, there are four different application procedures available for a marketing authorisation that will be valid in Denmark, which are the:

- Centralised procedure.
- Decentralised procedure.
- Mutual recognition authorisation procedure.
- National authorisation procedure under which the medicinal product is exclusively authorised in Denmark. The authorisation can then form the basis of applications in other EU (European Economic Area (EEA)) countries via the mutual recognition procedure.

**Regulatory authority**

The Danish Health and Medicines Authority (DHMA) is responsible for issuing Danish marketing authorisations under the national procedure, the decentralised procedure and mutual recognition authorisation procedure. The European Medicines Agency (EMA) is responsible for the centralised procedure.

### 4. IS THERE A SIMPLIFIED LICENCE PROCEEDING, OR RELAXED LICENSING CONDITIONS, FOR DRUGS WHICH HAVE ALREADY BEEN LICENSED FOR DISTRIBUTION IN ANOTHER JURISDICTION?

A medicinal product that has already been authorised in another EU (EEA) country is subject to a simplified procedure under mutual recognition authorisation rules.

A generic product that is identical to an already authorised product (reference product) can benefit from a simplified procedure by referring to the authorisation of the reference product.

A simple procedure also applies to parallel imported products, provided they are imported from another EU/EEA member state. Parallel imported medicinal products can obtain marketing authorisation by referring to the identical, directly distributed medicinal product with a marketing authorisation in Denmark. It is a condition that there are not any differences of therapeutic significance between the parallel imported and the directly distributed medicinal product.

### 5. IS VIRTUAL DRUG DISTRIBUTION POSSIBLE FROM YOUR JURISDICTION?

A national Danish marketing authorisation cannot be used outside Denmark. A product authorised under the centralised procedure can be virtually distributed to other EU/EEA member states.

## 6. WHAT IS THE PROCEDURE TO APPEAL (LEGAL REMEDY) A LICENSING DECISION?

The Danish Health and Medicines Authority's (DHMA) decisions regarding marketing authorisation applications can be appealed to the Ministry of Health. Ultimately, decisions made by the DHMA and the Ministry can be brought before the courts. It should, however, be noted that both the Ministry and the courts will be reluctant to set aside the medicinal assessment of a drug made by the DHMA.

## 7. WHAT ARE THE COSTS OF OBTAINING LICENSING?

An application fee must be paid upon submission of an application, and an annual fee must be paid as long as the authorisation is upheld. The size of the fees depends on the type of authorisation procedure. The 2015 fees are listed in Executive Order No. 1571 of the 16 December 2013 on the Fees on Medicinal Products. The fees for applying for the first authorisation for a product with ordinary documentation requirements include:

- National procedure: DKK82,930.
- Mutual recognition procedure (non-reference country): DKK70,714.
- Mutual recognition procedure (reference country): DKK74,668 (a national authorisation from another EU member state must be obtained).
- Decentralised procedure (non-reference country): DKK167,247.
- Decentralised procedure (reference country): DKK262,967.

## DISTRIBUTION TO CONSUMERS

## 8. WHAT ARE THE DIFFERENT CATEGORIES OF DRUGS FOR DISTRIBUTION?

For distribution purposes, medicinal products are divided into the following categories:

- Prescription-only medicines.
- Over-the-counter medicines.
- Hospital-only medicines.
- Pharmacy-restricted medicines.
- Non-pharmacy-restricted medicines.

## 9. WHO IS AUTHORISED TO DISTRIBUTE PRESCRIPTION DRUGS AND OVER-THE-COUNTER DRUGS TO CONSUMERS?

**Prescription drugs**

Pharmacies have the exclusive right to sell prescription-only medicines to consumers. Running a pharmacy requires a licence from the Danish Health and Medicines Authority (DHMA). A licence is issued to a private individual (the proprietary pharmacist) to run a pharmacy at a specific location. The staff working in Danish pharmacies are pharmacists and pharmaconomists.

**DENMARK**

### Over-the-counter drugs

All over-the-counter medicines can be sold in pharmacies. In addition, a selection of over-the-counter medicines is available in retail stores (for example, supermarkets), which have been authorised by the DHMA to sell such over-the-counter medicines.

The DHMA decides whether a medicine is suitable for sale outside pharmacies based on whether the medicine can be used by consumers without the advice given at pharmacies and the risk of individuals abusing or using the medicine incorrectly.

Retail shops must keep a basic range of products, including painkillers, cough suppressants, lozenges for a sore throat and nicotine chewing gum. The staff employed at shops that are outside the pharmacy sector are not required to have a pharmaceutical education.

### 10. WHAT DRUGS CAN AN ATTENDING PHYSICIAN DISTRIBUTE AND UNDER WHAT CIRCUMSTANCES?

Physicians are not allowed to distribute medicinal products directly to consumers.

### 11. WHO IS AUTHORISED TO PRESCRIBE PRESCRIPTION DRUGS TO CONSUMERS?

Only authorised physicians are allowed to prescribe prescription medicines.

### 12. IS DIRECT MAILING/DISTANCE SELLING OF DRUGS PERMITTED IN YOUR JURISDICTION?

### Conditions

Licensed pharmacies can upon notification to the Danish Health and Medicines Authority (DHMA) sell medicinal products to consumers on the internet subject to section 43(a) of Act No. 279 of 6 June 1984 (as amended) (Pharmacy Act). Retail stores that have been authorised by the DHMA to sell certain over-the-counter medicines can also sell these products on the internet subject to section 41 of the Medicines Act (*see Question 9*).

### Cross-border sales

Subject to EU rules, products can also be sold to consumers in other EU member states.

### 13. WHAT REGULATORY AUTHORITY IS RESPONSIBLE FOR SUPERVISING DISTRIBUTION ACTIVITIES?

The Danish Health and Medicines Authority (DHMA) is responsible for supervising distribution activities (*section 44, Medicines Act*) and will regularly inspect the premises of retailers. Retailers (pharmacies) must be inspected every four to five years. The timing of inspections is determined based on a risk assessment after each individual inspection. However, the DHMA can inspect a pharmacy earlier than planned if there is reason to believe that something is wrong, for example, due to complaints.

## DENMARK

### 14. WHAT IS THE PROCEDURE TO APPEAL (LEGAL REMEDY) A DISTRIBUTION DECISION?

The Danish Health and Medicines Authority's (DHMA) distribution decisions can be appealed to the Ministry of Health, whose decisions can be brought before the ordinary courts.

### 15. WHAT ARE THE LEGAL CONSEQUENCES OF NON-COMPLIANCE WITH CONSUMER DISTRIBUTION LAWS?

The Danish Health and Medicines Authority (DHMA) can suspend or withdraw an authorisation in the case of material non-compliance with general regulations or any specific term imposed in the individual authorisation.

Fines or imprisonment for up to one year and six months can be imposed for violations. The level of fines are not fixed by law, but decided by the ordinary courts based on the circumstances of the case.

According to Danish criminal law, natural persons within a company can be subject to liability only if they have a leading role and have acted by intent or gross negligence.

## WHOLESALE DISTRIBUTION

### 16. WHAT IS THE LEGAL REGIME REGARDING WHOLESALE DISTRIBUTION OF DRUGS?

Companies that distribute medicinal products through wholesale must be authorised by the Danish Health and Medicines Authority (DHMA) under section 39 of the Medicines Act. In order to be authorised, the company must have facilities that are suitably equipped and a person responsible for quality who is to ensure that the activities carried out comply with good distribution practice.

A wholesaler in Denmark is only permitted to receive medicines from either Denmark or other EU/EEA countries. An authorisation for wholesale distribution does not permit the importation of medicines from non-EU/EEA countries (third countries). Such importation requires a separate authorisation.

Even though wholesalers in Denmark are not permitted to import medicines from third countries, the company can obtain authorisation to export (supply) medicines to third countries.

An authorisation for wholesale distribution issued before 1 September 2012 is valid for up to three years. The authorisation can be renewed on application. An authorisation issued from 1 September 2012 has no expiry date.

The DHMA can also attach specific terms to the authorisation, including granting the authorisation for a limited period of time (*section 39a(2), Medicines Act*).

### 17. WHAT REGULATORY AUTHORITY IS RESPONSIBLE FOR SUPERVISING WHOLESALE DISTRIBUTION ACTIVITIES?

**Regulatory authority**

Companies authorised to distribute medicines by wholesale are supervised regularly by the Danish Health and Medicines Authority (DHMA) (*section 44, Medicines Act*).

### DENMARK

**Supervision**

Wholesalers are generally inspected every four to five years. However, if the DHMA has reason to believe that something is wrong, for example due to complaints, the wholesaler will be inspected earlier than planned. The time of the next inspection is determined based on a risk assessment after each individual inspection so that the wholesaler can be inspected more frequently if necessary.

**Rights of appeal**

The DHMA's decisions can be appealed to the Ministry of Health. Decisions by the Ministry of Health can be brought before the ordinary courts.

### 18. WHAT ARE THE LEGAL CONSEQUENCES OF NON-COMPLIANCE WITH WHOLESALE DISTRIBUTION LAWS?

The Danish Health and Medicines Authority (DHMA) can, at any time, suspend or withdraw an authorisation if the company infringes the general regulations or any specific term imposed in the individual authorisation. Fines or imprisonment for up to one year and six months can be imposed for violations.

The size of such fines are not provided for by law, but decided by the ordinary courts on a case-by-case basis.

According to Danish criminal law, natural persons within a company can only be subject to liability if they have a leading role in the company and have acted by intent or gross negligence.

## MARKETING

### PROMOTION

### 19. WHAT IS THE GENERAL LEGAL REGIME FOR THE MARKETING OF DRUGS?

**Legal regime**

Advertising is regulated by the:

- Medicines Act and the Executive Order No. 1153, 22 October 2014
- Advertising for Medicinal Products and Executive Order No. 1244, 12 December 2005 on the Supply of Medicinal Product Samples.

The rules implement the Directive 2001/83/EC on the Community code relating to medicinal products for human use (Code for Human Medicines Directive), as amended.

In section 1(1) of the Executive Order on Advertising for Medicinal Products, advertising is defined as any form of door-to-door information, canvassing activity or inducement designed to promote the prescription, supply, sale or consumption of medicinal products, including media activities designed for these purposes.

The definition does not specify that the entity advertising for a medicinal product must have a special interest (typically financial) in promoting the sale of a medicinal product. If a person or company via public communication clearly acts to induce others to buy a certain medicinal product, and such communication appears as advertising in form, this is tantamount to advertising for medicinal products regardless of whether the person or company is acting on its own initiative and is fully independent, in law and in fact, from the company holding the marketing authorisation for the product concerned.

Under section 2 of the Executive Order on Advertising for Medicinal Products, the following information is not considered to be advertising:

- The label of the medicinal product and the patient information leaflet.
- Individual correspondence answering specific questions about a certain medicinal product.
- Necessary and concrete information or documentation serving safety and non-commercial purposes.
- Price lists, product catalogues of the company's own products.
- Disease awareness campaigns, provided no specific drugs are mentioned.
- Press releases providing concise information about a medicinal product.

The regulations prohibit the advertising of:

- Medicinal products that are not legally sold or dispensed in Denmark.
- Medicinal products prepared for an individual person on instructions from a doctor.
- Medicinal products sold or dispensed under a special compassionate use permit (*section 29, Medicines Act*).
- Sera, vaccines, specific immune globulins and other immunological investigational medicinal products that are not covered by a marketing authorisation and are sold or dispensed from the State Serum Institute or the National Veterinary Institute, Technical University of Denmark (*section 30, Medicines Act*).

### Limits to marketing activities

Advertising for medicinal products must be adequate, objective, compatible with the approved summary of product characteristics, and must not mislead or exaggerate the qualities of the medicinal product. Additionally, advertising must contain a number of compulsory details about the product (for example, name, field of application, adverse effects and risks, price, among others). Specific rules address information requirements in relation to outdoor advertising, advertising in films, on the radio, on television and on monitors in sales outlets.

The holder of a marketing authorisation for a medicinal product has a duty to keep a copy of other documentation for all advertising material related to a medicinal product for at least two years. The material must be made available to the Danish Health and Medicines Authority (DHMA) on request.

## 20. ARE THERE OTHER CODES OF CONDUCT FOR THE MARKETING OF DRUGS (FOR EXAMPLE, BY PROFESSIONAL OR INDUSTRIAL ORGANISATIONS)?

The Danish Association of the Pharmaceutical Industry (Lif) has issued an Ethical Code on the Promotion of Medicines to Healthcare Professionals (Lif Code).

Members of the association are subject to the terms of the Code. Lif has also established a self-regulatory board (Ethical Board for the Pharmaceutical Industry), that supervises and enforces the Lif Code.

A decision made by the self-regulatory board cannot be appealed to the Danish Health and Medicines Authority (DHMA).

However, a party can bring a case before the DHMA even if it has already been before the self-regulatory board. The DHMA is not bound by the decision passed by the self-regulatory body, but will take it into consideration when assessing the case.

## MARKETING TO CONSUMERS

### 21. WHAT IS THE LEGAL REGIME FOR MARKETING TO CONSUMERS?

**Legal regime**

Under the Medicines Act and the Executive Order on Advertising for Medicinal Products, advertisements directed at the public must be presented in such a way that it is clear that it is an advertisement and that the product being advertised is a medicinal product. Any form of surreptitious advertising for a medicinal product is prohibited, for example, advertising camouflaged as editorial text in a journal, product placement in television and films or games on the internet with an underlying advertising message.

Certain information is explicitly prohibited in advertising aimed at non-healthcare professionals. For example, the advertisement must not:

- Give the impression that it is unnecessary to consult a doctor or veterinarian.
- Give the impression that the effect of the medicinal product is guaranteed, that it has no side effects or is better than or equivalent to the effect of another treatment, including another medicinal product.
- Suggest that the health of the person can be enhanced by taking the medicinal product.
- Suggest that the health of the person can be deteriorated by not taking the medicinal product.
- Be exclusively or principally directed at children.
- Make recommendations by healthcare professionals, scientists or persons, associations of persons, institutions, companies, who, because of their expertise or standing could encourage consumption of medicinal products.
- Compare the medicinal product with a foodstuff, cosmetic or other consumer product.
- Give the impression that the safety or efficacy of the medicinal product is due to the fact that its active ingredients are natural.
- Give information that could lead to erroneous self-diagnosis.
- Contain exaggerated, alarming or misleading claims of recovery.
- Use improper, alarming or misleading terms, pictorial representations of changes in the human body caused by disease or injury, or of the action of a medicinal product on the human body or parts thereof.
- Mention that the medicinal product has been granted a marketing authorisation by the authorities.
- Mention, either directly or indirectly, serious diseases or symptoms of serious diseases.

- Refer to analysis, literature, journals, among others.

Due to the prohibition against content indicating that the effect of a medicinal product is better than or equivalent to the effect of another treatment, including another medicinal product, advertising targeting the general public must not compare the effects of several medicinal products.

**Products**

The Danish Medicines Act prohibits advertising to the general public for:

- Prescription only medicinal products.
- Medicinal products that are inappropriate for use unless the patient has first consulted a doctor to obtain a diagnosis or for monitoring of the treatment.
- Psychotropic drugs.

### 22. WHAT KINDS OF MARKETING ACTIVITIES ARE PERMITTED IN RELATION TO CONSUMERS AND THE PRODUCTS WHICH MAY BE ADVERTISED TO THEM?

Marketing can include advertising in pharmacies and retail stores selling over-the-counter medicines, window displays, outdoor advertising, advertising in films and on the radio and advertising on television.

In connection with the advertising of medicinal products and professional information about medicinal products, hospitality in the form of payment of expenses for meals, travelling, accommodation and the likes must not be offered or given, regardless of extent and value.

### 23. IS IT PERMITTED TO PROVIDE CONSUMERS WITH FREE SAMPLES? ARE THERE PARTICULAR RESTRICTIONS ON SPECIAL OFFERS (FOR EXAMPLE, "BUY-ONE-GET-ONE-FREE")?

Distribution of free of charge samples to the public is prohibited. However, the Danish Health and Medicines Authority (DHMA) can authorise free distribution that does not have a promotional purpose, for example, distribution in connection with non-promotional information activities.

Bonuses or other economic advantages must not be paid or offered to users of medicinal products in connection with the sale of a pharmacy-only medicinal product.

### 24. ARE THERE PARTICULAR RULES OF PRACTICE ON THE USE OF THE INTERNET/SOCIAL MEDIA REGARDING DRUGS AND THEIR ADVERTISING?

Medicinal product advertising on the internet must meet the same requirements as advertisements in other media, but must also take into consideration the special characteristics of the internet.

Advertising on the internet, on pages generally accessible to the public, must comply with the requirements on advertising to the public.

The rules governing advertising to healthcare professionals apply to internet pages that are only accessible for healthcare professionals and persons engaged in the sale of medicinal products outside pharmacies. The access to such pages must be securely restricted by user identification, for example a unique user name or authorisation ID in combination with an associated personal password.

The self-regulatory board has issued a guide on the use of social media.

## 25. WHAT REGULATORY AUTHORITY IS RESPONSIBLE FOR SUPERVISING MARKETING ACTIVITIES TO CONSUMERS?

**Regulatory authority**

The Danish Health and Medicines Authority (DHMA) supervises marketing activities to consumers.

**Supervision**

The DHMA is entitled to request disclosure of all necessary information from the party responsible for the advertisement in order to check compliance with regulations.

**Rights of appeal**

Decisions made by the DHMA can be appealed to the Danish Ministry of Health. Decisions by the Ministry of Health can be brought before the ordinary courts.

## 26. WHAT ARE THE LEGAL CONSEQUENCES OF NON-COMPLIANCE WITH CONSUMER MARKETING LAWS?

The Danish Health and Medicines Authority (DHMA) can require illegal advertising for a medicinal product to be withdrawn. The DHMA can also order the party responsible for illegal advertising to publish the decision stating that the advertising must be stopped or to publish a corrective statement in relation to the advertisement. The form and content of such publications are decided by the DHMA.

Illegal advertising may in more severe cases be sanctioned with fines or imprisonment of up to four months. The level of fines are not fixed by law, but decided by the ordinary courts based on the circumstances of the case.

## MARKETING TO PROFESSIONALS

## 27. WHAT KINDS OF MARKETING ACTIVITIES ARE PERMITTED IN RELATION TO PROFESSIONALS?

Any information material about a medicinal product that is sent or handed over to healthcare professionals with the purpose of promoting sales must as a minimum contain the information specified in section 11(1) of the Executive Order on Advertising of Medicinal Products (the compulsory information, see *Question 19*) and the date when the material was last prepared or last updated.

Under section 13(2) of the Executive Order on Advertising all information in the material must be exact, current, verifiable and adequately detailed to enable the recipient to form their own opinion about the therapeutic value of the medicinal product. Any quotations, tables and illustrations taken from medical journals, scientific works, among others, used in the material must be reproduced loyally and the exact source must be referenced (*section 13(3), Executive Order on Advertising*).

The summary of product characteristics is considered as the basic documentation for the qualities of a medicinal product.

It is legal to advertise for prescription-only medicines in professional journals targeted at healthcare professionals. This is because advertising in such media is not considered to be targeted at the general public, regardless of the fact that the journal, by its nature, may be read by people other than healthcare professionals. A journal is deemed to be a professional journal when its content is predominantly technical and the vast majority of the readers and subscribers are healthcare professionals.

## 28. ARE THERE ANY RESTRICTIONS ON MARKETING TO PROFESSIONALS?

Advertising medicinal products that do not have a marketing authorisation in Denmark is prohibited. Providing off-label information promoting claims outside the scope of the authorisation will qualify as advertising for a medicinal product not having received the relevant marketing authorisation and is consequently prohibited.

Only clinical trials that have been subject to an independent assessment and published in recognised and independent works, professional journals, among others can be used in marketing activities as documentation for the properties of a medicinal product. "Independent" means that the entity publishing the work or journal has no interest in the sale or other form of promotion of medicinal products.

"Abstracts" and "data on file" (the final and signed study report setting out the results of the study) cannot be used as documentation since they do not meet the requirement of having been subject to an independent assessment. However, "data on file" that has undergone an independent assessment similar to the assessment made prior to the inclusion in recognised scientific journals and having been recognised as reliable by the independent assessment can be used until it has been published or rejected.

Benefits such as gifts and bonuses must not be offered or given to healthcare professionals as part of advertising or otherwise with the intention of promoting the sale of a medicinal product. The prohibition does not extend to the remuneration to healthcare professionals for services, when such remuneration is proportionate with the services offered.

Competitions and prizes must not be offered to healthcare professionals. The nature of the competition and value of the prize are unimportant. Whether or not a competition is held by a pharmaceutical company in direct relation to the promotion of a certain medicinal product has no bearing on this assessment.

Affiliation of healthcare professionals with pharmaceutical companies is regulated in section 202a of Act No. 1202 of the 14 November 2014 (Health Act), under which healthcare professionals must obtain approval from the Danish Health and Medicines Authority (DHMA) in order to acquire greater than DKK200,000 worth of securities in a pharmaceutical company at the time of the acquisition. Further, approval must be obtained in order for the healthcare professional to be affiliated with a pharmaceutical company, unless the affiliation is due to teaching or research-based tasks carried out for or with the pharmaceutical company.

The specifics are regulated in Executive Order No. 1154 of the 22 October 2014 on Health Care Professionals and their Affiliation with Pharmaceutical Medico Companies.

**Frequency**

There are no specific restrictions on the targeting of sales representatives. The Lif Code specifies that representatives must ensure that the frequency, time and duration of visits to healthcare professionals, pharmacies, hospitals and other healthcare facilities, together with the manner in which they are made, do not cause inconvenience. The Lif Code further stipulates that the sales representative must act ethically and responsibly in the carrying out of visits.

**Provision of hospitality**

The Executive Order on Advertising of Medicinal Products allows the giving or offering of the below listed financial benefits to healthcare professionals:

- **Hospitality.** Hospitality in the form of payment of direct expenses for meals, travel and accommodation in connection with the advertising for or professional information about medicinal products.
- **Professional information.** Professional information about and training related to medicinal products in the form of payment of direct expenses in connection with courses, congresses and other professional activities in which the health professional participates or arranges.

The above benefits must be kept at a reasonable level and must be closely linked to the main purpose of the meeting. Such hospitality must not cover anyone other than healthcare professionals, for example the spouse of a health professional.

If promotional or professional activities are held abroad, payment of the benefits can only take place if the holding of the event abroad is justified by material content-related, practical or financial circumstances.

Pharmaceutical companies cannot as part of advertising activities pay expenses for healthcare professionals' participation in purely social or cultural events, for example theatre, a museum or a football match.

### 29. WHAT INFORMATION IS IT LEGALLY REQUIRED TO INCLUDE IN ADVERTISING TO PROFESSIONALS?

Advertising targeting healthcare professionals must include the following information:

- The name of the medicinal product and its common name (for example, international non-proprietary name (INN)).
- The name of the marketing authorisation holder.
- Indicative text as specified in the summary of product characteristics.
- Contraindications.
- Adverse reactions and risks.
- Dosage.
- Pharmaceutical forms.
- Pack sizes.
- Dated price (registered price) including VAT.
- Dispensing group.

According to section 12 of the Executive Order on Advertising of Medicinal Products, advertisement requirements can be limited to the name of the medicinal product and its common name (Reminder Rule).

## 30. ARE THERE RULES ON COMPARISONS WITH OTHER PRODUCTS THAT ARE PARTICULARLY APPLICABLE TO DRUGS?

Advertising that compares a product with other medicinal products (including price comparisons) must clearly indicate which medicinal products (including strengths and pack sizes, among others) are compared and must be based on the particulars of the summaries of product characteristics for the products concerned.

Comparisons must only be made for medicinal products, including strengths and pack sizes, which are relevant to compare from an objective point of view (that is, medicinal products that are used for the same indication).

A comparison is only adequate if it covers all generic (and parallel imported) medicinal products that neither differ in terms of package form, therapeutic form or strength nor differ substantially in terms of pack size. However, products with an insignificant market share can be left out.

## 31. WHAT OTHER ITEMS, FUNDING OR SERVICES ARE PERMITTED TO BE PROVIDED TO PROFESSIONALS?

### Discounts

Financial benefits must not be offered or given to healthcare professionals as part of advertising or otherwise with the intention of promoting the sale of a medicinal product. Discounts can generally not be offered to healthcare professionals.

However, under section 36 of the Executive Order on Advertising of Medicinal Products, the prohibition does not apply to cost-related discounts to, for example, a wholesaler, that is, discounts that reflect cost-savings for the supplier as a direct consequence of purchase behaviour exhibited by the buyer.

Hospital products are purchased through public tenders and the companies are generally free to decide the price of their offer.

It should be noted that discounts may have implications under Danish or EU competition law.

### Free samples

Free samples of medicinal products can only be distributed if the following conditions are met:

- The receiving persons are qualified to prescribe the medicinal product, and are permitted to use the product as part of their activities within the medical field.
- One sample only of each medicinal product can be distributed to every doctor. If the medicinal product is available in several pharmaceutical forms and strengths, a sample for each form and strength can be distributed.
- The sample of medicinal product cannot be larger than the smallest pack available on the market.
- The pack must be marked "Free medical sample – not for resale".
- Medical samples must be distributed only in response to a written request, signed and dated by the recipient.
- Medical samples can only be supplied by the holder of the marketing authorisation or his representative. Samples cannot be distributed from a pharmacy.

- Each medical sample must be accompanied by its related summary of product characteristics.
- Samples of medicinal products covered by the Act No. 748 of 1 July 2008 on Euphoriants (narcotic drugs and psychotropic substances) (as amended) must not be distributed. The holder of a marketing authorisation or his representative must keep a record of the number of medical samples supplied for each medicinal product, stating the pharmaceutical form and strength. Such record, including the requests received from the recipients must be stored for at least two years during which period it must be available to the DHMA (*section 2, Executive Order No. 1244 of 12 December 2005 on the Distribution of Samples of Medicinal Products*).

Medical samples must only be used by doctors, dentists or veterinarians in their practice. In addition, the Lif Code stipulates that if the product is introduced on or after 1 January 2012, samples can only be distributed during the first two years following the introduction of the medicinal product.

### Sponsorship of professionals

Sponsoring of individual healthcare professionals or groups of healthcare professionals is generally not allowed. The prohibition is likely to apply even if the offer is made to a hospital, which then chooses the recipients. Financial support can be provided within the limits described under *Question 28*.

### Other items, funding or services

The regulations do not specifically allow other types of indirect incentives.

## 32. WHAT REGULATORY AUTHORITY IS RESPONSIBLE FOR SUPERVISING MARKETING ACTIVITIES REGARDING PROFESSIONALS?

### Regulatory authority

The Danish Health and Medicines Authority (DHMA) supervises marketing activities aimed at healthcare professionals.

### Supervision

The DHMA is entitled to request disclosure of all necessary information from the party responsible for the advertisement in order to secure compliance with regulations.

### Rights of appeal

Decisions made by the DHMA can be appealed to the Danish Ministry of Health. Complaints regarding marketing activities aimed at healthcare professionals may also be brought before the self-regulatory board (*see Question 20*).

## 33. WHAT ARE THE LEGAL CONSEQUENCES IN CASE OF NON-COMPLIANCE WITH PROFESSIONAL MARKETING LAWS?

The Danish Health and Medicines Authority (DHMA) can require that illegal advertising of a medicinal product be withdrawn.

The DHMA can also order the party responsible for illegal advertising to publish the decision stating that the advertising must be withdrawn and/or to publish a corrective statement in relation to the advertisement. The form and content of such publications are decided by the DHMA.

Illegal advertising can in more severe cases be sanctioned with fines or imprisonment. The sanction is determined by the ordinary courts. The self-regulatory board can impose fines up to DKK300,000.

# ENGAGEMENT WITH PATIENT ORGANISATIONS

## 34. WHAT KINDS OF ACTIVITIES ARE PERMITTED IN RELATION TO ENGAGEMENT WITH PATIENT ORGANISATIONS? WHAT ARE THE RESTRICTIONS THAT ARE IMPOSED ON RELATIONSHIP WITH PATIENT ORGANISATIONS?

Financial support for or collaboration with patient organisations is subject to the general advertising rules.

Additionally, the Danish Association of the Pharmaceutical Industry (Lif) has issued the Ethical Rules for Collaboration between Patient Groups and the Pharmaceutical Industry (Patient Group Code). The Code provides that all agreements concerning funding must be clear and in writing and must be published on the websites of the pharmaceutical companies.

In principle, support can be granted for all activities, projects and purposes within the sphere of the organisation's work, but professional activities must always be at the core of the collaboration and there must be a reasonable relationship between the support or services provided and received. Events must be held at suitable locations that contribute to the main purpose of events and which are not known for their entertainment facilities and are not too extravagant. It also follows from the Patient Group Code that catering or hospitality associated with events must be limited to expenses for transport, meals, overnight accommodation and fees for participation.

The Patient Group Code specifies that:

- Financial contributions must not be conditional on the organisation taking specific stands on professional and political issues.
- The pharmaceutical industry must not, as part of an agreement, require organisations to favour specific products.
- The pharmaceutical company must never use the organisation's logo or name, or otherwise refer to collaboration with the organisation, except by prior written agreement.
- No exclusive agreements can be made. Organisations are therefore always free to collaborate with several pharmaceutical companies, and likewise pharmaceutical companies can collaborate with one or several organisations.
- In order to avoid suspicion of improper dependency, agreements cannot be made for issues where the independence of the parties may be open to challenge.

# DENMARK

- The pharmaceutical company must always ensure that employees or elected representatives of the organisation only perform tasks for the pharmaceutical company if this has been reported to a superior or another executive within the organisation.
- Employees of the pharmaceutical industry must not hold positions of trust within organisations unless it is evident that there is no conflict of interest.

Further, patient groups must publish any economic benefits received under Executive Order No. 1155 of 22 October 2014 on Advertisement of Medicinal Equipment.

## REFORM

### 35. ARE THERE ANY PLANS TO REFORM THE LAW ON THE DISTRIBUTION AND PROMOTION OF DRUGS IN YOUR JURISDICTION?

There are currently no explicit plans to reform the law on the distribution and promotion of drugs.

# EUROPEAN UNION

Alison Dennis, FIELDFISHER

## DISTRIBUTION

### PRE-CONDITIONS FOR DISTRIBUTION

### 1. WHAT ARE THE LEGAL PRE-CONDITIONS FOR A DRUG TO BE DISTRIBUTED WITHIN THE JURISDICTION?

Drugs cannot be marketed in the EU unless they are the subject of an EU or national marketing authorisation. Drugs cannot be distributed in the EU unless they are the subject of an authorisation or exemption.

**Authorisation**

The term "medicinal product" is used in the EU rather than "drug", and is defined as:

- Any substance or combination of substances presented for treating or preventing disease in human beings.
- Any substance or combination of substances which can be administered to human beings with a view to making a medical diagnosis or to restoring, correcting or modifying physiological functions in human beings.

In the EU, there are essentially four different procedures for obtaining a marketing authorisation, although these can be linked. These are the:

- Centralised procedure.
- Decentralised procedure.
- Mutual recognition procedure.
- National procedure of each individual member state.

The centralised procedure is available for a limited range of products listed in the annex of Regulation (EC) 726/2004 on the authorisation and supervision of medicinal products and establishing a European Medicines Agency (EMA Regulation).

The centralised procedure is compulsory for the following drugs:

- Drugs for the treatment of human immunodeficiency virus (HIV) or acquired immune deficiency syndrome (AIDS), cancer, diabetes, neurodegenerative diseases, auto-immune and other immune dysfunctions, and viral diseases.
- Drugs derived from biotechnology processes, such as genetic engineering.
- Advanced therapy drugs, such as gene therapy, somatic cell therapy or tissue-engineered drugs.

- Officially designated "orphan drugs" (that is, drugs used for rare human diseases).

The centralised procedure is optional for the following drugs (which will otherwise be authorised nationally):

- Drugs that are a significant therapeutic, scientific or technical innovation.
- Drugs whose authorisation would be in the interest of public health.

Applications through the centralised procedure are submitted to the European Medicine Agency (EMA). The EMA's scientific committees take up to 210 active days (plus "clock stops") to adopt an opinion on whether the drug should be marketed or not. This opinion is transmitted to the European Commission, which is then responsible for granting the marketing authorisation.

Directive 2001/83/EC on the Community code relating to medicinal products for human use (Code for Human Medicines Directive) is the legal basis for both the mutual recognition and decentralised procedures. These are intended to allow applicants to obtain authorisations in multiple member states of the EU more rapidly and/or with a lower administrative burden than would be the case if each application were examined completely separately in each and every member state. They are different from a centralised authorisation in that each member state issues its own authorisation, which means that pharmacovigilance reporting and variations to authorisations must be made separately in each member state.

The mutual recognition procedure allows applicants, once they have obtained an authorisation in one member state, to request that other member states, on an individual basis, "recognise" an earlier granted authorisation from a member state, subject to meeting local requirements for labelling and patient information leaflets. The decentralised procedure is available if there is no authorisation in any country of the EU, and allows for one application to be made with a list of countries in which authorisation is sought, and for one reference member state to make a decision for and on behalf of all member states in which the application is made. In both the mutual recognition and the decentralised procedures, divergences of opinion about whether a product should or should not to be authorised are arbitrated by the Committee for Medicinal Products for Human Use (CHMP).

**Application procedure.** The procedure and content requirements for applications, including for national applications in the EU, are set out in volume 2 of "The Rules Governing Medicinal Products in the European Union". This document contains a list of regulatory guidelines related to procedural and regulatory requirements, including:

- Renewal procedures.
- Dossier requirements for Type IA/IB variation notifications.
- Summary of product characteristics.
- Package information and classification for the supply.
- Readability of the label.
- Package leaflet requirements.

The process is intended to be, in its essential elements, the same in all EU member states. There is also a 210-day limit on the time taken to authorise a drug in the EU, although this time limit is extended if more information is requested. For a drug for which an application is made via the centralised procedure and which is of "major interest" from the point of view of public interest and therapeutic innovation, an accelerated assessment can be requested, reducing the time limit to 150 days instead of 210 days (*Article 14(9), EMA Regulation*).

Article 21 of the Code for Human Medicines Directive requires that member states make the details of the application and the decision publicly available. Details of marketing authorisations granted through the centralised procedure are published in the Official Journal.

Marketing authorisations are normally initially valid for a period of five years, and must then be renewed and subject to a further risk/benefit analysis. At that point they can, if renewed, be subject to a further five-year renewal, or will otherwise continue indefinitely. If there are concerns about the product, then a one-year authorisation can be granted, subject to meeting specified conditions for a renewal thereafter.

A marketing authorisation for products that are not placed on the relevant market in the first three years of the authorisation will automatically cease.

**Other regulatory regimes (herbal medicinal products, food products and cosmetics).** There are other regulatory regimes that can apply to products that in other countries could be considered as drugs. There are separate regulatory regimes for "food products" (including food and dietary supplements) and "herbal medicinal products". Case-by-case guidance might be needed from national competent authorities to help determine which regime applies for "borderline" products. Which category a product falls into can depend on its mode of action, its ingredients and/or the claims made about the product in labelling and/or its promotion.

"Food products" are defined in Regulation 178/2002/EC as "any substance or product, whether processed, partially processed or unprocessed, intended to be, or reasonably expected to be ingested by humans". "Food supplements" are defined as "foodstuffs the purpose of which is to supplement the normal diet and which are concentrated sources of nutrients or other substances with a nutritional or physiological effect, alone or in combination, marketed in dose form". A product can be classed as a food supplement rather than a medicinal product if it would be chosen by consumers for its nutritional value or combination of vitamins and minerals, and is not marketed or sold with any claims to treat, prevent or cure disease.

"Herbal medicines" are defined in the Directive 2004/24/EC on traditional herbal medicinal products (Traditional Herbal Medicines Directive) as: "any medicinal product, exclusively containing as active ingredients one or more herbal substances or one or more herbal preparations, or one or more such herbal substances in combination with one or more such herbal preparations".

For example, any medicine that contains algae, fungi or a plant part as an active ingredient is a herbal medicinal product.

Marketing authorisations are required within the EU for all medicinal products and herbal medicinal products. The only exception to this is the simplified registration procedure that exists for traditional herbal medicinal products if the applicant can demonstrate that the constituent(s) of the product have a well established medical use and safety level. In contrast, the requirements for authorisation of a food supplement will largely fall within the scope of the relevant food standards agency in each jurisdiction.

Cosmetics are defined in Regulation (EC) 1223/2009 on cosmetic products (cosmetic Products Regulation) as "any substance or mixture intended to be placed in contact with the external parts of the human body (epidermis, hair system, nails, lips and external genital organs) or with the teeth and the mucous membranes of the oral cavity with a view exclusively or mainly to cleaning them, perfuming them, changing their appearance, protecting them or keeping them in good condition or correcting body odours".

**Generic products.** Generic products are defined as products that have the same qualitative and quantitative composition and active substances, and the same pharmaceutical form, as a "reference medicinal product". A reference medicinal product is a product being that has already been authorised under the Code for Human Medicines Directive and on whose clinical efficacy and safety data the applicant for the generic intends to rely. Applicants for a marketing authorisation for a generic product have the advantage of not being required to provide the results of pre-clinical tests and of clinical trials. However, there is a period of time during which generics cannot take advantage of the data already in the regulators' files. This is known as the period of data or market exclusivity.

Originator applications for marketing authorisations made after 30 October 2005, whether under the centralised, mutual recognition or decentralised procedures, benefit from:

- Eight years of data exclusivity, during which no applications can be made citing the clinical data supplied with the originator application.
- A further two years of market exclusivity, during which the generic product cannot be placed on the market, giving ten years of protection in total.
- An additional year (extending the protection to 11 years) if (*Article 10(1), Code for Human Medicines Directive*):
  - a new indication is added that is of significant clinical benefit in comparison with existing therapies; or
  - there is a change of classification supported by additional and significant pre-clinical tests or clinical trials within the first eight years.

Separately, orphan products benefit from ten years of total regulatory exclusivity (although this can be reduced if market conditions change), which can be extended to 12 years if the requirement for data on the product's use in the paediatric population is fully met.

## EXCEPTIONS

See *Questions 2* and *6*.

## 2. DO ANY TYPES OF NAMED PATIENT AND/OR COMPASSIONATE USE PROGRAMMES OPERATE? IF SO, WHAT ARE THE REQUIREMENTS FOR PRE-LAUNCH ACCESS?

**National authorisations under EU law**

To increase the availability of drugs, in particular on smaller markets in the EU, Article 126a of Directive 2001/83/EC on the Community code relating to medicinal products for human use (Code for Human Medicines Directive) allows, in the absence of a marketing authorisation or of a pending application for a medicinal product that has already been authorised in another member state, a member state to authorise the placing on the market of that medicinal product for justified public health reasons. In such cases, the competent authority of the member state must inform the marketing authorisation holder in the member states in which the medicinal product concerned is authorised of the proposal to authorise the placing on the market under this Article. The competent authority of the member state applying Article 126a must notify the Commission of drugs authorised, or which cease to be authorised, under this provision. Each member state has enacted its own specific mechanisms to implement this provision.

The publicly available register of drugs authorised to be placed on the market under Article 126a is available on the European Commission's website: *http://pharmacos.eudra.org/*.

EUROPEAN UNION

**Compassionate use**

Whilst compassionate use programmes are within the remit of the member states, the Committee for Medicinal Products for Human Use (CHMP) can, at the request of a member state, provide recommendations to all EU member states on how to administer, distribute and use certain medicines for compassionate use. The CHMP can also provide recommendations when it becomes aware that compassionate use programmes with a given medicine are being set up in a number of member states. The recommendations are optional only and do not create any legal obligation in the EU member states.

**Named patient basis**

Under Article 5 of the Directive 2001/83/EC on the Community code relating to medicinal products for human use (Code for Human Medicines Directive), the provision of drugs on a named patient basis is the responsibility of the doctor and must be for an individual named patient only. The doctor concerned will be in direct contact with the manufacturer.

Patients can sometimes enter "expanded access programmes". A company that makes a promising drug can choose to run one of these programmes to allow early access to its drug and to widen its use to patients who can benefit from it. For example, patients who have been treated with the drug during a clinical trial and wish to continue treatment may be able to do so via an expanded access programme. These programmes are often authorised by national authorities in the same way as clinical trials, and patients are followed in the same way as patients in a clinical trial.

**EU level exceptions**

**Conditional marketing authorisations.** The European Medicines Agency (EMA) can issue conditional marketing authorisations on an exceptional basis under Regulation (EC) 507/2006 on the conditional marketing authorisation for medicinal products (Conditional Marketing Authorisation Regulation) for drugs that would otherwise, if the clinical data were complete and acceptable, be subject to the centralised authorisation process. These drugs must meet unmet medical needs and satisfy one of the following conditions:

- Aim at the treatment, the prevention or the medical diagnosis of seriously debilitating diseases or life-threatening diseases.
- Be for use in emergency situations, in response to public health threats duly recognised either by the World Health Organization or by the Community in the framework of Decision No 2119/98/EC.
- Be designated as orphan drugs in accordance with Article 3 of Regulation (EC) 141/2000 on orphan medicinal products (Orphan Medicinal Products Regulation). The CHMP Guideline EMEA/509951/2006 of 5 December 2006 applies to these authorisations. This is currently being rewritten and is likely to be reissued in a revised form before the end of 2015.

**Marketing authorisations in "exceptional circumstances".** In circumstances where comprehensive data cannot be provided under normal conditions of use, an authorisation can be granted in "exceptional circumstances" (*Article 14(8), Regulation (EC) 726/2004 on the authorisation and supervision of medicinal products and establishing a European Medicines Agency (EMA Regulation)*). There are three reasons why such data may not be available:

- The condition is too rare.
- The present state of scientific knowledge does not allow it to be collected.
- It would be unethical to collect the data.

Authorisations granted in exceptional circumstances are distinct from conditional authorisations, for which the data will be provided but cannot be provided in the immediate future.

## LICENSING

**3. WHAT IS THE PROCEDURAL STRUCTURE REGARDING LICENSING A DRUG FOR DISTRIBUTION?**

See *Question 1*.

**4. IS THERE A SIMPLIFIED LICENCE PROCEEDING, OR RELAXED LICENSING CONDITIONS, FOR DRUGS WHICH HAVE ALREADY BEEN LICENSED FOR DISTRIBUTION IN ANOTHER JURISDICTION?**

The holder of a wholesale dealer's licence has the right to parallel export the product from one EU member state where there is a marketing authorisation in place for the product to another EU member state where there is a marketing authorisation in place for a similar product. Where the original manufacturer of the product owns intellectual property rights, including trade mark rights, in the product, they are not permitted to exercise their rights to oppose the importation of a product that has been lawfully placed on the market in another member state by, or with the consent of, the proprietor of that right. Because of cultural and, in particular, language differences, products that are parallel traded are frequently repackaged. Such activities have been the subject of a substantial number of court decisions, including many from the European Court of Justice (ECJ). The conclusion of these cases is essentially that the trade mark proprietor cannot use his right to prevent repackaging of a product imported in parallel when:

- The use of the trade mark right by the owner, having regard to the marketing system that it has adopted, will contribute to the artificial partitioning of the markets between member states.
- The repackaging cannot adversely affect the original condition of the product.
- The name of the repackaging company is stated on the new packaging.
- The presentation of the repackaged product is not such as to be liable to damage the reputation of the trade mark and its owner.
- The proprietor of the trade mark receives prior notice before the repackaged product is put on sale.

The European Commission has outlined its view of the law on parallel imports and repackaging in its Communication on Parallel Imports of Proprietary Drugs for Which Marketing Authorisations Have Already Been Granted (*COM(2003) 839*).

**5. IS VIRTUAL DRUG DISTRIBUTION POSSIBLE FROM YOUR JURISDICTION?**

This area is governed by the national law of the EU member states.

## 6. WHAT IS THE PROCEDURE TO APPEAL (LEGAL REMEDY) A LICENSING DECISION?

Applications for EU central authorisations are reviewed by a scientific committee of the European Medicines Agency (EMA), but the authorisation is granted by the European Commission. If the Commission refuses to grant authorisation, recourse must be made through the European Courts.

## 7. WHAT ARE THE COSTS OF OBTAINING LICENSING?

For a centralised marketing authorisation application to the European Medicines Agency (EMA) for approval to market a medicine within the EU (single strength, one pharmaceutical form, one presentation), fees start at EUR278,200. Details on fees can be found here: *www.ema.europa.eu/ema/index.jsp?curl=pages/regulation/document_listing/document_listing_000327.jsp&mid=WC0b01ac0580024596*.

## DISTRIBUTION TO CONSUMERS

## 8. WHAT ARE THE DIFFERENT CATEGORIES OF DRUGS FOR DISTRIBUTION?

There are three categories of drugs:

- Prescription-only medicines (POM).
- Pharmacy medicines (P).
- General sales list (GSL) medicines.

## 9. WHO IS AUTHORISED TO DISTRIBUTE PRESCRIPTION DRUGS AND OVER-THE-COUNTER DRUGS TO CONSUMERS?

Authorisations for the provision of drugs to consumers are regulated at national level. There are significant differences in the way in which prescribing is handled in the 28 EU member states.

## 10. WHAT DRUGS CAN AN ATTENDING PHYSICIAN DISTRIBUTE AND UNDER WHAT CIRCUMSTANCES?

This area is governed by the national law of the EU member states.

## 11. WHO IS AUTHORISED TO PRESCRIBE PRESCRIPTION DRUGS TO CONSUMERS?

This area is governed by the national law of the EU member states.

## 12. IS DIRECT MAILING/DISTANCE SELLING OF DRUGS PERMITTED IN YOUR JURISDICTION?

Directive 2011/62/EC relating to falsified medicinal products (Falsified Medicines Directive) contains provisions on online sales of medicinal products in Europe, including provisions on:

- The requirements applicable to persons selling drugs to consumers online.
- Controls by member states.
- An EU-wide logo scheme.

### EUROPEAN UNION

#### 13. WHAT REGULATORY AUTHORITY IS RESPONSIBLE FOR SUPERVISING DISTRIBUTION ACTIVITIES?

This area is governed by the national law of the EU member states.

#### 14. WHAT IS THE PROCEDURE TO APPEAL (LEGAL REMEDY) A DISTRIBUTION DECISION?

This area is governed by the national law of the EU member states.

#### 15. WHAT ARE THE LEGAL CONSEQUENCES OF NON-COMPLIANCE WITH CONSUMER DISTRIBUTION LAWS?

This area is governed by the national law of the EU member states.

### WHOLESALE DISTRIBUTION

#### 16. WHAT IS THE LEGAL REGIME REGARDING WHOLESALE DISTRIBUTION OF DRUGS?

Articles 77 to 85 of Directive 2001/83/EC on the Community code relating to medicinal products for human use (Code for Human Medicines Directive) require that member states regulate, and in particular issue, authorisations to wholesalers of medicinal products after checking and inspecting the wholesaler's premises. Inspections can also be carried out at any time after authorisation. If a wholesale dealer's authorisation is withdrawn by a member state, then the European Commission must be informed of this.

The Code for Human Medicines Directive requires that no more than 90 days is taken for the examination of applications for authorisation. This period is suspended on any requests for additional information.

Key conditions are:

- Suitable premises.
- Installations and equipment for the protection and distribution of the medicinal products.
- Properly trained staff, including a designated qualified person.

Wholesale dealers must only obtain medicinal products from other persons that are authorised to process and distribute those products (for example, a marketing authorisation holder or another wholesale dealer). They can only supply medicinal products to another wholesale dealer or persons that are authorised to supply the medicinal products to the public.

Wholesale dealers must have emergency plans in place to effect recalls, whether instituted by the competent authority, manufacturer or marketing authorisation holder.

Wholesale dealers must keep records of all sales and purchases for at least five years. These records must be available at all times for inspection by the national competent authority that has granted the authorisation and must include at least the following information:

- Date.
- Name of the medicinal product.
- Quantity received or supplied.
- Name and address of the supplier or consignee.

# EUROPEAN UNION

Information must be provided by the wholesale dealer to its onward purchasers, which provides a certain level of traceability through information including the supplier, and the name, pharmaceutical form and quantity of the medicinal product supplied.

The EU also publishes its own guidelines on good distribution practice, with which wholesale dealers must comply.

Member states can impose public service obligations on wholesale dealers, such as obligations to help maintain supplies of medicinal products. These must be applied to any wholesale dealer operating in the member state, including under authorisations issued by another member state.

**17. WHAT REGULATORY AUTHORITY IS RESPONSIBLE FOR SUPERVISING WHOLESALE DISTRIBUTION ACTIVITIES?**

This area is governed by the national law of the EU member states.

**18. WHAT ARE THE LEGAL CONSEQUENCES OF NON-COMPLIANCE WITH WHOLESALE DISTRIBUTION LAWS?**

This area is governed by the national law of the EU member states.

# MARKETING

## PROMOTION

**19. WHAT IS THE GENERAL LEGAL REGIME FOR THE MARKETING OF DRUGS?**

Articles 85 to 100 of Directive 2001/83/EC on the Community code relating to medicinal products for human use (Code for Human Medicines Directive) contain the general principles governing advertising of drugs in the EU. Supervision and enforcement of the laws on advertising and promotion are devolved to member states. Member states are required to have in place procedures that allow them to order particular advertising to cease or, in the case of pre-vetting, to not be published, and to have an accelerated procedure for doing so. Member states are permitted, but not required, to publish the decision and/or a corrective notice. Member states can give self-regulatory bodies the authority to regulate pharmaceutical advertising.

General principles included in the Code for Human Medicines Directive are that:

- Drugs that are not authorised cannot be advertised to any person (including the medical profession).
- Prescription-only drugs and drugs containing ingredients that are psychotropic or narcotic must not be advertised to the public.
- All permitted advertising must conform to the summary of product characteristics.
- All permitted advertising must encourage rational use, and must not be misleading.
- Member states can choose to ban the advertising to the public of drugs that are reimbursed.
- Companies must establish their own scientific service. They must retain copies of

advertisements published and must provide those to the authorities on request.

In addition to the directives and regulations that relate specifically to the pharmaceutical industry, the following four general directives and regulations apply:

- Directive 2005/29/EC concerning unfair business-to-consumer commercial practices in the internal market (Unfair Commercial Practices Directive), which regulates advertising to consumers.
- Directive 2006/114/EC concerning misleading and comparative advertising (Misleading and Comparative Advertising Directive).
- Council Directive 2010/13/EU concerning the provision of audiovisual media service (Audiovisual Media Services Directive).
- Regulation (EC) No 2006/2004 on cooperation between national authorities responsible for the enforcement of consumer protection laws (Consumer Protection Co-operation Regulation).

## 20. ARE THERE OTHER CODES OF CONDUCT FOR THE MARKETING OF DRUGS (FOR EXAMPLE, BY PROFESSIONAL OR INDUSTRIAL ORGANISATIONS)?

Companies operating in Europe refer to applicable codes of practice, in particular the European Federation of Pharmaceutical Industries and Associations (EFPIA) Code on the Promotion of Prescription-Only Drugs to, and Interactions with, Healthcare Professionals, and the EFPIA Code of Practice on Relationships between the Pharmaceutical Industry and Patient Organisations.

## MARKETING TO CONSUMERS

## 21. WHAT IS THE LEGAL REGIME FOR MARKETING TO CONSUMERS?

**Legal regime**

Articles 87 and 88 of Directive 2001/83/EC on the Community code relating to medicinal products for human use (Code for Human Medicines Directive) requires member states to prohibit advertising:

- Of drugs without a marketing authorisation.
- To consumers of drugs available on prescription only.
- To consumers for products containing psychotropic or narcotic substances.

Drugs intended to be used without intervention of a medical practitioner can be advertised to the public but must:

- Clearly indicate that product being advertised is a medicinal product.
- Include the name of the product and its common name if the medicinal product contains only one active substance (member states have the option to derogate from this and to allow reference to the name of the product and the international non-proprietary name (INN) only).
- Include information necessary for correct use of the product.
- Include an express legible invitation to read carefully the instructions on the leaflet or packaging.

Advertising to the public must not:

- Give the impression that a medical consultation or surgical operation is unnecessary.
- Suggest that the effects are guaranteed, without adverse reactions or better than or equivalent to those of another treatment or product.
- Suggest that health will be enhanced by taking the product.
- Suggest that health could be affected by not taking the product (except for vaccination campaigns).
- Be directed exclusively or principally at children.
- Refer to a recommendation by persons such as scientists, health professionals or celebrities which could encourage consumption.
- Suggest that the product is a food, cosmetic or other consumer product.
- Suggest that the safety or efficacy of the medicinal product is due to the fact that it is natural.
- Lead to erroneous self-diagnosis, due to a description of a case history.
- Refer in improper, alarming or misleading terms to claims of recovery.
- Use improper, alarming or misleading terms, or pictorial representations of changes in the human body caused by disease or injury or action of a product on the human body.

Apart from the rules above, the advertising of drugs is regulated nationally.

**22. WHAT KINDS OF MARKETING ACTIVITIES ARE PERMITTED IN RELATION TO CONSUMERS AND THE PRODUCTS WHICH MAY BE ADVERTISED TO THEM?**

See *Question 21*.

**23. IS IT PERMITTED TO PROVIDE CONSUMERS WITH FREE SAMPLES? ARE THERE PARTICULAR RESTRICTIONS ON SPECIAL OFFERS (FOR EXAMPLE, "BUY-ONE-GET-ONE-FREE")?**

This area is governed by the national law of the EU member states.

**24. ARE THERE PARTICULAR RULES OF PRACTICE ON THE USE OF THE INTERNET/SOCIAL MEDIA REGARDING DRUGS AND THEIR ADVERTISING?**

This area is governed by the national law of the EU member states.

**25. WHAT REGULATORY AUTHORITY IS RESPONSIBLE FOR SUPERVISING MARKETING ACTIVITIES TO CONSUMERS?**

This area is governed by the national law of the EU member states.

**26. WHAT ARE THE LEGAL CONSEQUENCES OF NON-COMPLIANCE WITH CONSUMER MARKETING LAWS?**

This area is governed by the national law of the EU member states.

# EUROPEAN UNION

## MARKETING TO PROFESSIONALS

### 27. WHAT KINDS OF MARKETING ACTIVITIES ARE PERMITTED IN RELATION TO PROFESSIONALS?

**Promotional materials**

Advertising to healthcare professionals (including all supporting documentation included as part of the promotion) must:

- Be accurate.
- Be up-to-date.
- Be verifiable.
- Be sufficiently complete to enable the recipient to form their own opinion of the therapeutic value.
- Contain essential information compatible with the summary of product characteristics.
- Indicate the supply classification of the medicinal product and the date when it was drawn up or last revised.

Quotations and tables or illustrations from medical journals must be faithfully reproduced and sources indicated. Member states have the option to require advertising to healthcare professionals to include the selling price or indicative price of the various presentations and the conditions for reimbursement by social security bodies. Member states also have the option to permit reminder items to include only the name of the product or the international non-proprietary name (INN).

**Activities of sales representatives**

It is the responsibility of the company employing sales representatives to ensure that they are adequately trained and knowledgeable to provide complete and accurate information about the medicinal products they are selling. At each visit, they must provide a summary of product characteristics and, if permitted by national legislation, the product's price and reimbursement status. If a healthcare practitioner shares their experience of the use of the product, this must be transmitted to the scientific service of the company.

No gifts of advantages must be provided to healthcare professionals, except for gifts that are inexpensive and relevant to the practice of medicine or pharmacy.

**Provision of hospitality**

Article 94 of Directive 2001/83/EC on the Community code relating to medicinal products for human use (Code for Human Medicines Directive) requires that hospitality at sales promotion events is strictly limited to the main purpose of the events and not extended to persons other than healthcare professionals. Hospitality can be offered at events for purely professional and scientific purposes, strictly limited to the main scientific objective of the event. EU law does not deal with sponsorship of professionals at educational events, as this is regulated at a national level.

### 28. ARE THERE ANY RESTRICTIONS ON MARKETING TO PROFESSIONALS?

See *Question 27*.

### 29. WHAT INFORMATION IS IT LEGALLY REQUIRED TO INCLUDE IN ADVERTISING TO PROFESSIONALS?

See *Question 27*.

### 30. ARE THERE RULES ON COMPARISONS WITH OTHER PRODUCTS THAT ARE PARTICULARLY APPLICABLE TO DRUGS?

Directive 2006/114/EC concerning misleading and comparative advertising (Misleading and Comparative Advertising Directive) applies to all comparative advertising, but without specific reference to medicinal products. This area is governed in more detail specific to medicinal products by the national law of the EU member states.

### 31. WHAT OTHER ITEMS, FUNDING OR SERVICES ARE PERMITTED TO BE PROVIDED TO PROFESSIONALS?

Under Article 95 of Directive 2001/83/EC on the Community code relating to medicinal products for human use (Code for Human Medicines Directive), free samples can only be provided exceptionally for medicinal products that do not contain psychotropic or narcotic substances, and only to persons qualified to prescribe such products if the following conditions are met:

- The number of samples for each medicinal product each year must be limited.
- Any supply of samples must be in response to a written request, signed and dated, from the prescribing individual.
- Persons supplying samples must maintain an adequate system of control and accountability.
- Each sample must be no larger than the smallest presentation on the market.
- Each sample must be marked: "free medical sample – not for sale" or any equivalent wording.
- Each sample must be accompanied by a copy of the summary of product characteristics.

### 32. WHAT REGULATORY AUTHORITY IS RESPONSIBLE FOR SUPERVISING MARKETING ACTIVITIES REGARDING PROFESSIONALS?

Member states are responsible for supervising marketing activities regarding professionals. Member states have more detailed legislation than is provided at EU level.

### 33. WHAT ARE THE LEGAL CONSEQUENCES IN CASE OF NON-COMPLIANCE WITH PROFESSIONAL MARKETING LAWS?

This area is governed by the national law of the EU member states.

## ENGAGEMENT WITH PATIENT ORGANISATIONS

**34. WHAT KINDS OF ACTIVITIES ARE PERMITTED IN RELATION TO ENGAGEMENT WITH PATIENT ORGANISATIONS? WHAT ARE THE RESTRICTIONS THAT ARE IMPOSED ON RELATIONSHIP WITH PATIENT ORGANISATIONS?**

This area is governed by the national law of the EU member states.

## REFORM

**35. ARE THERE ANY PLANS TO REFORM THE LAW ON THE DISTRIBUTION AND PROMOTION OF DRUGS IN YOUR JURISDICTION?**

There are currently no major plans to reform the law on the distribution and promotion of drugs at EU level.

# FINLAND

*Mikael Segercrantz, Johanna Lilja and Elina Saxlin-Hautamäki, ROSCHIER*

## DISTRIBUTION

### PRE-CONDITIONS FOR DISTRIBUTION

**1. WHAT ARE THE LEGAL PRE-CONDITIONS FOR A DRUG TO BE DISTRIBUTED WITHIN THE JURISDICTION?**

**Authorisation**

To be distributed in Finland a drug must have a marketing authorisation granted nationally by the Finnish Medicines Agency (FIMEA) or, alternatively, centrally by the EU Commission after evaluation by the European Medicines Agency (EMA).

**Exceptions**

As exceptions to this, compassionate use of a product is allowed under certain circumstances, and the EU scheme for licensing parallel imports is also followed.

**2. DO ANY TYPES OF NAMED PATIENT AND/OR COMPASSIONATE USE PROGRAMMES OPERATE? IF SO, WHAT ARE THE REQUIREMENTS FOR PRE-LAUNCH ACCESS?**

Some products have been authorised by the Finnish Medicines Agency (FIMEA) under the compassionate use exception, for example, zenamivir for the treatment of certain influenzas of pandemic nature.

Article 5(1) of Directive 2001/83/EC on the Community code relating to medicinal products for human use (Code for Human Medicines Directive) has been implemented in Finland under:

- Chapter 4, section 21(f) of the Medicines Act (*395/1987*).
- Section 10(b) of the Medicines Decree (*693/1987*).

Accordingly, the preconditions for the pre-launch use of a product are that either:

- No other means are available to treat an individual patient or an available treatment would not yield the desired result.
- No authorised drug is available to treat a group of patients or population, or to prevent an illness, and there are particularly notable reasons for granting the special authorisation.

The decision on pre-launch use is subject to any advice issued by the European Medicines Agency's Committee for Medicinal Products for Human Use.

FINLAND

In addition, when a product is supplied pre-launch, the supplier must ensure that the user of the product receives sufficient instructions on the product's correct and safe use and storage, as well as other necessary instructions.

## LICENSING

### 3. WHAT IS THE PROCEDURAL STRUCTURE REGARDING LICENSING A DRUG FOR DISTRIBUTION?

**Structure**

Marketing authorisations can be granted through any of the national, mutual recognition, decentralised or centralised procedures. The common EU application form is used in all of these procedures.

National decision making takes place following consideration of the application at the regular co-ordination and quality assurance meetings. The processing time of the application varies depending on the procedure followed.

**Regulatory authority**

The Finnish Medicines Agency (FIMEA) is responsible for the licensing of drugs in Finland.

### 4. IS THERE A SIMPLIFIED LICENCE PROCEEDING, OR RELAXED LICENSING CONDITIONS, FOR DRUGS WHICH HAVE ALREADY BEEN LICENSED FOR DISTRIBUTION IN ANOTHER JURISDICTION?

The mutual recognition procedure based on Directive 2001/83/EC on the Community code relating to medicinal products for human use (Code for Human Medicines Directive) has been implemented in Finland. Accordingly, an authorisation granted by another member state can be recognised by the Finnish Medicines Agency (FIMEA).

Parallel imports are subject to their own procedure. The product in respect of which parallel importation is to take place must have a marketing authorisation in Finland. Similarly, the product to be imported must have an authorisation in the country of acquisition, which must be an EU member state. In processing the application, FIMEA confirms these matters with the relevant authorities. A sample package stating the country of acquisition and a proposal for labelling and packaging leaflets must be attached to the application.

### 5. IS VIRTUAL DRUG DISTRIBUTION POSSIBLE FROM YOUR JURISDICTION?

The Finnish drugs delivery chain is linear, in that manufacturers and wholesalers can only sell products to each other or to licensed pharmacies, while licensed pharmacies or their separately authorised virtual equivalents (*see Question 12*), in turn, are the only places for consumers to purchase drugs.

However, on implementation in Finland of Directive 2011/62/EC amending Directive 2001/83/EC on the Community code relating to medicinal products for human use, as regards the prevention of the entry into the legal supply chain of falsified medicinal products (Falsified Medicinal Products Directive), as of 1 January 2014 the brokering of drugs has become possible under Section 34a of the Medicines Act. Accordingly, sales of authorised drugs, other than wholesale distribution, that do not include the physical handling of the product and take place on behalf of another legal or natural person, are now allowed under certain conditions. The broker engaging in these activities must have a permanent address within the EU area. If in Finland, the broker must present a notification to the Finnish Medicines Agency (FIMEA) to register its operation before pursuing its activities. FIMEA publishes a list of all registered brokers on its website and can impose additional regulations concerning such brokering. No brokers have so far been registered in Finland, nor has additional regulation relating to brokering of drugs been set out by FIMEA.

The virtual wholesaling of drugs is not addressed by the Finnish legislation. While it has not been explicitly prohibited, the reception and distribution of orders requires a wholesale licence issued by FIMEA under the Medicines Act. Best practice guidelines for these wholesale activities are set out in FIMEA Regulation No. 5/2013, which follows the EU Guidelines 2013/C 68/01 on Good Distribution Practice of Medicinal Products for Human Use (GDP Guidelines). Accordingly, a holder of the wholesale licence must appropriately confirm the quality of its products on reception. If the distributed products never physically enter the Finnish jurisdiction, making such an acceptance inspection would not be possible, meaning that virtual distribution would violate the wholesalers' duty of care and would therefore be inconsistent with Finnish legislation.

## 6. WHAT IS THE PROCEDURE TO APPEAL (LEGAL REMEDY) A LICENSING DECISION?

Licensing decisions can be appealed under the general provisions concerning appeals in administrative matters. In accordance with the Administrative Judicial Procedure Act, an appeal must be filed at the Administrative Court within 30 days from the date on which the decision was served to the appellate. The decision of the Administrative Court can be appealed to the Supreme Administrative Court, subject to a leave of appeal granted by the court.

## 7. WHAT ARE THE COSTS OF OBTAINING LICENSING?

The government fees for marketing authorisations are set out in Decree 252/2014 of the Ministry of Health and Social Affairs. In the national procedure, the costs for obtaining a marketing authorisation for a product concerning a new pharmaceutical compound, combination product or biologically similar product are:

- EUR13,000 for the first authorisation.
- EUR8,000 for subsequent medicine forms and strengths.

For generic products, applications in which reference to documentation of the original authorisation holder is made with its consent and mixed-type abridged applications referred to in Article 10(3) of Directive 2001/83/EC on the Community code relating to medicinal products for human use (Code for Human Medicines Directive), the fee is EUR8,000 for each authorisation or registration.

In a mutual recognition and decentralised procedure in which Finland is a concerned member state (CMS), the fee is:

- EUR10,000 for the first authorisation for a product concerning a new pharmaceutical compound, combination product or biologically similar product.
- EUR6,000 for subsequent medicine forms and strengths.

**FINLAND**

For generic products, applications in which reference to documentation of the original authorisation holder is made with its consent and mixed-type abridged applications referred to in Article 10(3) of the Code for Human Medicines Directive, the fee is EUR6,000 for each authorisation or registration.

In a mutual recognition and decentralised procedure in which Finland is the reference member state (RMS), the processing fee is EUR12,000 including all forms and strengths of the trade name authorised.

For authorisation concerning parallel imports, the fee is:

- EUR1,900 for the first country.
- EUR1,100 for subsequent countries.

## DISTRIBUTION TO CONSUMERS

### 8. WHAT ARE THE DIFFERENT CATEGORIES OF DRUGS FOR DISTRIBUTION?

There are two main categories of drugs:

- Prescription drugs.
- Over-the-counter drugs.

### 9. WHO IS AUTHORISED TO DISTRIBUTE PRESCRIPTION DRUGS AND OVER-THE-COUNTER DRUGS TO CONSUMERS?

**Prescription drugs**

Prescription drugs can only be distributed by pharmacies, hospital pharmacies and dispensaries. The required pharmacy licences are granted by the Finnish Medicines Agency (FIMEA). The number of licences granted annually is based on an objectively assessed need for new pharmacies in each geographic area.

**Over-the-counter drugs**

Over-the-counter drugs can only be distributed by pharmacies. However, homeopathic products and nicotine products can also be distributed by other entities, such as retail stores.

### 10. WHAT DRUGS CAN AN ATTENDING PHYSICIAN DISTRIBUTE AND UNDER WHAT CIRCUMSTANCES?

Under the Medicines Act, only licensed pharmacies are allowed to distribute drugs to patients. However, the attending physician can give the patient a starter pack of the prescribed medication should this be necessary for the immediate start of the treatment. Such packs must be given free of charge.

### 11. WHO IS AUTHORISED TO PRESCRIBE PRESCRIPTION DRUGS TO CONSUMERS?

Under the Act on Health Care Professionals (*559/1994*), prescription drugs can only be prescribed by qualified physicians and dentists, or students of medicinal and dental sciences temporarily acting in the position of a physician/dentist, to the extent the drugs are prescribed for their own patients. Qualified nurses and midwives also have a limited right to prescribe certain drugs for their own patients provided that the medicine in question is on a list approved by the physician in charge of the health centre or hospital district. Under Decree 1088/2010 of the Ministry of Health and Social Affairs, a further precondition for prescription is that the person prescribing the drug has personally attended to the patient during the last calendar year or can otherwise confirm the need for medication based on patient data.

## 12. IS DIRECT MAILING/DISTANCE SELLING OF DRUGS PERMITTED IN YOUR JURISDICTION?

### Conditions

Under the Medicines Act, distance selling is allowed in Finland, as of 1 February 2011. However, only a licensed pharmacist providing its main service in person can provide drugs virtually, and it requires an internet page where all the information about the products is available to customers. When opening a virtual pharmacy, the Finnish Medicines Agency (FIMEA) must be notified in advance. There are currently more than 100 legally established virtual pharmacies in Finland.

Under FIMEA Regulation 2/2011, there are strict conditions for the storage and delivery of drugs, including that:

- The consistency of the storage conditions described in the marketing authorisation must be documented and the products and their delivery controlled by a pharmacist.
- The drugs cannot be delivered before the pharmacist has ensured that the customer has received all the necessary information on the use of the product.
- If the drug mainly affects the central nervous system, only the smallest packages can be sold online.
- If a prescription is required for the drug, it must be written by an authorised physician (in Finland) and must be included in the Finnish system of electronic prescriptions. This excludes all foreign prescriptions.

### Cross-border sales

Cross-border sales of non-prescription drugs is allowed if carried out by registered virtual pharmacies. The conditions for this follow the content of Directive 2011/62/EC amending Directive 2001/83/EC on the Community code relating to medicinal products for human use, as regards the prevention of the entry into the legal supply chain of falsified medicinal products (Falsified Medicinal Products Directive), which has been implemented in Finland as from 1 January 2014. According to Section 52b of the Medicines Act, the pharmacy responsible for the online service must ensure that the marketing of the drug in question complies with the laws in the country of destination. It must also display on its website a hyperlink to FIMEA's website where a list of registered Finnish virtual pharmacies is presented, as well as the common European logo referred to in the Falsified Medicinal Products Directive. In addition, the general provisions on the distance sale of goods under the Consumer Protection Act apply also to distance sale of drugs.

### 13. WHAT REGULATORY AUTHORITY IS RESPONSIBLE FOR SUPERVISING DISTRIBUTION ACTIVITIES?

The Finnish Medicines Agency (FIMEA) supervises the manufacture, import and distribution of drugs. After licences have been granted, the supervision takes place mainly through inspections. FIMEA can conduct necessary inspections in co-operation with the European Medicines Agency (EMA).

The National Supervisory Authority for Welfare and Health (VALVIRA) supervises the prescription of drugs to consumers in accordance with the Act on Health Care Professionals. The main focus is on advance supervision taking place through licensing. VALVIRA grants, on application, the right to practise as a licensed or authorised professional, and authorises the use of the occupational title of the healthcare professional. After licensing, supervision takes place mainly based on notifications by patients and healthcare entities as well as through inspections.

### 14. WHAT IS THE PROCEDURE TO APPEAL (LEGAL REMEDY) A DISTRIBUTION DECISION?

Under the Medicines Act, orders given by an inspector in connection with an inspection cannot be appealed, but a request for rectification can be presented to the Finnish Medicines Agency (FIMEA). The request must be made in writing and presented to FIMEA within 30 days from the date on which the order was given. The decision issued by FIMEA can later be appealed.

The decisions of FIMEA and the National Supervisory Authority for Welfare and Health (VALVIRA) can be appealed in accordance with the general procedure concerning administrative appeals as defined in the Administrative Judicial Procedure Act. The appeal is addressed to the Administrative Court. The decision of the Administrative Court can then be appealed to the Supreme Administrative Court if leave of appeal is granted.

### 15. WHAT ARE THE LEGAL CONSEQUENCES OF NON-COMPLIANCE WITH CONSUMER DISTRIBUTION LAWS?

Non-compliance with the provisions of the Medicines Act relating to, for example, the import, storage, sale or distribution of drugs, is punishable by fine as a medicines infringement. Criminal liability under medicines offences can also follow, mainly for intentional misconduct, in which case the penalty is either a fine or a maximum of one year's imprisonment.

The Finnish Medicines Agency (FIMEA) also has the right to prohibit the import, manufacture, distribution, sale or other release for consumption of a drug if it becomes apparent that the conditions for granting the marketing authorisation no longer exist or if the requirements and obligations concerning the manufacture or import of the drug are no longer met. Similarly, it can suspend the distribution, sale or other release to consumption of a drug and order its withdrawal from the markets if there is reason to suspect that the product is counterfeit or otherwise defective.

For non-compliance by healthcare professionals in relation to the distribution of drugs, the possible legal consequences include:

- A written warning issued by the National Supervisory Authority for Welfare and Health (VALVIRA).
- VALVIRA suspending the licence of the persons in question, or otherwise prohibiting them from acting in the position of a healthcare professional for the duration of the examination of the matter.

# FINLAND

## WHOLESALE DISTRIBUTION

### 16. WHAT IS THE LEGAL REGIME REGARDING WHOLESALE DISTRIBUTION OF DRUGS?

The wholesale distribution of drugs is regulated under:

- The Medicines Act.
- The Medicines Decree.
- The Finnish Medicines Agency (FIMEA) regulation No. 5/2013 on good distribution practice of medicinal products.

In Finland, the wholesale of drugs can only be carried out under a licence granted by FIMEA. To obtain a licence, applicants must have appropriate facilities, equipment and personnel for their operations and for the storage of drugs. Wholesalers must also have a defined "responsible person" who ensures that all action is taken in line with the applicable legislation. The responsible person must be a qualified pharmacist.

The wholesale of drugs can be made to:

- Pharmaceutical manufacturers.
- Other pharmaceutical wholesalers.
- Pharmacies.
- Subsidiary pharmacies.
- Military pharmacies.
- Hospital pharmacies or dispensaries.
- Veterinary surgeons for the purposes of veterinary medication.

Drugs that are not restricted to sales to pharmacies (that is, nicotine and homeopathic products) can also be sold to other retailers. Active pharmaceutical ingredients can also be sold to other businesses for production purposes and to universities, institutions of higher education and other scientific research institutions for research purposes.

In Finland, the distribution of drugs is operated through a single channel (or direct-to-pharmacy) system. This means that nearly all pharmaceutical companies make exclusive distribution agreements with only one wholesaler at a time and their products are therefore available only through that channel. In the single channel system, the wholesalers of drugs are mainly responsible for the storage and distribution of drugs under their agreements with the pharmaceutical companies, and pharmaceutical companies set the prices of their products to pharmacies.

### 17. WHAT REGULATORY AUTHORITY IS RESPONSIBLE FOR SUPERVISING WHOLESALE DISTRIBUTION ACTIVITIES?

**Regulatory authority**

The Finnish Medicines Agency (FIMEA) supervises wholesale and distribution activities. When necessary, it can co-operate with the European Medicines Agency (EMA).

### Supervision

Supervision is mainly through inspections, during which the inspecting official has the right to take copies of necessary documentation, collect samples and take photographs in the premises of the wholesaler. The inspector can give orders concerning necessary improvements, which must be executed immediately.

### Rights of appeal

Orders given by the inspector in connection with an inspection cannot be appealed but a request for rectification can be presented to FIMEA. The request must be made in writing and presented to FIMEA within 30 days from the date on which the order was given.

Decisions made by FIMEA can be appealed in turn in accordance with the general procedure for administrative appeals under the Administrative Judicial Procedure Act. The appeal is addressed to the Administrative Court. The decision of the Administrative Court can later be appealed to the Supreme Administrative Court if leave of appeal is granted.

## 18. WHAT ARE THE LEGAL CONSEQUENCES OF NON-COMPLIANCE WITH WHOLESALE DISTRIBUTION LAWS?

The Finnish Medicines Agency (FIMEA) can revoke in part or in full a licence for the manufacture or wholesale of drugs if any of the requirements for granting the licence are no longer met or if an obligation essential to safety or quality has not been met. Non-compliance with the provisions of the Medicines Act relating to, for example, the import, storage, sale or distribution of drugs, is punishable by fines as a medicines infringement. Criminal liability under medicines offences can also follow, mainly for intentional misconduct, in which case the penalty is either a fine or a maximum of one year's imprisonment. See *Question 15*.

# MARKETING

## PROMOTION

## 19. WHAT IS THE GENERAL LEGAL REGIME FOR THE MARKETING OF DRUGS?

### Legal regime

The marketing of drugs is regulated under the Medicines Act and Medicines Decree. In addition, general legislation applicable to all marketing must be considered when undertaking marketing activities, such as:

- The Consumer Protection Act (when targeted at consumers).
- The Unfair Business Practices Act (when targeted at businesses).

### Limits to marketing activities

All promotional activities must be conducted on a transparent basis and encourage the appropriate use of drugs. All necessary information on a product must be given in accordance with the valid marketing authorisation, and the provision of misleading information is prohibited.

## 20. ARE THERE OTHER CODES OF CONDUCT FOR THE MARKETING OF DRUGS (FOR EXAMPLE, BY PROFESSIONAL OR INDUSTRIAL ORGANISATIONS)?

Pharma Industry Finland has its own Code of Ethics (PIF Code), which contains detailed regulations on marketing, and has been drafted and implemented by the representatives of the pharmaceutical industry. The European Federation of Pharmaceutical Industries and Associations' (EFPIA) Code of Practice on the Promotion of Medicines influenced the drafting of the PIF Code. All members of the Pharma Industry Finland (in practice most major innovative pharmaceutical companies acting in Finland) have undertaken to comply with the code. Therefore, the code can be considered to constitute customary regulation of the industry and complements the applicable legislation.

## MARKETING TO CONSUMERS

## 21. WHAT IS THE LEGAL REGIME FOR MARKETING TO CONSUMERS?

**Legal regime**

For the general legal regime, see *Question 19*.

**Products**

Only products authorised in Finland can be marketed, while the marketing of prescription-only drugs to consumers is prohibited.

## 22. WHAT KINDS OF MARKETING ACTIVITIES ARE PERMITTED IN RELATION TO CONSUMERS AND THE PRODUCTS WHICH MAY BE ADVERTISED TO THEM?

Permitted marketing activities have not been separately defined in the applicable regulations. However, the general limits must be considered when undertaking marketing activities (*see Question 19*). Marketing materials must include the trade name of the product as well as its active ingredient if the product only contains one active ingredient. Necessary information on the correct and safe use of the drug (such as indications, possible adverse effects or patient safety issues) must also be presented in accordance with the summary of product characteristics as well as a specific and clear request to carefully read the separate instructions for the use of the drug. Advertising must not give in any manner an exaggerated or misleading impression on the effect of the drug, or information that may lead to its incorrect use. In addition, under the Pharma Industry Finland Code of Ethics (PIF Code), marketing must not involve price competition.

Prohibited claims are further specified in Section 25b of the Medicines Decree. Accordingly, marketing directed at the general public must not contain material that:

- Gives the impression that visiting a physician or that any treatment recommended by a physician is not necessary.
- Suggests that the effects of taking the medicine are guaranteed or that there will be no adverse effects or that the effects are as good as or better than those of another treatment or medication.
- Suggests that the health of a person may be improved with a drug, or that changes may occur in a person's state of health if the drug is not taken (with the exception of certain

# FINLAND

vaccination campaigns).
- Is directed solely or primarily at children.
- Refers to recommendations made by scientists, healthcare professionals or public figures.
- Suggests that a drug is a foodstuff, cosmetic or other consumer product.
- Suggests that the efficacy of a drug or its safety is based on the product's natural origin.
- Could, in self-care, lead to an incorrect diagnosis or treatment on account of the inclusion of a detailed case description.
- Refers to claims of recovery with inappropriate, alarming or misleading expressions.
- Contains inappropriate, alarming or misleading pictorial representations of the changes that a disease or injury causes to the human body or of the effect of a drug on the human body or part thereof.
- States that the drug has been granted a marketing authorisation.

### 23. IS IT PERMITTED TO PROVIDE CONSUMERS WITH FREE SAMPLES? ARE THERE PARTICULAR RESTRICTIONS ON SPECIAL OFFERS (FOR EXAMPLE, "BUY-ONE-GET-ONE-FREE")?

Distribution of free samples to the public is prohibited. Similarly, giving discounts on drugs is prohibited, so that "buy-one-get-one-free" type offers would not be allowed. Offering other kinds of giveaways (such as other products or benefits) for non-prescription drugs is allowed but, under the Pharma Industry Finland Code of Ethics (PIF Code), this should not encourage the unnecessary purchase or use of drugs or endanger the appropriate communication of the correct and safe use of the product to consumers.

### 24. ARE THERE PARTICULAR RULES OF PRACTICE ON THE USE OF THE INTERNET/SOCIAL MEDIA REGARDING DRUGS AND THEIR ADVERTISING?

The same rules apply to internet advertising as to advertising through other media. Marketing or advertising of products which are to be sold by prescription, or which contain narcotics or psychotropic substances, are prohibited, unless aimed at persons entitled to prescribe those drugs. Where prescription drugs are marketed at those entitled to prescribe them, appropriate measures must be taken to ensure that the general public is not able to access such marketing material. Such a limited access system can be created by, for example, using passwords and other registration requirements.

Should a link to an independent webpage be presented on the company sponsored webpage, the page linked to must also comply with the relevant Finnish regulations, even if available information would be presented in a language other than Finnish or Swedish. A marketing authorisation holder is responsible for the content of an independent webpage that is accessible through a link displayed its own webpage.

### 25. WHAT REGULATORY AUTHORITY IS RESPONSIBLE FOR SUPERVISING MARKETING ACTIVITIES TO CONSUMERS?

**Regulatory authority**

The Finnish Medicines Agency (FIMEA) is primarily responsible for supervising drugs marketing activities. The Consumer Ombudsman also supervises marketing activities based on the Consumer Protection Act. The Supervisory Commission for the Marketing of Medicinal Products (PIF Supervisory Commission), as well as two inspection boards under its supervision, acting under Pharma Industry Finland, supervise their member companies' compliance with the Pharma Industry Finland Code of Ethics (PIF Code). Inspection board 1 supervises marketing targeted at consumers, while inspection board 2 supervises marketing to healthcare professionals and monitors the activities of medical sales representatives.

**Supervision**

Under the Medicines Decree, holders of a marketing authorisation for a drug must, on request, submit to FIMEA:

- The material used in marketing and an account of the recipients of the material.
- The method of its distribution and the starting date for the distribution.
- Other information and documentation that may be needed for the supervision of marketing activities.

The examination of cases by the PIF Inspection Boards is initiated by the board's own control initiatives, complaints by PIF's member companies, or based on preliminary inspections. Cases examined by the supervisory commission are, in turn, initiated on the basis of appeals by a party to the case, referrals by one of the inspection boards or requests of opinion.

If a case is already being examined by the authorities, neither the supervisory commission nor the inspection boards can proceed with the examination in accordance with the PIF Code. Instead, the matter is examined afterwards in light of the authorities' decision.

Companies can request a preliminary inspection of their marketing material by the inspection board 1 to ensure its compliance with the PIF Code. Radio and TV advertisements of drugs are subject to obligatory preliminary inspection under the PIF Code. The company must comply with the opinion of the inspection board. For other materials, if a decision rendered by the inspection board is not followed, the matter can be taken up by the board through its own supervisory proceedings if deemed necessary.

**Rights of appeal**

Decisions made by FIMEA can be appealed in accordance with the general procedure concerning administrative appeals under the Administrative Judicial Procedure Act. The appeal is addressed to the Administrative Court. The decision of the Administrative Court can later be appealed to the Supreme Administrative Court if leave of appeal is granted. Within Pharma Industry Finland, the decisions of the inspection boards can be appealed to the supervisory commission.

### 26. WHAT ARE THE LEGAL CONSEQUENCES OF NON-COMPLIANCE WITH CONSUMER MARKETING LAWS?

Under the Medicines Act, the Finnish Medicines Agency (FIMEA) can forbid the continuation or renewal of marketing and order the company in question to correct marketing if this is considered necessary in terms of patient safety. This prohibition or order can be enforced with a conditional fine.

A person that intentionally or due to gross negligence acts in violation of the Medicines Act or Medicines Decree or FIMEA's prohibition or order can be sentenced to fines or imprisonment of up to one year. For acts due to negligence, the person is subject only to fines.

Under the Pharma Industry Finland Code of Ethics (PIF Code), if a promotion is found to be non-compliant, the PIF member may in more minor cases be issued an admonition for future reference accompanied with a reasonable deadline by which the marketing materials must be revised. The request to cease an activity concerns more severe cases of breach, where the company must refrain from this activity immediately after the request to do so has been served. In such a case, the material in question must be immediately withdrawn from the market. In addition, at their discretion, the inspection boards or the supervisory commission can impose a fine ranging from the minimum of EUR1,000 to the maximum of EUR100,000 on a company that has violated the PIF Code. In the case of continuing misbehaviour, the inspection boards or the supervisory commission can also submit the case to the review of authorities or impose a contractual penalty on the company that has violated the code ranging from EUR20,000 to EUR300,000.

## MARKETING TO PROFESSIONALS

### 27. WHAT KINDS OF MARKETING ACTIVITIES ARE PERMITTED IN RELATION TO PROFESSIONALS?

Promotional activities targeted at healthcare professionals are strictly regulated. All benefits and gifts must relate to the professional activities and be moderate in nature. Under the Medicines Act, the holder of the marketing authorisation or other entity undertaking marketing activities must also maintain a publicly available list on all economic and other supportive measures (direct and indirect) it has taken in favour of health related associations and patient organisations.

### 28. ARE THERE ANY RESTRICTIONS ON MARKETING TO PROFESSIONALS?

**Marketing activities**

All benefits and gifts to healthcare personnel must be inexpensive and relate to their professional activities. Companies must not offer or otherwise give direct or indirect financial incentives or inducements to healthcare professionals. Sales promotions must not be inappropriate or potentially endanger the general public's trust that the prescription, use or assignment of drugs is independent. Additional benefits can be considered a bribe if they are significant and could induce the recipient to make acquisitions that would not otherwise be justifiable for the person or institution in question.

Prohibited types of marketing activities have not been further specified in the medicines legislation or other applicable regulation. However, compensation for participating, for example, in a non-interventional study must be of reasonable economic value. In addition, under the Pharma Industry Finland Code of Ethics (PIF Code), any study results included in the material for the marketing of drugs must have been published in article form in a scientific journal. The use of unpublished materials, such as abstracts, posters or similar materials that have not been published in scientific journals, is prohibited. However, as an exception, reference can be made to unpublished study results if this new information refers to a serious disease and there is clear proof that the new treatment is superior to the earlier treatments. The unpublished study results must in any case meet the same quality criteria applied to published results and involve explicit information on the trial arrangements (for example, in vivo, in vitro, animal testing). In addition, the use of such material is subject to the consent of the responsible investigator and additional information on the contents of that material must be given on request.

## Frequency

The PIF Code incorporates the Code for the Good Medical Sales Representation Practices. Although the code states that the ultimate decision on the arrangement of medical sales representation events is taken by the management of the relevant healthcare unit, certain general principles to follow are provided. For example:

- Visits must be organised in advance.
- Companies must follow the instructions given by the healthcare unit regarding the booking of visits, for the avoidance of unnecessary contacts that might disturb their operation.
- Sales representation activities must be fitted in as a flexible part of the working day of the healthcare unit and the physicians working there, so that they enhance proper pharmacotherapy without disturbing the operation of the unit or the patients.

Medical sales representation activities can be arranged in the healthcare unit premises or elsewhere. If arranged in the premises of the healthcare unit, they must take place in the physician's consulting room, the medical staff's common room or other similar premises assigned by the healthcare unit for presentation purposes to allow for the presentation to take place in privacy, without disturbing the other activities of the healthcare unit.

## Provision of hospitality

Hospitality at meetings with groups of professionals must be reasonable and secondary to the purpose of the event. According to the PIF Code, events organised or sponsored by the pharmaceutical industry must be consistent with the customary local norms of hospitality. Catering and other hospitality measures must be moderate and suit the occasion, and not compromise the objectivity of physicians in prescribing drugs or endanger the public trust in the neutrality of medicine subscription and supply. In addition, hospitality must not exceed what typical participants in the event would be prepared to pay if they had to cover their own expenses.

## 29. WHAT INFORMATION IS IT LEGALLY REQUIRED TO INCLUDE IN ADVERTISING TO PROFESSIONALS?

Advertising of drugs to healthcare professionals must only contain essential information on the drug and its use. In particular, such advertising must include:

- Essential information, in accordance with the summary of product characteristics, on the purpose of use, recommended use, effect and safety of the product.
- Legal conditions of supply.
- Conditions of reimbursement under the health insurance system, average treatment costs, where possible, and retail prices of different packages.
- The date when the advertisement was prepared or revised.

All information given in marketing must:

- Correspond to the approved summary of product characteristics.
- Be accurate, up-to-date, verifiable and clear enough to enable the reader to form an opinion of the therapeutic value of the product.

Quotations, as well as tables and other illustrative matter taken from medicinal journals or scientific research must be faithfully reproduced and their precise sources indicated.

### 30. ARE THERE RULES ON COMPARISONS WITH OTHER PRODUCTS THAT ARE PARTICULARLY APPLICABLE TO DRUGS?

The Medicines Act stipulates that marketing must not provide a misleading or exaggerated picture of the formula, origin or pharmaceutical significance of a product, or be inappropriate in any other similar way. In addition, the Unfair Business Practices Act contains general provisions regarding comparative advertising that may be applicable to the marketing of drugs. The Pharma Industry Finland Code of Ethics (PIF Code) stipulates that comparisons between different drugs, active ingredients, excipients or other characteristics must be accurate and reliable.

The graphic comparison and price comparison of the product must be clearly justifiable. The object of the comparison must be clearly recognisable. The packages and dosages used in price comparisons must be comparable to each other. When the prices of products are compared, the drugs covered by the comparison and their trade names must be clearly indicated. When using a comparison in marketing, the time of the comparison or the date of publication must be disclosed. The comparison must give special weight to the objectivity of the marketing and the correctness of the information.

### 31. WHAT OTHER ITEMS, FUNDING OR SERVICES ARE PERMITTED TO BE PROVIDED TO PROFESSIONALS?

**Discounts**

Pharmaceutical companies are not permitted to grant discounts to individual pharmacies, and the wholesale price must be the same for all pharmacies. The wholesale price must include all rebates, refunds and other benefits that are granted to a pharmacy. These restrictions do not apply to drugs that can be sold in places other than pharmacies, such as nicotine replacements. However, it is permitted for pharmaceutical companies to grant discounts to welfare and health units, such as hospital districts and individual hospital pharmacies.

**Free samples**

Samples of drugs can be distributed only to the persons entitled to prescribe and supply them. If the prescription is subject to restrictions on supply, the sample can be given only to a physician entitled to prescribe that product. Only one sample per recipient per year can be given of each strength and composition of a drug. A sample can be distributed only on the basis of a written, signed and dated request, and pharmaceutical companies must keep records of the free samples given in each calendar year. A sample must be the smallest package size available on the market. Each sample must be accompanied by a summary of product characteristics. Narcotics, including psychotropic substances and substances that mainly affect the central nervous system, cannot be distributed as samples.

**Sponsorship of professionals**

Under the Pharma Industry Finland Code of Ethics (PIF Code), making donations or giving grants to individual healthcare professionals is prohibited. As an exception to this, grants for investigator-initiated clinical trials with an appropriate study protocol, which have been approved by the regulatory authorities and ethics committee and which otherwise comply with the requirements set in the legislation for clinical trials, are allowed.

From 1 January 2014, the PIF Code obliges companies to carefully document and publish information on all economic benefits targeted at healthcare professionals, including all direct and indirect transfers of economic value either in cash or other forms of benefit.

**Other items, funding or services**

Healthcare professionals must not be offered or otherwise provided with any kind of indirect economic incentives or inducements. See *Questions 27* and *28*.

**32. WHAT REGULATORY AUTHORITY IS RESPONSIBLE FOR SUPERVISING MARKETING ACTIVITIES REGARDING PROFESSIONALS?**

**Regulatory authority**

The Finnish Medicines Agency's (FIMEA) and Pharma Industry Finland's role in supervising pharmaceutical marketing also applies to marketing targeted at companies or other entities (*see Question 25*).

**Supervision**

Under the Medicines Act, the National Supervisory Authority for Welfare and Health (VALVIRA) and the regional state administrative agencies supervise the prohibition on healthcare professionals accepting gifts or benefits that are contrary to the medicines legislation.

**Rights of appeal**

See *Question 25*.

**33. WHAT ARE THE LEGAL CONSEQUENCES IN CASE OF NON-COMPLIANCE WITH PROFESSIONAL MARKETING LAWS?**

See *Question 26*.

## ENGAGEMENT WITH PATIENT ORGANISATIONS

**34. WHAT KINDS OF ACTIVITIES ARE PERMITTED IN RELATION TO ENGAGEMENT WITH PATIENT ORGANISATIONS? WHAT ARE THE RESTRICTIONS THAT ARE IMPOSED ON RELATIONSHIP WITH PATIENT ORGANISATIONS?**

Pharmaceutical companies can give financial support to patient organisations and engage in other kinds of co-operation with them by, for example, arranging promotional events.

The patient organisation's logo can be used in the company's own operations solely based on the written consent of the organisation covering the purpose and means of use of the materials. Pharmaceutical companies must not try to influence the contents of the materials published by a sponsored patient organisation for the promotion of its own commercial interests. In addition, a pharmaceutical company cannot be the only founding member of a patient organisation or require it to be the sole funder of the organisation or of a certain significant form of its activities.

Under the Medicines Act and the Pharma Industry Finland Code of Ethics (PIF Code), a holder of a marketing authorisation or other entity undertaking marketing activities must also maintain a publicly available list on all economic and other supportive measures (direct and indirect) it has provided to health related associations and patient organisations (*see Question 31*).

## REFORM

**35. ARE THERE ANY PLANS TO REFORM THE LAW ON THE DISTRIBUTION AND PROMOTION OF DRUGS IN YOUR JURISDICTION?**

No significant reforms are expected in the near future in the field of distribution and promotion of drugs in Finland.

# FRANCE

*Olivier Lantrès, FIELDFISHER*

## DISTRIBUTION

### PRE-CONDITIONS FOR DISTRIBUTION

**1. WHAT ARE THE LEGAL PRE-CONDITIONS FOR A DRUG TO BE DISTRIBUTED WITHIN THE JURISDICTION?**

**Authorisation**

Under the Code of Public Health a medicinal product can only be sold and distributed in France if it has been:

- Authorised for sale (marketing authorisation (MA)).
- Registered (for homeopathic products sold under the generic name).
- Authorised or registered in another state in the European Economic Area

Medicines authorised in another EU jurisdiction must have an import licence or a parallel import licence to be imported in France from another Member State, unless they have an EU-wide MA.

**Exceptions**

Unauthorised medicinal products without MA can be distributed through a compassionate use programme, the provisions of which were recently modified by the law on the improvement of medicines safety (the Bertrand Law) on 29 December 2011. The medicinal product must obtain a "temporary use authorisation", from the National Security Agency of Medicines and Health Products (*Agence Nationale de Sécurité de Médicament et des Produits de Santé*).

There are also exceptions to the authorisation requirement for medicines which are produced at a pharmacy and which are intended for a specific patient.

The Bertrand Law also authorises the French Drug Agency to impose a new indication to an already authorised product, in the event that the new indication is already in use in practice outside its official scope of indication. This is generally challenged by pharmaceutical companies. It is known as RTU (*recommandation temporaire d'utilisation*). In 2014, three examples of RTUs were officially recognised by the French Drug Agency.

## 2. DO ANY TYPES OF NAMED PATIENT AND/OR COMPASSIONATE USE PROGRAMMES OPERATE? IF SO, WHAT ARE THE REQUIREMENTS FOR PRE-LAUNCH ACCESS?

A "temporary use authorisation" (ATU) allows early access to new promising drugs or to old drugs that are not covered by a marketing authorisation (MA) in France, when there is an unmet need. ATU is for treatment, prevention or diagnosis (not for investigation) of a rare or serious disease, when no satisfactory alternative method is available in France. There must be adequate proof of efficacy and safety and benefit must be anticipated for the patient. The patient must not be included in a clinical trial.

There are two kinds of ATU:

- **Nominative ATU.** The nominative ATU is only for one patient, on a named basis, on the request and responsibility of the physician.
- **Cohort ATU.** The cohort ATU is for a group of patients, for one indication. It is applied by the pharmaceutical company which commits to submit an MA.

In 2014, 18,000 patients were treated in the framework of nominative ATUs and 12,000 in the framework of cohort ATU.

## LICENSING

## 3. WHAT IS THE PROCEDURAL STRUCTURE REGARDING LICENSING A DRUG FOR DISTRIBUTION?

### Structure

To obtain a marketing authorisation (MA) for a drug, an application for an MA must be submitted to the National Security Agency of Medicines and Health Products (ANSM).

Four different procedures exist:

- National procedure.
- Mutual recognition procedure.
- Decentralised procedure, where the ANSM is competent to grant the MA.
- Centralised procedure for which the application is submitted to the European Medicines Agency (EMEA).

For additional details, see *Distribution and marketing of drugs in the EU: overview*.

For the national procedure, an application is needed for each single pharmaceutical formulation and strength. The application must follow the specific form supplied by the ANSM. Under Article R.5121-35 of the French Code of Public Health, the ANSM has 210 days to assess the application starting from the date where a complete application is filed. A technical and scientific evaluation of the data communicated by the company is carried out by the MA Commission from the ANSM. This assessment relies on criteria of quality, efficacy and safety of the medicinal product. If the requirements for authorisation are met, an MA is granted. The authorisation may be subject to conditions.

The ANSM cannot autonomously grant a national commission of marketing authorisation (*Autorisation de Mise sur le Marché*) (AMM) for a drug if it has already been authorised in another member state or if an AMM request has been submitted in one or more member states.

### 4. IS THERE A SIMPLIFIED LICENCE PROCEEDING, OR RELAXED LICENSING CONDITIONS, FOR DRUGS WHICH HAVE ALREADY BEEN LICENSED FOR DISTRIBUTION IN ANOTHER JURISDICTION?

If a drug is already authorised for sale in another European Economic Area state, the mutual recognition procedure will apply and the National Security Agency of Medicines and Health Products (ANSM) must recognise this authorisation and grant an equivalent French one.

Since 2004, there has been a specific procedure for parallel imports. This procedure relates to the import of a drug from another EU member state in order to sell it in France where there is an identical drug which has obtained a marketing authorisation (MA). The parallel importer must notify the MA owner of its intention to import and must obtain authorisation from the ANSM within 90 days from the request. Silence on the part of the ANSM is considered an implicit rejection. In practice, the procedure is longer and can last almost a full year in some cases (for example, if the ANSM asks for information related to the pharmaceutical product from another national health authority in another jurisdiction).

### 5. IS VIRTUAL DRUG DISTRIBUTION POSSIBLE FROM YOUR JURISDICTION?

A marketing authorisation (MA) obtained in France gives the MA holder the right to sell the authorised drug in France. The question of whether or not the medicinal product can be distributed in another country based on the French authorisation must be answered based on that country's law as there is no specific French legislation governing this issue.

### 6. WHAT IS THE PROCEDURE TO APPEAL (LEGAL REMEDY) A LICENSING DECISION?

Licensing decisions can be appealed before the administrative courts.

### 7. WHAT ARE THE COSTS OF OBTAINING LICENSING?

The application fees depend on the procedure. Fees for obtaining a marketing authorisation:

- Decentralised procedure: EUR50,000.
- Mutual recognition procedure: EUR34,000.
- National procedure: EUR34,000.

Up-to-date information on fees is available on the ANSM website (*www.ansm.sante.fr*).

## DISTRIBUTION TO CONSUMERS

### 8. WHAT ARE THE DIFFERENT CATEGORIES OF DRUGS FOR DISTRIBUTION?

The following different classifications are made of drugs for distribution:

- Non-prescription medicinal products.
- Prescription medicinal products that can be:
  - prescription-only;
  - exclusively for hospital use; or
  - reserved for certain specialist physicians.

These are also drugs which are reimbursable and those which are not.

## 9. WHO IS AUTHORISED TO DISTRIBUTE PRESCRIPTION DRUGS AND OVER-THE-COUNTER DRUGS TO CONSUMERS?

**Prescription drugs**

In order to be permitted to sell prescription drugs to consumers, an authorisation is required. Only open care pharmacies can obtain such an authorisation. The authorisation is granted by the Regional Health Agency (*Agence régionale de santé*). The pharmacy must be owned by a pharmacist who is duly registered with the French Society of Pharmacists. Hospital pharmacies can also sell specific products to patients, in particular those suffering from AIDS or rare diseases.

Lastly, in the event that there is no pharmacist in a large area, medical doctors are allowed to sell pharmaceutical products but this situation is rare (*see Question 10*). However in all other situations, medical practitioners cannot give drugs to patients.

**Over-the-counter drugs**

Over-the-counter medicinal products can only be distributed to consumers by pharmacies.

## 10. WHAT DRUGS CAN AN ATTENDING PHYSICIAN DISTRIBUTE AND UNDER WHAT CIRCUMSTANCES?

Under the Code of Public Health, physicians settled in urban areas where there is no pharmacist can be granted permission from the Regional Health Agency to store drugs and to dispense them to persons they treat. This involves reimbursed and non-reimbursed drugs necessary for treatment.

## 11. WHO IS AUTHORISED TO PRESCRIBE PRESCRIPTION DRUGS TO CONSUMERS?

Authorised doctors have a general authority to prescribe drugs and medicinal products to patients. Dental surgeons and midwives have limited authority to prescribe medicinal products to patients.

Under the Code of Public Health (CSP), and since the law called *Loi Hôpital, patients, santé et territoires* from 21 July 2009 codified in the French CSP, pharmacists can renew prescriptions of certain drugs and medicinal products, after informing the physician.

## 12. IS DIRECT MAILING/DISTANCE SELLING OF DRUGS PERMITTED IN YOUR JURISDICTION?

**Conditions**

Thanks to the Ordonnance of 19 December of 2012 and a decree of 31 December 2012, French law formally allows the distance selling of drugs. However, according to ethical rules, pharmacists must:

- Provide information and advice to patients.
- Personally carry out their business.
- Verify the authenticity of the prescription and its duration.

The internet site must be run by a pharmacy (and not just a virtual pharmacist).

Only non-prescription medicines can be sold on these websites. The website must be authorised by the Regional Health Agency and the Council of Pharmacists must be informed by the retail pharmacist who wants to create the website. Retail pharmacists based in the EU but outside France are allowed to sell medicines through websites to French patients in France.

## CROSS-BORDER SALES

### 13. WHAT REGULATORY AUTHORITY IS RESPONSIBLE FOR SUPERVISING DISTRIBUTION ACTIVITIES?

The French Society of Pharmacists, the National Security Agency of Medicines and Health Products and the Regional Health Agency are responsible for supervising the compliance of the Code of Public Health with the distribution activities regarding consumers.

Additionally, the Directorate General for Competition, Consumer Affairs and Prevention of Fraud (*Direction générale de la concurrence, de la consummation et de la répression des fraudes*), the government department responsible for fair competition, also regularly supervises pharmacies and pharmaceutical companies. The authorities can request, for example:

- Access to information and documents.
- Access to facilities used for the distribution.

They can also issue injunctions and prohibitions they consider necessary to ensure compliance. Fines for non-compliance are also imposed, with a maximum fine of EUR30,000 (EUR150,000 for a company).

### 14. WHAT IS THE PROCEDURE TO APPEAL (LEGAL REMEDY) A DISTRIBUTION DECISION?

Decisions on injunctions, prohibitions and fines can be appealed with the dispute section of the Council of Pharmacists when the decision is taken by this body, or at the Administrative Court.

### 15. WHAT ARE THE LEGAL CONSEQUENCES OF NON-COMPLIANCE WITH CONSUMER DISTRIBUTION LAWS?

In case of non-compliance, an authorisation to distribute drugs or medicinal products to consumers can be withdrawn. Additionally, anyone who distributes medicinal products to consumers without the necessary authorisation can face criminal charges.

Illegal exercise of pharmaceutical activity is considered as a criminal offence and is punishable by two years imprisonment and a fine of EUR30,000. A pharmacist who does not comply with his or her deontological obligations can face a ban on practising.

## WHOLESALE DISTRIBUTION

### 16. WHAT IS THE LEGAL REGIME REGARDING WHOLESALE DISTRIBUTION OF DRUGS?

Wholesale distribution of drugs or medicinal products is governed by French legislation. Wholesale distribution of drugs or medicinal products is permitted for companies with a wholesale trade authorisation granted by the National Security Agency of Medicines and Health Products (ANSM).

When applying for an authorisation, the pharmaceutical company must demonstrate that it has the ability to fulfil the requirements set out in the Code of Public Health, for example, that the wholesale authorisation holder must have appropriate facilities and a qualified person, who is a pharmacist in France, responsible for the safety and the quality of the medicinal products. In the last couple of years, some wholesale authorisations have been withdrawn by the ANSM, because the wholesales did not comply with French legislation.

### 17. WHAT REGULATORY AUTHORITY IS RESPONSIBLE FOR SUPERVISING WHOLESALE DISTRIBUTION ACTIVITIES?

**Regulatory authority**

The National Security Agency of Medicines and Health Products (ANSM) is responsible for supervising compliance with provisions regarding wholesale distribution from the Code of Public Health. The ANSM can, for example, demand access to information and documents necessary for the supervision as well as demand access to facilities used for the distribution. The ANSM can also issue injunctions and prohibitions necessary to ensure compliance. Fines for non-compliance might also be imposed.

Decisions on injunctions and prohibitions can be appealed with the Administrative Court located where the distribution facility is established. Since the *Mediator* case in 2011, in which it was considered that the previous healthcare agency did not verify pharmaceutical entities by being rigorous enough, the ANSM has been increasingly rigorous in its control of pharmaceutical companies.

Some wholesalers, the authorisations of which were withdrawn because they did not comply with the national mandatory law governing pharmaceutical wholesalers, brought the case before the court, but without success.

The French Drug Agency can also order injunctions against pharmaceutical wholesalers, which are published on the French Drug Agency website. The company must comply with the injunction. If not, the authorisation can be withdrawn.

Almost 50 injunctions have already been issued in 2014 and half of 2015.

### 18. WHAT ARE THE LEGAL CONSEQUENCES OF NON-COMPLIANCE WITH WHOLESALE DISTRIBUTION LAWS?

In case of non-compliance, the wholesale trade authorisation can be withdrawn (*see Question 17*). Additionally, anyone who pursues wholesale trade without the necessary authorisation can face criminal charges and be punished by a maximum fine of EUR30,000 (for individuals), and up to EUR150,000 for companies (legal persons), as well as two years in prison for individuals.

The French Drug Agency can also decide injunctions against pharmaceutical wholesalers, which are published on the French Drug Agency website. Almost 50 injunctions have already been issued in 2014 and half of 2015.

# MARKETING

## PROMOTION

### 19. WHAT IS THE GENERAL LEGAL REGIME FOR THE MARKETING OF DRUGS?

**Legal regime**

Drug advertising is only possible for drugs which are authorised for sale in France.

All advertising must comply with the provisions of the marketing authorisation and the therapy guidelines recommended by the French Health Authority (*Haute Authorité de Santé*). It must present the drug objectively and encourage proper use. It must not be misleading and must not adversely impact the protection of public health.

Further to this basic provision, the Code of Public Health also provides detailed rules on drug advertising based on whether the advertising is destined for professionals or the general public.

**Limits to marketing activities**

The National Security Agency of Medicines and Health Products (ANSM) and the National Agency for the Safety of Health Products) (*Agence française de sécurité sanitaire des produits de santé*) before the setting up of the ANSM, have always been very rigorous in their control of advertising and have regularly to prohibited specific advertisements.

Advertising of prescription drugs must not be aimed towards the general public, with the exception of campaigns for vaccination against human infectious diseases. Since the new law on medicinal products on 29 December 2011, all advertising is subject to prior authorisation.

Additionally, the general provisions from the French Consumer Code regarding advertising, which are applicable to advertising of all kinds of products and services, including drugs, set out a general requirement that all advertising must be fair towards consumers, and must be in French. The Consumer Code also sets out specific rules on, among other things, misleading advertising, comparative advertising and special offers.

### 20. ARE THERE OTHER CODES OF CONDUCT FOR THE MARKETING OF DRUGS (FOR EXAMPLE, BY PROFESSIONAL OR INDUSTRIAL ORGANISATIONS)?

The National Security Agency of Medicines and Health Products has issued guidelines clarifying and specifying the rules governing the advertising of medicinal products for human use in France.

Although not legally binding, the guidelines are widely recognised by the pharmaceutical industry and applied by courts. Those guidelines include prohibitions on, among other things, advertisement of prescription drugs to the general public, off-label advertisement and pre-launch marketing. They also list rules with respect to for example, authorised support for advertising, misleading or incomplete information and disguised advertisements.

MARKETING TO CONSUMERS

### 21. WHAT IS THE LEGAL REGIME FOR MARKETING TO CONSUMERS?

There is an explicit prohibition on the advertising of prescription-only and reimbursable drugs or medicinal products to the general public, with the exception of vaccination campaigns against human infectious diseases if they are on a specific list, and cessation-smoking aids.

Additionally, the marketing authorisation or the registration must not include any prohibition or restriction due to a possible risk for public health, in particular where the drug cannot be used without the involvement of a physician for the diagnosis, commencing or monitoring of treatment (*Article L.5122-6, Code of Public Health (CSP)*).

All drug advertising to the general public is controlled before its publication and an authorisation called "visa GP" must be granted by the National Security Agency of Medicines and Health Products.

### 22. WHAT KINDS OF MARKETING ACTIVITIES ARE PERMITTED IN RELATION TO CONSUMERS AND THE PRODUCTS WHICH MAY BE ADVERTISED TO THEM?

There are no specific restrictions under French law regarding the kinds of marketing activities to consumers that are permitted. However, all marketing activities must comply with the restrictions outlined in the Code of Public Health and the National Security Agency guidelines.

However, correspondence which is necessary to answer a specific question on a medicinal product or information about human health is not considered as an advertisement and is not controlled.

### 23. IS IT PERMITTED TO PROVIDE CONSUMERS WITH FREE SAMPLES? ARE THERE PARTICULAR RESTRICTIONS ON SPECIAL OFFERS (FOR EXAMPLE, "BUY-ONE-GET-ONE-FREE")?

Free samples of drugs or medicinal products that have been authorised for sale in France must only be provided to persons qualified to prescribe the product, or to pharmacists of hospital pharmacies, on request only. The sample must not be larger than the smallest pack available on the market. The sample must be similar to the medicines and must bear the words "free samples".

Special offers to consumers such as "buy-one-get-one-free" constitute promotion and are therefore not permitted regarding prescription-only medicinal products. The Code of Public Health also prohibits pharmaceutical companies from distributing medicines to patients.

### 24. ARE THERE PARTICULAR RULES OF PRACTICE ON THE USE OF THE INTERNET/SOCIAL MEDIA REGARDING DRUGS AND THEIR ADVERTISING?

Internet advertising of medicinal products is subject to the same rules as advertising in any other French media. The Code of Public Health and the National Security Agency of Medicines and Health Products (ANSM) guidelines on advertising are therefore also applicable to advertisements published on the internet or on social media.

Additionally, the ANSM has issued a Charter for Communication on the Internet by Pharmaceutical Industries on the interpretation of provisions on advertisement of medicinal products in relation to the internet.

## 25. WHAT REGULATORY AUTHORITY IS RESPONSIBLE FOR SUPERVISING MARKETING ACTIVITIES TO CONSUMERS?

**Regulatory authority**

The National Security Agency of Medicines and Health Products (ANSM) and Directorate General for Competition Consumer Affairs and Prevention of Fraud are responsible for supervising marketing activities. The ANSM can demand access to information and documents necessary forsupervision as well as demand access to facilities. The ANSM can also take action in case of non-compliance.

The ANSM can issue a prohibitive injunction subject to fines upon non-compliance. Decisions by the ANSM can be appealed before the administrative courts.

## 26. WHAT ARE THE LEGAL CONSEQUENCES OF NON-COMPLIANCE WITH CONSUMER MARKETING LAWS?

The normal sanction under the Code of Public Health (CSP) for failing to comply with the rules governing advertising is a prohibitive injunction subject to fines for non-compliance of up to EUR37,000 and two years in prison (EUR187,500 for a company).

The CSP provides for several remedies and sanctions, depending on the nature of the violation. The specific rules deal with misleading advertisements, the absence of authorisation or the distribution of free samples to consumers, which are punishable by a maximum fine of EUR30,000 (EUR150,000 for legal entities) and two years imprisonment.

Advertisement for reimbursed or prescription medicinal products is punishable by a maximum fine of EUR37,500 (EUR187,500 for legal entities). Most cases regarding pharmaceutical companies' advertising of medicinal products are handled by the National Security Agency of Medicines and Health Products.

### MARKETING TO PROFESSIONALS

## 27. WHAT KINDS OF MARKETING ACTIVITIES ARE PERMITTED IN RELATION TO PROFESSIONALS?

There are no specific restrictions under French law in respect of what kinds of marketing activities are permitted with regard to professionals. However, all marketing activity must comply with the restrictions outlined in the Code of Public Health and the National Security Agency of Medicines and Health Products Guidelines.

## 28. ARE THERE ANY RESTRICTIONS ON MARKETING TO PROFESSIONALS?

**Marketing activities**

The Code of Public Health contains provisions called the "anti-gift law" according to which pharmaceutical companies are forbidden to make any gifts to health professionals. The new law on medicinal products from 29 December 2011 has extended this prohibition to medical students. However, the anti-gift law does not apply when:

- The amount of the gift is reasonable (up to EUR60).
- A contract has been signed for a clinical trial (or research activity in general).
- For hospitality offered for scientific events.

Moreover, according to the French Criminal Code, any person who gives, promises, or offers any improper remuneration to an employee in respect of his services, can be held guilty of bribery.

Under the National Security Agency of Medicines and Health Products Guidelines, a number of media is authorised such as booklets, posters, agendas. Survey or observational studies are also authorised as long as they are compliant with the marketing authorisation of the product, and are scientifically useful.

**Frequency**

There are no specific rules on the number of times professionals might be targeted by sales representatives. However, the Economic Committee for Medicinal Products (*Comité Economique des Produits de Santé*) (CEPS) has published a Charter containing detailed rules regarding how such contact might be made. In practice, the infringement of the Charter means that CEPS will reduce the medicine's price.

Legislation regarding sales representatives' visits was modified in 2011 by the Bertrand Law in order to further control this practice. The Bertrand Law provides that such visits carried out in health institutions must be done only collectively to a number (the precise number is yet to be published) of health professionals (and not only one as was the case under previous law), under the conditions set out in an agreement concluded between each health institution and the employer of the health professional. This limitation does not deal with sales representatives' visits concerning medicinal products reserved for hospital use and those reserved for prescription-only medication. The law also provides that these mechanisms will eventually be extended to community-based medicine.

However, these new provisions concerning sales representatives' visits are not applicable as such because to date the implementing orders have not been published. Procedural requirements will be defined in a state order (*arrêté*). Currently, these provisions are subject to controversy because their implementation raises a certain number of questions, and it seems unlikely that they will really be applicable as they are currently. It is even more unlikely that they will be applicable to community-based medicine.

**Provision of hospitality**

The accepted level of benefits which might be provided to professionals is very low in France and great care must therefore be taken when hospitality is offered to health professionals. The prohibitions on bribery and under the French Criminal Code are also applicable to the offering of hospitality.

According to the anti-gift law, all hospitality offered to physicians attending meetings arranged by a company selling reimbursed medicinal products must be of such a kind and on such a scale that there is no risk that the recipients will let themselves be influenced thereby in the execution of their professional duties. The choice of location for an event must be reasonable in relation to the purpose of the event.

The body representing pharmaceutical companies (*Les Entreprises du Médicament*) (LEEM) and the French Society of Practitioners (*Conseil national de l'ordre des médecins*) (CNOM) have published some guidelines regarding the anti-gift law. Generally, companies cannot arrange or provide financial support for events held abroad unless it is justified in relation to the purpose of the event. The airplane ticket must be an economy class ticket except for travel exceeding five hours. Moreover, the choice of location for an event must be reasonable, which implies that locations that are known for leisure activities or other activities such as winter sports, motor and golf competitions, must be avoided. Hospitality agreements must be communicated to the CNOM for its opinion. Two month's notice is required for the opinion. In practice, in 2014 and 2015, the CNOM issued many unfavourable opinions concerning hospitality.

## 29. WHAT INFORMATION IS IT LEGALLY REQUIRED TO INCLUDE IN ADVERTISING TO PROFESSIONALS?

Written information must contain at least the following data:

- The name of the medicinal product.
- The name and address of the company responsible for the marketing of the medicinal product.
- Its dosage form and, if required, its strength.
- Names of its active ingredients, stated by a generic name, as well as quantities of such ingredients.
- Marketing authorisation number.
- A balanced statement of the product characteristics, including particulars of pharmacological group or other accepted group affiliation and indication or area of indications.
- The dosage.
- Potential drug interaction and side effects.
- Required warnings or limitations applicable to the use of the medicinal product.
- The status of the product and if the product is part of the social security benefits system (including possible restrictions) and the sale price.

If the advertisement contains quotations, numerical data or diagrams taken from a scientific study, or makes a comparison between drugs that are based on such a study, reference must always be made to the documentation. It must also state the date of the establishment or revision of the advertisement material. The information provided must be correct, up-to-date, verifiable and as detailed as possible in order for the recipient to get an opinion of the product's value for treatment. The National Security Agency of Medicines and Health Products applies rigorous controls of advertising.

## 30. ARE THERE RULES ON COMPARISONS WITH OTHER PRODUCTS THAT ARE PARTICULARLY APPLICABLE TO DRUGS?

The National Security Agency of Medicines and Health Products Guidelines provide for rules on comparisons with other medicinal products. They state that comparisons between effects, active ingredients and costs of treatment, among others, of drugs must be objectively and truthfully presented and give a fair overall picture of the compared products. This means among other things that the medicinal products must:

- Have the same properties.
- Be clearly specified (including the complete name and generic designation, if necessary).

The comparison must also give a comprehensive and fair picture of the properties compared, with efficacy and safety criteria.

## 31. WHAT OTHER ITEMS, FUNDING OR SERVICES ARE PERMITTED TO BE PROVIDED TO PROFESSIONALS?

**Discounts**

For drug marketing, the Code of Public Health (CSP) prohibits offering or promising a bonus or financial or material advantages to persons authorised to prescribe or dispense them, except where this is of negligible value.

Such arrangements can in certain circumstances have competition law implications, and there are also restrictions regarding discounts in respect of medicinal products included in the national reimbursement scheme.

In detail, the French Code of Social Security provides that a 2.5% decrease is allowed to pharmacists for prescription drugs and 40 per cent for generic products, since the law of 23 December 2013 and Order of 22 August 2014.

**Free samples**

According to the CSP, free samples of medicinal products that have been authorised for sale in France can only be provided to persons qualified to prescribe the product, or to pharmacists of hospital pharmacies, on their request.

The sample can only be supplied during the first two years after the product is marketed and in response to a written request, which has been signed and dated. The request must be kept and filed by the company. The company must also carefully check that the person sending the request is authorised to prescribe or dispense medicinal products.

Only one packet of the smallest size must normally be supplied on each occasion and the number of samples of each product each year to the same recipient must be limited. The implementation decree of the Bertrand Law states four products a year per doctor. The sample must be marked with "free sample". It is not permitted to distribute free samples of medicinal products listed as narcotics by the National Security Agency of Medicines and Health Products.

**Sponsorship of professionals**

Financial support to the healthcare sector, although not prohibited, is a sensitive issue in France, particularly since the publication of the new law on medicinal products, and great care must be taken in order not to challenge the integrity and independent relationship between the pharmaceutical industry and the medicinal profession. The offer to sponsor must never be addressed to individual physicians, but must always be targeted to and approved by the employer or principal concerned. Any sponsoring must be clearly documented in writing.

## 32. WHAT REGULATORY AUTHORITY IS RESPONSIBLE FOR SUPERVISING MARKETING ACTIVITIES REGARDING PROFESSIONALS?

**Regulatory authority**

The National Security Agency of Medicines and Health Products and also the Directorate General for Competition, Consumer Affairs and Prevention of Fraud are responsible for supervising marketing activities regarding professionals. They are entitled to conduct investigations and transmit their report to the prosecutor who will decide whether a case will be brought before the court.

The French Society of Practitioners can also take action in cases of non-compliance and can order temporary suspension of physicians from practising for a period of ten years.

## 33. WHAT ARE THE LEGAL CONSEQUENCES IN CASE OF NON-COMPLIANCE WITH PROFESSIONAL MARKETING LAWS?

The court can impose a maximum fine of EUR75,000 and a temporary ten-year suspension from practising against doctors, and a fine of EUR375,000 against pharmaceutical companies. The National Security Agency of Medicines and Health Products can prohibit any advertising campaign and the Economic Committee for Medicinal Products is also allowed to fine pharmaceutical companies.

# ENGAGEMENT WITH PATIENT ORGANISATIONS

## 34. WHAT KINDS OF ACTIVITIES ARE PERMITTED IN RELATION TO ENGAGEMENT WITH PATIENT ORGANISATIONS? WHAT ARE THE RESTRICTIONS THAT ARE IMPOSED ON RELATIONSHIP WITH PATIENT ORGANISATIONS?

There are no specific restrictions in respect of what kinds of activities are permitted. However, any activity must comply with the rules provided under the Code of Public Health (CSP). According to the CSP and guidelines published by the LEEM, agreements between a patient organisation and a pharmaceutical company must always be made in writing and be available to third parties. Financial support can only be given for special projects or activities, on the condition that the co-operation must be conducted in such a manner that the parties' independent positions in relation to each other cannot be questioned.

The pharmaceutical company must declare to the French Health Authority (HAS), before 30 June of each year, the list of patient organisations that they support and the amount of this support. The information is published by the HAS. Some pharmaceutical companies also work with patient associations through patient following programmes.

Lastly, all the links of interests between patient organisations and pharmaceutical companies must also be disclosed by the latter on a specific and public Ministry of Health website.

## REFORM

**35. ARE THERE ANY PLANS TO REFORM THE LAW ON THE DISTRIBUTION AND PROMOTION OF DRUGS IN YOUR JURISDICTION?**

At the present time, the French Ministry of Health and the French Parliament are preparing a significant bill concerning the health sector. Among the main aspects, there are provisions governing class actions and access to health data owned by the French Social security. They are not supposed to impact directly the distribution and promotion of drugs.

# GERMANY

*Dr Cord Willhöft, FIELDFISHER*

## DISTRIBUTION

### PRE-CONDITIONS FOR DISTRIBUTION

**1. WHAT ARE THE LEGAL PRE-CONDITIONS FOR A DRUG TO BE DISTRIBUTED WITHIN THE JURISDICTION?**

**Authorisation**

According to section 21(1) of the Medical Products Act (*Arzneimittelgesetz*) (AMG), a finished medicinal product can only be placed on the market after a marketing authorisation has been issued by the competent German higher federal authority or the European Commission. Finished medicinal products as defined in section 4(1) of the AMG are medicinal products which are manufactured in advance and placed on the market in packaging intended for distribution to the consumer. Finished medicinal products are not intermediate products intended for further processing by a manufacturer.

Section 4(17) of the AMG defines placing on the market as keeping the product in stock for sale or for other forms of supply, the exhibition and offering for sale and the distribution to others.

**Exceptions**

Two types of medicinal products described in section 21(2) of the AMG can be placed on the market without a marketing authorisation:

- The first are medicinal products for which the essential manufacturing stages are carried out in a pharmacy and no more than 100 packages in one day are produced, and are permitted by the pharmacy operating licence. Currently, the author represents a community pharmacy in a case in which the European Court of Justice (ECJ) has to decide on whether this exemption is in line with Directive 2001/83/EC on the Community code relating to medicinal products for human use, or whether such medicinal products can only be dispensed by pharmacies on basis of a physician's prescription (*ECJ C-267/15*).
- The second are medicinal products that are intended for use in clinical trials on human beings.

Section 21(2) No. 6 of the AMG permits the provision of medicinal products to patients for a compassionate use (that is, if patients have a seriously debilitating disease or whose disease is life-threatening, and who cannot be treated satisfactorily with an authorised medicinal product) to be made available free of charge. The Federal Ministry of Health (*Bundesgesundheitsministerium*) issued the Ordinance for Compassionate Use

(*Arzneimittel-Härtefall-Verordnung*) in 2010 which sets up the legal requirements for placing unlicensed medicinal products on the market in Germany before a marketing authorisation has been obtained by the pharmaceutical company. See *Question 2*.

## 2. DO ANY TYPES OF NAMED PATIENT AND/OR COMPASSIONATE USE PROGRAMMES OPERATE? IF SO, WHAT ARE THE REQUIREMENTS FOR PRE-LAUNCH ACCESS?

There are provisions under German law for both named patient supplies and/or compassionate use programs.

Article 5(1) of Directive 2001/83/EC on the Community code relating to medicinal products for human use on named patient supplies is implemented into German law, inter alia, by section 73(3) of the Medical Products Act (*Arzneimittelgesetz*) (AMG) and from the judgement of the ECJ in case C-143/06, *Rosenapotheke*. This legal provision stipulates the following requirements for distributing medicinal products under the conditions of named patient supply:

- The medicinal product in question is a finished medicinal product.
- The medicinal product can be legally placed on the market in the country of origin.
- The ordering and acquisition of the medicinal product is carried out by a pharmacy.
- The medicinal product is imported only in small quantities.
- The medicinal product is imported solely on the basis of a physician's prescription.
- A supply deficit exists, that is, no identical medicinal products with respect to active substances, and no comparable medicinal products with respect to the strength, are available.

Separately, compassionate use programmes are in place for patients suffering life-threatening disease or a disease leading to severe disability, such as some types of cancer, pulmonary infections and life-threatening types of influenza. The conduct of compassionate use programmes must be notified beforehand to the higher federal authority, which is either the Federal Institute for Drugs and Medical Devices (*Bundesinstitut für Arzneimittel und Medizinprodukte*) (BfArM) or the Federal Institute for Vaccines and Biomedicines (*Paul-Ehrlich-Institut*) (PEI).

Otherwise, the requirements for compassionate use programmes are, among others, as follows:

- The patients suffer from a life-threatening disease or a disease leading to severe disability.
- There is no other satisfying treatment option with medicinal products approved in the European Community.
- An authorisation application for the medicinal product is pending or clinical trials (Phase III) with this medicinal product are still ongoing.

## LICENSING

## 3. WHAT IS THE PROCEDURAL STRUCTURE REGARDING LICENSING A DRUG FOR DISTRIBUTION?

### Structure

The Federal Institute for Drugs and Medical Devices (*Bundesinstitut für Arzneimittel und Medizinprodukte*) (BfArM) is the competent authority for the authorisation of finished medicinal products in Germany, unless either the Federal Institute for Vaccines and Biomedicines (*Paul-Ehrlich-Institut*) (PEI) or the Federal Office of Consumer Protection and Food Safety (*Bundesministerium für Ernährung, Landwirtschaft und Verbraucherschutz*) (BMELV) is competent.

According to section 77(2) of the Medical Products Act (*Arzneimittelgesetz*) (AMG), the PEI is competent for the licensing of sera, vaccines, blood preparations, bone marrow preparations, tissue preparations, allergens, gene transfer medicinal products, somatic cell therapy products, xenogenic cell therapy products and blood components manufactured using genetic engineering.

The BMELV is responsible for the authorisation of medicinal products that are intended for administration to animals only (*section 77(3), AMG*).

Any product placed on the market in Germany and that is the subject of a marketing authorisation, whether from the German authorities or the European Medicines Agency (EMA), must have reports on all the results of confirmatory clinical trials substantiating the efficacy and safety of the medicinal product at the disposal of the competent higher federal authority. These reports must be made available within six months following the granting of the marketing authorisation/centralised marketing authorisation. This obligation applies regardless of whether or not any trial sites used were located in Germany.

## 4. IS THERE A SIMPLIFIED LICENCE PROCEEDING, OR RELAXED LICENSING CONDITIONS, FOR DRUGS WHICH HAVE ALREADY BEEN LICENSED FOR DISTRIBUTION IN ANOTHER JURISDICTION?

As it is part of the European Union three different marketing authorisation procedures apply in Germany:

- Centralised procedure.
- Mutual recognition procedure.
- Decentralised procedure.

Any of these can be used, as well as a standalone national authorised procedure.

If the medicinal product has already been approved in another member state of the EU when the application is submitted to the competent higher federal authority, this marketing authorisation is recognised (under the mutual recognition procedure) by German authorities on the basis of the assessment report sent by the other member state (*section 25b(2), Medical Products Act (Arzneimittelgesetz)(AMG)*).

There is a simplified licence proceeding for parallel import drugs which have already been licensed for national distribution in another country within the EU. The European Medicines Agency (EMA) has to be notified about the parallel import. According to section 13 of the AMG, the parallel importer needs a manufacturing authorisation for repacking, labelling and adding the package leaflet to the medicinal product.

For generics, a simplified licence proceeding is described in section 24b(1) of the AMG. When applying for a marketing authorisation of the generic product, reference can be made to the documents, including the expert report for the previous applicant's medicinal product (reference medicinal product). The previous applicant's agreement with the use of the reference documents is not necessary. There is a restriction that the reference medicinal product must have already been authorised for at least eight years before such an application will be considered.

## 5. IS VIRTUAL DRUG DISTRIBUTION POSSIBLE FROM YOUR JURISDICTION?

A marketing authorisation obtained in Germany gives the market authorisation holder the right to sell the authorised medicinal product in Germany. The question whether or not the medicinal product may be distributed in another country based on the German authorisation must be answered based on the law of that country.

## 6. WHAT IS THE PROCEDURE TO APPEAL (LEGAL REMEDY) A LICENSING DECISION?

There is the possibility of appealing (*Widerspruch*) against the federal drug administration's decision not to grant a licence. The competent authority will give judgment itself on the appeal by either rejecting it or declaring it to be founded. Furthermore an action might be brought before the local administrative courts (*Verwaltungsgericht*).

## 7. WHAT ARE THE COSTS OF OBTAINING LICENSING?

The costs of obtaining a centralised marketing authorisation as laid down by the

European Medicines Agency (EMA) are:

- A basic fee of EUR251,600 per application based on a completed dossier. This fee will be increased by EUR25,200 for each additional dosage/ pharmaceutical form.
- A reduced fee of EUR97,600 for an application regarding a generic pharmaceutical product.
- A special reduced fee of EUR162,600 for biological medicinal products. There could be additional charges up to EUR75,500 for the amendment/extension of an already existing authorisation.

The costs for obtaining a national marketing authorisation vary, depending on the nature of the product. The maximum fee is EUR57,500.

### DISTRIBUTION TO CONSUMERS

## 8. WHAT ARE THE DIFFERENT CATEGORIES OF DRUGS FOR DISTRIBUTION?

In Germany there are four different categories of drugs for distribution:

- General sales list medicines (*freiverkäufliche Arzneimittel*) which do not need to be sold in pharmacies.
- Medicines which are subject to sale by pharmacists only (*apothekenpflichtig*).
- Prescription drugs (*verschreibungspflichtig*) which are available by a doctor's prescription only.
- Narcotic drugs (*Betäubungsmittel*) which are available by special narcotic prescription only.

## 9. WHO IS AUTHORISED TO DISTRIBUTE PRESCRIPTION DRUGS AND OVER-THE-COUNTER DRUGS TO CONSUMERS?

**Prescription drugs**

According to section 43(3) of the Medical Products Act (*Arzneimittelgesetz*) (AMG) medicinal products can only be dispensed by pharmacies upon prescription. Pharmacies must have an authorisation as described in the Pharmacy Act (*Apothekengesetz*) (ApoG). The authorisation is granted by the competent higher federal authority of the state where the pharmacy is established. The applicant needs to fulfil certain criteria such as being licensed to practise pharmacy and being sufficiently reliable to operate a pharmacy. The authorisation to distribute prescription drugs in pharmacies can be granted as well if the applying pharmacist states that he or she operates a pharmacy in another member state of the EU.

**Over-the-counter drugs**

When talking about over-the-counter drugs, a distinction has to be made between general sales list medicines (*freiverkäufliche*) and medicines which are subject to sale by pharmacists only (*apothekenpflichtige*) medicines.

General sales list medicines (*freiverkäufliche Arzneimittel*) can be retailed outside of pharmacies provided that the owner is in possession of the necessary expert knowledge (*section 50(1), AMG*). To be considered as possessing the necessary expert knowledge, the person in question must furnish proof of experience and skill in respect of the proper filling, packaging, labelling, storing and marketing of medicinal products which are released for trade outside of pharmacies. Furthermore knowledge of the existing regulations applicable to these medicinal products is required.

Only pharmacies are entitled to distribute *apothekenpflichtige* drugs to consumers. Generally there is no price reimbursement for over-the-counter-drugs by statutory health insurance (*section 34(1), Social Code Book 5 (Sozialgesetzbuch V)(SGB V)*).

## 10. WHAT DRUGS CAN AN ATTENDING PHYSICIAN DISTRIBUTE AND UNDER WHAT CIRCUMSTANCES?

Physicians are not allowed to distribute drugs. There is only an exception for free samples which are handed on to the patients when consulting a physician.

## 11. WHO IS AUTHORISED TO PRESCRIBE PRESCRIPTION DRUGS TO CONSUMERS?

Under section 1 of the ordinance regarding the prescription of medicinal products (*Arzneimittelverschreibungsverordnung*) drugs can only be prescribed by physicians or dentists within their professional field. Please note that costs of medicinal products are only reimbursed by statutory health insurance if the prescription is made by a physician/dentist who has a contract with the statutory health insurance provider.

Unlike in other countries, in Germany nurses are not allowed to write prescriptions. Physicians working in hospitals are only allowed to make prescriptions for the duration of the patient's stay in hospital.

## 12. IS DIRECT MAILING/DISTANCE SELLING OF DRUGS PERMITTED IN YOUR JURISDICTION?

**Conditions**

Under section 11a Pharmacy Act (*Apothekengesetz*) (ApoG), an authorisation for direct mailing/distance selling of medicinal products can be granted by the federal higher state authority if the applicant already holds a permission to distribute drugs to consumers and confirms in writing that:

- Direct mailing/distance selling will take place in addition to the normal course of the pharmacy.
- A quality assurance system is established to assure that:
  - medicinal products are packed, transported and delivered properly in order to obtain the quality and the efficacy of the drugs;
  - shipped medicinal products are delivered only to the person listed in the order form;
  - patients are asked to consult a physician if they have any problems related to the consume/use of the medicinal product; and
  - an advisory service is provided to patients in German.

Furthermore pharmacies have to ensure that:

- Medicinal products are mailed out to the patient within two days after the receipt of the customer order.
- A system is established to inform patients about risks of medicinal products.
- A tracking system is maintained.
- Transport insurance is arranged.

**Cross-border sales**

Medicinal products only available on prescription can only be mailed to other member states of the EU. Over-the-counter drugs can be mailed to patients worldwide, but the import regulations of the receiving country should be verified in advance.

### 13. WHAT REGULATORY AUTHORITY IS RESPONSIBLE FOR SUPERVISING DISTRIBUTION ACTIVITIES?

Federal higher state authorities are responsible for the supervision of distribution of drugs to consumers.

### 14. WHAT IS THE PROCEDURE TO APPEAL (LEGAL REMEDY) A DISTRIBUTION DECISION?

Depending on the state where the drugs are distributed, there might be the possibility of an appeal against the competent federal higher state authority's decision. Additionally, an action might be brought before the local administrative courts.

### 15. WHAT ARE THE LEGAL CONSEQUENCES OF NON-COMPLIANCE WITH CONSUMER DISTRIBUTION LAWS?

In case of non-compliance, the penalties can include imprisonment or a fine. In particularly serious instances, the penalty can be imprisonment from one to ten years. In addition there might be administrative fines up to EUR25,000.

## WHOLESALE DISTRIBUTION

### 16. WHAT IS THE LEGAL REGIME REGARDING WHOLESALE DISTRIBUTION OF DRUGS?

Any person/company that engages in the wholesale trading of medicinal products, test sera or test antigens, requires an authorisation to do so (*section 52a(1), Medicinal Products Act (Arzneimittelgesetz)(AMG)*). The wholesale of drugs is defined in section 4(22) of the AMG as any professional or commercial activity for the purpose of doing business which consists of the procuring, storing, dispensing or exporting of medicinal products, with the exception of the dispensing of medicinal products to consumers other than physicians, dentists, veterinarians or hospitals.

The applicant must:

- Name the specific sites for which the authorisation is to be issued.
- Submit evidence that he or she is in possession of suitable and adequate premises, installations and facilities in order to ensure the proper storage and distribution and, where envisaged, proper decanting, packaging and labelling of medicinal products.
- Appoint a responsible person who possesses the required expert knowledge to perform the activity.
- Enclose a statement in which he or she commits himself in writing to observe the regulations governing the proper operation of a wholesale enterprise.

The decision on granting the authorisation is taken by the competent federal higher state authority of the state in which the wholesale is established. The authorisation can be refused if facts justify the assumption that the applicant or the person responsible for the wholesale does not possess the necessary reliability to perform the activity.

### 17. WHAT REGULATORY AUTHORITY IS RESPONSIBLE FOR SUPERVISING WHOLESALE DISTRIBUTION ACTIVITIES?

**Regulatory authority**

The federal higher state authorities of the state in which the wholesale is established supervise the distribution activities.

**Supervision**

See *above*.

**Rights of appeal**

Depending on the state where the drugs are wholesaled, there might be the option of an appeal against the competent federal higher state authority's decision. In addition, an action might be brought before the local administrative courts.

### 18. WHAT ARE THE LEGAL CONSEQUENCES OF NON-COMPLIANCE WITH WHOLESALE DISTRIBUTION LAWS?

In case of non-compliance, penalties can be imprisonment for a term not exceeding three years or a fine. In particularly serious instances, the penalty can be imprisonment from one to ten years. In addition there can be administrative fines up to EUR25,000.

# MARKETING

## PROMOTION

### 19. WHAT IS THE GENERAL LEGAL REGIME FOR THE MARKETING OF DRUGS?

**Legal regime**

The Advertisement of Healthcare Products Act (*Heilmittelwerbegesetz*) (HWG) contains the legal requirements for marketing activities of pharmaceutical companies addressed to healthcare professionals or consumers. In general, a marketing activity falls within the scope of the HWG only if the marketing activity is product-related and intended to increase sales of a respective product. Provided that the marketing activity is solely company-related, for example if no direct and/or indirect product-related information is given and only the general research activity of the company is mentioned, the rules of the Act Against Unfair Competition (*Gesetz gegen den unlauteren Wettbewerb*) (UWG) are applicable.

Finally, the Medicinal Products Act (*Arzneimittelgesetz*) (AMG) also imposes legal requirements for interactions with healthcare professionals and patient organisations.

**Limits to marketing activities**

The legal limits for product-related marketing activities addressed to healthcare professionals and/or the general public are outlined below.

### 20. ARE THERE OTHER CODES OF CONDUCT FOR THE MARKETING OF DRUGS (FOR EXAMPLE, BY PROFESSIONAL OR INDUSTRIAL ORGANISATIONS)?

There are several industry guidelines applicable to product or company-related marketing activities of pharmaceutical companies. Those industry guidelines are either addressed to healthcare professionals or the general public. Particularly relevant are the:

- AKG Code of Conduct (*Arzneimittel und Kooperation im Gesundheitswesen e.V.*), issued by the German Pharmaceutical Industry Association (*Bundesverband der Pharmazeutischen Industrie*) (BPI)
- FSA Code of Conduct of Health Care Professionals (*Freiwillige Selbstkontrolle für die Arzneimittelindustrie*), issued by the Association of Research based Pharmaceutical Companies (*Verband forschender Arzneimittelhersteller e.V.*) (VfA).

For members of the BPI and the VfA, the industry guidelines mentioned above are binding, and the compliance is monitored and sanctioned by the FSA and AKG arbitration board. In case of non-compliance, fines might be imposed by one of the arbitration boards, of up to EUR400,000. In particularly serious cases the arbitration board can publicly rebuke the pharmaceutical company.

Industry codes are not compulsory but serve as a means of interpretation for the courts when assessing whether a marketing activity infringes the applicable legal provisions or not. For this reason, judges have found them useful and refer to them in judgments on breaches of the law. However, recent decisions have questioned the general application of such industry guidelines also for non-members of the VfA. It is possible that judges will continue to use such conclusive guidelines to assess if specific practices in the field of the pharmaceutical industry infringe the general legal provisions (which apply also to other industry sectors).

## MARKETING TO CONSUMERS

### 21. WHAT IS THE LEGAL REGIME FOR MARKETING TO CONSUMERS?

**Legal regime**

The Advertisement of Healthcare Products Act (*Heilmittelwerbegesetz*) (HWG) describes in detail which advertising activities are permitted with regard to consumers.

**Products**

According to section 10(1) of the HWG, prescription drugs can only be advertised to healthcare professionals. In addition, treatments against insomnia and sleep disorders cannot be advertised to consumers. Under section 3(a) of the HWG, marketing activities for unlicensed medicines are prohibited, as well as marketing activities regarding off-label use of licensed medicines.

### 22. WHAT KINDS OF MARKETING ACTIVITIES ARE PERMITTED IN RELATION TO CONSUMERS AND THE PRODUCTS WHICH MAY BE ADVERTISED TO THEM?

The following marketing activities in relation to consumers are prohibited, among others (*section 11(1), Advertisement of Healthcare Products Act (Heilmittelwerbegesetz) (HWG)*):

- Marketing activities referring to scientific studies and professional publications.
- Marketing activities referring to an individual's medical history.
- Marketing activities which can give rise to uncertainty and anxiety.
- Promotional contests, drawings, raffles.

According to section 4(3) of the HWG, all marketing activities to consumers have to include the following notice: "For information on risks and side-effects please read the pack-insert and ask your doctor or pharmacist".

### 23. IS IT PERMITTED TO PROVIDE CONSUMERS WITH FREE SAMPLES? ARE THERE PARTICULAR RESTRICTIONS ON SPECIAL OFFERS (FOR EXAMPLE, "BUY-ONE-GET-ONE-FREE")?

It is not permitted to provide consumers with free samples of drugs (*section 11(1) No.14, Advertisement of Healthcare Products Act (Heilmittelwerbegesetz) (HWG)*).

Under Article 7(1) of the HWG, special offers such as "buy-one-get-one-free" are prohibited. The Federal Supreme Court (*Bundesgerichtshof*) ruled that discounts and bonuses are only permissible regarding insignificant gratuities such as consumer magazines or small advertising gifts whose value is below EUR1. Applicable industry guidelines draw the line at below EUR5.

For general sales list medicines, only special offers and discounts in kind such as "buy-one-get-one-free" are permitted.

### 24. ARE THERE PARTICULAR RULES OF PRACTICE ON THE USE OF THE INTERNET/SOCIAL MEDIA REGARDING DRUGS AND THEIR ADVERTISING?

Generally speaking, there are no specific rules on the use of the internet/social media in respect of drugs and their advertising. Only section 1(6) of the Advertisement of Healthcare Products Act (*Heilmittelwerbegesetz*) (HWG) states that the HWG will not apply on the order forms of online pharmacies regarding the information necessary for ordering of drugs online.

### 25. WHAT REGULATORY AUTHORITY IS RESPONSIBLE FOR SUPERVISING MARKETING ACTIVITIES TO CONSUMERS?

**Regulatory authority**

The competent authorities for supervision/marketing activities are the higher regional authorities in the federal states in which the pharmaceutical company is established.

Infringements of rules for the protection of fair competition by pharmaceutical manufacturers can be pursued by the competent national authorities. According to section 64(3) of the Medicinal Products Act (*Arzneimittelgesetz*) (AMG), the competent authority must ensure that the provisions relating to advertisements of medicines are observed. In practice, the higher regional authorities rarely pursue pharmaceutical manufacturers for infringements of unfair competition law. Instead the German market for medicinal products is mainly self-regulated, and it is common practice that competitors apply for preliminary injunctions or initiate regular court proceedings if a competitor fails to comply with the rules for the protection of fair competition.

**Supervision**

See *above*.

**Rights of appeal**

In case of an infringement, the competent authority will issue a prohibition order. This enforcement act might be objected by the addressee, first in an administrative procedure (*Widerspruch*) and subsequently, if necessary, by a court procedure (*Anfechtungsklage*).

### 26. WHAT ARE THE LEGAL CONSEQUENCES OF NON-COMPLIANCE WITH CONSUMER MARKETING LAWS?

In case of misleading marketing activities to consumers, the infringing company respectively the person in charge can be punished with imprisonment up to one year or with fines. In cases of non-compliance it would be more likely that a competitor would apply for a preliminary injunction or initiate regular court proceedings if a pharmaceutical company fails to comply with the rules of the Advertisement of Healthcare Products Act (*Heilmittelwerbegesetz*) (HWG) (see *Question 25*).

## MARKETING TO PROFESSIONALS

### 27. WHAT KINDS OF MARKETING ACTIVITIES ARE PERMITTED IN RELATION TO PROFESSIONALS?

Product-related advertisements (*section 3, Advertisement of Healthcare Products Act (Heilmittelwerbegesetz) (HWG)*) and company-related advertisements (*section 5, Act Against Unfair Competition (Gesetz gegen den unlauteren Wettbewerb) (UWG)*) addressed to healthcare professionals must not be misleading or unfair, namely, the promotional statement must be correct and, if necessary, verifiable. HWG and UWG contain concrete examples of misleading or unfair advertisements.

As far as product-related advertisements are concerned, the law requires, among others, that the promoted medicinal product must not be ascribed therapeutic efficacy or effects that it does not possess, and that the advertisement gives no false impression that success is guaranteed or that the recommended use has no side effects (*section 3 No.1 and No.2, HWG*).

A list of legal examples is set out in the UWG, which applies to company-related advertising statements (*sections 4 and 5, UWG*). In addition, as further main principles applying to product-related advertisements, the advertisement must always mention the mandatory information regarding the promoted medicine, and the promoted indications must be in line with the marketing authorisation, the summary of product characteristics and the package leaflet.

### 28. ARE THERE ANY RESTRICTIONS ON MARKETING TO PROFESSIONALS?

**Marketing activities**

The legal requirements for the collaboration of pharmaceutical companies with healthcare professionals are partly laid down in the Advertisement of Healthcare Products Act (*Heilmittelwerbegesetz*)(HWG) and the Act Against Unfair Competition (*Gesetz gegen den unlauteren Wettbewerb*) (UWG). These statutes apply to healthcare professionals working in the outpatient sector as well as to healthcare professionals working in hospitals.

Healthcare professionals are, according to section 2 of the HWG, any members of healthcare professions and healthcare occupations, organisations that serve human health, and other persons insofar as they are involved in the legal trade of medicinal products, procedures, treatment methods, objects or use such products in the course of their professional activity.

In addition, the German Criminal Code (*Strafgesetzbuch*) (StGB) sets out in section 299 and 331 legal requirements regarding attempts to influence healthcare professionals who work in public hospitals. In June 2012 the Federal Supreme Court ruled that pharmaceutical companies cannot be punished for bribery in public affairs under current legislation when offering money or so-called benefit programmes to physicians. Similarly statutory health insurance physicians who accept money and gifts from pharmaceutical companies or sales representatives cannot be charged for bribery in public affairs. According to the Federal Supreme Court physicians contracted by statutory health insurance companies are neither civil servants nor representatives of a state institution and so cannot be charged with bribery in public affairs. However, employed physicians working in medical institutions could be guilty of fraud *(section 263, StGB)* and breach of trust *(section 266, StGB)* when receiving kickback payments from pharmaceutical companies. The German legislator is currently closing this legal gap and a respective amendment of the StGB is expected for October 2015.

The Professional Code for Physicians *(Musterberufsordnung für Ärzte)* in its sections 33 to 35 stipulates rules and principles for the interactions of physicians, either from the in-patient or the hospital sector, with the pharmaceutical industry.

In addition, several industry guidelines govern the interaction between pharmaceutical manufacturers and healthcare professionals. These are the FSA Code of Conduct of Healthcare Professionals, the respective AKG Code of Conduct, and the Common Position Concerning the Consideration of Co-operation between Industry, Medical Institutions and Staff from the Aspect of Criminal Law. These industry guidelines are binding for members of the relevant industry associations, and must be observed by non-members since they serve as a means of interpretation for German courts when assessing if a certain collaboration with healthcare professionals infringes the respective legal provision *(see Question 20)*.

As stipulated in the introduction of the FSA Code of Conduct, all interactions and measures of collaborations with healthcare professionals "must remain within certain appropriate bounds and in accordance with the law". In this respect, the principles of separation, transparency, documentation equivalence (as stipulated in the Common Position Concerning the Consideration of Cooperation between Industry, Medical Institutions and Staff from the Aspect of Criminal Law) outline valuable reference points for the collaboration of the pharmaceutical industry with healthcare professionals from the outpatient sector or those working in the hospital. The collaboration between pharmaceutical manufacturers and healthcare professionals must meet the following requirements:

- According to the separation principle, the fees paid by the pharmaceutical manufacturer for the service provided by the healthcare professional must not constitute an incentive to recommend, prescribe, purchase, supply, sell or administer specific medicinal products.
- According to the transparency principle, all co-operation between pharmaceutical manufacturers and healthcare professionals must be notified to the administration of the professional's medical association; usually, a prior approval is required.
- According to the documentation principle, all collaborations between pharmaceutical companies and healthcare professionals must be recorded in writing.
- According to the equivalence principle, the fee paid by the pharmaceutical manufacturer for the service provided by the healthcare professional must correspond to the market value of the service.

**Frequency**

There is no legal provision regarding how, when, where or how often healthcare professionals can be visited by sales representatives of pharmaceutical companies.

Only the AKG Code of Conduct states that sales representatives should not unreasonably contact doctors during normal practice opening hours *(section 25(5), AKG Code of Conduct)*.

**Provision of hospitality**

In most instances contraventions result from travel and accommodation granted to healthcare professionals by pharmaceutical manufacturers under the scope of medical conferences. For instance, healthcare professionals attending a job-related training event cannot be invited to accommodation and hospitality that exceeds a reasonable limit. Taking this into account, a dinner must not exceed the value of EUR60 (*cipher 5.1, FSA Code of Conduct*), and the hotel accommodation must be classified within business class, not luxury class, and should not provide any extraordinary entertainments or services (*cipher 5.3, FSA Code of Conduct*).

### 29. WHAT INFORMATION IS IT LEGALLY REQUIRED TO INCLUDE IN ADVERTISING TO PROFESSIONALS?

Marketing to professionals must contain the following product information:

- Name of the medicinal product.
- The therapeutic target area.
- Warning notices.
- Pharmaceutical companies.
- The composition of the drug.
- If applicable, the rating as a prescription drug.
- Contraindications.
- Possible side effects.

### 30. ARE THERE RULES ON COMPARISONS WITH OTHER PRODUCTS THAT ARE PARTICULARLY APPLICABLE TO DRUGS?

Provisions regarding comparisons to other medicinal products can be found in section 12 of the Advertisement of Healthcare Products Act (*Heilmittelwerbegesetz*) (HWG). Under this, comparisons with other medicinal products are allowed when used for the purpose of marketing to professionals only. When advertising a product to consumers, comparisons with other medicinal products are not permitted.

### 31. WHAT OTHER ITEMS, FUNDING OR SERVICES ARE PERMITTED TO BE PROVIDED TO PROFESSIONALS?

**Discounts**

Discounts in kind and special offers are permitted on general sales list medicines only (*see Question 23*). Cash discounts are permitted on over-the-counter drugs only. This applies to marketing activities to professionals as well as to consumers. According to a judgment of the Higher Regional Court of Cologne, the promotion of drugs using rebates is only permissible if the rebates are product-related and not granted on products other than the promoted ones (*Higher regional court of Cologne, judgment of 23 February 2011, ref. no. 6 W 2/11*).

**Free samples**

Only medicinal sales representatives are allowed to provide healthcare professionals with free samples of medicinal products. According to section 47(4) of the Medicinal Products Act (*Arzneimittelgesetz*) (AMG), the number of samples per medicinal product and per healthcare professional is limited to two samples per year and can only be supplied in response to a written request. The samples cannot be larger than the smallest presentation of the medicinal product on the market. An adequate system to maintain control and accountability has to be established which contains information about the date of supply and the amount of supply.

### Sponsorship of professionals

The sponsoring of individuals is not allowed according to the applicable industry guidelines. If a pharmaceutical company sponsors a clinical, hospital or a medical association, it is only permitted if the legal requirements are fulfilled, and additionally, if the financial benefit serves a medical purpose (for example, public health), it is documented and does not constitute an undue influence on the prescription behaviour of healthcare professionals.

### Other items, funding or services

It is quite common for pharmaceutical manufacturers to infringe the equivalence principle when co-operating with healthcare professionals (*see Question 28*). In many cases, the fee paid for the services provided by healthcare professionals is inconsistent with the market value of the service. According to a decision of the FSA Board of Arbitration, a remuneration of EUR80.45 for a 30 minute qualified consulting service rendered by a healthcare professional is considered appropriate and reasonable (*FSA Board of Arbitration decision of 3 February 2009 (2008.1-220)*). However, this decision can only serve as a benchmark for an assessment of the appropriate market value of such a service. The respective assessment must be carried out on a case-by-case basis and in consideration of numerous factors, such as the difficulty of the service and the qualification of the healthcare professional. The amount decided in the FSA Board of Arbitration decision above is, at the time of writing, the highest sum considered appropriate in Germany.

With respect to the FSA Board of Arbitration, many cases result from gifts or services offered by pharmaceutical companies to healthcare professionals. As a general rule, the Advertisement of Healthcare Products Act (*Heilmittelwerbegesetz*) (HWG) and the respective industry guidelines prohibit the offering of products or services unless they are inexpensive and relevant to the practice of human medicine. According to the FSA Board of Arbitration and cipher 9.2 of the FSA Guidelines pursuant to section 6(2) of the FSA Code of Conduct (*FSA Leitlinien*), a gift is considered as "inexpensive" if it does not exceed the value of EUR5 (purchase price).

## 32. WHAT REGULATORY AUTHORITY IS RESPONSIBLE FOR SUPERVISING MARKETING ACTIVITIES REGARDING PROFESSIONALS?

### Regulatory authority

Medical associations (*Ärztekammer*) and associations of statutory health insurance registered doctors (*Kassenärztliche Vereinigung*) are responsible for the supervision of marketing activities to professionals.

### Supervision

See *above*.

### Rights of appeal

In serious cases of breaches, disciplinary procedures can be started. Opposition to these procedures is possible as well as an appeal to the administrative courts (*Verwaltungsgericht*) against the decisions of the medical associations and the associations of statutory health insurance registered doctors.

### 33. WHAT ARE THE LEGAL CONSEQUENCES IN CASE OF NON-COMPLIANCE WITH PROFESSIONAL MARKETING LAWS?

Disciplinary procedures of medical associations and associations of statutory health insurance registered doctors can lead to administrative fines.

## ENGAGEMENT WITH PATIENT ORGANISATIONS

### 34. WHAT KINDS OF ACTIVITIES ARE PERMITTED IN RELATION TO ENGAGEMENT WITH PATIENT ORGANISATIONS? WHAT ARE THE RESTRICTIONS THAT ARE IMPOSED ON RELATIONSHIP WITH PATIENT ORGANISATIONS?

Activities with respect to engagement with patient organisations are regulated in the relevant industry codes. Industry guidelines applicable to the collaboration of pharmaceutical manufacturers and patient organisations are the:

- FSA Code of Conduct on Patient Organisations.
- AKG Code of Conduct on Patient Organisations.

These codes of conduct define the term "patient organisations" as "voluntary, non-profit organisations of patients and/or their families, whose activities involve group support in coping with diseases, disseminating information about diseases and therapy options, lobbying in healthcare and social policy, publishing of media to inform and support patients and/or providing advisory services".

The term "patient organisation" is also defined by the European Federation of Pharmaceutical Industries and Associations (EFPIA).

In the authors' view, the scope of the definition set out by the FSA and the AKG is broader than the definition laid down in the EFPIA Code of Conduct on Relationships between the Pharmaceutical Industry and Patient Organisations (EFPIA Code of Conduct). Therefore, it has to be assumed that the German national Codes of Conduct also apply to interactions between patient organisations and pharmaceutical companies that are not subject to the EFPIA Code of Conduct.

As a main rule for the collaboration of the pharmaceutical industry with patient organisations, it is stipulated in the AKG and FSA Code of Conduct Patient Organisations that a pharmaceutical company cannot establish any patient organisation on their own (the separation principle). In addition, the pharmaceutical manufacturer is obliged to respect the neutrality and independence of the patient organisation, in particular regarding the events organised by the patient organisation (the principle of neutrality).

Apart from these principles, pharmaceutical companies must observe the principle of transparency, namely that the collaboration and support must be executed in a transparent and open manner. As a result, pharmaceutical companies must make available to the public a list of the patient organisations that are financially supported in Germany and throughout Europe, or that receive indirect or non-financial benefits. Accordingly, the collaboration can only proceed on the basis of a written agreement that spells out its basic elements.

Monetary contributions by member companies to patient organisations can only be made on the basis of a written request describing the fundamentals for collaboration. Contributions made by member companies of the AKG and the FSA need to be specified and described in detail.

Member companies need to make available to the public a list of self-help organisations to whom they provide financial support or non-financial contributions.

## REFORM

**35. ARE THERE ANY PLANS TO REFORM THE LAW ON THE DISTRIBUTION AND PROMOTION OF DRUGS IN YOUR JURISDICTION?**

There are currently no plans to reform the law on the distribution and promotion of drugs in Germany.

# INDONESIA

*Eri Raffaera Budiarti and Muhammad Iqsan Sirie*
ASSEGAF HAMZAH & PARTNERS

## DISTRIBUTION

### PRE-CONDITIONS FOR DISTRIBUTION

### 1. WHAT ARE THE LEGAL PRE-CONDITIONS FOR A DRUG TO BE DISTRIBUTED WITHIN THE JURISDICTION?

**Authorisation**

All medicines that will be distributed in Indonesia must be registered with the Food and Medicine Supervisory Board (*Badan Pengawas Obat dan Makanan*) (BPOM). The BPOM will issue a distribution licence (*izin edar*) for the registered medicines on registration.

**Exceptions**

Medicines that are used for special purposes are exempted from the registration requirement and include:

- Medicines as requested by physicians.
- Donated medicines.
- Medicines for clinical sampling.
- Sample medicines.

### 2. DO ANY TYPES OF NAMED PATIENT AND/OR COMPASSIONATE USE PROGRAMMES OPERATE? IF SO, WHAT ARE THE REQUIREMENTS FOR PRE-LAUNCH ACCESS?

There are no specific laws and regulations relating to named patient and/or compassionate use programmes in Indonesia.

## LICENSING

### 3. WHAT IS THE PROCEDURAL STRUCTURE REGARDING LICENSING A DRUG FOR DISTRIBUTION?

**Structure**

The Ministry of Health Regulation No. 1010/Menkes/Per/XI/2008 on Registration of Medicines, as amended by Ministry of Health Regulation No. 1120/Menkes/Per/XII/2008 (Regulation No. 1010/2008) provides that a medicine to be distributed in Indonesia must be registered with the Food and Medicine Supervisory Board (*Badan Pengawas Obat dan Makanan*) (BPOM). The BPOM will issue a distribution licence if the medicine meets the following criteria:

- Produces a benefit and is safe, as proven through animal testing and clinical examination trials or other scientific evidence.
- Its quality fulfills the requirements of, and its production is in accordance with Good Medicine Manufacturing Practices (*Cara Pembuatan Obat Yang Baik*) (CPOB), as provided for by BPOM Decree No. HK.00.05.3.02152 of 2002.
- The relevant product information contains complete and objective information to ensure its correct, rational and safe use.
- It satisfies a public need.

**Registration procedure**

The registration documents are submitted to the BPOM together with the official fee. A medicine produced in Indonesia (whether for domestic use or for export) is registered by the relevant pharmaceutical producer (that must have an industrial business licence). An imported medicine is registered by a domestic pharmaceutical producer that has obtained written approval from the foreign pharmaceutical producer. The written approval must provide for a transfer of technology so that the medicine can be produced locally within a five-year period, except if it is patented. The foreign pharmaceutical producer must also comply with the CPOB, as evidenced by relevant documents or an inspection by the Indonesian authorities. The documents must be attached to the application, together with the latest data on inspections conducted by the relevant local authorities (that is, for at least the last two years). The BPOM either approves or rejects the application for the distribution licence based on the recommendation of the committees. The BPOM reports the issuance of the distribution licence to the Ministry of Health (MOH) annually. If the registration is rejected, the applicant can submit a request for re-examination.

Once a distribution licence has been issued, the distribution licence holder must produce/import and circulate the medicine within a one-year period from the date of issuance.

**Regulatory authority**

The BPOM is authorised to issue the distribution licence.

## 4. IS THERE A SIMPLIFIED LICENCE PROCEEDING, OR RELAXED LICENSING CONDITIONS, FOR DRUGS WHICH HAVE ALREADY BEEN LICENSED FOR DISTRIBUTION IN ANOTHER JURISDICTION?

There are no simplified procedures for medicines that have already been licensed/approved in other jurisdictions. The medicines must still be registered with and obtain a distribution licence from the Food and Medicine Supervisory Board (*Badan Pengawas Obat dan Makanan*).

## 5. IS VIRTUAL DRUG DISTRIBUTION POSSIBLE FROM YOUR JURISDICTION?

Virtual distribution of medicines (that is, the physical products never enter the country but are distributed using the authorisation obtained in Indonesia) from Indonesia is not allowed, because under Indonesian law distributing medicines without actually having any control over the product is illegal.

## 6. WHAT IS THE PROCEDURE TO APPEAL (LEGAL REMEDY) A LICENSING DECISION?

If an applicant's registration is rejected by the Food and Medicine Supervisory Board (*Badan Pengawas Obat dan Makanan*) (BPOM), the applicant can re-register the same medicine using the same process for registration. However, if the applicant objects to the BPOM's decision to reject its application, the applicant only has the opportunity to appeal once (*peninjauan kembali*).

The applicant can lodge an appeal up to six months from the date of the BPOM's rejection letter. The appeal can be in the form of a hearing, and the appeal process must not exceed 100 calendar days from the submission date of the appeal documents.

## 7. WHAT ARE THE COSTS OF OBTAINING LICENSING?

A non-tax state revenue (*pendapatan negara bukan pajak*) applies with amounts ranging from IDR50,000 to IDR30 million per medicine, depending on the type of medicine that will be registered.

## DISTRIBUTION TO CONSUMERS

## 8. WHAT ARE THE DIFFERENT CATEGORIES OF DRUGS FOR DISTRIBUTION?

There are three main categories of medicine:

- Over-the-counter medicines.
- Hard medicines (or prescription medicines).
- Narcotic and psychotropic drugs.

**INDONESIA**

### 9. WHO IS AUTHORISED TO DISTRIBUTE PRESCRIPTION DRUGS AND OVER-THE-COUNTER DRUGS TO CONSUMERS?

**Prescription drugs**

Pharmacies, hospital pharmacies, clinics, drug stores and community health centres (*Puskesmas*) are authorised to distribute prescription medicines directly to customers.

**Over-the-counter drugs**

Over-the-counter medicines can be distributed by pharmacies and drug stores.

### 10. WHAT DRUGS CAN AN ATTENDING PHYSICIAN DISTRIBUTE AND UNDER WHAT CIRCUMSTANCES?

There are no specific regulations that set out the types of drugs that doctors can distribute directly to patients. However, in performing their duties as a doctor, they must observe the Indonesian Doctoral Code of Ethics issued by the Indonesian Association of Medical Doctors (*Ikatan Dokter Indonesia*). The Indonesian Doctoral Code of Ethics contains provisions prohibiting doctors from:

- Giving free samples of medicines that they receive from pharmaceutical companies.
- Encouraging patients to purchase certain medicines in return for commission paid by the relevant pharmaceutical company.
- Directly or indirectly promoting certain drugs, medical devices or other medical substances for the purpose of receiving benefits from third parties.

### 11. WHO IS AUTHORISED TO PRESCRIBE PRESCRIPTION DRUGS TO CONSUMERS?

Prescription medicines can be prescribed by doctors. Midwives working in remote areas (where no doctors are available) also have the right to prescribe medicines.

### 12. IS DIRECT MAILING/DISTANCE SELLING OF DRUGS PERMITTED IN YOUR JURISDICTION?

**Conditions**

Direct mailing of drugs has not been regulated in Indonesia. Distance selling is permitted for the export of medicine, provided that the legal entity exporting the medicine has obtained the following licences/documents:

- Exporter licence in accordance with the prevailing laws and regulations.
- Declaration from the Ministry of Health stating that the medicines have passed a quality, safety and benefit inspection.

**Cross-border sales**

See *above*.

## 13. WHAT REGULATORY AUTHORITY IS RESPONSIBLE FOR SUPERVISING DISTRIBUTION ACTIVITIES?

The Ministry of Health (MOH) periodically carries out inspections to protect the public from possible dangers posed by medicines that are distributed in the market. If the inspection findings do not satisfy the quality, safety and/or benefit requirements, the distribution licence can be revoked, and the product must be withdrawn from circulation by the producer/importer and be destroyed. The MOH is required to inform the general public in such cases.

## 14. WHAT IS THE PROCEDURE TO APPEAL (LEGAL REMEDY) A DISTRIBUTION DECISION?

There are no specific regulations providing a legal remedy in the event a party's distribution licence is revoked by the Ministry of Health (MOH) following inspection by the MOH (see *Question 12*). However, the party whose distribution licence is revoked can file a claim to the Administrative Court (*Pengadilan Tata Usaha Negara*) if it considers that the MOH's decision is arbitrary or a loss or damage was suffered by the party.

## 15. WHAT ARE THE LEGAL CONSEQUENCES OF NON-COMPLIANCE WITH CONSUMER DISTRIBUTION LAWS?

The Ministry of Health (MOH) can impose administrative sanctions on pharmaceutical distributors that violate the relevant laws and regulations on the distribution of medicines. The sanctions include:

- Warnings.
- Temporary prohibitions on distribution and/or instructions to withdraw products from distribution.
- Instructions to destroy products.
- Temporary or permanent revocation of the distribution licence.

In addition, criminal sanctions apply for certain acts as provided in the Health Law and its ancillary regulations. The Indonesian National Police Force and authorised officials from the MOH are responsible for investigating suspected criminal acts under the Health Law. The criminal offences established by the Health Law and its ancillary regulations include the following:

- Any person who produces and/or distributes medicines that do not satisfy the requirements of the Health Law is subject to imprisonment for a term of up to ten years and/or a fine of up to IDR1 billion.
- Any person who distributes medicines without a distribution licence is subject to imprisonment for a term of up to 15 years and/or a fine of up to IDR1.5 billion.

If the offences above are committed by a legal entity, the company is also subject to a fine three times the amount referred to above and can also have its business licence and/or corporate entity status revoked. This is in addition to the terms of imprisonment and fines that are imposed on the management of the company.

## WHOLESALE DISTRIBUTION

### 16. WHAT IS THE LEGAL REGIME REGARDING WHOLESALE DISTRIBUTION OF DRUGS?

In Indonesia, wholesale distribution of drugs is carried out by "large pharmaceutical distributors" (*Pedagang Besar Farmasi*), which must secure a licence issued by the Ministry of Health (MOH), specifically the Director General of Pharmaceuticals and Medical Equipment (DGPM). The licence is valid for five years and can be extended if certain requirements are fulfilled. In addition, only a limited liability company or co-operative can apply for such licence.

Pharmaceutical producers and pharmaceutical wholesalers cannot sell medicines to end customers. However, they are allowed to sell medicines to other large pharmaceutical distributors, pharmacies, hospital pharmacies, clinics, drug stores and community health centres (*Puskesmas*).

Under the Negative Investments List, there are restrictions on foreign investment in distribution of medicine activities. Only a company that is wholly owned by locals can sell medicines in Indonesia, except if the distribution is carried out by a pharmaceutical production company, in which case foreign investors can partially own shares in the company (that is, not more than 85%).

### 17. WHAT REGULATORY AUTHORITY IS RESPONSIBLE FOR SUPERVISING WHOLESALE DISTRIBUTION ACTIVITIES?

**Regulatory authority**

The Food and Medicine Supervisory Board (*Badan Pengawas Obat dan Makanan*) (BPOM) supervises the manufacture and distribution of medicines in Indonesia.

**Supervision**

The BPOM's supervision is mainly implemented through periodical reports submitted by large pharmaceutical distributors.

**Rights of appeal**

See *Question 13*.

### 18. WHAT ARE THE LEGAL CONSEQUENCES OF NON-COMPLIANCE WITH WHOLESALE DISTRIBUTION LAWS?

See *Question 14*.

INDONESIA

# MARKETING

## PROMOTION

### 19. WHAT IS THE GENERAL LEGAL REGIME FOR THE MARKETING OF DRUGS?

**Legal regime**

Marketing of medicines is regulated in a Food and Medicine Supervisory Board (*Badan Pengawas Obat dan Makanan*) regulation (No. HK.00.05.3.02706 of 2002 on Medicine Promotions). However, general legislation applicable to marketing must be considered when undertaking marketing activities. For example the:

- Consumer Protection Law must be observed when targeting consumers.
- Anti-Monopoly Law must be taken into consideration when marketing activities are targeted to businesses.

**Limits to marketing activities**

In general, the limits to marketing activities are as follows:

- Medicine promotions in the form of sponsorship are only allowed for scientific purposes.
- Provision of medicines to an institution (but not to professionals) for free or as a donation must not come with an obligation for the recipient to prescribe or use the medicines.
- Pharmaceutical producers/distributors must not:
  - enter into a co-operation with pharmacies or medicine prescribers (for example, doctors);
  - organise a group specifically to increase the use of certain medicines for marketing purposes;
  - promote certain medicines by using prizes as the reward (for example, quizzes or returning a medicine's packaging).

In addition, all promotional activities must be conducted on a transparent basis, and the medicines must provide written product information that is objective, complete and correct. The product information must contain the following minimum information:

- Trade/product name.
- Name of the producer/importer.
- Main ingredients/components.
- Directions for use.
- Warnings and side effects.
- Expiry date.

### 20. ARE THERE OTHER CODES OF CONDUCT FOR THE MARKETING OF DRUGS (FOR EXAMPLE, BY PROFESSIONAL OR INDUSTRIAL ORGANISATIONS)?

The Association of the Indonesian Pharmaceutical Company (*Gabungan Perusahaan Farmasi Indonesia*) and the Assoctiaton of International Pharmaceutical Manufacturers Group (*Perkumpulan International Pharmaceutical Manufacturers Group*) have their own codes of ethics:

- Code of Ethics on Marketing in Indonesian Pharmaceutical Industry (*Kode Etik Pemasaran Usaha Farmasi di Indonesia*).
- Code of Ethics on Pharmaceutical Product Marketing Practices (*Kode Etik Praktek Pemasaran Produk Farmasi*).

Both contain detailed regulation on the marketing of drugs. In addition, there are codes of ethics that are issued by the respective doctor and pharmacist associations, which contain provisions on the marketing of medicines.

All relevant parties have undertaken to comply with the codes, and the codes can be considered as constituting customary regulation of the industry and complementing the applicable laws and regulations.

## MARKETING TO CONSUMERS

### 21. WHAT IS THE LEGAL REGIME FOR MARKETING TO CONSUMERS?

**Legal regime**

See *Question 18*.

**Products**

Only products that have been registered in Indonesia and have obtained a distribution licence can be marketed. The marketing of prescription drugs to consumers is prohibited.

### 22. WHAT KINDS OF MARKETING ACTIVITIES ARE PERMITTED IN RELATION TO CONSUMERS AND THE PRODUCTS WHICH MAY BE ADVERTISED TO THEM?

The relevant laws and regulations have not defined the permitted marketing activities in Indonesia. However, the limits provided in *Question 18* must be considered when undertaking marketing activities.

### 23. IS IT PERMITTED TO PROVIDE CONSUMERS WITH FREE SAMPLES? ARE THERE PARTICULAR RESTRICTIONS ON SPECIAL OFFERS (FOR EXAMPLE, "BUY-ONE-GET-ONE-FREE")?

The provision of free samples of medicines and special offers are not a permitted marketing method.

### 24. ARE THERE PARTICULAR RULES OF PRACTICE ON THE USE OF THE INTERNET/SOCIAL MEDIA REGARDING DRUGS AND THEIR ADVERTISING?

There are no specific rules on the use of the internet/social media regarding drugs and their advertising. However, the laws and regulations on the use of the internet will apply. For example, the Electronic Information and Transaction Law prohibits any party transmitting or distributing any content on the internet that violates public decency and/or contains misleading information that may lead to consumer loss.

INDONESIA

## 25. WHAT REGULATORY AUTHORITY IS RESPONSIBLE FOR SUPERVISING MARKETING ACTIVITIES TO CONSUMERS?

**Regulatory authority**

See *Question 16*.

**Supervision**

See *Question 16*.

**Rights of appeal**

See *Question 16*.

## 26. WHAT ARE THE LEGAL CONSEQUENCES OF NON-COMPLIANCE WITH CONSUMER MARKETING LAWS?

See *Question 14*.

MARKETING TO PROFESSIONALS

## 27. WHAT KINDS OF MARKETING ACTIVITIES ARE PERMITTED IN RELATION TO PROFESSIONALS?

See *Question 18*.

## 28. ARE THERE ANY RESTRICTIONS ON MARKETING TO PROFESSIONALS?

**Marketing activities**

See *Question 18*.

**Frequency**

There are no laws and regulations specifically governing how, when, where or how often professionals can be targeted by sales representatives. However, in marketing their products to professionals, sales representatives must comply with the codes of ethics and the limitations to marketing activites (*see Question 19*).

**Provision of hospitality**

The Code of Ethics on Marketing in Indonesian Pharmaceutical Industry (*Kode Etik Pemasaran Usaha Farmasi di Indonesia*) and the Code of Ethics on Pharmaceutical Product Marketing Practices (*Kode Etik Praktek Pemasaran Produk Farmasi*) requires that any type of event targeting professionals must only be organised for the purpose of:

- Disseminating information about the pharmaceutical company organising the event.
- Providing accurate and propotionate scientific and education information.

The event must not involve the provision of any kind of appreciation, door prize, incentive, or monetary compensation to the professionals attending the event. The codes also regulate the bugdet, moderator/speaker fee, venue, and type of entertainment that is allowed when organising or sponsoring an event where the audience are professionals.

### 29. WHAT INFORMATION IS IT LEGALLY REQUIRED TO INCLUDE IN ADVERTISING TO PROFESSIONALS?

See *Question 18*.

### 30. ARE THERE RULES ON COMPARISONS WITH OTHER PRODUCTS THAT ARE PARTICULARLY APPLICABLE TO DRUGS?

See *Question 18*.

### 31. WHAT OTHER ITEMS, FUNDING OR SERVICES ARE PERMITTED TO BE PROVIDED TO PROFESSIONALS?

**Discounts**

See *Question 18*.

**Free samples**

See *Question 18*.

**Sponsorship of professionals**

See *Question 18*.

**Other items, funding or services**

See *Question 18*.

### 32. WHAT REGULATORY AUTHORITY IS RESPONSIBLE FOR SUPERVISING MARKETING ACTIVITIES REGARDING PROFESSIONALS?

**Regulatory authority**

See *Question 16*.

**Supervision**

See *Question 16*.

**Rights of appeal**

See *Question 16*.

**33. WHAT ARE THE LEGAL CONSEQUENCES IN CASE OF NON-COMPLIANCE WITH PROFESSIONAL MARKETING LAWS?**

See *Question 14*.

## ENGAGEMENT WITH PATIENT ORGANISATIONS

**34. WHAT KINDS OF ACTIVITIES ARE PERMITTED IN RELATION TO ENGAGEMENT WITH PATIENT ORGANISATIONS? WHAT ARE THE RESTRICTIONS THAT ARE IMPOSED ON RELATIONSHIP WITH PATIENT ORGANISATIONS?**

Prospective programmes that are held with patient organisations must be based on a written agreement and in line with the code of ethics of the pharmaceutical company. Pharmaceutical companies can only provide financial support to patient organisations if the financial support is intended to be used for professional, educational and scientific purposes.

## REFORM

**35. ARE THERE ANY PLANS TO REFORM THE LAW ON THE DISTRIBUTION AND PROMOTION OF DRUGS IN YOUR JURISDICTION?**

The Indonesian legislative body (*Dewan Perwakilan Rakyat*) (DPR) has proposed two new laws relating to:

- Pharmaceuticals practice.
- Supervision of food and medicines.

Both new laws contain legal provisions on the distribution of pharmaceutical supplies (including medicines) in the list of legislation that the DPR will pass during the period from 2014 to 2019. Unfortunately, the laws are not part of the 37 prioritised legislations that the DPR will pass and enact during this period.

## THE REGULATORY AUTHORITIES

**MINISTRY OF HEALTH OF REPUBLIC OF INDONESIA (*KEMENTERIAN KESEHATAN REPUBLIC INDONESIA*) (MOH)**

**W** www.depkes.go.id/index.php

**Principal responsibilities.** The MOH is responsible for formulating national policy, implementation and technical policy in the field of health. It is also in charge of issuing licences in the healthcare industry.

**FOOD AND MEDICINE SUPERVISORY BOARD** (*BADAN PENGAWAS OBAT DAN MAKANAN*)

**W** www.pom.go.id/new/

**Principal responsibilities.** The Board is responsible for implementing specific policies in the food and drug industry, including but not limited to the supervision of the implementation of such specific policies in the industry.

## ONLINE RESOURCES

**W** www.hukumonline.com

**Description.** The website is maintained by PT Justika Siar Publika (JSP), a private company unaffiliated to the government, and is the only web portal in Indonesia providing an organised and systematic collection of laws, regulations and court cases. The website provides English translations for some laws and regulations and is generally up-to-date.

# ITALY

*Laura Opilio and Maria Letizia Patania,*
*CMS ITALY (CMS ADONNINO ASCOLI & CAVASOLA SCAMONI)*

## DISTRIBUTION

### PRE-CONDITIONS FOR DISTRIBUTION

**1. WHAT ARE THE LEGAL PRE-CONDITIONS FOR A DRUG TO BE DISTRIBUTED WITHIN THE JURISDICTION?**

#### Authorisation

Drugs can be distributed in Italy if they are either:

- Licensed by the Italian Medicine Agency (*Agenzia Italiana del Farmaco*) (which involves a national procedure) as provided in Directive 2001/83/EC on the Community code relating to medicinal products for human use (Code for Human Medicines Directive) (implemented in Italy by Article 8 of the Legislative Decree No. 219/2006).
- Licensed according to:
  - Regulation (EC) 726/2004 on the authorisation and supervision of medicinal products and establishing a European Medicines Agency (EMA Regulation) (which is a mutual recognition procedure); or
  - Regulation 1394/2007 on advanced therapy medicinal products and amending the Code for Human Medicines Directive and the EMA Regulation (which is a decentralised procedure).

All the procedural requirements listed in Article 28 of the Code for Human Medicines Directive (implemented in Italy by Articles 41 to 49 of the Legislative Decree No. 219/2006) apply.

#### Exceptions

Parallel imported drugs must be licensed by the Italian Medicine Agency according to Ministerial Decree dated 29 August 1997 (*see Question 3*).

**2. DO ANY TYPES OF NAMED PATIENT AND/OR COMPASSIONATE USE PROGRAMMES OPERATE? IF SO, WHAT ARE THE REQUIREMENTS FOR PRE-LAUNCH ACCESS?**

#### Licensing

A non-authorised drug can be requested from the manufacturing company for use outside a clinical trial when there is no valid therapeutic alternative for the treatment of:

- Serious illnesses.
- Rare illnesses.
- Illnesses which put the patient's life in danger.

The request can be made only if the trial drug has been or will be included in phase III clinical trials or, in the case of terminally ill patients, the drug has been induced in phase II clinical trials.

Such a drug can only be requested from the manufacturer by:

- The doctor, for a specific patient who is not subject to clinical trials.
- More doctors operating in different centres or multi-centre collaborative groups.
- Doctors or collaborative groups whose patients participated in a clinical trial and demonstrated a profile of efficacy and tolerability such as to make it necessary for the ones who participated in the trial to use it as soon as possible.

Following the request, the producer can provide the drug on the basis of a protocol in which the following are present and documented:

- The clinical motivation for the request.
- The relevant data regarding efficacy and tolerability.
- The comparability rate of the patients included in the trial and the ones for which the request was formulated.
- The modalities of information of the patient, that is, the practical way in which the patient has been informed about the drug, the state of the trial and possible side effects, to be established through a paper of informed consent.
- The method of data collection.

The protocol must be:

- Submitted for urgent approval from an ethical committee by a doctor, accompanied by a note in which the doctor takes responsibility for the treatment.
- Notified to the Ministry of Health.

Approval from the ethical committee must be presented for the drug to enter through customs.

## 3. WHAT IS THE PROCEDURAL STRUCTURE REGARDING LICENSING A DRUG FOR DISTRIBUTION?

**Structure**

Italy applies the national, mutual recognition and centralised procedures (*see Question 4*). The application is made to the Italian Medicine Agency (*see below, Regulatory authority*). A decision must be taken by the competent authority within the term of 210 days, from the reception of a valid application. The technical and scientific assessment is completed by the Technical Scientific Commission, with the co-operation of experts belonging to the National Institute of Health. Other experts with well-known experience who belong to the Italian academic and health community are also consulted.

**Regulatory authority**

The Italian Medicine Agency is the national body responsible for licensing new drugs or varying already granted licences.

### 4. IS THERE A SIMPLIFIED LICENCE PROCEEDING, OR RELAXED LICENSING CONDITIONS, FOR DRUGS WHICH HAVE ALREADY BEEN LICENSED FOR DISTRIBUTION IN ANOTHER JURISDICTION?

Both the mutual recognition and centralised procedures apply in the EU. The procedures set out under Article 28 of Directive 2001/83/EC on the Community code relating to medicinal products for human use (Code for Human Medicines Directive) (implemented in Italy by Articles 41 to 49 of Legislative Decree No.219/2006) apply, depending on whether Italy acts as a reference member state or not. The mutual recognition procedure is where a company that has a drug authorised in one EU member state can apply for this authorisation to be recognised in Italy. The centralised procedure is where an application is made to the European Medicines Agency for a single authorisation which applies in all EU member states.

The above procedures apply also to parallel imports/exports. When there is parallel export of drugs licensed according to the mutual recognition procedure, the Italian Medicine Agency provides the requesting regulatory authorities from other member states with information regarding some of the identification elements of the drugs licensed in Italy.

In the case of parallel import of drugs already licensed in Italy, the procedure set out in Ministerial Decree dated 29 August 1997 applies. The importer must apply for authorisation by submitting an application to the Italian Medicine Agency providing:

- Details of the importer and the relevant member state.
- The name of the drugs to be imported.
- Qualitative and quantitative composition.
- Therapeutic specifications, contra-indications and side-effects.
- Dosage, medication, and so on.
- Summary of the product specifications and handout of the packaging both translated into Italian.

The Italian Medicine Agency must provide its authorisation (or refusal) within 45 days from the date the application was submitted.

There are no simplified licence proceedings or relaxed licensing conditions for drugs already authorised outside the EU. Therefore, the standard procedure of authorisation must be followed before such product can be distributed.

### 5. IS VIRTUAL DRUG DISTRIBUTION POSSIBLE FROM YOUR JURISDICTION?

Virtual distribution is only allowed for non-prescription drugs. Pharmacies and stores that wish to sell non-prescription drugs are authorised by the competent region or autonomous province (or other competent authorities) to remotely distribute the drugs.

It is a condition for virtual distribution that the following information be communicated to the relevant authority:

- Name, VAT number and full address of the logistics site.
- Date of the beginning of the remote sale activity to the public.

- Website address used for selling and all the necessary information to identify the website. The website must contain:
- The address of the competent authority.
- A hyperlink to the competent authority's website.
- A common logo, clearly visible on each page of the website of the pharmacy or store.

### 6. WHAT IS THE PROCEDURE TO APPEAL (LEGAL REMEDY) A LICENSING DECISION?

If the licence application is refused, the Italian Medicine Agency must notify the applicant of this decision. The applicant is then entitled to submit an opposition to the agency. This opposition must be decided within 90 days.

Appeals against agency decisions are made to the Regional Administrative Courts within 60 days of the receipt of the decision.

### 7. WHAT ARE THE COSTS OF OBTAINING LICENSING?

The costs of obtaining a licence in Italy range between EUR21,600 or EUR36,000 for a new marketing authorisation not supported by a full dossier, to EUR55,680 for a new marketing authorisation supported by a full dossier.

## DISTRIBUTION TO CONSUMERS

### 8. WHAT ARE THE DIFFERENT CATEGORIES OF DRUGS FOR DISTRIBUTION?

The different categories of drugs for distribution can be summarised as follows:

- Prescription drugs.
- Renewable delivery prescription drugs.
- Special prescription drugs.
- Restricted prescription drugs.
- Drugs distributable to consumers only under healthcare rules.
- Drugs usable only within healthcare rules.
- Drugs usable only by specialists.
- Non-prescription drugs.
- Over-the-counter drugs.
- All other drugs that do not require a medical prescription.

### 9. WHO IS AUTHORISED TO DISTRIBUTE PRESCRIPTION DRUGS AND OVER-THE-COUNTER DRUGS TO CONSUMERS?

**Prescription drugs**

Pharmacists are entitled to distribute prescription drugs to consumers. To be a pharmacist, an individual must have gained the relevant qualifications and be enrolled on a public register. Individuals can obtain a licence to operate on a physical premises after competitive state examinations and through, for example, acquisition or inheritance.

**Over-the-counter drugs**

Over-the-counter drugs can be distributed to consumers within pharmacies or supermarkets and other commercial shops. In the latter two cases, a pharmacist must always be present during store hours.

### 10. WHAT DRUGS CAN AN ATTENDING PHYSICIAN DISTRIBUTE AND UNDER WHAT CIRCUMSTANCES?

Attending physicians are not allowed to distribute drugs.

### 11. WHO IS AUTHORISED TO PRESCRIBE PRESCRIPTION DRUGS TO CONSUMERS?

Doctors are entitled to prescribe drugs to consumers. Dentists who graduated before 1985 are also allowed to prescribe since they are doctors who are specialised in dentistry. Dentists who graduated after 1985 are only entitled to prescribe drugs connected with their profession.

### 12. IS DIRECT MAILING/DISTANCE SELLING OF DRUGS PERMITTED IN YOUR JURISDICTION?

**Conditions**

Distance selling is not allowed for prescription drugs. Pharmacies and stores that wish to sell non-prescription drugs are authorised by the competent region or autonomous province (or other competent authorities) to remotely distribute the drugs (*see Question 5*).

**Cross-border sales**

In relation to parallel imports/exports, see *Question 4*.

### 13. WHAT REGULATORY AUTHORITY IS RESPONSIBLE FOR SUPERVISING DISTRIBUTION ACTIVITIES?

Local health authorities (*Aziende Sanitarie Locali*) are responsible for supervising the distribution and prescription of drugs to consumers.

The supervision is carried out through sample checks in the pharmacies and through the publication (after the verification of the provided data), on the national pharmacovigilance database, of the possible reporting made by professionals on the malfunctioning of a drug. The report must also be communicated to the relevant company.

### 14. WHAT IS THE PROCEDURE TO APPEAL (LEGAL REMEDY) A DISTRIBUTION DECISION?

Appeals against decisions made by the local health authorities must be made before the Regional Administrative Courts (*Tribunale Amministrativo Regionale*) within 60 days from the date when the decision was notified to the interested party or the latter became aware of it.

### 15. WHAT ARE THE LEGAL CONSEQUENCES OF NON-COMPLIANCE WITH CONSUMER DISTRIBUTION LAWS?

In cases of non-compliance, the local health authorities report to the Ministry of Health and to the Italian Medicine Agency. Penalties of up to EUR3,000 can be imposed and the pharmacy/commercial shop can be closed for a period of up to 30 days.

## WHOLESALE DISTRIBUTION

### 16. WHAT IS THE LEGAL REGIME REGARDING WHOLESALE DISTRIBUTION OF DRUGS?

The wholesale distribution of drugs is provided for by Articles 79 and 80 of Directive 2001/83/EC on the Community code relating to medicinal products for human use (Code for Human Medicines Directive) (implemented in Italy by Articles 101 to 104 of Legislative Decree No. 219/2006). The wholesale distributor must keep a record of all drugs that are distributed.

The wholesale distributor must employ a "qualified person" as set out in Article 79(b) of the Code for Human Medicines Directive, who must be a graduate in pharmaceuticals, chemistry, industrial chemistry or pharmaceutical and chemical technologies. This person must have a clean criminal record and should not be linked to the unlawful trade of pharmaceutical products. If a wholesale distributor owns more than one wholesale outlet, he or she is not required to employ more than one qualified person provided that the appointed qualified person is able to fulfil his or her tasks within reasonable working hours.

The competent authorities responsible for authorising wholesale distribution are the regions or the autonomous provinces where the wholesale activity will be carried out. In the case of wholesale distribution in more than one region, authorisation for each region is required. The authorisation must be granted within 90 days of receipt of the application, although time to grant varies depending on the region. Each region is entitled to ask for certain documents and certificates with the application, however the following certificates are required as standard:

- Fitness for use of the buildings issued by the territorially competent municipality.
- Enrolment on the Companies' Register.
- Prevention of fire.
- Wiring system compliance (and others such as atmospherics and grounding safety certificates).

The internal procedures covering points 2 to 6 of the Guidelines of 19 March 2015 on Good Distribution Practice of active substances for medicinal products for human use must also be submitted. It is important to bear in mind that authorisation requirements will differ from region to region.

### 17. WHAT REGULATORY AUTHORITY IS RESPONSIBLE FOR SUPERVISING WHOLESALE DISTRIBUTION ACTIVITIES?

**Regulatory authority**

In addition to the territorially competent region, both the Ministry of Health and the Italian Medicine Agency are entitled to undertake inspections of the wholesale distributors' premises.

## Supervision

In cases of non-compliance, penalties of up to EUR18,000 can be imposed on wholesale distributors.

## Rights of appeal

Appeals against decisions made by the authorities can be made before the Regional Administrative Courts within 60 days from the date when the decision was notified to the interested party or the date the latter became aware of it.

### 18. WHAT ARE THE LEGAL CONSEQUENCES OF NON-COMPLIANCE WITH WHOLESALE DISTRIBUTION LAWS?

In cases of non-compliance, penalties of up to EUR18,000 can be imposed on wholesale distributors (*see Question 16*).

# MARKETING

## PROMOTION

### 19. WHAT IS THE GENERAL LEGAL REGIME FOR THE MARKETING OF DRUGS?

## Legal regime

Drugs can be marketed if they have been duly licensed either pursuant to the national procedure or to the mutual recognition and decentralised procedures.

The marketing authorisation holders must establish a scientific service within their company which will be responsible for co-ordinating information about the drugs. This information must in turn be managed by a Qualified Person under Article 79(b) of Directive 2001/83/EC on the Community code relating to medicinal products for human use (Code for Human Medicines Directive) who is a graduate of medicine, pharmaceuticals or chemistry.

Through the scientific service, the licence holder must comply with all of the following obligations:

- Ensuring that the promotion of drugs is compliant with the regulations.
- Verifying that pharmaceutical sales representatives employed by the company have been adequately trained and act in compliance with the regulations.
- Providing assistance to the authorities and complying with their rules.

All members of the marketing team must comply with these obligations.

When advertising to consumers and healthcare professionals, there are special restrictions on some promotional activities.

## Limits on marketing activities

Promotional information must always be truthful as to the exact nature of the drug and must:

- Aim to encourage the rational use of the drug, presenting it in an objective way and without exaggerating its properties.
- Not be misleading.

When advertising to consumers and healthcare professionals there are special restrictions on some promotional activities.

Regarding the limitations regarding advertisement to consumers, it is forbidden to:

- Advertise prescription drugs to consumers.
- Make the intervention of a doctor appear as superfluous.
- Induce the consumer to think that the drug has superior effects than it actually does.
- Aim the advertisement to children.
- Advertise the product through a widely known person.
- Compare the drug to a cosmetic, a food product or another consumer product.
- Induce to a wrong auto-diagnosis.
- Connect the security or efficacy of the drug to its "natural" nature.
- Make abusive, shocking or misleading reference to certificates of healing and to visual representations of the human body's alterations due to an illness, and the action of the drug on the body or one of its parts.
- Indicate that the drug has received an authorisation for distribution.

For the advertisement before professionals, it can only be made to these professionals entitled to prescribe it and by the companies which are authorised for the distribution of the drug or their Italian representative if the company is foreign. The advertisement must always include the description of the drug and its class of reference.

If the use of scientific reports, papers or materials is made during the advertisement, such material must be presented integrally and not just in reference to some parts of it.

## 20. ARE THERE OTHER CODES OF CONDUCT FOR THE MARKETING OF DRUGS (FOR EXAMPLE, BY PROFESSIONAL OR INDUSTRIAL ORGANISATIONS)?

In addition to the legal regime, and separate from the codes of conduct implemented by each company, there are also guidelines concerning the promotion of drugs set out in the Farmindustria Ethics Code (Code). Farmindustria is the Italian pharmaceutical companies' trade association. The Code represents the commitment of the industry not only to abide by specific laws in force but also to operate on the basis of transparent standards of conduct that regulate the various circumstances in which corporate activities take place. The Code is a voluntary agreement entered into by pharmaceutical companies belonging to Farmindustria, and is designed to regulate relations not only between companies but also between companies and the health industry.

All members of Farmindustria must accept and comply with the provisions of the Code. The Code is considered to be a reference guideline for companies that are not necessarily members of Farmindustria.

## MARKETING TO CONSUMERS

### 21. WHAT IS THE LEGAL REGIME FOR MARKETING TO CONSUMERS?

**Legal regime**

A specific application for each advertisement (even if this advertisement is released through several different media) must be submitted to the Ministry of Health for authorisation to market drugs to consumers.

If the Ministry of Health does not provide this authorisation within 45 days from the date of the application, it is deemed to have been granted. The authorisation lasts for 24 months.

Authorisation is not required when:

- The promotional message is included in newspapers or periodical press and reproduces in full the information provided in the patient information leaflet.
- It consists of a picture of the package put on price tags.

Italian regulations require that promotion to consumers:

- Is clear that the message is a promotion and about a drug.
- Includes the following minimum information:
  - the name of the drug as well as the name of the active ingredient (if the drug contains only one active ingredient);
  - the information necessary for correct use of the drug;
  - an express and legible invitation to read carefully the instructions on the package leaflet or on the outer packaging. For promotional messages included in newspapers or periodical press, this invitation must be in font size nine.

**Products**

Promotion of drugs to consumers is only permitted if the drugs are non-prescription or do not need the intervention of a doctor for diagnostic purposes.

The following kinds of drugs must not be promoted to consumers at all:

- Drugs which are available on medical prescription only.
- Drugs which contain psychotropic or narcotic substances.
- Drugs which are totally or partially reimbursed by the National Health System.

### 22. WHAT KINDS OF MARKETING ACTIVITIES ARE PERMITTED IN RELATION TO CONSUMERS AND THE PRODUCTS WHICH MAY BE ADVERTISED TO THEM?

See *Question 19, Limits on marketing activities*.

### 23. IS IT PERMITTED TO PROVIDE CONSUMERS WITH FREE SAMPLES? ARE THERE PARTICULAR RESTRICTIONS ON SPECIAL OFFERS (FOR EXAMPLE, "BUY-ONE-GET-ONE-FREE")?

It is not permitted to give consumers free samples or to give them promotional offers on drugs.

## 24. ARE THERE PARTICULAR RULES OF PRACTICE ON THE USE OF THE INTERNET/SOCIAL MEDIA REGARDING DRUGS AND THEIR ADVERTISING?

No specific legal provisions are provided on the use of the internet in respect of advertising drugs. The general principles concerning marketing to consumers apply, including the authorisation procedure for advertising. The only specific provision is provided for in the Farmindustria Ethics Code. This requires that websites opened by an Italian company or a company operating in Italy which is addressed either to consumers or to healthcare professionals must clearly identify the:

- Company on whose behalf the advertising is placed.
- Source of all information provided on the site.
- Designated recipients of such information and the objectives of the site.

In all cases, access to sections providing promotional information on the company's products must be exclusively reserved to healthcare professionals for products which are not permitted to be advertised to consumers or for which authorisation to advertise has not yet been granted.

## 25. WHAT REGULATORY AUTHORITY IS RESPONSIBLE FOR SUPERVISING MARKETING ACTIVITIES TO CONSUMERS?

### Regulatory authority

The Ministry of Health is the authority responsible for supervising marketing activities to consumers.

### Supervision

In cases of non-compliance, the Ministry of Health is entitled to order the immediate termination of promotional activities as well as circulation of a press release containing a retraction. As a general rule, fines from EUR2,600 to EUR15,600 can be imposed. Higher amounts are imposed in cases of infringement of the prohibition against showing a drug in a non-advertising context to indirectly promote its use. Fines ranging from EUR10,000 to EUR60,000 can be imposed, for example, if the drug is shown in movies or television shows.

### Rights of appeal

Appeals against decisions made by the authorities can be made before the Regional Administrative Courts within 60 days from the date the decision was notified to the interested party or the date the latter became aware of it.

## 26. WHAT ARE THE LEGAL CONSEQUENCES OF NON-COMPLIANCE WITH CONSUMER MARKETING LAWS?

See *Question 25, Supervision*.

## MARKETING TO PROFESSIONALS

### 27. WHAT KINDS OF MARKETING ACTIVITIES ARE PERMITTED IN RELATION TO PROFESSIONALS?

Marketing activities can only be directed to healthcare professionals who are authorised to prescribe or supply the relevant drugs. Marketing material must first be submitted to the Italian Medicine Agency and ten days later can be delivered to healthcare professionals. No actual authorisation is required, there is only a duty to submit it to the Italian Medicine Agency. If the Italian Medicine Agency prohibits it, it cannot be used.

In general terms the following kinds of marketing activities (some of which will be better examined in the following questions) are permitted with regard to healthcare professionals, provided that the relevant material meets the above-mentioned requirements:

- Verbal information.
- Delivery of promotional material.
- Free samples.
- Scientific congresses and conventions.
- Refresher courses.
- Visits to companies' laboratories.
- Investigators' meetings.
- Scholarships and scientific consultancy.

### 28. ARE THERE ANY RESTRICTIONS ON MARKETING TO PROFESSIONALS?

**Marketing activities**

Exaggerated statements, universal and exaggerated claims and comparisons without any objective basis are not permitted. Use of e-mail, automated calling systems and other electronic communication aimed at divulging promotional material regularly approved by the Italian Medicine Agency is prohibited, unless the company holds a prior written and informed consent from the healthcare professionals to whom the material is addressed.

**Frequency**

There is no provision concerning frequency of marketing activities.

**Provision of hospitality**

The Italian Medicine Agency must be informed at least 60 days before the start date of any event, meeting, conference (or similar) organised or funded by an Italian drugs company. This includes both in Italy and abroad and applies to any gathering designed to discuss matters related to the use of drugs that are an occasion for pharmaceutical companies to meet healthcare professionals. The following information must be provided to the Italian Medicine Agency:

- Details of the pharmaceutical company.
- Location and date of the event.

- The matters to be discussed during the event.
- The possible attendees.
- Speakers' qualifications.
- A detailed estimate of the costs.

Any positive opinion from the Italian Medicine Agency will be issued within 45 days.

Should the event be held abroad or involve costs higher than EUR25,822.85, specific authorisation must be granted by the Italian Medicine Agency for events in Italy or involving Italian healthcare professionals before the commencement date as well as the payment of a rate equal to EUR1,859.24.

During the events, no kind of display and/or distribution of samples for promotional purposes is permitted with the exception of leaflets and other information-bearing conference materials.

As far as hospitality is concerned, pharmaceutical companies may only offer economy-class air travel to Italian healthcare professionals invited to conference events in Italy or abroad. Any category of paid-for hotel accommodation must not exceed four stars. In addition, the same healthcare professionals cannot be invited by the same pharmaceutical company more than twice a year. This restriction does not apply to speakers or moderators.

No events may be directly or indirectly organised by a pharmaceutical company outside Italy if it is to be mainly attended by Italian healthcare professionals.

The duration and the venue of the event are also subject to specific conditions. Events must be held in places and venues chosen for logistical, scientific and organisational reasons, which excludes restaurants. If the conference is to be held in a location popular with tourists, the following restrictions apply:

- No conferences are to be held at seaside resorts during 1 June to 30 September.
- No conferences are to be held in mountain resorts during 1 December to 1 March, and 1 July to 31 August.

The hospitality offered to the participants cannot exceed a 12-hour period before and immediately after the event and the hospitality must be secondary to the technical and/or scientific content of the event. No hospitality of any kind can be offered to guests of the invited healthcare professionals.

### 29. WHAT INFORMATION IS IT LEGALLY REQUIRED TO INCLUDE IN ADVERTISING TO PROFESSIONALS?

Marketing statements must always be substantiated by documented and verifiable evidence. The minimum particulars that must be included in all advertising are:

- The information listed in the summary of the product characteristics.
- The supply category of the drug.
- The selling price and the conditions under which it can be reimbursed by the national health system.

The promotional material may also include the name of the drug and the name of the active ingredient, together with the name of the licence holder and of the co-promoter, if any.

### 30. ARE THERE RULES ON COMPARISONS WITH OTHER PRODUCTS THAT ARE PARTICULARLY APPLICABLE TO DRUGS?

Comparisons without an objective basis are not permitted (*see Question 28, Marketing activities*).

### 31. WHAT OTHER ITEMS, FUNDING OR SERVICES ARE PERMITTED TO BE PROVIDED TO PROFESSIONALS?

**Discounts**

No discounts from the sale price are permitted. Promotion to healthcare professionals must be carried out by pharmaceutical sales representatives who belong to the scientific service of the company. This service must be independent of the company's marketing service.

**Free samples**

Free samples of drugs can only be supplied to healthcare professionals qualified to prescribe them and then only exclusively by pharmaceutical sales representatives. Healthcare professionals are required to keep the samples according to the instructions on the packaging or in the patient information leaflet.

The following strict criteria must be followed:

- Any supply of samples must be in response to a written request, signed, stamped and dated by the healthcare professional.
- In the first 18 months after the first marketing of the drugs, only two samples for each drug can be supplied to one healthcare professional during each visit and in any case no more than eight samples per year.
- After this time period, only four samples of each drug can be supplied to each healthcare professional during each visit and in no case more than ten samples per year.
- Each sample must be equal to or less than the smallest package put on the market, provided that this is expressly stated on the sample's label.
- Each sample must always be supplied together with a summary of the products' characteristics.
- Each sample must be marked with "free sample – not for sale" or other similar wording.
- No samples of drugs containing psychotropic or narcotic substances can be supplied.

Pharmaceutical companies must train their pharmaceutical sales representative in accordance with the above criteria and keep records of requests made to them for free samples over an 18-month period.

**Sponsorship of professionals**

Pharmaceutical companies may work with healthcare professionals as consultants for services such as speakers and moderators at conferences, or may invite them to participate in observational studies or training and education services. Based on the Farmindustria Ethics Code, the following criteria must be fully complied with:

- A written agreement must be signed between the healthcare professional and the pharmaceutical company specifying the nature of the service. The need for the service must be clearly identified and stated.

- The agreement must also state that the healthcare professional undertakes to disclose his or her relationship with the pharmaceutical company whenever he or she writes or speaks in public on the subject matter to which the co-operative relationship refers. The same obligation also applies in the event that the pharmaceutical company employs practising healthcare professionals on a part-time basis.
- The company is required to keep the documentation on the services provided by healthcare professionals for at least three years.
- The fees paid by pharmaceutical companies for the services must meet cost-performance criteria and reflect their market value. The initiative must guarantee coherence and appropriateness in respect of the pursued objectives and it must be capable of being fully documented.

**Other items, funding of services**

No other indirect incentives are permitted.

## 32. WHAT REGULATORY AUTHORITY IS RESPONSIBLE FOR SUPERVISING MARKETING ACTIVITIES REGARDING PROFESSIONALS?

**Regulatory authority**

The Italian Medicine Agency is the authority responsible for supervising marketing activities to healthcare professionals.

**Supervision**

In cases of non-compliance, the Italian Medicine Agency is entitled to order the immediate termination of the promotional activities and require circulation of a press release containing a retraction to be uploaded to the corporate website. Fines from EUR2,600 to EUR15,600 can be imposed. Higher amounts are imposed if free samples are marketed without the indication "free sample – not for sale" (from EUR5,000 to EUR30,000) (*see Question 31, Free samples*).

**Rights of appeal**

Appeals against decisions made by the authorities can be made before the Regional Administrative Courts within 60 days from the date the decision was notified to the interested party or the date the interested party became aware of it.

## 33. WHAT ARE THE LEGAL CONSEQUENCES IN CASE OF NON-COMPLIANCE WITH PROFESSIONAL MARKETING LAWS?

See *Question 32, Supervision*.

## ENGAGEMENT WITH PATIENT ORGANISATIONS

**34. WHAT KINDS OF ACTIVITIES ARE PERMITTED IN RELATION TO ENGAGEMENT WITH PATIENT ORGANISATIONS? WHAT ARE THE RESTRICTIONS THAT ARE IMPOSED ON RELATIONSHIP WITH PATIENT ORGANISATIONS?**

Any form of economic support (whether direct or indirect) by pharmaceutical companies to a patient organisation must comply with the following criteria (*Farmindustria Ethics Code*):

- A specific and preliminary agreement aimed at regulating the amount of and reasons for financing must be reached. For this reason, each pharmaceutical company must develop a standard internal procedure for approving this category of agreements.
- Any public utilisation by a pharmaceutical company of the logo or material owned by a patient organisation must be authorised in advance by the organisation. To acquire that authorisation, the objectives for, and the manner of use of the logo, must be clearly defined.
- Any form of sponsorship by pharmaceutical companies given to patient organisations must be transparent and without promotional objectives.
- No company can ask to be the sole financier of a patient organisation.
- In all cases in which journeys or other forms of hospitality are provided, the above provisions, as also set out in the Farmindustria Ethics Code, must apply.
- Companies must publish on their websites a list of all patient organisations that were financially supported by it in the previous year. This list must detail the monetary value of the support and must be publicly available for a period of three months coinciding with the first three months of each year.

Agreements between pharmaceutical companies and patient organisations under which the organisations provide any type of services to the companies are only allowed if the services are aimed at supporting healthcare activities or research. Patient organisations may be engaged as experts and advisors for services such as participation at advisory board meetings and speaker services. A written agreement must be executed in advance in order to specify the nature of these services and the basis of payment for them. A legitimate need for the services must be clearly identified and documented in advance of requesting them. Compensation for the services must be reasonable and not exceed the fair market value of the services provided. Companies are required to publish an annual list of the patient organisations which they have engaged to provide services.

## REFORM

**35. ARE THERE ANY PLANS TO REFORM THE LAW ON THE DISTRIBUTION AND PROMOTION OF DRUGS IN YOUR JURISDICTION?**

There are no plans to reform the law on the distribution and promotion of drugs in Italy.

# JAPAN

*Shinya Tago, Atsushi Ueda, Landry Guesdon and Ryohei Kudo, IWATA GODO LAW OFFICES*

## DISTRIBUTION

### PRE-CONDITIONS FOR DISTRIBUTION

**1. WHAT ARE THE LEGAL PRE-CONDITIONS FOR A DRUG TO BE DISTRIBUTED WITHIN THE JURISDICTION?**

**Authorisation**

The placing of pharmaceutical products on the market in Japan is regulated by the Law on Securing Quality, Efficacy and Safety of Pharmaceuticals, Medical Devices, Regenerative and Cellular Therapy Products, Gene Therapy Products, and Cosmetics (PMDL) formerly known as the Pharmaceutical Affairs Law. Drugs must be authorised prior to their distribution and a marketing authorisation (MA) is required from the Minister of the Ministry of Health, Labour, and Welfare (MHLW). The term "marketing" used in the PMDL refers to the retail, rental or handover of drugs (excluding active pharmaceutical ingredients) that a person has manufactured (including through subcontracting) or imported.

A person intending to start a drug manufacturing/marketing business must obtain a manufacturing/marketing business licence from the prefectural governor depending on the type of business to be conducted. Two new pharmaceutical business categories were created in 2014:

- In vitro diagnostics.
- Regenerative medical products (that is, cellular and tissue-based products).

Manufacturers intending to manufacture drugs overseas and export them to Japan are required to be accredited by the MHLW as "accredited foreign manufacturers". Foreign manufacturers must have an in-country representative (that can be an affiliate) known as the Japanese marketing authorisation holder (MAH) to import and commercialise drugs in Japan. The MAH must be licensed by the MHLW to act in this capacity.

The main licences needed for the manufacture, importation and marketing of medicinal products in Japan are as follows:

- Marketing business licence for MAH (*Article 12, PMDL*).
- Manufacturing business licence (*Article 13(1), PMDL*).
- Accreditation as foreign manufacturer (of drugs manufactured overseas) (*Article 13 (3), PMDL*).
- MA for each product (*Article 14, PMDL*).

### Exceptions

There are limited exceptions to the MA requirement (for example, if the drug is intended to be used in a clinical trial or in a named patient programme (*see Question 2*)).

## 2. DO ANY TYPES OF NAMED PATIENT AND/OR COMPASSIONATE USE PROGRAMMES OPERATE? IF SO, WHAT ARE THE REQUIREMENTS FOR PRE-LAUNCH ACCESS?

Japan has created provisions for granting access to drugs prior to approval for patients who have exhausted alternative treatment options. Certain rules define access criteria, promotion, and the control of drug distribution in this context. Exceptions to the licensing requirement include imports by doctors for use by their own patients. Under the relevant Minister of the Ministry of Health, Labour, and Welfare (MHLW) guidelines, imports by doctors can be permitted when:

- There is an emergency that necessitates a treatment.
- No alternative product is distributed in Japan.
- The products are solely to be used for their own patients' diagnosis or treatment.

There is a restricted approval system under Article 14 (3) of the Law on Securing Quality, Efficacy and Safety of Pharmaceuticals, Medical Devices, Regenerative and Cellular Therapy Products, Gene Therapy Products, and Cosmetics (PMDL). The restricted approval system is a special procedure for importing a medicinal product that is urgently needed to prevent a dangerous disease from reaching epidemic proportions and has received a foreign marketing authorisation.

## LICENSING

## 3. WHAT IS THE PROCEDURAL STRUCTURE REGARDING LICENSING A DRUG FOR DISTRIBUTION?

### Structure

The marketing authorisation (MA) application must be filed with the Minister of the Ministry of Health, Labour, and Welfare (MHLW) through the Pharmaceuticals and Medical Devices Agency (PMDA). A number of conditions must be satisfied before an MA can be delivered by the MHLW Minister. This includes set criteria relating to:

- Quality.
- Efficacy.
- Safety of the drug.
- The applicant's marketing business licence.
- The proposed manufacturer's manufacturing business licence or accreditation as a foreign manufacturer.

The drug must be manufactured using a method that complies with the manufacturing control and quality control standards based on a proper quality and safety management system as generally applied in Japan. Appropriateness for healthcare usage is determined in light of state of the art medical and pharmaceutical technology. In the process, the MHLW will review the product including:

- Name.
- Ingredients.
- Composition.
- Dosage and administration.
- Indications.
- Adverse reactions.

A good manufacturing practice (GMP) compliance review is carried out to ensure that the manufacturer complies with manufacturing control and quality control standards. An MA is granted to products meeting these standards.

Clinical trials must be conducted using the standards provided by the MHLW. If the standards are satisfied, clinical trials can also be conducted in a foreign country.

The standard time period from filing an application until the grant of the MA for a new drug is approximately one year. However, an abridged procedure and shorter standard review time can apply to generic products subject to the satisfaction of certain conditions.

### Regulatory authority

The MA is ultimately delivered by the MHLW, but the approval review process is conducted by the Pharmaceuticals and Medical Devices Agency (PMDA), an independent administrative organisation. The PMDA's activities can be divided into three main categories:

- Offering guidance and conducting scientific reviews of MA applications.
- Monitoring post-marketing safety.
- Providing relief compensation to those who have suffered from adverse drug reactions or infections caused by pharmaceuticals or biological products.

## 4. IS THERE A SIMPLIFIED LICENCE PROCEEDING, OR RELAXED LICENSING CONDITIONS, FOR DRUGS WHICH HAVE ALREADY BEEN LICENSED FOR DISTRIBUTION IN ANOTHER JURISDICTION?

Drug approval reviews are normally processed in the order of application. However, the following can be given review priority:

- Drugs labeled as orphan drugs (a drug that has been developed specifically to treat a rare medical condition).
- Other drugs considered to be of particular importance from a medical standpoint (that is, new drugs for the treatment of serious diseases).

An approval can be secured under the restricted approval system without the need to comply with ordinary approval review procedures (*see Question 1*). The system applies to drugs that are:

- Already marketed overseas.
- Needed in an emergency to prevent the spread of disease (that can have a major effect on public health) and are specifically defined by an administrative order.

In 2014, a new approval system was introduced for regenerative medical products. Under the system, non-uniform quality tissue-engineered medical products can be approved earlier than under the standard approval system if they are assumed to be effective and proven to be safe.

# JAPAN

### 5. IS VIRTUAL DRUG DISTRIBUTION POSSIBLE FROM YOUR JURISDICTION?

It is possible to distribute drugs virtually from Japan. A Japanese manufacturer/distributor/wholesaler can carry out distribution/wholesale activities (under a Japanese marketing authorisation) in/into another country subject to compliance with the laws and regulations of the country where the medicinal products are distributed.

### 6. WHAT IS THE PROCEDURE TO APPEAL (LEGAL REMEDY) A LICENSING DECISION?

Where an application is refused, an applicant can appeal the decision to the Minister of the Ministry of Health, Labour, and Welfare (MHLW) under the Administrative Appeal Act. Alternatively, the applicant may seek a judicial review of the Pharmaceuticals and Medical Devices Agency's (PMDA's) decision-making procedure by filing an administrative action with the Japanese district courts under the Administrative Case Litigation Act.

### 7. WHAT ARE THE COSTS OF OBTAINING LICENSING?

The marketing authorisation (MA) application fee differs depending on the type of drugs. The MA application fee for a new medicinal product ranges from JPY2 million to JPY50 million.

## DISTRIBUTION TO CONSUMERS

### 8. WHAT ARE THE DIFFERENT CATEGORIES OF DRUGS FOR DISTRIBUTION?

Pharmaceutical products are defined as the products listed in the Japanese pharmacopoeia in addition to certain other materials intended for use in the diagnosis, treatment, or prevention of disease and substances intended to affect the structure or functions of the body (excluding equipment and instruments).

The Law on Securing Quality, Efficacy and Safety of Pharmaceuticals, Medical Devices, Regenerative and Cellular Therapy Products, Gene Therapy Products, and Cosmetics (PMDL) categorises pharmaceutical products into two categories according to use and supply:

- Prescription (or ethical) drugs that can only be dispensed with a prescription issued by a medical practitioner or a dentist.
- Drugs that can be sold without a prescription (over-the-counter (OTC) drugs) and that are intended for use by consumers at their discretion through direct purchase in a pharmacy or a drugstore under the guidance of a pharmacist or a person duly licensed to retail drugs.

Prescription drugs are described by the Minister of the Ministry of Health, Labour, and Welfare (MHLW) as:

- Drugs that cannot be used effectively or safely without proper selection based on a doctor's prescription.
- Drugs that require periodic medical checks to prevent serious adverse effects.
- Drugs that can be used for other improper uses.

OTC drugs can be divided into three subcategories (in addition to the "behind-the-counter drugs" category (*see Question 9*) based on the potential risk of an adverse effect:

- Type 1 (high risk). Type 1 drugs require special attention for use.
- Type 2 (moderate risk).

- Type 3 (relatively low risk). Type 3 drugs are OTC drugs other than Type 1 and Type 2 (for example, vitamin B and C tablets and digestive aids).

Certain conventional OTC drugs have been newly categorised as "drugs requiring instructions" and the sale of which requires a consultation with a pharmacist (*Question 9*).

## 9. WHO IS AUTHORISED TO DISTRIBUTE PRESCRIPTION DRUGS AND OVER-THE-COUNTER DRUGS TO CONSUMERS?

### Prescription drugs

Prescription drugs can only be distributed to consumers by a person conducting a retail pharmacy business as a pharmacy owner licensed by the governor of the prefecture where the pharmacy is located (or by medical institutions). The drugs must be dispensed by or under the supervision of a registered pharmacist. No special permission is required for the provision of prescription drugs by medical institutions.

In 1956, the Act on the Partial Amendment of the Medical Practitioners Act, Dentist Act, and Pharmaceutical Affairs Law (the so-called law for the separation of dispensing and prescribing functions) came into effect, making it mandatory for prescriptions to be issued by medical doctors and dentists.

### Over-the-counter drugs (OTC drugs)

OTC drugs can be purchased directly at:

- Pharmacies from a pharmacist.
- Drugstores from a person who is duly licensed to retail drugs (A*rticle 24, Law on Securing Quality, Efficacy and Safety of Pharmaceuticals, Medical Devices, Regenerative and Cellular Therapy Products, Gene Therapy Products, and Cosmetics (PMDL)*).

Licences to retail drugs are divided into (*Article 25, PMDL*):

- **Licences to retail drugs at a store.** This refers to the business of selling non-prescription drugs at a store. The store retailer must appoint a pharmacist or a retail person authorised by a prefecture governor as having the knowledge and experience necessary to engage in retail activities (*Article 28, PMDL*).
- **Licences to retail drugs by way of household distribution.** This refers to the business of selling non-prescription drugs (with a relatively long shelf life) door-to-door by visiting customers' homes, delivering the drugs and returning to replenish the stock of drugs, and collect payment for any used drugs.
- **Licences for the wholesale of drugs.**

The subject of the sales of OTC drugs on the internet has sparked a heated debate. As a result, the PMDL was amended in 2013 and now permits the sale of all OTC drugs. The amendment also led to the establishment of a new category of drugs called "drugs requiring guidance (behind-the-counter drugs)". These drugs include powerful drugs and the so-called "switch OTC drugs" (that is, items that have just been switched from prescription drugs to OTC drugs), and whose risks as OTC drugs have yet to be identified. All the drugs must be sold in person by pharmacists. Internet sales of these drugs will be permitted after three years has passed following their change of status and once the risks have been assessed.

## 10. WHAT DRUGS CAN AN ATTENDING PHYSICIAN DISTRIBUTE AND UNDER WHAT CIRCUMSTANCES?

A medical practitioner can distribute any drug to a patient subject to compliance with applicable laws and regulations, including prescription medicines (and drugs for which a marketing authorisation is yet to be delivered under a named patient programme).

## 11. WHO IS AUTHORISED TO PRESCRIBE PRESCRIPTION DRUGS TO CONSUMERS?

Prescription drugs can be only be prescribed by medical practitioners or dentists.

## 12. IS DIRECT MAILING/DISTANCE SELLING OF DRUGS PERMITTED IN YOUR JURISDICTION?

**Conditions**

The supply of prescription drugs in Japan by mail order (including online sales) is prohibited and prescription drugs must be sold in person. Since the 2013 revision to the Law on Securing Quality, Efficacy and Safety of Pharmaceuticals, Medical Devices, Regenerative and Cellular Therapy Products, Gene Therapy Products, and Cosmetics (PMDL) (*see Question 9*) over-the-counter drugs can be sold online (with a few exceptions).

**Cross-border sales**

Cross-border sales can be conducted by any business or individual by mail from Japan to a foreign country if the drugs have been approved under the PMDL and are sold without any change to the packaging.

The importation of drugs for business purposes is subject to a marketing authorisation and other licensing requirements. In principle, the importation of drugs by an individual for personal use (private imports) requires a filing with the Regional Health and Welfare Bureau to obtain a certificate confirming that the import is not for business purposes.

Licences are needed for export business (a manufacturing business licence must be held by a local manufacturer). Drugs must also comply with Japanese good manufacturing practice even if they are intended for export and distribution outside of Japan.

## 13. WHAT REGULATORY AUTHORITY IS RESPONSIBLE FOR SUPERVISING DISTRIBUTION ACTIVITIES?

The distribution of drugs to consumers is supervised by the Minister of the Ministry of Health, Labour, and Welfare (MHLW) and the competent prefectural governor. A prefectural governor can:

- Request a pharmacy, a licensed retailer of drugs at a store, or a retailer carrying out household distribution in his prefecture, to submit a status report as specified under MHLW Ministerial Ordinance on their compliance with the applicable laws and ordinances.
- Send officers to carry out on-site inspections of premises at which the distribution of a drug is being carried out. The officers can inspect buildings and facilities, audit records and question employees or other personnel (*paragraph 2, Article 69, Law on Securing Quality, Efficacy and Safety of Pharmaceuticals, Medical Devices, Regenerative and Cellular Therapy*

Products, Gene Therapy Products, and Cosmetics (PMDL)).

- Order a pharmacy, a retailer at a store, or a door-to-door retailer to make certain improvements when quality assurance or post-marketing surveillance procedures do not comply with the standards provided in the MHLW Ministerial Ordinance (*Article 72, PMDL*). He can suspend all or part of a business until completion of the improvements.

The MHLW Minister can revoke the licence of a marketing authorisation holder or drug manufacturer or order the suspension of their business, while a prefecture governor can do the same for a pharmacy owner or drug retailer for violations of the PMDL (*paragraph 1, Article 75, PMDL*). Through delegation of authority from the MHLW, the Pharmaceuticals and Medical Devices Agency (PMDA) can conduct inspections, question staff, collect materials and samples and thereafter submit its investigation report to the Minister in accordance with the MHLW Ministerial Ordinance.

The regulator can monitor drugs subject to a marketing authorisation (MA) and new drugs are subject to reexamination. Manufacturing/marketing authorisation holders must perform post-marketing surveys on new drugs so that safety can be reconfirmed by the MHLW's reexamination for a specified period after the MA grant. All drugs, including those that have been reexamined must undergo a reevaluation to check their efficiency, safety, and quality in accordance with progress in medical and pharmaceutical sciences.

## 14. WHAT IS THE PROCEDURE TO APPEAL (LEGAL REMEDY) A DISTRIBUTION DECISION?

A distribution decision can include an order by the regulator to dispose of, recall medicinal products or take some other measure for:

- The protection of public health.
- A licence cancellation.
- A temporary shutdown of operations/business.

The steps (whether taken by the Minister of the Ministry of Health, Labour, and Welfare (MHLW) or a prefectural governor) can be appealed under the Administrative Appeal Act. Alternatively, the applicant can seek a judicial review of the decision by filing an administrative action with the Japanese courts under the Administrative Case Litigation Act.

## 15. WHAT ARE THE LEGAL CONSEQUENCES OF NON-COMPLIANCE WITH CONSUMER DISTRIBUTION LAWS?

Under Article 84 of The Law on Securing Quality, Efficacy and Safety of Pharmaceuticals, Medical Devices, Regenerative and Cellular Therapy Products, Gene Therapy Products, and Cosmetics (PMDL) provides that a person who is guilty of participating in drug retail without a license will be liable to either or both:

- A fine not exceeding JPY3 million.
- Imprisonment for a term of up to three years.

In addition, if a person licensed to market drugs violates any of the marketing methods prescribed by the PMDL (*see Question 9*), he will be liable to either or both:

- A fine not exceeding JPY2 million.
- Imprisonment for a term of up to two years.

## WHOLESALE DISTRIBUTION

### 16. WHAT IS THE LEGAL REGIME REGARDING WHOLESALE DISTRIBUTION OF DRUGS?

The wholesale distribution of drugs is mainly governed by the Law on Securing Quality, Efficacy and Safety of Pharmaceuticals, Medical Devices, Regenerative and Cellular Therapy Products, Gene Therapy Products, and Cosmetics (PMDL). Any company wanting to wholesale drugs in Japan must hold a wholesaler's licence issued by the prefectural governor competent for each business establishment (*Article 25 and paragraph 1, Article 31, PMDL*). Supplying wholesale refers to selling or supplying drugs to the proprietor of a pharmacy, a marketing authorisation holder, a manufacturer, a retailer of drugs, or a hospital, a clinic, or any other such persons or places (other than the end-user of the medicinal product). Wholesale supply will be permitted if there is a marketing authorisation in place for the drug in Japan. A wholesaler can wholesale drugs that are non-prescription drugs to store retailers and door-to-door retailers engaged in household distribution (*Article 156, PMDL Enforcement Regulations*). In principle, a wholesaler must have a pharmacist based at each business establishment in charge of overseeing the business establishment (*paragraphs 1 and 2, Article 35, PMDL*).

### 17. WHAT REGULATORY AUTHORITY IS RESPONSIBLE FOR SUPERVISING WHOLESALE DISTRIBUTION ACTIVITIES?

**Regulatory authority**

The Minister of the Ministry of Health, Labour, and Welfare (MHLW) and the competent prefectural governor are responsible for overseeing the wholesale supply of drugs in Japan. Some authority can also be delegated to the Pharmaceuticals and Medical Devices Agency (PMDA).

**Supervision**

A prefectural governor can request a wholesaler located in his prefecture to submit a status report as specified under the MHLW Ministerial Ordinance. It can also send officers to enter and carry out on-site inspections of premises where the distribution of a medicinal product is being carried out. The officers can inspect buildings and facilities, audit records and question the employees or other personnel involved (*paragraph 2, Article 69, Law on Securing Quality, Efficacy and Safety of Pharmaceuticals, Medical Devices, Regenerative and Cellular Therapy Products, Gene Therapy Products, and Cosmetics (PMDL)*). A prefectural governor can order a wholesaler to make certain improvements when quality assurance or post-marketing surveillance procedures do not comply with the standards provided in the MHLW Ministerial Ordinance (*Article 72, PMDL*) or the governor can suspend all or part of a business until completion of the improvements. In cases of violations of the PMDL and related laws and ordinances, the MHLW Minister can revoke the licence of a marketing authorisation holder or drug manufacturer or order the suspension of their business, while a prefectural governor can do the same for a wholesale dealer (*paragraph 1, Article 75, PMDL*).

**Rights of appeal**

See *Question 14*.

## 18. WHAT ARE THE LEGAL CONSEQUENCES OF NON-COMPLIANCE WITH WHOLESALE DISTRIBUTION LAWS?

The wholesaler's licence can be revoked or suspended. A breach of the requirements applicable to wholesalers can also constitute a criminal offence under the Law on Securing Quality, Efficacy and Safety of Pharmaceuticals, Medical Devices, Regenerative and Cellular Therapy Products, Gene Therapy Products, and Cosmetics (PMDL). Under Article 84 of the PMDL, a person who is guilty of the offence of participating in drug wholesale without a licence will be liable to either or both:

- A fine not exceeding JPY3 million.
- Imprisonment for a term of up to three years.

If a wholesaler is in breach of the obligation to have a pharmacist supervise each of its business locations, it will be liable to either or both (*paragraph 1, Article 1, PMDL*):

- A fine not exceeding JPY1 million.
- Imprisonment (for the representative of a juridical person, or an agent, an employee, or any other worker in the service of a juridical person) for up to one year.

# MARKETING

## PROMOTION

## 19. WHAT IS THE GENERAL LEGAL REGIME FOR THE MARKETING OF DRUGS?

**Legal regime**

The Law on Securing Quality, Efficacy and Safety of Pharmaceuticals, Medical Devices, Regenerative and Cellular Therapy Products, Gene Therapy Products, and Cosmetics (PMDL) and other relevant laws and ordinances regulate marketing activities applicable to drugs. Promotional activities are not expressly regulated by the PMDL, except for drug information or the advertising of drugs. The PMDL and the Standards for Fair Advertising Practices concerning Medicinal Products (PAB Notice No. 1339 of 9 October 1980) (MHLW Guidelines) set basic standards for the advertising of drugs. The expression "advertising" is defined in the PMDL as referring to advertisements clearly intended to induce consumers, specifying the name of a medicinal product and recognisable as such by the general public.

General competition laws can also be relevant, in particular the:

- Act on the Prohibition of Private Monopolisation and the Maintenance of Fair Trade (Antimonopoly Act).
- Unfair Competition Prevention Act (UCPA).
- Act against Unjustifiable Premiums and Misleading Representations (AUPMR).
- Criminal Code.
- National Public Service Ethics Act.

### Limits to marketing activities

The AUPMR regulates premiums and representations relating to transactions of goods and services to ensure fair competition and protect the interests of consumers. The Act prohibits unjustifiable premiums and misleading representations, including through advertisements (*Articles 3 and 4, AUPMR*). Industry organisations have established self-imposed industry standards in pursuance of Article 11 of the AUPMR (*see Question 20*).

Articles 66 to 68 of the PMDL prohibit the advertising of or dissemination of false or exaggerated statements on the:

- Name, manufacturing method, indications or performance of a drug.
- Endorsement by healthcare professionals.
- Advertising of drugs for specially designated diseases (treating cancer, sarcoma and leukaemia).
- Advertising of the name, manufacturing method and/or indications of a drug before the grant of a marketing authorisation.

The MHLW Guidelines prohibit the advertisement of prescription drugs aimed at the general public. They include specific restrictions on advertisements under the PMDL and also limit the use of premiums, prizes and awards in this context.

### 20. ARE THERE OTHER CODES OF CONDUCT FOR THE MARKETING OF DRUGS (FOR EXAMPLE, BY PROFESSIONAL OR INDUSTRIAL ORGANISATIONS)?

The marketing of drugs is governed by a combination of legislation and codes of practice. Various industry self-regulations apply to promotional activities. The Japan Pharmaceutical Manufacturers' Association (JPMA) is a voluntary industry group that unites and represents large pharmaceutical companies that are present in Japan. It is active through its self-regulation initiatives supplementing laws and regulations. The JPMA requires its members to comply with its code of practices for the promotion of prescription drugs to the healthcare professionals (HCP) sector (Promotion Code). The code is part of the JPMA Code of Practice established in 2013 following amendments to the International Federation of Pharmaceutical Manufacturers and Associations (IFPMA) Code of Practice that provides guidance to pharmaceutical companies on how to interact with HCPs, institutions and patient organisations. The IFPMA is a global voluntary organisation that represents the research-based pharmaceutical industry and its code applies to JPMA members.

In addition, the Fair Trade Council of the Ethical Pharmaceutical Drugs Marketing Industry has adopted a code for fair competition and fair trade that limits the benefits and premiums that can be offered for the promotion of ethical drugs (Fair Competition Code). The Fair Competition Code (along with corresponding guidelines and interpretive commentary) has been approved by the Japan Fair Trade Commission (JFTC). It is a voluntary code but has semi-legal binding aspects and the JFTC can step in to prevent violations. The Fair Competition Code is, to some extent, a specific adaptation for the pharmaceutical industry of the wider body of rules contained in the Act against Unjustifiable Premiums and Misleading Representations (AUPMR).

The JPMA Promotion Code and the Fair Competition Code are among the most significant codes of conduct. The JPMA Code of Practice gives a number of basic principles regarding members' materials (brochures, adverts in medical journals, websites targeting HCPs, audiovisual materials) in addition to the fact that the statements contained therein must be correct, objective and based on scientific data. For example:

- Statements regarding indications, dosage and administration, and any other statements, must not deviate from the approved items.
- No false, exaggerated, or misleading labels, layout or expression can be used regarding efficiency and safety.
- Fair statements must be made by presenting both efficiency data and safety data, including adverse reactions.
- Comparisons with other drugs must be based on scientific data, in principle made using generic names.
- Competitors or competitors' drugs must not be slandered or defamed.
- Extraordinary data must not be presented to give the impression that the data has universal value.
- Where an advertisement is aimed mainly at promoting only the name of a drug, the items described in an advertisement must include the:
  - brand name;
  - therapeutic category (product title);
  - regulatory classification;
  - non-proprietary name;
  - national health insurance (NHI) price listing status; and
  - contact details to request more detail.

In addition, the Japan Generic Medicines has adopted its own code of practice for the promotion of generic drugs (JGA Promotion Code). For over-the-counter (OTC) drugs, the Federation of Pharmaceutical Manufacturers' Associations of Japan (FPMAJ) and the Japan Self-Medication Industry (JSMI) jointly issued a Voluntary Code for OTC Medicine Advertising. Although voluntary, the Voluntary Code is considered by the Minister of the Ministry of Health, Labour, and Welfare (MHLW) as the most appropriate advertising standard for the industry. These codes apply to association members but they are also carefully scrutinised by other industry players as the rules can serve as reliable indicators of the views of the MHLW, the JFTC or the Consumer Affairs Agency (the Japanese consumer protection authority) on topics that deserve clarification or benchmarking.

## MARKETING TO CONSUMERS

### 21. WHAT IS THE LEGAL REGIME FOR MARKETING TO CONSUMERS?

**Legal regime/ Products**

The advertising of prescription drugs to the general public is prohibited (*see Question 19*) under the:

- Law on Securing Quality, Efficacy and Safety of Pharmaceuticals, Medical Devices, Regenerative and Cellular Therapy Products, Gene Therapy Products, and Cosmetics (PMDL).
- Standards for Fair Advertising Practices concerning Medicinal Products (PAB Notice No. 1339 of 9 October 1980).

In addition, misleading representations to the effect that the use of a particular drug will cure cancer, diabetes, hyperlipidaemia, heart diseases, hepatitis or other diseases which generally require a medical practitioner's diagnosis and treatment, are prohibited in advertisements targeting consumers.

By contrast, over-the-counter (OTC) drugs can be freely advertised in Japan like other consumer goods. This is because OTC drug advertising is regarded as an important means of conveying useful health-related information to the general public. This (relative) freedom is subject to strict compliance with certain regulatory and voluntary checks. OTC drug advertising control in Japan has two key features:

- Control is post-publication or post-broadcast (not a unique feature as the same applies to other drugs).
- Existence of a Voluntary Code that is well established and strictly observed by the industry.

## 22. WHAT KINDS OF MARKETING ACTIVITIES ARE PERMITTED IN RELATION TO CONSUMERS AND THE PRODUCTS WHICH MAY BE ADVERTISED TO THEM?

There are no particular restrictions on the kinds of marketing activities that are permitted. The choice of media can include newspapers, magazines, television commercials, the internet or social media.

## 23. IS IT PERMITTED TO PROVIDE CONSUMERS WITH FREE SAMPLES? ARE THERE PARTICULAR RESTRICTIONS ON SPECIAL OFFERS (FOR EXAMPLE, "BUY-ONE-GET-ONE-FREE")?

The Standards for Fair Advertising Practices concerning Medicinal Products (PAB Notice No. 1339 of 9 October 1980) permit the provision of free samples to consumers if the drugs are:

- For external use.
- Headache medication.
- Antidiarrheal products.
- Vitamin supplements.
- Commonly used at home.

The following is prohibited:

- The provision of free samples of powerful drugs or prescription drugs.
- Advertising drugs as a premium/prize or award.
- Advertising that free drugs will be given in exchange for empty containers or packages of drugs.

## 24. ARE THERE PARTICULAR RULES OF PRACTICE ON THE USE OF THE INTERNET/SOCIAL MEDIA REGARDING DRUGS AND THEIR ADVERTISING?

See *Question 22*.

## 25. WHAT REGULATORY AUTHORITY IS RESPONSIBLE FOR SUPERVISING MARKETING ACTIVITIES TO CONSUMERS?

**Regulatory authority**

The following are responsible for the supervision of marketing activities to consumers:

- Minister of the Ministry of Health, Labour, and Welfare (MHLW).
- Consumer Affairs Agency (CAA).
- Prefectural governors are responsible for the supervision of marketing activities to consumers.

**Supervision**

See *Question 13*.

In addition, if an entrepreneur acts in violation of Articles 3 and 4 of the Act against Unjustifiable Premiums and Misleading Representations (AUPMR) the Prime Minister (or Secretary General of the CAA by delegation) can:

- Order that the entrepreneur stops the violating act (*Article 6, AUPMR*).
- Take the measures necessary to prevent the reoccurrence of the violation (*Article 12, AUPMR*).

This is in addition to the right to request compliance reports from the offender, conduct on-site inspections, and to question staff. The prefectural governor can also give instructions to the entrepreneur on the necessary measures to be taken.

**Rights of appeal**

If an entrepreneur is subject to an administrative sanction for a breach and the punishment is illegal or unreasonably harsh, the entrepreneur can appeal the decision (*see Question 6*).

## 26. WHAT ARE THE LEGAL CONSEQUENCES OF NON-COMPLIANCE WITH CONSUMER MARKETING LAWS?

Breaches of the Law on Securing Quality, Efficacy and Safety of Pharmaceuticals, Medical Devices, Regenerative and Cellular Therapy Products, Gene Therapy Products, and Cosmetics (PMDL) and the texts governing advertising is subject to administrative punishment by the Minister of the Ministry of Health, Labour, and Welfare (MLHW). Serious breaches of the PMDL can trigger criminal sanctions of:

- Imprisonment for a term of up to two years.
- A fine of up to JPY2 million.
- Both a fine of up to JPY2 million and imprisonment for a term of up to two years for certain offences including (*Article 85, PMDL*):
  – false and exaggerated claims and advertising (*Article 66, PMDL*);
  – advertising before delivery of a marketing authorisation (MA) (*Article 68, PMDL*).

Violations of the Act against Unjustifiable Premiums and Misleading Representations (AUPMR) are punishable by:

- Imprisonment for a term of up to two years, and/or a fine not exceeding JPY3 million (*Article 16, AUPMR*).
- A fine up to JPY300 million (for corporations) (*Article 18, AUPMR*).

A 2014 amendment introduced the imposition of an administrative fine for a business that has made the following misleading representations (*Article 4, AUPMR*):

- Where the quality or standard of goods is portrayed to general consumers as being much better than that of the actual goods, or much better than those supplied by other businesses.

- If the price or any other trade terms of the goods can be misunderstood by general consumers to be much more favourable than the actual goods supplied, or to be much more favourable than those supplied by other businesses.

The following can take measures to stop or prevent breaches of the Fair Competition Code:

- Fair Trade Council of the Ethical Pharmaceutical Drugs Marketing Industry.
- Japan Fair Trade Commission (JFTC).
- Consumer Affairs Agency (CAA).

In the case of breaches of voluntary standards by industry organisations, corrective measures or disciplinary sanctions can be taken by the industry organisations against their respective members. For example, for breaches of the Japan Pharmaceutical Manufacturers' Association (JPMA) Code of Practices, the Promotion Code Committee of the JPMA can take action (within the limits of its authority as a self-governing regulatory body).

## MARKETING TO PROFESSIONALS

### 27. WHAT KINDS OF MARKETING ACTIVITIES ARE PERMITTED IN RELATION TO PROFESSIONALS?

Marketing activities relating to healthcare professionals are not expressly prohibited. However, they must comply with the:

- Applicable laws and regulations (*see Question 19*).
- Fair Competition Code and the relevant industry self-regulations applicable to promotional activities (where applicable) (see *Question 20*).

### 28. ARE THERE ANY RESTRICTIONS ON MARKETING TO PROFESSIONALS?

**Marketing activities**

See *Questions 19* and *20*.

Article 68 of the Law on Securing Quality, Efficacy and Safety of Pharmaceuticals, Medical Devices, Regenerative and Cellular Therapy Products, Gene Therapy Products, and Cosmetics (PMDL) provides that no person can advertise the name, manufacturing process, indications or performance of a drug before the granting of a market authorisation (MA). In accordance with commentary of the Japan Pharmaceutical Manufacturers' Association (JPMA) Promotion Code, this should not deprive medical/pharmaceutical experts (or the general public) of the right to know about scientific advancements. For example, the provision does not restrict the:

- Appropriate exchange of scientific information about a drug through the presentation of research findings in a meeting of an academic society or scientific journal.
- Display of scientific exhibition materials about a drug yet to be approved in Japan in accordance with separate guidelines at a meeting of an international academic society.
- Supply of peer-reviewed scientific literature, such as a reprint of a research paper at the request of a doctor.
- Lawful disclosure of medical information on products under development to the pharmaceutical company's shareholders. This also applies to off-label information. Article 5(2) of the Fair Competition Code authorises the supply of information or explanatory materials concerning medical data or a drug manufactured by a company.

In certain special circumstances, gifts and promotional items can be offered to healthcare professionals (HCPs) but they must comply with good ethical practices and remain within the limits of decency imposed by the pharmaceutical industry and its core objectives. In accordance with the Fair Competition Code, inappropriate financial benefit or benefit in-kind should not be offered to medical practitioners to induce them to prescribe drugs. This does not preclude the supply of after-sales services in the ordinary course of business. Article 3 of the Fair Competition Code provides that a Japanese marketing authorisation holder (MAH) cannot provide premiums to HCPs, such as hospitals or pharmacies, as a means of unjustly inducing transactions.

The JPMA Promotion Code generally prohibits its members from offering any gift or cash that could potentially affect the appropriate use of drugs to HCPs. The impact of the gift or cash offering must be considered, in particular whether the practice may:

- Affect the proper use of drugs.
- Be perceived by the public as interfering with neutral, independent and scientifically based prescription methods and consequently undermine the social role of drugs.

The JPMA Promotion Code requires member companies to set clear standards for gifts and cash offerings in their own in-house codes and strictly observe them in accordance with the principles of the JPMA Promotion Code and the International Federation of Pharmaceutical Manufacturers and Associations (IFPMA) Code of Practice. Seasonal gifts must not be offered even when they are customary because, depending on value and frequency, they can be seen as interfering with the independence of an HCP's decision to prescribe, recommended or purchase drugs.

If a pharmaceutical company makes inappropriate gifts or donations of money to, or entertains, a Japanese medical practitioner who is also a public official, the pharmaceutical company and the medical practitioner may be charged with bribery under the Criminal Code or the National Public Official Moral Code. Under the Unfair Competition Prevention Act, the provision of gifts, travel expenses, meals or entertainment to foreign public officials can be treated as bribery in the same way as the provision of cash or any other benefits.

**Frequency**

There is no clear restriction set by laws or ordinances. The industry self-regulations provide that medical representatives visiting a medical institution must act in an orderly manner and observe the rules established by the institution.

**Provision of hospitality**

Various industry self-regulations apply to promotional activities relating to pharmaceutical products and medical devices. The JPMA Promotion Code requires that seminars for members' products be held at appropriate venues and, if food and drinks or any social event or gift is offered in conjunction with a seminar, they must not be extravagant. The IFPMA Code of Practice provides that refreshments and meals incidental to the event can be offered only when they are restrained and reasonable by reference to local standards. In the JPMA Promotion Code commentary, "restrained and reasonable" is interpreted as the amount of money usually payable by healthcare professionals and considered as a first impression by the general public not to be extremely high. The Fair Competition Code contains similar provisions.

## 29. WHAT INFORMATION IS IT LEGALLY REQUIRED TO INCLUDE IN ADVERTISING TO PROFESSIONALS?

The Standards for Fair Advertising Practices concerning Medicinal Products (PAB Notice No. 1339 of 9 October 1980) (MHLW Guidelines) (see *Question 19*) require certain minimum information to be provided to healthcare professionals, including the:

- Product's name for distribution.
- Generic classification name.
- Product's indications and effects.
- Method of administration.
- Information regarding adverse reactions, precautions and contraindications, and dosage.
- Contact address for further information.
- Date of preparation of the advertisement.

## 30. ARE THERE RULES ON COMPARISONS WITH OTHER PRODUCTS THAT ARE PARTICULARLY APPLICABLE TO DRUGS?

The Act against Unjustifiable Premiums and Misleading Representations (AUPMR) does not prohibit comparative advertising. However, in accordance with the Guidelines for Comparative Advertising under the AUPMR issued by the Japan Fair Trade Commission, the following comparative advertising is considered as misleading representations and likely to affect the appropriate selection of products by consumers:

- Comparison by indicating matters that have not been proven and are incapable of being proven.
- Comparison based on unfair grounds, for example, by putting the emphasis on the importance of certain aspects that are inconsequential to product selection by consumers, or on an arbitrary selection of the products compared.
- Advertising that disparages competitors or their products.

The Standards for Fair Advertising Practices concerning Medicinal Products (PAB Notice No. 1339 of 9 October 1980) (MHLW Guidelines) prohibit a pharmaceutical company from disparaging other companies' products in relation to quality, potency/effect, safety, or other drug-related aspects.

The Japan Pharmaceutical Manufacturers' Association Code of Practices provides that comparisons with other drugs must be conducted properly and based on scientific data, in principle made using generic names. Competitors' drugs must not be slandered or defamed. Under the Code's commentary, comparing new drugs with drugs that have been previously used and finding out where and in what way they differ is extremely important in deciding which drug to use. Therefore, it is imperative that they be introduced based on accurate data with scientific backing, in compliance with the Guidelines for Specifying Product Information Summaries for Prescription Drugs, while avoiding ambiguous expressions that may lead to misunderstandings. When making a comparison with another drug, the drug that is being compared against, must be referred to using its generic name (the use of rival manufacturers' logos or brands is prohibited unless their consent has been received and this is unlikely to happen).

## 31. WHAT OTHER ITEMS, FUNDING OR SERVICES ARE PERMITTED TO BE PROVIDED TO PROFESSIONALS?

**Discounts**

There is no express statutory restriction or prohibition dealing with discounts for drugs.

**Free samples**

The provision of free samples is permitted under the:

- Japan Pharmaceutical Manufacturers Association Promotion Code.
- Japan Generic Medicines Association Promotion Code.

However, only the minimum requisite number of samples should be supplied (together with information on the drug).

The Fair Competition Code includes detailed provisions on the supply of samples. A medical institution is prohibited from providing free medical drugs as a means of inducing the institution to buy drugs (*Article 4(2), Fair Competition Code*). However, the provision of free drugs is permitted for clinical trial purposes in order to test the quality, effectiveness, safety, and characteristics of a medicinal product. Free samples can also be supplied to medical institutions at the time of the product launch to allow medical staff to become familiar with the formulation, colour, taste, appearance or other characteristics of the product prior to use (*Article 5 (3) and Article 2, Implementing Regulation of the Fair Competition Code*).

**Sponsorship of professionals**

The Fair Competition Code provides for the:

- Payment of compensation and costs and expenses for medical or pharmaceutical studies/research that are entrusted to a medical institution (for example, post-marketing surveillance studies, clinical trials, other medical or pharmaceutical research) (*Article 5(4), Fair Competition Code*).
- Donation of equipment or supply of services to medical institutions (as long as they are not luxurious or excessive) for use in lectures relating to the company's own drugs (*Article 5(5), Fair Competition Code*).

Pharmaceutical companies must comply with the Fair Competition Code guidelines (in particular the Standards for Premiums and Standards for donations) issued by the Japan Fair Trade Commission (JFTC) and the Consumer Affairs Agency (CAA).

Under Article 5 (5) of the Fair Competition Code, it is possible to:

- Pay reasonable *honoraria* (payment given for professional services that are rendered nominally without charge).
- Reimburse out-of-pocket expenses (for example, travelling and accommodation) for conference speakers and presenters.
- Bear some of the expenses of an attending medical practitioner.

These payments must be kept at a modest level.

**Other items, funding or services**

The Fair Competition Code states that the provision of the following is permissible (conditional on the purchase of drugs):

- Equipment or services necessary for the use of the offeror's own prescription drugs by medical institutions (*Article 5(1)*).
- Equipment or services that enhance the efficiency and benefit of the drugs (*Article 5(1)*).
- Medical or pharmaceutical information and explanatory materials on the company's own drugs (*Article 5 (2)*).

### 32. WHAT REGULATORY AUTHORITY IS RESPONSIBLE FOR SUPERVISING MARKETING ACTIVITIES REGARDING PROFESSIONALS?

See *Question 25*.

### 33. WHAT ARE THE LEGAL CONSEQUENCES IN CASE OF NON-COMPLIANCE WITH PROFESSIONAL MARKETING LAWS?

For a breach of the Fair Competition Code, the Fair Trade Council can (*Article 10, Fair Trade Council*):

- Issue a warning.
- Impose a penalty up to JPY1 million.
- Order the expulsion of the violator.

If the Fair Trade Council decides to impose a penalty or order the expulsion of a member company, it must first submit its decision as a draft to the company. The company then has ten days to file an objection (*Article 11 (2), Fair Trade Council*). The Fair Trade Council will give the company the opportunity to submit its own arguments before making a final decision on the measures to be taken (*Article 11 (3), Fair Trade Council*).

See *Question 26* for criminal punishments for violations of laws and ordinances and breaches of self-imposed industry standards.

## ENGAGEMENT WITH PATIENT ORGANISATIONS

### 34. WHAT KINDS OF ACTIVITIES ARE PERMITTED IN RELATION TO ENGAGEMENT WITH PATIENT ORGANISATIONS? WHAT ARE THE RESTRICTIONS THAT ARE IMPOSED ON RELATIONSHIP WITH PATIENT ORGANISATIONS?

There is no specific restriction placed by laws or ordinances. The Japan Pharmaceutical Manufacturers Association Code of Practice provides that member companies must act ethically and respect the independence of patient groups in all types of collaboration with patient organisations. Member companies collaborating with patient organisations must establish guidelines for their own companies on the basis of the Guideline on Collaboration with Patient Organisations. When providing financial support to patient organisations, each member company must ensure transparency by:

- Making it clear that it is involved.

- Secure written consent for the objectives.
- Keep records.

Other support to a patient group must be established in the members' own guidelines based on the Patient Group Transparency Guidelines. Similarly, with respect to relationships with patient organisations, the Guidelines for Transparency of Relationship between Corporate Activities and Patient Organisations (Patient Group Transparency Guidelines) trigger spend disclosure obligations on members.

## REFORM

### 35. ARE THERE ANY PLANS TO REFORM THE LAW ON THE DISTRIBUTION AND PROMOTION OF DRUGS IN YOUR JURISDICTION?

Healthcare laws, regulations and industry self-regulations are currently evolving at a fast pace to deal with political and demographic (ageing population) pressures and to follow technological and scientific progress and international trends. This includes strengthening drug safety, introducing rules dealing with regenerative medicines, including a specific approval system, and the treatment of patients with cell therapy and gene therapy products.

# THE NETHERLANDS

*Willem Hoorneman, Rogier de Vrey, Bart Essink and Anastasia Chistyakova, CMS Derks Star Busmann*

## DISTRIBUTION

### PRE-CONDITIONS FOR DISTRIBUTION

**1. WHAT ARE THE LEGAL PRE-CONDITIONS FOR A DRUG TO BE DISTRIBUTED WITHIN THE JURISDICTION?**

**Authorisation**

Before a drug can be introduced into the market it must be authorised (also referred to as having received a marketing authorisation) by the Medicines Evaluation Board (*College ter beoordeling van Geneesmiddelen*) (MEB). The MEB is part of the Ministry of Health, Welfare and Sport.

The MEB evaluates the drug based on criteria cited in the Medicines Act 2007 (*Geneesmiddelenwet*) and sets the conditions for authorising the product for marketing in The Netherlands. The responsibility for the evaluation, authorisation and pharmacovigilance of medicinal products for human use (including homeopathic and herbal medicines) rests with the MEB, which consists of doctors, pharmacists and scientists. The MEB has independent authority to take decisions on the availability of these medicinal products. The MEB is responsible for both the authorisation and monitoring of effective and safe medicinal products and is jointly responsible for the approval of the medicinal products throughout the EU.

**Exceptions**

There are several exceptions to the obligation to acquire a marketing authorisation. No marketing authorisation is required for:

- Any drug prepared in a pharmacy in accordance with a medical prescription for an individual patient.
- Any drug that is prepared in a pharmacy in accordance with the prescriptions of a pharmacopoeia and is intended to be supplied directly to the patients served by the pharmacy in question.
- Drugs intended for research and development trials.
- Whole blood, plasma or blood cells of human origin, except for plasma that is prepared by a method involving an industrial process.
- Intermediate products intended for further processing by an authorised manufacturer.

## 2. DO ANY TYPES OF NAMED PATIENT AND/OR COMPASSIONATE USE PROGRAMMES OPERATE? IF SO, WHAT ARE THE REQUIREMENTS FOR PRE-LAUNCH ACCESS?

Article 5(1) of Directive 2001/83/EC on the Community code relating to medicinal products for human use (Code for Human Medicines Directive), as regards the prevention of the entry into the legal supply chain of falsified medicinal products has been transposed by the Netherland's legislator. At the national level, the legal conditions have been included in the Medicines Act 2007 (*Geneesmiddelenwet*). "Named patient" is an individual patient and falls under the jurisdiction of the Healthcare Inspectorate (*Inspectie voor de Gezondheidszorg*). The Medicines Evaluation Board (*College ter beoordeling van Geneesmiddelen*) (MEB) can approve compassionate use programmes.

### Named patient

Permission to supply a pharmaceutical product without marketing authorisation must be obtained from the Healthcare Inspectorate (*Article 3:17, Medicines Act Regulation (Regeling Geneesmiddelenwet)*). Such permission can be sought by a manufacturer, distributor, established pharmacist or a general practitioner that administers his own pharmacy. A separate application form must be completed for each product. The application must state the condition that the product is intended to treat. The first application must be accompanied by a declaration signed by the doctor wishing to prescribe the product. The manufacturer remains liable for the safety of the product at all times.

### Compassionate use programmes

Permission to supply a pharmaceutical product without a marketing authorisation must be obtained from the MEB (*Article 3:17, Medicines Act Regulation*).

A company must submit a request to the MEB for implementing a compassionate use programme. This request must indicate how the cohort of patients will be defined and which patients fall under this definition.

The application must include:

- A clear aspect of compassion in case there is no registered alternative medicine.
- Confirmation that the criteria under Article 83(2) of Regulation (EC) 726/2004 laying down Community procedures for the authorisation and supervision of medicinal products for human and veterinary use and establishing a European Medicines Agency are fulfilled and there is therefore a need to set up a compassionate use programme.
- An overview of the available (pre-) clinical data and, if necessary, quality data.
- An overview of any studies still running and how the company guarantees that the compassionate use programme will not interfere with this.
- Information about which phase the possible marketing authorisation process is in (there should be a successful registration in the near future).
- Whether a compassionate use programme has been started in other EU countries.
- Whether a marketing authorisation dossier has been submitted to the Committee for Medicinal Products for Human Use (CHMP) or whether the CHMP has given an opinion on a compassionate-use programme.

The MEB assesses the request (taking into account the CHMP recommendation where available). If the board decides to allow the request for a compassionate use programme, then the company is notified. The Healthcare Inspectorate is then informed that a compassionate use programme has been approved and the conditions under which this was done. If the board decides to reject the request then both the company and the Healthcare Inspectorate are informed of this decision.

Both positive and negative decisions of the board concerning the permission of a compassionate use programme are published on the MEB website. The Healthcare Inspectorate is responsible for supervising the implementation of the compassionate use programme.

## LICENSING

### 3. WHAT IS THE PROCEDURAL STRUCTURE REGARDING LICENSING A DRUG FOR DISTRIBUTION?

**Structure**

Applicants can request two forms of marketing authorisation for a drug:

- A national marketing authorisation.
- A European marketing authorisation.

There are four different procedures by which marketing authorisation can be obtained:

- The national procedure.
- Decentralised procedure (DCP).
- The centralised procedure (for a European marketing authorisation).
- The mutual recognition procedure (MRP).

**Regulatory authority**

The Medicines Evaluation Board (*College ter beoordeling van Geneesmiddelen*) (MEB) concentrates on the efficacy, safety and quality of the drug when performing its assessment. Homeopathic drugs on the other hand are assessed for safety and quality, but not for efficacy. Once the MEB has assessed and approved a medicinal product then it issues a marketing authorisation. The drug is then added to the Register of Medicinal Products. The "Summary of Product Characteristics" or product information is part of the marketing authorisation. This is the scientific text that contains all the key data about the product. Package leaflets are based on this text. Manufacturers submit a draft for these texts but the final version is drawn up by the MEB.

### 4. IS THERE A SIMPLIFIED LICENCE PROCEEDING, OR RELAXED LICENSING CONDITIONS, FOR DRUGS WHICH HAVE ALREADY BEEN LICENSED FOR DISTRIBUTION IN ANOTHER JURISDICTION?

As an EU member state, in The Netherlands, the simplified licence procedures of the decentralised procedure (DCP) and mutual recognition procedure (MRP) are available. These procedures are based on the principle that member states recognise marketing authorisations issued in another EU member state. The assessment report of the country that granted the first marketing authorisation for the drug in question is made available to other member states.

# THE NETHERLANDS

There is also a simplified procedure for parallel imports. Parallel imports are defined in Article 48 of the Medicines Act 2007 (*Geneesmiddelenwet*). This provision sets out the conditions for the parallel importation of medicines for which a marketing authorisation has already been granted in The Netherlands. A person in The Netherlands who wants to introduce a pharmaceutical product that has been put on the market in another member state of the EU or European Economic Area (EEA) can, at his request, be registered by the Medicines Evaluation Board (*College ter beoordeling van Geneesmiddelen*) (MEB) as a parallel marketing authorisation holder.

During the processing of a request for a parallel marketing authorisation, it must be evaluated whether the product that is to be parallel imported differs from the Dutch reference product in relation to safety and efficacy. The parallel product must be interchangeable with the Dutch reference product.

## 5. IS VIRTUAL DRUG DISTRIBUTION POSSIBLE FROM YOUR JURISDICTION?

Virtual drug distribution is possible. For example, a distributor with a Dutch wholesale licence could use a logistic service provider based in another country, for example Germany. The distributor can distribute drugs from the warehouse in Germany towards another country, for example the UK. Physical products never enter The Netherlands but are distributed using the authorisation obtained in The Netherlands.

## 6. WHAT IS THE PROCEDURE TO APPEAL (LEGAL REMEDY) A LICENSING DECISION?

The refusal to grant a marketing authorisation is a decision open to appeal (*Article 1:3, General Administrative Law Act (Awb)*).

The notice of appeal must be submitted to the authority that took the decision within six weeks of the date that the decision was announced. A decision must be reached within six weeks of receipt of the notice of appeal (*Article 7:10, Awb*). The decision can be postponed for a maximum of four weeks.

The Medicines Evaluation Board (*College ter beoordeling van Geneesmiddelen*) (MEB) has delegated hearings in the context of the appeals procedure to an internal committee, which is the appeals committee.

The appeals committee does not make any decisions during the hearing, but reports to the MEB in the form of an opinion. The MEB then reaches a decision on the appeal.

The MEB has drafted a policy appeal document (*Bezwaarschriftenprocedure*) (latest update 5 November 2012) on the subject. The decision of the MEB is open to appeal too. The notice of appeal must be submitted to the administrative court. The appeal must be lodged no later than six weeks after being notified of the decision of the MEB.

## 7. WHAT ARE THE COSTS OF OBTAINING LICENSING?

The fee for a first national application of a new active substance is EUR43,900. The fee for an application via the mutual recognition procedure (MRP) with The Netherlands as the reference member state (RMS) is EUR19,570. The fee for an application via the decentralised procedure (DCP) with The Netherlands as the RMS is EUR63,470.

All fees can be found on the website of the Medicines Evaluation Board (*College ter beoordeling van Geneesmiddelen*) (MEB) (*http://english.cbg-meb.nl/human/for-marketing-authorisation-holders/contents/technical-requirements/product-types-and-fees*).

## DISTRIBUTION TO CONSUMERS

### 8. WHAT ARE THE DIFFERENT CATEGORIES OF DRUGS FOR DISTRIBUTION?

The availability of drugs is divided into two main groups:

- Medicines available only on prescription from a doctor or specialist (PO).
- Medicines available without prescription (over-the-counter) (OTC).

The Medicines Evaluation Board (*College ter beoordeling van Geneesmiddelen*) (MEB) determines whether a drug requires a PO or not.

### 9. WHO IS AUTHORISED TO DISTRIBUTE PRESCRIPTION DRUGS AND OVER-THE-COUNTER DRUGS TO CONSUMERS?

**Prescription drugs**

Prescription drugs are only dispensed at pharmacies (*apotheken*).

Under certain conditions, a GP can distribute prescription drugs to patients, if they are a dispensing GP or for other GPs in case of emergency.

**Over-the-counter drugs**

Since the enactment of the Medicines Act 2007 (*Geneesmiddelenwet*), over-the-counter (OTC) medicines have been divided into three categories of legal status of supply. The aim of the legislator was to ensure a good balance between availability and risks. These categories are:

- Pharmacy only (PH): medicines with a relatively mild potential risk. These can only be obtained from a pharmacy.
- Pharmacy and drugstore (that does not require employment of a pharmacist) (PDO): medicines with a relatively low potential risk. These can only be obtained from a pharmacy or drugstore.
- Without restriction (GS): medicines with a very low potential risk. These drugs are available not only from pharmacists and chemists, but also from other sales channels such as supermarkets or service stations.

### 10. WHAT DRUGS CAN AN ATTENDING PHYSICIAN DISTRIBUTE AND UNDER WHAT CIRCUMSTANCES?

Under certain conditions, a GP can distribute prescription drugs to consumers, such as a dispensing GP or in an emergency.

### 11. WHO IS AUTHORISED TO PRESCRIBE PRESCRIPTION DRUGS TO CONSUMERS?

The provision of the authorisation to prescribe prescription drugs to consumers is regulated by the Individual Healthcare Professions Act (*Wet op de beroepen in de individuele gezondheidszorg*) (*Wet BIG*). According to the Wet BIG the following healthcare professionals can prescribe prescription drugs to consumers:

- Doctors, such as a GP or hospital doctor.

THE NETHERLANDS

- Dentists.
- Obstetricians.
- Physician assistants.
- Nurse specialists for somatic disorders.
- Specialised diabetes nurse.
- Specialised long nurse.
- Specialised oncology nurse.

## 12. IS DIRECT MAILING/DISTANCE SELLING OF DRUGS PERMITTED IN YOUR JURISDICTION?

### Conditions

Prescription drugs can only be prescribed by qualified physicians and can only be supplied to consumers by authorised pharmacists operating from qualified premises. Physicians can only prescribe prescription drugs online to patients if the physician and the patient have previously met in person and the medication history of the patient is available to the physician. If those requirements are met, drugs can, in principle, be ordered by a consumer using the internet, provided that the prescription is in writing, on paper and submitted to the pharmacist.

When offering drugs through the internet, Directive 2000/31/EC on certain legal aspects of information society services, in particular electronic commerce, in the Internal Market (Electronic Commerce Directive) and Directive 97/7/EC on the protection of consumers in respect of distance contracts (Distance Selling Directive) (both implemented in the Civil Code) provide that certain information must be provided, such as the contact details, price and main characteristics of the drugs.

### Cross-border sales

In principle it is possible to sell drugs over The Netherlands' border, but it depends on the local legislation.

## 13. WHAT REGULATORY AUTHORITY IS RESPONSIBLE FOR SUPERVISING DISTRIBUTION ACTIVITIES?

The Healthcare Inspectorate can monitor compliance with the marketing authorisations and can exercise its powers if required. Under the Medicines Act 2007 (*Geneesmiddelenwet*), the Healthcare Inspectorate can impose an "administrative fine" for any breach.

The Healthcare Inspectorate can impose a fine if, for example:

- The guidelines for preparation of medicines are not followed.
- A product is offered for sale without the required marketing authorisation.
- Trials of a drug are conducted without the necessary licences and permits.

The amount of the fine depends on a number of factors, including the:

- Seriousness of the incident.
- Potential risk to public health.
- Size of the company in question.

Indicative tables of the fine amounts can be found in the Policy Guidelines on Administrative Fines (*Beleidsregels Bestuurlijke Boete*).

### 14. WHAT IS THE PROCEDURE TO APPEAL (LEGAL REMEDY) A DISTRIBUTION DECISION?

Any party whose interests are directly affected by a decision (that is an interested party) can submit a notice of appeal (*Article 7:1, General Administrative Law Act (Awb)*). The notice of appeal must be submitted to the Healthcare Inspectorate within six weeks of the date that the decision was announced. A decision must be reached within six weeks of receipt of the notice of appeal (*Article 7:10, Awb*). The decision can be postponed for a maximum of four weeks.

The decision of the Healthcare Inspectorate is open to appeal too. The notice of appeal must be submitted to the administrative court. The appeal must be lodged no later than six weeks after being notified of the decision of the Healthcare Inspectorate.

### 15. WHAT ARE THE LEGAL CONSEQUENCES OF NON-COMPLIANCE WITH CONSUMER DISTRIBUTION LAWS?

Marketing a drug without a marketing authorisation is a criminal offence, which can be punished with imprisonment of up to six months or a fine of up to EUR450,000 depending on whether, for example:

- The breach was committed intentionally.
- It concerned a legal entity.
- The breach was a repeat offence.

The Minister of Health can impose an administrative fine for breach of the marketing authorisation's terms. The maximum fine under the Minister's policy rules for a first offence is EUR4,500 for infringements, except those concerning advertising, where the standard fine for large companies (50 employees or more) is EUR150,000. Indicative tables of the fine amounts can be found in the Policy Guidelines on Administrative Fines (*Beleidsregels Bestuurlijke Boete*).

## WHOLESALE DISTRIBUTION

### 16. WHAT IS THE LEGAL REGIME REGARDING WHOLESALE DISTRIBUTION OF DRUGS?

Distributors and importers of drugs intended for human use must hold a wholesale licence. A wholesale licence is required to be allowed to obtain, store or resell drugs within the European Economic Area (EEA) (that is, the EU countries plus Norway, Iceland and Liechtenstein) and the delivery of them. For the import of drugs from outside the EEA, a manufacturer permit is required. A wholesale dealer can provide drugs to any of the following parties:

- Pharmacists.
- GPs that administer his or her own pharmacy.
- Other holders of a wholesale license.

Farmatec, a unit of the Ministry of Health, deals with applications for manufacturing, import and wholesale authorisations, as well as the decision-making procedures relating to pricing and reimbursement. The Healthcare Inspectorate also advises the Minister of Health on issuing or revising manufacturing or wholesale licenses.

# THE NETHERLANDS

## 17. WHAT REGULATORY AUTHORITY IS RESPONSIBLE FOR SUPERVISING WHOLESALE DISTRIBUTION ACTIVITIES?

**Regulatory authority**

The Healthcare Inspectorate enforces this legal obligation in The Netherlands.

**Supervision**

The inspections are primarily concerned with compliance of the Good Distribution Practice (GDP) guidelines. The Healthcare Inspectorate focuses on storage and other elements of the GDP guidelines during inspection for the wholesale licence.

**Rights of appeal**

The notice of appeal must be submitted to the Healthcare Inspectorate within six weeks of the date that the decision was announced. A decision must be reached within six weeks of receipt of the notice of appeal (*Article 7:1, General Administrative Law Act (Awb)*). The decision can be postponed for a maximum of four weeks.

The decision of the Healthcare Inspectorate is open to appeal too. The notice of appeal must be submitted to the administrative court. The appeal must be lodged no later than six weeks after being notified of the decision of the Healthcare Inspectorate.

## 18. WHAT ARE THE LEGAL CONSEQUENCES OF NON-COMPLIANCE WITH WHOLESALE DISTRIBUTION LAWS?

Under the Medicines Act 2007 (*Geneesmiddelenwet*), the Healthcare Inspectorate can impose an administrative fine for any non-compliance. Indicative tables of the fine amounts are to be found in the Policy Guidelines on Administrative Fines (*Beleidsregels Bestuurlijke Boete*). Breach of the terms of a wholesale licence could lead to an administrative fine of up to EUR450,000. It is also considered as a crime punishable by imprisonment.

# MARKETING

## PROMOTION

## 19. WHAT IS THE GENERAL LEGAL REGIME FOR THE MARKETING OF DRUGS?

**Legal regime**

The marketing requirements set out in Directive 2001/83/EC on the Community code relating to medicinal products for human use (Code for Human Medicines Directive) have been implemented in Articles 83 to 96 of the Medicines Act 2007 (*Geneesmiddelenwet*). The Healthcare Inspectorate has also issued policy rules that further explain the rules stipulated in the Medicines Act regarding two subjects:

- Provision of inducements.

- Administrative penalty.

**Limits to marketing activities**

The Medicines Act sets out the following general limits to marketing activities directed at the general public and at healthcare professionals:

- Marketing of drugs for which a marketing authorisation has not been granted is prohibited.
- Prescription drugs cannot be marketed to the general public in any media.
- Marketing of prescription drugs to healthcare professionals is permitted, but is also subject to strict conditions.
- Marketing of over-the-counter (OTC) medicines to the general public is permitted, but is subject to strict conditions.
- Providing objective information on drugs is allowed, but is also subject to strict conditions.

### 20. ARE THERE OTHER CODES OF CONDUCT FOR THE MARKETING OF DRUGS (FOR EXAMPLE, BY PROFESSIONAL OR INDUSTRIAL ORGANISATIONS)?

The rules stipulated in the Medicines Act 2007 (*Geneesmiddelenwet*) have been included and refined in a voluntary Code of Conduct for Pharmaceutical Advertising (*Gedragscode Geneesmiddelenreclame*), a regulation of the self-governing Foundation for the Code for Pharmaceutical Advertising (*Stichting Code Geneesmiddelenreclame*) (CGR). The CGR has also issued explanatory notes regarding the way the Code is to be interpreted. The Code of Conduct on Marketing Directed at the General Public (*Code voor de Publieksreclame van Geneesmiddelen*) (CPG) forms an integral part of the Code of Conduct for Pharmaceutical Advertising.

## MARKETING TO CONSUMERS

### 21. WHAT IS THE LEGAL REGIME FOR MARKETING TO CONSUMERS?

**Legal regime**

The rules on marketing to consumers are set out in the Medicines Act 2007 (*Geneesmiddelenwet*) and the Code of Conduct on Marketing Directed at the General Public (*Code voor de Publieksreclame van Geneesmiddelen*)(CPG).

**Products**

The Medicines Act and CPG state that any marketing of drugs for which a marketing authorisation has not been granted is prohibited. An exception to this rule is for marketing in a strictly international context that is not at all directed at the Dutch market (for example, in scientific journals). Marketing of prescription drugs and over-the-counter (OTC) medicines that contain substances as referred to in list I and II of the Dutch Opium Act directed at consumers is prohibited under all circumstances. Marketing of homeopathic drugs without approved therapeutic indications is prohibited. Marketing of OTCs to consumers is permitted, but is subject to strict conditions.

## THE NETHERLANDS

### 22. WHAT KINDS OF MARKETING ACTIVITIES ARE PERMITTED IN RELATION TO CONSUMERS AND THE PRODUCTS WHICH MAY BE ADVERTISED TO THEM?

Marketing directed at consumers is only permitted for over-the-counter (OTC) medicines. Such marketing must:

- Make clear that it concerns an advertisement of a drug.
- Contain the name of the drug and a generic name of the active ingredient in the event the drug contains only one active ingredient.
- Contain information that is necessary for proper use of the drug, such as indications and contraindications.
- Contain an explicit request to read the instruction leaflet or the text on the outer package.

All marketing to consumers must be approved by the Inspection Board for the Advertising of Medicinal Products to the General Public (*Keuringsraad Openlijke Aanprijzing Geneesmiddelen*) (KOAG).

The Medicines Act 2007 (*Geneesmiddelenwet*) and Code of Conduct on Marketing Directed at the General Public (*Code voor de Publieksreclame van Geneesmiddelen*)(CPG) set out further rules on marketing to consumers. All the rules apply to marketing in writing. Some exceptions to the rules are made for marketing in radio broadcasts and for recollection advertisements. For example, the generic name of the active ingredient does not have to be mentioned in a radio broadcast advertisement. A recollection advertisement only needs to contain the name of the drug and, if applicable, the generic name of the active ingredient.

Pharmaceutical companies cannot sponsor activities of a third party (such as healthcare professionals, patient organisations and pharmaceutical service providers) that offers marketing of prescription drugs to consumers in return.

Testimonials are allowed as long as they represent an accurate overview of the user experience. Testimonials cannot contain any direct or indirect promotion by scientists, healthcare professionals or celebrities.

Pharmaceutical companies can provide "objective" information on prescription drugs. The CPG contains specific guidelines regarding provision of information to consumers on prescription drugs. These guidelines are applicable to the provision of objective information about a disease, its clinical features and treatment, whereby a prescription drug is mentioned directly or indirectly, as well as general and technical information about the use of a prescription drug without a specific request by a patient to provide such information. The second category of information cannot be generally available to the public. With the internet, such information must be protected by a password. All communication must mention the name and address of the person or entity responsible for the provision of this information and the date on which the information was updated for the last time.

### 23. IS IT PERMITTED TO PROVIDE CONSUMERS WITH FREE SAMPLES? ARE THERE PARTICULAR RESTRICTIONS ON SPECIAL OFFERS (FOR EXAMPLE, "BUY-ONE-GET-ONE-FREE")?

The Code of Conduct on Marketing Directed at the General Public (*Code voor de Publieksreclame van Geneesmiddelen*)(CPG) stipulates that marketing that does not encourage the rational use of a medicine is prohibited. Therefore it is not permitted to:

- Give samples of medicines free of charge.
- Make direct or indirect price offers, provide coupons or organise "refund campaigns".

THE NETHERLANDS

- Make the purchase of the medicine a condition for participation in competitions and games and to receive small gifts.

The distribution of small gifts is only permitted as long as there is no obligation to purchase and the words "no purchase obligation" are incorporated in a readable font in the corresponding advertisement.

Price offers such as "now for ...", "buy three, get fourth free", "in our shop only for..." or those that suggest a price offer by mentioning the price of the drug in a large font or by introducing the word "only" preceding the price, are prohibited. General (price) offers for certain ranges of drugs, such as savings systems or a reduction on the total range are permitted.

## 24. ARE THERE PARTICULAR RULES OF PRACTICE ON THE USE OF THE INTERNET/ SOCIAL MEDIA REGARDING DRUGS AND THEIR ADVERTISING?

The marketing of prescription drugs to consumers is prohibited under all circumstances. This rule applies to all marketing activities, including marketing via internet and social media.

The Code of Conduct on Marketing Directed at the General Public (*Code voor de Publieksreclame van Geneesmiddelen*)(CPG) contains specific rules regarding the provision of objective information on prescription drugs to consumers via the internet. For example, it can use the name of the pharmaceutical company, the indication or the trade mark of a prescription drug in the name of the website. This website can only contain a complete insert of the drug and clinical features that are concise and subordinate in nature. The website must also state the name and address of the person or entity responsible for the content of the website and the date on which the information was updated for the last time. The website can also contain an e-mail address that the consumers can use to request additional information. Hyperlinking is permitted so long as the website to which the link is provided complies with the rules of the CPG and it is obvious to the internet user that the original website is left on clicking on the hyperlink.

The Inspection Board for the Advertising of Medicinal Products to the General Public (*Keuringsraad Openlijke Aanprijzing Geneesmiddelen*) (KOAG) has issued specific guidelines on marketing prescription drugs to consumers via social media (*Handleiding KOAG/KAG inzake Digitale communicatie/Social Media*). The general rule of thumb is that the rules for offline advertising are also applicable to online communication. In practice this means that if a pharmaceutical company advertises via digital media (for example, via Facebook, LinkedIn or Twitter) then it has an obligation to pre-screen on a daily basis, and, if necessary, remove posts of the public that are in violation of the CPG. Any company or product related website, Facebook or LinkedIn page and any digital advertising has to be pre-approved by the KOAG.

For marketing over-the-counter (OTC) medicines to consumers via social media, the general rules set out by the Dutch Advertising Code Authority in the Advertising Code for Social Media (*Reclamecode Social Media*) apply. Generally, any advertising via social media must be clearly recognisable as such. Any relationship between the advertiser and the distributor of the post must be disclosed.

For further rules with regard to sale of drugs via the internet, see *Question 12*.

## 25. WHAT REGULATORY AUTHORITY IS RESPONSIBLE FOR SUPERVISING MARKETING ACTIVITIES TO CONSUMERS?

### Regulatory authority

The Healthcare Inspectorate is responsible for supervising marketing activities to consumers.

### Supervision

In practice, the Healthcare Inspectorate leaves it to the Inspection Board for the Advertising of Medicinal Products to the General Public (*Keuringsraad Openlijke Aanprijzing Geneesmiddelen*) (KOAG), the Inspection Board for the Promotion of Health Products (*Keuringsraad Aanprijzing Gezondheidsproducten*) (KAG) as well as the Advertising Code Committee (*Reclame Code Commissie*) (RCC) (both self-regulatory bodies) to supervise marketing activities directed at consumers. The RCC has jurisdiction over complaints filed against an advertisement by consumers. The Code Committee (*Codecommissie*) of the KOAG and KAG has jurisdiction over complaints filed by others than consumers.

### Rights of appeal

Appeals against the decisions of the RCC can be filed with the Board of Appeal of the RCC. Appeals against the decisions of the Code Committee of KOAG and KAG can be filed with the Committee of Appeal of the KOAG and KAG.

## 26. WHAT ARE THE LEGAL CONSEQUENCES OF NON-COMPLIANCE WITH CONSUMER MARKETING LAWS?

For violation of the Code of Conduct on Marketing Directed at the General Public (*Code voor de Publieksreclame van Geneesmiddelen*)(CPG), the Advertising Code Committee (*Reclame Code Commissie*) (RCC) will recommend that the advertiser discontinues the advertising. The compliance department monitors compliance with the RCC's decision. With non-compliance of the RCC decision, the RCC publishes its decision on its website under non-compliance, which will attract the attention of the authorities.

Where the Code Committee of the KOAG and the KAG decides on whether to allow the complaint it can impose disciplinary measures on the advertiser, ranging from a reprimand to an order to rectify the advertisement and a recall of all material containing the advertisement. The Code Committee of the KOAG and KAG cannot impose a fine. However, it can decide that the advertiser has to refund the court fee of the complainant (amounting to EUR500) and/or has to compensate the costs of the assessment of the complaint made by the Code Committee. These costs are set on a yearly basis.

Although the KOAG and KAG and the RCC are primarily responsible for supervising marketing activities directed towards consumers, the Minister of Health is authorised by the Medicines Act 2007 (*Geneesmiddelenwet*) to impose an administrative fine up to EUR450,000 for violation of the provisions of the Medicines Act regarding marketing to consumers. The maximum fine under the Minister's policy rules for a first offence is set at EUR150,000. Indicative tables of the standard fine amounts can be found in the Policy Guidelines on Administrative Fines (*Beleidsregels Bestuurlijke Boete*). Where the advertiser is fined twice for the same violation within a period of 24 months, this violation constitutes a criminal act and can be punished by six months imprisonment or a criminal fine amounting to EUR8,100.

## MARKETING TO PROFESSIONALS

### 27. WHAT KINDS OF MARKETING ACTIVITIES ARE PERMITTED IN RELATION TO PROFESSIONALS?

The following types of marketing activities with respect to professionals are permitted:

- Marketing of prescription drugs to healthcare professionals is permitted, but is subject to strict conditions.
- Marketing of non-interventional studies that are not subject to the Medical Scientific Research with Humans Act (*Wet Medisch Wetenschappelijk Onderzoek met Mensen*) (WMO) and therefore do not need to be approved in advance by an official Medical Ethic Testing Committee (*Medisch Ethische Toetsing Commissie*) (METC) is permitted, but is subject to strict conditions.

### 28. ARE THERE ANY RESTRICTIONS ON MARKETING TO PROFESSIONALS?

**Marketing activities**

The following types of marketing activities to professionals are not permitted:

- Any marketing of drugs for which a marketing authorisation has not been granted is prohibited. The one exception to this rule is for marketing to professionals in a strictly international context, that is not in any way directed at the Dutch market (for example, in scientific journals).
- Sponsoring of individual healthcare professionals is prohibited (*see Question 31*).
- Provision of inducements, meaning holding out the prospect of, offering or granting money or valuable goods or services for the purpose of inducement of prescription, supply or use of specific drugs, is prohibited. The Netherlands Healthcare Inspectorate (*Inspectie voor de Gezondheidszorg*) (IGZ) has issued policy rules that relate to the provision of inducements. Exceptions are made for the provision of hospitality, gifts, discounts and bonuses and services (*see Question 31*).

**Frequency**

The Code of Conduct on Marketing Directed at the General Public (*Code voor de Publieksreclame van Geneesmiddelen*)(CPG) contains some general rules on promotional activities by sales representatives. Medical sales representatives must ensure that the frequency, scheduling and duration of the visits to healthcare professionals or hospitals, as well as the manner in which these visits occur, do not cause any inconvenience.

Oral advertising by telephone is not permitted, except by prior appointment with the relevant healthcare professional.

**Provision of hospitality**

The Medicines Act 2007 (*Geneesmiddelenwet*), the CPG and policy rules regarding provision of inducements, set out restrictions on meetings or manifestations with groups of professionals and the provision of hospitality.

Under the CPG a distinction is made between the provision of hospitality at meetings and at manifestations:

- A meeting is an event with a scientific objective that has been accredited by a recognised body, such as a scientific organisation. If the event has not been accredited, it can still qualify as a meeting if either:
  - the organisation is independent;
  - it is organised by a pharmaceutical company and the Foundation for the Code for Pharmaceutical Advertising (*Stichting Code Geneesmiddelenreclame*) (CGR) has first reviewed and approved its content and hospitality to be provided there.
- A manifestation is an event with a programme that provides for the information needs of healthcare professionals but does not qualify as a meeting.

The CPG provides that the place, duration and date of the meeting or manifestation cannot lead to confusion or doubt regarding its nature. Hospitality has to fulfil the following requirements:

- It must remain within reasonable limits.
- It must be subordinate to the main purpose of the meeting or manifestation.
- It cannot be provided to anyone other than participants of the scientific part of the meeting or manifestation.

Hospitality in meetings held in The Netherlands is deemed to remain within reasonable bounds if either:

- The costs do not exceed EUR500 per occasion and EUR1,500 per year per healthcare professional and per therapeutic class (the limit of EUR1,500 per year includes amounts received for a different meeting organised by a third party for the same therapeutic class).
- The healthcare professional bears at least 50% of all the costs (travel and accommodation and the costs of participation).

Hospitality at manifestations held in The Netherlands is within reasonable bounds when the costs for the account of the pharmaceutical company do not exceed EUR75 per healthcare professional per therapeutic classification per occasion and EUR225 per year.

For providing a meal in The Netherlands, the limit is set at EUR75.

These rules apply both to meetings and manifestations directly or indirectly organised by a pharmaceutical company and meetings or manifestations that are sponsored by a pharmaceutical company.

The provision of hospitality (unless travel and accommodation costs are not compensated), must be set out in writing in advance and must contain an exact description of the project or activity and the rights and obligations of the parties. The contract also must specify the location, date and length of the meeting or manifestation as well as which costs are compensated. Information about agreements exceeding a value of EUR500 a year must be made available to the Healthcare Transparency Register (*Transparantieregister Zorg*) within three months of the end of the calendar year and be disclosed on its website.

### 29. WHAT INFORMATION IS IT LEGALLY REQUIRED TO INCLUDE IN ADVERTISING TO PROFESSIONALS?

According to the Foundation for the Code for Pharmaceutical Advertising (*Stichting Code Geneesmiddelenreclame*) (CGR), all marketing material in written form must state:

- The name of the drug.
- The name and address of the entity responsible for putting the drug on the market.
- The qualitative and quantitative composition of the active ingredients.

- The pharmacotherapeutic group, where applicable.
- The pharmaceutical form and the main therapeutic indications.
- The most important side effects (based on frequency and gravity).
- The most important warnings (precautionary measures regarding use).
- All contra-indications.
- The supply qualification of the drug.
- Conditions for reimbursement by social security bodies.
- The date on which it was drawn up or last revised.

Some exceptions to the above-mentioned requirements are made for recollection advertisements.

All marketing materials in written form have to be approved by an internal scientific department of the pharmaceutical company.

## 30. ARE THERE RULES ON COMPARISONS WITH OTHER PRODUCTS THAT ARE PARTICULARLY APPLICABLE TO DRUGS?

The Code of Conduct on Marketing Directed at the General Public (*Code voor de Publieksreclame van Geneesmiddelen*)(CPG) contains specific rules on comparative advertising. Any comparative advertising that explicitly or by implication makes reference to a competitor or competing drugs or substances must comply with the following conditions. The comparison:

- Cannot be misleading.
- Cannot be detrimental to the value of the drugs in question.
- Cannot discredit or denigrate the competitor or its trademarks or trade names.
- Cannot create confusion between the drugs and their trade marks or between the pharmaceutical companies involved and their trade names.
- Cannot present the drugs in question as imitations or replicas of drugs that are protected by trade marks of trade names.
- Cannot take unfair advantage of the reputation of a trade mark, trade name or other distinguishing marks of a competitor.
- Must be demonstrably scientifically correct and in line with the most recent state of the science (this must be demonstrated by means of one or more scientific studies).
- Must be complete with regard to the effects, side-effects, indications and contra-indications and all other relevant information.

## 31. WHAT OTHER ITEMS, FUNDING OR SERVICES ARE PERMITTED TO BE PROVIDED TO PROFESSIONALS?

### Discounts

Discounts in the form of gifts (such as bonus deliveries of other drugs or other products from a different industry) are prohibited. This rule does not apply to discounts made for the delivery of drugs by the pharmaceutical companies to healthcare professionals (such as pharmacists and general practitioners), provided that it concerns bonus deliveries of the same drug or a discount in cash, insofar as explicitly stated in writing (for example, in an invoice or a credit note).

Generally, pharmaceutical companies must refrain from:

- Offering or promising gifts.
- Waives of payment.
- Bonuses.
- Any other benefits in cash or in kind.

It is also not permissible to make the price of a certain drug dependent on the purchase of other drugs or products. This does not apply to gifts that are of minor value and are relevant to the practice of the healthcare professional. The Foundation for the Code for Pharmaceutical Advertising (*Stichting Code Geneesmiddelenreclame*) (CGR) has indicated that a gift is presumed to be minor in value if the value does not exceed EUR50 (based on shop value and including VAT) per time, with a maximum of EUR150 per year, per healthcare professional, per pharmaceutical company and per therapeutic class.

**Free samples**

Provision of free samples of drugs to healthcare professionals is prohibited, unless:

- A healthcare professional qualified to prescribe drugs has filed a request, personally signed and dated, to that extent with the pharmaceutical company.
- The sample is no larger than the smallest presentation of the drug available on the market.
- A healthcare professional cannot receive more than two samples of the same drug per calendar year.
- The sample itself is marked with the text that it is "free of charge" and "not for sale".
- A copy of the summary of product characteristics of the drug is provided with the sample.
- The entity or person providing the samples must keep records of the professionals that requested the samples, on which date and in which quantities for a period of five years.

Each healthcare professional can only receive free samples of a particular drug for two years after he first requested samples of that particular drug. It is also prohibited to provide free samples of drugs containing substances as referred to in lists I and II of the Dutch Opium Act to healthcare professionals.

**Sponsorship of professionals**

The Code of Conduct on Marketing Directed at the General Public (*Code voor de Publieksreclame van Geneesmiddelen*)(CPG) contains specific rules regarding sponsorship. These rules apply to sponsorship by pharmaceutical companies of professionals and associations of professionals. The CPG stipulates that the provision of financial support or any other monetary support for individual professionals, with the exception of sponsorship of a doctoral thesis, is prohibited unless it meets strict conditions as set out below. Any type of support (for example, a donation) is qualified as sponsoring under these rules.

Sponsoring of healthcare professionals is allowed under the following strict conditions. Briefly, these conditions relate to sponsoring, transparency and integrity. The parties involved must be able to demonstrate that the purpose of sponsoring is:

- To support innovative and/or quality-improving activities.
- Directed at the direct or indirect improvement of the healthcare of patients or the promotion of medical science.
- Does not concern activities that can be funded in part or in whole in any other way (for example, by the government, healthcare insurers or subsidies).

Sponsoring cannot, under any circumstances, lead to personal gain of the healthcare professional or constitute an inducement to recommend, prescribe, purchase, supply, sell or administer specific drugs.

The sponsorship contract must be set out in writing before the sponsoring commences and must contain an exact description of the project or activity and the rights and obligations of the parties. Structural sponsorship exclusivity (a conscious decision to limit sponsoring to only one sponsor) is prohibited. The CPG also stipulates that certain information about sponsorship contracts exceeding a value of EUR500 per calendar year must be made available to the Healthcare Transparency Register within three months of the end of the calendar year and will be disclosed on its website.

**Other items, funding or services**

Pharmaceutical companies can use healthcare professionals as consultants and advisors. Compensation for such services must be reasonable and must reflect the fair market value of the services provided. A written contract must be agreed in advance of the commencement of the services and must specify the purpose and the nature of the services to be provided.

The CPG stipulates that if the value of the contract exceeds EUR500 per calendar year then information regarding the contract must be made available to the Healthcare Transparency Register within three months of the end of the calendar year and will be disclosed on its website.

## 32. WHAT REGULATORY AUTHORITY IS RESPONSIBLE FOR SUPERVISING MARKETING ACTIVITIES REGARDING PROFESSIONALS?

**Regulatory authority**

The Healthcare Inspectorate is responsible for supervising marketing activities to healthcare professionals.

**Supervision**

In practice, the Healthcare Inspectorate leaves it to the self-regulatory body that is the Code Committee of the Foundation for the Code for Pharmaceutical Advertising (*Stichting Code Geneesmiddelenreclame*) (CGR) to supervise marketing activities regarding professionals.

**Rights of appeal**

Appeals against the decisions of the Code Committee of CGR can be filed with the Committee of Appeal of CGR.

## 33. WHAT ARE THE LEGAL CONSEQUENCES IN CASE OF NON-COMPLIANCE WITH PROFESSIONAL MARKETING LAWS?

Where the Code Committee of the Foundation for the Code for Pharmaceutical Advertising (*Stichting Code Geneesmiddelenreclame*) (CGR) decides to allow the complaint, it can impose disciplinary measures on the advertiser, ranging from a reprimand to an order to rectify the advertisement and a recall of all advertising material containing the advertisement. The Code Committee of CGR cannot impose a fine. However, it can decide that the advertiser has to compensate the costs of the assessment of the complaint made by the Code Committee of CGR and to refund the court fee of the complainant (ranging from nothing to EUR1,250 in the first instance, depending on the persona of the complainant). The costs of assessment of the case are set on a yearly basis.

Although the CGR is primarily responsible for supervising marketing activities directed towards professionals, the Minister of Health is authorised by the Medicines Act 2007 (*Geneesmiddelenwet*) to impose an administrative fine up to EUR450,000 for violation of the provisions of the Medicines Act regarding marketing to professionals. The maximum fine under the Minister's policy rules for a first offence is set at EUR150,000. Indicative tables of the standard fine amounts can be found in the Policy Guidelines on Administrative Fines (*Beleidsregels Bestuurlijke Boete*). If the advertiser is fined twice for the same violation within a period of 24 months, this violation constitutes a criminal act and can be punished by six months imprisonment or a criminal fine amounting to EUR8,100.

## ENGAGEMENT WITH PATIENT ORGANISATIONS

### 34. WHAT KINDS OF ACTIVITIES ARE PERMITTED IN RELATION TO ENGAGEMENT WITH PATIENT ORGANISATIONS? WHAT ARE THE RESTRICTIONS THAT ARE IMPOSED ON RELATIONSHIP WITH PATIENT ORGANISATIONS?

Because members of the general public participate in patient organisations, the general rules on marketing to consumers are applicable. Therefore, only the following activities are permitted with respect to engagement with patient organisations:

- Marketing of over-the-counter (OTCs) is permitted under strict conditions.
- Provision of objective information on drugs is permitted under strict conditions.
- Financial support (for example, sponsoring, subsidising or support in kind) is permitted, but is subject to strict conditions. Generally, financial support cannot compromise the independence of the patient organisation, its policy or activities.

Prescription drugs cannot be marketed through patient organisations under any circumstances. Sponsorship exclusivity is not permitted, unless it concerns a specific, short term project, such as a publication or organising a meeting.

## REFORM

### 35. ARE THERE ANY PLANS TO REFORM THE LAW ON THE DISTRIBUTION AND PROMOTION OF DRUGS IN YOUR JURISDICTION?

The Code of Conduct on Marketing Directed at the General Public (*Code voor de Publieksreclame van Geneesmiddelen*)(CPG) is reviewed by the Foundation for the Code for Pharmaceutical Advertising (*Stichting Code Geneesmiddelenreclame*) (CGR) on a regular basis. The most recent changes were made in January 2015 as a result of the implementation of the Disclosure Code of the European Federation of Pharmaceutical Industries and Associations (EFPIA). No specific reforms of the CPG are planned in the foreseeable future.

# POLAND

Marcin Matczak, Tomasz Kaczyński and Krzysztof Kumala,
DOMAŃSKI ZAKRZEWSKI PALINKA SP. K.

## DISTRIBUTION

### PRE-CONDITIONS FOR DISTRIBUTION

**1. WHAT ARE THE LEGAL PRE-CONDITIONS FOR A DRUG TO BE DISTRIBUTED WITHIN THE JURISDICTION?**

#### Authorisation

In principle, only products which have obtained a marketing authorisation can be distributed in Poland. Prior to the distribution of a drug, the marketing authorisation holder (MAH) must apply for an authorisation from the President of the Office for Registration of Medicinal Products, Medical Devices and Biocidal Products (Registration Office).

Authorisation is usually issued for five years, with a possible extension or shortening of the period on an application of the marketing authorisation holder.

Obtaining the authorisation is subject to a fee, as specified by the appropriate regulation of the Minister of Health.

#### Exceptions

Products which are exempt from the authorisation include:

- Medicinal products used by manufacturers.
- Medicinal products used in clinical trials, registered in the Central Register of Clinical Trials.
- Pharmaceutical raw materials produced for further use in the manufacturing process.

In exceptional circumstances, medicinal products can also be introduced on the Polish market through direct import, on conditional authorisation or during a state of emergency (see Question 4).

**2. DO ANY TYPES OF NAMED PATIENT AND/OR COMPASSIONATE USE PROGRAMMES OPERATE? IF SO, WHAT ARE THE REQUIREMENTS FOR PRE-LAUNCH ACCESS?**

At present, compassionate use programmes are not operated in Poland. The institution of compassionate use as outlined in Regulation (EC) 726/2004 on the authorisation and supervision of medicinal products and establishing a European Medicines Agency (EMA Regulation) has not been implemented, nor has Article 5(1) of Directive 2001/83/EC on the Community code relating to medicinal products for human use (Code for Human Medicines

Directive). The Ministry of Health is working on an amendment to the Pharmaceutical Law Act of 6 September 2001 (Pharmaceutical Act) relating to clinical trials, which aims at the implementation of the EMA Regulation. It is understood that the project, which is to be published by the end of 2015, will introduce compassionate use programmes. Regardless of the provisions of the Pharmaceutical Act, the Minister of Health may issue a decision approving the use of an unregistered medicinal product in certain cases and/or within a compassionate use programme in individual cases justified by a threat to the patient's health or life.

## LICENSING

### 3. WHAT IS THE PROCEDURAL STRUCTURE REGARDING LICENSING A DRUG FOR DISTRIBUTION?

**Structure**

Applications for marketing authorisations must be submitted to the President of the Registration Office. A detailed description of the content of the application is laid down in the Pharmaceutical Act.

Submission of the application begins the administrative proceedings for marketing authorisation. The proceedings must be concluded within 210 days from the date of the submission.

A template of the application was issued in a regulation of 10 January on the specimen application for an authorisation for a medicinal product issued by the Minister of Health. The applicant must pay a fee for an application for authorisation.

Applications for parallel import permits must also be submitted to the President of the Registration Office, accompanied by:

- The packaging design and the content of the label.
- A copy of the manufacturing permit issued by the responsible body of the relevant EU member state.
- Confirmation of the fee paid for the application.

In the case of medicinal products registered under the centralised procedure, the European Medicines Agency issues a permit for parallel distribution from the member state where such a product was marketed.

**Regulatory authority**

The national body responsible for issuing marketing authorisations, that is, licensing drugs for distribution, is the Office for Registration. Licences are issued by way of an administrative decision of the President of the Office.

### 4. IS THERE A SIMPLIFIED LICENCE PROCEEDING, OR RELAXED LICENSING CONDITIONS, FOR DRUGS WHICH HAVE ALREADY BEEN LICENSED FOR DISTRIBUTION IN ANOTHER JURISDICTION?

The following procedures are available:

- **Decentralised procedure.** Under this procedure, a previously unregistered product is registered in a member state (reference state), and subsequently registered in secondary member states where the applicant would like the product to be marketed. This procedure is used as an alternative to the centralised procedure (*see Question 3*) and enables a product to be registered in selected member states at the same time. The President of the Registration Office must issue a marketing authorisation within 30 days after acknowledging an assessment report prepared by the relevant body of the reference country.
- **Mutual recognition procedure.** This procedure applies where a medicinal product is marketed in the EU and the applicant applies for it to be registered in another member state. The President of the Registration Office must issue the marketing authorisation within 30 days after acknowledging an assessment report prepared by the relevant body of the reference country.
- **Direct import.** Under this procedure, a medicinal product that is unavailable in Poland but authorised in another country may be directly imported to Poland if it is required for saving the life or health of the patient and there is no existing equivalent with marketing authorisation on the Polish market. In such a case, the hospital or doctor in charge must make an official request for the product. This then needs to be endorsed by the national or district consultant of the appropriate speciality.
- **State of emergency.** Under Polish pharmaceutical law, in the event of a natural disaster or other danger to the life and health of the people, the Minister of Health can issue an authorisation for the import of medicinal products, subject to conditions specified by law.
- **Conditional authorisation.** The European Commission can grant conditional authorisation in the case of the outbreak of diseases for which a limited number of therapies is available on the market, when full clinical data is not yet available.
- **Generic drugs.** Polish pharmaceutical law allows a relaxation of rules with regard to registration of generic drugs. There is no requirement to provide reports on mandatory trials when applying for a marketing authorisation, under the condition that the reference medicinal product (of which the given generic drug is the equivalent) has already received such authorisation.

## 5. IS VIRTUAL DRUG DISTRIBUTION POSSIBLE FROM YOUR JURISDICTION?

Polish pharmaceutical law does not explicitly prohibit the virtual distribution of drugs. However, in practice, the pharmaceutical supervision authorities hold that virtual distribution is impossible, and they require that the invoiced recipient be the entity to which the product is delivered. In this way, the pharmaceutical wholesalers must physically trade in medicinal products, rather than merely issuing sales invoices. The view of the authorities is that the invoice must "follow" the goods.

## 6. WHAT IS THE PROCEDURE TO APPEAL (LEGAL REMEDY) A LICENSING DECISION?

Under Polish pharmaceutical law, a marketing authorisation is issued by the President of the Registration Office through an administrative decision. Therefore, the appropriate appeal mechanism in such cases will be based on the Polish Code of Administrative Procedure. A decision of the President of the Registration Office can be challenged in the Voivodeship Administrative Court, or subsequently by a complaint lodged with the Supreme Administrative Court.

## 7. WHAT ARE THE COSTS OF OBTAINING LICENSING?

The cost of obtaining a marketing authorisation for medicinal products is provided for in a regulation issued by the Minister of Health on the method of determining and the payment of fees for the marketing authorisation of a medicinal product.

The fee for the application for a marketing authorisation of one medicinal product has been set at PLN87,500 for registration in the centralised procedure.

In the case of registering products from parallel import, the cost of obtaining a licence at the Registration Office was set at PLN6,388.

## DISTRIBUTION TO CONSUMERS

## 8. WHAT ARE THE DIFFERENT CATEGORIES OF DRUGS FOR DISTRIBUTION?

The categories of drugs for distribution are differentiated on the basis of their legal status. Pharmaceutical law establishes the following categories of medicinal products:

- Available without prescription (over-the-counter (OTC)).
- Available on prescription only (Rp).
- Available on prescription only, for restricted use (Rpz).
- Available on prescription only, containing narcotic drugs or psychotropic substances specified in separate regulations (Rpw).
- For hospital use only (Lz).

## 9. WHO IS AUTHORISED TO DISTRIBUTE PRESCRIPTION DRUGS AND OVER-THE-COUNTER DRUGS TO CONSUMERS?

### Prescription drugs

Retail distribution of prescription drugs is conducted by pharmacies and pharmacy outlets. Under pharmaceutical law, an entity intending to open a pharmacy or a pharmacy outlet must apply for an authorisation from the district pharmaceutical inspector.

### Over-the-counter (OTC) drugs

OTC drugs can be distributed by pharmacies and pharmacy outlets, as in the case of prescription drugs. Additionally, pharmaceutical law allows certain OTC drugs to be distributed by:

- Herbal and medical shops.
- Specialised stores for medical supplies.
- General shops.

The criteria regarding appropriate premises and equipment for non-pharmacy outlets, as well as qualifications required for the persons dispensing the products, are regulated in detail in regulations issued by the Minister of Health. In addition, lists of OTC medicinal products eligible for distribution by non-pharmacy outlets are published in the Ministry of Health regulation issued on 22 October 2010.

## 10. WHAT DRUGS CAN AN ATTENDING PHYSICIAN DISTRIBUTE AND UNDER WHAT CIRCUMSTANCES?

The distribution of medicinal products must always be conducted on the basis of the provisions of the Pharmaceutical Act. The direct use on patients of medicinal products and medicinal products which are part of anti-shock treatment kits, intended to be used in conjunction with the medicinal service provided, must not be treated as retail trade. The Ministry of Health regulation issued on 12 January 2011 specifies the:

- Rules on distribution including circumstances in which drugs can be distributed.
- List of medicinal products which can be supplied on an as-needed basis.
- List of medicinal products included in life-saving anti-shock treatment kits.

The lists of these medicinal products are categorised separately for attending physicians and nurses/midwives.

## 11. WHO IS AUTHORISED TO PRESCRIBE PRESCRIPTION DRUGS TO CONSUMERS?

The only persons authorised to prescribe prescription drugs to patients are doctors and dentists (*Act of 5 December 1996 on the professions of doctor and dentist*). However, from 1 January 2016 nurses and midwives will also be able to prescribe prescription drugs.

In special cases, in the event of a sudden threat to life or health, a pharmacy manager can dispense drugs on a pharmaceutical prescription only and without a doctor's or dentist's prescription. Such prescriptions can apply only to medicinal products normally available on prescription in the smallest therapeutic packs, excluding narcotic substances, psychotropic substances and I-R group precursors.

## 12. IS DIRECT MAILING/DISTANCE SELLING OF DRUGS PERMITTED IN YOUR JURISDICTION?

**Conditions**

The direct mailing of drugs is permitted in Poland.

Retail pharmacies and dispensaries are allowed to sell non-prescription medicinal products by mail order. Specific conditions related to the direct mailing of drugs (that is, the methods by which medicinal products are supplied to the recipient, the conditions to be met concerning the premises of retail pharmacies and dispensaries) are designated in the Ministry of Health regulation of 26 March 2015 on the direct mailing of drugs. Information about retail pharmacies and dispensaries that carry out the direct mailing of drugs is placed in the National Register of Authorisations for Running Retail Pharmacies and Dispensaries and in the Register of Consents to Run Hospital Pharmacies, Institutional Pharmacies and Hospital Pharmacy Departments. Any website on which medicinal products are offered for sale by mail order must display the logo referred to in paragraph 85c(3) of Directive 2001/83/EC on the Community code relating to medicinal products for human use.

**Cross-border sales**

The direct mailing of drugs is possible beyond the borders of Poland.

### 13. WHAT REGULATORY AUTHORITY IS RESPONSIBLE FOR SUPERVISING DISTRIBUTION ACTIVITIES?

The State Pharmaceutical Inspectorate, including the Main Pharmaceutical Inspector and Voivodeships Pharmaceutical Inspectors, is mainly responsible for supervising distribution activities. The duties of the State Pharmaceutical Inspectorate include:

- Inspecting the quality of medicinal products in trade.
- Inspecting pharmacies and other entities conducting retail trade and wholesale distribution of medicinal products.
- Inspecting the quality of prescription and over-the-counter drugs prepared in pharmacies.
- Inspecting the labelling and advertising of medicinal products.
- Supervising the export of medicinal products from Poland.

The President of the Registration Office has additional duties in connection with the supervision of distribution activities, such as:

- Gathering reports on single occurrences of adverse reactions reported, among others, by patients.
- Analysing and preparing reports, including cause and effect assessments of all the single occurrences of adverse reactions.
- Publishing announcements on the safety of use of medicinal products intended for and directly addressed to medicinal practitioners or the general public.
- Issuing permission for the parallel import of medicinal products.

If there are any suspicions that a specific medicinal product does not meet the approved requirements:

- The voivodeship pharmaceutical inspector issues decisions on suspending the turnover of particular batches of a medicinal product within its voivodeship.
- The Main Pharmaceutical Inspector issues decisions on suspending the turnover of particular batches of a medicinal product in the entire country.

When such decisions are announced, the turnover of the particular batches of a specific medicinal product is suspended in all wholesale stores and pharmacies, until laboratory tests have been conducted on them.

If the laboratory test results confirm a quality defect, the Main Pharmaceutical Inspector issues a decision to recall the medicinal product.

Further, in the case of a justified suspicion that a particular medicinal product could cause severe adverse reactions, the Main Pharmaceutical Inspectorate can issue a decision (at the request of the President of the Registration Office):

- Ordering a temporary prohibition on marketing a specific product.
- Suspending the turnover of a specific product.
- Recalling a specific product.

Additionally, if there is a possible risk to public health caused by medicinal products, the Main Pharmaceutical Inspector, at the request of the Minister of Health or the President of the Registration Office, can issue such a decision.

## 14. WHAT IS THE PROCEDURE TO APPEAL (LEGAL REMEDY) A DISTRIBUTION DECISION?

For every decision issued by the State Pharmaceutical Inspectorate, there is a legal remedy (*Polish Code of Administrative Procedure*).

Regarding a decision of a voivodeship pharmaceutical inspector, there is a right to appeal to the Main Pharmaceutical Inspector, whose decision can further be appealed against in the provincial administrative court.

While a decision of the Main Pharmaceutical Inspector cannot be appealed against, a motion for it to be reconsidered can be brought. After a second decision of the Main Pharmaceutical Inspector it is also possible to appeal to the Voivodeship Administrative Court in Warsaw.

## 15. WHAT ARE THE LEGAL CONSEQUENCES OF NON-COMPLIANCE WITH CONSUMER DISTRIBUTION LAWS?

The legal consequences for non-compliance with consumer distribution laws vary and depend on the kind of inconsistency.

Some have already been mentioned (*see Question 13*):

- Temporary prohibition on marketing a specific product.
- Decisions on suspending the distribution of particular batches of a medicinal product.
- Decisions to recall a medicinal product.

The State Pharmaceutical Inspectorate can also refuse or revoke authorisation to carry out retail trade or wholesale distribution. The Pharmaceutical Act stipulates penal provisions and fines for non-compliance with consumer distribution laws.

## WHOLESALE DISTRIBUTION

## 16. WHAT IS THE LEGAL REGIME REGARDING WHOLESALE DISTRIBUTION OF DRUGS?

Wholesale distribution of medicinal products can only be carried out by authorised pharmaceutical wholesalers. Before the wholesale distribution of medicinal products can commence, the authorisation of the Main Pharmaceutical Inspector is required. The wholesale distribution of narcotic and psychotropic substances and I-R group precursors requires an additional authorisation. There is a fee charged for the grant of authorisation to carry out the wholesale distribution of medicinal products.

A wholesaler can only supply medicinal products to a producer, importer, other wholesalers, pharmacies and other authorised entities; direct supply to the general public is excluded.

The Pharmaceutical Act stipulates specific requirements with respect to applying for authorisation to carry out wholesale distribution. There is also a need to obtain an opinion on the suitability of the premises, issued by the State Sanitary Inspection appropriate for the location of the warehouse. Additionally, during the authorisation procedure, the Main Pharmaceutical Inspector assesses the suitability of the premises with respect to carrying out wholesale distribution of medicinal products.

A wholesaler engaged in the wholesale distribution of medicinal products must have the appropriate facilities for this activity, employ a qualified staff and fulfil the obligations set forth in the Pharmaceutical Act and in accordance with the principles of good distribution practice. Some details are included in European principles and guidelines on good manufacturing practices in relation to medicinal products.

The inspector of wholesale distribution from the Main Pharmaceutical Inspectorate must verify at intervals not exceeding three years that a given wholesale distributor meets the obligations imposed by applicable laws. In the event of a justified suspicion that a wholesale distributor is not applying mandatory requirements, an immediate inspection can be carried out.

The Main Pharmaceutical Inspector will revoke the authorisation for operating a pharmaceutical wholesale facility if the business entity concerned conducts sales of medicinal products without a marketing authorisation, or breaches its obligation to conduct retail trade in reimbursed medicinal products, as required by patients' quantitative needs.

The Pharmaceutical Act also specifies other circumstances in which the Main Pharmaceutical Inspector can revoke an authorisation, for example:

- Despite notice, the wholesaler makes it impossible or difficult for the Main Pharmaceutical Inspectorate to carry out its obligations.
- The wholesaler does not comply with storage conditions set out in the marketing authorisation.
- The wholesaler does not comply with organisational obligations regarding the warehouse, or stocks products obtained from unauthorised entities.

## 17. WHAT REGULATORY AUTHORITY IS RESPONSIBLE FOR SUPERVISING WHOLESALE DISTRIBUTION ACTIVITIES?

### Regulatory authority

The Main Pharmaceutical Inspector is principally responsible for supervising wholesale distribution activities. The Main Pharmaceutical Inspector issues authorisations for the wholesale distribution of medicinal products; it may also refuse or revoke such authorisations. Other duties of the Main Pharmaceutical Inspector are to inspect the wholesale distribution of medicinal products, to issue certificates of compliance with good manufacturing practice, and to supervise the export of medicinal products from Poland. New legal rules require that wholesalers intending to export medicinal products from Poland will in some cases need to obtain clearance for export from the Main Pharmaceutical Inspector.

The Chairman of the Office for Registration of Medicinal Products, Medical Products and Biocidal Products issues permits for the parallel import of medicinal products.

The Ministry of Health is responsible for supervision of the distribution of reimbursed medicinal products, in amounts as required by patients' quantitative needs.

### Supervision

The entities responsible for supervising wholesale distribution activities are the Main Pharmaceutical Inspector, the Chairman of the Registration Office, and the Minister of Health (*see above*).

Supervision depends on the individual case and the kind of medicinal product.

POLAND

**Rights of appeal**

There is no right of appeal with respect to a decision of the Main Pharmaceutical Inspector, the Chairman of the Office for Registration of Medicinal Products, Medical Products and Biocidal Products or the Ministry of Health; the applicable law (the Polish Code of Administrative Procedure) does however allow a motion for it to be reconsidered. After a second decision there is also the possibility to appeal to the Voivodeship Administrative Court in Warsaw, and later even lodge a complaint with the Supreme Administrative Court.

### 18. WHAT ARE THE LEGAL CONSEQUENCES OF NON-COMPLIANCE WITH WHOLESALE DISTRIBUTION LAWS?

Non-compliance with wholesale distribution laws boil results a refusal by the Main Pharmaceutical Inspector to issue an authorisation to carry out the wholesale distribution of medicinal products, and the revocation of that authorisation. After an inspection, the Main Pharmaceutical Inspector may refuse to issue a certificate of compliance with GMP, or revoke an existing certificate, making notification to the European database EuraGMDP.

The Pharmaceutical Act also stipulates penal provisions and fines for non-compliance with wholesale distribution laws.

# MARKETING

### PROMOTION

### 19. WHAT IS THE GENERAL LEGAL REGIME FOR THE MARKETING OF DRUGS?

**Legal regime**

The advertisement of medicinal products is regulated in two legal acts:

- The Pharmaceutical Law Act of 6 September 2001.
- The Regulation of the Minister of Health of 21 November 2008 on the advertisement of medicinal products.

**Limits to marketing activities**

Marketing activities regarding the promotion of medicinal products are limited (*see Questions 22 to 34*).

### 20. ARE THERE OTHER CODES OF CONDUCT FOR THE MARKETING OF DRUGS (FOR EXAMPLE, BY PROFESSIONAL OR INDUSTRIAL ORGANISATIONS)?

The Polish Employers' Union of Innovative Pharmaceutical Companies (INFARMA) has issued a self-regulation document, entitled "The Code of Good Marketing Practices of the Pharmaceutical Industry", setting out detailed provisions on the advertising of medicinal products. The Code establishes a requirement that, for example, clinical assessments, post-marketing monitoring programmes and analyses as well as post-marketing authorisation studies cannot constitute forms of hidden advertisement. It also regulates the procedure concerning the provision of free product samples. In some cases the Code stipulates even stricter regulations for companies affiliated within INFARMA. For example, the provision of free samples of medicinal products is limited to a maximum of four samples (instead of five under the Pharmaceutical Act), and only for five years after the date of the first marketing authorisation of a particular product.

## MARKETING TO CONSUMERS

### 21. WHAT IS THE LEGAL REGIME FOR MARKETING TO CONSUMERS?

**Legal regime**

The advertisement of medicinal products to consumers is regulated in two legal acts:

- The Pharmaceutical Law Act of 6 September 2001.
- The Regulation of the Minister of Health of 21 November 2008 on the advertisement of medicinal products.

**Products**

There is a prohibition on advertising to the general public medicinal products that:

- Are available on medical prescription only.
- Contain psychotropic or narcotic substances.
- Have been placed on the lists of reimbursed medicines in accordance with separate regulations and can be dispensed over the counter with a name identical to those on these lists.

The prohibition also applies to the advertising of any medicinal product whose name is identical to that of a medicinal product dispensed only on prescription. However it does not apply to preventive vaccinations specified in a communication from the Chief Sanitary Inspector.

### 22. WHAT KINDS OF MARKETING ACTIVITIES ARE PERMITTED IN RELATION TO CONSUMERS AND THE PRODUCTS WHICH MAY BE ADVERTISED TO THEM?

Marketing activities towards consumers are permitted only with respect to over-the-counter medicinal products. Marketing activities are in practice limited to advertising via press, radio, television, internet and other written material. The Pharmaceutical Act prohibits the advertising of a medicinal product involving the offer or promise of any benefits, either directly or indirectly, in exchange for purchasing a medicinal product or providing proof that a medicinal product was purchased.

The advertising of medicinal products is prohibited, if (*chapter 4, Pharmaceutical Act*):

- A marketing authorisation has not been granted in Poland in respect of the advertised medicinal product.
- The products have been approved for sale but the "direct import" authorisation has not been obtained.
- The advertising contains information which is inconsistent with the approved Summary of Medicinal Product Characteristics.

Further, the advertising of the medicinal product must not be misleading, and must present the drug in an objective fashion and provide information on its sensible use.

In general, the advertising of a medicinal product must not be directed at children, nor include any element directed at them. The advertising of a medicinal product which resembles a complete advertisement, in addition to its proprietary name and common name, may include a trade mark, but without any reference to its therapeutic qualities, pharmaceutical form, dose, advertising lines or other advertising content.

There are certain further restrictions on the content of advertising of a medicinal product to the general public, for example, it must not involve:

- The presentation of a medicinal product by public persons, scientists, persons with medical or pharmaceutical education or purporting to have such education.
- Reference to the recommendation of public persons, scientists, persons with medical or pharmaceutical education or purporting to have such education.

The advertising of a medicinal product to the general public must not contain any content which:

- Suggests that:
  - a medical consultation or surgical operation is unnecessary, in particular based on a diagnosis or by suggesting treatments by mail;
  - the health of a healthy person can be enhanced by taking the medicinal product;
  - the health of the person may deteriorate by not taking the medicinal product (except for vaccination campaigns announced by the Main Sanitary Inspection);
  - the medicinal product is a foodstuff, cosmetic or other consumer product;
  - the efficacy or safety of the medicinal product results from its natural origin; and
  - the effects of taking the medicinal product are guaranteed, are unaccompanied by adverse reactions or are better than or equivalent to those of another treatment or medicinal product.
- Could, by a description or detailed presentation of a case history or disease symptoms, lead to erroneous self-diagnosis.
- Refers to therapeutic qualities in an inappropriate, frightening or misleading form.
- Uses improper, alarming or misleading terms, pictorial representations of changes in the human body caused by disease or injury, or the action of a medicinal product on the human body or parts of the body.

Further, the advertising of a medicinal product to the general public must not promise directly or indirectly any material or immaterial benefits.

The Pharmaceutical Act specifies several types of medicinal products that must not be advertised to consumers, such as:

- Medicinal products that are available on medical prescription only.
- Medicinal products containing narcotic or psychotropic substances.
- Medicinal products indicated in the reimbursement lists, in accordance with separate regulations, or that are available without prescription under a name indicated in the name of a medicinal product indicated in such a list.
- Medicinal products the name of which is identical to the name of a medicinal product available on medicinal prescription only.

Only drugs that are not set out in these restrictions can be advertised to the general public.

## 23. IS IT PERMITTED TO PROVIDE CONSUMERS WITH FREE SAMPLES? ARE THERE PARTICULAR RESTRICTIONS ON SPECIAL OFFERS (FOR EXAMPLE, "BUY-ONE-GET-ONE-FREE")?

Under Polish pharmaceutical law, the provision of free product samples is a form of advertisement. The law implicitly prohibits the provision of free samples of medicinal products to the general public and only allows such conduct towards professionals authorised to write prescriptions. In addition, a sample can only be given to a person authorised to write prescriptions under the following conditions:

- The person authorised to write prescriptions has asked in written form to obtain a sample from the sales or medical representative.
- The person providing the sample keeps a record of samples provided.
- Each sample provided can be no bigger than that which is contained in the smallest packaging of a product authorised for marketing in the territory of Poland.
- Each sample provided bears the description "free sample – not for sale".
- Each sample is accompanied by a summary of product characteristics.
- No more than five samples of the same medicinal product can be provided to the same person over a one-year period. INFARMA's code (*see Question 20*) limits the number of free samples provided to healthcare professionals to four, with an additional reservation that such actions are permitted only for five years after the date of the first marketing authorization of a particular product. This additional rule refers only to companies affiliated with INFARMA.

Medicinal products containing narcotic drugs or psychotropic substances may not be provided as free samples.

## 24. ARE THERE PARTICULAR RULES OF PRACTICE ON THE USE OF THE INTERNET/SOCIAL MEDIA REGARDING DRUGS AND THEIR ADVERTISING?

There is no distinction under pharmaceutical law between advertisements on the internet/social media and others. Every kind of medicinal product advertisement must contain all the obligatory information; this also applies to social media/internet advertising.

The law allows the mail order of medicinal products available without prescription in pharmacies and pharmacy outlets. Particular requirements for premises, methods of delivery, period of storage of the documentation related to mail ordering as well as the minimum level of information that must be placed on websites enabling the sale of medicinal products are published in regulations by the Minister of Health. Regulations also establish the extent of access to documentation enabling Pharmaceutical Inspection officers appropriate supervision of mail ordering operations.

## 25. WHAT REGULATORY AUTHORITY IS RESPONSIBLE FOR SUPERVISING MARKETING ACTIVITIES TO CONSUMERS?

**Regulatory authority**

The Main Pharmaceutical Inspector is responsible for supervising marketing activities to consumers. Compliance with the regulations on advertising of medicinal products is monitored.

POLAND

**Supervision**

The Main Pharmaceutical Inspector can issue a decision ordering:

- The cessation of displaying or running advertisements of medicinal products which are not in compliance with the provisions of the Pharmaceutical Act relating to advertising.
- The publication of such a decision in the places where the advertisement violating the law was published, and the publication of a corrective statement regarding such false advertisement.
- The removal of the violation.

The general rules concerning advertising under the Act on Combating Unfair Competition 1993 also apply.

A person who does not comply with the regulations on advertising of a medicinal product is liable to a fine imposed by the Main Pharmaceutical Inspector.

**Rights of appeal**

With respect to decisions issued by the Main Pharmaceutical Inspector, the applicable law (the Polish Code of Administrative Procedure) allows a motion for it to be reconsidered. After a second decision there is also the possibility to appeal to the Provincial Administrative Court in Warsaw.

## 26. WHAT ARE THE LEGAL CONSEQUENCES OF NON-COMPLIANCE WITH CONSUMER MARKETING LAWS?

The Main Pharmaceutical Inspector can order that the recipient of the decision:

- Ceases advertising the medicinal product.
- Displays the decision on the breach in the places where the advertisement appeared, and publishes a retraction.
- Rectifies the breach.
- Pays a fine.

## MARKETING TO PROFESSIONALS

## 27. WHAT KINDS OF MARKETING ACTIVITIES ARE PERMITTED IN RELATION TO PROFESSIONALS?

The catalogue of admissible marketing activities is vast, and such marketing is permitted as long as it stays in compliance with pharmaceutical law. In this regard for example it is permitted to:

- Organise visits by medical or sales representatives to persons authorised to write prescriptions or persons that distribute medicinal products.
- Supply samples of medicinal products.
- Sponsor promotional meetings for persons authorised to write prescriptions or persons that distribute medicinal products.
- Sponsor conferences, conventions and scientific congresses for persons authorised to write prescriptions, or persons that distribute medicinal products.

## 28. ARE THERE ANY RESTRICTIONS ON MARKETING TO PROFESSIONALS?

**Marketing activities**

It is prohibited to direct at persons authorised to write prescriptions, and persons that distribute medicinal products, advertising involving gifts, offers or promises of material benefits, presents or other inducements, prizes, trips or the organisation and financing of meetings to promote medicinal products during which hospitality exceeds the main purpose of the meeting. Accepting such benefits is also prohibited. However, these prohibitions do not apply to the giving or accepting of items bearing a mark advertising a given firm or medicinal product and valued at under PLN100, and that are relevant to the practice of medicine or pharmacy.

Further, pharmaceutical law limits to five a year the number of medicinal product samples that can be delivered to professionals (*see Question 31*).

Advertising that involves the free supply of samples of the product must not be applied to medicinal products containing psychotropic or narcotic substances. Additionally it is prohibited to advertise a medicinal product that has no marketing authorisation approval, or is beyond its Summary of Medicinal Product Characteristics.

**Frequency**

There are no general restrictions regarding the frequency with which professionals might be targeted by sales representatives.

**Provision of hospitality**

There are restrictions on meetings with groups of professionals and the provision of hospitality. Such restrictions include trips and the organisation and financing of meetings to promote medicinal products during which hospitality exceeds the main purpose of the meeting (*Article 58, Pharmaceutical Act*).

## 29. WHAT INFORMATION IS IT LEGALLY REQUIRED TO INCLUDE IN ADVERTISING TO PROFESSIONALS?

The legal requirements for advertising to professionals are listed in the Pharmaceutical Act and the Regulation of the Ministry of Health of 21 November 2008. According to these acts it is necessary to include:

- The name of the medicinal product and the name commonly used.
- The product's qualitative and quantitative composition in respect of active substances and the excipients which are essential for the proper use of the product.
- The pharmaceutical form.
- An indication or therapeutic indications for use.
- The dosage and method of administration.
- Contraindications.
- Special warnings and precautions for use.
- Adverse reactions.
- Identification of the marketing authorisation holder (MAH).

- The number of the marketing authorisation and the name of the authority that issued it.
- Information on the reimbursement category, and in the case of medicinal products on the lists of reimbursed medicines information on the official retail price and the maximum price.
- Information as to when the particular marketing material was drafted or revised.

## 30. ARE THERE RULES ON COMPARISONS WITH OTHER PRODUCTS THAT ARE PARTICULARLY APPLICABLE TO DRUGS?

There are no special rules under Polish pharmaceutical law, apart from legal definitions regarding particular products and the day-to-day practice of public authorities. Nevertheless there are several rules on comparative advertising. Eight different requirements must be fulfilled under the Act on Combating Unfair Competition. These requirements for comparative advertisements are:

- It is not misleading advertising referred in the Act on Combating Unfair Competition.
- In a fair and verifiable way compares products or services meeting the same needs or intended for the same purpose.
- Objectively compares one or several material, characteristic, verifiable and typical features of these products and services, including price.
- It does not lead to confusion on the market place between the advertiser and his competitor nor between their products or services, trademarks, trade names or other distinguishing marks.
- It does not discredit products, services, activities, trademarks, trade names, products, services, activities or circumstances of a competitor.
- In relation to products with geographical regional designation, it relates always to products with the same designation.
- It does not take unfair advantage of the reputation of a trade mark, trade name or other distinguishing marks of the competitor or of the geographical regional designation of competing products.
- It does not present product or service as imitation or replica of product or service bearing the protected trademark or another distinguishing designation.

## 31. WHAT OTHER ITEMS, FUNDING OR SERVICES ARE PERMITTED TO BE PROVIDED TO PROFESSIONALS?

It is permitted to provide professionals with indirect incentives, such as sponsorships, educational activities, free samples of medicinal products, scientific research and contracts. These contracts must comply with the provisions of the Pharmaceutical Act.

### Discounts

Discounts are permitted on unreimbursed medicinal products. Discounts can be provided to wholesalers and retail sellers on the basis of a separate commercial agreement. The provision of discounts on reimbursed products is not allowed with respect to fixed prices and wholesale margins.

**Free samples**

Free samples can be provided to professionals, to a maximum of five a year. Pharmaceutical companies affiliated within the Employers Union of Innovative Pharmaceutical Companies (INFARMA) have under INFARMA's regulations limited this number to four free samples a year, and only for five years after the date of the first marketing authorisation of a particular product.

**Sponsorship of professionals**

It is permitted to provide a professional with sponsorship. Pharmaceutical law permits the sponsorship of conferences, conventions and scientific congresses for persons authorised to write prescriptions, or persons that distribute medicinal products. The hospitality during such events must not exceed the main purpose of the meeting (*Pharmaceutical Act*).

It is necessary that an appropriate sponsorship agreement be concluded between the professional and the pharmaceutical company or any other entity acting in its name.

**Other items, funding or services**

Other indirect incentives are also allowed. Examples of such incentives are:

- The organisation of visits by medical or sales representatives to persons authorised to write prescriptions or persons that distribute medicinal products.
- The supply of samples of medicinal products.
- The sponsorship of promotional meetings for persons authorised to write prescriptions, or persons that distribute medicinal products.
- The sponsorship of conferences, conventions and scientific congresses for persons authorised to write prescriptions or persons that distribute medicinal products.

## 32. WHAT REGULATORY AUTHORITY IS RESPONSIBLE FOR SUPERVISING MARKETING ACTIVITIES REGARDING PROFESSIONALS?

**Regulatory authority**

The Main Pharmaceutical Inspector is responsible for supervising marketing activities to professionals, and monitoring compliance with the regulations on advertising of a medicinal product.

**Supervision**

The Main Pharmaceutical Inspector who supervises marketing activities to professionals can issues a decision ordering:

- The cessation of displaying or running advertisements of medicinal products which are not in compliance with the provisions of the Pharmaceutical Act relating to advertising.
- The publication of such decision in the places where the advertisement violating the law was published, and the publication of a corrective statement regarding such false advertisement.
- Removal of the violation.

The general rules concerning advertising under the Act on Combating Unfair Competition 1993 also apply.

A person who does not comply with the regulations on advertising a medicinal product is liable to a fine imposed by the Main Pharmaceutical Inspector.

**Rights of appeal**

With respect to a decision issued by the Main Pharmaceutical Inspector, the applicable law (the Polish Code of Administrative Procedure) allows a motion for it to be reconsidered. After a second decision there is also the possibility to appeal to the Provincial Administrative Court in Warsaw.

33. **WHAT ARE THE LEGAL CONSEQUENCES IN CASE OF NON-COMPLIANCE WITH PROFESSIONAL MARKETING LAWS?**

The Main Pharmaceutical Inspector can order that the recipient of the decision:

- Cease advertising the medicinal product.
- Display the decision on the breach in the places where the advertisement was shown and publishes a retraction.
- Rectify the breach.

Additionally, incentives breaching the provisions of the Pharmaceutical Act might also be recognised as bribery activities, and as a result be the subject of criminal liability.

## ENGAGEMENT WITH PATIENT ORGANISATIONS

34. **WHAT KINDS OF ACTIVITIES ARE PERMITTED IN RELATION TO ENGAGEMENT WITH PATIENT ORGANISATIONS? WHAT ARE THE RESTRICTIONS THAT ARE IMPOSED ON RELATIONSHIP WITH PATIENT ORGANISATIONS?**

The nature of permissible actions is similar to those that may be taken with regard to consumers (*see Question 22*).

## REFORM

35. **ARE THERE ANY PLANS TO REFORM THE LAW ON THE DISTRIBUTION AND PROMOTION OF DRUGS IN YOUR JURISDICTION?**

At present, two projects on reform have been implemented in recent months or soon will be:

- New regulations concerning falsified medicinal products, and rules on good distribution practice in relation to medicinal products and their export to other countries were introduced at the beginning of 2015. These new regulations implement EU directives in this field. The new regulations introduce new obligations for business entities, especially concerning the management of supply chains, the prohibition on selling medicinal products

by pharmacies to entities other than patients, and providing notifications to the Main Pharmaceutical Inspector concerning selling medicinal products abroad.
- From 1 January 2016 nurses and midwives gain new competences in the field of prescribing medicinal products. In effect they may be recognised as an addressee of advertisements for medicinal products, with all the accompanying effects. Further, national and regional health consultants must now disclose most of the transfers of value that they have received from the industry or by co-operating with other entities. Additionally, several provisions have been made concerning conflicts of interest between consultants and entities with which they co-operate. As a result, business entities must modify their internal procedures and approach towards consultants, nurses and midwives to remain in compliance with the legal regime.

# PORTUGAL

Fernanda Matoso and Eduardo Maia Cadete,
MORAIS LEITÃO, GALVÃO TELES, SOARES DA SILVA & ASSOCIADOS,
SOCIEDADE DE ADVOGADOS, R.L.

## DISTRIBUTION

### PRE-CONDITIONS FOR DISTRIBUTION

**1. WHAT ARE THE LEGAL PRE-CONDITIONS FOR A DRUG TO BE DISTRIBUTED WITHIN THE JURISDICTION?**

**Authorisation**

The Portuguese Medicine Act, enshrined in Decree Law No. 176/2006, 30 August 2006, as amended (Medicine Act), establishes the national legal framework applicable to medicines for human use. The Medicine Act implements Directive 2001/83/EC on the Community code relating to medicinal products for human use (Code for Human Medicines Directive) (as amended) at national level.

Under the Medicine Act, a medicinal product to be distributed in Portugal must hold a marketing authorisation obtained via any of the following methods:

- The centralised procedure before the European Medicines Agency.
- The Decentralised Procedure.
- The Mutual Recognition Procedure.
- A strictly national procedure.

See *Question 4*.

**Exceptions**

Under special and exceptional circumstances, medicines without a marketing authorisation (including medicines for compassionate use) can be allowed to be used to treat patients in Portugal. This is subject to an authorisation granted with a temporary and transitory nature by the Portuguese Medicine Regulatory Authority (*Autoridade Nacional dos Medicamentos e de Produtos de Saúde*) (INFARMED) (www.infarmed.pt).

The rules applicable to the authorisation of medicinal products for compassionate use are provided in Articles 92 and 93 of the Medicine Act and in INFARMED Decision 139/CD/2014, 6 November 2014. See also *Question 2*.

## 2. DO ANY TYPES OF NAMED PATIENT AND/OR COMPASSIONATE USE PROGRAMMES OPERATE? IF SO, WHAT ARE THE REQUIREMENTS FOR PRE-LAUNCH ACCESS?

There are several programmes in place, which are mainly internal and reserved to specific patients of healthcare institutions that are part of the National Health Service (NHS), and this type of information is not publicly disclosed to the general public. The Portuguese Medicine Regulatory Authority (INFARMED) can authorise the pre-launch access by patients to such medicines when any of the following conditions are met:

- Where, for reasons of urgency and clinical justification, the medicines are considered to be indispensable for the treatment or diagnosis of certain pathologies.
- Where the medicines are necessary to avoid a suspected or confirmed spread of pathogenic agents, toxins, chemical agents or nuclear radiation, any of which could cause harm.
- In exceptional cases, where the medicines are acquired by a pharmaceutical service or a hospital pharmacy and are dispensed to a specific patient.

Article 5(1) of Directive 2001/83/EC on the Community code relating to medicinal products for human use (Code for Human Medicines Directive) (as amended) has been enacted in Portugal and is reflected in Article 92 of the Medicine Act. The rules applicable to the authorisation of medicinal products for compassionate use are set in INFARMED Decision 139/CD/2014, 6 November 2014.

## LICENSING

## 3. WHAT IS THE PROCEDURAL STRUCTURE REGARDING LICENSING A DRUG FOR DISTRIBUTION?

**Structure**

The applicant's request for a marketing authorisation must include the information and documentation listed and detailed in Chapter II of the Medicine Act. Such information includes the following data (among others):

- The name or corporate name and permanent address of the applicant and (where applicable) the manufacturer.
- The proposed name of the medicinal product.
- The qualitative and quantitative particulars of all the constituents of the medicinal product, including active substances and excipients.
- The therapeutic indications, contra-indications and adverse reactions.
- The posology, pharmaceutical form, method and route of administration and expected shelf life.
- The reasons for any precautionary and safety measures to be taken for the storage of the medicinal product, its administration to patients and for the disposal of waste products, together with an indication of potential risks presented by the medicinal product for the environment.
- A summary of the product characteristics, and a mock-up of the outer and inner packaging.
- A copy of a manufacturing licence valid in Portugal or, if the medicine is not manufactured in Portugal, a certificate of a valid manufacturing licence by the manufacturer in the applicable country.

- The data regarding the medicine manufacturing, including description of the manufacturing method.
- The description of the control methods employed by the manufacturer.
- A written confirmation that the manufacturer of the medicinal product has verified compliance of the manufacturer of the active substance with principles and guidelines of good manufacturing practice by conducting audits. Such written confirmation must contain a reference to the date of the most recent audit and a declaration that the outcome of the audit confirms that the manufacturing complies with the principles and guidelines of good manufacturing practice.
- The results of pharmaceutical, pre-clinical and clinical trials.
- A summary of the applicant's pharmacovigilance system.
- A risk management plan describing the risk management system which the applicant will introduce for the medicinal product concerned (together with a related summary).
- A statement to the effect that clinical trials carried out outside the EU meet the ethical requirements applicable to clinical trials.
- A copy of any authorisation, obtained in another member state or in a third country, to place the medicinal product on the market, a summary of the safety data including the data contained in the periodic safety update reports, where available, and suspected adverse reactions reports, together with a list of those member states in which an application for authorisation is under examination.
- A report on potential environmental risks posed by the medicinal product, accompanied, when deemed needed, by specific arrangements to limit such risks.
- A copy of any designation of the medicinal product as an orphan medicinal product under Regulation (EC) 141/2000 on orphan medicinal products (Orphan Medicinal Products Regulation).
- Proof of payment of the applicable fee to the Portuguese Medicine Regulatory Authority (INFARMED).

On receiving the authorisation request, the INFARMED must make a final decision on a complete marketing authorisation application within a period of 210 days, without prejudice to potential time suspensions (for example, where the INFARMED requests further information from the applicant due to detected deficiencies in the submitted file).

The marketing authorisation is initially granted for a period of five years. After the first renewal, the marketing authorisation will, as a rule, be valid for an indefinite period of time.

**Regulatory authority**

The INFARMED is the national licensing agency for medicinal products.

### 4. IS THERE A SIMPLIFIED LICENCE PROCEEDING, OR RELAXED LICENSING CONDITIONS, FOR DRUGS WHICH HAVE ALREADY BEEN LICENSED FOR DISTRIBUTION IN ANOTHER JURISDICTION?

There are simplified licensing proceedings where the Portuguese Medicine Regulatory Authority (INFARMED), in accordance with the Medicine Act, participates in the Mutual Recognition Procedure or the Decentralised Procedure as a "Reference Member State".

For parallel imports, there is a legal presumption that a medicine subject to EU parallel trade will have the same qualitative and quantitative composition, pharmaceutical form and indications, and will therefore not represent a risk to public health. This presumption is applicable either:

- When the medicine to be imported has a common origin.
- Where there is a connection between the companies that hold the marketing authorisation in Portugal and in the member state of origin.

The outcome is that an applicant must only declare (not demonstrate) that any differences in any inactive carrier substances (excipients) do not affect the medicines' therapeutic value or endanger public health. The parallel import authorisation is granted within a period of 45 days from the date the application is submitted before the INFARMED.

### 5. IS VIRTUAL DRUG DISTRIBUTION POSSIBLE FROM YOUR JURISDICTION?

"Virtual" distribution does not appear to be possible under the rules of the Medicine Act. This is because, under the applicable provisions:

- The distribution activity must be physically carried out in the national territory.
- The distributor, through the maintenance of an adequate stock, must be capable of immediately supplying the Portuguese market.

### 6. WHAT IS THE PROCEDURE TO APPEAL (LEGAL REMEDY) A LICENSING DECISION?

The licensing decisions of the Portuguese Medicine Regulatory Authority (INFARMED) can be subject to judicial review before administrative courts. The appeal must be filed before the INFARMED within a period of three months from the date the decision is notified to the addressee.

### 7. WHAT ARE THE COSTS OF OBTAINING LICENSING?

Pursuant to Order No. 377/2005, 4 April 2005, which establishes the fees for the services rendered by the Portuguese Medicine Regulatory Authority, the applicable base fees are the following (among others):

- Marketing authorisation requests under the national procedure (per dosage and pharmaceutical form) cost about EUR2,916.
- Marketing authorisation requests that Portugal be the Reference Member State cost about EUR7,673 (per dosage and pharmaceutical form).
- Marketing authorisation requests for the parallel import of a medicine costs about EUR1,760 (per dosage and pharmaceutical form).

## DISTRIBUTION TO CONSUMERS

### 8. WHAT ARE THE DIFFERENT CATEGORIES OF DRUGS FOR DISTRIBUTION?

In terms of access by the general public, medicines for distribution are classified into two main categories:

- Medicines subject to medical prescription.
- Over-the-counter medicines (that is, medicines not subject to medical prescription).

## Prescription drugs

Medicines are classified as "subject to medical prescription" if any of the following are applicable:

- They are likely to present a danger (directly or indirectly) even when used correctly, if utilised without medical supervision.
- They are frequently and to a very wide extent used incorrectly, and as a result are likely to present a direct or indirect danger to human health.
- They contain substances or preparations thereof, the activity and/or adverse reactions of which require further investigation.
- They are normally prescribed by a doctor.

Medicines subject to medical prescription can be further classified as:

- **Medicines subject to a renewable medical prescription.** These are medicines that address specific diseases or prolonged treatments that may, in compliance with safety in their use, be acquired more than once, without requiring a new medical prescription (as the original medical prescription, contains two identical copies, which can be used within a period of six months).
- **Medicines subject to a special medical prescription.** These are medicines that meet one of the following criteria:
  - the medicinal product contains, in a non-exempt quantity, a substance classified as a narcotic or a psychotropic substance within the applicable legislation;
  - the medicinal product is likely, if incorrectly used, to present a substantial risk of medicinal abuse, or to lead to addiction or be misused for illegal purposes; or
  - the medicinal product contains a substance which, by reason of its novelty or properties, could be considered as belonging to the group envisaged in the second indent as a precautionary measure.
- **Medicines restricted to a medical prescription, reserved for use in certain specialised areas.** These are medicines that meet one of the following conditions:
  - the medicinal product, because of its pharmaceutical characteristics or novelty or in the interests of public health, is reserved for treatments which can only be followed in a hospital environment;
  - the medicinal product is used in the treatment of conditions which must be diagnosed in a hospital environment or in institutions with adequate diagnostic facilities, although administration and follow-up may be carried out elsewhere; or
  - the medicinal product is intended for outpatients, but its use may produce very serious adverse reactions requiring a prescription to be drawn-up as required by a specialist and special supervision throughout the treatment.

## Over-the-counter drugs

Medicines which do not fulfil the conditions provided in the previous paragraphs are classified as over-the-counter medicines.

## 9. WHO IS AUTHORISED TO DISTRIBUTE PRESCRIPTION DRUGS AND OVER-THE-COUNTER DRUGS TO CONSUMERS?

**Prescription drugs**

According to Decree Law 307/2007, 31 August 2007, as last amended by Decree-Law 109/2014, 10 July 2014, which governs the rules applicable to pharmacies, the sale of prescription drugs to consumers can only be made through pharmacies.

Pharmacies are subject to strict monitoring and supervision and must be registered with the Portuguese Medicine Regulatory Authority (INFARMED). Each pharmacy must have a pharmaceutical technical director and an additional pharmacist.

For pharmacies, a serious offence to the applicable legal regime (and without prejudice to any tort, contractual or criminal liability) can be subject to misdemeanour fine of up to 10% of its annual turnover or EUR75,000 (whichever is the lower).

**Over-the-counter drugs**

Over-the-counter medicinal products can be distributed by pharmacies and over-the-counter medicine retailers (the latter are also subject to registration with the INFARMED).

Over-the-counter medicine retailers are governed by the rules of Decree Law 134/2005, 16 August 2005, as last amended by Law 51/2014, 25 August 2014, and also subject to the supervision of the INFARMED.

For over-the-counter medicine retailers, a serious non-compliance with the governing rules (and without prejudice to potential contractual, tort or criminal liability) is sanctionable with a misdemeanour fine of up to 30% of its annual turnover or EUR100,000 (whichever is lower).

## 10. WHAT DRUGS CAN AN ATTENDING PHYSICIAN DISTRIBUTE AND UNDER WHAT CIRCUMSTANCES?

In accordance with the Portuguese Medical Association Code of Ethics, physicians must not sell medicines or other medical articles or products to the respective patients.

Free-of-charge supply can only be made in strict and duly justified cases, notably in an emergency situation.

## 11. WHO IS AUTHORISED TO PRESCRIBE PRESCRIPTION DRUGS TO CONSUMERS?

In accordance with the Medicine Act, a prescription drug can be prescribed by a doctor or, in cases specifically provided in the legislation, a dentist or an orthodontist (*odontologista*).

## 12. IS DIRECT MAILING/DISTANCE SELLING OF DRUGS PERMITTED IN YOUR JURISDICTION?

**Conditions**

Home delivery of medicines is allowed, specifically by pharmacies in relation to medicines subject to medical prescription and by over-the-counter retailers regarding over-the-counter medicines (*Order 1427/2007, 2 December 2007*). Therefore, drugs can be sold at a pharmacy/

over-the-counter retailer or through a pharmacy/over-the-counter retailer distance selling system. Delivery to a patient's residence or workplace can be arranged by telephone, fax, online or via e-mail.

**Cross-border sales**

Cross-border sales are allowed. However, such activity is subject to prior communication to the Portuguese Medicine Regulatory Authority (INFARMED), as detailed in Decree Law 307/2007, 31 August 2007, as last amended by Decree-Law 109/2014, 10 July 2014. In a cross-border sale, the destination country rules must also be taken into account by the supplying entity.

### 13. WHAT REGULATORY AUTHORITY IS RESPONSIBLE FOR SUPERVISING DISTRIBUTION ACTIVITIES?

The Portuguese Medicine Regulatory Authority (INFARMED) is the agency responsible for the supervision and enforcement of the provisions applicable to distribution activities.

The INFARMED ensures that the legal requirements governing medicinal products are complied with through the use of:

- Inspections of the facilities of pharmacies or over-the-counter retailers (which may be unannounced if necessary).
- Audit and reporting requirements, including of adverse reactions under the pharmacovigilance rules.

In the use of its supervision and enforcement powers, the INFARMED can adopt decisions, including interim measures, leading to the suspension or revocation of medical authorisations.

### 14. WHAT IS THE PROCEDURE TO APPEAL (LEGAL REMEDY) A DISTRIBUTION DECISION?

Decisions from the Portuguese Medicine Regulatory Authority (INFARMED) can be subject to judicial review before national courts.

As a rule, if the subject matter of the INFARMED's decision is the application of a misdemeanour fine, the criminal courts are competent to review the decision. In addition, administrative courts are competent to review cases of INFARMED decisions related to the grant, suspension or revocation of authorisations or licences.

In such setting, interim measures can be triggered by the addressee of the INFARMED decision before administrative courts, which are followed by the main proceedings.

### 15. WHAT ARE THE LEGAL CONSEQUENCES OF NON-COMPLIANCE WITH CONSUMER DISTRIBUTION LAWS?

Non-compliance with consumer distribution laws may cause the non-compliant entity to be subject to misdemeanour fines and accessory sanctions by the Portuguese Medicine Regulatory Authority (INFARMED) (the product owner and/or distributor may also be subject to criminal, contractual, tort or disciplinary liability).

The INFARMED's fines can reach 15% of the infringing company's annual turnover or EUR180,000 (whichever is the lower) per each piece of illicit conduct committed.

## PORTUGAL

## WHOLESALE DISTRIBUTION

### 16. WHAT IS THE LEGAL REGIME REGARDING WHOLESALE DISTRIBUTION OF DRUGS?

The Medicine Act sets out the rules applicable to the wholesale distribution of medicinal products. Wholesale distribution of medicinal products is subject to prior authorisation from the Portuguese Medicine Regulatory Authority (INFARMED).

To obtain a distribution authorisation, the applicant must fulfil the following minimum requirements:

- The applicant must have suitable and adequate premises, installations and equipment to ensure proper conservation and distribution of the medicinal products.
- The applicant must have staff, and in particular, a qualified technical director designated as responsible.
- The applicant must undertake to fulfil the following obligations:
  - to make the premises, installations and equipment accessible at all times to the person responsible for inspecting them;
  - to obtain medicinal products supplies only from persons who are themselves in possession of the distribution authorisation or who are exempt from obtaining such authorisation under the applicable derogation;
  - to supply medicinal products only to persons who are themselves in possession of the distribution authorisation or who are authorised or entitled to supply medicinal products to the public;
  - to have an emergency plan which ensures effective implementation of any recall from the market ordered by the INFARMED or carried out in co-operation with the manufacturer or medical authorisation holder for the medicinal product concerned;
  - to keep records in the form of purchase/sales invoices, or on computer, or in any other form, giving for any transaction in medicinal products received or dispatched at least the following information: the date, name of the medicinal product, quantity received or supplied, name and address of the supplier or consignee, as appropriate;
  - to keep the records of the information referred to in the point above that are available to the INFARMED, for inspection purposes, for a period of five years; and
  - to comply with the principles and guidelines of Good Distribution Practice for medicinal products as set out in Order 348/98, 15 June 1998.

The wholesale supply of medicinal products can only be executed to either:

- Persons who are themselves in possession of the distribution authorisation (that is, other distributors).
- Persons who are authorised or entitled to supply medicinal products to the public (for example, pharmacies, over-the-counter retailers, and healthcare centres authorised to acquire medicines directly from distribution wholesalers).

## 17. WHAT REGULATORY AUTHORITY IS RESPONSIBLE FOR SUPERVISING WHOLESALE DISTRIBUTION ACTIVITIES?

### Regulatory authority

The Portuguese Medicine Regulatory Authority (INFARMED) is the agency responsible for the supervision and enforcement of the provisions applicable to wholesale distribution activities.

The INFARMED ensures that the legal requirements governing the wholesale distribution of medicinal products are complied with, by means of:

- Inspections (which may be unannounced if necessary) of the facilities of pharmacies and over-the-counter retailers.
- Audit and reporting requirements, including under the national guidelines of Good Distribution Practice for medicinal products as provided in Order 348/98, 15 June 1998.

When using its supervision and enforcement powers, the INFARMED can adopt decisions, including interim measures, leading to the suspension, withdrawal and revocation of wholesale distribution authorisations.

### Supervision

See above, *Regulatory authority*.

### Rights of appeal

INFARMED decisions in the setting of wholesale distribution authorisations can be subject to judicial review before administrative or criminal courts, depending on the factual matter and legislation taken into account in the relevant decision.

## 18. WHAT ARE THE LEGAL CONSEQUENCES OF NON-COMPLIANCE WITH WHOLESALE DISTRIBUTION LAWS?

The legal consequences of non-compliance with wholesale distribution laws are the same as for non-compliance with consumer distribution laws (*see Question 15*).

# MARKETING

## PROMOTION

## 19. WHAT IS THE GENERAL LEGAL REGIME FOR THE MARKETING OF DRUGS?

### Legal regime

The marketing of medicines is regulated by:

- The Medicine Act.
- Portuguese Medicine Regulatory Authority (INFARMED) Decision 44/CD/2008, 7 February 2008.

- The National Advertising Code, established in Decree Law 330/90, 23 October 1990 (as amended) (Advertising Code).

The following activities are not considered to be "advertising":

- The labelling of the medicinal product and the accompanying package leaflets.
- Any correspondence to answer a specific question about a particular medicinal product.
- Any factual, informative announcements and reference material relating to the medicinal product (for example, information relating to pack modifications, adverse-reaction warnings as part of general drug precautions, trade catalogues and price lists), provided such information does not include any product claims.
- Any statements relating to human health or diseases, provided there is no reference, even indirect, to medicinal products.

In addition, any measures or commercial practices related to margins, prices and discounts are not subject to the advertising rules of the Medicine Act.

**Limits to marketing activities**

The following cannot be marketed to the general public, and can only be marketed to healthcare professionals (doctors, pharmacists and nurses and so on):

- Medicines subject to medical prescription (*see Question 8, Prescription drugs*).
- Medicinal products which contain psychotropic or narcotic substances.
- Medicines subject to reimbursement by the National Health Service (NHS).

However, over-the-counter medicines can be advertised to the general public.

Advertising of any of the categories of medicinal products identified above, before the applicable addresses, must fulfil the following requirements:

- The advertising must comply with the particulars listed in the summary of product characteristics.
- The advertising must encourage the rational use of the medicinal product, by presenting it objectively and without exaggerating its properties.
- The advertising must not be misleading.

In addition, all advertising activities to the general public of an over-the-counter medicine must:

- Be set out in such a way that it is clear that the message is an advertisement and that the product is clearly identified as a medicinal product.
- Include the following minimum information:
  - the name of the medicinal product, and the common name if the medicinal product contains only one active substance;
  - the information necessary for the correct use of the medicinal product; and
  - an explicit, legible invitation to read the instructions on the package leaflet carefully or outer packaging.

The advertising of a medicinal product to the general public must not contain any material which:

- Gives the impression that a medical consultation or surgical operation is unnecessary (for example, by offering a diagnosis or suggesting treatment by mail).
- Suggests that the effects of taking the medicine are guaranteed, are unaccompanied

by adverse reactions or are better than, or equivalent to, those of another treatment or medicinal product.
- Suggests that the health of the subject can be enhanced by taking the medicine.
- Suggests that the health of the subject could be affected by not taking the medicine (however, this does not apply to vaccination campaigns provided in the Medicine Act).
- Is directed exclusively or principally at children.
- Refers to a recommendation by scientists, health professionals or persons who are neither of the foregoing but who, because of their celebrity, could encourage the consumption of medicinal products.
- Suggests that the medicinal product is a foodstuff, a cosmetic or other consumer product.
- Suggests that the safety or efficacy of the medicinal product is due to the fact that it is natural.
- Could, by a description or detailed representation of a case history, lead to erroneous self-diagnosis.
- Refers, in improper, alarming or misleading terms, to claims of recovery.
- Uses, in inadequate, alarming or misleading terms, pictorial representations of changes in the human body caused by disease or injury, or of the action of a medicinal product on the human body or human body parts.

Advertising of a medicinal product to persons qualified to prescribe or supply such products must include:

- Essential information compatible with the summary of product characteristics.
- The supply classification of the medicinal product.
- The conditions for reimbursement by the NHS.

In accordance with Article 164(4) of the Medicine Act and INFARMED's Decision 44/CD/2008, 7 February 2008, advertising elements regarding prescription drugs and over-the-counter medicines, addressed to healthcare professionals, must be communicated to the INFARMED within ten days, counting from the date the marketing campaign is initiated.

## 20. ARE THERE OTHER CODES OF CONDUCT FOR THE MARKETING OF DRUGS (FOR EXAMPLE, BY PROFESSIONAL OR INDUSTRIAL ORGANISATIONS)?

Since 1987, the Portuguese Association of the Pharmaceutical Industry (*Associação Portuguesa da Indústria Farmacêutica*) (API) has developed a Code of Ethics for Promotion Practices of the Pharmaceutical Industry and Interactions with Healthcare Professionals and Institutions, Organisations or Associations comprising Healthcare Professionals (API Code).

The current version of the API Code, which entered into force on 1 January 2014, takes into account and is aligned with the rules of:

- The Medicine Act.
- The International Federation of Pharmaceutical Manufacturers Code.
- The European Federation of Pharmaceutical Industries and Associations Code on promotion of prescription-only medicines to, and interactions with, healthcare professionals.

Compliance with the provisions of API's Code by the respective associated members is monitored and supervised by the association Council of Ethics. In the case of an alleged breach, the complaint is submitted by the associated member to the API's Council of Ethics. If it is found that a company did not act in accordance with the provisions of the API Code, the API can request the associated member to cease the irregular activity and to undertake, in writing not to repeat such practice. A breach of the API Code by a company is considered a disciplinary offence and the applicable sanctions are provided for in API statutes. Where a breach is found, the applied sanction, as well as the nature of the offence, can be publicised by the API.

## MARKETING TO CONSUMERS

### 21. WHAT IS THE LEGAL REGIME FOR MARKETING TO CONSUMERS?

**Legal regime**

The relevant rules are set out in the Medicines Act and in Portuguese Medicine Regulatory Authority (INFARMED) Decision 44/CD/2008, 7 February 2008, which approves the regulation governing specific issues related to medicines marketing.

**Products**

The following products cannot be marketed to the general public and can only be marketed to healthcare professionals (doctors, pharmacists and nurses):

- Prescription drugs.
- Over-the-counter medicines subject to reimbursement by the National Health Service.
- Medicinal products which contain psychotropic or narcotic substances.

Over-the-counter medicines can be marketed to the general public.

In accordance with the INFARMED's Decision 44/CD/2008, 7 February 2008, all advertising elements regarding medicines addressed to healthcare professionals must be communicated to the INFARMED within a period of ten days, counting from the date in which the marketing campaign is initiated. See also *Question 19*.

### 22. WHAT KINDS OF MARKETING ACTIVITIES ARE PERMITTED IN RELATION TO CONSUMERS AND THE PRODUCTS WHICH MAY BE ADVERTISED TO THEM?

Over-the-counter medicines can be subject to most common types of marketing activities, including through the use of communication platforms such as television, internet, radio, magazines and newspapers.

### 23. IS IT PERMITTED TO PROVIDE CONSUMERS WITH FREE SAMPLES? ARE THERE PARTICULAR RESTRICTIONS ON SPECIAL OFFERS (FOR EXAMPLE, "BUY-ONE-GET-ONE-FREE")?

Consumers cannot be provided with free samples of medicinal products. Samples can only be provided to healthcare professionals under strict conditions (*see Question 31*).

A special offer of the type "buy-one-get-one-free" could potentially be qualified as a breach of the samples regime and as an incentive for the non-rational use of medicinal products. Therefore, such a special offer is not permitted under the Medicine Act.

However, pharmacies can grant discounts to consumers when acquiring medicinal products, as discounts are not subject to the advertising rules of the Medicine Act.

Furthermore, Decree Law 97/2015, 1 June 2015, which regulates (among others) the price regime for medicines subject to medical prescription and over-the-counter medicines reimbursed by the National Health Service (NHS), specifically states that discounts are allowed in all stages of medical distribution, from the manufacturer to the retailer. The Decree Law also provides that discounts applied by pharmacies to the price of medicines partially reimbursed by the NHS are applicable only to the part of the price not subject to reimbursement.

## 24. ARE THERE PARTICULAR RULES OF PRACTICE ON THE USE OF THE INTERNET/SOCIAL MEDIA REGARDING DRUGS AND THEIR ADVERTISING?

There are no specific rules on the use of the internet or social media other than the rules provided in relation to consumers above (*see Questions 21 to 23*).

In relation to healthcare professionals, the Code of Ethics for Promotion Practices of the Pharmaceutical Industry and Interactions with Healthcare Professionals and Institutions, Organisations or Associations comprising Healthcare Professionals (API Code) specifically states that the internet promotion of medicinal products targeting healthcare professionals must be based on technical, scientific and professional principles. The API Code also provides that pharmaceutical companies should adopt measures to guarantee that the promotion is accessed exclusively by healthcare professionals (and not by the general public).

## 25. WHAT REGULATORY AUTHORITY IS RESPONSIBLE FOR SUPERVISING MARKETING ACTIVITIES TO CONSUMERS?

**Regulatory authority**

The Portuguese Medicine Regulatory Authority (INFARMED) is the agency responsible for the supervision and enforcement of the provisions applicable to consumer marketing activities.

The INFARMED ensures that the legal requirements applicable to advertising rules are complied with. If the INFARMED has suspicions of non-compliant promotional activities, the INFARMED can open an inquiry (on its own initiative or based on a complaint). Such an inquiry can potentially lead to the application of significant misdemeanour fines, per illicit conduct, and/or the loss of licences, authorisations or permits.

**Supervision**

See above, *Regulatory authority*.

**Rights of appeal**

A decision of the INFARMED relating to marketing activities can be subject to judicial review before the competent national court.

## 26. WHAT ARE THE LEGAL CONSEQUENCES OF NON-COMPLIANCE WITH CONSUMER MARKETING LAWS?

The legal consequences for non-compliant marketing activities vary depending on the specificities of each case. The activities will be subject to investigation from the Portuguese

Medicine Regulatory Authority (INFARMED), which may order misdemeanour fines and accessory sanctions for the activities, including a ban on advertising the medicine for a period of up to two years (the non-compliant entity may also be subject to criminal, contractual, tort or disciplinary liability). The fine, per illicit conduct, can reach 15% of the infringing company's annual turnover or EUR180,000 (whichever is the lower).

In addition, in the case of a medicine subject to reimbursement by the National Health Service, the breach of the relevant advertising provisions can also lead to the medicine being excluded from the applicable public reimbursement regime.

## MARKETING TO PROFESSIONALS

### 27. WHAT KINDS OF MARKETING ACTIVITIES ARE PERMITTED IN RELATION TO PROFESSIONALS?

The Medicine Act allows for the following types of marketing activities:

- Advertisements in publications exclusively addressed to healthcare professionals (in the case of prescription drugs).
- Visits by sales representatives to healthcare professionals (however, restrictions apply, see *Question 28*).
- Promotional events, including meetings, congresses, conferences, and symposia attended by persons qualified to prescribe or supply medicinal products.
- Supply of samples (however, restrictions apply, see *Question 31*).
- Benefits-in-kind can be given or offered to professionals, but only if those benefits have a low cash value (no more than EUR60 (*Ministry of Health Dispatch 12284/2014, 6 October 2014*)) and are relevant for the practice of medicine or pharmacy and/or involve a benefit for the patient.

In addition, the Code of Ethics for Promotion Practices of the Pharmaceutical Industry and Interactions with Healthcare Professionals and Institutions, Organisations or Associations comprising Healthcare Professionals (API Code) specifically allows the use of fax, e-mail, automatic call systems, text messaging and other means of electronic communication to contact professionals with the previous authorisation or request of the healthcare professional.

### 28. ARE THERE ANY RESTRICTIONS ON MARKETING TO PROFESSIONALS?

**Marketing activities**

The Medicine Act states that the provision of inducements to prescribe or supply medicinal products by gift, offer or promise of any benefit or bonus, whether in money or in kind, are strictly prohibited. However, an exception may apply if the intrinsic value of the offer is minimal and cumulatively it is relevant for the medical practice. For example, where the value:

- Does not exceed EUR60 (*Ministry of Health Dispatch 12284/2014, 6 October 2014*).
- Is no more than EUR25, if one takes into account the Code of Ethics for Promotion Practices of the Pharmaceutical Industry and Interactions with Healthcare Professionals and Institutions, Organisations or Associations comprising Healthcare Professionals (API Code), and cumulatively the offer to the healthcare professional is relevant for the practice of medicine or pharmacy and/or involves a benefit for the patient.

There are also limits on interactions by sales representatives when addressing healthcare professionals active in establishments of the National Health Service (NHS). In the case of healthcare professionals who provide their services in establishments of the NHS, sales representatives must be registered with the Portuguese Medicine Regulatory Authority (INFARMED) and their contact with the professionals are governed by strict rules (*INFARMED Dispatch 8213-B/2013, 24 June 2013*).

**Frequency**

Pharmaceutical companies, in relation to institutions of the NHS, can only make six visits per year to each institution or service (though in specific circumstances, eight visits may be allowed). Also, in principle, and in relation to the NHS, each sales representative should not visit more than eight healthcare professionals per day.

Furthermore, the maximum number of daily visits permitted is:

- Two sales representatives per NHS hospital service.
- Three sales representatives in the case of other NHS services.

On such visits, each pharmaceutical company can only have one sale representative present. The sales representative's visits to the NHS must take place in a location suitable for the purpose of the meeting and cannot be held in:

- Emergency services.
- Areas where patients are accommodated.
- Internment services.

Visits to healthcare professionals must also take place outside of consultation hours.

Non-compliance with the applicable rules can lead the sales representative and respective pharmaceutical company being banned from performing visits to healthcare professionals at NHS institutions for up to three years.

**Provision of hospitality**

Under the Medicine Act, only educational, informative, scientific or promotional events can be addressed to healthcare professionals. The entities which promote or organise the event can only support the hospitality costs of healthcare professionals which are participants (support is strictly limited to the main purpose of the event).

Under the Medicine Act, hospitality, registration, travel and accommodation costs are considered to be acceptable expenses during an event. However, the supported accommodation costs must not:

- Exceed the period between the day prior to the beginning of the event and the day after the end of it.
- Include any social events that may impede participation in the sessions of the event.

The location of the event is subject to strict criteria from both a professional and a logistical standpoint, most notably in terms of hospitality and financial costs.

In addition, the API Code further states that:

- Any meeting, congress, conference, symposium or other event of a promotional, scientific or professional nature, organised or sponsored by a company which is the holder of a marketing authorisation or promoter of a medicinal product must take place in a suitable venue.

- The companies which are holders of a marketing authorisation or the promoters of a medicinal product should not choose places and/or tourist complexes which are known for their leisure, entertainment or sport facilities to hold a scientific or an educational event.
- The event should be held in Portugal, unless it is logistically more reasonable to hold the event in another country, taking into account:
  - the home countries of most of the guests; or
  - the location of the resources or relevant knowledge which are the main topic of the event.
- When the event is held in another country (international event) the following rules must be complied with:
  - where a prescription drug is promoted within the scope of the event, the rules of the Code of Ethics in force in the country where the promotion takes place are applicable, except if the rules of the Code of Ethics of the country of the home country of the company which organises or sponsors the event are more stringent, in which case the latter will apply; and
  - in relation to interactions with healthcare professionals within the scope of the event, the rules of the Code of Ethics in force in the country where the healthcare professional works.

The API Code also provides that the sponsorship of any promotional, scientific or educational event should take into consideration the following principles:

- The sponsorship should be preceded by a written request of the beneficiary entity, dated and signed, addressed to the company which grants the sponsorship.
- The sponsorship should be clearly announced prior to the event and during its duration.
- The payment of fees and the reimbursement of expenses (including travel, meals and accommodation for the speakers and moderators of the events) should be deemed suitable.
- Any and all material or information resulting from the event must be accurate and honestly reflect the talks and discussions.

### 29. WHAT INFORMATION IS IT LEGALLY REQUIRED TO INCLUDE IN ADVERTISING TO PROFESSIONALS?

Under the Medicines Act, any advertising of a medicinal product to persons qualified to prescribe or supply such products must include:

- The medicine's name.
- Supply classification of the medicinal product.
- The conditions for reimbursement by the National Health Service.
- Essential information compatible with the summary of product characteristics.

When the advertising is a mere reminder of the medicinal products' international non-proprietary name, where this exists, or the trade mark, the conditions provided above may not be applicable.

Portuguese Medicine Regulatory Authority (INFARMED) Decision 44/CD/2008, 7 February 2008 further states that advertising elements addressed to healthcare professionals must also include information on the following:

- The quantitative and qualitative composition.
- The pharmaceutical form.
- The therapeutic indications.

- The dosage and mode of application.
- The contra-indications (that is, the situations in which the medicine should not be used because it may be harmful to the patient).
- The side effects.

In accordance with INFARMED Decision 44/CD/2008, the following elements must also be included, if deemed relevant from a clinical point of view:

- Warnings and special precautions for use.
- Information on interactions with other medicinal products and other forms of interaction.

## 30. ARE THERE RULES ON COMPARISONS WITH OTHER PRODUCTS THAT ARE PARTICULARLY APPLICABLE TO DRUGS?

The Medicine Act does not allow comparative advertising of medicines before the general public.

The Code of Ethics for Promotion Practices of the Pharmaceutical Industry and Interactions with Healthcare Professionals and Institutions, Organisations or Associations comprising Healthcare Professionals provides that:

- Comparative advertising is only permitted among healthcare professionals.
- Comparisons among different medicinal products should be based on relevant and comparative aspects and should not be deceitful or defamatory.

Furthermore, comparisons among different medicinal products can only be made based on the elements included in the respective summary of the medicinal products' characteristics, respective instructions for use and technical documentation or on credible clinical data.

The Advertising Code also provides rules applicable to comparative advertising. Under these rules, comparative advertising is generally permitted when all of the following conditions are met:

- It is not misleading.
- It compares goods or services meeting the same needs or intended for the same purpose.
- It objectively compares one or more material, relevant, verifiable and representative features of those goods and services, which may include price.
- It does not create confusion in the market place between the advertiser and a competitor or between the advertiser's trade marks, trade names, other distinguishing marks, goods or services and those of a competitor.
- It does not discredit or denigrate the trade marks, trade names, other distinguishing marks, goods, services, activities, or circumstances of a competitor.
- It does not take unfair advantage of the reputation of a trade mark, trade name or other distinguishing mark of a competitor or of the designation of origin of competing products.
- It does not present goods or services as imitations or replicas of goods or services bearing a protected trade mark or trade name.

## 31. WHAT OTHER ITEMS, FUNDING OR SERVICES ARE PERMITTED TO BE PROVIDED TO PROFESSIONALS?

**Discounts**

Decree Law 97/2015, 1 June 2015, specifically states that discounts are allowed at all stages of the distribution chain, from the manufacturer to the retailer. This Decree Law further states that discounts applied by pharmacies to the price of medicines partially reimbursed by the National Health Service are applicable only to the part of the price not subject to reimbursement. Therefore, discounts can be granted by the manufacturer to the wholesale distributor and by the wholesale distributor to the retailer (pharmacy or over-the-counter retailer).

**Free samples**

Free samples can be provided on an exceptional basis and only to healthcare professionals qualified to prescribe them on the following conditions:

- The number of samples for each medicinal product must be limited to 12 units per year.
- Any supply of samples must be in response to a written request, signed and dated, from the prescribing agent.
- Those supplying samples must maintain an adequate system of control and accountability.
- Each sample must be identical to the smallest presentation on the market;
- Each sample must be marked *"amostra gratuita"* (free sample) or *"venda proibida"* (not for sale) or marked with other wording having the same meaning.
- Each sample must be accompanied by a copy of the summary of product characteristics.
- No samples of medicinal products containing psychotropic or narcotic substances within the meaning of international conventions can be supplied.
- In the case of medicines subject to a medical prescription, the samples can only be provided in the first two years from the effective date of the respective placement of the medicinal product on the market for commercialisation.

**Sponsorship of professionals**

The Medicine Act provides strict rules in relation to the sponsorship of healthcare professionals.

The Medicine Act provides and allows the payment of fees to healthcare professionals for their active participation through, for example:

- The presentation of scientific communication in events related to healthcare.
- Training and promotion sessions of medicinal products.

However, the payment for the participation must not be directly or indirectly dependent upon the professional prescribing or dispensing medicinal products.

In addition, the Code of Ethics for Promotion Practices of the Pharmaceutical Industry and Interactions with Healthcare Professionals and Institutions, Organisations or Associations comprising Healthcare Professionals (API Code) states that donations and subsidies and benefits in kind granted to institutions, organisations or associations of healthcare professionals and/or professionals providing healthcare or engaged in research will be authorised if all of the following apply:

- They are made for the purpose of supporting health care provision or research.
- They are documented and recorded by the donor.
- They do not constitute an incentive to the recommendation, prescription, purchase, supply, sale or administration of certain medicinal products.

The API Code further provides that no donations or subsidies should be granted to healthcare professionals individually.

### Other items, funding or services

The Medicine Act does not allow indirect incentives to healthcare professionals.

### 32. WHAT REGULATORY AUTHORITY IS RESPONSIBLE FOR SUPERVISING MARKETING ACTIVITIES REGARDING PROFESSIONALS?

### Regulatory authority

Medicines marketing activities are subject to the supervision of the Portuguese Medicine Regulatory Authority (INFARMED). Under its supervising competences, the INFARMED can open investigations based on the results of audits, complaints by competitors or publicly available information on potential non-compliant marketing activities.

### Supervision

See above, *Regulatory authority*.

### Rights of appeal

The INFARMED's decisions regarding alleged non-compliant actions in the setting of marketing activities can be subject to judicial review.

### 33. WHAT ARE THE LEGAL CONSEQUENCES IN CASE OF NON-COMPLIANCE WITH PROFESSIONAL MARKETING LAWS?

Non-compliance with consumer distribution laws may cause the product owner to be subject to misdemeanour fines and accessory sanctions (including an advertisement ban on the medicine for a period of up to two years) by the Portuguese Medicine Regulatory Authority (INFARMED) (the product owner may also be subject to criminal, contractual, tort or disciplinary liability).

The INFARMED's fines can reach 15% of the infringing company's annual turnover or EUR180,000 (whichever is the lower) per each piece of illicit conduct.

In addition, in the case of a medicine subject to reimbursement by the National Health Service, the breach of the relevant marketing provisions can also lead to the medicine being excluded from the applicable public reimbursement regime.

## ENGAGEMENT WITH PATIENT ORGANISATIONS

### 34. WHAT KINDS OF ACTIVITIES ARE PERMITTED IN RELATION TO ENGAGEMENT WITH PATIENT ORGANISATIONS? WHAT ARE THE RESTRICTIONS THAT ARE IMPOSED ON RELATIONSHIP WITH PATIENT ORGANISATIONS?

The Medicine Act does not entail any provisions applicable exclusively to interactions with patient organisations (however, the restrictions identified in *Questions 21 to 26* apply).

Subsidies, sponsorships, subventions or any other amount, product or right determinable in cash, granted to patients organisations must be reported to the Portuguese Medicine Regulatory Authority (INFARMED) by the grantor and the beneficiary within a 30-day period from the date the benefit was granted (*Medicine Act*). All benefits with a value above EUR60 are subject to such communication to the INFARMED (*Ministry of Health Dispatch 12284/2014, 6 October 2014*).

The Code of Ethics for Promotion Practices of the Pharmaceutical Industry and Interactions with Healthcare Professionals and Institutions, Organisations or Associations comprising Healthcare Professionals (API Code) provides that member companies must also comply with the provisions of API's Code of Conduct for the relations between the Pharmaceutical Industry and Patient Organisations (Patients Code), based on the (similar) European Federation of Pharmaceutical Industries and Associations Code.

Under the Patients Code, companies that aim to provide direct or indirect financial support and significant non-financial support to patients' organisations should draft it in writing, by means of an agreement duly signed by both parties. The agreement should mention the express amount of the financing, as well as its purpose or a description of the significant non-financial support as the case may be. Each company should also establish internal proceedings to formally approve the agreements.

In addition, companies and patients' organisations can agree contracts under which patients' organisations can provide services to companies for the purpose of supporting health and/or research.

Companies are also allowed to contract patients' organisations to be speakers, experts and/or consultants during meetings held by them. In this context, the following criteria should be complied with:

- The parties must specify the nature of services to be provided and the payment conditions.
- The parties must identify, in a clear way, the legitimate need for such service.
- The criteria to select the service should relate directly to the need identified above and the person responsible for its selection should have the suitable experience and knowledge to assess if the speaker, expert and/or consultant meet those criteria.
- The extent of the service provided cannot exceed what is reasonably necessary to meet the identified needs.
- The contracting company should keep the records regarding the services provided and use that information in a suitable way.
- The agreements signed with patients' organisations cannot be an incentive for the recommendation of a particular medicinal product.
- The payment of the service provided should be reasonable and reflect the market practice in a fair manner.
- The agreement should include the obligation for patients' organisations to declare that

they provide paid services to a company every time they write or speak in public on subjects covered by the agreement or matters related to the company.

Furthermore, the list of patients' organisations sponsored by each company within the scope of the agreements above should be disclosed each year, in the manner identified below, and should mention:

- The nature of the provided support.
- The monetary value of the provided support.
- The benefits received, as far as significant non-financial support which no monetary value can be ascribed are concerned.

Companies should ensure the information on the sponsorship of patient's organisations is presented in a clear and transparent manner, and is available on request of any stakeholder or through the institutional website of the company, until 31 May each year (Patients Code).

# REFORM

### 35. ARE THERE ANY PLANS TO REFORM THE LAW ON THE DISTRIBUTION AND PROMOTION OF DRUGS IN YOUR JURISDICTION?

Between 2011 and 2014, Portugal was under an EU/IMF Financial Assistance Programme (FAP) which involved an extensive set of initiatives including structural measures relating to public finances, financial stability and competitiveness. In relation to the health sector, the FAP, which ceased in 2014, involved:

- Reorganisation and rationalisation of the public hospital network through specialisation, concentration and downsizing of hospital services, joint management and joint operation of hospitals.
- Reduction of debt due to suppliers of the National Health Service (NHS), (including pharmaceutical companies).
- Improvements to the billing and collection of revenues from NHS moderating fees (*taxas moderadoras*), insurance companies and fees for the treatment of cross-border/foreign patients.
- Improvements to the monitoring and assessment system of doctors' prescription behaviour regarding medicines and diagnostic in terms of volume and value and as against prescription guidelines and peers.
- Additional centralised public tenders for active substances and medical devices, and establishment of an observatory for prices and acquisitions.
- Compulsory e-prescription and international non-proprietary name (INN) prescription.
- Changes in pharmacies' margins in the international reference price system and in the pricing of generics.
- Removal of administrative and legal hurdles to enhance the use of generic medicines.
- Regulation of medicines cross-border sales by pharmacies to the general public.

Although FAP ceased in 2014, part of the referred measures will continue to be adjusted and monitored during 2015 by national public authorities.

# RUSSIAN FEDERATION

*Vsevolod Tyupa, CMS, RUSSIA*

## DISTRIBUTION

### PRE-CONDITIONS FOR DISTRIBUTION

**1. WHAT ARE THE LEGAL PRE-CONDITIONS FOR A DRUG TO BE DISTRIBUTED WITHIN THE JURISDICTION?**

#### Authorisation

In order to be distributed in Russia, a drug must receive approval from the Ministry of Health. This authorisation requires a completed registration procedure involving:

- The submission of a registration dossier and expert review of the drug.
- Clinical trials.
- Other regulatory steps.

#### Exceptions

Non-authorised medicines can only be distributed for a particular patient on the basis of a named permission issued by the Ministry of Health ("named patient basis"). Non-registered medicines can also be imported by individuals for their personal use.

**2. DO ANY TYPES OF NAMED PATIENT AND/OR COMPASSIONATE USE PROGRAMMES OPERATE? IF SO, WHAT ARE THE REQUIREMENTS FOR PRE-LAUNCH ACCESS?**

The "named patient basis" is the only exception for commercial distribution of a non-authorised medicine (*see Question 1*). The importer must obtain permission from the Ministry of Health. Permission is issued based on an application supported by documents listed in the Regulations on Performance of the State Function of Issuance of Permissions for the Importation of a Particular Batch of Non-Authorised Medicines into the Territory of the Russian Federation adopted by the Order of the Ministry of Health of the Russian Federation dated 2 August 2012 No. 58n, including, among others:

- A resolution from the Council of Physicians.
- Justification for the quantity of units of medicine (vials, blisters, and so on).
- A quality certificate.

The application must be reviewed by the Ministry of Health within five business days and is valid for six months.

## LICENSING

### 3. WHAT IS THE PROCEDURAL STRUCTURE REGARDING LICENSING A DRUG FOR DISTRIBUTION?

**Structure**

From 1 July 2015, original drugs (except for orphan and paediatric ones) as well as the fourth and further generics of the same original drug must be authorised within 160 business days from the date of application. "Orphan" drugs in Russia are those intended exclusively for diagnostics and pathogenetic treatment of rare (orphan) diseases. The first three generics of an original drug, orphan drugs and paediatric drugs (that is, intended solely for minors) benefit from a streamlined registration procedure for authorisation within 80 business days. However, each of the above terms does not include clinical trials.

The drugs are authorised based on an application filed with the regulatory authority and supported by the registration dossier containing of the documents listed in the law including:

- Normative documentation.
- Pre-clinical trials report.
- Draft of clinical trial report.
- Draft of patient information leaflet.

Once the regulatory authority receives the application and supporting documents, ethical and medical experts review the documents. If the review is positive, a permit for clinical trials is granted and the clinical trials can begin.

Under the Good Clinical Practice standards, clinical trials must be made with the agreement of authorised medical institutions (the list is held by the authority and publicly available online, see *http://grls.rosminzdrav.ru/Ree_orgCl2.aspx*).

When the clinical trials are completed, a clinical trial report is submitted to the regulatory authority. The drugs in question are then subject to a drug quality analysis and a risk-benefit analysis. Specialised expert institutions, approved by the regulatory authority, must conduct these reviews. The regulatory authority's expert committee then evaluates the results of the reports when deciding on whether or not to authorise a drug licence for distribution.

**Regulatory authority**

The regulatory authority for the licensing of a drug for distribution is the Ministry of Health.

### 4. IS THERE A SIMPLIFIED LICENCE PROCEEDING, OR RELAXED LICENSING CONDITIONS, FOR DRUGS WHICH HAVE ALREADY BEEN LICENSED FOR DISTRIBUTION IN ANOTHER JURISDICTION?

There is no simplified authorisation procedure for a drug already authorised in another jurisdiction or for parallel imports.

A simplified authorisation procedure is available for orphan drugs, the first three generics of the original drug and paediatric drugs, irrespective of whether or not these medicines have been registered in any other jurisdiction (*see Question 2*).

## 5. IS VIRTUAL DRUG DISTRIBUTION POSSIBLE FROM YOUR JURISDICTION?

The Russian authorisation procedure requires the provision of drug samples to the regulatory authority, which are then registered. Therefore the virtual distribution, in which the physical products never enter the country, is not possible.

## 6. WHAT IS THE PROCEDURE TO APPEAL (LEGAL REMEDY) A LICENSING DECISION?

Under Russian procedural law, a decision of a state authority (including Ministry of Health) can be appealed in a state commercial arbitration court. The appeal must be based on applicable laws and regulations that, in the appellant's view, were breached by the authority when making a licensing decision. The court must consider the appeal within three months from the date of its submission.

## 7. WHAT ARE THE COSTS OF OBTAINING LICENSING?

The major part of the costs required for drug authorisation is the sponsorship of clinical trial. This cost can vary depending on, among others:

- The number of hospitals and patients involved.
- The type of disease.
- The area of medicine.

The authorisation of a drug distribution licence also involves the payment of several kinds of state fees. The main state fees are:

- Ethical and medical review of the documents to receive permission for a clinical trial: RUB110,000 (about EUR1,800).
- Fee for permission for a clinical trial: RUB5,000 (about EUR80).
- Fee for a drug quality analysis and a risk-benefit analysis: RUB325,000 (about EUR5,400).
- Fee for issuance of the drug registration certificate (paper original): RUB10,000 (about EUR160).
- Fee for analysis of a possibility to consider a drug as orphan one (if applicable and requested): RUB25,000 (about EUR400).

In addition, other related expenses (for example, notarisation and translation) must be considered when applying for a drug distribution licence. In particular, when registering a foreign drug, the applicant must present all the required documents to the regulatory authority in Russian. This usually involves the translation of the registration dossier into Russian and the payment of relevant translation fees.

## DISTRIBUTION TO CONSUMERS

## 8. WHAT ARE THE DIFFERENT CATEGORIES OF DRUGS FOR DISTRIBUTION?

Russia uses the following categorisation of drugs for distribution:

- Over-the-counter (OTC) (consumer) drugs.
- Prescription drugs.

Additionally, the medicines are separated into:

- Those listed on the Essential Drug List (EDL), which are subject to pricing limitation by means of state registration of a maximum sale price and limitation of allowable mark-ups.
- Drugs not included into the EDL that are not subject to pricing limitation and suppliers can set prices for these drugs as they do on a free market.

## 9. WHO IS AUTHORISED TO DISTRIBUTE PRESCRIPTION DRUGS AND OVER-THE-COUNTER DRUGS TO CONSUMERS?

### Prescription drugs

Only pharmacies are authorised to distribute prescription drugs to consumers. The pharmacy must hold a licence for pharmaceutical retail activity.

### Over-the-counter drugs

Only pharmacies are authorised to distribute over-the-counter (OTC) drugs to consumers. The pharmacy must hold a license for pharmaceutical retail activity. Currently, retail shops are not allowed to sell OTC medicines in Russia. However, this right may be granted in the future (*see Question 35*).

## 10. WHAT DRUGS CAN AN ATTENDING PHYSICIAN DISTRIBUTE AND UNDER WHAT CIRCUMSTANCES?

An attending physician must not sell drugs himself. He can only recommend over-the-counter (OTC) drugs or prescribe prescription drugs.

## 11. WHO IS AUTHORISED TO PRESCRIBE PRESCRIPTION DRUGS TO CONSUMERS?

Only physicians are authorised to prescribe prescription drugs to consumers.

## 12. IS DIRECT MAILING/DISTANCE SELLING OF DRUGS PERMITTED IN YOUR JURISDICTION?

### Conditions

Distance selling of drugs (including by means of postal delivery) is not permitted. From 1 July 2015, the authorities are entitled to block websites offering the distance selling of drugs without a court decision.

### Cross-border sales

Not permitted, see above, *Conditions*.

## 13. WHAT REGULATORY AUTHORITY IS RESPONSIBLE FOR SUPERVISING DISTRIBUTION ACTIVITIES?

The Federal Service for Surveillance on Consumers Rights Protection and Human Wellbeing (*Rospotrebnadzor*) supervises all consumer-related distribution activities (including distribution of drugs). The *Rospotrebnadzor*:

- Considers and reacts to consumer claims on violations of the consumers' rights.
- Conducts scheduled and unscheduled audits of retail and other companies interacting with consumers.
- Imposes penalties to individuals and companies breaching consumer rights.
- Issues recommendations to rectify breaches.

Furthermore, the *Rospotrebnadzor* supervises the compliance with sanitary and epidemiological requirements.

The Russian Federal Service on Surveillance in Healthcare (*Roszdravnadzor*) also supervises distribution of drugs to consumers by monitoring compliance with rules on retail of drugs and relevant licensing requirements, auditing pharmacies, detection of drugs whose quality or labelling fail to comply with the law.

## 14. WHAT IS THE PROCEDURE TO APPEAL (LEGAL REMEDY) A DISTRIBUTION DECISION?

The procedure is the same as for appealing a licensing decision (*see Question 6*). The appeal is submitted to a state commercial arbitration court.

## 15. WHAT ARE THE LEGAL CONSEQUENCES OF NON-COMPLIANCE WITH CONSUMER DISTRIBUTION LAWS?

As a general rule, a breach of consumer rights protection laws can lead to a penalty of up to RUB20,000 (about EUR330) for each violation unless a particular breach is subject to more serious sanctions directly specified in the law. Potential breaches of consumer rights protection laws include:

- Failing to provide the consumer with full and accurate information on the goods being sold.
- Use of unreasonably disadvantageous contractual conditions in the sale and purchase agreement with the consumer.

In particular, selling a counterfeit, falsified or unregistered drugs or drugs of improper quality to a consumer could lead to a maximum prison term of eight or ten years, depending on the statutory requirements breached. Those convicted may also have to pay a fine of up to RUB3 million (about EUR49,000) or equal to their personal income for a period of up to three years.

Some offences can also result in the offender's disqualification from the holding of certain positions for a maximum of three or five years, depending on the breach. If the commission of the offence has led to the death of two or more persons, then the maximum prison term, fine and/or disqualification period prescribed by law will be even higher than those stated above.

Additionally, failing to comply with pharmaceutical retail licence requirements (for example, holding duly equipped premises for pharmacy retail, employment of required number of pharmacists) can lead to a licence revocation.

## WHOLESALE DISTRIBUTION

### 16. WHAT IS THE LEGAL REGIME REGARDING WHOLESALE DISTRIBUTION OF DRUGS?

Only the companies holding a licence for conducting a pharmaceutical wholesale are allowed to wholesale drugs. The wholesale of drugs is permitted to:

- Other companies undertaking the wholesale of drugs.
- Manufacturers of drugs for manufacturing purposes.
- Pharmacies.
- Research institutions for scientific and research activities.
- Individual entrepreneurs holding a licence for pharmaceutical activity or medical activity.
- Medical institutions.

The wholesale of drugs must be made using a sale and purchase agreement, provided that the medicines being sold are duly authorised in Russia, of proper quality and do not violate the intellectual property rights of third parties.

### 17. WHAT REGULATORY AUTHORITY IS RESPONSIBLE FOR SUPERVISING WHOLESALE DISTRIBUTION ACTIVITIES?

**Regulatory authority**

The regulatory authority responsible for supervising wholesale distribution is the Russian Federal Service on Surveillance in Healthcare (*Roszdravnadzor*).

**Supervision**

The *Roszdravnadzor* issues licences for wholesale and retail pharmaceutical activities and supervises compliance with the licence requirements by license holders.

Additionally, the *Roszdravnadzor* investigates claims of improper, counterfeit or unregistered drugs distributed via wholesale activities. It can issue an order to withdraw these drugs from circulation and have them destroyed.

**Rights of appeal**

An authority's decision can be appealed in the state commercial arbitration court.

If a company disagrees with the *Roszdravnadzor's* order to destroy improper drugs and/or refuses to perform such an order, the *Roszdravnadzor* can bring a court action.

### 18. WHAT ARE THE LEGAL CONSEQUENCES OF NON-COMPLIANCE WITH WHOLESALE DISTRIBUTION LAWS?

Wholesale of counterfeit, falsified or unregistered drugs or drugs of an improper quality is subject to the same criminal sanctions as the sale of the same drugs to consumers (*see Question 15*).

Failure to comply with pharmaceutical wholesale licence requirements (for example, holding duly equipped pharmaceutical warehouse) can lead to a licence revocation.

# MARKETING

## PROMOTION

### 19. WHAT IS THE GENERAL LEGAL REGIME FOR THE MARKETING OF DRUGS?

**Legal regime**

Over-the-counter (OTC) drugs can be advertised and promoted in public, subject to restrictions provided for in the laws of advertising. OTC drugs can also be subject to special offers, discounts and other similar marketing activities. Prescription drugs can only be promoted among healthcare professionals (HCPs) in compliance with laws governing advertising and interactions with HCPs. Advertising in Russia is governed by the Federal Law of the Russian Federation, dated 13 March 2006, No. 38-FZ "On Advertising" (Law on Advertising).

**Limits to marketing activities**

Provided the marketing activities are compliant with the applicable legal requirements, there are no limits to the frequency or budgets of marketing campaigns provided for in the law.

However, under Russian tax legislation the company's expenses on drugs advertising may be deductible for the purposes of corporate profit tax only if such expenses do not exceed 1% of the company's turnover. The advertising costs exceeding this limit are not tax-deductible.

### 20. ARE THERE OTHER CODES OF CONDUCT FOR THE MARKETING OF DRUGS (FOR EXAMPLE, BY PROFESSIONAL OR INDUSTRIAL ORGANISATIONS)?

Marketing of drugs in Russia may also be subject to the Code of Practice of the Association of International Pharmaceutical Manufacturers (AIPM). The AIPM Code sets out certain rules for, among others:

- Advertising and marketing drugs.
- Interaction with healthcare professionals (HCPs).

Compliance with the Code is mandatory for companies who are members of the AIPM. However, it is not a statutory law and, therefore, not mandatory under Russian legislation. The companies failing to comply with the AIPM Code can lose their membership in the AIPM without return of the paid membership fee. However, they cannot be penalised by the Russian authorities for actions breaching the AIPM Code unless these actions also breach Russian legislation.

## MARKETING TO CONSUMERS

### 21. WHAT IS THE LEGAL REGIME FOR MARKETING TO CONSUMERS?

**Legal regime**

Over-the-counter (OTC) drugs can be advertised to and promoted among consumers subject to limitations provided for in the Law on Advertising.

Prescription drugs must not be advertised to consumers.

## PRODUCTS

### 22. WHAT KINDS OF MARKETING ACTIVITIES ARE PERMITTED IN RELATION TO CONSUMERS AND THE PRODUCTS WHICH MAY BE ADVERTISED TO THEM?

Over-the-counter (OTC) drugs can be promoted to consumers through:

- Advertising in media, internet, billboards and in other lawful forms (provided the applicable restrictions are complied with).
- Disease awareness campaigns and similar educational materials.
- Special offers, discounts and other similar selling marketing activities (*see Question 23*).

### 23. IS IT PERMITTED TO PROVIDE CONSUMERS WITH FREE SAMPLES? ARE THERE PARTICULAR RESTRICTIONS ON SPECIAL OFFERS (FOR EXAMPLE, "BUY-ONE-GET-ONE-FREE")?

The provision of free samples to consumers is permitted for over-the-counter (OTC) drugs. However, the drugs must not contain narcotic or psychotropic substances.

### 24. ARE THERE PARTICULAR RULES OF PRACTICE ON THE USE OF THE INTERNET/SOCIAL MEDIA REGARDING DRUGS AND THEIR ADVERTISING?

There are no particular rules of practice on the use of the internet and/or social media for drug advertising in Russia. This advertising is subject to general rules and restrictions.

### 25. WHAT REGULATORY AUTHORITY IS RESPONSIBLE FOR SUPERVISING MARKETING ACTIVITIES TO CONSUMERS?

**Regulatory authority**

The Federal Anti-monopoly Service (FAS) is responsible for supervising advertising and fair competition in Russia.

**Supervision**

The FAS conducts the following activities:

- Reviewing and assessing advertising materials and advertising campaigns from the point of compliance with law.
- Imposing penalties for breaches of the laws on advertising.
- Issuing orders to remedy a breach (including the deletion or destruction of improper advertising materials or suspending the distribution of incompliant advertising).

**Rights of appeal**

The FAS consists of the head federal office and regional subdivisions. Both are entitled to supervise advertising activities. However, a decision of regional subdivision of the FAS may be appealed to the Head Office in Moscow. Furthermore, both decisions of regional and federal FAS may be appealed to a state commercial arbitration court irrespective of whether or not a decision of regional FAS has been appealed to the federal FAS.

26. WHAT ARE THE LEGAL CONSEQUENCES OF NON-COMPLIANCE WITH CONSUMER MARKETING LAWS?

A breach of the laws on advertising can lead to the imposition of a fine from RUB200,000 (about EUR3,300) to RUB500,000 (about EUR8,250). The fine is supported by an order to remedy the breach (for example, destruction of the advert stop distributing the materials breaching the advertising laws).

If the regulatory authority decides that a violation is minor, it has can issue an order only to remedy the breach, not to pay the fine.

MARKETING TO PROFESSIONALS

27. WHAT KINDS OF MARKETING ACTIVITIES ARE PERMITTED IN RELATION TO PROFESSIONALS?

The permitted forms of marketing activities relating to healthcare professionals (HCPs) include:

- Advertising of drugs (including prescription drugs) in professional print media intended to HCPs solely and in the frames of professional events for HCPs (for example, conferences, congresses and symposia).
- Provision of reprints, scientific and educational materials (including articles and brochures).
- Educational seminars in hospitals organised in accordance with the internal policies and procedures and agreed with the hospital's management.
- Educational video conferences, webinars or other similar activities.
- Distribution of small items/souvenirs with company's brand (for example, pens and pencils), provided that the distribution is made at a public event on a de-personalised basis and no items are given to an HCP personally.

### 28. ARE THERE ANY RESTRICTIONS ON MARKETING TO PROFESSIONALS?

**Marketing activities**

The following marketing activities are prohibited in relation to healthcare professionals (HCPs) in Russia:

- Visits.
- Provision of gifts (including gifts of an insignificant value and educational nature).
- Provision of samples for further distribution among patients.
- Engagement in market research or any kinds of marketing activities.
- Inducement to use prescription forms containing information of a promotion nature.

**Frequency**

There are no restrictions on targeting HCPs via emails or phone. However, personal face-to-face visits are prohibited.

**Provision of hospitality**

There are no particular restrictions with respect to the amount of hospitality, but the hospitality must always be reasonable, modest and secondary to the main purpose of the meeting.

### 29. WHAT INFORMATION IS IT LEGALLY REQUIRED TO INCLUDE IN ADVERTISING TO PROFESSIONALS?

There are no requirements to include any particular information when advertising to healthcare professionals (HCPs).

However, any information included in the drug advertising must be correct, accurate and limited to the indications included in the instruction on application.

### 30. ARE THERE RULES ON COMPARISONS WITH OTHER PRODUCTS THAT ARE PARTICULARLY APPLICABLE TO DRUGS?

There are no specific rules on comparisons with other products in Russian legislation that are particularly applicable to drugs.

The Code of Practice of the Association of International Pharmaceutical Manufacturers (AIPM Code) states that "the comparative advertising should be correct, compare identical characteristics, and should not mislead consumers through the absence of any significant information in the advertisement" (*clause 2.3.6, AIPM Code*).

Under the general advertising rules, any comparison must be correct. An incorrect comparison of advertised goods may be interpreted as activities of unfair competition and penalised. From a practical standpoint such a comparison supposes:

- The same parameters of comparison.
- The comparison of all the parameters which are to be of importance for the compared goods.
- Using the same and correct methodology of comparison.

## 31. WHAT OTHER ITEMS, FUNDING OR SERVICES ARE PERMITTED TO BE PROVIDED TO PROFESSIONALS?

### Discounts

Healthcare professionals (HCPs) must not procure drugs from pharmaceutical companies themselves (unless they are acting as consumers outside of their job responsibilities). Therefore, any discounts are not applicable. Discounts to medical institutions are permitted subject to negotiations between seller and buyer and granted on the basis of respective contractual conditions.

### Free samples

It is permitted to provide professionals with free samples, provided that the samples are intended for the professional's information only. Provision of samples for further transfer to patients is prohibited.

### Sponsorship of professionals

As a general rule, direct sponsorship of HCP is prohibited as it could be considered as a gift to HCP, which is prohibited.

Direct sponsorship of HCPs is only possible if such sponsorship is a part of mutually binding agreement between a pharmaceutical company and HCP setting out mutual consideration from both parties. For example, delivering a lecture by an HCP in return of sponsorship of his/her attendance of a scientific event for upgrade of his/her professional level and improvement of the quality of scientific services to be rendered by the HCP.

### Other items, funding or services

Pharmaceutical companies may engage HCPs in provision of scientific or pedagogical services or participation in clinical trials on a remuneration basis.

Provision of scientific services is lawful if it leads to obtaining new fundamental or practical knowledge. Scientific services can be rendered in the form of lecture delivering, article writing and other similar forms by well-qualified HCPs whose experience and professional knowledge enable them to achieve new scientific knowledge.

The pedagogical services may be rendered in collaboration with educational institutions in the frames of adopted educational programmes.

In order to be involved in clinical trials, an HCP must meet certain professional requirements (for example, the principal investigator must have a medical speciality relevant to the clinical trial to be performed and have no less than three years of professional experience in clinical trials).

However, under the Code of Practice of the Association of International Pharmaceutical Manufacturers (AIPM Code), all payments made by AIPM members to HCPs must be made publicly available and provided that the requirements of legislation on personal data are complied with.

## 32. WHAT REGULATORY AUTHORITY IS RESPONSIBLE FOR SUPERVISING MARKETING ACTIVITIES REGARDING PROFESSIONALS?

**Regulatory authority**

The *Roszdravnadzor* is responsible for supervising marketing activities regarding healthcare professionals (*see Question 13*).

**Supervision**

The authority supervises the compliance with the rules on interactions between pharmaceutical companies and healthcare professionals by both sides (companies and physicians).

**Rights of appeal**

As in other cases, an authority's decision can be appealed to a state commercial arbitration court.

## 33. WHAT ARE THE LEGAL CONSEQUENCES IN CASE OF NON-COMPLIANCE WITH PROFESSIONAL MARKETING LAWS?

Currently, the liability for breaching the rules on interactions between pharmaceutical companies and healthcare professionals has not yet been established. However, physicians breaching these rules may be subject to job disciplinary responsibility in accordance with the employer's policies and regulations. The consequences for the company are generally limited to reputational damage and orders to stop the improper marketing activity.

Meanwhile, the distribution of advertising intended to healthcare professionals (HCPs) which breaches applicable requirements is subject to the same sanctions as other breaches of pharmaceutical advertising rules (*see Question 26*).

# ENGAGEMENT WITH PATIENT ORGANISATIONS

## 34. WHAT KINDS OF ACTIVITIES ARE PERMITTED IN RELATION TO ENGAGEMENT WITH PATIENT ORGANISATIONS? WHAT ARE THE RESTRICTIONS THAT ARE IMPOSED ON RELATIONSHIP WITH PATIENT ORGANISATIONS?

There are no specific restrictions on engagement with patient organisations in Russia, apart from a general limitation that a patient organisation being a non-commercial entity must not be involved in commercial activities (for example, sales and marketing, among others) and can only carry out those activities that are relevant to charter purposes of the patient organisation.

Pharmaceutical companies may collaborate with patient organisations in different non-commercial projects contributing to the achievement of the goals of patient organisation (for example, charitable donations to patients and educational projects in the sphere of certain diseases).

Following the transparency requirements provided for in the Code of Practice of the Association of International Pharmaceutical Manufacturers (AIPM Code), all payments made by the AIPM members to patient organisations must be made publicly available.

# REFORM

**35. ARE THERE ANY PLANS TO REFORM THE LAW ON THE DISTRIBUTION AND PROMOTION OF DRUGS IN YOUR JURISDICTION?**

Significant amendments to the Russian laws on circulation of drugs entered into force on 1 July 2015. In particular, these amendments have:

- Adopted the new rules for the calculation and registration of the maximum sale price of Essential Drug List (EDL) drugs.
- Introduced the concepts of drug interchangeability and marketing authorisation holder.
- Provided for three new grounds for a drug authorisation to be cancelled by the Ministry of Health, namely:
- where the drug has not been marketed in Russia for three or more years;
    - where there has been a failure by the marketing authorisation holder or its authorised representative to take measures to ensure the safety of the drug;
    - where there has been a refusal by the marketing authorisation holder or its authorised representative to edit the medicine information leaflet to reflect new confirmed data that the risks of adverse effects of the medicine are higher than previously stated.
- Required the authorities to provide details of approved good distribution practice (there still no such document or its analogue in Russia).

These amendments are intended to improve the rules for the registration, manufacture and quality control of medicines. However, they also aim to harmonise Russian laws on the distribution of drugs with international standards.

In terms of future reform, there are upcoming limitations for public procurement of drugs originating outside of Russia (that is, state preferences to local products). There is also a proposal to allow the retail of drugs through non-pharmacy shops. However, this is still under development.

# SOUTH AFRICA

Danie Dohmen, Alexis Apostolidis, Jenny Pienaar and Natasha Wright,
ADAMS & ADAMS

## DISTRIBUTION

### PRE-CONDITIONS FOR DISTRIBUTION

### 1. WHAT ARE THE LEGAL PRE-CONDITIONS FOR A DRUG TO BE DISTRIBUTED WITHIN THE JURISDICTION?

The distribution of medicines in South Africa is governed strictly by:

- The Medicines and Related Substances Act No.101 of 1965, as amended (Medicines Act).
- Other pieces of legislation governing the movement of medicines in the supply chain and persons authorised to distribute medicines within the supply chain including the:
  - Pharmacy Act No. 53 of 1974, as amended;
  - Health Professions Act No.56 of 1974, as amended (HPA).

**Authorisation**

The distribution of medicine requires a licence that must be obtained from the Medicines Control Council (MCC). The MCC also issues licences to wholesalers, importers and retailers of medicines.

**Exceptions**

The use of medicines outside of the licensing regime is permitted in certain circumstances for compassionate use (*see Question 2*). The MCC can use its discretion to decide whether or not:

- To grant a licence.
- A medicine can be sold.

### 2. DO ANY TYPES OF NAMED PATIENT AND/OR COMPASSIONATE USE PROGRAMMES OPERATE? IF SO, WHAT ARE THE REQUIREMENTS FOR PRE-LAUNCH ACCESS?

Access to medicines in a compassionate use programme is granted on a case- by-case basis. Therefore, there are no named compassionate use systems, models or programmes that rely on named patients or any other basis.

However, the Medicines Control Council (MCC) has the right to use its discretion to allow compassionate use of unlicensed medicines or medicines by unlicensed persons. Pre-launch access is required, and access to an unlicensed medicine or to a medicine by an unlicensed person must be approved by the MCC.

Failure to obtain approval will result in an offence under the Medicines Act. For further information see the requisite application form at *www.mccza.com/genericdocuments/6.12_ section_21_application_form_feb04_v1_1.doc*.

## LICENSING

### 3. WHAT IS THE PROCEDURAL STRUCTURE REGARDING LICENSING A DRUG FOR DISTRIBUTION?

**Structure**

The structure for the procedure is set out in the Medicines Act. The Medicines Act (read together with the General Regulations) provides details about the particular forms, application fees and information as required by the Medicines Control Council (MCC).

Licensees are required to provide the requisite information in the application forms and also provide information that is stipulated in the General Regulations regarding the substance to be licensed. The application is then delivered to the MCC and deliberated by the MCC. A decision is then made about whether or not to license the medicine for distribution, and the implementation of conditions that will be applicable to the medicine for distribution purposes (including its scheduled status).

**Regulatory authority**

The MCC is responsible for the licensing of drugs in South Africa.

### 4. IS THERE A SIMPLIFIED LICENCE PROCEEDING, OR RELAXED LICENSING CONDITIONS, FOR DRUGS WHICH HAVE ALREADY BEEN LICENSED FOR DISTRIBUTION IN ANOTHER JURISDICTION?

Simplified or expedited licensing procedures exist under section 15 of the Medicines Act. However, the regimes are not really used in practice, due to frequent delays at the Medicine Control Council (MCC) in relation to the processing of licence applications.

There are provisions in the Medicines Act for parallel imports to be accepted, provided that the Minister of Health, (who is ultimately responsible for the enforcement of the Medicines Act) agrees to the parallel import based on a need or requirement of public health. Section 15C of the Medicines Act provides that:

- Any patented medicine can be imported if already registered in South Africa.
- A person or company that wishes to import a patented medicine must apply to the Minister of Health for a permit to parallel import a medicine.
- The holder of a certificate of registration for a medicine in South Africa is not entitled to prevent the medicine's importation into South Africa or its sale, on account of the certificate of registration or the existence of a patent on the medicine.
- The parallel importer is responsible and liable for the parallel imported medicines, for example, he must notify the MCC in the event of a recall or adverse event.
- The parallel importer is responsible for destroying any expired, parallel imported medicines (for the duration of the permit and also after the parallel importation permit has expired).

Section 15C of the Medicines Act has not been used to date.

# SOUTH AFRICA

## 5. IS VIRTUAL DRUG DISTRIBUTION POSSIBLE FROM YOUR JURISDICTION?

There is no specific provision contained in the Medicines Act or any other piece of legislation regarding the virtual distribution of medicines. The Medicines Act assumes that all factors and elements of the distribution of the medicine are physically present within South Africa, including the distributor and the substance being distributed.

It is unlikely that the Medicine Control Council (MCC) would recognise virtual drug distribution. This is because the structure of the Medicines Act provides the MCC with direct jurisdictional control over the process of distributing and selling medicines in South Africa.

## 6. WHAT IS THE PROCEDURE TO APPEAL (LEGAL REMEDY) A LICENSING DECISION?

There is an appeal provision within the Medicines Act that allows applicants for a licence to appeal the decisions of the Medicine Control Council (MCC) if they are dissatisfied with the outcome of the application. The appeal provisions are strengthened by the provisions relating to procedurally fair administrative law contained in section 33 of the Constitution of the Republic of South Africa 1996, read together with the:

- Provisions of the Promotion of Administrative Justice Act No.3 of 2000.
- Various pronouncements in the common law, most notably by the Constitutional Court of South Africa.

The appeal procedure is governed by the provisions of the General Regulations provided in relation to the Medicines Act. Any person aggrieved by a decision of the MCC can appeal under section 24 of the Medicines Act.

## 7. WHAT ARE THE COSTS OF OBTAINING LICENSING?

The costs will vary depending on the nature of the licence that is required. The costs are published, from time to time, by the Medicine Control Council (MCC) in the *Government Gazette*. The *Government Gazette* must be consulted when the licence application is made to the MCC with regard to the costs of a particular licence.

## DISTRIBUTION TO CONSUMERS

## 8. WHAT ARE THE DIFFERENT CATEGORIES OF DRUGS FOR DISTRIBUTION?

The categories of the medicines are determined by the Medicine Control Council.

The primary method for categorising medicines is based on schedules that range from Schedule 0 to Schedule 7. Various conditions attach to the distribution and sale of the medicine depending on the nature of the schedule that is applied. For example:

- Schedule 0 medicines are available off the shelf or without prescription in a supermarket.
- Schedule 5 medicines are only available from a pharmacist on prescription by an authorised prescriber.

SOUTH AFRICA

## 9. WHO IS AUTHORISED TO DISTRIBUTE PRESCRIPTION DRUGS AND OVER-THE-COUNTER DRUGS TO CONSUMERS?

The sale of medicines to consumers is determined by:

- **Section 22C of the Medicines Act.** A person holding a dispensing licence can sell medicines to consumers.
- **Pharmacy Act.** A person who is registered as a pharmacist can sell medicines directly to consumers.

Certain categories of medicines can be sold directly to consumers "off the shelf" and can be sold by anyone including retailers. The licensing requirements under the Medicines Act provide that:

- A written application must be made.
- The applicant must adhere to certain criteria as determined by the Medicine Control Council.

The sale of over-the-counter medicines to consumers is restricted to pharmacists who are licensed and registered under the provisions of the Pharmacy Act, and persons licensed under the provisions of section 22C of the Medicines Act. It should be noted that corporate ownership of pharmacies is permitted in terms of section 22A of the Pharmacy Act, provided that the existence of a pharmacy, within the confines of, for example, a retailer or other non-pharmacy setting, is governed by provisions in the Medicines Act and supervised by the Department of Health.

### Over-the-counter drugs

The sale of over-the-counter medicines to consumers is restricted to:

- Pharmacists who are licensed and registered under the provisions of the Pharmacy Act.
- Persons licensed under the provisions of section 22C of the Medicines Act (see above).

Corporate ownership of pharmacies is allowed under section 22A of the Pharmacy Act, provided that the existence of a pharmacy is governed by provisions in the Medicines Act and supervised by the Department of Health.

## 10. WHAT DRUGS CAN AN ATTENDING PHYSICIAN DISTRIBUTE AND UNDER WHAT CIRCUMSTANCES?

Any substance that is registered as a medicine under the provisions of the Medicines Act is available for sale or distribution by an attending physician and can be provided to a consumer/patient by an attending physician.

The Medicines Act and the Pharmacy Act allow for the sale of medicines by attending physicians in circumstances where the medicine is needed to treat the consumer/patient's condition and the attending physician completes the correct prescription for the sale of that medicine. However, a generic substitution is required by law where a generic alternative exists for a branded or prescribed medicine.

## 11. WHO IS AUTHORISED TO PRESCRIBE PRESCRIPTION DRUGS TO CONSUMERS?

Authorised prescribers can prescribe medicines under the provisions of the Medicines Act and the Health Professions Act No.56 of 1974 (HPA). The term "authorised prescriber" is defined in the HPA and recognised by the Medicines Act as persons who are admitted as medical practitioners.

The following persons are allowed to prescribe medicines:

- Medical practitioners.
- Psychiatrists.
- Dentists.
- Other persons authorised in accordance with the licensing provisions of the Medicines Act and the Pharmacy Act read together with the HPA.

## 12. IS DIRECT MAILING/DISTANCE SELLING OF DRUGS PERMITTED IN YOUR JURISDICTION?

### Conditions

Distance selling of medicines is permitted, and various courier-type pharmacies exist that specialise in the movement of medicines across large distances. Typically, such arrangements exist within the context of private medical funding. Therefore, a medical scheme (being the vehicle for private medical funding) generally has an arrangement with a courier pharmacy that creates an obligation on the pharmacy to transport medicines within South Africa.

### Cross-border sales

Cross-border sales are not normally authorised unless the:

- Receiving state has authorised the entry of medicines into the country through its own licensing regimes.
- Persons operating the importation of medicines into that state are authorised and licensed accordingly.

In addition, under the Pharmacy Act, the distributor must be licensed to move medicines over distances, in a courier format.

## 13. WHAT REGULATORY AUTHORITY IS RESPONSIBLE FOR SUPERVISING DISTRIBUTION ACTIVITIES?

Distribution activities are supervised by the:

- Medicine Control Council in relation to applications for licence for a medicines distributor.
- South African Pharmacy Council in relation to the dispensing functions of pharmacists.

## 14. WHAT IS THE PROCEDURE TO APPEAL (LEGAL REMEDY) A DISTRIBUTION DECISION?

Provisions exist in the Medicines Act and the Pharmacy Act for an applicant to appeal a decision by the Medicine Control Council or the South African Pharmacy Council in relation to an application for a distribution licence or the existence of a distribution licence.

SOUTH AFRICA

### 15. WHAT ARE THE LEGAL CONSEQUENCES OF NON-COMPLIANCE WITH CONSUMER DISTRIBUTION LAWS?

There are various legal consequences for a person who does not have the correct licence to distribute medicines or who sells medicines in circumstances that contravene the Medicines Act, the Pharmacy Act or the Health Professions Act No.56 of 1974 (HPA).

Penalties include civil and criminal liability. The level of fine or imprisonment will depend on the nature of the offence and the statutory requirement that has been violated. In addition, persons who endanger consumers/patients through the sale of medicines without the appropriate licenses can also contravene the Consumer Protection Act No.68 of 2008 (CPA). The CPA provides for additional penalties.

## WHOLESALE DISTRIBUTION

### 16. WHAT IS THE LEGAL REGIME REGARDING WHOLESALE DISTRIBUTION OF DRUGS?

The wholesale of medicines is governed by the Medicines Act and a licensing structure imposed by the Medicine Control Council (MCC). Any person who wishes to engage in the wholesale of medicines must be licensed to do so by the MCC in accordance with the requirements contained in the Medicines Act and the General Regulations provided in the Medicines Act. Any person can apply to be a wholesaler of medicines subject to requirements that prohibit the existence of a wholesale licence within certain commercial companies that have a direct or indirect beneficial interest in a retail pharmacy.

### 17. WHAT REGULATORY AUTHORITY IS RESPONSIBLE FOR SUPERVISING WHOLESALE DISTRIBUTION ACTIVITIES?

**Regulatory authority**

The Medicine Control Council (MCC) is responsible for supervising wholesale distribution activities.

**Supervision**

The MCC is empowered through an inspectorate, created by virtue of provisions in the Medicines Act, to ensure that wholesale activities occur within the confines of the law.

**Rights of appeal**

A person has a legal right under the Medicines Act to appeal any decisions made by the MCC or its inspectorate. The right to appeal is reinforced by the:

- Administrative law provisions set out in section 33 of the Constitution.
- Provisions of the Promotion of Administrative Justice Act No.3 of 2000.
- Applicable pronouncements in the common law including those by the Constitutional Court of South Africa.

## 18. WHAT ARE THE LEGAL CONSEQUENCES OF NON-COMPLIANCE WITH WHOLESALE DISTRIBUTION LAWS?

A person can be subject to criminal liability in the form of fines and imprisonment for the wholesale distribution of medicines without the required licence. The applicable penalties are provided in the Medicines Act and vary on a case by case basis depending on the nature of the offence committed.

# MARKETING

## PROMOTION

## 19. WHAT IS THE GENERAL LEGAL REGIME FOR THE MARKETING OF DRUGS?

**Legal regime**

The Medicines Act and its Regulations, govern the marketing of medical substances and devices in South Africa. The Code of Marketing Practice (Code) and its Guidelines provided under the Medicines Act were drafted to regulate the ethical marketing of medicines and medical devices in South Africa.

In particular, the Code regulates:

- Medical devices.
- Registered health products (including scheduled and unscheduled medication).
- All advertising and promotional activities where members of the medical field are influenced to purchase, prescribe, supply, administer, loan or lease a health product.

**Limits to marketing activities**

The Medicines Act provides that no person can advertise any medicine or scheduled substance for sale unless the advertisement complies with the prescribed requirements. The Medicines Act also prohibits the publication or distribution of any false or misleading advertisement relating to any medicine.

The Regulations under the Medicines Act provide that only the following can be advertised to the public:

- Medicines that do not contain a scheduled substance.
- Medicines that contain a substance appearing in Schedule 0 or Schedule 1 (*see Question 8*).

Medicines that contain a substance appearing in Schedules 2 to 6 (*see Question 8*) can be advertised for information purposes to:

- Medical practitioners.
- Dentists.
- Veterinarians.
- Pharmacists and other persons authorised to prescribe medicines.
- Persons in receipt of certain publications containing the advertising.

## SOUTH AFRICA

The Code deals with the appropriate advertising of medicines and regulates:

- Truthful advertising.
- Comparative advertising.
- Disparaging references.
- Inducements, gifts and promotional items and competitions.

In general, advertisements must not be misleading or disparaging (either directly or by implication). Information, claims and comparisons must be accurate, balanced, fair, objective, unambiguous and supportable and must be based on an up-to-date evaluation of all the evidence and reflect that evidence clearly. The use of medical terminology is acceptable provided that it does not confuse or mislead the consumer.

### 20. ARE THERE OTHER CODES OF CONDUCT FOR THE MARKETING OF DRUGS (FOR EXAMPLE, BY PROFESSIONAL OR INDUSTRIAL ORGANISATIONS)?

The Code of Marketing Practice (Code) was enacted by the Minister of Health, in consultation with the Medicine Control Council (MCC) and other stakeholders.

The Code is enforced by the Marketing Code Authority (MCA), which is also the body responsible for adjudicating complaints and disputes relating to the Code. The Code is based on the principle of self-regulation through the health industry. However, it is legally binding, as national legislation recognises the self-regulatory Code's principles and procedures.

The Code is adopted by companies in the health industry, for example, the health products trade associations and the South African Medical Device Industry Association, in order to ensure that the marketing of health products to healthcare professionals (HCP) and the public is carried out in a reasonable, ethical and professional manner, based on information that is practical and scientifically validated.

## MARKETING TO CONSUMERS

### 21. WHAT IS THE LEGAL REGIME FOR MARKETING TO CONSUMERS?

**Legal regime**

The Medicines Act and the Code of Marketing Practice (Code) govern the marketing of medicinal products to consumers.

The Consumer Protection Act of 2008 (CPA) promotes and advances the social and economic welfare of South African consumers. The CPA:

- Is applicable to all goods marketed for human consumption.
- Prohibits the application of a trade description to a product that is likely to mislead consumers.
- Provides that goods cannot be marketed in such a way that is reasonably likely to imply a false or misleading representation. When marketing a product, a supplier:
    - cannot make a false, misleading or deceptive representation to consumers regarding the material facts relating to a product;
    - must correct any misapprehension on the part of consumers.

The Advertising Standard Authority Code (ASA Code) is the guiding document of the Advertising Standard Authority of South Africa and mainly regulates commercial advertising in South Africa. The Preamble of the ASA Code provides that advertising must be:

- Legal.
- Decent.
- Honest.
- Truthful.

The provisions of the ASA Code and the CPA are incorporated to a great extent in the Code and the Medicines Act and its Regulations. For this reason, only the relevant portions of the Code and the Medicines Act are discussed further. However, a complainant is not prohibited from seeking relief under the CPA and the ASA Code, if it believes that the marketing of a medicine contravenes any of the relevant provisions.

### Products

The following can be advertised to the public:

- Medicines that do not contain a scheduled substance.
- Medicines that contain a substance appearing in Schedule 0 or Schedule 1 (*see* Question 8).

## 22. WHAT KINDS OF MARKETING ACTIVITIES ARE PERMITTED IN RELATION TO CONSUMERS AND THE PRODUCTS WHICH MAY BE ADVERTISED TO THEM?

### The Medicines Act

Under the Medicines Act, the term "advertisement" includes any written, pictorial, visual or other descriptive matter or verbal statement or reference that is intended to promote the sale of that medicine or scheduled substance by:

- Appearing in any newspaper, magazine, pamphlet or other publication.
- Being distributed to members of the public.
- Being brought to the notice of members of the public in any manner whatsoever.

The term "advertise" has a corresponding meaning.

### The Code of Marketing Practice (Code)

Advertising and/or promotion and promotional materials or activities, includes the following:

- Advertorials.
- Branded materials relating to product sponsorship.
- Aerial promotions, for example hot air balloons.
- Booklets.
- Cinema commercials.
- Consumer leaflets.
- Consumer broadsheets.
- Direct mail materials.
- Website and other internet materials, including press releases intended for internet publication.

- Outdoor advertising.
- Point of sale materials and posters.
- Print advertisements (for example, for use in newspapers and magazines).
- Promotional aids including those used for direct selling activities.

In the marketing and/or advertising of Schedules 0 and 1 medicines (see Question 8), the Code provides that advertisements to the general public must be consistent with the requirements of the Medicines Act and other applicable legislation.

Compliance with the Medicines Act includes that all advertising and/or promotional material:

- Must give the information necessary for the correct use of a product as approved by the medicines regulatory authority.
- Cannot deviate from, be in conflict with or go beyond the evidence submitted in the application for registration of the medicine (and that has been approved by the Medicines Control Council and incorporated in the approved package insert).
- Must not be misleading or disparaging (either directly or by implication).
- Must not be misleading as to the nature of the product, its ingredients or indications.
- Must not contain any other express or implied exaggerated claims as to the benefits that can be obtained from use of the health product.
- Must not cause consumers unwarranted anxiety with regard to any condition.
- Must not use language which causes fear or distress.
- Must not suggest that using a health product can enhance normal good health or be a substitute for a healthy diet and lifestyle.
- Must not be aimed principally or exclusively at children (under 12 years of age).
- Must not show children using, or within reach of health products without adult supervision.
- Must not encourage individuals to exclusively self-diagnose, particularly where medical intervention is required.
- Must not encourage consumers to discontinue the use of prescribed health products.
- Must not include a recommendation by a person who, because of his celebrity status, can encourage consumers to use a particular health product.

Advertising and/or promotion must not unfairly defame or discredit (either directly or by implication) a competitor product, ingredient or treatment type, or suggest that a product's effects are better than or equal to another identifiable product or treatment.

Testimonials are allowed, provided that the testimonial complies with the approved package insert and the testimonial is not more than three years old. The use of healthcare professionals (HCPs) for marketing, promotion, endorsements or testimonials is allowed, provided that it takes place within the scope set by the professional codes applicable to such professionals.

## 23. IS IT PERMITTED TO PROVIDE CONSUMERS WITH FREE SAMPLES? ARE THERE PARTICULAR RESTRICTIONS ON SPECIAL OFFERS (FOR EXAMPLE, "BUY-ONE-GET-ONE-FREE")?

### The Medicines Act

Part A of the Code of Marketing Practice (Code), which deals with the marketing of health products to healthcare professionals (HCPs), prohibits the supply of samples beyond the conditions provided under the Medicines Act.

The Medicines Act provides that no person must provide a sample of any medicine. A "sample" means the free supply of medicines by a manufacturer or wholesaler or its agent to a pharmacist, medical practitioner, dentist, veterinarian, practitioner, nurse or other person registered under the Health Professions Act 1974. It does not include the free supply of medicines for the purposes of clinical trials, donations of medicines to the state, tendering to the state and quality control by inspectors. Part A of the Code does not expressly prohibit the provision of free samples to consumers.

### The Code

The Code provides that the provision of medical goods that will enhance patient care or benefit the South African health system are acceptable. The provision of such goods must not be done in such a way as to be an inducement to prescribe, supply, administer or buy any health product or to recommend its use, prescription or purchase. However, it is unclear if the term "medicinal goods" means medicines or if it relates to medical equipment or promotional items, for example, desk pads and pens.

The Code provides that banded packs for Schedule 0 medicinal products (*see Question 8*) are permitted. The medicinal products that are banded together must be the same product that is two lots of product "X" lozenges.

It is not permissible to band together different dosage forms or products (that is product X syrup and product X lozenges).

Giveaway items, for example plastic dosage spoons for Schedule 0 products must be of a nominal value and not mislead the patient or encourage the inappropriate use of the health product.

The branding of children's medicines must not advertise or encourage the use of medicines by children.

## 24. ARE THERE PARTICULAR RULES OF PRACTICE ON THE USE OF THE INTERNET/SOCIAL MEDIA REGARDING DRUGS AND THEIR ADVERTISING?

The advertising of Schedules 0 and 1 medicines to the public is permitted. Therefore, E-pharmacies are restricted to the promotion and online sale of Schedule 0 and Schedule 1 medicines.

The Code of Marketing Practice (Code) provides that internet access to promotional materials of Schedule 2 to Schedule 6 medicine that is directed at the South African public must be limited through a password protection scheme to healthcare professionals (HCPs).

Information or promotional material relating to Schedule 2 to Schedule 6 medicines that is placed on the internet outside of South Africa will be regarded as falling within the scope of the Code if:

- It was placed on the internet by a South African company or an affiliate of a South African company, or at the instigation or with the authority of a South African company or an affiliate of a South African company.
- It makes specific reference to the availability or use of the medicine in South Africa.

Schedule 2 to Schedule 6 medicines can be advertised in relevant, independently produced electronic journals that are intended for HCPs or appropriate administrative staff, provided that the electronic journals cannot be accessed by non-HCPs.

Package inserts of Schedule 2 to Schedule 6 medicines can be made available on the internet and accessed by members of the public, provided that the package inserts are not presented in such a way as to be promotional in nature.

In addition, it must be made clear to an internet user:

- That he is leaving any of the company sites.
- When he is leaving any sites sponsored by the company.
- That he is being directed to a site that is not that of the company.

The promotion of all medicines by e-mail is prohibited, unless the option to opt out is given and the decision is respected. The opt out option must also be provided on all subsequent communications, even if the addressee has not opted out after the first point of contact.

## 25. WHAT REGULATORY AUTHORITY IS RESPONSIBLE FOR SUPERVISING MARKETING ACTIVITIES TO CONSUMERS?

**Regulatory authority**

The Medicines Control Council (MCC) is the body authorised to supervise the marketing of medicines under the Medicines Act.

The Code of Marketing Practice (Code) is enforced by the Marketing Code Authority (MCA), which is also responsible for settling complaints and disputes under the Code. The Code is based on the principle of self-regulation through the health industry. However, it is legally binding, as national legislation recognises the self-regulatory Code's principles and procedures.

**Supervision**

**The Medicines Act.** The MCC is empowered through an inspectorate, created in accordance with the Medicines Act, to ensure that wholesale distribution activities occur within the confines of the law.

Under the Medicines Act, an inspector can enter any premises if he suspects, on reasonable grounds that an offence under the Medicines Act is being, or may be committed in the future. The inspector can also inspect any medicine or scheduled substance, any book, record or documents that he believes, on reasonable grounds, to contain any information relevant to the administration or enforcement of the Medicines Act.

**The Code.** The MCA can process any dispute or complaint relating to the provisions of the Code, and an aggrieved party can, after exhausting all internal remedies in the Code, approach the MCC for resolution of the matter. The MCA also has the authority to refer any matter to the MCC if it considers that the matter warrants the referral.

## Rights of appeal

Under the Medicines Act, any person aggrieved by a decision of the MCC can appeal against the decision to an appeal committee.

Under the Code, it is possible to appeal against the decision of the Adjudication Committee. Appeals can, at the discretion of the Adjudication Committee, and depending on the complexity of the matter, be a face-to-face hearing, or a paper-based appeal. A decision against the Adjudication Committee must lie with an Appeal Committee and no other body.

## 26. WHAT ARE THE LEGAL CONSEQUENCES OF NON-COMPLIANCE WITH CONSUMER MARKETING LAWS?

### The Medicines Act

It is an offence to contravene the provisions of the Medicines Act, including those that prohibit the misleading advertising of medicines. Any person who is convicted of an offence will be liable to a fine, or to imprisonment for a period of up to ten years.

The court that convicts any person of an offence can declare that any medicine or scheduled substance in relation to the offence committed can be forfeited to the state. Any medicine or scheduled substance forfeited to the state must be destroyed or otherwise dealt with as the Director-General may direct.

### The Code of Marketing Practice (Code)

A complainant can lodge a written, formal complaint with the Executive Officer of the Marketing Code Authority (MCA) setting out the details of the complaint. The respondent can then respond to the complaint. The complaint is then forwarded to the Adjudication Committee. Legal representation is only allowed if the Adjudication Committee considers it appropriate, based on the facts of the matter. If the Adjudication Committee finds in favour of the complainant, the Committee can impose one of the following sanctions:

- A reprimand, caution or warning.
- A fine (the amount is determined from time to time by the MCA).
- A directive ordering the infringing party to audit its internal policies and procedures to be in line with those prescribed by the Code.
- A directive prescribing that any offending promotional activity, material or advertisement is ceased and/or withdrawn.
- An order that the infringing party provides a written undertaking that it will avoid similar breaches in future.
- An order that the infringing party must make a public statement correcting its non-compliance with the Code.
- An appropriate costs order, including the costs of the complainant.

**SOUTH AFRICA**

MARKETING TO PROFESSIONALS

### 27. WHAT KINDS OF MARKETING ACTIVITIES ARE PERMITTED IN RELATION TO PROFESSIONALS?

All forms of advertising and promotional activities must conform to the provisions of the Medicines Act and its Regulations. The following forms of marketing activities (although not exhaustive) to healthcare professionals (HCPs) are permitted:

- Journal advertising.
- Distribution of promotional material, including promotional aids and gifts.
- Hosting or sponsoring meetings and events.
- Hosting competitions.

### 28. ARE THERE ANY RESTRICTIONS ON MARKETING TO PROFESSIONALS?

**Marketing activities**

**Reprints.** Under the Code of Marketing Practice (Code), reprints of articles in journals must not be provided to any healthcare professional unless the articles have been published in a peer reviewed publication in line with good principles of scientific review and publication. When providing a reprint of an article about a health product, it must be accompanied by prescribing information.

**Distribution of promotional material.** Promotional material must only be sent or distributed to categories of persons whose need or interest in the particular information can reasonably be assumed.

**Frequency**

A company must respect any requests by an addressee to cease or limit the volume of promotional material. Mailing lists must be kept up to date. Requests from healthcare professionals (HCPs) to be removed from promotional mailing lists must be complied with promptly and no name can be restored except at their request or with their permission.

**Provision of hospitality**

Companies, organisations or individuals are permitted to organise or sponsor meetings and events provided that:

- The merit and focus of the meeting is clearly scientific and/or educational.
- The venue and hospitality is secondary to the meeting (both in the allocation of time and focus).
- The venue is appropriate and beneficial to the scientific or educational objectives and the purpose of the event or meeting.
- Hospitality, meals and entertainment are modest. As a general rule, hospitality must not exceed what the HCPs would normally pay for themselves.
- Invitations are not extended to spouses or other guests, except if they are HCPs or administrative staff and form part of the trainees or invited attendees at the meeting/event.
- Inappropriate financial benefit or material benefits (including excessive hospitality) is not offered and/or extended to HCPs.

SOUTH AFRICA

- Reasonable payment and reimbursement for out-of-pocket expenses, including travel, are permissible for speakers (provided it is included in the terms of a written contract).

Meetings organised for patients, the general public, individual or groups of doctors, other HCPs and/or for administrative staff that are wholly or mainly of an entertainment, leisure, social or sporting nature are not permitted.

## 29. WHAT INFORMATION IS IT LEGALLY REQUIRED TO INCLUDE IN ADVERTISING TO PROFESSIONALS?

All advertising and/or promotional material must be based on the current approved South African package insert. Under the Medicines Act, the advertising and promotion of health products must:

- Conform to the applicable regulations under the Medicines Act.
- Form part of the promotional material and not be separate.
- Be included in all promotional material (except for promotional items such as promotional aids, on which limited information must appear).
- Be provided in a clear and legible manner.
- Be consistent with the most recently approved package insert for the medicine.

The statement "For full prescribing information refer to the package insert approved by the medicines regulatory authority" must appear or be stated in all forms of advertising and/or promotion (written, audio, audio-visual and the internet, except for promotional items such as promotional aids).

## 30. ARE THERE RULES ON COMPARISONS WITH OTHER PRODUCTS THAT ARE PARTICULARLY APPLICABLE TO DRUGS?

The Code of Marketing Practice (Code) provides that a comparison in the marketing and promotion of health products is only permitted in promotional material if:

- It is not misleading or disparaging.
- Health products or services for the same needs or intended for the same purpose are compared.
- One or more material, relevant and representative feature(s) are compared.
- No confusion is created between the health product advertised and that of a competitor, or between the advertisers' trademarks, proprietary names, other distinguishing marks and those of a competitor.
- The trade marks, proprietary names, other distinguishing marks, health products, services, activities or circumstances of a competitor are not discredited or defamed.
- The trade marks or company names of another company are only mentioned with written permission from the other company.
- No unfair advantage is taken of the reputation of a brand, trademark, proprietary name or other distinguishing mark of another company.
- Health products or services are not presented as imitations or replicas of goods or services bearing another company trademark or trade name.
- Hanging (open-ended) comparisons are not used.

Price comparisons must be accurate, fair and must not mislead.

SOUTH AFRICA

### 31. WHAT OTHER ITEMS, FUNDING OR SERVICES ARE PERMITTED TO BE PROVIDED TO PROFESSIONALS?

The Medicine Act provides that no person can supply any medicine according to a bonus system, rebate system or any other incentive scheme.

The Code Marketing Practice (Code) provides that there must be no personal enrichment of healthcare professionals (HCPs) or other healthcare providers. No gift, benefit in kind, rebate, discount, kickback or any other pecuniary advantage can be offered or given to HCPs, administrative staff, government officials, or the general public as an inducement to prescribe, lease, loan, supply, stock, dispense, administer or buy any health product.

**Discounts**

Discounts are not permitted under the Medicines Act.

**Free samples**

The Medicines Act provides that no manufacturer or wholesaler or its agent can supply free of charge medicine to a pharmacist, medical practitioner, dentist, veterinarian, practitioner, nurse or other person registered under the Health Professions Act 1974. This exclusion does not include the provision of medicine, free of charge, for the purposes of clinical trials, donations of medicines to the state, tendering to the state and quality control by inspectors.

**Sponsorship of professionals**

The sponsorship of professionals is regulated largely under the Code, particularly dealing with the attendance of HCPs at conferences or meetings.

The Code provides that the rationale for any meeting or sponsorship of a professional to attend a meeting must be transparent, valid and clear.

Payment of registration fees, travel and accommodation must be made to the professional associations/organisers and not directly to the HCP, unless proof is received that the amount spent is in the name of the sponsored person and corresponds to each and every line item as per the agreed sponsorship.

Sponsored speakers can receive reasonable payments.

**Other items, funding or services**

**Gifts.** Occasional gifts to HCPs are acceptable provided that they are:

- Inexpensive and of modest intrinsic value.
- Not for personal use, for example, no entertainment CDs/DVDs, electronic items for entertainment, tickets to attend sporting events or other forms of entertainment.
- Educational and/or of scientific value.

**Competitions.** Competitions must fulfil the following criteria:

- The competition is based on medical/product knowledge or the acquisition of scientific knowledge.
- The individual prizes or educational items offered are within the price limit set from time to time by the Marketing Code Authority (MCA).
- Entry into a competition must not be dependent on prescribing, ordering or recommending a product and no such condition must be made or implied.

## 32. WHAT REGULATORY AUTHORITY IS RESPONSIBLE FOR SUPERVISING MARKETING ACTIVITIES REGARDING PROFESSIONALS?

The Medicine Control Council and the Marketing Code Authority (MCA) are responsible for supervising marketing activities to healthcare professionals (HCPs).

See *Question 22* for further details.

## 33. WHAT ARE THE LEGAL CONSEQUENCES IN CASE OF NON-COMPLIANCE WITH PROFESSIONAL MARKETING LAWS?

See *Question 23*.

# ENGAGEMENT WITH PATIENT ORGANISATIONS

## 34. WHAT KINDS OF ACTIVITIES ARE PERMITTED IN RELATION TO ENGAGEMENT WITH PATIENT ORGANISATIONS? WHAT ARE THE RESTRICTIONS THAT ARE IMPOSED ON RELATIONSHIP WITH PATIENT ORGANISATIONS?

### Written agreements

When companies provide financial support, significant indirect support and/or significant non-financial support to patient organisations, they must have in place a written agreement that states the amount of funding and also the purpose.

### Use of logos and proprietary materials

The public use of a patient organisation's logo and/or proprietary material by a company requires written permission from that organisation.

### Editorial control

Companies must not seek to influence the text of any patient organisation material that they sponsor in a manner that is favourable to their own commercial interests. This does not preclude companies from correcting factual inaccuracies.

### Contracted services

Contracts between companies and patient organisations where they provide any type of services to companies are only allowed if the services are provided for the purpose of supporting healthcare or research.

### Events and hospitality

All events sponsored or organised by or on behalf of a company including scientific, business or professional meetings must comply with the requirements that deal with the appropriate provision of hospitality and the hosting of meetings and events.

Hospitality can only be extended to persons who qualify as participants in their own right. In exceptional cases, in case of clear health needs (for example, disability), the travel meals, accommodation and registration fees of an accompanying person considered to be a care giver can be provided.

## REFORM

### 35. ARE THERE ANY PLANS TO REFORM THE LAW ON THE DISTRIBUTION AND PROMOTION OF DRUGS IN YOUR JURISDICTION?

In 2008, amendments to the Medicines Act were passed by parliament and are known as the "Prelex" to the Medicines Act. The amendments provide for the:

- Registration and regulation of medical devices.
- Establishment of the South African Health Products Regulatory Authority (SAHPRA) (which will replace the current Medicines Control Council).
- Appointment of a CEO of SAHPRA.

It was thought that the amendments would come into effect in mid 2013. However, the amendments, which still deal, to a large extent, with the registration, licensing, and advertising of medical devices, have not been passed or come into effect yet and it is uncertain when the Medicines Act will be amended.

The General Regulations to the Medicines Act were amended in November 2013 to include the registration of complementary medicines. The amendments, relating to the registration of complementary medicines came into effect in November 2013.

# SOUTH KOREA

Hyeong Gun Lee and Jin Hwan Chung, LEE & KO

## DISTRIBUTION

### PRE-CONDITIONS FOR DISTRIBUTION

**1. WHAT ARE THE LEGAL PRE-CONDITIONS FOR A DRUG TO BE DISTRIBUTED WITHIN THE JURISDICTION?**

#### Authorisation

Under the Pharmaceutical Affairs Act (PAA) a product approval (that is, market authorisation) must be obtained from the Ministry of Food and Drug Safety (MFDS) to manufacture, import or market a medicinal product within South Korea.

For pharmaceutical products, an application with supporting documents (including clinical trial data and a good manufacturing practice (GMP) certificate) must be submitted to the MFDS for approval. However, some products are exempt from the MFDS approval procedure (for example, products set out under the South Korean Pharmacopoeia, an official book of medicinal products recognised by the MFDS). In exemption cases, a report must be submitted to the MFDS before the manufacture, importing or marketing of the products. The MFDS will review the report to ensure that the exemption requirements are satisfied.

#### Exceptions

Certain orphan drugs (that is, pharmaceutical agents developed specifically to treat a rare medical condition) and drugs requested by the Ministry of Defence for military use can be imported and distributed prior to obtaining a market authorisation under the PAA.

**2. DO ANY TYPES OF NAMED PATIENT AND/OR COMPASSIONATE USE PROGRAMMES OPERATE? IF SO, WHAT ARE THE REQUIREMENTS FOR PRE-LAUNCH ACCESS?**

The named patient programme/compassionate programme has not been officially introduced in South Korea. However, certain products (for example, orphan drugs and drugs requested by the Defence Minister for military use) can be imported and distributed prior to obtaining a market authorisation under the PAA (*see Question 1*).

## LICENSING

### 3. WHAT IS THE PROCEDURAL STRUCTURE REGARDING LICENSING A DRUG FOR DISTRIBUTION?

**Structure**

An import business licence is not currently required for licensing a drug for distribution. However, a registration as an import business with the local branch of the Ministry of Food and Drug Safety (MFDS) is required in practice. In any case, from 29 September 2015, an entity wanting to import drugs as part of its business will be required to file an import business notification to the MFDS in addition to obtaining a product approval (*see Question 1*).

A wholesaler is required to obtain a wholesale licence from the local municipal government. A pharmacy is established and operated by a licensed pharmacist only upon making a filing with the local municipal government.

**Regulatory authority**

See *above, Structure*.

### 4. IS THERE A SIMPLIFIED LICENCE PROCEEDING, OR RELAXED LICENSING CONDITIONS, FOR DRUGS WHICH HAVE ALREADY BEEN LICENSED FOR DISTRIBUTION IN ANOTHER JURISDICTION?

In principle, a simplified licence proceeding and relaxed licensing conditions are not recognised under the Pharmaceutical Affairs Act.

### 5. IS VIRTUAL DRUG DISTRIBUTION POSSIBLE FROM YOUR JURISDICTION?

Virtual drug distribution is not possible from South Korea.

### 6. WHAT IS THE PROCEDURE TO APPEAL (LEGAL REMEDY) A LICENSING DECISION?

The procedure to legal remedy a licensing decision is either to:

- File an administrative appeal with the Administrative Tribunal under the Administrative Appeals Act.
- File an administrative litigation with the courts under the Administrative Litigation Act.

### 7. WHAT ARE THE COSTS OF OBTAINING LICENSING?

The costs of obtaining licensing are as follows:

- **Fees for product approval:**
  - for a new drug up to KRW3.726 million (online application) and KRW4.140 million (in-person application);
  - for an orphan drug up to KRW1.863 million (online application) and KRW1.260 million (in-person application);

- for other drugs up to KRW1.134 million (online application) and KRW1.26 million (in-person application).
- **Import licence filing fee.** Not yet determined.
- **Wholesaler licence filing fee.** KRW20,000.

## DISTRIBUTION TO CONSUMERS

### 8. WHAT ARE THE DIFFERENT CATEGORIES OF DRUGS FOR DISTRIBUTION?

The different categories of drugs for distribution are as follows:

- **Prescription drugs.** These are sold at pharmacies with a physician's prescription.
- **Over-the-counter drugs.** These are sold at pharmacies without a physician's prescription.
- **Safe and readily available drugs.** These can be sold at 24-hour convenience stores without a physician's prescription.

### 9. WHO IS AUTHORISED TO DISTRIBUTE PRESCRIPTION DRUGS AND OVER-THE-COUNTER DRUGS TO CONSUMERS?

**Prescription drugs**

A licensed wholesaler can distribute prescription drugs to pharmacies. A pharmacy established and operated by a licensed pharmacist can sell prescription drugs to patients with a physician's prescription.

**Over-the-counter drugs**

A licensed wholesaler can distribute over-the-counter drugs to pharmacies. A pharmacy established and operated by a licensed pharmacist can sell over-the-counter drugs to consumers without a physician's prescription. Certain over-the-counter drugs are designated by the Ministry of Food and Drug Safety as "safe and readily available drugs" which can be sold at 24-hour convenience stores without a physician's prescription.

### 10. WHAT DRUGS CAN AN ATTENDING PHYSICIAN DISTRIBUTE AND UNDER WHAT CIRCUMSTANCES?

In principle, a physician is not allowed to directly dispense drugs to patients except in the following cases:

- Where he dispenses drugs in an area where no pharmacy exists.
- Where he dispenses drugs for the purpose of disaster relief because pharmacies become virtually non-existent due to a natural disaster.
- Where he dispenses drugs for an emergency patient or a patient suffering from mental illness, for example schizophrenia and manic-depressive insanity, and who is feared to harm himself or a third party.
- Where he dispenses drugs to the following:
  - in-patients;
  - patients suffering from a Type 1 infectious disease under the Infectious Disease Control

and Prevention Act; or
- a person admitted to a social welfare facility under the Social Welfare Services Act (where a person does not board and lodge in the social welfare facility, it will be limited only to the dispensing of drugs during the period for which he utilises the facility).
- Where he gives injections.
- Where he administers medication, including vaccines to prevent infectious diseases, drugs for medical examinations, and other drugs prescribed by the Ordinance of the Ministry of Health and Welfare (MOHW).
- Where he dispenses drugs for patients while serving in a public health centre or its branch office under the Regional Public Health Act (excluding ambulatory care services for residents within the jurisdiction of a public health centre and a public health branch office designated by the MOHW).
- Where he dispenses drugs for:
  - veterans with disability ratings (from 1 to 3) under the Act on the Honorable Treatment and Support of Persons of Distinguished Services to the State and its Enforcement Decree;
  - persons with disability ratings (from 1 to 4) among those wounded in the 18 May democratisation movement under the Act on the Honorable Treatment of Persons of Distinguished Service to the 18 May Democratisation Movement;
  - persons with severe disabilities under the Act on Assistance to Patients from Actual or Potential Aftereffects of Defoliants and its Enforcement Decree;
  - persons with disability ratings (1 and 2) under the Act on Welfare of Persons with Disabilities and its Enforcement Decree; or
  - patients suffering from Parkinson's disease or Hansen's disease.
- Where he dispenses drugs for the treatment of persons having undergone surgery involving an internal organ transplant and for the treatment of patients suffering from AIDS.
- Where he dispenses drugs for:
  - active service persons in the course of discharging a military duty;
  - riot police officers;
  - security guards of any correctional institution; or
  - other persons who are held in correctional institutions under the Administration and Treatment of Correctional Institution Inmates Act and the Act on the Execution of Criminal Penalties in the Armed Forces and the Treatment of Military Prison Inmates, protected juvenile accommodation facilities under the Act on the Treatment of Protected Juveniles and internment facilities under the Immigration Control Act.
- Where he administers drugs for the treatment of tuberculosis under the Tuberculosis Prevention Act (limited to public health centres, public health branches and subsidiary hospitals of the Korean National Tuberculosis Association).
- Where he dispenses drugs for community service activities.
- Where he is prohibited from disclosing prescriptions for the confidentiality of information related to national security.
- Other cases prescribed by the Presidential Enforcement Decree of the Pharmaceutical Affairs Act.

## 11. WHO IS AUTHORISED TO PRESCRIBE PRESCRIPTION DRUGS TO CONSUMERS?

Licensed physicians are authorised to prescribe prescription drugs to consumers.

## 12. IS DIRECT MAILING/DISTANCE SELLING OF DRUGS PERMITTED IN YOUR JURISDICTION?

Direct mailing/distance selling is not allowed in principle. However, in practice a patient may be allowed to import a small amount of drugs (other than narcotics drugs) for his own personal use (that is, not for resale or distribution).

## 13. WHAT REGULATORY AUTHORITY IS RESPONSIBLE FOR SUPERVISING DISTRIBUTION ACTIVITIES?

The main regulatory authority is the Ministry of Food and Drug Safety (MFDS). The MFDS monitors drug distribution activities and is allowed to conduct on-site inspections and impose certain administrative sanctions under the Pharmaceutical Affairs Act.

## 14. WHAT IS THE PROCEDURE TO APPEAL (LEGAL REMEDY) A DISTRIBUTION DECISION?

See *Question 6*.

## 15. WHAT ARE THE LEGAL CONSEQUENCES OF NON-COMPLIANCE WITH CONSUMER DISTRIBUTION LAWS?

Administrative sanctions can be imposed on a wholesaler or pharmacist who has violated the Pharmaceutical Affairs Act in distributing drugs. Sanctions include the suspension of sales activities or revocation of the distribution licence.

A criminal penalty can also be imposed if an importer, a wholesaler or a pharmacist distributes or sells a drug without the requisite licence.

## WHOLESALE DISTRIBUTION

## 16. WHAT IS THE LEGAL REGIME REGARDING WHOLESALE DISTRIBUTION OF DRUGS?

The standard pharmaceutical wholesale licence covers medicinal products as a whole, and does not provide for limitations on specific classes of drugs (provided that Article 53 of the Pharmaceutical Affairs Act (PAA) is complied with). Article 53 provides that in order to sell state-authorised drugs such as vaccines, anti-venom, and plasma derivatives, a review and inspection of materials on the manufacturing and quality control processes by and subsequent sales approval of the Ministry of Food and Drug Safety is required.

A wholesaler must maintain an office and storage area of at least a certain area size. The storage facility must have:

- Refrigeration and protection from light.
- Preventative measures against vermin.
- Temperature and humidity control to prevent degradation of medicinal products.
- Designated storage facilities for biopharmaceutical products (including containers for transportation).
- Storage instructions (if necessary).

The PAA requires a certain amount of capital for wholesalers of pharmaceutical products (paid-in capital or equity capital of KRW500 million or more).

### 17. WHAT REGULATORY AUTHORITY IS RESPONSIBLE FOR SUPERVISING WHOLESALE DISTRIBUTION ACTIVITIES?

Under the Pharmaceutical Affairs Act (PAA), the Ministry of Food and Drug Safety has the general authority to supervise wholesalers and ensure that they comply with the regulations provided in the PAA. Certain supervisory rights are delegated to municipal governments.

The regulatory authority is allowed to conduct on-site inspections and to ask a wholesaler to submit certain documents and information relating to its activities.

Certain administrative sanctions can be imposed if a wholesaler fails to comply with regulations, which can be challenged by the wholesaler (*see Question 6*).

### 18. WHAT ARE THE LEGAL CONSEQUENCES OF NON-COMPLIANCE WITH WHOLESALE DISTRIBUTION LAWS?

Non-compliance with wholesale distribution laws can result in:

- Administrative sanctions (for example, suspension of business and/or revocation of the wholesaler licence).
- Criminal sanctions in certain cases (for example, distribution of drugs without a licence and provision of undue economic values to healthcare professionals for the promotion of drugs).

## MARKETING

### PROMOTION

### 19. WHAT IS THE GENERAL LEGAL REGIME FOR THE MARKETING OF DRUGS?

Drug marketing is regulated by the Pharmaceutical Affairs Act (PAA) and supervised by the Ministry of Food and Drug Safety (MFDS). In addition, the Fair Labelling and Advertising Act that governs advertising activities in general and is supervised by the Korea Fair Trade Commission may also apply (in theory).

The general limitations under the PAA are as follows:

- Advertising is only allowed for MFDS-approved products.
- Advertising must comply with the MFDS's approved indications, efficacies and other conditions.
- False, deceitful, exaggerating or slanderous advertising is prohibited.
- Absolute expressions such as "the best" cannot be used.
- A gift cannot be provided to consumers purchasing drugs.
- Individual healthcare professionals cannot be recommended.
- Direct-to-consumer advertising must be reviewed in advance by the MFDS or its designated body (the authority to review is delegated to the Korea Pharmaceutical Manufacturers

Association under the PAA).
- Direct-to-consumer advertising for prescription drugs is not allowed.

In addition, the PAA prohibits pharmaceutical companies and wholesalers from providing undue economic values to healthcare professionals for the purpose of promoting drugs (that is, the prohibition of kickbacks).

## 20. ARE THERE OTHER CODES OF CONDUCT FOR THE MARKETING OF DRUGS (FOR EXAMPLE, BY PROFESSIONAL OR INDUSTRIAL ORGANISATIONS)?

There are two industry codes in Korea:

- Korea Pharmaceutical Manufacturers Association (KPMA) Fair Competition Code.
- Korea Research-based Pharmaceutical Industry Association (KRPIA) Fair Competition Code.

The KPMA is an industry association and most members are local pharmaceutical companies, whereas the KRPIA consists of multinational pharmaceutical companies doing business in Korea.

The KPMA Code and the KRPIA Code are generally seen as voluntary industry codes without statutory enforcement. However, both codes have been reviewed and endorsed by the Korea Fair Trade Commission under Article 23 of the Monopoly Regulation and Fair Trade Act. It is generally recognised that both codes act as quasi-statutory regulations. The main purpose of the codes is to prevent pharmaceutical companies from providing undue economic values to healthcare professionals for the purpose of promoting their products.

## MARKETING TO CONSUMERS

## 21. WHAT IS THE LEGAL REGIME FOR MARKETING TO CONSUMERS?

Drug marketing is regulated by the Pharmaceutical Affairs Act (PAA) and supervised by the Ministry of Food and Drug Safety (MFDS). In addition, the Fair Labelling and Advertising Act which governs advertising activities in general and is supervised by the Korea Fair Trade Commission may also apply (in theory).

The general limitations under the PAA are as follows:

- Advertising is only allowed for MFDS-approved products.
- Advertising must comply with the MFDS's approved indications, efficacies and other conditions.
- False, deceitful, exaggerating or slanderous advertising is prohibited.
- Absolute expressions such as "the best" cannot be used.
- A gift cannot be provided to consumers purchasing drugs.
- Individual healthcare professionals cannot be recommended.
- Direct-to-consumer advertising must be reviewed in advance by the MFDS or its designated body (the authority to review is delegated to the Korea Pharmaceutical Manufacturers Association under the PAA).
- Direct-to-consumer advertising for prescription drugs is not allowed.

## 22. WHAT KINDS OF MARKETING ACTIVITIES ARE PERMITTED IN RELATION TO CONSUMERS AND THE PRODUCTS WHICH MAY BE ADVERTISED TO THEM?

For over-the-counter products, direct-to-consumer advertising is allowed under the Pharmaceutical Affairs Act (*see Question 21*).

Direct-to-consumer advertising for prescription drugs is not allowed, although a pharmaceutical company can post information about a prescription drug on its website. A website dedicated to a specific prescription drug is not allowed unless access to the website is limited to healthcare professionals.

## 23. IS IT PERMITTED TO PROVIDE CONSUMERS WITH FREE SAMPLES? ARE THERE PARTICULAR RESTRICTIONS ON SPECIAL OFFERS (FOR EXAMPLE, "BUY-ONE-GET-ONE-FREE")?

A pharmaceutical company can provide a sample in the minimum packaging unit to healthcare professionals under the Pharmaceutical Affairs Act. However, no sample or special offer can be provided to general consumers (patients).

## 24. ARE THERE PARTICULAR RULES OF PRACTICE ON THE USE OF THE INTERNET/SOCIAL MEDIA REGARDING DRUGS AND THEIR ADVERTISING?

The Pharmaceutical Affairs Act applies in general, but no specific statutory regulation has been established yet.

## 25. WHAT REGULATORY AUTHORITY IS RESPONSIBLE FOR SUPERVISING MARKETING ACTIVITIES TO CONSUMERS?

The Ministry of Food and Drug Safety has the general authority to supervise marketing activities to consumers.

See *Question 6* for rights of appeal.

## 26. WHAT ARE THE LEGAL CONSEQUENCES OF NON-COMPLIANCE WITH CONSUMER MARKETING LAWS?

If a pharmaceutical company fails to comply with the regulations, the following can be imposed:

- Administrative sanctions, such as the suspension of advertising activities of the relevant drug and revocation of the market approval of the relevant drug.
- Criminal sanctions (up to one year's imprisonment or a fine of up to KRW10 million).

### MARKETING TO PROFESSIONALS

## 27. WHAT KINDS OF MARKETING ACTIVITIES ARE PERMITTED IN RELATION TO PROFESSIONALS?

The following are examples of the kind of marketing activities that are allowed:

- Provision of samples.
- Detailing (marketing technique used by pharmaceutical companies, for example, sales calls).
- Product presentation.

## 28. ARE THERE ANY RESTRICTIONS ON MARKETING TO PROFESSIONALS?

### Marketing activities

The following marketing restrictions apply:

- Provision of medical journals or medical books is not allowed, but article reprints are allowed.
- Provision of gifts or educational items is not allowed in principle.
- Sponsorship of non-interventional studies is allowed, but only on the condition that there is a legitimate business need (that is, not for promotional purposes).

### Frequency

The provision of:

- Samples is generally once in the lifetime of the drug.
- Detailing (marketing technique used by pharmaceutical companies) is up to four times a month, if meals or drinks are provided.

### Provision of hospitality

The provision of hospitality is prohibited unless the Pharmaceutical Affairs Act and the industry codes (that is, the Korea Pharmaceutical Manufacturers Association (KPMA) and the Korea Research-based Pharmaceutical Industry Association Code (KRPIA)) specifically allow otherwise:

- For a multi-centre product presentation, meals (up to KRW100,000 per meal), travel expenses (economy class), lodging and souvenirs (up to KRW50,000) can be provided or supported with the prior approval of the KPMA or the KRPIA.
- Provision of hospitality at an academic conference can be provided with the prior approval of the KPMA or the KRPIA.
- A gift whose value does not exceed KRW10,000 can be provided to healthcare professionals at detailing.

## 29. WHAT INFORMATION IS IT LEGALLY REQUIRED TO INCLUDE IN ADVERTISING TO PROFESSIONALS?

For the provision of samples, the word "sample" must be marked. There are no other statutory requirements.

### 30. ARE THERE RULES ON COMPARISONS WITH OTHER PRODUCTS THAT ARE PARTICULARLY APPLICABLE TO DRUGS?

Under the Fair Labelling and Advertising Act, comparison advertising must be fair, factual and substantiated by objective evidence.

### 31. WHAT OTHER ITEMS, FUNDING OR SERVICES ARE PERMITTED TO BE PROVIDED TO PROFESSIONALS?

**Discounts**

Early payment discounts are allowed if the requirements provided in the Pharmaceutical Affairs Act (PAA) are satisfied. In addition, a volume discount made within the ordinary course of business is allowed.

**Free samples**

See *Question 28*.

**Sponsorship of professionals**

All academic grants must be made through the Korea Pharmaceutical Manufacturers Association or the Korea Research-based Pharmaceutical Industry Association with their prior review and approval. The same principle applies to the sponsorship of physicians' attendance at academic congresses.

**Other items, funding or services**

Any other indirect incentives for the purpose of promoting drugs are, in principle, not permitted under the PAA.

### 32. WHAT REGULATORY AUTHORITY IS RESPONSIBLE FOR SUPERVISING MARKETING ACTIVITIES REGARDING PROFESSIONALS?

The Ministry of Health and Welfare has the general authority under the Pharmaceutical Affairs Act. However, the Korea Fair Trade Commission can investigate pharmaceutical companies and healthcare professionals under Article 23 of the Monopoly Regulation and Fair Trade Act which prohibits unfair inducement of customers (that is, kickbacks). In addition, given that certain criminal sanctions can be imposed, the Prosecutors' Office can also conduct an investigation.

If a pharmaceutical company provides undue economic values to healthcare professionals the following can be imposed:

- Administrative sanctions (for example, the suspension of sales of the relevant drug and revocation of product approval of the relevant drug).
- Criminal sanctions (for example, imprisonment of up to two years or a fine of up to KRW30 million).

See *Question 6* for rights of appeals.

## 33. WHAT ARE THE LEGAL CONSEQUENCES IN CASE OF NON-COMPLIANCE WITH PROFESSIONAL MARKETING LAWS?

See *Question 32*.

# ENGAGEMENT WITH PATIENT ORGANISATIONS

## 34. WHAT KINDS OF ACTIVITIES ARE PERMITTED IN RELATION TO ENGAGEMENT WITH PATIENT ORGANISATIONS? WHAT ARE THE RESTRICTIONS THAT ARE IMPOSED ON RELATIONSHIP WITH PATIENT ORGANISATIONS?

No statutory regulation has been established yet. However, the general principles are that:

- Interactions with patient organisations are only for the well-being of patients, and not for the company's pursuit of profits.
- No advertising for prescription drugs is allowed.
- A sponsorship to patient organisations must not be used as a mechanism to disguise the provision of undue benefits to healthcare professionals.

# REFORM

## 35. ARE THERE ANY PLANS TO REFORM THE LAW ON THE DISTRIBUTION AND PROMOTION OF DRUGS IN YOUR JURISDICTION?

The government has not announced any specific plans for reform.

# SPAIN

*Teresa Paz-Ares and Beatriz Cocina, URÍA MENÉNDEZ ABOGADOS S.L.P*

## DISTRIBUTION

### PRE-CONDITIONS FOR DISTRIBUTION

**1. WHAT ARE THE LEGAL PRE-CONDITIONS FOR A DRUG TO BE DISTRIBUTED WITHIN THE JURISDICTION?**

**Authorisation**

In order to be placed on the Spanish market, drugs must obtain a prior marketing authorisation from the Spanish Medicinal Products and Medical Devices Agency (*Agencia Española de Medicamentos y Productos Sanitarios*) (AEMPS) or the European Medicines Agency (EMA) and be registered with the medicines registry within the AEMPS. Before marketing a prescription medicine, the pharmaceutical company must have offered it to the national health authorities for inclusion in the reimbursed medicines public health system.

Drugs can only be sold by pharmaceutical companies holding the appropriate marketing authorisation and their local representatives, or by licensed wholesalers.

**Exceptions**

As an exception to the requirement of holding a marketing authorisation as a precondition for its distribution in Spain, the AEMPS can authorise the prescription and use (and import, where necessary) of investigational medicines (for compassionate use) or of medicines authorised in countries other than Spain.

**2. DO ANY TYPES OF NAMED PATIENT AND/OR COMPASSIONATE USE PROGRAMMES OPERATE? IF SO, WHAT ARE THE REQUIREMENTS FOR PRE-LAUNCH ACCESS?**

Unauthorised medicines can be supplied in special situations (*Article 5(1), Directive 2001/83/EC*). Accordingly, further to Article 24 of Royal Legislative Decree 1/2015, (approving the revised text of the Law on Guarantees and Rational Use of Medicines and Medical Devices (Medicines Law), as developed by Royal Decree 1015/2009 on the availability of medicines in special situations (Royal Decree 1015/2009)) the Spanish Medicinal Products and Medical Devices Agency (AEMPS) can authorise:

- Access to unauthorised medicines that:
  - have been the subject-matter of an application for a marketing authorisation; and
  - are undergoing clinical trials.

- Access can be authorised for patients suffering from chronic, severely debilitating or life-threatening conditions that cannot be satisfactorily treated with authorised medicines.
- Access to medicines that are not authorised in Spain, provided that there is no authorised medicine in Spain with the same composition or form and there is no appropriate alternative medicine authorised in Spain (this includes supply shortages).

In both cases, the AEMPS can grant authorisations on a named patient only basis or under a general protocol applicable to a category of patients.

## LICENSING

### 3. WHAT IS THE PROCEDURAL STRUCTURE REGARDING LICENSING A DRUG FOR DISTRIBUTION?

**Structure**

The national authorisation procedure is regulated by Royal Decree 1345/2007 on the procedure for the authorisation, registration and conditions for dispensation of industrial human medicines and requires the submission of a detailed application that covers all aspects of the medicine and the results of preclinical, clinical and pharmaceutical investigations, as well as relevant expert reports. The documentation is evaluated by the Spanish Medicinal Products and Medical Devices Agency (AEMPS), which can request additional information. The AEMPS issues a reasoned evaluation report that, if unfavourable, is submitted to the applicant before the adoption of the decision.

In accordance with EU law, as implemented in Spain, the AEMPS decision must be issued within 210 calendar days following the submission of a valid application. This term can be extended for three, or, exceptionally, six months, if additional documentation is requested from the applicant.

**Regulatory authority**

The AEMPS is in charge of granting national marketing authorisations for medicines in Spain and can do so under the national, mutual recognition or decentralised procedures. Drugs can also be licensed by the European Medicines Agency (EMA) (*see Question 1*).

### 4. IS THERE A SIMPLIFIED LICENCE PROCEEDING, OR RELAXED LICENSING CONDITIONS, FOR DRUGS WHICH HAVE ALREADY BEEN LICENSED FOR DISTRIBUTION IN ANOTHER JURISDICTION?

Medicines that have been authorised in another EU member state can be authorised in Spain following the mutual recognition procedure. Additionally, simplified procedures are in place under the Spanish legislation implementing EU Directive 2001/83/EC for:

- Generics of medicines that have been authorised in other jurisdictions for at least eight years (even if not authorised in Spain).
- Active principles that are regarded as having had a "well-established use" in the EU for ten years and are acknowledged as being effective and safe.

See *Question 3*.

## 5. IS VIRTUAL DRUG DISTRIBUTION POSSIBLE FROM YOUR JURISDICTION?

Royal Decree 782/2013 on the Distribution of Medicines (Royal Decree on Distribution) established, for the first time, obligations to be fulfilled by "brokers", that is entities that are involved in the sale and purchase of medicinal products without selling or purchasing the products themselves and without owning or physically handling the medicinal products. The Royal Decree on Distribution is in line with Directive 2011/62/EU of the European Parliament and of the Council, amending Directive 2001/83/EC on the Community Code relating to medicinal products for human use, as regards preventing falsified medicines from entering the supply chain. According to this regulation, brokers must notify their activity to the Spanish Medicinal Products and Medical Devices Agency (AEMPS) and comply with specific obligations concerning:

- Traceability.
- Record keeping.
- Complaints handling.
- Quality management.
- Management of recalls.

Anyway, neither a Spanish marketing authorisation nor a Spanish distribution or brokering authorisation covers the activity of distributing medicines beyond Spain's borders. The necessary authorisations must be assessed based on the legislation of the countries where the marketing and distribution takes place.

## 6. WHAT IS THE PROCEDURE TO APPEAL (LEGAL REMEDY) A LICENSING DECISION?

As with any other decision taken by a public body, the decisions of the Spanish Medicinal Products and Medical Devices Agency (AEMPS) on medicine marketing authorisations can be challenged. An administrative claim can be filed before the Ministry of Health within one month from the date the AEMPS's decision is notified to the applicant. The decision settling this claim can also be appealed before the contentious-administrative courts within a term of two months from its notification to the claimant.

## 7. WHAT ARE THE COSTS OF OBTAINING LICENSING?

The administrative fees for applying for a medicine marketing authorisation from the Spanish Medicinal Products and Medical Devices Agency (AEMPS) and its subsequent registration are EUR20,529.17. For generics, traditional herbal medicines, homeopathic medicines and medicinal gases, the fees are EUR8,350.71. Additional fees apply to:

- Modifications.
- Transfers and renewals of marketing authorisations.
- Certain on-going obligations (such as the submission of periodic safety reports).
- Authorisations for parallel distribution.

## DISTRIBUTION TO CONSUMERS

## 8. WHAT ARE THE DIFFERENT CATEGORIES OF DRUGS FOR DISTRIBUTION?

Medicines for distribution can be divided into two main categories:

- Prescription medicines.
- Non-prescription medicines (over-the-counter) (OTC) drugs.

Prescription medicines can be classified as:

- Medicines subject to a renewable prescription.
- Medicines subject to a special prescription. These are medicines that:
    - contain any amount of a substance considered a narcotic or psychotropic according to international conventions;
    - if used incorrectly, may result in a substantial risk of medicine abuse that could ultimately lead to addiction or to other illegal uses; or
    - contain any substance that, due to its novelty or properties, must be included in this category for precautionary reasons.
- Medicines subject to restricted prescription, which includes:
    - medicines for use in hospitals;
    - medicines used in hospital diagnosis and that can only be prescribed by specialist doctors; and
    - medicines that are subject to special medical controls.

## 9. WHO IS AUTHORISED TO DISTRIBUTE PRESCRIPTION DRUGS AND OVER-THE-COUNTER DRUGS TO CONSUMERS?

### Prescription drugs

The distribution of prescription medicines to patients (technically, "dispensing") is reserved by law to:

- Authorised retail pharmacies open to the public.
- Pharmacies in hospitals, health centres, primary healthcare facilities of the National Health Service and medicine deposits (*botiquín*).

In Spain, only individual pharmacists can own and run retail pharmacies. Retail pharmacies must be in possession of an authorisation granted by the appropriate authority in the autonomous region where the pharmacy is located, which is issued according to a quota system based on geographic location and population.

### Over-the-counter drugs

There are no special regulations on over-the-counter (OTC) drugs. The rules for prescription drugs apply to all drugs.

## 10. WHAT DRUGS CAN AN ATTENDING PHYSICIAN DISTRIBUTE AND UNDER WHAT CIRCUMSTANCES?

Traditionally, except within the context of healthcare assistance provided at hospitals (whether public or private), attending physicians (for example, those in private individual practice) were prevented from dispensing or applying medicines to patients in Spain.

However, echoing reiterated requests from healthcare professionals, the Royal Decree on Distribution opened a window and instructed the Spanish Medicinal Products and Medical Devices Agency (AEMPS) to compile a list of medicines that can be sold directly to physicians, dental practitioners or chiropodists (among other healthcare professionals) within the framework of their professional activity, so that they can be administered to patients. On 11 March 2015, the AEMPS issued a resolution establishing the medicines that can be acquired by healthcare professionals for use in their clinics or health centres. This list includes, for example, local anaesthesia products used in odontology clinics.

Therefore, further to the Royal Decree on Distribution, healthcare professionals, dental practitioners and chiropodists are now legally entitled to purchase the medicines they need to carry out their activities from retail pharmacies, manufacturers and wholesalers.

## 11. WHO IS AUTHORISED TO PRESCRIBE PRESCRIPTION DRUGS TO CONSUMERS?

Prescriptions (both public and private) can only be issued by doctors, dental practitioners or chiropodists.

The Law on Guarantees and Rational Use of Medicines and Medical Devices (Medicines Law) states that nurses can indicate the use of, apply and authorise dispensation of non-prescription medicines and the government can pass further regulations on this. Royal Decree 1718/2010 on medical prescription and dispensation orders already establishes that nurses can issue "dispensation orders" for certain prescription medicines once the relevant nurses have obtained the corresponding accreditation. However, the framework within which nurses can carry out such activities (conditions and requirements) has to be further regulated.

Under no circumstances can professionals other than doctors, dental practitioners or chiropodists (for example, pharmacists or nurses) prescribe prescription-only medicines. However, in certain limited circumstances (medicines formally included in "homogeneous groupings" or during shortages) pharmacists can substitute the medicine prescribed by a physician and dispense a different one to the patient.

## 12. IS DIRECT MAILING/DISTANCE SELLING OF DRUGS PERMITTED IN YOUR JURISDICTION?

**Conditions**

Direct mailing, distance and online selling of prescription medicines is prohibited (*Article 3, Law on Guarantees and Rational Use of Medicines and Medical Devices(Medicines Law)*). However, this does allow for sales of non-prescription medicines through these channels, subject to the approval of secondary regulations that define the applicable requirements.

These requirements were defined by Royal Decree 870/2013 of 8 November 2013 on distance selling to the public through websites of non-prescription human use medicines, which establishes the following regarding distance selling through websites:

- Authorised operators are authorised pharmacies that have notified the regional health authorities that they intend to engage in online sales.
- Sales must be made by a pharmacist from his pharmacy and only after appropriate advice has been given to the user.
- Medicine sales can only be made directly from the pharmacy, without any intermediaries.
- No gifts, discounts or bonuses can be given as a means of promoting medicines on a website.

**Cross-border sales**

Distance selling to purchasers in other EU member states must comply with the above requirements and those applicable under the corresponding local laws.

## 13. WHAT REGULATORY AUTHORITY IS RESPONSIBLE FOR SUPERVISING DISTRIBUTION ACTIVITIES?

Spain is divided into seventeen autonomous regions that have broad powers in relation to healthcare matters and are responsible for, among other things, supervising the dispensing of medicinal products (that is, retail supply to patients).

The regional health authorities generally establish their inspection priorities on an annual basis. Inspectors can visit pharmacy premises unannounced and carry out any inspection they deem necessary to monitor compliance with applicable regulations. Among other things, they can:

- Take product samples.
- Request originals and copies of documentation.
- Conduct interviews.

## 14. WHAT IS THE PROCEDURE TO APPEAL (LEGAL REMEDY) A DISTRIBUTION DECISION?

As with any other decision of a public body, the decisions of the regional health authorities regarding dispensation, supervision and licensing (including penalties) can be challenged before a higher administrative body. This appeal must be filed within one month from the date the decision is notified. The decision settling this claim can also be appealed before the contentious-administrative courts within a term of two months from its notification.

## 15. WHAT ARE THE LEGAL CONSEQUENCES OF NON-COMPLIANCE WITH CONSUMER DISTRIBUTION LAWS?

The breach of regulations regarding the distribution and dispensation of medicines can result in fines and the amount depends on how serious the infringement is (and could vary from one autonomous region to another). According to the general regulations applicable on a national scale:

- Minor infringements can be penalised with fines ranging from EUR6,000 to EUR30,000. Dispensing expired medicines is an example of a minor infringement.
- Serious infringements can be penalised with fines ranging from EUR30,000 to EUR90,000. Dispensing medicines without holding the relevant authorisation is an example of a serious infringement.
- Very serious infringements can be penalised with fines ranging from EUR90,000 to EUR1,000,000 or even up to five times the value of the products or services involved in the infringement. The distribution of medicines by retail pharmacies to other pharmacies, wholesalers or the shipment of medicines by pharmacies beyond national borders are examples of very serious infringements.

Each level of offence has minimum, standard and maximum penalties, which depend on elements such as:

- Negligence.
- Intention.

- Fraud.
- Connivance.
- Breach of prior warnings.
- Turnover.
- Number of persons affected.
- Harm caused.
- Profits made from the offence.
- Persistence or duration of the breach.
- Recurrence.

Infringements can also be penalised with the confiscation by the Public Treasury (*Tesoro Público*) of the profits obtained as a consequence of the infringement. For very serious infringements, the establishment or premises can even be closed for up to five years.

## WHOLESALE DISTRIBUTION

### 16. WHAT IS THE LEGAL REGIME REGARDING WHOLESALE DISTRIBUTION OF DRUGS?

The Royal Decree 782/2013 on the Distribution of Medicines (Royal Decree on Distribution) regulates the obligations of entities involved in the distribution of medicines, including wholesalers and pharmaceutical companies and third parties that undertake distribution activities on behalf of wholesalers and pharmaceutical companies (*almacén por contrato*).

The Royal Decree on Distribution regulates the brokering of medicines for the first time, establishing the requirements that must be met by those involved in the distribution chain but that do not acquire or physically handle medicines (*see Question 5*).

Wholesale distributors of medicines and medical substances that supply pharmacies require the prior authorisation of the health authorities of the autonomous region in which their main place of business is located. Wholesale distributors must also notify their activities to the health authorities of all autonomous regions in which they carry out these activities.

The Royal Decree on Distribution further develops Article 67 of the Law on Guarantees and Rational Use of Medicines and Medical Devices (Medicines Law), acknowledging that medicines can be distributed by wholesale distributors or directly by the holder of the marketing authorisation. The health authorities and the courts have repeatedly and expressly stated that the commercialisation of medicinal products through wholesalers is free and voluntary, and pharmaceutical companies can, if they so decide, operate without the services of intermediary wholesalers and directly supply pharmacies and hospitals. Both pharmaceutical companies that supply their products directly and wholesalers are subject to certain public service obligations for the medicines that they distribute.

The Royal Decree on Distribution details the basic obligations of entities involved in the distribution of medicines (be it wholesalers or pharmaceutical laboratories that carry out distribution activities). Supplying pharmacies in the national territory is established as the priority and the essential function of these entities, which must ensure that all orders are delivered to pharmacies and other pharmaceutical services within 24 hours.

The Royal Decree on Distribution also establishes a restriction with unquestionable practical significance: wholesalers can only accept returns from pharmacies and pharmaceutical services if they previously supplied the relevant medicines directly to the returning entity.

This restriction has been imposed to tackle a rather widespread practice that hindered the traceability of medicines.

Medicines can only be purchased from and distributed to entities that are legally authorised to acquire them (that is, pharmaceutical wholesalers, pharmacies and hospitals).

The Royal Decree on Distribution also reinforces the control, monitoring and pharmacovigilance measures that must be put in place if third parties are engaged to perform parts of the distribution activity.

### 17. WHAT REGULATORY AUTHORITY IS RESPONSIBLE FOR SUPERVISING WHOLESALE DISTRIBUTION ACTIVITIES?

The same supervisory authority, inspection procedures and decision making processes apply as for dispensation activities. See *Question 13*.

### 18. WHAT ARE THE LEGAL CONSEQUENCES OF NON-COMPLIANCE WITH WHOLESALE DISTRIBUTION LAWS?

Distributing medicines without holding the necessary authorisation or to those not authorised to purchase them are considered serious administrative infringements. Distributing medicines without observing the applicable conditions is considered a very serious infringement. The same penalties apply as for infringements by pharmacies (*see Question 15*).

## MARKETING

### PROMOTION

### 19. WHAT IS THE GENERAL LEGAL REGIME FOR THE MARKETING OF DRUGS?

**Legal regime**

The statutory and self-regulatory frameworks are generally fairly restrictive in terms of pharmaceutical companies' promotional activities and their interactions with healthcare professionals.

The main regulations governing the promotion of medicines in Spain are contained in the Law on Guarantees and Rational Use of Medicines and Medical Devices (Medicines Law) and Royal Decree 1416/1994, which governs the advertising of medicines for human use (Royal Decree on Advertising), in line with Directive 2001/83/EC.

The Ministry of Health and the autonomous regions of Madrid and Catalonia (where most Spanish pharmaceutical companies are based) have approved guidelines on certain provisions of the Royal Decree on Advertising in relation to promotional activities.

With the promotion of medicines addressed to healthcare professionals, the main purpose of these regulations is to ensure that healthcare professionals are not influenced in an improper way by their relationships with any pharmaceutical company when performing their duties (particularly when prescribing or administering medicines).

To guarantee independence, the notion of "promotion of medicines" for the purpose of these regulations comprises, among other things:

- Promotion addressed to persons qualified to prescribe or dispense medicines.
- Sales calls by sales representatives to healthcare professionals (*visitas médicas*).
- Sponsoring promotional meetings and scientific meetings.
- Bearing associated travel and hotel expenses and offering or granting certain types of benefits.

**Limits to marketing activities**

The main limits to marketing activities under the current legal framework are the following:

- Only specific categories of medicines can be advertised to the public (*see Question 21*).
- All elements of the promotion of a medicine must be compatible with the approved summary of product characteristics (SPC) and must favour its rational use, present it in an objective manner and without exaggerating its properties. Promotional materials must provide the technical information necessary for the reader to be in a position to independently assess the therapeutic value of the medicine and must include the essential information on the product according to the information contained in the SPC.
- The autonomous regions' guidelines are very detailed and regulate, for example:
    - the use of certain terminology or phrases;
    - how to reproduce bibliographic references in promotional materials;
    - how to manage the delivery of information that refers to indications or characteristics not contained in the SPC approved in Spain ("off-label" information) in international scientific meetings.
- The purpose of the visits by medical sales representatives (sales calls) must be to provide objective and technical knowledge. Medical sales representatives must be given adequate training and have sufficient scientific knowledge to be able to provide information that is as precise and as complete as possible about the medicines that they are promoting. Medical sales representatives must also relay any information about the use of the medicinal products they advertise and, in particular, adverse reactions, to the relevant department within the pharmaceutical company. Some autonomous regions have restricted the number and frequency of these visits.
- Essentially, promotional materials (including both published advertising and brochures given to healthcare professionals during visits by medical sales representatives) should be scientific. They must be notified to the regional authorities before their distribution, attaching an express declaration that they have been reviewed by the appropriate department of the pharmaceutical company and that they are compatible with the information contained in the SPC.
- No incentives, discounts, rewards or gifts can be offered by those who have direct or indirect interests in the production, manufacture or commercialisation of medicines to healthcare professionals involved in the prescription, dispensation and administration of medicines or any of their relatives. Not only physicians, but also pharmacies (as healthcare establishments) fall under the scope of this prohibition as, according to the law, they can only be owned and run by individual pharmacists (who are considered healthcare professionals). The Royal Decree on Advertising clarifies that this prohibition is not an impediment to pharmaceutical companies offering reasonable hospitality within the framework of professional scientific meetings.

By way of exception, wholesalers are expressly allowed to offer "volume and prompt payment discounts" to pharmacies, provided that all of the following conditions are met (*Article 4.6, Medicines Law*):

- For reimbursed medicines (therefore excluding, among others, non-prescription medicines), the discount cannot exceed 10% of the price.
- The discount does not encourage the purchase of a particular product over competing products.
- The discount is properly reflected in the relevant invoice.

## 20. ARE THERE OTHER CODES OF CONDUCT FOR THE MARKETING OF DRUGS (FOR EXAMPLE, BY PROFESSIONAL OR INDUSTRIAL ORGANISATIONS)?

Self-regulation has further interpreted and elaborated the general regulations (*see Question 19*). In 1991, the Spanish Pharmaceutical Companies Trade Association (*Asociación Nacional Empresarial de la Industria Farmacéutica; Farmaindustria*) approved the Code of Good Practice for the Pharmaceutical Industry (the Code), which has subsequently been amended on a number of occasions, most recently in June 2014.

The scope of the Code covers promotional practices (*see Question 19*) except for those linked to commercial transactions by pharmaceutical companies with wholesalers, pharmacies or hospitals. However, the Code regulates other kinds of interactions with healthcare professionals that could result in any kind of payment being made, such as services agreements or the performance of observational studies. The Code also sets out detailed rules regarding:

- The contents of promotional documentation.
- Pecuniary or in kind benefits granted to healthcare professionals.
- Hospitality and meals.
- Consulting arrangements and other types of relationship that could result in payments being made to doctors (which must be reasonable, adjusted to market value and documented in writing).
- The performance of observational studies (which cannot be aimed at promoting the prescription or use of a given medicine and where the involvement of sales representatives is limited to purely logistical aspects).

The 2014 version of the Code has also incorporated the transparency rules adopted by the European Federation of Pharmaceutical Industry Associations (EFPIA) in the Code on disclosure of transfers of value from pharmaceutical companies to healthcare professionals and healthcare organisations. These rules provide for the disclosure of any "transfers of value" by pharmaceutical companies to healthcare professionals and healthcare organisations. The first reporting period is 2015.

The Code must be observed by all pharmaceutical companies that are members of Farmaindustria. Although the Code is not binding, it is considered a useful tool to help interpret and flesh out the regulations in force.

Accordingly, the regulations contained in the Code, including its Implementation Guidelines and the FAQ Brochure, have been expressly endorsed by certain healthcare authorities, which have in some instances made adherence to the Code a prerequisite for pharmaceutical companies to be allowed to carry out certain promotional activities in their territories (particularly, sales calls). Despite the voluntary nature of the Code, there are cases where the courts have also relied on the Code to interpret more generic mandates set out in laws and regulations.

## MARKETING TO CONSUMERS

### 21. WHAT IS THE LEGAL REGIME FOR MARKETING TO CONSUMERS?

**Legal regime**

Consumer advertising is regulated in Article 80 of the Law on Guarantees and Rational Use of Medicines and Medical Devices (Medicines Law) and the Royal Decree 1416/1994, which governs the advertising of medicines for human use (Royal Decree on Advertising). Further to a recent amendment to the Medicines Law, advertising to consumers no longer requires prior authorisation.

Advertising must include the following:

- The name of the medicine.
- The essential information needed to encourage its rational use.
- A specific message advising consumers that they should read the information leaflet and consult their pharmacist if in doubt.

In any event, the promotional nature of the message and the fact that it refers to a medicine must be clearly stated.

Advertising aimed at consumers cannot refer to recommendations of scientists, healthcare professionals or other persons that could:

- Encourage the consumption of medicines.
- Suggest certainty as to the product's effects, lack of side-effects or enhanced efficacy as opposed to other treatments.
- Infer that the use of the medicine may improve health or boost sporting performance.

Advertising addressed exclusively or primarily to children is not allowed.

Guidelines on the advertising of medicines to the public issued by the Ministry of Health provide additional detailed information on the permitted content in advertising messages aimed at the general public. According to these guidelines, comparative advertising is only allowed for medicines that belong to the same pharmaceutical company and they cannot suggest that the effect of a medicine is equal to or better than that of a different treatment or medicine.

**Products**

Advertising to consumers is only allowed for medicines that:

- Are not included in the public reimbursement system.
- Are not subject to medical prescription.
- Do not contain narcotic or psychotropic substances.

## 22. WHAT KINDS OF MARKETING ACTIVITIES ARE PERMITTED IN RELATION TO CONSUMERS AND THE PRODUCTS WHICH MAY BE ADVERTISED TO THEM?

Advertising can take the form of inserts in published, audiovisual or online media (newspapers, radio, TV or the internet), leaflets and outdoor advertising.

## 23. IS IT PERMITTED TO PROVIDE CONSUMERS WITH FREE SAMPLES? ARE THERE PARTICULAR RESTRICTIONS ON SPECIAL OFFERS (FOR EXAMPLE, "BUY-ONE-GET-ONE-FREE")?

Pharmacies cannot provide free samples to consumers.

With special offers, pharmacies can only apply discounts of up to 10% of the retail price, and only in relation to medicines that can be advertised to the public. No other offers are allowed.

## 24. ARE THERE PARTICULAR RULES OF PRACTICE ON THE USE OF THE INTERNET/SOCIAL MEDIA REGARDING DRUGS AND THEIR ADVERTISING?

There are no specific rules on the use of the internet or social media for medicines and their advertising. This practice is subject to the general rules governing the advertising of medicines to the public. Conversely, companies must ensure that promotional materials on medicines that are to be advertised solely to healthcare professionals are only accessible to them and not to the general public. It is generally considered that websites for healthcare professionals must be password protected and that the healthcare professionals must previously evidence their status as such.

## 25. WHAT REGULATORY AUTHORITY IS RESPONSIBLE FOR SUPERVISING MARKETING ACTIVITIES TO CONSUMERS?

**Regulatory authority**

The healthcare authorities of each autonomous region are in charge of supervising marketing activities aimed at consumers.

**Supervision**

Supervision is basically carried out through the monitoring of promotional materials aimed at consumers to ensure that their contents comply with regulatory requirements and that they respect the technical and scientific conditions imposed in marketing authorisations. The healthcare authorities can also limit, condition or prohibit the advertising of medicines to consumers on safety or public health grounds.

In addition to the monitoring measures, each year pharmaceutical companies must submit a list of all the marketing activities they have carried out to the authorities. This applies both to consumer marketing activities as well as to promotional activities addressed to healthcare professionals (*see Question 32*).

The healthcare authorities can impose sanctions for infringing advertising and can, through a reasoned decision, request the cessation or rectification of any advertising considered misleading that poses a risk to health and safety or otherwise infringes applicable regulations. They can also request the suspension of the advertising if it poses an immediate and extraordinary risk to health.

**Rights of appeal**

All decisions of the health authorities on these matters can be appealed before the relevant higher administrative body and ultimately before the courts.

## 26. WHAT ARE THE LEGAL CONSEQUENCES OF NON-COMPLIANCE WITH CONSUMER MARKETING LAWS?

Advertising medicines in breach of applicable regulations constitutes a very serious administrative infringement that can be sanctioned with fines ranging from EUR90,000 to EUR1 million or even up to five times the value of the products or services involved in the infringement and the confiscation by the Public Treasury (*Tesoro Público*) of unlawful profits obtained as a consequence of the infringement. For very serious infringements, the registered office or company premises can also be closed for up to five years.

## MARKETING TO PROFESSIONALS

## 27. WHAT KINDS OF MARKETING ACTIVITIES ARE PERMITTED IN RELATION TO PROFESSIONALS?

The applicable regulations specifically refer to the following types of promotional activities aimed at healthcare professionals:

- Documentary advertising.
- Distribution of free samples.
- Visits by sales representatives.
- Sponsorship of scientific or promotional events.

Generally, "promotion" means any offer of information, prospection or encouragement regarding the prescription, supply, sale, administration or consumption of medicinal products. This definition is construed broadly, and any information provided by a pharmaceutical company that directly or indirectly refers to branded or unbranded medicinal products can be considered promotional, and is therefore subject to the rules and restrictions on the promotion of medicines.

For example, publications in the form of "expert opinions", "expert interviews", "sections", "lines of treatment" or "current situation in the treatment of..." published in any format are considered promotional if there is a specific, direct or indirect contractual relationship between the pharmaceutical company that holds the marketing authorisation of the relevant medicine and the author or the company responsible for the publication and are therefore subject to all regulations governing promotion.

## 28. ARE THERE ANY RESTRICTIONS ON MARKETING TO PROFESSIONALS?

**Marketing activities**

"Independence guarantees" apply to the prescription and dispensation of medicines (*Article 4, Law on Guarantees and Rational Use of Medicines and Medical Devices (Medicines Law)*). These guarantees prohibit the direct or indirect offer of any incentives by those that have a direct or indirect interest in the manufacture or commercialisation of medicines to healthcare professionals involved in the prescription or dispensation of the same.

The Code of Good Practice for the Pharmaceutical Industry (the Code) prohibits gifts to healthcare professionals, except for those related to the practice of medicine or consisting of stationery items provided that:

- They do not relate to a prescription-only medicine.
- They are worth no more than EUR10.

The direct or indirect provision of information or educational materials to healthcare professionals is also limited under the Code. For materials to be compliant with the Code, they must:

- Be inexpensive (that is worth less than EUR60).
- Relate to the practice of medicine or pharmacy.
- Enhance patient care.

With items of medical utility, they must:

- Be inexpensive (that is worth less than EUR60).
- Not alter routine professional practices of the recipient.

Non-interventional studies are allowed in Spain (and are specifically regulated), provided that they are not used as a tool to increase the prescription or sale of a particular medicine. Therefore, they should not be considered or used as marketing tools.

The same applies to the engagement of healthcare professionals to provide services to a pharmaceutical company or to grants and charitable contributions made by a pharmaceutical company to entities formed by healthcare professionals or engaged in the provision of healthcare assistance or research. Even though these rules are not expressly contemplated in the applicable regulations, they clearly stem from the spirit of the same and have been expressly included in the Code.

**Frequency**

Some autonomous regions have regulations limiting the number, duration and frequency of sales calls by sales representatives to healthcare professionals. Some of these regulations have established a quota of visits per pharmaceutical company and year (for example, four yearly visits to each healthcare centre), while others merely establish specific days and times when calls are allowed. Some regions require that sales calls be made collectively to panels of doctors.

It appears that enforcement of these restrictions is generally quite relaxed. Some of these regional regulations have also been annulled by the courts on the basis of formal infringements.

**Provision of hospitality**

The Royal Decree 1416/1994, which governs the advertising of medicines for human use (Royal Decree on Advertising) clarifies that the prohibition on gifts is not an impediment to pharmaceutical companies offering reasonable hospitality within the scope of scientific meetings, provided that the hospitality is reasonable and secondary to the main purpose of the meeting and does not extend to persons other than the healthcare professionals themselves.

The Code provides very detailed guidelines on how much hospitality is allowed within the scope of scientific meetings, including venue selection, hotel categories, entertainment programmes and duration:

- Hospitality must be limited to the payment of travel, registration and maintenance expenses, which must be reasonable and not disproportionate and limited to the days when the scientific meeting is taking place. Hospitality is considered "reasonable" if its cost does not exceed what recipients would normally be prepared to pay for themselves in the same circumstances.
- Expenses must be paid for directly by pharmaceutical companies. Travel grants in cash or the reimbursement of expenses in cash are not allowed, except for minor travel expenses (for example, taxi fares). This means that expenses can be paid by the pharmaceutical company but only directly to the supplier of the services.
- Hospitality must always be secondary to the main purpose of the meeting so the scientific goals must constitute the main focus of the organisation of the meetings. Social or cultural aspects can never take precedence over scientific issues.
- Hospitality must not extend to persons other than healthcare professionals that qualify as participants in the meeting in their own right. Spouses or other companions cannot attend these events even if they pay their own expenses.
- Pharmaceutical companies cannot directly or indirectly pay physicians or groups of physicians the cost of renting rooms to be used for meetings unless it is evidenced that the payments are made to lease rooms for this purpose.
- Scientific goals must be the main focus of the meetings, and social or cultural aspects cannot interfere or prevail over scientific issues. The scientific content of congresses and meetings should occupy at least 60% of each working day (presuming an eight-hour working day, excluding travel time). Cultural or social events must not coincide with the scientific programme. Hospitality provided by a pharmaceutical company must never include the sponsorship or organisation of leisure events (for example, sports or entertainment).
- Healthcare professionals must not be remunerated merely for attending the event. Only speakers and moderators can be paid reasonable fees.
- Generally, pharmaceutical companies cannot organise or promote events to be held outside Spain (international events) when the majority of attendees practise in Spain, unless an international location proves to be more convenient from a logistical standpoint.
- The fact that the meeting is sponsored by a pharmaceutical company must be clearly disclosed in all documents relating to the meetings.

## 29. WHAT INFORMATION IS IT LEGALLY REQUIRED TO INCLUDE IN ADVERTISING TO PROFESSIONALS?

Promotional materials addressed to healthcare professionals must include:

- Essential information on the product, in line with the summary of product characteristics (SPC), including:
  - its name;
  - composition;
  - full clinical data;
  - incompatibilities;
  - side effects and contraindications;

- instructions for use and handling; and
- the name and address of the holder of the marketing authorisation.
- The date on which the information was created or last reviewed.
- The different presentations, dosages and forms.
- The prescription and dispensation conditions of the product.
- The selling price or indicative price of the various presentations and the conditions for reimbursement by social security bodies and, where possible, information on the cost of the treatment.

Advertising for the sole purpose of reminding people of the product's name is exempted from these rules. However, reminder advertising is only allowed once the product has been authorised for at least two years.

### 30. ARE THERE RULES ON COMPARISONS WITH OTHER PRODUCTS THAT ARE PARTICULARLY APPLICABLE TO DRUGS?

Comparative advertising is generally governed by the principles contained in unfair competition and advertising regulations. The guidelines issued by the Ministry of Health and some autonomous regions concerning the advertising of medicines have also introduced specific rules:

- Comparative advertising that suggests that the effect of a medicine is equal to or better than that of a different treatment or medicine is not allowed.
- A comparison must be scientifically evidenced and must refer to medicines of comparable safety and efficacy and equivalent therapeutic effect.
- Sources of the data used must be readily available to the health authorities (and, according to the Code of Good Practice for the Pharmaceutical Industry (the Code) to competitors).
- Relevant information (such as the statistical relevance of results) cannot be omitted.
- Results from different studies cannot be compared in the same graph or chart, unless a meta-analysis has been conducted.

### 31. WHAT OTHER ITEMS, FUNDING OR SERVICES ARE PERMITTED TO BE PROVIDED TO PROFESSIONALS?

There is a general prohibition set out in Article 4.6 of the Law on Guarantees and Rational Use of Medicines and Medical Devices (Medicines Law) on the direct and indirect offering of any incentives (including bonuses, discounts, premiums and gifts) by those that have a direct or indirect interest in the manufacture or commercialisation of medicines to healthcare professionals involved in the prescription or dispensation of the same.

**Discounts**

As an exception to the general prohibition on all incentives and discounts, wholesalers are expressly allowed (this is understood to include pharmaceutical companies that engage in the direct distribution of their products) to offer pharmacies volume and prompt payment discounts, provided that (*Article 4.6., Medicines Law*):

- They do not encourage the prescription of a particular product instead of a competing product.
- The discounts are properly reflected in the relevant invoice.

In any event, with reimbursed medicines, these discounts cannot exceed ten per cent of the regular price of the medicine.

**Free samples**

Samples can only be offered during the first two years following the granting of the medicines' marketing authorisation. Each healthcare professional can be offered a maximum of ten samples per year (unless otherwise stated by the relevant authority).

Samples cannot be larger than the smallest presentation of the medicine, must be labelled "free medical sample – not for sale" and cannot bear the reimbursement label.

Delivery of samples must include the authorised summary of product characteristics (SPC) and information on price, reimbursement conditions and, whenever possible, the estimated cost of treatment. Companies must have an adequate system in place to control and keep track of the samples distributed.

**Sponsorship of professionals**

Prizes, scholarships, contributions and financial assistance to attend meetings, congresses and similar activities are allowed provided that they relate exclusively to scientific activities and do not represent an incentive for the recommendation, prescription, purchase, supply, sale or administration of medicines. Sponsoring healthcare professionals' attendance at scientific events is allowed subject to the hospitality rules (*see Question 28*).

When meetings, congresses, symposia and similar events are sponsored by pharmaceutical companies, that fact must be disclosed in all of the papers relating to the meetings and in any published paper, speech or document related to such meetings.

Also, according to the Code of Good Practice for the Pharmaceutical Industry (the Code), when any kind of prizes are given, the rules governing the prizes must be publicly available and indicate, among other things:

- The entities organising or sponsoring the prize.
- The conditions for participation.
- Dates.
- Type and amount of the prize.
- The entity responsible for selecting the winners.

**Other items, funding or services**

Direct and indirect incentives are prohibited (*see Question 28*). However, the Code allows objects such as medical or pharmaceutical books or other materials on optical, magnetic, electronic or similar media to be given to healthcare professionals. The provision of other gifts (whose value exceeds EUR10 or which are not of a scientific or technical nature) is not allowed. The direct or indirect provision of portable electronic devices for personal use, even if they may also have a professional use, is also not permitted.

## 32. WHAT REGULATORY AUTHORITY IS RESPONSIBLE FOR SUPERVISING MARKETING ACTIVITIES REGARDING PROFESSIONALS?

### Regulatory authority

The health authorities of each autonomous region are in charge of supervising consumer marketing activities.

### Supervision

With marketing to healthcare professionals, pharmaceutical companies must submit a copy of all promotional materials they use (including printed or audiovisual) to the healthcare authorities at the time of their publication or release, indicating:

- Who they are aimed at.
- How they will be published.
- The date they will be first released.

Each year pharmaceutical companies must also submit a list of all the marketing activities they have carried out to the healthcare authorities.

The healthcare authorities can impose sanctions on infringing advertising and can, through a reasoned decision, request the cessation or rectification of any advertising:

- Considered misleading.
- That poses a risk to health and safety.
- That otherwise infringes applicable regulations.

They can also request the suspension of advertising if it poses an immediate and extraordinary risk to health.

### Rights of appeal

Any decisions of the health authorities on these matters can be appealed before the relevant higher administrative body and ultimately before the courts.

## 33. WHAT ARE THE LEGAL CONSEQUENCES IN CASE OF NON-COMPLIANCE WITH PROFESSIONAL MARKETING LAWS?

Advertising medicines in breach of applicable regulations constitutes a very serious administrative infringement with various consequences (*see Question 26*).

The offering of bonuses, premiums, incentives, gifts or discounts linked to the promotion or sale of medicines to the public also qualifies as a very serious infringement with the same consequences.

The infringement of requirements imposed by autonomous regions regarding visits to healthcare professionals is a minor infringement that can be sanctioned with fines ranging from EUR6,000 to EUR30,000. Finally, the offering or granting of unlawful gifts or incentives to healthcare professionals in the framework of the promotion of medicines qualifies as a serious infringement, which can be sanctioned with fines ranging from EUR30,000 to EUR90,000.

# ENGAGEMENT WITH PATIENT ORGANISATIONS

### 34. WHAT KINDS OF ACTIVITIES ARE PERMITTED IN RELATION TO ENGAGEMENT WITH PATIENT ORGANISATIONS? WHAT ARE THE RESTRICTIONS THAT ARE IMPOSED ON RELATIONSHIP WITH PATIENT ORGANISATIONS?

There are no specific regulations on interactions between the pharmaceutical industry and patient organisations.

The law foresees certain "incentives for patronage", which are tax benefits applicable to donors when contributions are made to entities considered "beneficiaries of patronage". Associations that have been declared to be of public interest (*declaración de utilidad pública*), which is the case of most patient organisations, are considered "beneficiaries of patronage". These contributions could be channelled through donations, or through collaboration agreements, where the organisation receives funds to be used for its public interest activities and undertakes to disclose the financial assistance received from the grantor for these activities.

In 2014, Farmaindustria incorporated provisions in the Code of Good Practice for the Pharmaceutical Industry (the Code) on interactions between the pharmaceutical industry and patient organisations (that previously were the subject matter of another code specifically aimed at patient organisations). The Code sets out certain rules and standards aimed at guaranteeing the independence of these organisations and the transparency of their interactions with the industry. The Code expressly contemplates, in addition to the provision of financial support:

- Contracts under which patient organisations provide pharmaceutical companies with services related to healthcare or research.
- The engagement of patient organisations as experts and advisors for services such as participating in advisory board meetings and speaking at meetings or events.
- The sponsorship of events organised by patient organisations.
- The provision of hospitality in events organised by the patient organisation or by the pharmaceutical company.

According to the Code:

- Collaboration between pharmaceutical companies and patient organisations must be documented in a written agreement that covers:
    - the activities to be carried out;
    - the amount and sources of funding;
    - the purpose of funding;
    - relevant indirect support;
    - any other type of significant non-financial support.
- Pharmaceutical companies must not seek to influence the text of a patient organisation's materials that they sponsor. This does not mean that companies cannot correct factual inaccuracies.
- Arrangements that cover consultancy or other services must be documented in writing. A legitimate need for the services must have been clearly identified and documented in advance and the criteria for selecting services and their providers must be directly related to the identified need and assessed by persons who have the expertise necessary to evaluate whether the particular experts and advisors meet those criteria. The contracting company

must keep a record of, and make appropriate use of, the services. Compensation for the services must be:
- based on market criteria;
- proportionate to the time dedicated, the work done and the responsibilities assumed;
- properly documented.
- Companies must also publish a list of patient organisations with which they have engaged to provide remunerated services.
- Generally with hospitality, the standards established in the Code on interactions with healthcare professionals must be observed. Companies must pay all expenses to patient organisations and never directly to patients on an individual basis.

## REFORM

### 35. ARE THERE ANY PLANS TO REFORM THE LAW ON THE DISTRIBUTION AND PROMOTION OF DRUGS IN YOUR JURISDICTION?

No noteworthy changes are expected in the near future concerning the law on the distribution and promotion of drugs.

# SWEDEN

*Helén Waxberg and Maja Edlund,*
*MANNHEIMER SWARTLING ADVOKATBYRÅ*

## DISTRIBUTION

### PRE-CONDITIONS FOR DISTRIBUTION

### 1. WHAT ARE THE LEGAL PRE-CONDITIONS FOR A DRUG TO BE DISTRIBUTED WITHIN THE JURISDICTION?

**Authorisation**

Under the Medicinal Products Act a medicinal product can only be sold and distributed in Sweden if it has been either:

- Authorised for sale either through a national application or by way of a European Economic Area (EEA) mutual recognition or decentralised application.
- Registered. Registration is only available for homeopathic medicinal products and herbal medicinal products and is based on Directive 2001/83/EC.

**Exceptions**

Unauthorised medicinal products can be distributed through a compassionate use programme or by a pharmacy under a specific licence. There are also exceptions from the authorisation requirement for medicinal products that are produced at a pharmacy and are intended for a specific patient.

### 2. DO ANY TYPES OF NAMED PATIENT AND/OR COMPASSIONATE USE PROGRAMMES OPERATE? IF SO, WHAT ARE THE REQUIREMENTS FOR PRE-LAUNCH ACCESS?

Unauthorised medicinal products can be sold to an individual patient on a named patient basis by a pharmacy under a licence granted by the Medical Products Agency (MPA) provided that the patient's need for medicine cannot be met by any medicinal product already authorised in Sweden. However, there are no requirements in relation to the severity of the disease.

The named patient use of the medicinal product under a licence is initiated by the prescribing physician who issues a prescription and justifies the named patient use of the medicinal product by stating the reasons for the named patient use. The licence is based on the pharmacy's application and the prescribing physician's justification and is valid for a maximum period of one year.

Selling unauthorised medicinal products with a licence is based on Article 5(1) of Directive 2001/83/EC.

From 1 July 2012, unauthorised medicinal products can be made available to patients through a compassionate use programme. The possibility of compassionate use programmes is based on Article 83 of Regulation 726/2004/EC which provides that a compassionate use programme must be aimed towards a group of patients:

- With a chronically or seriously debilitating disease.
- Whose disease is considered to be life threatening and cannot be treated satisfactorily by an authorised medicinal product.

In addition, the relevant medicinal product must belong to the categories referred to in Article 3(1) and (2) of Regulation 726/2004/EC and must either be:

- The subject of an application for a marketing authorisation under Article 6 of Regulation 726/2004/EC.
- Undergoing clinical trials.

There must also be satisfactory evidence for the medicinal product's safety and efficacy and the benefits must be advantageous for the concerned patient group in relation to the risks.

The medicinal product that is provided through the programme must be made available to the patients until it is placed on the market.

## LICENSING

### 3. WHAT IS THE PROCEDURAL STRUCTURE REGARDING LICENSING A DRUG FOR DISTRIBUTION?

**Structure**

An application for marketing authorisation must be submitted to the Medical Products Agency (MPA) for a medicinal product. An application is needed for each single pharmaceutical formulation and strength. The application must be made on a specific form supplied by the MPA. The MPA has 210 days to assess the application starting from the date a complete application is filed.

The conditions that must be satisfied by the applicant under the national procedure are set out in regulations issued by the MPA and include the requirements provided under EU law. These also apply if Sweden is the reference member state under a mutual recognition procedure (MRP) or a decentralised procedure (DCP). The applicant must demonstrate that the medicinal product does not have any harmful effects disproportionate to its intended effect and is of satisfactory quality, safety and efficacy. If the requirements for authorisation are met, a marketing authorisation is granted. The authorisation can be subject to conditions.

**Regulatory authority**

The MPA is responsible for granting marketing authorisations under MRPs and DCPs.

## 4. IS THERE A SIMPLIFIED LICENCE PROCEEDING, OR RELAXED LICENSING CONDITIONS, FOR DRUGS WHICH HAVE ALREADY BEEN LICENSED FOR DISTRIBUTION IN ANOTHER JURISDICTION?

There is no simplified authorisation procedure for medicinal products that have already been authorised in another jurisdiction outside of the European Economic Area (EEA).

If a medicinal product is already authorised for sale in another EEA state, the mutual recognition procedure (MRP) must be applied. Therefore, under the Medicinal Products Act, if a medicinal product is already authorised for sale in another EEA state, a regular marketing authorisation application submitted to the Medical Products Agency (MPA) will be dismissed unless the applicant requests that the authorisation obtained in that EEA state be recognised in Sweden. Such an authorisation must be recognised unless the medicinal product involves a serious risk to the public. When an authorisation has been recognised, the relevant medicinal product will be regarded as authorised in Sweden.

## 5. IS VIRTUAL DRUG DISTRIBUTION POSSIBLE FROM YOUR JURISDICTION?

A wholesale trade authorisation obtained in Sweden gives the authorisation holder the right to distribute the medicinal product in Sweden. Whether the medicinal product can be distributed in another country based on the Swedish authorisation must be answered based on that country's law.

## 6. WHAT IS THE PROCEDURE TO APPEAL (LEGAL REMEDY) A LICENSING DECISION?

Licensing decisions can be appealed before the Administrative Court in Uppsala.

## 7. WHAT ARE THE COSTS OF OBTAINING LICENSING?

To obtain a licence, the following costs apply:

- Application fee of SEK400,000.
- Annual fee of SEK46,000.

Up-to-date information on fees is available on the Medicinal Products Agency (MPA) website (*www.lakemedelsverket.se*).

## DISTRIBUTION TO CONSUMERS

## 8. WHAT ARE THE DIFFERENT CATEGORIES OF DRUGS FOR DISTRIBUTION?

The following different categories of drugs can be distributed:

- Prescription-only medicinal products.
- Non-prescription medicinal products.

### 9. WHO IS AUTHORISED TO DISTRIBUTE PRESCRIPTION DRUGS AND OVER-THE-COUNTER DRUGS TO CONSUMERS?

**Prescription drugs**

Under the Act on Trade with Medicinal Products, an authorisation is required to sell prescription only medicinal products to consumers. Only open care pharmacies (regular pharmacies in Sweden) can obtain authorisation. The authorisation is granted by the Medicinal Products Agency (MPA).

**Over-the-counter drugs**

Medicinal products can be distributed to consumers by open care pharmacies. In addition, under the Act on Trade with some Non-Prescription Medicinal Products, other sales outlets (other than open care pharmacies) can sell the following medicinal products to consumers:

- Nicotine drugs.
- Other non-prescription medicinal products for human use that have not been prescribed if:
  - the medicinal product is suitable for self-care;
  - serious adverse reactions are rare; or
  - it is appropriate considering patient safety and the protection of the public health.

The MPA decides which medicinal products fulfil these requirements. The proprietor of the sales outlet must notify the MPA prior to entering into the distribution of medicinal products.

### 10. WHAT DRUGS CAN AN ATTENDING PHYSICIAN DISTRIBUTE AND UNDER WHAT CIRCUMSTANCES?

Under the Medical Products Agency Regulation 2009:13, at the time of a treatment session, a prescriber can provide a patient with medicinal products in small doses to cover the patient's need for the medicinal product (until it can be dispensed at an open care pharmacy). Only medicinal products that are included in the prescriber's right to prescribe can be distributed this way by the prescriber. The medicinal products cannot be sold to the patient by the prescriber (that is, the medicinal product must be provided for free). Otherwise this will constitute trade with medicinal products which requires an authorisation under the Act on Trade with Medicinal Products.

### 11. WHO IS AUTHORISED TO PRESCRIBE PRESCRIPTION DRUGS TO CONSUMERS?

Authorised doctors have a general authority to prescribe medicinal products to patients. Trained nurses, dentists, dental hygienists and midwives have limited authority to prescribe medicinal products to patients.

### 12. IS DIRECT MAILING/DISTANCE SELLING OF DRUGS PERMITTED IN YOUR JURISDICTION?

**Conditions**

Medicinal products can be sold to consumers via direct mailing/distance selling if all the requirements under the Act on Trade with Medicinal Products and the Act on Trade with some

Non-Prescription Medicinal Products are met. For example, the selling is permitted under the same conditions as distribution of medicinal products to consumers in general.

Medicinal products can be sold via direct mailing/distance selling by open care pharmacies. Other sales outlets can also sell non-prescription medicinal products that are approved by the Medicinal Products Act (MPA) to be sold via direct mailing/distance selling.

**Cross-border sales**

Medicinal products can be sold beyond the Swedish borders, subject to the laws of the country to which the medicinal products are sold.

### 13. WHAT REGULATORY AUTHORITY IS RESPONSIBLE FOR SUPERVISING DISTRIBUTION ACTIVITIES?

The Medicinal Products Agency (MPA) is responsible for supervising the compliance of the Act on Trade with Medicinal Products and the Act on Trade with some Non-Prescription Medicinal Products. As part of its supervisory responsibilities, the MPA can demand access to:

- Information and documents.
- Facilities used for the distribution.

The MPA can also issue injunctions and prohibitions to ensure compliance. Fines can be issued if the injunctions and prohibitions are not complied with. There is no specific limit regarding the level of the fines but must be proportionate in relation to the relevant rule and company.

For sales outlets that are permitted to distribute medicinal products to consumers under the Act on Trade with some Non-Prescription Medicinal Products, their local municipality has some authority regarding their supervision.

### 14. WHAT IS THE PROCEDURE TO APPEAL (LEGAL REMEDY) A DISTRIBUTION DECISION?

Decisions on injunctions and prohibitions can be appealed to the Administrative Court in Uppsala.

### 15. WHAT ARE THE LEGAL CONSEQUENCES OF NON-COMPLIANCE WITH CONSUMER DISTRIBUTION LAWS?

An authorisation to distribute medicinal products to consumers can be withdrawn in cases of non-compliance. In addition, anyone who distributes medicinal products to consumers without the necessary authorisation can face criminal charges. Sales outlets (other than open care pharmacies) that fail to notify the Medicinal Products Agency (MPA) of its distribution of non-prescription medicinal products can also face criminal charges.

## WHOLESALE DISTRIBUTION

### 16. WHAT IS THE LEGAL REGIME REGARDING WHOLESALE DISTRIBUTION OF DRUGS?

The wholesale of medicinal products is governed by the Act on Trade with Medicinal Products, which includes the provisions of the EU Directive 2001/83/EC. The lawful wholesale of medicinal products requires a wholesale trade authorisation granted by the Medicinal Products Agency (MPA). The applicant must demonstrate that it has the ability to fulfil the requirements set out in the Act on Trade with Medicinal Products when applying for an authorisation. The requirements include that the wholesale authorisation holder must have appropriate facilities and an expert responsible for the safety and the quality of the medicinal products. The wholesale authorisation holder is also required to distribute the medicinal products included in its authorisation. The medicinal products must be distributed as soon as possible by sufficient and consecutive deliveries. The MPA can issue injunctions and prohibitions for failure to distribute. Such injunctions and prohibitions can be subject to fines for non-compliance. In addition, the wholesale trade authorisation can be withdrawn by the MPA.

## 17. WHAT REGULATORY AUTHORITY IS RESPONSIBLE FOR SUPERVISING WHOLESALE DISTRIBUTION ACTIVITIES?

### Regulatory authority

The Medicinal Products Agency (MPA) is responsible for supervising compliance with the Act on Trade with Medicinal Products.

### Supervision

The MPA can demand access to:

- Information and documents necessary for the supervision of wholesale distribution activities.
- Facilities used for the distribution.

The MPA can also issue injunctions and prohibitions necessary to ensure compliance. Such injunctions and prohibitions may be subject to fines for non-compliance.

### Rights of appeal

Decisions on injunctions and prohibitions can be appealed to the Administrative Court in Uppsala.

## 18. WHAT ARE THE LEGAL CONSEQUENCES OF NON-COMPLIANCE WITH WHOLESALE DISTRIBUTION LAWS?

The wholesale trade authorisation can be withdrawn in the event of non-compliance. In addition, anyone who pursues wholesale trade without the necessary authorisation can face criminal charges.

# MARKETING

## PROMOTION

### 19. WHAT IS THE GENERAL LEGAL REGIME FOR THE MARKETING OF DRUGS?

**Legal regime**

The Medicinal Products Act includes provisions required by the EU Directive 2001/83/EC and a basic provision that all advertising of medicinal products must be kept up-to-date, factual, balanced and must not be misleading. Advertising of medicinal products must also be compatible with good marketing practice, and the Medicinal Products Act provides detailed rules on the advertising of medicinal products. The Medicinal Products Agency (MPA) has issued a regulation clarifying and specifying the rules governing the advertising of medicinal products for human use in Sweden.

In addition, the general provisions of the Market Practices Act are applicable to advertising of all kinds of products and services, including medicinal products. The Market Practices Act provides a general requirement that all marketing activities must be compatible with good marketing practice and fair towards consumers and the industry. The Market Practices Act also sets out specific rules on misleading advertising, comparative advertising and special offers.

**Limits to marketing activities**

The following is prohibited:

- Advertising of medicinal products or indications that are not authorised for sale in Sweden.
- Advertising of medicinal products that are aimed at children.
- Advertising of medicinal products that are only available on prescription to the general public (with the exception of campaigns for vaccinations against human infectious diseases).

### 20. ARE THERE OTHER CODES OF CONDUCT FOR THE MARKETING OF DRUGS (FOR EXAMPLE, BY PROFESSIONAL OR INDUSTRIAL ORGANISATIONS)?

Detailed rules relating to pharmaceutical advertising are provided in the Ethical Rules for the Pharmaceutical Industry (LER Rules) issued by the Swedish Association of the Pharmaceutical Industry (LIF), last amended on 16 February 2015. The LER Rules are widely recognised by the pharmaceutical industry and applied by courts as an expression of fair and ethical marketing, although not legally binding. The LER Rules:

- Include prohibitions on the advertisement of prescription drugs to the general public, off-label advertisements and pre-launch marketing.
- List rules relating to comparative advertising, misleading, incomplete or unsubstantiated information and disguised advertisements.

## MARKETING TO CONSUMERS

### 21. WHAT IS THE LEGAL REGIME FOR MARKETING TO CONSUMERS?

**Legal regime**

The advertisement of non-prescription medicinal products to the general public is permitted in accordance with the regulatory framework (*see Question 19*).

**Products**

There is an explicit prohibition in the Medicinal Products Act on the advertising of prescription-only medicinal products to the general public (with the exception of vaccination campaigns against human infection diseases).

The Ethical Rules for the Pharmaceutical Industry (LER Rules) prohibit advertising for prescription-only medicinal products to the general public. However, companies can provide information from Patient-FASS (the Swedish Medicines Information Engine, operated by the Swedish Association of the Pharmaceutical Industry (LIF)) and provide aids (for example, brochures) intended to be given to patients by healthcare professionals to facilitate the correct use of their medicinal product.

### 22. WHAT KINDS OF MARKETING ACTIVITIES ARE PERMITTED IN RELATION TO CONSUMERS AND THE PRODUCTS WHICH MAY BE ADVERTISED TO THEM?

There are no specific restrictions under Swedish law on what kinds of marketing activities are permitted relating to consumers. However, any marketing activity must comply with the restrictions outlined in the Medical Products Act, the Market Practices Act and the Ethical Rules for the Pharmaceutical Industry (LER Rules).

### 23. IS IT PERMITTED TO PROVIDE CONSUMERS WITH FREE SAMPLES? ARE THERE PARTICULAR RESTRICTIONS ON SPECIAL OFFERS (FOR EXAMPLE, "BUY-ONE-GET-ONE-FREE")?

Under the Medical Products Agency Regulation LVFS 2009:6 on the marketing of medicinal products for human use and the Ethical Rules for the Pharmaceutical Industry (LER Rules), free samples of medicinal products that have been authorised for sale in Sweden can only be provided to:

- Persons qualified to prescribe the product.
- Those with a pharmacy authorisation.
- Those persons responsible for medicinal products in pharmacies.
- Other retailers authorised to sell medicinal products.
- Pharmacists of hospital pharmacies (the sample can only be distributed by the healthcare professional).

Medicinal products that are included in the pharmaceutical benefits scheme can only be sold by pharmacies at the sales price set by the Dental and Pharmaceutical Benefits Agency (TLV). Therefore, special offers such as buy-one-get-one-free in relation to the medicinal products are not permitted.

Special offers to consumers (such as buy-one-get-one-free) constitute promotion and are therefore not permitted in relation to prescription-only medicinal products.

There is no explicit prohibition against these kinds of offers with regard to non-prescription medicinal products that are not included in the pharmaceutical benefits scheme. However, there is a risk that the Medicinal Products Agency (MPA) may consider them to qualify as a promotion that does not constitute an appropriate use of the medicinal product, in violation of the Medicinal Products Act.

## 24. ARE THERE PARTICULAR RULES OF PRACTICE ON THE USE OF THE INTERNET/ SOCIAL MEDIA REGARDING DRUGS AND THEIR ADVERTISING?

Internet advertising of medicinal products is subject to the same rules as advertising in any other Swedish media. The Medicinal Products Act, the Market Practices Act and the Ethical Rules for the Pharmaceutical Industry (LER Rules) are therefore applicable to advertisements published on the internet/ social media. In addition, the Swedish Association of the Pharmaceutical Industry (LIF) has issued an interpretative document on how the LER Rules must be interpreted with regard to social media.

## 25. WHAT REGULATORY AUTHORITY IS RESPONSIBLE FOR SUPERVISING MARKETING ACTIVITIES TO CONSUMERS?

### Regulatory authority

The Medicinal Products Agency (MPA) is responsible for supervising marketing activities.

### Supervision

The MPA can demand access to:

- Information and documents necessary for the supervision.
- Facilities.

The MPA can take action in cases of non-compliance, but will normally seek a voluntary solution. If an amicable solution is not found, the MPA can:

- Issue a prohibitive injunction (non-compliance of which can lead to fines).
- Notify the Consumer Ombudsman who is authorised to issue prohibitive injunctions (non-compliance of which can lead to fines) or initiate action in the Market Court.

In relation to marketing activities by pharmaceutical companies, the majority of all cases regarding advertising of medicinal products never reach court, but are handled by the Swedish Association of the Pharmaceutical Industry (LIF) through its two self-regulatory bodies:

- The Pharmaceutical Industry's Information Examiner (IGM), who is a physician.
- The Information Practises Committee (NBL), which is a court-like body.

### Rights of appeal

Decisions by the MPA can be appealed to the County Administrative Court in Uppsala. Decisions by the Market Court cannot be appealed. A decision by the IGM can be appealed to the NBL.

## 26. WHAT ARE THE LEGAL CONSEQUENCES OF NON-COMPLIANCE WITH CONSUMER MARKETING LAWS?

Under the Medicinal Products Act, the general sanction for failing to comply with the rules governing advertising is a prohibitive injunction, with additional fines in the event of non-compliance.

The Market Practices Act provides for several sanctions, depending on the nature of the violation. For example, the specific rules on misleading advertisements and special offers carry the following sanctions:

- Prohibitive injunctions subject to fines on non-compliance.
- Market disruption fees between SEK5,000 and SEK5 million.
- Third party damages.

Only prohibitive injunctions are available for the violation of the general clause on unfair marketing.

An action before the Market Court or the Stockholm District Court can be initiated by the Consumer Ombudsman, a competitor, a consumer/patient or a trade or consumer association. Most cases regarding pharmaceutical companies' advertising of medicinal products are handled by the two self-regulatory bodies:

- The Pharmaceutical Industry's Information Examiner (IGM), who is a physician.
- The Information Practises Committee (NBL), which is a court-like body.

The IGM monitors the market and can open a case without a formal complaint, or refer a case to the NBL. Private individuals and pharmaceutical companies, including competitors, are also entitled to bring an action before the IGM. The IGM and the NBL have contractual authority to fine member companies who violate the Ethical Rules for the Pharmaceutical Industry (LER Rules). The maximum fine is SEK500,000 by both the IGM and the NBL.

## MARKETING TO PROFESSIONALS

## 27. WHAT KINDS OF MARKETING ACTIVITIES ARE PERMITTED IN RELATION TO PROFESSIONALS?

There are no specific restrictions in relation to the kinds of marketing activities that are permitted regarding professionals. However, any marketing activity must comply with the restrictions in the Medicinal Products Act and the Ethical Rules for the Pharmaceutical Industry (LER Rules) (*see Question 28*).

## 28. ARE THERE ANY RESTRICTIONS ON MARKETING TO PROFESSIONALS?

**Marketing activities**

Gifts cannot be supplied, offered or promised to healthcare professionals. Information and educational material can be provided if they are:

- Below the value of SEK450.
- Directly relevant to the practice of the healthcare professional.
- Directly beneficial to the care of patients.

Items for medical use can be provided to educate healthcare professionals and for the care of patients if the item is:

- Below the value of SEK450.
- Not routinely used in the recipient's business.

**Frequency**

There are no specific rules on the amount of times that professionals can be targeted by sales representatives. However, the Ethical Rules for the Pharmaceutical Industry (LER Rules) contain detailed rules about how contact can be made. Meetings for communicating verbal information must aim to present facts and objective data and the meetings must be arranged to co-ordinate with the duties of the healthcare professional. When a meeting is planned, the pharmaceutical company must notify the professionals' concerned in advance and the LER Rules provide for detailed guidance on what information the notifications must contain.

**Provision of hospitality**

The provision of benefits is not generally accepted in Sweden and great care must be taken when any hospitality is offered to both public and private healthcare professionals. The prohibitions on bribery and bribe-taking under the Swedish Criminal Code are also applicable to the offering of hospitality.

The LER Rules provide that the basis for all cooperation between the industry and healthcare professionals is documentation, transparency and reasonability, and must be of benefit to all parties.

In addition, the LER Rules provide for specific requirements with regards to refreshments and meals. In general, meals provided must be very modest and can only be offered in connection with meetings. Alcoholic drinks (in the form of wine and beer) can only be offered in limited quantities and only as table drink. The offering of spirits is not allowed.

Recreational activities, including various forms of entertainment, cannot be financed by pharmaceutical companies or requested by healthcare employees in connection with meetings or other forms of interaction. Simple social activities will not be considered as an offering by the pharmaceutical company provided that they have not been organised, requested or paid for by the pharmaceutical company.

The possibility of offering hospitality abroad is limited. The choice of location for an event must be reasonable in relation to the purpose of the event. Locations at which major international events are being staged at the same time as, or in connection with, the pharmaceutical event must be avoided. Pharmaceutical companies must also not contribute financially to events that are located in such places.

### 29. WHAT INFORMATION IS IT LEGALLY REQUIRED TO INCLUDE IN ADVERTISING TO PROFESSIONALS?

If the FASS catalogue text or the Summary of Product (Characteristic) (SmPC) is not reproduced, written information must contain at least the following data in relation to the medicinal product:

- The name.
- Its dosage form and, if required its strength (it is required when the relevant medicinal product is available in different strengths or if the strength otherwise must be stated).

- Names of its active ingredients, stated by a generic name, as well as quantities of the ingredients.
- A balanced statement of the product characteristics, including particulars on the pharmacological group or other accepted group affiliation and indication or area of indications.
- Required warnings or limitations applicable to the use of the medicinal product.
- Information about the date on which the documentation and SmPC were compiled or reviewed, the status of the product and if the product is part of the benefits system (including possible restrictions) and the sale price.

In addition, the advertisement must clearly show the name, and address or telephone number or web address of the pharmaceutical company responsible for the marketing of the medicinal product in Sweden, or of its representative in Sweden. In addition, a reference to "FASS.se" must be made for additional information. If the advertisement contains quotations, numerical data or diagrams taken from a scientific study, or makes a comparison between drugs that are based on such a study, reference must always be made to the source. Otherwise, it is not normally necessary to make references to documentation that support statements contained in the advertisement. It must also state the date of the establishment or revision of the advertisement material. The information provided must be correct, up-to-date, verifiable and as detailed as possible in order for the recipient to get an opinion of the product's value for treatment.

## 30. ARE THERE RULES ON COMPARISONS WITH OTHER PRODUCTS THAT ARE PARTICULARLY APPLICABLE TO DRUGS?

There is no particular provision on comparative advertising in the Medicinal Products Act. However, under the general provision of the Act, advertising must be kept up-to-date, factual, balanced and must not be misleading.

Under the Ethical Rules for the Pharmaceutical Industry (LER Rules) comparisons between a drug's effects, active ingredients and cost of treatment must be objectively and accurately presented and give a fair overall picture of the compared products.

This means, among other things, that the:

- Objects included in the comparison must be selected in a correct manner and be relevant for the comparison.
- Objects included in the comparison must be clearly specified (including the complete name and generic designation, if necessary).
- Facts which the comparison is intended to clarify and the limitations of the comparison must be clearly presented.
- Comparisons of properties of synonymous drugs, or of drugs with the same indications, must give a comprehensive and fair picture of the properties compared.
- Presentation must not induce incorrect or misleading conclusions regarding properties not covered by the comparison.

If required for clarity, the complete name and generic designation of the compared drugs must be stated.

## 31. WHAT OTHER ITEMS, FUNDING OR SERVICES ARE PERMITTED TO BE PROVIDED TO PROFESSIONALS?

**Discounts**

The Swedish rules on advertising do not prevent the offering of discounts to healthcare providers. However, such arrangements can have competition law implications, in certain circumstances. There are also restrictions regarding discounts in respect of medicinal products included in the national reimbursement scheme.

**Free samples**

Under the Medical Products Agency Regulation LVFS 2009:6 on the marketing of medicinal products for human use and the Ethical Rules for the Pharmaceutical Industry (LER Rules), free samples of medicinal products that have been authorised for sale in Sweden can only be provided to:

- Persons qualified to prescribe the product.
- Those with a pharmacy authorisation.
- Responsible persons for medicinal products in pharmacies.
- Other retailers authorised to sell medicinal products.
- Pharmacists of hospital pharmacies (the sample can only be distributed by the healthcare professional).

The sample can only be supplied in response to a written request, which has been signed and dated. The request must be kept and filed by the company. The company must also carefully check that the person sending the request is authorised to prescribe or dispense medicinal products.

Samples must only be distributed with great restraint. Medical samples of prescription medicinal products for human can only be of new products. Only one package of the smallest available size must be supplied on each occasion and the number of samples of each product to the same recipient must be limited to one sample per year. The sample must be marked with "medicinal sample, not for sale" and the expiry date, and it must be accompanied by a copy of the Summary of Product (Characteristic) (SmPC). The sample cannot be used for the treatment of humans or animals. It is not permitted to distribute free samples of medicinal products that have been listed as narcotics by the Medicinal Products Agency.

**Sponsorship of professionals**

Financial support to the healthcare sector is a sensitive issue in Sweden and great care must be taken to not challenge the integrity and independent relationship between the pharmaceutical industry and the medicinal profession. The offer to sponsor must not be addressed to individual physicians. Under certain circumstances it is possible to sponsor meetings arranged by or on behalf of the healthcare provider or an association that organises employees in the healthcare sector. In such cases, the scientific and professional programme must be the purpose of the meeting. Pharmaceutical companies can only offer sponsorship to meetings that have a connection with the company's own business areas. Sponsorship of ordinary activities and internal activities of healthcare providers or associations cannot occur.

The income generated to healthcare providers or associations by sponsorship can only cover actual, documented, reasonable and direct costs that are necessary to carry out the professional parts of a meeting. For example, expenses for speakers, venues, moderate meals, or the cost for training materials. Sponsorship of meetings where the meal is the only actual cost cannot be requested or offered. Travel, accommodation, and participation fees for professionals cannot be paid for by pharmaceutical companies or requested by individual participants. The booking of travel and accommodation cannot be provided by pharmaceutical companies. Any sponsorship must clearly be documented in writing and be made transparent by the company.

**Other items, funding or services**

See *Question 28*.

## 32. WHAT REGULATORY AUTHORITY IS RESPONSIBLE FOR SUPERVISING MARKETING ACTIVITIES REGARDING PROFESSIONALS?

**Regulatory authority**

The Medicinal Products Agency (MPA) monitors the pharmaceutical market, including advertising and other marketing activities of pharmaceutical companies.

**Supervision**

The MPA can take action in cases of non-compliance, but will normally seek a voluntary solution. If an amicable solution is not found, the MPA can issue a prohibitive injunction (subject to fines for non-compliance) or refer the case to the Information Practises Committee (NBL) (*see below*).

**Rights of appeal**

Decisions by the MPA can be appealed to the Administrative Court in Uppsala. In addition, action can be brought before the Pharmaceutical Industry's Information Examiner (IGM) and NBL. See *Questions 25* and *26*.

## 33. WHAT ARE THE LEGAL CONSEQUENCES IN CASE OF NON-COMPLIANCE WITH PROFESSIONAL MARKETING LAWS?

Under the Medicinal Products Act, the general sanction for failing to comply with the rules on advertising is a prohibitive injunction (subject to fines for non-compliance).

The Pharmaceutical Industry's Information Examiner (IGM) and the Information Practises Committee (NBL) have contractual authority to fine member companies who violate the LER Rules. The maximum fine is SEK500,000 by the IGM and SEK500,000 by the NBL.

## ENGAGEMENT WITH PATIENT ORGANISATIONS

**34. WHAT KINDS OF ACTIVITIES ARE PERMITTED IN RELATION TO ENGAGEMENT WITH PATIENT ORGANISATIONS? WHAT ARE THE RESTRICTIONS THAT ARE IMPOSED ON RELATIONSHIP WITH PATIENT ORGANISATIONS?**

The Ethical Rules for the Pharmaceutical Industry (LER Rules) cover co-operation with all kinds of patient organisations (for example, disability organisations, patient organisations, organisations for relatives and associations for senior citizens). The LER Rules provide that agreements between a patient organisation and a pharmaceutical company must:

- Be made in writing.
- Be available to third parties.
- Only give financial support for special projects or activities.
- Be conducted in such a manner that the parties' independent positions in relation to each other cannot be questioned and that it must always be clearly evident that the parties are co-operating.

## REFORM

**35. ARE THERE ANY PLANS TO REFORM THE LAW ON THE DISTRIBUTION AND PROMOTION OF DRUGS IN YOUR JURISDICTION?**

There are no plans for reform.

# SWITZERLAND

Markus Schott, *BÄR & KARRER AG*

## DISTRIBUTION

### PRE-CONDITIONS FOR DISTRIBUTION

**1. WHAT ARE THE LEGAL PRE-CONDITIONS FOR A DRUG TO BE DISTRIBUTED WITHIN THE JURISDICTION?**

#### Authorisation

Distribution of drugs in Switzerland is almost exclusively regulated at the federal level, primarily by Articles 23 to 30 of the Therapeutic Products Act (HMG).

The distribution of a drug in Switzerland (irrespective of whether the drug requires a prescription or can be sold over the counter) requires a marketing authorisation from the Swiss Agency for Therapeutic Products (Swissmedic) (*Article 9, HMG*).

This marketing authorisation is issued if the applicant can prove (*Article 10, HMG*):

- That the drug or the process is of high quality, safe and effective.
- That it has a licence for manufacture, import or wholesale trade.
- That its registered address or office is in Switzerland or that it has set up a subsidiary in Switzerland.

The marketing authorisation is valid for five years but can be renewed as long as the conditions for issuing the marketing authorisation are met (*Article 16, HMG*).

#### Exceptions

Besides the ordinary licence procedure, the law provides for a simplified licence procedure (*Article 14, HMG*). In particular, for generic and orphan drugs, the simplified application procedure applies if this is compatible with the quality, safety and efficacy requirements provided for by the law (*Article 14, HMG*).

**2. DO ANY TYPES OF NAMED PATIENT AND/OR COMPASSIONATE USE PROGRAMMES OPERATE? IF SO, WHAT ARE THE REQUIREMENTS FOR PRE-LAUNCH ACCESS?**

The Swiss Agency for Therapeutic Products (Swissmedic) can authorise, for a limited period, the distribution or dispensing of unauthorised drugs to treat life-threatening diseases if (*Article 9, Therapeutic Products Act (HMG)*):

- This authorisation is compatible with the protection of health.

# SWITZERLAND

- A significant therapeutic benefit is to be expected from the administration of these drugs.
- No comparable other drug exists.

## LICENSING

### 3. WHAT IS THE PROCEDURAL STRUCTURE REGARDING LICENSING A DRUG FOR DISTRIBUTION?

**Structure**

The distribution of a drug requires an application with the Swiss Agency for Therapeutic Products (Swissmedic) for a marketing authorisation for the drug to be distributed in Switzerland. The application for a marketing authorisation must contain all of the data and documents necessary for its assessment. In particular, the following information has to be provided (*Article 11, Therapeutic Products Act (HMG)*):

- The name of the drug.
- The name of the manufacturer and the distribution company.
- The process of manufacture, the composition, the quality and stability of the drug.
- The therapeutic effects and undesirable effects.
- The labelling, the medical information (patient information as well as information for professionals), the method of supply and the method of administration.
- The results of physical, chemical, galenic and biological or microbiological tests, the results of the pharmacological and toxicological tests.
- The results of the clinical trials.

Under certain conditions, test and trial results are not required for an application regarding generic drugs (*Article 12, HMG*).

Following the submission of the required documents, the application is examined by Swissmedic that decides whether the marketing authorisation is to be issued or not based on the quality of the manufacturing, the drug's efficacy and its safety (*Article 16, HMG*). The entire authorisation procedure (ordinary licence procedure) takes between ten and 12 months or between four and five months if the expedited procedure is chosen by the applicant.

**Regulatory authority**

Swissmedic is responsible for issuing the marketing authorisation.

### 4. IS THERE A SIMPLIFIED LICENCE PROCEEDING, OR RELAXED LICENSING CONDITIONS, FOR DRUGS WHICH HAVE ALREADY BEEN LICENSED FOR DISTRIBUTION IN ANOTHER JURISDICTION?

Swiss law provides for a simplified licence procedure for certain kinds of drugs, including (*Article 14, Therapeutic Products Act (HMG)*):

- Generic drugs.
- Orphan drugs.
- Authorisation of an additional distributor to market drugs already licensed for marketing in

Switzerland, but imported from another country (parallel imports).

The simplified licence procedure is applicable for parallel imports, if the following conditions are fulfilled:

- The drug must be imported from a country with a marketing authorisation system equivalent to the one in Switzerland.
- The drug must satisfy the same requirements as the drug already approved in Switzerland, in particular for the labelling and product information.
- The parallel importer can guarantee the same safety and quality requirements as the original applicant.

Possible patent claims are not considered in the licence procedure. However, patent owners can use civil actions for defending their patent rights.

If a drug is not yet licensed for marketing in Switzerland, but has been licensed in another country with a similar marketing authorisation system, the Swiss Agency for Therapeutic Products (Swissmedic) takes the results of the respective tests into account (*Article 13, HMG*).

## 5. IS VIRTUAL DRUG DISTRIBUTION POSSIBLE FROM YOUR JURISDICTION?

It is possible to distribute drugs virtually from Switzerland. However, trading these drugs in foreign countries from Switzerland, without the drugs entering Switzerland, requires a licence from the Swiss Agency for Therapeutic Products (Swissmedic) (*Article 18, Therapeutic Products Act (HMG)*). This licence is issued if:

- The necessary professional and operational conditions are fulfilled.
- An appropriate system of quality assurance exists.

## 6. WHAT IS THE PROCEDURE TO APPEAL (LEGAL REMEDY) A LICENSING DECISION?

If the Swiss Agency for Therapeutic Products (Swissmedic) rejects an application, the applicant can appeal to the Federal Administrative Tribunal, whose decisions can finally be appealed at the Federal Supreme Court.

## 7. WHAT ARE THE COSTS OF OBTAINING LICENSING?

The fees for a licence depend on the licensing procedure:

- The fees for licensing a drug with a new active substance are CHF70,000 or CHF110,000 if the expedited procedure is used.
- The fees for licensing a drug with an existing registered active substance are between CHF15,000 and CHF28,000 (depending on whether there is an inventive step) if using the simplified licence procedure and between CHF27,500 and CHF47,000 if the expedited procedure is used.
- For renewing an existing authorisation the fees are CHF500.

## DISTRIBUTION TO CONSUMERS

## 8. WHAT ARE THE DIFFERENT CATEGORIES OF DRUGS FOR DISTRIBUTION?

The law differentiates between two categories of drugs:

- Prescription drugs.
- Non-prescription drugs.

These two categories of drugs have been further divided into five sub-categories (categories A to E) depending on the degree of perceived risk represented by the product. Each drug is classified in the authorisation process by the Swiss Agency for Therapeutic Products (Swissmedic):

- Category A drugs are subject to a more stringent prescription requirement that means that a medical prescription only allows for a one-time supply of the prescribed drug.
- Category B drugs are subject to a prescription that allows for a repeated supply of the prescribed drug.
- Category C drugs do not need a prescription but can only be supplied after the advice of a medical person has been obtained.
- For category D drugs no prescription is necessary. However, category D drugs can only be supplied after expert advice has been obtained.
- Category E drugs can be supplied without any restrictions.

## 9. WHO IS AUTHORISED TO DISTRIBUTE PRESCRIPTION DRUGS AND OVER-THE-COUNTER DRUGS TO CONSUMERS?

**Prescription drugs**

Pharmacists can distribute prescription-only drugs on prescription of a physician but also in justified exceptional cases (for example, in case of an emergency) without prescription. The distribution of prescription drugs to patients requires an authorisation that is issued by the cantonal authorities and not by the Swiss Agency for Therapeutic Products (Swissmedic).

Physicians can also distribute prescription drugs to consumers if the cantonal regulations allow for so-called self-distribution. Therefore, whether a physician is allowed to distribute prescription drugs depends on cantonal law. Some cantons do not allow physicians to distribute prescription drugs at all, others stipulate some restrictions. In the cantons where physicians are not allowed to distribute prescription drugs, only pharmacists can distribute prescription drugs (on prescription by a physician).

All duly trained professionals can also distribute prescription drugs, provided that they are supervised either by a pharmacist or a physician. Therefore, nurses in hospitals can also distribute prescription drugs provided that a physician or a hospital pharmacist supervises the nurse.

**Over-the-counter drugs**

Everyone that is entitled to distribute prescription drugs to patients can also distribute over-the-counter (OTC) drugs. Therefore, pharmacists as well as physicians can distribute OTC drugs to consumers, if cantonal law permits.

Druggists that hold a federal diploma can distribute OTC drugs of categories D and E but not OTC drugs of category C. All duly trained professionals can distribute the respective non-prescription drugs, provided that they are supervised either by a pharmacist, a physician or a druggist. Those with a federally recognised education in complementary medicine can also distribute certain OTC drugs.

## 10. WHAT DRUGS CAN AN ATTENDING PHYSICIAN DISTRIBUTE AND UNDER WHAT CIRCUMSTANCES?

Generally, a physician can prescribe any drug provided that he observes the recognised rules of pharmaceutical and medical science and does not endanger the health of the patient. A drug can only be prescribed if the state of the health of the patient is known.

However, distribution of drugs by the physician to patients directly depends on whether the canton of the physician's domicile allows self-distribution of drugs by physicians (*see Question 9*).

## 11. WHO IS AUTHORISED TO PRESCRIBE PRESCRIPTION DRUGS TO CONSUMERS?

Prescription drugs can only be prescribed by physicians.

## 12. IS DIRECT MAILING/DISTANCE SELLING OF DRUGS PERMITTED IN YOUR JURISDICTION?

### Conditions

In principle, direct mailing or distance selling of drugs is not permitted, except for drugs of category E. However, for all other drugs (categories A to D) the cantons can issue an authorisation for direct mailing or distance selling if all of the following requirements are met (*Article 27, Therapeutic Products Act (HMG)*):

- The drug has been prescribed by a physician.
- No safety requirements prohibit direct mailing.
- Appropriate consultation with a physician is guaranteed.
- Sufficient medical supervision of the effect of the drug is guaranteed.

The issuing of the authorisation for direct mailing or distance selling of drugs requires a cantonal retail trade licence for the operation of a pharmacy as well as the implementation of a quality assurance system. These requirements also apply to the distribution of drugs over the internet.

### Cross-border sales

Sales can be made beyond the borders of Switzerland. However, the export of drugs requires a licence from the Swiss Agency for Therapeutic Products (Swissmedic) (*Article 18, Therapeutic Products Act (HMG)*). This licence is issued if:

- The necessary professional and operational conditions are fulfilled.
- An appropriate system of quality assurance exists.

However, the export of drugs and their foreign trade from Switzerland is prohibited if either:

- The drugs are prohibited in the destination country.
- Or if circumstances suggest that the drugs could be intended for an illegal purpose.

Anyone exporting drugs (pre-packaged or not) must provide the recipient with the appropriate basic medical and pharmaceutical information.

### 13. WHAT REGULATORY AUTHORITY IS RESPONSIBLE FOR SUPERVISING DISTRIBUTION ACTIVITIES?

The Swiss Agency for Therapeutic Products (Swissmedic) and the competent cantonal authorities (generally the respective department of health) are responsible for the supervision of the distribution activities. They supervise the Swiss market in general as well as the individuals distributing the drugs. A specific investigation is opened either if Swissmedic or the cantonal authorities discover any violation during their supervision or if a violation is notified to them.

Swissmedic and the cantonal authorities can perform any necessary investigation into a specific incident and the parties involved must fully co-operate in this investigation. In particular, Swissmedic or the cantonal authorities can:

- Take samples.
- Demand information and essential documents.
- Request any necessary help for this purpose.

Swissmedic, or in case of a serious and immediate threat to health the cantonal authorities, takes all necessary administrative measures to remedy a breach.

### 14. WHAT IS THE PROCEDURE TO APPEAL (LEGAL REMEDY) A DISTRIBUTION DECISION?

Orders of the Swiss Agency for Therapeutic Products (Swissmedic) can be appealed to the Federal Administrative Tribunal and finally to the Federal Supreme Court. Criminal prosecution falls either within the competence of Swissmedic or in the competence of the cantonal authorities. In both cases, court appeals are possible.

### 15. WHAT ARE THE LEGAL CONSEQUENCES OF NON-COMPLIANCE WITH CONSUMER DISTRIBUTION LAWS?

If the violation is committed intentionally, the criminal liability is imprisonment of up to three years or a fine of up to CHF200,000. If the responsible person acted in his professional capacity, the punishment is imprisonment for up to five years and a fine of up to CHF500,000. For negligence, the law provides for imprisonment of up to six months or a monetary fine of up to CHF100,000.

## WHOLESALE DISTRIBUTION

### 16. WHAT IS THE LEGAL REGIME REGARDING WHOLESALE DISTRIBUTION OF DRUGS?

The wholesale of drugs requires a licence (*Article 28, Therapeutic Products Act (HMG)*). This licence is issued by the Swiss Agency for Therapeutic Products (Swissmedic) if:

- The necessary professional and operational conditions are fulfilled.
- An appropriate system of quality assurance exists.

If the applicant is already in possession of a manufacturing or import licence for drugs, it is also eligible for a wholesale licence. The licence cannot be transferred to anyone else or to any other site. It is valid for a period of five years but can be extended. An extension of the licence is granted if the conditions for issuing a licence are still fulfilled. The wholesale of drugs is only permissible for drugs that have a marketing authorisation for Switzerland. As well as the requirements for the issuance of the licence, a company that is engaged in the wholesale trade of drugs must also respect the recognised principles of Good Distribution Practice.

The wholesale of drugs is permitted by anyone in possession of a licence. A licence holder can wholesale drugs to persons that are allowed to trade with, process, distribute or apply drugs.

## 17. WHAT REGULATORY AUTHORITY IS RESPONSIBLE FOR SUPERVISING WHOLESALE DISTRIBUTION ACTIVITIES?

### Regulatory authority

The Swiss Agency for Therapeutic Products (Swissmedic) is responsible for the issuance of the licence for the wholesale distribution of drugs. Depending on the nature of the drug, either Swissmedic or the respective cantonal authorities are responsible for the supervision of wholesale distribution activities.

### Supervision

Either Swissmedic or the respective cantonal authority can perform inspections and verify whether the requirements for the issuance of the licence are fulfilled. If the authorities discover any violations, they can take all administrative measures that are necessary in order to re-establish compliance with the law. In particular, the authorities can:

- Raise objections and fix an appropriate time period for the re-establishment of compliance with the law.
- Suspend or withdraw establishment licences and marketing authorisations.
- Close establishments.
- Seize, hold in official storage or destroy therapeutic products that endanger health or that do not comply with the legal requirements.

### Rights of appeal

Orders of Swissmedic can be appealed to the Federal Administrative Tribunal and finally to the Federal Supreme Court. Orders of cantonal authorities can be appealed to the competent cantonal courts and finally to the Federal Supreme Court.

## 18. WHAT ARE THE LEGAL CONSEQUENCES OF NON-COMPLIANCE WITH WHOLESALE DISTRIBUTION LAWS?

If the violation has been committed intentionally, the criminal liability is imprisonment of up to three years or a monetary fine of up to CHF200,000. If the person responsible acted in his professional capacity, the punishment is imprisonment for up to five years and a monetary fine of up to CHF500,000. For negligence, the law provides for imprisonment of up to six months or a monetary fine of up to CHF100,000.

# MARKETING

## PROMOTION

### 19. WHAT IS THE GENERAL LEGAL REGIME FOR THE MARKETING OF DRUGS?

**Legal regime**

Marketing of drugs is exclusively regulated at the federal level, primarily by Articles 31 to 33 of the Therapeutic Products Act (HMG), and by the Ordinance on Advertising for Medicinal Products (AWV), which implements and specifies in more detail the statutory requirements of the HMG. These legal texts contain a comprehensive regime regarding marketing of ready-to-use drugs to consumers and to professionals as well as its enforcement by the Swiss Agency for Therapeutic Products (Swissmedic). The regime is applicable to all drugs that are being marketed in Switzerland.

**Limits to marketing activities**

Generally, prescription drugs can only be marketed to professionals but non-prescription drugs can also be marketed to consumers (*Article 31, HMG*).

For drugs that are being listed on the Swiss List of Specialities (SL) and that are therefore reimbursed by the mandatory health insurance, additional rules contained in the Health Insurance Act (KVG) and the Ordinance on Health Insurance (KVV) apply. In particular, all marketing to consumers is prohibited for drugs that are reimbursed within this framework. Non-compliance with this prohibition can lead to delisting of the respective drug.

Apart from the above-mentioned drug-specific regimes, the general legal framework regarding advertising is also applicable to marketing of drugs. In particular, the Act Against Unfair Competition (UWG) prohibits any kind of unfair marketing activities such as:

- False statements.
- Unnecessary debasement of competitors.
- Causation of confusion.
- Aggressive marketing techniques.

The UWG also prohibits bribery of employees, directors or other staff of competitors, suppliers and customers.

### 20. ARE THERE OTHER CODES OF CONDUCT FOR THE MARKETING OF DRUGS (FOR EXAMPLE, BY PROFESSIONAL OR INDUSTRIAL ORGANISATIONS)?

The Code of Conduct of the Pharmaceutical Industry in Switzerland (dated 4 December 2003, last revision of 6 September 2013) (the Pharma Code) has been drafted by five associations of the Swiss pharmaceutical industry and has been signed by around 120 Swiss pharmaceutical companies. The Pharma Code is based on the respective codes of the International Federation of Pharmaceutical Manufacturers and Associations (IFPMA) and the European Federation of Pharmaceutical Industries and Associations (EFPIA). It is applicable to marketing activities and financial contributions regarding professionals but not to marketing activities regarding consumers. The Pharma Code also includes rules on the co-operation between pharmaceutical companies and healthcare professionals (and their organisations) on clinical trials and invitations to promotional events.

Based on the EFPIA Disclosure Code of June 2013, the Code of Conduct of the Pharmaceutical Industry in Switzerland on co-operation with Healthcare Professional Circles and Patient Organisations (dated 6 September 2013) (the Pharma Co-operation Code) was drafted by the same associations that drafted the Pharma Code. The Pharma Co-operation Code includes rules on the co-operation between pharmaceutical companies and healthcare professionals, healthcare organisations and patient organisations. It requires disclosure (in accordance with Swiss data protection law) of pecuniary benefits granted by pharmaceutical companies to professionals and such organisations as of 1 January 2016. The Pharma Co-operation Code also specifies the implementation of the relevant obligations by the pharmaceutical companies and how compliance will be monitored. Violations of the Pharma Code or the Pharma Co-operation Code are investigated by a Code Secretariat (affiliated with one of the associations) that can order the member companies to cease non-compliant activities. Non-observance of this order means that the Secretariat brings the case to the Swiss Agency for Therapeutic Products' (Swissmedic) attention if the public health is at risk.

Besides the general rules on (un)fair competition in the Act Against Unfair Competition (UWG), there are the Principles for the Fair Competition in Commercial Communication (dated April 2008), which the Swiss Commission on Fair Competition has defined. According to Principle 2.4, healthcare professionals cannot be used in advertisements that refer to products that relate to health but that are not subject to governmental approval if such use is intended to make the product look like a drug.

In addition, based on Principle 5.7, marketing of products relating to personal care, hygiene and wellbeing cannot give the impression that such products actually have medical effects. The Commission on Fair Competition decides on complaints about violations of the principles, but it has no power to give binding orders.

## MARKETING TO CONSUMERS

### 21. WHAT IS THE LEGAL REGIME FOR MARKETING TO CONSUMERS?

Only non-prescription drugs can be marketed directly to consumers (DTC), that is categories C, D, and E (*Article 31, Therapeutic Products Act (HMG) and Article 14, Ordinance on Advertising for Medicinal Products (AWV)*). Additionally, advertising of non-prescription drugs to consumers is prohibited if such drugs either:

- Contain narcotic or psychotropic substances.
- Or if they cannot, because of their composition and intended use, be used without the intervention of a physician for the relevant diagnosis, prescription or treatment.
- Or if the drugs are frequently the object of abuse or if they lead to addiction or dependence (*Article 32, HMG*).

It is also prohibited to advertise drugs that are reimbursed by mandatory health insurance (*Article 65, Ordinance on Health Insurance (KVV)*).

## 22. WHAT KINDS OF MARKETING ACTIVITIES ARE PERMITTED IN RELATION TO CONSUMERS AND THE PRODUCTS WHICH MAY BE ADVERTISED TO THEM?

Generally, all marketing activities must comply with the basic requirements of Article 32 of the Therapeutic Products Act (HMG). This means that advertising cannot be misleading or contrary to public order and morality and it cannot incite excessive, abusive or inappropriate use of drugs.

The following is a non-exhaustive list of permitted advertising methods that can be done directly to consumers (DTC) (*Article 15, Ordinance on Advertising for Medicinal Products (AWV)*):

- Advertisements in newspapers, magazines, books.
- Advertising on objects.
- Advertising by audiovisual means including the internet.
- Advertising statements made during home visits and presentations.
- Advertising statements in physicians' practices and pharmacies.
- Provision of samples.

The ordinance also defines advertising that is prohibited (*Articles 21 and 22, AWV*). In particular, the following are prohibited marketing practices:

- Advertising for indications or possible uses that require a diagnosis or treatment by a physician.
- Acceptance of orders for drugs during home visits, exhibitions, presentations, or promotional excursions.
- Individually addressed direct mailing.
- Provision of drugs for sales promotion purposes.
- Provision of vouchers for drugs.
- The organisation of competitions.
- Marketing that only or mainly targets children and adolescents.

However, some of these restrictions do not apply to drugs of category E.

## 23. IS IT PERMITTED TO PROVIDE CONSUMERS WITH FREE SAMPLES? ARE THERE PARTICULAR RESTRICTIONS ON SPECIAL OFFERS (FOR EXAMPLE, "BUY-ONE-GET-ONE-FREE")?

Drug samples given to the public must be clearly and permanently labelled as "free samples". These samples cannot contain more than one recommended daily dose and cannot be sold (*Article 19, Ordinance on Advertising for Medicinal Products (AWV)*). Samples of drugs of categories C and D can only be supplied to the public by the persons authorised to distribute these products to consumers. Regular packs of drugs cannot be given away as samples.

## 24. ARE THERE PARTICULAR RULES OF PRACTICE ON THE USE OF THE INTERNET/SOCIAL MEDIA REGARDING DRUGS AND THEIR ADVERTISING?

While advertising for drugs of categories C and D on radio, television, and in cinemas must be submitted to the Swiss Agency for Therapeutic Products (Swissmedic) for approval before appearing (*Article 23, Ordinance on Advertising for Medicinal Products (AWV)*), no such preliminary control procedure is required for marketing activities on the internet. The mandatory warnings that must be included at the end of television and cinema commercials, (for example, "This is a medicinal product. Please take advice from a health professional and read the patient information."), do not apply to advertisements on the internet.

## 25. WHAT REGULATORY AUTHORITY IS RESPONSIBLE FOR SUPERVISING MARKETING ACTIVITIES TO CONSUMERS?

### Regulatory authority

The Swiss Agency for Therapeutic Products (Swissmedic) is responsible for implementing and supervising compliance with the legal requirements in relation to marketing of drugs to consumers.

### Supervision

Advertising for drugs of categories C and D on radio, television and in cinemas must be submitted to Swissmedic for approval prior to appearing (*Article 23, Ordinance on Advertising for Medicinal Products (AWV)*). The same applies to advertisements in print and audiovisual media for analgesics, soporifics and sedatives, laxatives and anorectics. In all other cases, there are no preliminary control procedures, but rather ex-post control procedures based on information that Swissmedic has gathered itself or that it has received from third parties (*Article 24, AWV*). The holder of the marketing authorisation must designate a person that is responsible for the advertising of the drugs that are placed on the market (*Article 25, AWV*).

### Rights of appeal

Decisions of Swissmedic can be appealed before the Federal Administrative Tribunal whose judgments can then be appealed (if certain conditions are met) before the Federal Supreme Court.

## 26. WHAT ARE THE LEGAL CONSEQUENCES OF NON-COMPLIANCE WITH CONSUMER MARKETING LAWS?

Persons that have wilfully violated the provisions regarding advertising of drugs can be punished by detention or a fine of up to CHF50,000 (*Article 87, Therapeutic Products Act (HMG)*). Contraventions in a professional capacity can be punished by imprisonment of up to six months and a fine of up to CHF100,000. Negligent contraventions can be punished by a fine of up to CHF10,000.

The Swiss Agency for Therapeutic Products (Swissmedic) can also take all administrative measures necessary to re-establish compliance with the law (*Article 66, HMG*). In particular, Swissmedic can seize, hold in official storage, destroy or prohibit the use of non-compliant advertising media and publish the prohibition at the expense of the responsible parties.

Swissmedic can oblige authorisation holders that have violated the provisions regarding advertising of drugs either repeatedly or to a serious extent to then submit all planned advertising for prior approval.

## SWITZERLAND

### MARKETING TO PROFESSIONALS

**27. WHAT KINDS OF MARKETING ACTIVITIES ARE PERMITTED IN RELATION TO PROFESSIONALS?**

Generally, all marketing activities must comply with the basic requirements that advertising cannot be misleading or contrary to public order and morality and it cannot incite excessive, abusive or inappropriate use of drugs (*Article 32, Therapeutic Products Act (HMG)*).

The following is a non-exhaustive list of advertising methods (*Article 4, Ordinance on Advertising for Medicinal Products (AWV)*):

- Advertisements in newspapers, magazines and books.
- Advertising on objects.
- Advertising by audiovisual means including the internet.
- Advertising within the framework of scientific conferences or promotional events.
- The organisation of promotional events and financial support for such events.
- Hospitality provided within the framework of scientific conferences and promotional events.
- Advertising by mail.
- Visits by medical sales representatives.
- Provision of samples.

**28. ARE THERE ANY RESTRICTIONS ON MARKETING TO PROFESSIONALS?**

**Marketing activities**

According to section 141 in connection with section 47 of the Code of Conduct of the Pharmaceutical Industry in Switzerland (dated 4 December 2003, last revision of 6 September 2013) (the Pharma Code), non-interventional studies cannot constitute an inducement to recommend, prescribe, purchase, supply, sell or administer a particular drug. The company's medical representatives can only collaborate in non-interventional studies under the supervision of the scientific service of the company and for administrative purposes. Their collaboration cannot be associated with a promotion for drugs.

**Frequency**

The authorisation holder must ensure that medical sales representatives are adequately trained and have sufficient knowledge to provide all the necessary information (*Article 12, Ordinance on Advertising for Medicinal Products (AWV)*). The representatives have to use scientific literature and the latest product information approved by the Swiss Agency for Therapeutic Products (Swissmedic) as the basis for any statements. There are no restrictions regarding areas such as the time, frequency and place of the visits. However, the professional cannot be paid for receiving sales representatives.

**Provision of hospitality**

It is prohibited to grant, offer or promise material benefits to persons that prescribe or dispense drugs or to the organisations that employ them (and for such persons to accept or solicit such material benefits) (*Article 33, Therapeutic Products Act (HMG)*). However, material benefits of modest value and that are related to medical or pharmaceutical practice are allowed.

Hospitality provided within the framework of scientific conferences or promotional events must remain reasonable and remain secondary in relation to the main purpose of the event. Additionally, third parties (such as spouses) cannot be included in hospitality (*Article 11, AWV*).

The Pharma Code, the Code of Conduct of the Pharmaceutical Industry in Switzerland on co-operation with Healthcare Professional Circles and Patient Organisations (dated 6 September 2013) (the Pharma Co-operation Code) and a guideline published by Swissmedic in 2006 contain detailed additional requirements regarding hospitality.

## 29. WHAT INFORMATION IS IT LEGALLY REQUIRED TO INCLUDE IN ADVERTISING TO PROFESSIONALS?

All advertising must contain at least the following information (*Article 6, Ordinance on Advertising for Medicinal Products (AWV)*):

- The product name (brand).
- The active substances with their abbreviation.
- The name and address of the authorisation holder.
- At least one indication or possibility for use, plus the dosage and route of administration.
- A summary of restrictions regarding use, adverse reactions and interactions.
- The dispensing category.
- A reference to the fact that more detailed information can be found in the patient information or the published product information, citing the exact source.

All the information in the advertising intended for professionals must comply with the latest product information approved by the Swiss Agency for Therapeutic Products (Swissmedic). In particular, only those indications and possibilities for use that have been approved by Swissmedic can be advertised.

The texts within the advertising must comply with and reflect the current status of scientific knowledge. They can only refer to clinical trials that have been carried out in compliance with the requirements of Good Clinical Trial Practice (GCTP) and whose results have been published or accepted for publication. These publications must be cited faithfully, in full and state the exact source. Advertising intended for professionals must also state that the professionals can request a full copy of the trial report from the company concerned (*Article 5, AWV*).

## 30. ARE THERE RULES ON COMPARISONS WITH OTHER PRODUCTS THAT ARE PARTICULARLY APPLICABLE TO DRUGS?

Comparisons with other drugs are only permitted if they are scientifically correct and based on trials that fulfil the requirements of Good Clinical Trial Practice (GCTP) (*Article 7, Ordinance on Advertising for Medicinal Products (AWV)*).

## 31. WHAT OTHER ITEMS, FUNDING OR SERVICES ARE PERMITTED TO BE PROVIDED TO PROFESSIONALS?

**Discounts**

It is prohibited to grant, offer or promise material benefits to persons that prescribe or dispense drugs or to the organisations that employ them (and for such persons to accept or solicit such material benefits) (*Article 33, Therapeutic Products Act (HMG)*). However, commercially and economically justified discounts that directly reduce the price for the consumer or his health insurance are allowed.

Also, the healthcare professional must pass on to the debtor of the compensation all discounts he has received from suppliers of drugs (*Article 56, Health Insurance Act (KVG)*).

**Free samples**

Samples can only be supplied in small quantities and on written request by the professional. Samples cannot be larger than the smallest packaging available on the market. The sale of samples is prohibited (*Article 10, Ordinance on Advertising for Medicinal Products (AWV)*).

**Sponsorship of professionals**

According to section 141 in connection with section 222 of the Code of Conduct of the Pharmaceutical Industry in Switzerland on co-operation with Healthcare Professional Circles and Patient Organisations (dated 6 September 2013) (the Pharma Co-operation Code), pharmaceutical companies can support institutions, organisations or associations of healthcare professionals either financially or in some other way, in so far as the support:

- Is restricted to research and other services in the healthcare sector.
- Is confirmed in writing and the relevant documents are available in the company.
- Does not constitute an inducement to recommend, prescribe, purchase, supply, sell or administer certain drugs.

However, the financial or other sponsoring of individual healthcare professionals is not allowed.

In addition, section 4 of the Code of Conduct of the Pharmaceutical Industry in Switzerland (dated 4 December 2003, last revision of 6 September 2013) (the Pharma Code) contains detailed requirements regarding the sponsorship of clinical trials. The pharmaceutical companies are required to assure the transparency of the clinical trials sponsored by them.

Companies that sponsor clinical trials must ensure that the most objective trial results will be obtained and that the collaboration between sponsors and investigators is as transparent as possible. This is achieved by avoiding conflicts of interest and financial dependencies.

**Other items, funding or services**

According to the Pharma Code and the Pharma Co-operation Code, pharmaceutical companies can enter into agreements with institutions, organisations or associations of healthcare professionals, according to which the latter provide certain services to these companies, provided that these services are limited to research and other work in the healthcare sector and do not constitute an inducement to recommend, prescribe, purchase, supply, sell or administer certain drugs.

The pharmaceutical companies can also appoint healthcare professionals as consultants, in groups or individually, to undertake services such as providing reports and leading meetings, medical or scientific studies, clinical trials, training, consulting committees and market research. The companies can reimburse them appropriately for the associated expenditure according to the usual standards. The fact that consultants are used for services cannot constitute an inducement to recommend, prescribe, purchase, supply, sell or administer certain drugs. Also, consultancy arrangements allowing healthcare professionals to receive financial remuneration without having a duty to provide a service are explicitly prohibited.

### 32. WHAT REGULATORY AUTHORITY IS RESPONSIBLE FOR SUPERVISING MARKETING ACTIVITIES REGARDING PROFESSIONALS?

See *Question 25*.

Violations of the Code of Conduct of the Pharmaceutical Industry in Switzerland (dated 4 December 2003, last revision of 6 September 2013) (the Pharma Code) and the Code of Conduct of the Pharmaceutical Industry in Switzerland on co-operation with Healthcare Professional Circles and Patient Organisations (dated 6 September 2013) (the Pharma Co-operation Code) are being investigated by the Secretariat that can order the member companies to re-establish compliance with the Codes. Where there is non-observance of the order, the Secretariat brings the case to the Swiss Agency for Therapeutic Products's (Swissmedic) attention if the public health is at risk.

### 33. WHAT ARE THE LEGAL CONSEQUENCES IN CASE OF NON-COMPLIANCE WITH PROFESSIONAL MARKETING LAWS?

See *Question 26*.

## ENGAGEMENT WITH PATIENT ORGANISATIONS

### 34. WHAT KINDS OF ACTIVITIES ARE PERMITTED IN RELATION TO ENGAGEMENT WITH PATIENT ORGANISATIONS? WHAT ARE THE RESTRICTIONS THAT ARE IMPOSED ON RELATIONSHIP WITH PATIENT ORGANISATIONS?

Relationships between the pharmaceutical industry and patient organisations are regulated by section 3 of the Code of Conduct of the Pharmaceutical Industry in Switzerland on co-operation with Healthcare Professional Circles and Patient Organisations (dated 6 September 2013) (the Pharma Co-operation Code). According to the applicable rules, the pharmaceutical companies cannot ask patient organisations or accept offers from them to promote certain drugs. Companies cannot ask patient organisations to be their sole company support overall or for individual projects, whether financially or otherwise.

Contracts between companies and patient organisations under which they provide any type of services to companies are only allowed if such services are provided for the purpose of supporting healthcare or research. It is also permitted to engage patient organisations as experts and advisors for services such as participation at advisory board meetings and speaker services. In any event, the compensation for the services must be reasonable and cannot exceed the fair market value of the services provided. All forms of hospitality offered to patient organisations and their representatives must be reasonable, and strictly limited to the purpose of the respective event.

Each pharmaceutical company must publish on a website the patient organisations that it supports financially or otherwise to any significant extent. The disclosure must include a short description of the type of support that is sufficiently complete to enable the average reader to form an understanding of the significance of the support. The description must indicate the monetary value of financial support and of invoiced costs. The published information has to be updated at least once per year.

Each company must also publish the patient organisations to which it provides significant contracted services. This list must include a description of the nature of the services and be sufficiently complete to enable the average reader to form an understanding of the nature of the arrangement without the necessity to divulge confidential information. Companies must also make public the total amount paid per patient organisation over the reporting period.

# REFORM

### 35. ARE THERE ANY PLANS TO REFORM THE LAW ON THE DISTRIBUTION AND PROMOTION OF DRUGS IN YOUR JURISDICTION?

The Therapeutic Products Act (HMG) is currently being revised. The main objectives of the revision regarding drugs are the:

- Simplification of market access for some kinds of drugs.
- Improved safety of drugs.
- An increase in the transparency of information.
- Clarification of controversial regulations.
- The removal of legislative loopholes.

The changes suggested by the government affect the regulation of material benefits granted by pharmaceutical companies and the distribution of drugs by pharmacies and druggists.

Regarding the material benefits granted by pharmaceutical companies to professionals, the revised draft of the HMG aims to increase the transparency of these benefits and extends the circle of professionals covered by the regime on the one hand. On the other hand, it only covers prescription drugs (categories A and B) in contrast to today's provision that prohibits granting benefits for all drugs. Regarding the categories of drugs for distribution, the draft suggests allowing distribution of some prescription drugs by pharmacies without a physician's prescription. Also, druggists should be allowed to distribute all non-prescription drugs.

The proposed draft of the revised HMG is still under discussion in the Federal Parliament. The revised HMG is planned to enter into force by the end of 2017 at the earliest.

# THAILAND

Alan Adcock, Siraprapha Rungpry and Areeya Pornwiriyangkura,
TILLEKE & GIBBINS

## DISTRIBUTION

### PRE-CONDITIONS FOR DISTRIBUTION

**1. WHAT ARE THE LEGAL PRE-CONDITIONS FOR A DRUG TO BE DISTRIBUTED WITHIN THE JURISDICTION?**

**Authorisation**

Before distributing modern and traditional drugs into Thailand, a pharmaceutical company or its distributor must apply for an import licence or a manufacturing licence.

A modern drug is a "drug intended for use in the practice of modern medicine or the cure of an animal disease" (*Section 4 of the Drug Act, as amended*), whereas a traditional drug is "a drug intended for use in the practice of the traditional medicine or the cure of an animal disease which appears in a pharmacopoeia of traditional drug notified by the Minister of the Ministry of Public Health (Minister), or a drug notified by the Minister as a traditional drug, or a drug of which formula has been registered as that of a traditional drug" (*Section 4 of the Drug Act, as amended*).

The importer or manufacturer must:

- Be the owner of the business, and have sufficient assets and structure to be able to establish and operate the business.
- Be at least 20 years of age.
- Be a resident of Thailand.
- Not have been convicted for an offence against certain laws (for example, laws concerning narcotics and psychotropic substances).
- Have the premises to produce, sell, import or store drugs and equipment for use in the production, sale or storage of drugs and the control or maintenance of drug quality and quantity as prescribed in ministerial regulations.
- Use a trade name for the drug business that is not a repetition of, or similar to, the trade name used by another active licensee or a licensee whose licence has been suspended or revoked for less than a full year.

After the manufacturing licence or import licence is obtained, modern and traditional drugs must be registered with the Thai Food and Drug Administration (FDA) prior to be distributed in Thailand.

**Exceptions**

There are some rare exceptions under which certain drugs do not need product registration. According to section 79(4) of the Drug Act (BE 2510 (AD 1967)), a drug imported for research, analysis, exhibition or charitable purposes does not require registration if it complies with the requirements set up by the Notification of the Ministry of Public Health No.14 (BE 2532 (AD 1989)) regarding Bases, Procedures, and Conditions Respecting Importation of Medicines with No Need to Apply for Pharmacopeia Registration, as amended in 2009. Additionally, active pharmaceutical ingredients, semi-finished products, and sample drugs for registration purposes do not require product registration. With regard to the sale of drugs, the drug store requires a licence to sell, yet the hospitals or clinics can sell drugs directly to his or her patients without having applied for a licence to sell.

## 2. DO ANY TYPES OF NAMED PATIENT AND/OR COMPASSIONATE USE PROGRAMMES OPERATE? IF SO, WHAT ARE THE REQUIREMENTS FOR PRE-LAUNCH ACCESS?

Drugs sold by medical practitioners to their patients do not have to obtain a licence from the regulator (that is, the Thai Food and Drug Administration (FDA)) (*section 13(3), Drug Act BE 2510 (AD 1967)*). However, a doctor must still apply for an import licence. Only the following are allowed to import drug products without applying for an import licence or product licence (*section 13(5), Drug Act*):

- Ministries.
- Sub-ministries (in their official disease prevention and treatment duties).
- The Thai Red Cross Society.
- The Government Pharmaceutical Organisation.

Medicines can also be granted permission to be imported into Thailand based on the procedures and conditions prescribed by the Minister, with the approval of the Drug Board, a governmental body consisting, among others, of the (*section 79(4), Drug Act*):

- Permanent Secretary of the Ministry of Public Health (for example, the chairman).
- The Director-Generals of the Departments of Medical Services, Communicable Disease Control, Medical Sciences and Health.
- Not less than five but no more than nine qualified members appointed by the Minister of which at least two must be practitioners of traditional medicine.

The Notification of the Ministry of Public Health No.14 (BE 2532 (AD 1989)) Regarding Bases, Procedures, and Conditions in Respect to Importation of Medicines with No Need to Apply for Pharmacopeia Registration, as amended in 2009, states that medicines imported into Thailand can be exempted from product registration with the FDA if they are used for research, analysis, exhibition or charitable purposes. However, the right to import is limited to certain entities. For example, importation for research and analysis is limited to:

- A manufacturer.
- Importer.
- Ministry.
- Department with duties of prevention and treatment of diseases.
- The Thai Red Cross Society.
- The Government Pharmaceutical Organisation.

The importer must also submit the relevant application and supportive documents proving that it falls into the scope of the exception.

A drug that is imported into Thailand for clinical research purposes must have the following relevant supporting documentation:

- Labels for all containers.
- Investigator brochure.
- Patient information sheet in the Thai language.
- Synopsis of the clinical research in the Thai language.
- Complete information relating to the clinical research.
- Manufacturing and quality control of the drug.
- Approval as reported by the Institutional Review Board (IRB) or the Independent Ethics Committee (IEC) in Thailand. This process is quite burdensome, as it requires complying with lengthy administrative steps.

The relevant documents that are required when applying for importation of a drug for donation purposes are as follows:

- Labels of all of the containers.
- Package inserts.
- Certificate of free sale.

## LICENSING

### 3. WHAT IS THE PROCEDURAL STRUCTURE REGARDING LICENSING A DRUG FOR DISTRIBUTION?

**Structure**

Companies and individuals wishing to place a drug on the market must:

- Obtain a licence from the Thai Food and Drug Administration (FDA) to manufacture, sell or import drugs in Thailand. An import licence must be renewed every year and is valid from 1 January to 31 December.
- After obtaining the import licence, obtain an authorisation to manufacture or import drug samples.
- Submit a full marketing approval application, together with samples, to the FDA for review and registration. Registration requirements differ for general drugs (which include generics, new medicines, and new generics) and traditional drugs. A drug product licence does need to be renewed.

**Regulatory authority**

The regulation of drugs in Thailand is overseen by the Ministry of Public Health (MOPH). The Drug Control Division of the FDA, under the supervision of the MOPH, handles the four main aspects of drug regulation:

- Pre-marketing control (including licensing and registration).
- Post-marketing monitoring and surveillance.
- Consumer education and dissemination of information.
- Promotion of technological development and research for export.

## THAILAND

### 4. IS THERE A SIMPLIFIED LICENCE PROCEEDING, OR RELAXED LICENSING CONDITIONS, FOR DRUGS WHICH HAVE ALREADY BEEN LICENSED FOR DISTRIBUTION IN ANOTHER JURISDICTION?

Even if a company has already obtained a market authorisation issued in a foreign jurisdiction, it cannot benefit from a simplified or relaxed licensing and registration process. However, the application requires the applicant to inform the Thai Food and Drug Administration (FDA) of any approved and pending marketing authorisations for the product granted in other countries.

If the foreign marketing authorisation has been obtained in a country where the regulatory practice is credible and globally accepted, it would support the registration process and could be used as evidence to support the application for marketing approval.

Additionally, following the Association of Southeast Asian Nations (ASEAN) Harmonisation on Pharmaceutical Product Registration of 1 January 2009, the FDA implemented the ASEAN Common Technical Requirements and Dossier (ACTR or ACTD) on Quality, Safety and Efficacy, which provides guidelines on analytical and process validation, stability studies, and bioavailability or bioequivalence. It means that in the ASEAN, the same requirements exist for all drug products, which facilitates the registration process. However, some local specifics still remain.

Parallel imports are not regulated in Thailand, because the exhaustion of rights principle is recognised by most intellectual property laws in Thailand.

However, parallel imports are not permitted in the pharmaceutical sector, because it is mandatory for a company to preliminarily obtain an import licence and product registration locally. Also, the FDA will not accept an application for a product that has a trade mark that is identical to other products in the Thai market, unless this product has the same manufacturer and the manufacturer has given its authorisation to use and sell such product.

### 5. IS VIRTUAL DRUG DISTRIBUTION POSSIBLE FROM YOUR JURISDICTION?

It is not legally possible to market pharmaceutical products online, by e-mail or by mail order. If a company has applied for an import licence and a drug product licence, but does not actually import that product within two consecutive years, the company would have its product licence for that product withdrawn (*section 85, Drug Act BE 2510 (AD 1967)*).

### 6. WHAT IS THE PROCEDURE TO APPEAL (LEGAL REMEDY) A LICENSING DECISION?

If a licence is not being granted or if it is being revoked or withdrawn, the applicant has the right to appeal to the Minister of Public Health within 30 days from the date of the knowledge of the order (*section 99, Drug Act BE 2510 (AD 1967)*).

The decision of the Minister is final. The Minister can either dismiss the appeal or amend the order. There is no other official remedy against licensing decisions. In practice, companies would also contact the relevant officials and the head of each relevant group if a licence cannot be obtained.

### 7. WHAT ARE THE COSTS OF OBTAINING LICENSING?

The government fees for a drug import licence are THB10,000 per year. A drug import licence can cover different types of drugs, but cannot cover narcotics.

The government fees for the registration of pharmaceutical products are THB2,000 per product. There are no renewal fees.

## DISTRIBUTION TO CONSUMERS

### 8. WHAT ARE THE DIFFERENT CATEGORIES OF DRUGS FOR DISTRIBUTION?

Under the law, there are four main drugs categories:

- New drugs.
- New generic drugs.
- Generic drugs.
- Traditional drugs.

Other drug categories exist, namely biological drugs and narcotic drugs, but those are governed by a different sub-department at the Thai Food and Drug Administration (FDA), and have different requirements to comply with. For example, narcotic drugs in categories 1 and 2 have to go through a tender process. There is also an orphan drugs category with an easier registration process. However, the list of orphan drugs is strictly controlled and limited.

### 9. WHO IS AUTHORISED TO DISTRIBUTE PRESCRIPTION DRUGS AND OVER-THE-COUNTER DRUGS TO CONSUMERS?

**Prescription drugs**

The marketing authorisation holder or distributor that holds the drug import licence and product registration licences that have been approved by the Thai Food and Drug Administration (FDA) is responsible for the distribution of drug products to hospitals, clinical institutes or pharmacies.

The marketing authorisation holder or distributor must register its company to get the drug import licence. It must also register a drug product with the FDA before distributing the drug product to consumers in Thailand.

**Over-the-counter drugs**

The marketing authorisation holder or distributor that holds the drug import licence and product registration licences that have been approved by the FDA is responsible for the distribution of over-the-counter (OTC) drugs to hospitals, clinical institutes or pharmacies.

### 10. WHAT DRUGS CAN AN ATTENDING PHYSICIAN DISTRIBUTE AND UNDER WHAT CIRCUMSTANCES?

The attending physician can distribute non-registered drug products and registered drug products to patients for clinical research purposes only.

### 11. WHO IS AUTHORISED TO PRESCRIBE PRESCRIPTION DRUGS TO CONSUMERS?

Physicians and dentists can prescribe prescription drugs for human use to consumers.

# THAILAND

### 12. IS DIRECT MAILING/DISTANCE SELLING OF DRUGS PERMITTED IN YOUR JURISDICTION?

Direct mailing or the distance selling of drugs is not allowed under the Drug Act BE 2510 (AD 1967).

### 13. WHAT REGULATORY AUTHORITY IS RESPONSIBLE FOR SUPERVISING DISTRIBUTION ACTIVITIES?

The Thai Food and Drug Administration (FDA), under the supervision of the Ministry of Public Health, is responsible for supervising drug distribution activities to consumers in Thailand. The Drug Act BE 2510 (AD 1967) covers substantial aspects of drug regulation. The FDA is also responsible for licensing the sale of drugs. Applications for licences must be filed in accordance with the rules, measures and conditions prescribed in Ministerial Regulations.

### 14. WHAT IS THE PROCEDURE TO APPEAL (LEGAL REMEDY) A DISTRIBUTION DECISION?

The licensee can appeal the decision of the Thai Food and Drug Administration (FDA) to the Minister of Public Health within 30 days from the receipt of the decision.

### 15. WHAT ARE THE LEGAL CONSEQUENCES OF NON-COMPLIANCE WITH CONSUMER DISTRIBUTION LAWS?

The penalties for non-compliance by the product licensee under the Drug Act BE 2510 (AD 1967) include a suspension of the import licence and product registration licence, fines and imprisonment.

## WHOLESALE DISTRIBUTION

### 16. WHAT IS THE LEGAL REGIME REGARDING WHOLESALE DISTRIBUTION OF DRUGS?

The marketing authorisation holder or the legal distributor that holds the import licence, the sales licence or the product licence of a drug approved by the Thai Food and Drug Administration (FDA) is responsible for wholesale distribution of drug products to hospitals, clinical institutes or pharmacies.

### 17. WHAT REGULATORY AUTHORITY IS RESPONSIBLE FOR SUPERVISING WHOLESALE DISTRIBUTION ACTIVITIES?

**Regulatory authority**

The regulatory authority responsible for supervising wholesale distribution activities is the Thai Food and Drug Administration (FDA). As with other types of distribution, applications for licences must be conducted in accordance with the rules, measures and conditions prescribed in Ministerial Regulations.

## Supervision

As with the regime regarding consumers, responsibility for supervision of wholesale distribution activities falls on the FDA, which is also responsible for licensing the sale of pharmaceutical products. The Import and Export Inspection Division is also involved in the logistics and distribution activities at the border.

## Rights of appeal

Decisions of the FDA can be appealed to the Minister of Public Health within 30 days from the receipt of the decision.

### 18. WHAT ARE THE LEGAL CONSEQUENCES OF NON-COMPLIANCE WITH WHOLESALE DISTRIBUTION LAWS?

Under the Drug Act BE 2510 (AD 1967), non-compliance by the product licensee is punished by suspension of the import licence and product registration licence, fines and imprisonment.

# MARKETING

## PROMOTION

### 19. WHAT IS THE GENERAL LEGAL REGIME FOR THE MARKETING OF DRUGS?

## Legal regime

Sections 88 to 90 of the Drug Act regulate the advertising of medicinal products and are enforced by the Thai Food and Drug Administration (FDA). The authorities also take the Consumer Protection Act 1979 into consideration when regulating advertising practice. Further, pharmaceutical companies that are members of the Pharmaceutical Research and Manufacturers Association (PReMA) must comply with the PReMA Code. Although the PReMA Code is not considered to be law, and the FDA does not have the authority to enforce it, a violation of the PReMA Code can be reviewed by the PReMA Committee, which can sanction its members.

## Limits to marketing activities

Advertisements for prescription or pharmacy dispensed medicines can only be targeted to professionals. Drugs in the household remedy category can be advertised directly to consumers and the general public, but that advertising is subject to FDA review and approval before dissemination.

Dangerous drugs cannot be advertised directly to consumers and the general public. Most drugs are classified as dangerous drugs under Thai law and the Advertising must be approved by the FDA before dissemination (*section 88 bis, Drug Act*).

Advertisements must not (*section 88, Drug Act*):

- Boast that a medicine can miraculously or absolutely treat, cure or prevent disease or

illness.
- Exaggerate or falsely declare properties of the medicine.
- Give the impression that the drug has a substance as its chief or component ingredient that it either:
  - does not have; or
  - has in a lower quantity than believed to be present.
- Give the impression that it is an abortifacient or a strong emmenagogue.
- Give the impression that it is an aphrodisiac or a birth control drug.
- Advertise specially controlled drugs or dangerous drugs.
- Contain certification or endorsement of its therapeutic properties by any other person.
- Show its therapeutic properties as being capable of curing, mitigating, treating or preventing diseases (or symptoms of them) as notified by the Ministry of Public Health (MOPH) under section 77 of the Drug Act.

Further, advertisements must not (*FDA Internal Rules 2002*):

- Be contrary to traditions, for example, local beliefs, norms and morals.
- Persuade patients to consume the product more than necessary or create a misunderstanding that the product must be used regularly.
- Make a comparison that would defame other products.
- Cause consumers to misunderstand that the drug is equivalent to other products, such as food or cosmetics.
- Encourage acts or activities contrary to law.

Furthermore, advertisements must meet the FDA information requirements (for example, contain the drug name, ingredients and manufacturing source).

## 20. ARE THERE OTHER CODES OF CONDUCT FOR THE MARKETING OF DRUGS (FOR EXAMPLE, BY PROFESSIONAL OR INDUSTRIAL ORGANISATIONS)?

Pharmaceutical companies that are members of the Pharmaceutical Research and Manufacturers Association (PReMA) must comply with the PReMA Code of Sales and Marketing Practice 8th edition 2008 (PReMA Code). The PReMA Code provides the standards for the industry's practice of promotional activities, including organising conferences for healthcare professionals.

Many pharmaceutical companies, including non-members of PReMA, tend to follow the same standards as a courtesy and to ensure fair competition within the industry.

Although the PReMA Code is not considered to be law, and the Thai Food and Drug Administration (FDA) does not have the authority to enforce it, a violation of the PReMA Code can be reviewed by the PReMA Committee, which has the power to sanction its members.

# THAILAND

## MARKETING TO CONSUMERS

### 21. WHAT IS THE LEGAL REGIME FOR MARKETING TO CONSUMERS?

**Legal regime**

Only drugs in the household remedy category can be advertised directly to consumers and the general public. This advertising is subject to Thai Food and Drug Administration (FDA) review and approval before dissemination.

**Products**

Drugs that can be advertised directly to consumers and the general public must not be classified as dangerous drugs. However, most drugs are classified as dangerous drugs under the law. Also, drugs that are classified as dangerous must be dispensed by a pharmacist or doctor.

Drugs that are not classified as dangerous drugs are traditional drugs or household remedies that are specifically listed by the Ministry of Public Health as drugs that patients can buy without having a pharmacist dispense the drug. Traditional drugs or household remedies can be advertised to consumers but the advertisement and marketing activities must receive prior approval from the FDA.

### 22. WHAT KINDS OF MARKETING ACTIVITIES ARE PERMITTED IN RELATION TO CONSUMERS AND THE PRODUCTS WHICH MAY BE ADVERTISED TO THEM?

For a non-household remedy drug, marketing activity to consumers is limited to activities that help create disease awareness, patient education and basic healthcare education.

For the household remedy category that can be advertised directly to consumers and the general public, the law does not limit the types of activity. However, advertisements to sell drugs through radio, television, motion pictures or through printed matter:

- Must receive prior permission for the text, sound or picture used in the advertisement from the Thai Food and Drug Administration (FDA).
- Must follow the conditions (if any) set by the FDA (*section 88, Drug Act BE 2510 (AD 1967)*). The law further provides that no sale of drugs can be advertised impolitely or by means of singing and dancing or by showing the distress or suffering of a patient (*section 89, Drug Act*).

Although the Drug Act is silent about the restrictions on patient education, the general public must have access to information on medical conditions and the treatments that may be prescribed by their doctors. The Pharmaceutical Research and Manufacturers Association (PReMA) Code gives a guideline that patient education material should be distributed for educational purposes and should encourage patients to seek further information or explanation from the appropriate healthcare professional.

The following criteria must also be satisfied:

- The educational material must be current, accurate and balanced.
- The educational material cannot focus on a particular product, unless the material is intended to be given to the patient by a healthcare professional after the decision to prescribe that product has been made.

- The educational material can include descriptions of the therapeutic category, medical condition and a discussion of the relevant clinical parameters in general.
- The educational material must include the advice "please consult your physician" and the contact address and telephone number of the supplier of the material.

The educational material must include a statement directing the patient to seek further information about the condition or treatment from his or her doctor. Such statements must never be designed or made for the purpose of encouraging members of the public to ask their doctor to prescribe a product.

The tone of the message must not be presented in a way that unnecessarily causes alarm or misunderstanding in the community.

On all occasions, the information, whether written or communicated by other means, must be presented in a balanced way so as to avoid the risk of increasing unfounded hopes on a particular product.

Patient aids that are solely intended to provide information for the patient once a decision to prescribe that product has been made can be product-specific.

The content of such material must be designed to promote patient compliance by providing information that clarifies the method of administration, precautions and special instructions and similar information. It must not make comparisons or include promotional claims.

A "hotline" or "website" or other similar information service can be set up to provide general information useful to the public (for example, de-worming, travel, or smoking cessation). Such services must be general and cannot include any product promotional information or personal medical advice.

Drug companies can set up or participate in programmes that support patients already prescribed a prescription-only medicine to improve positive health outcomes. To ensure that such activities are not considered as promotional programmes, drug companies must ensure that any statements made or material provided to members of the general public are not promotional and cannot be considered as having the intention of promoting a prescription medicine to members of the general public.

### 23. IS IT PERMITTED TO PROVIDE CONSUMERS WITH FREE SAMPLES? ARE THERE PARTICULAR RESTRICTIONS ON SPECIAL OFFERS (FOR EXAMPLE, "BUY-ONE-GET-ONE-FREE")?

No sale of drugs can be advertised by a gift or lottery drawing (*section 90, Drug Act BE 2510 (AD 1967)*). The Thai Food and Drug Administration (FDA) has adopted a broad interpretation of this section, and has determined that the giving of free samples or "buy-one-get-one-free" offers is equivalent to advertising by giving a gift.

### 24. ARE THERE PARTICULAR RULES OF PRACTICE ON THE USE OF THE INTERNET/SOCIAL MEDIA REGARDING DRUGS AND THEIR ADVERTISING?

There are no particular rules or codes of practice on the use of the internet or social media for drug advertising. Information distributed on the internet that is intended for customers in Thailand must meet the same requirement as other media. According to the Thai Food and Drug Administration (FDA), most advertisements (more than 85%) on the internet are being run without permission, and the FDA has made it a priority to focus on this problem.

## 25. WHAT REGULATORY AUTHORITY IS RESPONSIBLE FOR SUPERVISING MARKETING ACTIVITIES TO CONSUMERS?

**Regulatory authority**

The agency responsible for supervising marketing activities to consumers is the Thai Food and Drug Administration (FDA) under the Ministry of Public Health (*Food and Drug Law BE 2510 (AD 1967)*).

**Supervision**

The FDA randomly visits hospitals and drug stores and monitors advertisements on TV, radio and the internet. The FDA also conducts investigations when it receives complaints from consumers or competitors. When the FDA finds that an advertiser has violated the advertising or marketing regulations, a notice is sent to the advertiser with a deadline to provide explanations or defend its case.

**Rights of appeal**

An appeal against the final decision can be filed with the Office of the Secretary General of the FDA.

## 26. WHAT ARE THE LEGAL CONSEQUENCES OF NON-COMPLIANCE WITH CONSUMER MARKETING LAWS?

The Secretary-General of the Thai Food and Drug Administration (FDA) can issue a written order to cease any advertisement deemed to be contrary to the Drug Act BE 2510 (AD 1967). If the advertisement led the public into a misunderstanding of information, the FDA can order the violator to issue a corrective advertisement.

Any violation of the Drug Act's marketing provisions is subject to a fine of not more than THB100,000. The calculation of the fine depends on the response time before the advertiser takes action after receiving a warning or notice of violation. The number of occurrences of wrongdoing is also taken into consideration when calculating the fine. For example, five posters and two gimmick gifts that have never been submitted for FDA approval, being used at a single promotional booth, could be considered as seven offences.

## MARKETING TO PROFESSIONALS

## 27. WHAT KINDS OF MARKETING ACTIVITIES ARE PERMITTED IN RELATION TO PROFESSIONALS?

Advertisements for prescriptions or pharmacy-dispensed medicines can only be targeted at professionals. As a result, marketing activities in the pharmaceutical industry in Thailand are mainly focused on the professional sector. The types of marketing activities to professionals are more open than those to consumers. However, only products that are registered in Thailand can be promoted to healthcare professionals. When promoting products, the information must be accurate, fair and objective and it must be presented in such a way as to conform not only to the legal requirements but also to high ethical standards. The information should also be in good taste. Claims cannot be stronger than the scientific evidence warrants and every effort should be made to avoid ambiguity and making off-label product claims. No pharmaceutical product can be promoted for use until the requisite approval for marketing for such use has been obtained (*Pharmaceutical Research and Manufacturers Association (PReMA) Code*).

## 28. ARE THERE ANY RESTRICTIONS ON MARKETING TO PROFESSIONALS?

**Marketing activities**

Advertisements of marketing activities cannot:

- Exaggerate or falsely declare properties of the medicine.
- Give the impression that the drug has a substance as its chief or component ingredient that it:
  - does not have;
  - has in a lower quantity than is believed to be present.
- Be advertised impolitely, by means of singing and dancing or by showing the distress or suffering of a patient.

The Pharmaceutical Research and Manufacturers Association (PReMA) Code also provides a broad guideline for promotional activities to ensure the transparency of such promotion. Clinical assessments, post-marketing surveillance and experience programmes and post-authorisation studies must not be disguised as promotion. Such assessments, programmes and studies must be conducted with a primary scientific or educational purpose. Material relating to pharmaceutical products and their uses, whether or not it is promotional in nature, which is sponsored by a company, must clearly indicate by whom it has been sponsored. Product information furnished to healthcare professionals must be current, accurate, balanced and cannot be misleading, either directly or by implication, omission or addition. Scientific data to support the claims and recommendations for use must be made available, on request, to healthcare providers.

Payment in cash or cash equivalents (such as a gift voucher) must not be offered to healthcare professionals and gifts for personal benefits of healthcare professionals are prohibited. However, gifts to healthcare professionals and institutions for customary and acceptable local occasions are allowed on an infrequent basis. The value of the gifts, the nature and type of which are related to the particular customary occasion, must not exceed THB3,000 per healthcare professional per occasion (*PReMA Code*).

**Frequency**

The restriction under the PReMA Code is that medical representatives must not employ any inducement or subterfuge to gain a sale. Neither can any fee be paid for that purpose.

**Provision of hospitality**

There are no explicit restrictions on the provision of hospitality. However, the PReMA Code provides a guideline that the medical representatives must ensure that the frequency, timing and duration of appointments, together with the manner in which they are made, are such that do not cause inconvenience to the doctors, pharmacists or nurses, especially in the out-patient department.

## 29. WHAT INFORMATION IS IT LEGALLY REQUIRED TO INCLUDE IN ADVERTISING TO PROFESSIONALS?

For printed promotional materials (with the exception of reminder (short) advertisements), the following information must be included:

- Name(s) of the active ingredient(s), using either International Non-Proprietary Names (INN) or the approved generic name of the drug.
- Brand name.
- Content of active ingredient(s) per dosage form or regimen.
- Name(s) of other ingredients known to cause problems.
- Approved therapeutic uses.
- Dosage form or regimen.
- Side effects and major adverse drug reactions.
- Precautions, contraindications and warnings.
- Major interactions.
- Name and address of manufacturer or distributor.
- Reference to scientific literature, as appropriate.
- Approval number granted by the Thai Food and Drug Administration (FDA) after approving the contents of the promotional material.

## 30. ARE THERE RULES ON COMPARISONS WITH OTHER PRODUCTS THAT ARE PARTICULARLY APPLICABLE TO DRUGS?

Comparisons with other products can be done to the extent that the comparison is fair and is not misleading. Any comparison implying a therapeutic advantage that is not in fact justified must be avoided. Disparaging references to other products or manufacturers must also be avoided (*Pharmaceutical Research and Manufacturers Association (PReMA) Code*).

## 31. WHAT OTHER ITEMS, FUNDING OR SERVICES ARE PERMITTED TO BE PROVIDED TO PROFESSIONALS?

### Discounts

Giving discounts and rebates is acceptable in Thailand. Such discounts or rebates associated with the sales of pharmaceutical products can only be made by account payee check, bank transfer to a bank account associated with the respective hospital, or by invoice (*Pharmaceutical Research and Manufacturers Association (PReMA) Code*).

### Free samples

The Drug Act BE 2510 (AD 1967) does not address the issue of free samples for professionals. However, the PReMA Code provides that samples of products can only be supplied to a healthcare professional on their consent. The size and quantity of the sample supplied should be appropriate for the following:

- Familiarisation with presentation and appearance of a product.
- Providing to patients for initiation of therapy.

- Conduct of an agreed on clinical evaluation of the product.

All samples delivered by sole distributors or medical representatives, or via mail or courier, must be securely packed and signed for by the receiver when received.

Under the PReMA Code, the term "drug sample" means a unit of a drug that is not intended to be sold and is intended for the reasons stated above. No one can sell or trade, or offer to sell or trade, any drug samples.

**Sponsorship of professionals**

It is acceptable and permissible to sponsor healthcare professionals to attend an international congress and to invite them to a satellite symposium at a congress they are already attending.

It is prohibited and not acceptable or appropriate to run an overseas stand-alone company-sponsored meeting for healthcare professionals where all (or nearly all) of the attendees or speakers are from Thailand.

Additionally, the PReMA Code contains the guideline that symposia or congresses (local and international) that are initiated by the company (locally only), the regional office or corporate headquarters, must devote a minimum of 75% of the total time to scientific sessions, outside of reasonable travel time. Any hospitality, entertainment or gimmick provided by drug companies, either directly or by sponsorship or assistance to the meeting organisers of educational meetings, must be secondary to the educational purpose and not capable of being seen as extravagant by local standards.

Invitations to attend medical and scientific meetings must only be given to healthcare professionals. Sponsorship is limited to the payment of travel, meals, accommodation and registration fees. Guests cannot be invited, nor can the expenses of persons accompanying the attendee be paid for.

Companies cannot provide direct sponsorship for healthcare professionals to attend sporting or other entertainment events, as this can be seen as inducement.

Donations can be made directly to the institution (not individuals) on the institution's request to support activities for healthcare professionals, as long as it can be demonstrated that there is a link to scientific education, patient benefit or charitable contribution that would benefit the improvement of healthcare services.

## 32. WHAT REGULATORY AUTHORITY IS RESPONSIBLE FOR SUPERVISING MARKETING ACTIVITIES REGARDING PROFESSIONALS?

**Regulatory authority**

The agency responsible for supervising marketing activities regarding professionals is the Thai Food and Drug Administration (FDA) under the Ministry of Public Health (*Food and Drug Law BE 2510 (AD 1967)*) (*see Question 25*). The Pharmaceutical Research and Manufacturers Association (PReMA) also takes an important role in supervising marketing activities that violate the Pharmaceutical Research and Manufacturers Association (PReMA) Code.

**Supervision**

PReMA supervises marketing activities that violate the PReMA Code. The Sales and Marketing Ethics Committee (SME) carries out a review of the provisions of the PReMA Code, after seeking input from interested parties, at least every three years. Besides regular review of the PReMA Code, the SME performs activities to create awareness of the PReMA Code.

If a complaint regarding a breach of the PReMA Code is filed by one of the members, the complaint is administered by the PReMA Chief Executive Officer and the Code of Conduct Committee (CCC).

**Rights of appeal**

When the allegedly breaching company or complainant disagrees with the decision of the CCC, they can request a second-instance ruling. The re-submission must be made in writing with any new evidence within ten days after receiving the notification from the PReMA's chief executive officer (CEO). If new evidence or arguments are put forward, the other party is invited to provide comments within 30 days. The decision of the CCC at this stage is regarded as final.

## 33. WHAT ARE THE LEGAL CONSEQUENCES IN CASE OF NON-COMPLIANCE WITH PROFESSIONAL MARKETING LAWS?

The legal consequences of non-compliance with professional marketing laws are the same as for non-compliance for consumer marketing laws (*see Question 26*).

In addition, the Pharmaceutical Research and Manufacturers Association's (PReMA) chief executive officer (CEO), on the decision of the Code of Conduct Committee (CCC), can order one or more of the following sanctions against a company found in breach of the PReMA Code:

- Refer the complaint to the International Federation of Pharmaceutical Manufacturers' Association (IFPMA).
- Refer the complaint and the CCC's findings to the head office and regional office of the offending company.
- Suspend the offending company's membership in PReMA for not more than three years.
- Debar the offending company from membership in PReMA.
- Require a written undertaking that the practice complained about will be discontinued on or before a date to be determined by the CCC.
- Require retraction statements, including corrective letters and advertising, to be issued by the company, subject to the approval of the CCC prior to release.

It is the company's responsibility to ensure that the requirements of the CCC are met and to immediately inform and provide evidence to PReMA of their fulfilment.

PReMA can also issue a fine to the company as follows:

- No more than THB100,000 for a first offence.
- No more than THB500,000 for a second offence within a 12-month period.

The imposed fine is to be paid within 30 days of being issued, subject to any appeal that might be lodged.

## ENGAGEMENT WITH PATIENT ORGANISATIONS

**34. WHAT KINDS OF ACTIVITIES ARE PERMITTED IN RELATION TO ENGAGEMENT WITH PATIENT ORGANISATIONS? WHAT ARE THE RESTRICTIONS THAT ARE IMPOSED ON RELATIONSHIP WITH PATIENT ORGANISATIONS?**

Pharmaceutical companies have limited freedom of action when promoting pharmaceutical products. Pharmaceutical companies can join patient support programmes that support patients that have already been prescribed a prescription-only medicine to improve positive health outcomes (*Article 4.11, Pharmaceutical Research and Manufacturers Association (PReMA) Code (that covers Promotion to Non-Healthcare (Medical) Professionals (or the general public))*).

However, pharmaceutical companies must ensure that their statements are not considered promotional and do not have the objective to promote a prescription drug. More specifically, they have to comply with the following requirements:

- Any payment for the work undertaken by a healthcare professional in such programmes is commensurate with the work undertaken.
- No incentives, other than material incentives that will enhance positive health outcomes and compliance, are provided to patients to become involved in these programmes.
- The programme complies with Thailand's privacy legislation.
- All information provided to patients must comply with sections 4.11.4 (Patient Education) and 4.11.5 (Patient Aid) of the PReMA Code. This means they must be educational (*see Question 20*).
- The data collected from these programmes is not used for any purpose other than to increase positive health outcomes, and never for promotional activities.
- The duration of these programmes is appropriate to the disease treated by the product involved.

## REFORM

**35. ARE THERE ANY PLANS TO REFORM THE LAW ON THE DISTRIBUTION AND PROMOTION OF DRUGS IN YOUR JURISDICTION?**

While Thailand currently has no comprehensive data protection legislation, a draft "Personal Data Protection Bill" and draft "Data Privacy Bill" have been approved by the Cabinet and will be considered by the National Legislative Assembly. These bills are expected to be passed by the National Legislative Assembly soon. The bills, as drafted, would dramatically change personal data privacy requirements and would require consent from the subject for some types of data collection.

This change could have an impact on the distribution and promotion of drugs, as those two aspects rely heavily on patient and more generally consumer data. After the bills are passed, this may be more difficult to acquire.

# TURKEY

Özge Atılgan Karakulak and Tuğçe Avcısert Geçgil, GÜN + PARTNERS

## DISTRIBUTION

### PRE-CONDITIONS FOR DISTRIBUTION

**1. WHAT ARE THE LEGAL PRE-CONDITIONS FOR A DRUG TO BE DISTRIBUTED WITHIN THE JURISDICTION?**

**Authorisation**

Under the Regulation on Licensing of Medicinal Products for Human Use (Licensing Regulation) (*Official Gazette No. 25705 of 19 January 2005*), no medicinal product for human use can be marketed unless it is licensed in Turkey. The licence is issued by the Pharmaceutical Product and Medical Device Institution (Institution) of the Turkish Ministry of Health (MoH).

For placing the product on the market, the following additional regulations must be considered:

- Regulation on Labelling and Packaging of Medicinal Products for Human Use (Labelling Regulation) (*Official Gazette No. 25904 of 12 August 2005*). It determines the procedures and essential information to be given on labels and packages.
- Regulation on Safety of Pharmaceuticals (Safety Regulation) (*Official Gazette No. 28973 of 15 April 2014*). The Safety Regulation lists the activities conducted for monitoring, research, recording, archiving and assessing the safety of medicinal products for human use which have been granted registration or permit, as well as natural or legal persons conducting such activities.

The principles for the inspections and examinations conducted by the MoH and the recall procedures for products posing threat to human health are also regulated in a variety of separate regulations.

**Exceptions**

In principle, off-label use of a pharmaceutical products is not allowed in Turkey and the related rules are set out in the Guideline on Off-Label Use of Pharmaceutical Products (Off-label Guideline) published by the MoH. Under the Off-label Guideline, the off-label use for the treatment of diseases which can be treated within the approved indications and doses of the licensed pharmaceutical products is not allowed. The off-label demand must be prepared and filed by the treating physician. The off-label prescription is only available after the MoH's approval. The required documentation includes the literature supporting the off-label use. The promotion of off-label use is strictly prohibited in Turkey.

Although the regulations set out the obligation to have a licence in order to distribute pharmaceuticals, there are alternative ways such as compassionate use or named patient use (*see Question 2*).

## 2. DO ANY TYPES OF NAMED PATIENT AND/OR COMPASSIONATE USE PROGRAMMES OPERATE? IF SO, WHAT ARE THE REQUIREMENTS FOR PRE-LAUNCH ACCESS?

The named patient use is defined as the special importation of pharmaceuticals which have no marketing authorisation in Turkey or which have marketing authorisation but are not present in the Turkish market. These products are imported from abroad on a named patient basis by the Turkish Pharmacists' Association (TEB). This importation is based on the Guidelines of Obtainment of Pharmaceuticals Abroad together with its Annexes and a protocol dated April 2007 signed by and between the SSI and TEB. TEB is authorised to import the products that are registered in the Imported Pharmaceuticals Provision System. This is an extendable list, therefore products can be added to this system on the approval of the Ministry of Health (MoH). Within the scope of these systems, products can be used by the patients in Turkey without the need for a licence to be granted by the MoH. The MoH has granted authorisation to 26 pharmaceutical warehouses to supply products this way.

In addition, Turkey has a compassionate use programme established under the Guideline on Compassionate Use Programme issued by the MoH. This programme is defined in as an arrangement that aims to provide free of charge pharmaceuticals which are not registered in Turkey and are registered or not registered in other countries, to patients whose treatment in Turkey has failed with the existing accessible products registered by the MoH and who suffer from a serious or urgent and life-threatening disease and have not been included in the scope of the clinical trials conducted in this field (*Article 1, the Guideline*).

In order for this program to be implemented, the treating physician of the patient must make a written commitment for taking over the responsibility of including the patient in this programme and report this to the MoH (*Article 2, the Guideline*).

Except for scientifically justifiable and very rare exceptional cases, pharmaceuticals for which at least Phase II studies have been completed and Phase III studies have been initiated across the world, are included in the programme. The studies do not need to be conducted in Turkey in order for a product to be included in this programme.

It is clearly stated that this programme is not a clinical trial and that the physician conducting the programme does not receive any payment under any name. This programme does not aim to collect information about the effectiveness of the drug and even if such information is collected, it will not be used in the procedures relating to the registration of the drug by the MoH. The Guideline explicitly states that compassionate use and off-label use cannot be conducted at the same time.

TURKEY

LICENSING

### 3. WHAT IS THE PROCEDURAL STRUCTURE REGARDING LICENSING A DRUG FOR DISTRIBUTION?

**Regulatory authority**

The Turkish Institution of Pharmaceuticals and Medical Devices of the Ministry of Health (MoH) is the national body responsible for licensing of pharmaceutical products in Turkey.

**Structure**

The requirements set out in the Licensing Regulation must be met in order to be granted a licence and initiate the marketing of the medicinal product for human use.

The persons applying for a pharmaceutical product licence must meet the following conditions of eligibility:

- Individuals must have a university degree from in pharmacy, medicine or chemical sciences and must be qualified to practise their profession in Turkey (*Article 7, Licensing Regulation*).
- Pharmacists must be Turkish citizens to practise their profession in Turkey (*Law on Pharmacists and Pharmacies No.6197*). There is no nationality requirement for chemists.
- Legal entities must employ an authorised person who meets the required conditions and experience of the product for which the application is submitted.

The Turkish MoH follows the European CTD format (including five modules) for the application files. Article 15 of the Licensing Regulation sets a 210-day period for the evaluation of the licence application by the MoH. However, in practice, this period can be extended even for a year or two, due to the workload of the MoH. The Good Manufacturing Practices (GMP) certificates required for the licensing are issued by the MoH after an on-site examination conducted by the MoH officials. This creates a lot of delays especially in the authorisation of imported products.

### 4. IS THERE A SIMPLIFIED LICENCE PROCEEDING, OR RELAXED LICENSING CONDITIONS, FOR DRUGS WHICH HAVE ALREADY BEEN LICENSED FOR DISTRIBUTION IN ANOTHER JURISDICTION?

An abridged application can be submitted as per Article 9 of the Licensing Regulation. In abridged applications, the applicant is not required to present the results of toxicological and pharmacological tests and clinical trials, if:

- The medicinal product is essentially similar to a medicinal product which has been previously registered in Turkey and the marketing registration holder of the original medicinal product consented to the use of the toxicological, pharmacological and/or clinical references contained in the dossier of the original medicinal product for the purpose of evaluating the referred application.
- Any constituent(s) of the medicinal product have a well-established medical use, determined by means of detailed scientific bibliography and with a reasonable efficiency and acceptable level of safety.
- The medicinal product is essentially similar to a registered medicinal product and has completed its data exclusivity period.

Data exclusivity applies to the original products:

- For which no generic registration application was submitted in Turkey before 1 January 2001.
- Registered for the first time in one of the countries within the Customs union Area after 1 January 2001.
- Registered for the first time in one of the countries within the Customs union Area after 1 January 2005.

The data exclusivity period lasts six years from the first registration date in the Customs union Area. Data exclusivity period for products which benefit from patent protection in Turkey is limited to this patent period.

Parallel import of pharmaceuticals is strictly forbidden under Turkish law. Pharmaceutical products for human use cannot be marketed unless they are (*Article 5, Licensing Regulation*):

- Registered by the Ministry of Health (MoH) under the provisions of the Licensing Regulation.
- Imported through the alternative ways as described above.

The pharmaceutical products can only be cleared from the Turkish customs by the marketing authorisation holder. In a Circular No. 2014/11 of 20 November 2014 the MoH explained that all measures will be taken to prevent the export of the imported pharmaceuticals which are supplied for Turkish citizens' needs. To the extent of authors' knowledge, to date no specific measures have been taken.

## 5. IS VIRTUAL DRUG DISTRIBUTION POSSIBLE FROM YOUR JURISDICTION?

This situation is not regulated under Turkish law and the licence given by the Ministry of Health is only effective on the Turkish territory, therefore it seems that virtual distribution is not possible.

## 6. WHAT IS THE PROCEDURE TO APPEAL (LEGAL REMEDY) A LICENSING DECISION?

The licensing decisions are considered as administrative decisions in nature. The Administrative Procedure Code regulates the application for cancellation of administrative decisions or application for indemnity.

Under the Code, the licensing decision can be challenged within 60 days after its notification before administrative courts or it is possible to request corrective actions from the authority as well as through an application made within the scope of Article 11 of the Code. The corrective action ceases the 60-day period for filing an action and the period starts to recount after the response of the related authority or the lapse of a 60-day period in case the authority does not give any response.

## 7. WHAT ARE THE COSTS OF OBTAINING LICENSING?

The fee tariff is announced on the website of the Turkish Institution of Pharmaceuticals and Medical Devices every year. There are a number of different fees to be paid depending on the nature of the application.

According to the 2015 fee tariff the fee for an application to obtain a pharmaceutical licence is TRL23,681.18.

Article 57 of the Decree Law No. 663 sets out a limit of TRL150,000 which cannot be exceeded in determining fees for licences.

## DISTRIBUTION TO CONSUMERS

### 8. WHAT ARE THE DIFFERENT CATEGORIES OF DRUGS FOR DISTRIBUTION?

Under Article 5 of the Regulation on the Classification of Medical Products for Human Use (Classification Regulation) (*Official Gazette of 17 February 2005, No. 25730*) drugs are categorised during the licensing procedure as being subject to a prescription or not. There is no categorisation of drugs based on distribution criteria.

### 9. WHO IS AUTHORISED TO DISTRIBUTE PRESCRIPTION DRUGS AND OVER-THE-COUNTER DRUGS TO CONSUMERS?

**Prescription drugs**

Only pharmacies can sell prescription drugs to consumers. There are eligibility conditions to obtain an authorisation to sell prescription drugs (*Article 3 of the Law on Pharmacies and Pharmacists No. 6197*). For example, to establish a pharmacy, the applicant must have Turkish citizenship and a pharmacy or medicine degree which is authorised by the Ministry of Health (MoH).

**Over-the-counter drugs**

The Classification Regulation defines in detail what a prescription drug is, but only defines non-prescription drugs as everything else. Due to the lack of a regulation of the over-the-counter (OTC) drugs, the number of non-prescription drugs in Turkey is considerably limited and therefore all kinds of pharmaceutical products must be sold in pharmacies.

### 10. WHAT DRUGS CAN AN ATTENDING PHYSICIAN DISTRIBUTE AND UNDER WHAT CIRCUMSTANCES?

Only pharmacists can distribute drugs to patients, attending physicians are not allowed to do so (*see Question 9*). However, physicians can give free samples to their patients.

### 11. WHO IS AUTHORISED TO PRESCRIBE PRESCRIPTION DRUGS TO CONSUMERS?

Only physicians or dentists can prescribe drugs (*Article 13, Law No.1219 on the Medical Practice and Related Arts*).

### 12. IS DIRECT MAILING/DISTANCE SELLING OF DRUGS PERMITTED IN YOUR JURISDICTION?

The movement of pharmaceuticals in the supply chain is tracked by the Ministry of Health. Hence, no direct mailing/distance selling is possible under the tracking system.

**TURKEY**

However, the online pharmaceutical track and trace system has been established in Turkey to trace the sales of drugs from the pharmaceutical companies to warehouses and from warehouses to hospitals and pharmacies within the scope of reimbursement. The barcode of the drugs purchased and sold in the pharmacies, as well as on all levels of the distribution chain must be registered and tracked.

Accordingly, for online selling there may be particular problems for the reimbursement of drugs, as it may not be possible to create an online system integrated with the track and trace system.

### 13. WHAT REGULATORY AUTHORITY IS RESPONSIBLE FOR SUPERVISING DISTRIBUTION ACTIVITIES?

The Regulation on the Procedure and Principles of the Ministry of Health's Market Surveillance and Inspection of 25 June 2007 sets out the general rules for market surveillance and inspection of pharmaceuticals and medical devices.

Drug distribution activities are supervised by the Institution of Pharmaceuticals and Medical Devices.

Additionally, in line with the Regulation on Withdrawal and Collection of Pharmaceutical and Medical Preparations, Substances, Materials, Mixtures and Herbal Preparations (*Official Gazette No. 19196 of 15 August 1986*), products which are found to pose a threat to patients and public health during the surveillance activities can be withdrawn, collected and destroyed if necessary. The aim of the Regulation is to maintain a market of quality and defect-free drugs and to prevent the distribution and usage of any defected products for the sake of consumer health and safety. This surveillance activity encompasses drug factories, laboratories, trading houses, warehouses and pharmacies.

### 14. WHAT IS THE PROCEDURE TO APPEAL (LEGAL REMEDY) A DISTRIBUTION DECISION?

The marketing authorisation grants its holder the right to distribute the relevant pharmaceutical. Therefore, there is no need to have any other administrative decision to distribute pharmaceuticals or to work with any distribution channels. However, all distribution activities are subject to control of the Institution of Pharmaceuticals and Medical Devices (IPMD), which can impose sanctions. The IPMD's decisions are considered administrative decisions and can be challenged (*see Question 6*).

### 15. WHAT ARE THE LEGAL CONSEQUENCES OF NON-COMPLIANCE WITH CONSUMER DISTRIBUTION LAWS?

Under the Regulation on the Procedure and Principles of the Ministry of Health's Market Surveillance and Inspection, the violation of the Regulation provisions can have the following consequences:

- Prohibition of marketing.
- Withdrawal, collection and destruction of the related products.
- Administrative monetary fines as stipulated in Law No.1262.

Under the Law No.1262, an administrative monetary fine can be given and the granted authorisation can be withdrawn if it is determined that:

- The substance entering into the composition of the preparation is impure.

- The substance does not conform to the formula for which the permit is granted.
- Preparations are made without permission and are sold knowingly.

Other acts violating the Regulation can be sanctioned with an administrative monetary fine as well (*Article 20, Law No. 1262*).

The withdrawal, collection and destruction decisions are implemented in line with the principles set out in the Regulation on Withdrawal and Collection of Pharmaceutical and Medical Preparations, Substances, Materials, Mixtures and Herbal Preparations. In case the withdrawn or collected defective products are damaging to health, the provisions of the Turkish Penal Code (TPC) (*Official Gazette of 12 October 2004, No.5237*) apply depending on the gravity of the damage.

In addition to these provisions, the Law Relating to the Preparation and Implementation of the Technical Legislation on the Products (*Official Gazette of 11 July 2001, No.4703*), implements severe administrative monetary fines. These fines are foreseen in case of a violation of this law which sets out the obligations of the producers and distributors of any product including drugs.

Under the TPC, the sale of decayed or otherwise damaged food or drugs and the production or selling of drugs that risk the life and health of others is a crime. Such a crime is punishable with imprisonment from one year to five years, as well as a punitive fine of up to 1500 daily units, which amounts to approximately up to TRL 150,000, paid to the state (*Articles 186 and 187, TPC*).

## WHOLESALE DISTRIBUTION

### 16. WHAT IS THE LEGAL REGIME REGARDING WHOLESALE DISTRIBUTION OF DRUGS?

Under Turkish law, wholesale distribution of drugs is regulated by:

- The Law on Pharmacists and Pharmacies (*Law No. 6197*) (*Official Gazette No. 8591 of 24 December 1953*).
- The Regulation on Pharmacies and Pharmacists (*Official Gazette No. 28970 of 12 April 2014*).
- The Good Distribution Practices Guidelines of the Pharmaceuticals and Products Stored in Warehouses.

Drugs cannot be sold directly from the pharmaceutical company to the consumers (patients).

In the Turkish pharmaceutical sector there are three major types of organisations in the distribution chain:

- Pharmaceutical companies, which sell their pharmaceutical products to warehouses.
- Warehouses.
- Pharmacies. All drugs must be sold to patients through pharmacies.

There is no specific rule requiring the manufacturers or importers to sell pharmaceutical products through wholesale.

The pharmacy trading houses can carry out wholesales or retail sales only to the pharmacies (*Article 11, Law No. 984 on Pharmacy Trading Houses (Official Gazette No. 575 of 12 March 1927)*). Manufacturers and importers can carry on stocking pharmaceutical products beyond promotional requirements provided that they comply with the rules concerning pharmacy trading houses (*Article 8/3, Law No.1262*).

To manage a warehouse a licence from the Pharmacy and Pharmaceutical Warehouse Office must be obtained. An agent pharmaceutical warehouse must comply with:

- The Regulation on Pharmaceutical Warehouses and Products Stored in Pharmaceutical Warehouses (Warehouses Regulation) (*Official Gazette No.23852 of 20 October 1999*) in terms of warehouse storage conditions.
- The Regulation on Manufacturing Plants of Medicinal Products for Human Use (*Official Gazette No.28630 of 27 April 2013*) in terms of provision of secondary packaging services.

### 17. WHAT REGULATORY AUTHORITY IS RESPONSIBLE FOR SUPERVISING WHOLESALE DISTRIBUTION ACTIVITIES?

The Institution is responsible for supervising wholesale distribution activities. Its decisions are considered to be administrative decisions and can be challenged (*see Question 6*).

### 18. WHAT ARE THE LEGAL CONSEQUENCES OF NON-COMPLIANCE WITH WHOLESALE DISTRIBUTION LAWS?

In case of a violation of the provisions set out by the Warehouses Regulation, the provisions regulated under the Law No. 6502 (*Official Gazette No. 28835 of 28 November 2013*) on Protection of Consumers or the TPC are applied depending on the gravity of the act. The Law on Protection of Consumers aims to protect the health, safety and economic interests of consumers. In case of sale of goods or services that can potentially endanger or harm a person's health or the environment, a warning must be added or written, in an easily visible and legible manner, on the packaging or included in the information leaflet (*Article 55/3*). In case of a violation of this obligation, an administrative monetary fine of TRL220 per unit of product will apply to the producers, importers and sellers.

Articles 186 and 187 TPC also apply (*see Question 15*).

## MARKETING

### PROMOTION

### 19. WHAT IS THE GENERAL LEGAL REGIME FOR THE MARKETING OF DRUGS?

**Legal regime**

In Turkey, the legal regime regarding marketing of drugs is contained in the Regulation on Promotional Activities of Human Medicinal Products (Promotion Regulation) (*Official Gazette No.28037 of 26 August 2011*).

**Limits to marketing activities**

Under the Regulation, as a general rule no promotion activities are permitted for drugs which are not licensed in Turkey. It is strictly prohibited to address general public in promotional activities. Moreover, neither marketing authorisation/licence holders nor their representatives can provide offers or promise benefits to the healthcare professionals by way of promotional activities. The marketing authorisation or licence holder company must not encourage the prescription of its products by offering any kind of benefit to a healthcare professional.

## 20. ARE THERE OTHER CODES OF CONDUCT FOR THE MARKETING OF DRUGS (FOR EXAMPLE, BY PROFESSIONAL OR INDUSTRIAL ORGANISATIONS)?

There are codes of conduct for professionals prepared by industry organisations which are applied together with the legal regime, for example:

- The Turkish Pharmacists Deontological Rules.
- The Turkish Pharmacists' Association Law.

In addition, there are three pharmaceutical associations in Turkey which have their own codes of practice:

- The Turkey Pharmaceuticals Industry Association (TISD).
- Association of Research-Based Pharmaceutical Companies (AIFD).
- Pharmaceuticals Manufacturers Association (IEIS).

These associations' rules establish standards for the companies in the respective sector and are considered auxiliary rules for the industry. AIFD is a member of EFPIA and its promotional code is in line with the EFPIA.

## MARKETING TO CONSUMERS

## 21. WHAT IS THE LEGAL REGIME FOR MARKETING TO CONSUMERS?

**Legal regime**

It is forbidden to promote medicinal products for human use to the general public in Turkey (*Article 13, Law No.1262 on Pharmaceutical and Medical Preparations and the Promotion Regulation*).

**Products**

No pharmaceutical product can be advertised to consumers. However, information can be provided to the general public on products that will be used in vaccination campaigns, organised actions to combat epidemics or other campaigns run by the Ministry of Health (MoH) to promote health (as they are important in safeguarding public health) upon permission of the MoH and within the scope of principles and procedures set by the MoH for such products.

## 22. WHAT KINDS OF MARKETING ACTIVITIES ARE PERMITTED IN RELATION TO CONSUMERS AND THE PRODUCTS WHICH MAY BE ADVERTISED TO THEM?

It is forbidden to advertise any kind of pharmaceutical products to the general public (*see Question 21*). Promotional activities can only be directed at healthcare professionals. Healthcare professionals are defined as physicians, dentists, pharmacists, nurses, midwives, and other professionals listed in additional Article 13 of the Law No. 1219.

### 23. IS IT PERMITTED TO PROVIDE CONSUMERS WITH FREE SAMPLES? ARE THERE PARTICULAR RESTRICTIONS ON SPECIAL OFFERS (FOR EXAMPLE, "BUY-ONE-GET-ONE-FREE")?

Under the Promotion Regulation, pharmaceutical companies cannot provide free samples to patients. Any offers such as "buy one get one free" will be considered as an infringement of this rule if they are introduced as a promotional activity. However, physicians can provide free samples to their patients.

"Buy-one-get-one-free offers" can be used by pharmaceutical companies to wholesalers and by wholesalers to pharmacies during their commercial activities. The Ministry of Health allows these kinds of commercial arrangements and currently there are no sanctions in place against such practices.

### 24. ARE THERE PARTICULAR RULES OF PRACTICE ON THE USE OF THE INTERNET/SOCIAL MEDIA REGARDING DRUGS AND THEIR ADVERTISING?

Promotional activities cannot be directed at the general public (*Article 13, Law No.1262*). Some regulations repeat this prohibition in order to emphasise its importance. However, promotion of licensed drugs is allowed if it is aimed at healthcare professionals and includes objective, informative and factual medical data in a way that enables the healthcare professionals to form their own opinion about the product.

There are no specific rules/codes prohibiting the use of internet/social media in respect of promotion activities directed at the health professionals. The general rules on promotion activities apply in this area.

### 25. WHAT REGULATORY AUTHORITY IS RESPONSIBLE FOR SUPERVISING MARKETING ACTIVITIES TO CONSUMERS?

**Regulatory authority**

The Institution of Pharmaceuticals and Medical Devices (IPMD), is entitled to inspect, *ex officio* or upon receipt of a complaint, promotional activities and any materials and methods employed in the context of such activities. The Ministry of Health (MoH) can require the marketing authorisation or the licence holder to cease, terminate or correct the information provided during any promotional activity which is found to be non-compliant with the Promotion Regulation or deemed inappropriate for public health. Any request by the MoH must be complied with without delay.

Also, since the Advertising Regulation and the Law on Establishment of Radio and Television Institutions and their Media Services (RTUK Law) (*Official Gazette No.6112 of 15 February 2011*) prohibit the advertisement of drugs, the Advertisement Board and the RTUK Council examine the advertisements and can impose sanctions.

The Advertisement Board, established within the Ministry of Customs and Trade, is the sole administrative authority controlling advertisements in Turkey. The Advertisement Board is entitled to conduct an investigation ex officio or upon an individual complaint and to impose administrative monetary fines.

The RTUK Council can also control radio and television advertisements in Turkey. The Council can warn, impose an administrative monetary fines and may cease the broadcast of programmes that violate the prohibition.

## Rights of appeal

The decisions of the IPMD, the Advertisement Board and the RTUK Council, are considered to be administrative decisions and can be challenged (*see Question 6*).

### 26. WHAT ARE THE LEGAL CONSEQUENCES OF NON-COMPLIANCE WITH CONSUMER MARKETING LAWS?

Other than the consequences mentioned under *Question 25*, under Article 13 of the Promotion Regulation anyone who acts or operates in violation of the provisions in the Regulation will be subjected to, depending on the nature of the violation, the applicable provisions of:

- TPC (*see Question 3*).
- Law No.6502 on Protection of Consumers (dated 28 November 2013).
- Law on Protection of Competition (dated 12 December 1994 and No.4054).
- RTUK Law.
- Other applicable regulatory provisions.

Such non-compliance can also be considered as leading to an unfair competition. In this case, the general rules of the Turkish Commercial Code apply and an indemnity depending on the damage may be claimed by the injured party.

Moreover, under Article 18 of the Law No. 1262 if, following the analyses mentioned in Article 10, it is detected that the substances into the composition of preparations are not pure or are incompliant with the approved formulation submitted for receiving registration or have been manufactured in a manner to derogate from or eliminate its curative properties, and if such act does not constitute a criminal offence, the registration holder and whoever sells, supplies or causes selling of the preparation knowing that it was manufactured in such state will be fined between TLR10,000 to 500,000. Those who promote and sell preparations in violation of this law, market them off-label and thus encourage generation of prescription in this direction will be subject to an administrative fine of up to five times of the relevant product's total sales of the last one year (not less than TLR100,000). If promotion and sales are performed via the Internet, the MoH will decide whether to block their access and such decision will be communicated to the Information Technologies and Communication Agency to enforce it. For those who promote and sell products with a health declaration without the permit of the competent authority or in violation of the permit issued will be subject to an administrative fine ranging from TRL20,000 to 300,000.

If a violation is determined, disciplinary action will be brought against healthcare professionals by their institutions and professional organisations. In case the promotion of a pharmaceutical product violates the Promotion Regulation's provisions, the marketing authorisation or the licence holder will receive a warning. In the event of recurrence, the holder will be banned from engaging in promotional activities. In case of further reoccurrence of the same breach, the marketing of the product will be suspended for three months, followed by a one year suspension, if the breach persists. Moreover, if a product representative violates the Promotion Regulation within the validity period of his proficiency certificate, the representative will receive a warning first, in case of reoccurrence, the proficiency certificate will be suspended for three months, and for one year, if the breach persists.

## MARKETING TO PROFESSIONALS

### 27. WHAT KINDS OF MARKETING ACTIVITIES ARE PERMITTED IN RELATION TO PROFESSIONALS?

The Promotion Regulation governs the relationship between the pharmaceutical companies and the healthcare professionals. The ethical principles drafted by medical associations which the healthcare professional is a member of also apply to this relationship. Under the Promotion Regulation, promotion to healthcare professionals occurs through publications given out or sold to healthcare professionals, or through publication in medical or professional journals with a scientific content, sponsoring or holding of scientific meetings, meeting of product representatives with physicians, dentists and pharmacists, and informing healthcare professionals on matters such as administration or side effects of products.

### 28. ARE THERE ANY RESTRICTIONS ON MARKETING TO PROFESSIONALS?

**Marketing activities**

Pharmaceutical products which are not licensed or authorised according to applicable regulations cannot be promoted to healthcare professionals, excluding promotional activities during international congresses held in Turkey (*Article 6, Promotion Regulation*). Promotion aimed at healthcare professionals must include objective, informative and factual medical data in a way that allows healthcare professionals to form their own opinions about the product. The promotional activities cannot be used to encourage unnecessary use of a product.

Healthcare professional must not act in promotional activities of such products without the permission of the Ministry of Health (MoH). Promotions cannot involve sweepstakes, lottery or similar schemes. The Promotion Regulation does not allow providing, offering or promising of any benefits, whether in cash or in kind, and the healthcare professionals must not accept or request any incentive during the course of such promotional activities.

Any kind of object or benefit received directly or indirectly which affects or is likely to affect a public officer's impartiality, decision or performance of duties is deemed to be a gift regardless of its economic value (*Article 15 of the Regulation on Ethical Principles for Public Officers and Implementation Procedure and Principles of Application (Official Gazette No.25785 of 13 April 2005)*). However, books, magazines, articles, cassettes, calendars and CDs are not considered to be gifts. Greeting, farewell or celebration gifts, scholarships, travel, complimentary accommodation and gift checks received from the persons that have a business, service or benefit from the relationship with the related institution are considered to be gifts. Although these provisions are directly binding for the public officers, not for the companies, non-compliance may also have consequences for companies under anti-bribery provisions of the TPC as they can be used in the interpretation of constitutes bribery.

It should be noted that industry association AIFD interprets the regulations more strictly and obliges its members to not provide any promotion materials to healthcare professionals. Gift or reminder material qualified as a gift or financial advantage in cash or kind, which may be perceived as an inducement in relation to a promotion or for prescribing, procuring, administering, recommending the administration of, selling or buying a prescription drug must not be supplied, given or promised to healthcare professionals or those in an administrative position (*Article 14, Ethics Code of the AIFD*).

## Frequency

Product promotion representatives (PPRs) can promote human medicinal products at public health institutions during working hours subject to the following rules (*Article 10, Promotion Regulation*):

- At the beginning of a meeting, the product promotion representative must show his product promotion representative identification card and disclose which marketing registration holder he is representing.
- Relevant administrative supervisors at every public health institution will designate the most suitable time period to enable meetings between PPRs and healthcare professionals for product promotion, taking account of the work schedules. Such designation cannot disrupt educational functions or provision of healthcare services to patients.
- Product promotion is prohibited at emergency rooms or at outpatient clinics during patient-seeing hours.
- Product promotion representatives calling on healthcare institutions to perform their promotional functions cannot be charged any fee, pecuniary or otherwise (for example, donations or others) for gaining access to the public health institution.

## Provision of hospitality

Scientific meetings and educational activities related to the promotion of a medicinal product for human use must not be used for any purpose other than transmitting the existing medical information and/or presenting new information (*Article 7, Promotion Regulation*). Marketing authorisation holders cannot cover, whether directly or indirectly, transportation or accommodation expenses of participants taking part in educational activities.

Marketing authorisation holders can sponsor healthcare professionals for participating in scientific meetings such as congresses or symposia taking place in or outside Turkey on the following conditions:

- Meetings are related to the specialty/role of the healthcare professional.
- A healthcare professional can benefit from such sponsorships three times within the same calendar year. Only two out of these three sponsorships can be provided by the same registration/permit holder and only one out of these three sponsorships can be used for a meeting abroad. This excludes meetings which healthcare professionals attend as a speaker, or as an investigator presenting a paper, with the sponsorship of registration/permit holder.
- Sponsorship is provided to the organisation holding the meeting, and not directly to an individual.

Marketing authorisation holders must notify the MoH of particulars of healthcare professionals to be sponsored in accordance with the Guidelines on Scientific and Educational Meetings.

Meetings of investigators, sponsored by the marketing authorisation holder, held in Turkey or abroad in connection with a national or international multicentre clinical trial, must not be considered as attendance at a congress or symposium.

Any application submitted to the MoH for such meetings must include a clear description of the meeting's nature and indicate the purpose of the meeting. Except international meetings that are held each time in a different country, it is not suitable to organise scientific meetings for physicians, dentists or pharmacists in water sports locations and resorts in coastal towns during summer months, and within or near winter sports facilities in winter months or to sponsor the meetings organised under these conditions. MoH does not regard it suitable for pharmaceutical companies to organise meetings and/or contribute to the scientific meetings organised in ski centres between 1 December and 1 March, and in coastal holiday resorts between 1 June and 1 September.

Non-healthcare professionals cannot be invited to the meetings, and their expenses cannot be covered. However, guests of honour are excluded from this provision.

At least 60% of all meetings lasting more than six hours, organised or contributed to by marketing authorisation holders within a calendar year, must include a session on the rational use of drugs, relevant to the topic of the meeting. The content of presentations delivered on during such sessions must be aligned with MoH-approved educational materials and diagnostic and therapeutic guidelines, and submitted to the MoH for review, as described in the guidelines.

Persons appointed by the MoH can attend these meeting for inspection purposes with or without prior notice.

## 29. WHAT INFORMATION IS IT LEGALLY REQUIRED TO INCLUDE IN ADVERTISING TO PROFESSIONALS?

Promotion of a product must be consistent with the information and data contained in such product's current summaries of product characteristics (SmPCs) (*Article 6/3, Promotion Regulation*). Since it is necessary to show the SmPCs in a licence application, the SmPCs is regulated under the Licensing Regulation. The Regulation lists all the information that must appear on the products.

Moreover, under Article 6/4 of the Promotion Regulation, promotion must include informative and factual medical data on a product's characteristics that will help healthcare professionals establish their own opinion on a product's therapeutic value.

The AIFD Ethics Code specifies that the following information must also be included in the promotional materials:

- The dosage.
- Mode of administration.
- Side effects.
- Precautions.
- "Inverted black triangle" symbol in drugs subject to additional monitoring, contra-indications and warnings.

These information must be placed in such a position on the promotional materials that it is easily seen by the reader. In addition, the name of the active substance of the drug must appear on the promotional materials in a legible size, immediately adjacent to the most prominent display of the commercial name.

- In audio-visual materials such as films, video recordings and information in interactive data systems, abbreviated SmPCs must be provided in A document which is made available to all persons to whom the material is shown or sent.
- The audio-visual recording or interactive data system itself.

## 30. ARE THERE RULES ON COMPARISONS WITH OTHER PRODUCTS THAT ARE PARTICULARLY APPLICABLE TO DRUGS?

The general provisions on comparative advertising under the Advertising Regulation apply to the promotional activities of pharmaceutical products. The name of the product compared must not be mentioned. The compared products must meet the same consumer needs and address the same purpose. It must be in conformity with the fair competition principles that prohibit misleading of the consumer.

According to the AIFD Ethics Code, comparisons between different medicinal products must include "comparative features". Comparison can be made in a promotional material under the following conditions, without making any reference to trade marks:

- It is not misleading.
- Drugs or services for the same needs and purposes are compared.
- Relevant, proven and significant features are compared.
- Comparisons are not used to create confusion on purpose.
- Pejorative or derogatory statements are not included regarding the competing product or brand.
- Unfair advantage of the reputation of a competitor is not taken.

## 31. WHAT OTHER ITEMS, FUNDING OR SERVICES ARE PERMITTED TO BE PROVIDED TO PROFESSIONALS?

### Discounts

Discounts are permitted under Turkish law. However, discounts cannot be linked to any promotional activities, it can be solely a commercial activity. Discounts can be provided by pharmaceutical companies to warehouses and by warehouses to pharmacies. Pharmacies may also provide discounts to patients.

### Free samples

Free samples can only be distributed to physicians, dentists or pharmacists provided that the following conditions are fulfilled (*Article 9, Promotion Regulation*):

- Marketing authorisation holders must set up and appoint qualified persons for an adequate system of records and control, for the production, importation and distribution of free promotional samples, to safely withdraw them where necessary. Upon demand, these records must be submitted to MoH officials electronically or in hardcopy in the format designated by the MoH.
- Free samples contain a quantity reduced in size. However, this requirement does not apply to enteral nutritional products and promotional samples of products which, for technical reasons, cannot be reduced.
- The statement, "Free promotional sample – not for sale" must visibly appear on the outer packaging of promotional samples on at least one surface. The same statement must be printed also on the inner package, where this is possible.
- A copy of the summaries of product characteristics (SmPCs) and the PIL, where available, mustbe provided with the promotional sample.
- Samples must not be provided or distributed of products containing psychotropic or

narcotic substances, (covered under the Single Convention on Narcotic Drugs of 1961 and the Convention on Psychotropic Substances of 1971) and of products subject to national control.
- In principle, there is no barcode/datamatrix on the packaging of promotional samples. If their inclusion is mandatory, permission will be requested from the MoH, offering sufficient justification, and their sale will be blocked in the Ministry's Drug Tracking System. Registration/marketing holders will establish a system to enable safe withdrawal of free samples where necessary.
- Free samples of medicinal products for human use can be distributed:
  - in the first calendar year as of the introduction date, up to 5% of the total annual sales on monitoring the monthly sales;
  - in the second calendar year up to 5% of total annual sales generated the preceding year;
  - in the third, fourth and fifth calendar years up to 3% of total sales generated the preceding year;
  - after the fifth calendar year, up to 1% of total sales generated the preceding year.

Enteral nutritional products with prioritised oral use, designated as taste samples are exempt from the decremental restriction of amount by years.

- Promotional samples may not be used as an investigational product during a clinical trial.

**Sponsorship of professionals**

Under Article 15 of the AIFD Ethics Code, donations and sponsorships can be provided under the following conditions to non-profit organisations, associations, foundations that are composed of physicians, dentists and pharmacists and/or organisations providing healthcare or conducting research:

- They are provided for the purpose of supporting research programme or the provision of a specific public health service.
- The donor/grantor documents them and keeps them on its official records.
- The written commitment from the institution is received, indicating that the donation/grant will appear on their books and will be disclosed to the public.
- It does not constitute an inducement to recommend, prescribe, purchase, supply, sell or administer specific medicinal products.
- A person or a group of persons chosen by the company will not exclusively benefit from a conditional grant to pay for their personal or scientific expenses.

No personal donation can be made directly or indirectly to healthcare professionals (*Article 6, Promotion Regulation*).

Sponsorship of healthcare professionals in their participation in national or international events are also subject to strict rules (*see Question 28*).

### OTHER ITEMS, FUNDING OR SERVICES

There are no other incentives allowed under Turkish law except the ones mentioned above. Donations are not considered incentives and are strictly regulated under the Promotion Regulation.

## 32. WHAT REGULATORY AUTHORITY IS RESPONSIBLE FOR SUPERVISING MARKETING ACTIVITIES REGARDING PROFESSIONALS?

**Regulatory authority**

The Institution of Pharmaceuticals and Medical Devices can examine, *ex officio* or upon receipt of a complaint, the promotional activities and any materials and methods employed in the context of such activities (*see Question 25*).

## 33. WHAT ARE THE LEGAL CONSEQUENCES IN CASE OF NON-COMPLIANCE WITH PROFESSIONAL MARKETING LAWS?

The legal consequences are the same as the ones listed in *Question 26*.

# ENGAGEMENT WITH PATIENT ORGANISATIONS

## 34. WHAT KINDS OF ACTIVITIES ARE PERMITTED IN RELATION TO ENGAGEMENT WITH PATIENT ORGANISATIONS? WHAT ARE THE RESTRICTIONS THAT ARE IMPOSED ON RELATIONSHIP WITH PATIENT ORGANISATIONS?

There are no regulations restricting the collaboration between the pharmaceutical industry and patient organisations. However, TISD, AIFD and IEIS have their own codes of practice which govern relations with patient organisations.

Under the AIFD Ethics Code, the pharmaceutical company can provide financial support or services to a patient organisation. A written agreement must be signed between the pharmaceutical company and the patient organisation and the amount of the financial support must be clearly defined. The non-financial, direct or indirect support must also be defined in the agreement. These service agreements can only be concluded if they aim to support public health or research. Every pharmaceutical company must declare the patient organisations they are supporting. This declaration must be clear and understandable to an average reader.

The logos of patient organisations can be used only on their approval. Pharmaceutical companies must not insist on being the sole supporter of a patient organisation or a big project. The Ethics Code repeats the prohibition to promote pharmaceuticals to the general public through patient organisations.

In case of a complaint based on a violation of these provisions, the pharmaceutical company can face sanctions depending on the gravity of the violation. The authority to examine the violation differs depending on the complainant. For example, if the complaint is made by a physician with regard to an AIFD member, the case is examined by TIDK (Promotion Principles Inspection Board of AIFD). The Ethics Code sets out the sanctions such as a warning sanction, a notification, reprobation, a suspension of the company's membership of the Association and permanent exclusion from the Association. In the case of a repetition of the same violation, there will be a heavier sanction.

## REFORM

**35. ARE THERE ANY PLANS TO REFORM THE LAW ON THE DISTRIBUTION AND PROMOTION OF DRUGS IN YOUR JURISDICTION?**

Amendments to the Promotion Regulation are currently under discussion before the Ministry of Health. A draft has been sent to the industry associations. The potential major amendment is disclosure of value transfers of pharmaceutical companies to healthcare professionals to the Institution. The industry has provided comments to the draft amendments and the draft is expected to be published by the end of 2015.

# UK (ENGLAND AND WALES)

*Alison Dennis, FIELDFISHER*

## DISTRIBUTION

### PRE-CONDITIONS FOR DISTRIBUTION

**1. WHAT ARE THE LEGAL PRE-CONDITIONS FOR A DRUG TO BE DISTRIBUTED WITHIN THE JURISDICTION?**

#### Authorisation

A drug must have a marketing authorisation that is effective in the UK, either by:

- A centralised application (applied for through the European Medicines Agency (EMA)).
- A national application, which may or may not have been obtained through either of the other EU mechanisms, which are the decentralised or mutual recognition procedures.

A company that holds a manufacturer's licence (*section 17, Human Medicines Regulations 2012 (THMR)*) can only sell the product to the holder of the marketing authorisation. Any other person wanting to trade in the product in the European Economic Area (EEA) and that is not the marketing authorisation holder or their contract manufacturer must hold a "wholesale dealer's licence" (*section 18, THMR*).

#### Exceptions

There are exceptions for parallel imports of drugs with no therapeutic difference from ones already licensed in the UK and compassionate use or "specials". A person can also sell wholesale drugs in the UK without a marketing authorisation, or wholesale dealer's licence, solely if those products are to be exported outside the EEA, so are considered to never fall within the regulatory regime of the EU (*section 19(5), THMR*).

**2. DO ANY TYPES OF NAMED PATIENT AND/OR COMPASSIONATE USE PROGRAMMES OPERATE? IF SO, WHAT ARE THE REQUIREMENTS FOR PRE-LAUNCH ACCESS?**

Unlicensed medicines can be supplied to meet the needs of individual patients (*section 167, Human Medicines Regulations 2012 (THMR)*). These are known as "specials" and are only permitted where the drug is:

- Supplied in response to an unsolicited order.
- Manufactured and assembled in accordance with the specification of a doctor, dentist, nurse independent prescriber, pharmacist independent prescriber or supplementary prescriber or for use under the supervision of a pharmacist in a registered pharmacy, a

hospital or a health centre and the drug is manufactured under that supervision.
- For use by a patient whose treatment requires the prescriber to be directly responsible for fulfilling the special needs of that patient.

If a "special" is manufactured in the UK or a country outside the European Economic Area (EEA), the manufacturer must hold a manufacturer's (specials) licence issued by the Medicines and Healthcare Products Regulatory Agency (MHRA). If the product is manufactured in the EEA, but not in the UK, then the manufacturer must have an authorisation to do so under EU legislation. If a "special" is distributed through a wholesale dealer, then that wholesale dealer must hold a licence in relation to that product. A "special" cannot be advertised and records must be kept and serious adverse drug reactions reported to the MHRA.

Separately, the UK has enacted the authorisation requirement under Article 126a Directive 2001/83/EC on the Community code relating to medicinal products for human use, under which the MHRA can grant such an authorisation if:

- No other marketing authorisation for a drug or a registration for a traditional herbal product is either in place or has been applied for and is pending.
- The MHRA considers that placing the product on the market in the UK is justified by public health reasons.
- The product is imported from another member state in which it is authorised.
- The applicant is established in the EU.

Since April 2014, the MHRA has put in place an early-access scheme for products treating, diagnosing or preventing life threatening, chronic or seriously debilitating conditions with a high unmet need. This scheme provides patients and prescribers with a means for checking the validity of claims that the benefits of a medicine outweighed the risks as a treatment for one of these conditions. It is seen as an interim measure to fill the gap between completion of phase III trials and the issue of a marketing authorisation. The Early Access to Medicines Scheme (EAMS) is voluntary and consists of a two-step evaluation process:

- The promising innovative medicine (PIM) designation.
- The early access to medicines scientific opinion.

The PIM can be applied for during clinical development where this shows that the product is likely to demonstrate significant benefit for patients suffering life-threatening or seriously debilitating conditions. The application can be for a new indication for an already marketed drug. The three conditions to be met are:

- The condition must be life-threatening or seriously debilitating.
- There is a high unmet need (that is, there is no available treatment or existing treatments have serious limitations).
- The potential adverse effects are likely to be outweighed by the benefits (based on preliminary scientific evidence).

Once a PIM has been obtained, then an early access to a medicines scientific opinion can be applied for. It is this opinion that is intended to support prescribers when making decisions about treating patients suffering conditions which are life-threatening or seriously debilitating. Following a positive scientific opinion, the MHRA publishes a public assessment report on the product and their opinion, with details including:

- Summaries of the key clinical studies.
- Risk or benefit analysis.
- Any uncertainties and measures to monitor and manage risk.

Regular updates must be provided to the MHRA and the scientific opinion must be renewed every 12 months, when any clinical or other data generated in the interim is considered.

## LICENSING

### 3. WHAT IS THE PROCEDURAL STRUCTURE REGARDING LICENSING A DRUG FOR DISTRIBUTION?

**Structure and regulatory authority**

Drugs must be licensed by a competent authority, which is either the:

- European Medicines Agency (EMA) through a centralised procedure (*see below*) where this is applicable to the particular products.
- National "competent authority", through a national procedure, for all other products and which in the UK is the Medicines and Healthcare Products Regulatory Authority (MHRA).

These national procedures may or may not be part of EU decentralised or mutual recognition procedures. Applications for a marketing authorisation are provided for in Part 5 of the Human Medicines Regulations 2012 (THMR). Applications must be made in accordance with Annex 1 of Directive 2001/83/EC on the Community code relating to medicinal products for human use.

The centralised procedure is compulsory for the following types of drugs:

- Drugs for the treatment of human immunodeficiency virus (HIV) or acquired immune deficiency syndrome (AIDS), cancer, diabetes, neurodegenerative diseases, auto-immune and other immune dysfunctions and viral diseases.
- Medicines derived from biotechnology processes, such as genetic engineering.
- Advanced-therapy medicines, such as gene-therapy, somatic cell-therapy or tissue-engineered medicines.
- Officially designated "orphan medicines" (medicines used for rare human diseases).

The centralised procedure is optional for the following types of drugs (and are otherwise authorised nationally):

- Drugs that are a significant therapeutic, scientific or technical innovation.
- Drugs whose authorisation is in the interest of public health.

Applications through the centralised procedure are submitted to the EMA. The EMA's scientific committees takes up to 210 active days plus "clock stops", at the end of which the committee adopts an opinion on whether the medicine should be marketed or not. This opinion is transmitted to the European Commission and they are then responsible for granting the marketing authorisation.

### 4. IS THERE A SIMPLIFIED LICENCE PROCEEDING, OR RELAXED LICENSING CONDITIONS, FOR DRUGS WHICH HAVE ALREADY BEEN LICENSED FOR DISTRIBUTION IN ANOTHER JURISDICTION?

There is a UK Parallel Import Licensing Scheme that allows drugs authorised in other EU member states to be marketed in the UK, provided the imported products have no therapeutic difference from the equivalent UK products (*section 172, Human Medicines Regulations 2012*

*(THMR), which refers to the EU parallel import licensing regime)*. An application is made to the Medicines and Healthcare Products Regulatory Agency (MHRA), who examines the licence given to the product in other jurisdictions and decides whether a parallel import licence should be granted.

There are three levels of "therapeutic similarity" for the purpose of a parallel import licence, each requiring a different complexity of application:

- A "simple" licence where the products being imported are made by the same group of companies or under licence from the same licensor that holds the UK marketing authorisation.
- A standard licence, where there is no common origin, but the application is not seen as complex.
- A "complex" licence which is required where there is no common origin and where any of a list of risk factors (being specific differences in manufacturing processes) applies.

For the standard and complex categories, the parallel importer is responsible for the pharmacovigilance for the product.

### 5. IS VIRTUAL DRUG DISTRIBUTION POSSIBLE FROM YOUR JURISDICTION?

A wholesale dealer's licence allows its holder to obtain supplies of drugs from the marketing authorisation holder or another EU member state-authorised dealer for that particular activity and where the products can be distributed "virtually", that is, without ever entering the UK. The Medicines and Healthcare Products Regulatory Agency (MHRA) has indicated that it is used to handling wholesale dealer licences where the physical product is in another European Economic Area (EEA) member state and never actually enters the UK. The wholesale dealer must nevertheless have a named qualified person to supervise and authorise the activities and the MHRA can check the records kept regarding the wholesale dealing activities. Although the products never enter the country, the guidance on ensuring the supply of drugs and meeting product shortages nevertheless apply. Whether the MHRA applies these rules to a virtual wholesale dealer has yet to be publicly tested.

### 6. WHAT IS THE PROCEDURE TO APPEAL (LEGAL REMEDY) A LICENSING DECISION?

If an applicant does not agree with the decision of the Medicines and Healthcare Products Regulatory Agency (MHRA) not to grant a marketing authorisation their recourse is to an administrative law procedure known as "judicial review". Under this process, the applicant must prove that the way the decision was made was not lawful, for example if the MHRA has failed to take specific information into account that should have been a part of the decision-making process.

### 7. WHAT ARE THE COSTS OF OBTAINING LICENSING?

Fees for obtaining licences are set by the Medicines and Healthcare Products Regulatory Agency (MHRA) and are updated in April every year:

- For 2015 to 2016 the fee for a UK Marketing Authorisation is GB£103,059.
- For a decentralised application where the UK is the reference member state, it is GB£143,134.

A full list of current fees can be found on the MHRA website (*www.gov.uk/government/publications/mhra-fees/*

# UK (ENGLAND AND WALES)

*current-mhra-fees#licence-applications-marketing-authorisations-including-extension-applications-fees*).

## DISTRIBUTION TO CONSUMERS

### 8. WHAT ARE THE DIFFERENT CATEGORIES OF DRUGS FOR DISTRIBUTION?

There are three categories of drugs:

- Only on prescription (POM).
- Only from a pharmacy (P).
- On general sale (GSL).

### 9. WHO IS AUTHORISED TO DISTRIBUTE PRESCRIPTION DRUGS AND OVER-THE-COUNTER DRUGS TO CONSUMERS?

Prescription-only drugs can be prescribed and supplied by:

- A doctor.
- A dentist.
- A supplementary prescriber, although there are conditions and limitations on giving injections (*section 215, Human Medicines Regulations 2012 (THMR)*).
- A nurse independent prescriber.
- A pharmacist independent prescriber.
- An optometrist independent prescriber (not medicines for injection or controlled drugs).
- A community practitioner nurse prescriber though there is a list of products that they are allowed to prescribe (*schedule 13, THMR*).
- A European Economic Area (EEA) health professional (not controlled drugs) (*section 214, THMR*).

Professionals that are "independent prescribers" or "supplementary prescribers" must have undergone specific training and have acquired specific qualifications and their registrations with their respective professional bodies must note they have achieved this status. However, a supplementary prescriber operates in a voluntary partnership with a doctor or dentist and prescribes drugs only where implementing an agreed patient-specific clinical management plan with the patient's agreement. For more detailed information, see "Improving Patients' Access to Medicines: A Guide to Implementing Nurse and Pharmacist Independent Prescribing within the NHS in England" (*Department of Health Gateway reference: 6429, April 2006*).

There is currently a proposal under discussion to allow radiographers, paramedics and dieticians to become independent prescribers and for exemptions to apply to orthoptists. If agreed by ministers, this could become law in 2016 (*www.england.nhs.uk/2015/02/26/access-to-medicines*).

Prescription-only medicines that have been prescribed by a person authorised as stated above can be supplied to consumers if the following three conditions are met:

- Supply is by a person lawfully conducting a retail pharmacy business (that is a qualified pharmacist with an appropriate registration with the General Pharmaceutical Council).
- Where the medicine is sold, supplied or offered for sale or supply on premises that are a

registered pharmacy.
- If the transaction is carried out on behalf of the registered pharmacist by another person and that other person is, or acts under the supervision of, the registered pharmacist (*section 220, THMR*).

There are also provisions in section 224 of the THMR for emergency sales of prescription-only drugs by a licensed pharmacist where a prescription is provided within 72 hours. An emergency supply for a more limited range of prescription-only drugs is possible, at the request of the patient (*section 225, THMR*).

**Over-the-counter drugs**

Over-the-counter (OTC) drugs (that is medicines that are only from a pharmacy (P) or on general sale (GSL)) can be distributed to consumers by any pharmacy registered with the General Pharmaceutical Council. GSL medicines can also be distributed from premises that the occupier can close so as to exclude the public and on the condition that the products are pre-packaged in advance of supply to those premises and supplied in packaging that has not been opened. There are also restrictions on the volume of analgesics packaged and available for general sale (*schedule 15, THMR*).

It is unlawful to sell drugs from an automatic machine except for GSL products.

### 10. WHAT DRUGS CAN AN ATTENDING PHYSICIAN DISTRIBUTE AND UNDER WHAT CIRCUMSTANCES?

Medicines legislation does not specifically address the issue of the administration of medicines. The restrictions on the sale or supply of prescription-only medicines do not apply to doctors or dentists registered to practise in the UK (and with limitations, the European Economic Area (EEA)) (*section 223(1), Human Medicines Regulations 2012 (THMR)*).

### 11. WHO IS AUTHORISED TO PRESCRIBE PRESCRIPTION DRUGS TO CONSUMERS?

See *Question 9*.

### 12. IS DIRECT MAILING/DISTANCE SELLING OF DRUGS PERMITTED IN YOUR JURISDICTION?

Over-the-counter (OTC) drugs can be sold via internet pharmacies based in the UK.

**Conditions**

Conditions imposed on distance selling require the sale to be made from lockable premises. There is also specific provision covering electronic prescriptions, allowing prescriptions to be transmitted via the internet so that a patient can be dispensed prescription-only medicines through direct mailing. All pharmacies, including internet-only pharmacies must be registered with the General Pharmaceutical Council (GPhC). The GPhC issues logos to internet sites supplying medicines if they are satisfied that they meet specific criteria, including those in its guidelines relating to the issue of the logo.

From 1 July 2015, anyone in the UK selling medicines to the public via a website also must be registered with the Medicines and Healthcare products Regulatory Agency (MHRA) and be on the MHRA's list of UK registered online retail sellers.

They must also display the new EU common logo on every page of their website offering medicines for sale, even if they display the GPhC voluntary logo. There is then a link from the registered EU common logo on their site to their entry in the MHRA's list of registered online sellers.

**Cross-border sales**

UK registered pharmacies can supply overseas patients through a UK-based internet pharmacy, subject to receipt of a lawfully issued prescription for prescription-only medicines. There are set requirements for prescriptions that can be lawfully filled by registered pharmacies in the UK (*sections 217 to 219, Human Medicines Regulations 2012 (THMR)*).

## 13. WHAT REGULATORY AUTHORITY IS RESPONSIBLE FOR SUPERVISING DISTRIBUTION ACTIVITIES?

The Medicines and Healthcare products Regulatory Agency (MHRA) supervises the distribution of drugs and can choose whether to resolve a matter directly with the individual or to undertake a criminal prosecution under the Human Medicines Regulations 2012 (THMR), the Trade Marks Act 1994 or the Proceeds of Crime Act 2002. The MHRA can also ask for an injunction to prevent sale or importation. This work is undertaken by the Defective Medicines Report Centre (DMRC), which is a unit of the Enforcement and Intelligence Group of the MHRA that takes action against illegal activities involving medicines and their availability, manufacture, import, sale, supply and administration. Sanctions include criminal prosecutions, which are usually tried in the Crown Court.

## 14. WHAT IS THE PROCEDURE TO APPEAL (LEGAL REMEDY) A DISTRIBUTION DECISION?

From the Crown Court there is an appeal to the Court of Appeal and then the Supreme Court as a second appeal, but only on a point of law.

If the matter is not dealt with via criminal proceedings but rather the MHRA take a decision (such as a refusal) which is not accepted by the company, this can be challenged through judicial review of the decision made.

## 15. WHAT ARE THE LEGAL CONSEQUENCES OF NON-COMPLIANCE WITH CONSUMER DISTRIBUTION LAWS?

If an unlicensed drug is distributed or if an unauthorised person distributes drugs, the Medicines and Healthcare products Regulatory Agency (MHRA) requires that all such sales cease and that a recall is put in place for products improperly distributed.

There are criminal penalties (*see Question 13*) available as well as civil actions by owners of patents, supplementary protection certificates and trade marks if any of these are infringed. These laws allow the rights' owners to work together with HM Customs and Revenues' (HMRC) Intellectual Property Authorisation Unit to stop counterfeit medicines at the border.

# UK (ENGLAND AND WALES)

## WHOLESALE DISTRIBUTION

### 16. WHAT IS THE LEGAL REGIME REGARDING WHOLESALE DISTRIBUTION OF DRUGS?

Any company or individual wishing to wholesale deal drugs within the EU must hold a wholesale dealer's licence (obtained from a national competent authority) that specifies the premises from which they can undertake their wholesale dealing operations. Supplying wholesale is defined as selling, supplying or procuring to anyone other than the end-user of the drug and is permitted where there is a marketing authorisation in place for the product in the UK or other country of the European Economic Area (EEA) in which the wholesale dealer is operating. Applications for wholesale dealers' licences in the UK are made to the Medicines and Healthcare products Regulatory Agency (MHRA) through their eSubmissions portal. The MHRA publishes the Orange Guide of the Rules and Guidance for Pharmaceutical Manufacturers and Distributors, which applies to the activities of wholesale dealers in the UK. There are currently no laws on securing the supply of drugs on to the UK market, but the MHRA has agreed with industry Guidelines on Best Practice for ensuring the efficient supply and distribution of medicines to patients, last published in January 2013. There is further guidance developed with the Department of Health and the pharmaceutical supply chain, which is the "Trading Medicines for Human Use: Shortages and Supply Chain Obligations", last updated in January 2013.

### 17. WHAT REGULATORY AUTHORITY IS RESPONSIBLE FOR SUPERVISING WHOLESALE DISTRIBUTION ACTIVITIES?

**Regulatory authority**

The Medicines and Healthcare products Regulatory Agency (MHRA) Inspection, Enforcement and Standards Division is responsible for supervising wholesale distribution activities and their policy unit advises on the interpretation of the law as well as developing policy relating to wholesale distribution activities.

**Supervision**

The MHRA can revoke, vary or suspend a licence where they find that the wholesaler is not meeting the conditions of the licence.

**Rights of appeal**

The licence holder can make written representations and appear before an adjudicator to request a review of the decision. They also have the right to request judicial review of the MHRA's decision through the courts.

### 18. WHAT ARE THE LEGAL CONSEQUENCES OF NON-COMPLIANCE WITH WHOLESALE DISTRIBUTION LAWS?

A wholesale dealers' licence whose terms are breached can be revoked, varied or suspended by the Medicines and Healthcare products Regulatory Agency (MHRA).

# MARKETING

## PROMOTION

**19. WHAT IS THE GENERAL LEGAL REGIME FOR THE MARKETING OF DRUGS?**

Pharmaceutical advertising is regulated through EU laws that are transposed into and supplemented by UK laws, specifically Part 14, Chapter 2 of Human Medicines Regulations 2012 (THMR), while Chapter 3 provides the enforcement regime.

In the EU, it is prohibited to advertise prescription-only drugs. For other drugs, it is prohibited to publish an advertisement unless the advertisement encourages the rational use of the product by presenting it objectively and without exaggerating its properties. Advertisements that are misleading cannot be published. It is a requirement to include a statement indicating:

- Those to whom the advertisement is addressed.
- The method of its publication.
- The date when it was first published.

The Cancer Act 1939 prohibits certain advertisements relating to treatments for cancer.

As well as the legislation that is specific to the advertisement of pharmaceuticals, other more generally applicable laws also apply. These include the Trade Descriptions Act 1968 and the Consumer Protection from Unfair Trading Regulations 2008 that implement the EU Directives on misleading and comparative advertising. The Director-General of Fair Trading is the supervisory body and enforcement is carried out at a local level by trading standards. Broadcast advertising is regulated by the Broadcasting Acts of 1990 and 1996 and the Communications Act 2003. There are also the general advertising rules laid down by the Advertising Standards Association through the Code of Advertising Practice (CAP) and the Broadcast Code of Advertising Practice (BCAP) Codes.

The Bribery Act 2010 also has to be taken into account in any interactions with healthcare professionals by the pharmaceutical industry.

The Medicines and Healthcare products Regulatory Agency (MHRA) publishes a "Blue Guide" to pharmaceutical advertising, currently in its third edition published in August 2012. This contains details of its opinions on the interpretation of pharmaceutical advertising legislation.

Pharmaceutical advertising is largely self-regulated. For prescriptions medicines, the Association of the British Pharmaceutical Industry (ABPI) publishes its code of practice and is administered and regulated by a separate body, the Pharmaceutical Medicines Code of Practice Authority (PMCPA).

For over-the-counter (OTC) medicines, the self-regulatory body is the Proprietary Association of Great Britain (PAGB), which publishes its own codes of practice and reviews all advertising of its members prior to publication.

**20. ARE THERE OTHER CODES OF CONDUCT FOR THE MARKETING OF DRUGS (FOR EXAMPLE, BY PROFESSIONAL OR INDUSTRIAL ORGANISATIONS)?**

The Secretary of State for Health has the primary responsibility for supervising marketing activities for pharmaceutical products. This responsibility is delegated to the Medicines and Healthcare products Regulatory Agency (MHRA). The MHRA allows self-regulation and

## UK (ENGLAND AND WALES)

maintains relationships with the Association of the British Pharmaceutical Industry (ABPI) and the Proprietary Association of Great Britain (PAGB), but still maintains its own ultimate authority over advertising. The MHRA's role is supervisory for companies that are members of those industry bodies and the MHRA continues to deal directly with companies and individuals that are not either members of the relevant self-regulatory industry bodies or signed-up to the relevant codes.

For prescription medicines, the self-regulatory body is the ABPI, which publishes its code of practice and is regulated by the Pharmaceutical Medicines Code of Practice Authority (PMCPA). Members of the ABPI have signed-up to the ABPI code, but non-members can also agree to abide by the ABPI code and then have their advertising subject to the same regime.

For over-the-counter (OTC) and on general sale (GSL) products advertised to consumers, the PAGB publishes its code of practice and pre-vets all its members' advertising.

Where complaints occur, the MHRA can require that future advertising of the perpetrator is pre-vetted by them. The MHRA also pre-vets advertising for new products whenever it considers it appropriate. They aim to give an opinion within five days from submission.

## MARKETING TO CONSUMERS

### 21. WHAT IS THE LEGAL REGIME FOR MARKETING TO CONSUMERS?

Only over-the-counter (OTC) and on general sale (GSL) products can be advertised to consumers, except for government controlled vaccination campaigns. No offers to treat or prescribe any remedy for the treatment of cancer can be made. Medicines containing psychotropic or narcotic substances cannot normally be advertised to the general public.

The following information must be included in advertising addressed to the public:

- Name of the drug.
- If the product contains only one active ingredient, the common name of the drug.
- Information for the product's correct use.
- An express and legible invitation to read carefully the instructions in the leaflet or on the label.
- For products with a traditional herbal registration only, the following statement: "Traditional herbal drug for use in [indications consistent with registration] exclusively based on long standing use as a traditional remedy".
- It must also be clear that the material is an advertisement and the product being advertised is a medicine.

### 22. WHAT KINDS OF MARKETING ACTIVITIES ARE PERMITTED IN RELATION TO CONSUMERS AND THE PRODUCTS WHICH MAY BE ADVERTISED TO THEM?

There are no restrictions on where advertising of over-the counter (OTC) drugs can be placed.

The content of advertising for authorised OTC drugs to consumers must not:

- Relate to a drug containing narcotic substances.
- State or imply that a medical consultation or surgery is unnecessary.
- Offer to provide a diagnosis or suggest a treatment by post or electronically.
- By a description or detailed representation of a case history, be likely to lead to erroneous self-diagnosis.

- Suggest that effects of the drug are guaranteed, better than or equivalent to those of another identifiable treatment or product or not accompanied by any adverse reaction.
- Uses in terms that are misleading or likely to cause alarm, pictorial representations of changes in the human body caused by disease or injury or the action of the drug on the human body.
- Refer to claims of recovery in terms that are misleading or likely to cause alarm.
- Suggest the health of a person not suffering from any disease or injury could be enhanced by taking the drug.
- Suggest the health of a person could be affected by not taking the drug.
- Suggest the drug is a food, cosmetic or other consumer product.
- Suggests that the drug's safety or efficacy is due to the fact it is natural.
- Refer to a recommendation by scientists, healthcare professionals or persons that because of their celebrity could encourage the use of the drug.
- Be directed principally at children.

The advertisement must make it clear it is an advertisement and the product must be clearly identified as a drug.

## 23. IS IT PERMITTED TO PROVIDE CONSUMERS WITH FREE SAMPLES? ARE THERE PARTICULAR RESTRICTIONS ON SPECIAL OFFERS (FOR EXAMPLE, "BUY-ONE-GET-ONE-FREE")?

The provision of free samples of drugs to consumers is prohibited (*Regulation 293, Human Medicines Regulations 2012 (THMR)*).

There are no specific restrictions on special offers but promotions that are more likely to encourage over or unnecessary use of medicines, and particularly those with known safety issues, are likely to be prohibited. That principle is reflected in the Proprietary Association of Great Britain (PAGB) "Guidelines on Consumer Promotions and Public Relations" (PAGB Guidelines) which provide additional guidance on its application.

The PAGB Guidelines on consumer special offers require that:

- The money off or price reduction should not be excessive.
- The proposed amount of discount or offer must be justified.
- Promotions must be for a sufficiently long duration to avoid encouraging over-purchasing unrequired medicines.
- The promotion must not amount to the drug being provided free-of-charge.

Similarly, points on loyalty cards must not be excessive in a way that could encourage purchases.

Free gifts are permitted if:

- The gift is of a sufficiently lower value than the price of the medicine (both the actual and perceived value) so as not to encourage purchase of the medicine to get the gift.
- The gift is related to the use of the medicine.
- Consumers are not required to purchase multiple medicines in order to obtain the gift.
- The gift is not attractive to children.
- The gift is not likely to result in the consumer needing to use more of the medicine.

Offers such as "two for the price of one" are permitted, but consumers must still have the choice of buying a single product. However, it is considered that promotions that encourage people to buy multiple packs of medicines that have known safety issues are undesirable. Any volume promotions relating to drugs must:

- Be intended for medium to long term use.
- Not contain ingredients that have the potential for misuse or accidental poisoning.

Drug packs must also not be banded together for sale unless that banding is authorised by the Medicines and Healthcare products Regulatory Agency (MHRA).

It is not considered ethical to require consumers to purchase a medicine to enter a prize promotion.

## 24. ARE THERE PARTICULAR RULES OF PRACTICE ON THE USE OF THE INTERNET/SOCIAL MEDIA REGARDING DRUGS AND THEIR ADVERTISING?

Advertising via the internet is subject to the same rules as other consumer advertising of drugs. However, given that advertising via the internet directed at, or available to, UK consumers can be made from anywhere in the world, this poses practical issues for enforcement.

Advertising posted on UK websites or aimed at the UK audience is subject to UK medicines advertising legislation.

## 25. WHAT REGULATORY AUTHORITY IS RESPONSIBLE FOR SUPERVISING MARKETING ACTIVITIES TO CONSUMERS?

### Regulatory authority

The Secretary of State for Health retains primary responsibility for supervising marketing activities for pharmaceutical products and whose responsibility is delegated to the Medicines and Healthcare products Regulatory Agency (MHRA).

### Supervision

The MHRA allows self-regulation of consumer advertising for over-the-counter (OTC) and general sales list products to the Proprietary Association of Great Britain (PAGB) but retains ultimate authority over advertising. Members of the PAGB must obtain approval for their adverts whatever the media. Clearcast is an additional approval body for TV commercials and the Radio Advertising Clearance Centre (RACC) for radio commercials and the Cinema Advertising Authority (CAA) for advertising in cinemas. The Advertising Standards Authority also exercises control over consumer advertising where this is in print, by direct marketing, sales promotions, radio, TV or over the internet. For TV or radio sponsorship Ofcom acts as the complaint body (as well as the MHRA).

### Rights of appeal

There is no right of appeal against the final determination by the MHRA of a breach of consumer advertising laws but the decision can be judicially reviewed through the administrative law process. For PAGB, Clearcast, the RACC and CAA, there is a requirement for prior authorisation for the advertisement. Therefore, any disputes are usually resolved by negotiation before advertising the product. The Advertising Standards Authority (ASA) on the other hand takes action post-marketing and there is a 21 day window from the date on the ASA's letter of notification of the ruling in which the advertiser can ask the Independent Reviewer of the Rulings of the ASA Council to review the case. Cases are only reviewed where there is a substantial and apparent flaw of process or ruling or if additional relevant evidence is available. Decisions can be challenged in the administrative law division of the high court using a judicial review process, but the circumstances for such reviews are limited.

## 26. WHAT ARE THE LEGAL CONSEQUENCES OF NON-COMPLIANCE WITH CONSUMER MARKETING LAWS?

Breaches of the law on pharmaceutical advertising are a criminal offence (*Regulation 303, Human Medicines Regulations 2012 (THMR)*). Fines can be levied to the statutory maximum and individuals can be imprisoned for up to two years as well as fined. If the offence falls under one of the following Regulations then this is a lesser or "summary offence" that is subject to a fine only:

- Regulation 298(1) of the THMR (free samples).
- Regulations 299(2) or (3) of the THMR (medical sales representatives).
- Regulation 300(4) of the THMR (solicitation or acceptance of inducements or hospitality).

Breaches of the Advertising Standards Authority (ASA) code are published by the ASA on its website and it can require that advertisers themselves publish in the media a statement noting the breach. Persistent offenders can be required to have some or all of the marketing communications vetted by the Code of Advertising Practice (CAP) Copy Advice team. Where the breach is online, the CAP can ask internet search engines to remove the company's paid-for search advertisements from linking to pages hosting non-compliant communication. The ASA can also feature an advertisement drawing attention to the breach.

The effect of the advertisement of the breach of advertising rules can lead to other companies including the media withholding services or denying access to space. Trading privileges (including direct mail discounts) and recognition can be revoked, withdrawn or temporarily withheld. Sometimes, the non-compliant party is referred to Trading Standards that enforces the Consumer Protection from Unfair Trading Regulations 2008 that includes criminal sanctions such as fines and imprisonment.

## MARKETING TO PROFESSIONALS

## 27. WHAT KINDS OF MARKETING ACTIVITIES ARE PERMITTED IN RELATION TO PROFESSIONALS?

The law does not prescribe the activities that can be undertaken, but instead covers the restrictions on activities (*see Question 28*).

## 28. ARE THERE ANY RESTRICTIONS ON MARKETING TO PROFESSIONALS?

There are limited legal provisions relating to advertising and marketing to professionals, including various restrictions (*sections 294 to 300, Human Medicines Regulations 2012 (THMR)*).

# UK (ENGLAND AND WALES)

For advertising to professionals the Association of the British Pharmaceutical Industry (ABPI) Code applies to prescription-only drugs and the Proprietary Association of Great Britain (PAGB) Professional Code for Medicines to over-the-counter (OTC) drugs.

### Marketing activities

Promotions cannot be accompanied by written materials, unless the required notices are included as set out in Schedule 30 of the THMR, as well as the date it was drawn up (*section 297, THMR*). The information must be accurate, up-to-date, verifiable and sufficiently complete to enable the recipient to form an opinion of the therapeutic value of the product. Illustrative material must be accurately reproduced and indicate the source.

The provision of unsolicited journal articles is prohibited unless they have been referred (*clause 10, ABPI Code*).

Free samples can be given to professionals qualified to prescribe them, for the purpose of acquiring experience in dealing with that product and are made in response to a request form signed and dated by the recipient (*section 298, THMR*). Free samples cannot contain narcotics or psychotropic substances. The sample must be:

- No larger than the smallest presentation available in the UK.
- Marked "free medical sample: not for resale".
- Accompanied by a copy of the Summary of Product Characteristics (SPCs).

The supplier must maintain an adequate system of control and accountability for its supply of free samples.

Sales representatives can visit prescribers but must provide a copy of the SPC for each product promoted. Any adverse reactions reported to the sales representatives must be reported to the marketing authorisation holder's scientific service.

### Frequency

The provision of samples is (by law) on an exceptional basis only and in any year only a limited number of samples of any particular product can be supplied to an individual prescriber.

The ABPI Code requires "restraint" in the frequency of distribution and volume of promotional material. It also requires non-interventional studies to be conducted for a scientific purpose and properly documented with a protocol. The results of the study must be published in the same way as any clinical trial (*section 13, ABPI Code*).

### Provision of hospitality

Hospitality limited to the main purpose of a meeting is permitted (*section 300, THMR*) and includes sponsorship for attendance and payment of travel and accommodation expenses.

The ABPI Code requires that hospitality can only be provided to health professionals at scientific or promotional meetings and that must be held in appropriate venues "conducive to the main purpose". Hospitality must be limited to subsistence only and cannot be more expensive than recipients would normally pay for themselves. There is a cap of GB£75 per person excluding VAT and gratuities, but the expectation is that on most occasions sums expended will be significantly lower.

The PAGB Code includes almost identical provisions, albeit only in relation to meetings for the purpose of advertising and promoting OTC products and without a specific limit on the cost of a meal.

## Gifts to professionals

Gifts, pecuniary advantages or benefits cannot be supplied, ordered or promised to those that prescribe or supply drugs, unless they are inexpensive and relevant to the practice of medicine or pharmacy (*section 300(1), THMR*).

Clause 18 of the ABPI Code is more restrictive in that it prohibits gifts, pecuniary advantages or benefits to be supplied, offered or promised to healthcare professionals or other decision makers in connection with the promotion of drugs or as an inducement in relation to drugs.

Exceptions to this are patient support items to be passed to patients as part of a formal patient support programme and that are inexpensive. Inexpensive notebooks, pens and pencils not bearing the names of any medicine can be provided at scientific meetings. If the meeting is organised by the company, then these items can bear the company name. If organised by a third party, then no company name can be included.

### 29. WHAT INFORMATION IS IT LEGALLY REQUIRED TO INCLUDE IN ADVERTISING TO PROFESSIONALS?

The list of particulars to be included in advertising to professionals includes (*schedule 30, Human Medicines Regulations 2012 (THMR)*):

- Marketing authorisation number.
- Name and address of the marketing authorisation holder.
- The product's name and classification.
- Active ingredients by common name.
- Indications consistent with the marketing authorisation.
- Succinct statement of the entries in the Summary of Product Characteristics (SPCs) relating to adverse reactions, precautions and contra-indications, dosage and method of use and (where not obvious) method of administration.
- Cost excluding VAT.

### 30. ARE THERE RULES ON COMPARISONS WITH OTHER PRODUCTS THAT ARE PARTICULARLY APPLICABLE TO DRUGS?

A comparison is only permitted in promotional material if (*clause 7.3, Association of the British Pharmaceutical Industry (ABPI) Code*):

- It is not misleading.
- Medicines or services for the same needs or intended for the same purpose are compared.
- One or more material, relevant, substantial and representative features are compared.
- No confusion is created between the medicine advertised and that of a competitor or between the advertiser's trade marks, trade names, other distinguishing marks and those of a competitor.
- The trade marks, trade names, other distinguishing marks, medicines, services, activities or circumstances of a competitor are not discredited or denigrated.
- No unfair advantage is taken of the reputation of a trade mark, trade name or other distinguishing marks of a competitor.
- Medicines or services are not presented as imitations or replicas of goods or services bearing a competitor's trade mark or trade name.

Rule 37 of the Proprietary Association of Great Britain (PAGB) Code does not permit denigration of another product or active ingredient. Any point of difference must also be sufficient to be significant to consumers. The PAGB Code also prohibits the use of a competitor product brand name without the permission of its owner (which is different from the general law on comparisons in advertising). Hanging comparisons are also prohibited. The bar for substantiation for comparative claims is high and claims of being the superior product are even more so. The supporting clinical or consumer research necessary to substantiate the claims made must be robust.

## 31. WHAT OTHER ITEMS, FUNDING OR SERVICES ARE PERMITTED TO BE PROVIDED TO PROFESSIONALS?

### Discounts

Normal commercial practices are permitted, whereas any practices designed to incentivise professionals to prescribe a particular product rather than the most appropriate one for the patient are prohibited.

### Free samples

This is the same as for discounts. Items such as samples are permitted, because they are not considered to be incentives. See *Question 28*.

### Sponsorship of professionals

See *Question 28*.

## 32. WHAT REGULATORY AUTHORITY IS RESPONSIBLE FOR SUPERVISING MARKETING ACTIVITIES REGARDING PROFESSIONALS?

### Regulatory authority

As with consumer advertising, the Medicines and Healthcare products Regulatory Agency (MHRA) has ultimate responsibility for supervising advertising to professionals, with the Pharmaceutical Medicines Code of Practice Authority (PMCPA) supervising self-regulation under the Association of the British Pharmaceutical Industry (ABPI) Code and Proprietary Association of Great Britain (PAGB) supervising self-regulation under the PAGB Code.

However, other activities in relation to professionals, such as sponsorship, hospitality and consultancy arrangements, can also infringe the Bribery Act 2010 and as such, the Serious Fraud Office (SFO) can become involved. The Bribery Act 2010 has extra-territorial effect, which means that activities undertaken in countries outside the UK by companies or individuals with certain connections to the UK can be investigated by the SFO and can lead to criminal prosecution in the UK.

All healthcare professionals with prescribing rights belong to a professional regulatory body. Each of these bodies has its own code of practice. Each one, in one form or another, requires that the professional acts in accordance with the interests of the patient and not in their own interest. Therefore, the healthcare professional can also be sanctioned in accordance with the rules of their professional body if it is found that their activities with any drug company amounts to an actual or perceived inducement to prescribe.

## Supervision

See above, *Regulatory authority*.

## Rights of appeal

Rights of appeal against MHRA decisions are by way of judicial review through the administrative law division of the High Court.

Decisions of the PMCPA in respect of the ABPI Code are appealed to the Code of Practice Appeal Board.

The SFO can pursue prosecutions through the criminal justice system that are then appealable through the normal court system via the Court of Appeal and the Supreme Court.

## 33. WHAT ARE THE LEGAL CONSEQUENCES IN CASE OF NON-COMPLIANCE WITH PROFESSIONAL MARKETING LAWS?

Generally, there are no legal consequences of non-compliance with professional marketing laws, as the UK system is mainly self-regulatory.

However, for breaches of the professional advertising laws, action can be taken by the Medicines and Healthcare products Regulatory Agency (MHRA) for Association of the British Pharmaceutical Industry (ABPI) and Pharmaceutical Medicines Code of Practice Authority (PMCPA) non-members, and the consequences are the same as for breaches of consumer advertising laws (*see Question 26*). The Advertising Standards Authority (ASA) and other general advertising bodies only deal with consumer advertising and therefore their authority is not engaged for professional advertising.

Breaches of the ABPI Code are considered by the PMCPA Code of Practice Panel. The Panel can require undertakings are given and there is broad scope for what can be included in undertakings, dependent on the nature of the breach. This can include undertakings to withdraw particular advertising or cease a particular activity and to take all reasonable steps to prevent a reoccurrence. The undertaking must be signed by the Chief Executive or Managing Director. An administrative charge is also levied, calculated on the number of breaches of the ABPI Code that are found.

The Panel can also report a company to the Appeal Board of the PMCPA if the breach is sufficiently serious or raises concerns about a company's procedures. The Appeal Board has additional powers to require audits of company activities, processes and procedures, and can require that marketing materials are pre-vetted. It can also require that the company publishes a corrective statement with the content, timing and placement to be agreed with the Appeal Board. If the breach of the Code is sufficiently serious, the company can be reported to the ABPI board that has the power to suspend or expel the company from the ABPI membership. All cases heard by the PMCPA Panel and Appeal Board are included in publicly available case reports via the PMCPA website.

UK (ENGLAND AND WALES)

## ENGAGEMENT WITH PATIENT ORGANISATIONS

### 34. WHAT KINDS OF ACTIVITIES ARE PERMITTED IN RELATION TO ENGAGEMENT WITH PATIENT ORGANISATIONS? WHAT ARE THE RESTRICTIONS THAT ARE IMPOSED ON RELATIONSHIP WITH PATIENT ORGANISATIONS?

Interaction with patient organisations is regulated by the general advertising and promotions laws outlined above (*see Questions 19 to 26*), and otherwise is only regulated in detail by clause 27 of the Association of the British Pharmaceutical Industry (ABPI) Code.

Pharmaceutical companies can interact with and support the work of patient organisations, but in doing so must:

- Respect their independence.
- Comply with the prohibition on advertising prescription only drugs to the public.
- Must be transparent about any sponsorship.

All significant work with patient organisations must be the subject of a written agreement that is precise about the relationship, including funding. If the patient organisation is to provide services, they can only be to support healthcare or research and paid for at fair market value. Companies cannot require exclusivity and must not influence the content of patient organisation material so as to favour its commercial interests.

The requirement for transparency means that a list of patient organisations supported by the pharmaceutical companies (updated at least annually) must be publicly available, and must include the amount of financial support and value of non-financial support the organisations receive.

## REFORM

### 35. ARE THERE ANY PLANS TO REFORM THE LAW ON THE DISTRIBUTION AND PROMOTION OF DRUGS IN YOUR JURISDICTION?

The requirements for transparency of interactions by companies with the healthcare industry continue to be under debate, and the Association of the British Pharmaceutical Industry (ABPI) Code is likely to be developed further in this regard in due course.

# UNITED STATES

Jamie K Wolszon & Andrew J Hull, HYMAN, PHELPS & MCNAMARA, PC

# DISTRIBUTION

## PRE-CONDITIONS FOR DISTRIBUTION

**1. WHAT ARE THE LEGAL PRE-CONDITIONS FOR A DRUG TO BE DISTRIBUTED WITHIN THE JURISDICTION?**

### Authorisation

The Federal Food, Drug & Cosmetic Act (FDC Act) requires approval by the federal Food and Drug Administration (FDA) for the drug's intended use prior to the introduction of a new prescription drug into interstate commerce.

Under FDA law, drugs are defined as articles which are:

- Intended for use in the diagnosis, cure, mitigation, treatment, or prevention of disease in man or other animals.
- Other than food, intended to affect the structure or any function of the body of man or other animals.
- Intended for use as a component of any articles specified above.

A drug can also be any article recognised in the United States Pharmacopeia or National Formulary, the official Homeopathic Pharmacopeia of the United States. FDA law states that a prescription drug is a drug that, because of its toxicity or other potential harmful effects, or the method of its use, or the collateral measures necessary to its use, is not safe for use except under the supervision of a practitioner licensed by law to administer such a drug, or the drug approval is limited to use under the supervision of a licensed practitioner. The FDA approves prescription drugs through one of the following routes:

- The full new drug application (NDA).
- A less comprehensive version of the full NDA known as a 505(b)(2) application.
- The abbreviated new drug application (ANDA) (that is, the approval for "generic drugs").

An over-the-counter (OTC) drug may come to market without requiring pre-market review if the product meets the conditions outlined in a monograph.

### Exceptions

The FDA has exceptions intended to speed the requisite approval, including expedited review and accelerated approval. Examples include Subpart E, Subpart H, Fast Track, Priority Review

UNITED STATES

and Breakthrough Therapy Designation. FDA also has a well-established compassionate use program (*see Question 2*).

## 2. DO ANY TYPES OF NAMED PATIENT AND/OR COMPASSIONATE USE PROGRAMMES OPERATE? IF SO, WHAT ARE THE REQUIREMENTS FOR PRE-LAUNCH ACCESS?

The Food and Drug Administration's (FDA) compassionate use programme includes:

- Expanded access for individual patients, including in emergencies.
- Expanded access for intermediate-size patient populations (smaller than those typical of a treatment for an Investigational New Drug (IND) (*see Question 3*) or treatment protocol).
- Expanded access treatment for an IND or treatment protocol.

For all three types of expanded access, the programme must meet the following general criteria:

- The patient or patients to be treated have a serious or immediately life-threatening disease or condition, and there is no comparable or satisfactory alternative therapy to diagnose, monitor, or treat the disease or condition.
- The potential patient benefit justifies the potential risks of the treatment use and those potential risks are not unreasonable in the context of the disease or condition to be treated.
- Providing the investigational drug for the requested use will not interfere with the initiation, conduct, or completion of clinical investigations that could support marketing approval of the expanded access use or otherwise compromise the potential development of the expanded access use.

Each subcategory has additional requirements.

## LICENSING

## 3. WHAT IS THE PROCEDURAL STRUCTURE REGARDING LICENSING A DRUG FOR DISTRIBUTION?

The Food and Drug Administration (FDA) is responsible for drug approval (*see Question 1*). As part of the full new drug application (NDA), the company must provide pre-clinical and clinical data to support the safety and efficacy of the new drug. The FDA's Investigational New Drug (IND) procedures allow a company to investigate an unapproved drug in humans. If the FDA does not comment within 30 days after the submission of an IND, the sponsor may initiate the clinical trial proposed in the IND. The FDA can order the discontinuation of a clinical trial at any time, or impose other sanctions, if it believes that the clinical trial either is not being conducted in accordance with FDA regulatory requirements or presents an unacceptable risk to the clinical trial patients.

Clinical trials to support NDAs for marketing approval are typically conducted in three phases:

- **Phase 1.** This involves the introduction of the drug into healthy human subjects or patients.
- **Phase 2.** This usually involves trials in a limited patient population to determine the effectiveness of the drug for a particular indication, dosage tolerance, and best dosage, and to identify common adverse effects and safety risks.
- **Phase 3.** These trials obtain additional information about clinical efficacy and safety in a larger number of patients, typically at geographically dispersed clinical trial sites, to permit the FDA to evaluate the overall benefit-risk relationship of the drug and to provide

adequate information for the labelling of the drug. The FDA typically requires two adequate and well-controlled Phase 3 clinical trials to demonstrate the efficacy of the drug.

After completion of the required clinical testing, an NDA is prepared and submitted to FDA. The NDA must include the following types of information:

- A summary that includes a general understanding of the application, and the drug type and rationale.
- Chemistry manufacturing and controls information including information on the drug substance and drug product.
- Non-clinical data that includes pharmacology/toxicology studies and a statement of compliance with Good Laboratory Practices.
- Pharmacokinetics and bioavailability in humans' data.
- A description of the statistical analysis.
- Required paediatric information.
- Clinical data.
- Case report forms.
- Patent information.
- Certifications.

The FDA has 60 days from its receipt of an NDA to determine whether the agency will accept the application for filing based on the agency's threshold determination that the application is sufficiently complete to permit substantive review. Once the submission is accepted for filing, the FDA begins an in-depth review. The FDA has agreed to certain performance goals in the review of NDAs. Most applications for standard review drug products are reviewed within ten to 12 months; most applications for priority review drugs are reviewed in six to eight months. The FDA can extend these reviews by three months. Priority review can be applied to drugs that the FDA determines offer major advances in treatment, or provide a treatment where no adequate therapy exists.

The FDA may refer applications to an advisory committee (a panel that includes clinicians and other experts) for review, evaluation, and a recommendation as to whether the FDA should approve the application. The FDA is not bound by the recommendation of an advisory committee, but it usually follows such recommendations. Before approving an NDA, the FDA will typically inspect one or more clinical sites to assure compliance with good clinical practices and will inspect the facility or the facilities at which the drug is manufactured to ensure satisfactory compliance with current good manufacturing practices (GMPs), a quality system regulating manufacturing.

A 505(b)(2) application is a hybrid between the full NDA and the abbreviated new drug application (ANDA). It relies on published studies and/or the FDA's previous safety and effectiveness findings. The sponsor of a 505(b)(2) application must establish a scientific "bridge" to the product that was the subject of the previously-approved NDA, which generally includes comparative bioavailability information. Meanwhile, for an ANDA, safety and efficacy are presumed if the generic drug is shown to be "the same as" the reference-listed drug including:

- Active ingredient(s).
- Dosage form.
- Strength.
- Route of administration.
- Conditions of use (labelling).

## 4. IS THERE A SIMPLIFIED LICENCE PROCEEDING, OR RELAXED LICENSING CONDITIONS, FOR DRUGS WHICH HAVE ALREADY BEEN LICENSED FOR DISTRIBUTION IN ANOTHER JURISDICTION?

There are no such simplified proceedings for drugs that have already been licensed for distribution in another jurisdiction. Nor is there a simplified procedure for parallel imports. However, there is an exemption that allows for the importation of a limited supply of a drug that is not approved in the United States for that individual's personal use.

## 5. IS VIRTUAL DRUG DISTRIBUTION POSSIBLE FROM YOUR JURISDICTION?

There is no such pathway within the United States. For products not manufactured in the United States and not distributed in the United States, there is no need for any authorisation. The strict regulatory and legal framework in the United States surrounding the distribution of drugs would make the attempt to obtain authorisation when the product will not be manufactured or distributed in the United States impractical.

## 6. WHAT IS THE PROCEDURE TO APPEAL (LEGAL REMEDY) A LICENSING DECISION?

The FDA must find that the full new drug application (NDA) contains data that provides substantial evidence that the drug is safe and effective in the studied indication before it will issue an approval letter. If the FDA decides not to issue an approval letter, it will issue a complete response letter that outlines the deficiencies in the submission including possibly substantial additional testing, or information, needed for the FDA to reconsider the application. Sponsors may appeal using one of several mechanisms, including FDA's Formal Dispute Resolution process.

## 7. WHAT ARE THE COSTS OF OBTAINING LICENSING?

The costs of obtaining approval of a full new drug application (NDA) are substantial and include the costs of pre-clinical and clinical testing, preparing and submitting the NDA, responding to any Food and Drug Administration (FDA) questions during the review of the NDA, preparation for an advisory committee meeting if the FDA decides to convene such a meeting, and preparation for any FDA pre-approval inspections. Submission of most NDAs is additionally subject to a substantial application user fee, currently exceeding US$2,335,000, and the manufacturer and/or sponsor under an approved new drug application are also subject to annual product and establishment user fees, currently exceeding US$110,000 per product and US$569,000 per establishment. These fees are typically increased annually.

## DISTRIBUTION TO CONSUMERS

## 8. WHAT ARE THE DIFFERENT CATEGORIES OF DRUGS FOR DISTRIBUTION?

There are two general categories of drug products that can be provided to consumers:

- Prescription drugs, which include controlled and non-controlled substances.
- Over-the-counter or non-prescription drugs (OTC). OTC drugs are generally defined as drugs that are safe and effective for use by the general public without the need for supervision by a healthcare practitioner and therefore without a prescription.

The federal Controlled Substances Act (CSA) defines a controlled substance as "a drug or other substance, or immediate precursor, included in schedule I, II, III, IV, or V [in the CSA or implementing regulations]". Drugs are included in schedules I to V based upon their history or potential for abuse and scientific evidence. Drugs included in schedule I have a high potential for abuse with no accepted medical use in the US. Drugs included in schedule II have a high potential for abuse, but there is a medically accepted use in the US. Drugs listed in schedules III-V have a lower potential for abuse (though still may be addictive), and they are used for medically accepted purposes in the US.

## 9. WHO IS AUTHORISED TO DISTRIBUTE PRESCRIPTION DRUGS AND OVER-THE-COUNTER DRUGS TO CONSUMERS?

### Prescription drugs

The preparation, packaging, labelling, record keeping, and transfer of a prescription drug to a patient or intermediary responsible for providing the drug to the patient is considered drug dispensing, which is generally part of the practice of pharmacy. The practice of pharmacy is primarily regulated by the states rather than the federal government. States generally limit the practice of pharmacy to licensed pharmacists and pharmacies. Therefore, licensed pharmacists (including those authorised to work under the supervision of a pharmacist) and pharmacies can provide prescription drugs directly to consumers. In most states, healthcare practitioners (such as physicians) licensed to prescribe or administer prescription drugs can also dispense them to patients under certain conditions. In addition, any healthcare practitioner, pharmacist, pharmacy, or other entity that dispenses controlled substances is required to obtain a registration from the United States Drug Enforcement Administration (DEA) and the appropriate state regulatory authority. Some states have restrictions or requirements on the dispensing of controlled substances in addition to the DEA's restrictions and requirements.

### Over-the-counter drugs

Generally, there are no licensing or registration requirements to distribute over-the-counter (OTC) drugs to consumers in the United States. However, some states require retail outlets providing OTC drugs to consumers to obtain a retail drug dispensing licence. In addition, some OTC drugs have dispensing restrictions. For example, OTC products containing ephedrine, pseudoephedrine, or phenylpropanolamine have federal daily sales limits of 3.6g per purchaser and 30-day purchase limits of 9g as described in the Combat Methamphetamine Epidemic Act of 2005.

## 10. WHAT DRUGS CAN AN ATTENDING PHYSICIAN DISTRIBUTE AND UNDER WHAT CIRCUMSTANCES?

The dispensing of drug products to patients is primarily regulated by the states rather than the Food and Drug Administration (FDA) (*see Question 9*). The vast majority of states allow physicians to dispense and/or administer prescription and over-the-counter (OTC) drugs, as well as controlled substances, to their patients as long as they are properly licensed to do so.

## 11. WHO IS AUTHORISED TO PRESCRIBE PRESCRIPTION DRUGS TO CONSUMERS?

States, rather than the federal government, generally regulate healthcare practitioners, including their prescribing authority. As such, the states determine which practitioners can prescribe drugs. Every state permits licensed physicians to prescribe drugs, but state law can vary widely with respect to the prescribing authority of other healthcare practitioners. Generally, in addition to licensed physicians, licensed physician assistants, nurse practitioners, and advanced registered nurse practitioners can prescribe drugs to patients. It should be noted that any healthcare practitioner that is entitled to prescribe controlled substances under state law must also have a valid Drug Enforcement Administration (DEA) registration before doing so. Federal and state law forbids a licensed practitioner from prescribing a controlled substance to a patient without a legitimate medical purpose and outside of the usual course of professional practice.

## 12. IS DIRECT MAILING/DISTANCE SELLING OF DRUGS PERMITTED IN YOUR JURISDICTION?

**Conditions**

The selling and dispensing of drugs via the mail and/or the internet is generally permitted in the US. For prescription drugs and controlled substances, there must be a valid prescription issued based on an established doctor-patient relationship. As discussed in *Question 9*, states regulate the practice of pharmacy, and the vast majority of states allow out-of-state pharmacies to dispense drugs to their residents through the mail and the internet as long as they are properly licensed. Every state requires pharmacies located within the state to be licensed, and the vast majority of states require out-of-state pharmacies dispensing drugs to consumers in their state to be licensed as well. As such, in order to dispense drugs to customers located outside the state where the pharmacy is based, a pharmacy must be licensed in both its home state as well as the state into which it is dispensing drugs. For example, a pharmacy located in Maryland can dispense drugs to patients in California as long as it holds a pharmacy licence from both the Maryland and California boards of pharmacy. It should be noted that a pharmacy dispensing controlled substances to customers located in another state must also be registered with the Drug Enforcement Administration (DEA) as well as applicable state authorities.

**Cross-border sales**

In order to ship drug products outside of the country, an entity must comply with Food and Drug Administration (FDA) export requirements. Exporting a drug requires that the drug must:

- Comply with the specifications of the foreign purchaser.
- Not be in conflict with the laws of the country where it is being exported to.
- Have a shipping package labelled for export.
- Not be sold or offered for sale in domestic commerce.

In addition, any entity seeking to export controlled substances from the United States must comply with DEA requirements. This includes obtaining an export permit or filing a declaration with the DEA depending upon the drug's schedule and complying with the necessary record keeping requirements. Generally, prescriptions cannot be filled for foreign patients.

# UNITED STATES

### 13. WHAT REGULATORY AUTHORITY IS RESPONSIBLE FOR SUPERVISING DISTRIBUTION ACTIVITIES?

The government agencies primarily responsible for regulating the dispensing of drugs to patients are the state boards of pharmacy or similar state authorities. Other state agencies can also be involved to the extent that other healthcare practitioners (such as physicians and nurses) dispense drugs. The dispensing of controlled substances is regulated by the Drug Enforcement Administration (DEA) at the federal level, and some states also have controlled substance regulatory authorities separate from their boards of pharmacy that are responsible for regulating the dispensing of controlled substances in that state.

### 14. WHAT IS THE PROCEDURE TO APPEAL (LEGAL REMEDY) A DISTRIBUTION DECISION?

The ability to appeal an adverse decision by a state agency varies by state, but dispensing entities can generally seek administrative and/or judicial appeals of adverse decisions. Entities aggrieved by administrative decisions by the Drug Enforcement Administration (DEA) can seek judicial review of such decisions.

### 15. WHAT ARE THE LEGAL CONSEQUENCES OF NON-COMPLIANCE WITH CONSUMER DISTRIBUTION LAWS?

Penalties for violating state laws related to drug dispensing vary depending on the state, but they may include a suspension, revocation, or denial of the pharmacy/professional healthcare licence, administrative fines, civil penalties, injunctions, or criminal penalties. If the Drug Enforcement Administration (DEA) determines that a pharmacy or healthcare practitioner is not operating in compliance with the Controlled Substances Act (CSA) or implementing regulations, it can seek to suspend, revoke, or deny a registration, and registrants can request an administrative hearing. The DEA can also impose civil penalties of up to US$10,000 or US$25,000 per violation, seek an injunction, or pursue criminal charges if applicable.

## WHOLESALE DISTRIBUTION

### 16. WHAT IS THE LEGAL REGIME REGARDING WHOLESALE DISTRIBUTION OF DRUGS?

**Federal prescription drug wholesale distribution requirements**

The Drug Supply Chain Security Act of 2013 (DSCSA) amended the Federal Food, Drug & Cosmetic Act (FDC Act) and governs the wholesale distribution of prescription drugs.

The DSCSA defines wholesale distribution as the "distribution of a drug...to a person other than a consumer or patient, or receipt of a drug...by a person other than the consumer or patient". A wholesale distributor is "a person (other than a manufacturer, a manufacturer's co-licensed partner, a third-party logistics provider, or repackager) engaged in wholesale distribution".

The DSCSA prohibits any person from engaging in wholesale distribution without:

- A licence in the state from which the prescription drugs are distributed (or from FDA if the state does not require a licence).
- A licence from any state in which the prescription drugs are distributed if the state requires a licence.

As applied to wholesale distributors, the DSCSA has several key provisions:

- It limits wholesale distributors of prescription drugs to transactions only between authorised trading partners that are appropriately licenced under federal and state law.
- It creates new drug-tracing requirements (also referred to as "track-and-trace") under which a wholesale distributor can only receive and transfer ownership of prescription drugs when the product is accompanied by certain product-tracing information, including the product's transaction history and transaction information, as well as a transaction statement. This product-tracing provision pre-empts all state pedigree requirements, including those enacted under the direction of the Prescription Drug Marketing Act of 1987 (PDMA).
- Wholesale distributors must report their licensing status and contact information to the Food and Drug Administration (FDA) on an annual basis.
- Wholesale distributors must put in place a system of:
  - verifying the legitimacy of all prescription drug products that they receive;
  - dealing with suspect and illegitimate product; and
  - properly notifying the FDA and appropriate trading partners.
- Finally, the DSCSA charges the FDA with instituting new minimum standards for the handling of prescription drugs by wholesale distributors to replace the current set of minimum standards introduced under the PDMA. As the FDA has until 27 November 2015 to promulgate such regulations but (as at the time of printing of this chapter) has yet to do so, the FDA's regulations under the PDMA set the current minimum standards that each state must create in order to licence a wholesale distributor (*see below*).

The FDA's regulations under the PDMA set out minimum required standards that states must comply with during the licensing process, as well as minimum qualifications wholesale distributors must meet in order to receive a state licence. Such minimum requirements for obtaining a licence include, but are not limited to:

- Name and contact information for the entity.
- Type of ownership.
- Names of the owners/operators of a facility.
- No convictions relating to drug samples or the distribution of prescription drugs or controlled substances.
- No felony convictions.
- Past experience in the manufacture or distribution of prescription drugs.
- No suspension or revocation of government licences related to the manufacture or distribution of prescription drugs.
- Compliance with the record keeping requirements under PDMA.

Once a state licence is obtained, a wholesale distributor must comply with the following minimum standards regarding personnel, security, storage and handling, recordkeeping, examination of products, and written policies and procedures.

**Personnel.** Wholesale distributors must employ personnel who have the appropriate education and/or experience to assume responsibility for compliance with state licensing requirements.

**Security.** All distribution facilities must be kept secure from unauthorised entry. This includes a well-lit perimeter and an alarm system. Additionally, access to prescription drugs must be limited to authorised personnel.

**Storage and handling.** The PDMA and associate regulations specify minimum standards for facilities that handle prescription drugs to ensure that they are stored under appropriate lighting, ventilation, temperature, sanitation, humidity, space, and equipment conditions.

**Record keeping.** Wholesale distributors must maintain records on all transactions, such as the identity, quantity, and dates of drugs received, distributed, and disposed of. Inventories and records must also be maintained and made available for inspection by government authorities for a period of three years. Records of temperature, thefts, losses and discrepancies must also be maintained.

**Examination of product.** All incoming shipments must be visually examined to identify products that are damaged, contaminated, or otherwise unfit for distribution. Outgoing drugs must be inspected to ensure they are accurately identified and have not been damaged in storage.

**Written policies and procedures.** Wholesalers must establish, maintain and adhere to written policies and procedures throughout the distribution process. This includes policies and procedures for the receipt, security, storage, inventory and distribution of drug products, as well as the reporting of thefts/losses.

The new regulations set to be established by the FDA before the end of 2015 will also require minimum standards for the states regarding the furnishing of a bond, mandatory background checks and fingerprinting of facility managers or designated representatives, mandatory physical inspections of facilities, and prohibitions of certain persons from maintaining a licence for wholesale distribution.

### Federal controlled substances wholesale distribution requirements

The distribution of prescription drugs that are classified as controlled substances under the Controlled Substances Act (CSA) and its implementing regulations are regulated by the Drug Enforcement Administration (DEA). Wholesale distributors of controlled substances must comply with registration, record keeping, reporting, and security requirements that vary depending on drug schedules, as discussed below.

**Registration.** Each facility that distributes or otherwise handles controlled substances must obtain a registration from the DEA specific to each activity and geographic location. The facility is only authorised to handle a drug in the schedules identified on its application for registration, which may be modified to add additional schedules. Additionally, a DEA manufacturing registration is required if the facility repackages or re-labels controlled substances.

**Records.** There are significant record-keeping requirements involved with the distribution of controlled substances. A registered facility must maintain a record of the quantity, location, and identification of the customer of all controlled substance distributions. Wholesale distributors must also maintain complete and accurate records of every controlled substance received, manufactured, and distributed or disposed of, as well as of certain List I chemicals. Each registered facility must maintain records for schedule I-II drugs separately from schedule III-V drugs.

**Inventories.** Every wholesale distributor must take a physical inventory of all controlled substances before engaging in distribution. Wholesale distributors must also take an inventory of all controlled substances every two years and maintain separate inventories of schedule I-II drugs from schedule III-V drugs.

**Reports.** A wholesale distributor must notify the DEA of any theft or significant loss upon discovery, and reporting in-transit losses is the supplier's responsibility. Additionally, distributors must report "suspicious orders", which include orders of unusual size, orders that deviate from the normal patterns, or orders of unusual frequency, and notify the DEA regarding the intended destruction of controlled substances (for example, damaged goods, returns).

**Security.** Wholesale distributors of schedule I and II drugs must store them in a safe, steel cabinet, or a vault, depending on the amount. Wholesale distributors of schedule III, IV, and V controlled substances must store such drugs in a safe, steel cabinet, vault, cage, or other secure enclosure as defined in the DEA regulations. In addition to physical security, the DEA requires electronic security for all storage areas. Other required security can include:

- Secure fencing around receiving, order picking and packaging areas;
- Key, pass code, or combination lock controls.
- On-site guard force.
- Local police protection.
- Employee screening and restriction is also required.

**State wholesale drug distribution requirements**

Although the DSCSA and PDMA establish minimum requirements for wholesale distributors of prescription drugs, many states have created their own requirements.

Many states have essentially adopted the federal requirements for distributors regarding personnel, security, storage, and record keeping, but most states license wholesale distribution facilities located within and outside of the state. The timeframe for obtaining state wholesale distributor licenses varies significantly from state to state. It should be noted that, while federal requirements only apply to the wholesale distribution of prescription drugs, some states enforce licensing requirements for the distribution of over-the-counter (OTC) drugs as well.

In addition to requiring wholesale distributors of prescription drugs to be licensed, several states also require distributors of controlled substances to obtain an additional registration. In those states, wholesale distributors of controlled substances (which are, by definition, also prescription drugs) must obtain a distributor licence as well as a state controlled substance registration. State controlled substance registrations are typically not difficult to obtain, provided that the wholesale distributor has a drug distributor licence in that state and a DEA registration. Most states have adopted the DEA's requirements regarding record keeping, inventories, security and reports for controlled substances distributors, but some states have developed additional requirements.

**17. WHAT REGULATORY AUTHORITY IS RESPONSIBLE FOR SUPERVISING WHOLESALE DISTRIBUTION ACTIVITIES?**

**Federal agencies.** The Food and Drug Administration (FDA) and Drug Enforcement Administration (DEA) are the federal agencies generally responsible for regulating the wholesale distribution of prescription drugs, including controlled substances. See *Question 16*.

**State agencies.** Each state is responsible for licensing and monitoring wholesale drug distributors operating in that state. See *Question 16*.

The state agency responsible for regulating wholesale distributors is usually the board of pharmacy, but that may vary depending on the state.

In some states, the same agency regulates distributors of both prescription drugs and controlled substances while those responsibilities are divided among different agencies in other states.

## 18. WHAT ARE THE LEGAL CONSEQUENCES OF NON-COMPLIANCE WITH WHOLESALE DISTRIBUTION LAWS?

Under the Drug Supply Chain Security Act of 2013 (DSCSA), no entity can operate as a drug wholesaler in the US unless it is licensed by the appropriate state(s).

Therefore, operating as a prescription drug wholesaler without the proper state licence can result in imprisonment of up to 10 years, a fine of up to US$250,000, or both. Other violations of requirements discussed in *Question 16* can result in up to a one-year prison sentence, a US$1,000 fine, or both. If a wholesaler violates a requirement with the intent to defraud or mislead, the potential penalty increases to a prison sentence of up to three years, a fine of up to US$10,000, or both. The Food and Drug Administration (FDA) can also seek an injunction against the wholesaler to prevent the activity at issue. A wholesaler can appeal adverse penalties through the courts.

The Drug Enforcement Administration (DEA) is the federal agency that registers wholesaler distributors of controlled substances, and no entity can operate as a wholesaler of controlled substances in the United States without a registration. If the DEA determines that a wholesaler is not operating in compliance with the Controlled Substances Act (CSA) or related regulations, it can seek to suspend, revoke, or deny a registration, and a registrant can contest such action through an administrative hearing. The DEA can also impose civil penalties of up to US$25,000 per violation, seek an injunction, or pursue criminal charges if applicable. Wholesalers can seek judicial review of any adverse decisions.

Penalties for violating state laws related to drug wholesale distribution vary depending on the state, but they can include a suspension, revocation, or denial of the wholesale licence, administrative fines, civil penalties, injunctions, or criminal penalties. The ability to appeal an adverse decision varies by state as well, but wholesalers can generally seek administrative and/or judicial appeals of adverse decisions.

# MARKETING

### PROMOTION

## 19. WHAT IS THE GENERAL LEGAL REGIME FOR THE MARKETING OF DRUGS?

The Food and Drug Administration (FDA) regulates the labelling and the advertising of prescription drugs. In addition, healthcare fraud and abuse laws including the federal anti-kickback statute and False Claims Act prevent certain marketing and promotional activities.

The Federal Food, Drug & Cosmetic Act (FDC Act) lists a number of "prohibited acts", for which penalties can be assessed. Introducing a drug in interstate commerce that is "misbranded" is a prohibited act. A drug is misbranded if, among other things, its labelling is false and misleading in any particular way. Labelling consists of "written, printed, or graphic matter" on or "accompanying" a drug. The material does not physically need to accompany the drug or device to be labelling. Labelling includes quotations by physicians or other third parties about drug products if made on behalf of the drug company. Although the statute refers to "written, printed, or graphic" materials, the FDA considers labelling to also include oral statements, which can include:

- Speeches by company officials.
- Statements by sales representatives.
- Presentations or discussions at trade shows.
- Speeches at certain Continuing Medical Education (CME) or other third party programmes.

As discussed above, the FDA approves a drug for a specific intended use. According to FDA regulations, a product's intended use is based on the "objective intent" of the manufacturer. A drug can be misbranded if it lacks adequate directions for use, and if a drug's intended use is for an off-label use, the FDA deems the drug to be misbranded under this section.

When the FDA approves a new drug application (NDA), it approves a package insert (PI). The sponsor can promote information that relates to, and is consistent with, the FDA-approved PI, which must include the indication and can include information about the drug's mechanism of action, clinical results, pharmacology, special populations, dosing, and safety information. The promotional materials must provide "fair balance", that is present information regarding both risks and benefits of the product presented in the material. All printed promotional labelling must be accompanied by the approved PI for the drug.

The FDC Act states that advertisements include those published in journals, magazines, other periodicals, and newspapers, and broadcast through media such as radio, television, and telephone communications systems. This list is illustrative and not exhaustive. Drug advertisements must contain a brief summary of the drug's risk information. A "brief summary" is a summary of the drug's side effects, warnings, precautions contraindications, cautions, special considerations, important notes, and effectiveness.

As for healthcare fraud and abuse laws, under the federal anti-kickback statute, it is a felony for a manufacturer of a prescription drug to offer anything of value to anyone if one purpose of the offer is to induce the person to:

- Purchase or order a product.
- Arrange for or recommend the purchase or order of a product covered under a federal health care program.

Many states have comparable anti-kickback statutes.

The False Claims Act (FCA) prohibits knowingly:

- Presenting or causing to be presented a false claim for payment.
- Using or causing to be used a false record or statement to get a false claim paid.

The FCA includes a *"qui tam"* provision that allows a whistle blower known as a relator to sue on behalf of him or herself and the government. A claim submitted for items or services, the provision of which resulted from a violation of the anti-kickback statute, is false under the FCA. Many states also have false claims acts.

In addition, the Federal Physician Payment Sunshine provisions of the Affordable Care Act require disclosure of certain promotional activities to the federal government starting in 2013. The Centers for Medicare & Medicaid Services (CMS), a sister agency of FDA, implements these provisions and recently finalised a regulation implementing that requirement. The first reports were due in 2014. On 30 September 2014, CMS posted the first round of data in searchable form on a public website. Failure to submit the required information can result in civil monetary penalties.

## 20. ARE THERE OTHER CODES OF CONDUCT FOR THE MARKETING OF DRUGS (FOR EXAMPLE, BY PROFESSIONAL OR INDUSTRIAL ORGANISATIONS)?

The Pharmaceutical Research and Manufacturers of America (PhRMA), the industry group that represents brand-name drug manufacturers, has published a Code on Interactions with Healthcare Providers (HCPs).

The Code includes the following limitations:

- No entertainment or recreational events for HCPs.
- Modest meals involving HCP can be offered as part of an educational programme or detail and can be held only in HCP's office or hospital by sales representatives.
- Consulting agreements must be bona fide.
- Consultant meetings/advisory boards cannot be held at resort locations.
- A drug manufacturer can occasionally give items of less than US$100 for education of HCP or patients.
- No practice-related items such as pens or flash drives.
- No gifts for personal benefit of HCP (floral arrangements, artwork, CDs, golf balls, tickets to sporting events).

Although the PhRMA Code is technically a voluntary code, the Department of Health and Human Services, Office of Inspector General has identified the Code as a minimum standard. Furthermore, a handful of states require that drug manufacturers adopt a compliance code that is at least as stringent as the PhRMA Code. In addition, certain states have directly adopted as law some of the provisions in the code, for instance gift prohibitions. Moreover, other states have adopted provisions more conservative than the code. For example, Massachusetts does not allow any meals outside a healthcare setting, and Vermont does not permit any meals.

## MARKETING TO CONSUMERS

## 21. WHAT IS THE LEGAL REGIME FOR MARKETING TO CONSUMERS?

The legal regime with respect to promoting and to consumers is generally the same as described in *Question 19*. There are no products that categorically cannot be advertised to consumers. All materials must be in consumer-friendly language. In addition, as described in *Question 19*, there are specific requirements pertaining to broadcast advertisements.

## 22. WHAT KINDS OF MARKETING ACTIVITIES ARE PERMITTED IN RELATION TO CONSUMERS AND THE PRODUCTS WHICH MAY BE ADVERTISED TO THEM?

The kinds of marketing activities permitted with regard to consumers and the products which might be advertised to them are generally the same as those for professionals. (*see Question 27*).

### 23. IS IT PERMITTED TO PROVIDE CONSUMERS WITH FREE SAMPLES? ARE THERE PARTICULAR RESTRICTIONS ON SPECIAL OFFERS (FOR EXAMPLE, "BUY-ONE-GET-ONE-FREE")?

Drug manufacturers can provide free samples of prescription drugs to physicians, under certain circumstances, who then have the right to provide those samples to their patients. The Prescription Drug Marketing Act of 1987 (PDMA) imposes certain record keeping and reporting requirements on the distribution of samples.

With certain exceptions, the anti-kickback act prevents the provision of items of value, including samples of product covered by federal healthcare programs, so the drug manufacturers cannot bill federal health care programmes for the samples (*see Question 19*). Drug manufacturers can establish patient assistance programmes if programmes abide by certain terms. They can also provide discounts and coupons for prescription drugs under certain circumstances.

### 24. ARE THERE PARTICULAR RULES OF PRACTICE ON THE USE OF THE INTERNET/SOCIAL MEDIA REGARDING DRUGS AND THEIR ADVERTISING?

There are no specific rules/codes of practice on the use of the internet/social media in respect of drugs and advertising. The Food and Drug Administration (FDA) considers product information posted on the internet to be labelling or advertising and restrictions apply, such as no off-label promotion and including fair balance.

In June 2014, the FDA published two draft guidance notes related to social media. It published guidance on how drug manufacturers can achieve fair balance on the internet or social media platforms with character space limitations. It also published guidance on correcting independent third-party information about drugs.

### 25. WHAT REGULATORY AUTHORITY IS RESPONSIBLE AUTHORITY IS RESPONSIBLE FOR SUPERVISING MARKETING ACTIVITIES TO CONSUMERS?

The Food and Drug Administration (FDA) regulates the labelling and the advertising of prescription drugs. For over-the-counter drugs, the FDA has jurisdiction over labelling, but the Federal Trade Commission has jurisdiction over advertising. The Office of Inspector General has jurisdiction over exclusions under the anti-kickback act, and the state attorneys general, acting in concert with the Department of Justice, can bring litigation under the False Claims Act (FCA).

### 26. WHAT ARE THE LEGAL CONSEQUENCES OF NON-COMPLIANCE WITH CONSUMER MARKETING LAWS?

The performance of a prohibited act under the Federal Food, Drug & Cosmetic Act (FDC Act) can result in untitled or warning letters, civil fines, seizure, injunction, and jail time.

The Food and Drug Administration (FDA) can issue untitled or warning letters on its own initiative. The Department of Justice (DOJ) brings actions such as seizure or injunction on behalf of the FDA.

Penalties under the anti-kickback act include jail time, criminal monetary penalties and exclusion from participation in all health care programs. The False Claims Act (FCA) allows for the recovery of US$5,500 to US$11,000 per claim plus three times the amount in damages.

## MARKETING TO PROFESSIONALS

### 27. WHAT KINDS OF MARKETING ACTIVITIES ARE PERMITTED IN RELATION TO PROFESSIONALS?

Drug manufacturers can promote their prescription drugs to professionals in accordance with their Food and Drug Administration-approved package insert (PI) in multiple venues including educational conferences, journal advertisements, trade conferences and webinars and so on.

### 28. ARE THERE ANY RESTRICTIONS ON MARKETING TO PROFESSIONALS?

**Marketing activities**

The dissemination of journal reprints has been a controversial topic in the United States that has not been entirely resolved. In *Washington Legal Foundation v Friedman* (13 F. Supp. 2d 51 (D.D.C. 1988)), a federal district court judge ruled that the Food and Drug Administration (FDA) could not prohibit the dissemination of truthful and non-misleading reprints of peer-reviewed articles, even if the articles describe off-label uses of the drugs, without violating the First Amendment of the US Constitution. The Court of Appeals vacated the decision without reaching the constitutional issue, leading to uncertainty.

In addition, in the more recent cases of *United States v Caronia* (703 F.3d 149 (2d 2012)), and *Amarin Pharma, Inc. v US Food & Drug Administration* (No. 15-CIV-3588 (S.D.N.Y. Aug. 7, 2015)), some federal courts in one federal jurisdiction have held that the dissemination of truthful and non-misleading information is protected by the First Amendment.

The FDA published draft guidance on good reprint practices in March 2015. Provision of and types of gifts have all been allegations in False Claims Act (FCA) or anti-kickback actions. In addition, as discussed in *see Question 20* above, the Pharmaceutical Research and Manufacturers of America (PhRMA) Code prohibits provision to Healthcare Professionals (HCPs) of all non-educational items, and even for educational items, there is a limit of less than US$100. In addition, certain states either have a code similar to the PhRMA Code or have adopted certain of the prohibitions directly into their laws (*see Question 20*). In addition, the Sunshine provisions of the Affordable Care Act require disclosure of certain promotional activities to the federal government.

**Frequency**

There are restrictions in terms of provision of items of value to healthcare professionals (*see Question 20*). In certain instances the Department of Justice (DOJ) and the state attorneys general have cited detailing practices as evidence of off-label promotion, that is, if the sales representatives are only detailing practices that specialise in medical areas not included in the package insert (PI). In addition, the FDA considers statements made by sales representatives to be labelling subject to FDA jurisdiction.

**Provision of hospitality**

The PhRMA code establishes several restrictions such as not allowing entertainment and limiting meals (*Question 20*). As previously discussed, several states either require adoption by companies of a code that is very similar to the PhRMA code or have incorporated into law

UNITED STATES

restrictions on the provision of hospitality. Also note that meals must be disclosed pursuant to the Sunshine provisions of the Affordable Care Act.

### 29. WHAT INFORMATION IS IT LEGALLY REQUIRED TO INCLUDE IN ADVERTISING TO PROFESSIONALS?

Information that is legally required includes a "brief summary" and "fair balance". For the concepts of the brief summary and fair balance for prescription drugs, see *Questions 19* and *24*. The package insert (PI) must be included (*see Question 19*).

### 30. ARE THERE RULES ON COMPARISONS WITH OTHER PRODUCTS THAT ARE PARTICULARLY APPLICABLE TO DRUGS?

A drug manufacturer must possess substantial evidence to make claims that its product is better or superior to another drug. Substantial evidence consists of two adequate well-controlled trials.

### 31. WHAT OTHER ITEMS, FUNDING OR SERVICES ARE PERMITTED TO BE PROVIDED TO PROFESSIONALS?

**Discounts**

Discounts for prescription drugs covered under federal health programmes are permitted under a "safe harbour" to the anti-kickback act if the following conditions are met:

- Reporting obligations for the buyer, seller and offeror.
- The buyer's requirements depend on the type of provider.
- The seller must fully report a discount on the invoice, coupon, or statement to the buyer, and inform the buyer of its obligation to report.
- Maintain a paper trail.
- Documentation that will permit accurate reporting to federal programmes.

**Free samples**

It is permitted to provide professionals with free samples if the conditions of the Prescription Drug Marketing Act of 1987 (PDMA) are followed and the company does not bill federal healthcare programmes for the samples. See *Question 23*.

### 32. WHAT REGULATORY AUTHORITY IS RESPONSIBLE FOR SUPERVISING MARKETING ACTIVITIES REGARDING PROFESSIONALS?

See *Question 25*.

### 33. WHAT ARE THE LEGAL CONSEQUENCES IN CASE OF NON-COMPLIANCE WITH PROFESSIONAL MARKETING LAWS?

See *Question 26*.

# ENGAGEMENT WITH PATIENT ORGANISATIONS

**34. WHAT KINDS OF ACTIVITIES ARE PERMITTED IN RELATION TO ENGAGEMENT WITH PATIENT ORGANISATIONS? WHAT ARE THE RESTRICTIONS THAT ARE IMPOSED ON RELATIONSHIP WITH PATIENT ORGANISATIONS?**

The activities permitted are the same as those for consumers.

# REFORM

**35. ARE THERE ANY PLANS TO REFORM THE LAW ON THE DISTRIBUTION AND PROMOTION OF DRUGS IN YOUR JURISDICTION?**

See *Question 16* regarding state prescription drug requirements.

# VIETNAM

*Tu Ngoc Trinh and Huong Lan Nguyen, TILLEKE & GIBBINS*

## DISTRIBUTION

### PRE-CONDITIONS FOR DISTRIBUTION

**1. WHAT ARE THE LEGAL PRE-CONDITIONS FOR A DRUG TO BE DISTRIBUTED WITHIN THE JURISDICTION?**

**Authorisation**

In order to be distributed in Vietnam, a drug must have a marketing authorisation (MA) number issued by the Drug Administration of Vietnam (DAV) under the Ministry of Health (MOH). Under the current regulations on drug registration, an MA number for a drug should be issued within six months of the receipt of a complete application dossier. In practice, the timeline for issuance of an MA number for a drug can range from one to two years. Drugs granted MA numbers can be imported into Vietnam without an import licence.

**Exceptions**

Drugs used for certain special purposes can be imported into and distributed in Vietnam without MA numbers if they are granted import licences.

The exceptions include:

- Finished drug products containing active ingredients (with or without MA numbers) which are in insufficient supply for treatment demands.
- Rare drugs and drugs used for the special treatment demands of certain hospitals.
- Drugs used for emergency demands of epidemic prevention or recovering from natural disasters.
- Drugs used for national health target programmes.
- Drugs for aid or humanitarian aid.

**2. DO ANY TYPES OF NAMED PATIENT AND/OR COMPASSIONATE USE PROGRAMMES OPERATE? IF SO, WHAT ARE THE REQUIREMENTS FOR PRE-LAUNCH ACCESS?**

Vietnam has no regulations for named patient or compassionate use programmes. However, there are some special cases in which drugs can be accessed before being granted marketing authorisation (*see Question 1*).

Among the special cases, the grant of an import licence for the following two cases is quite similar to the compassionate use programme in EU countries:

- Finished drug products containing active ingredients (with or without marketing authorisation (MA) numbers) which are in insufficient supply for treatment demands.
- Rare drugs and drugs used for the special treatment demands of certain hospitals.

However, there is no specific definition of which cases will be considered to be in "insufficient supply for treatment demands" or "used for special treatment demands". This depends on the evaluation of the Drug Administration of Vietnam (DAV).

In practice, "insufficient supply for treatment demands" often refers to situations where there is a shortage of drugs having particular active ingredients. A pharmaceutical company can apply for an import licence for its drug if its active ingredient has the potential to be considered as being in "insufficient supply for treatment demands". If this is the case, the drug can be circulated in Vietnam after being granted an import licence, with no accompanying conditions.

In contrast, "used for special treatment demands" often refers to situations of unmet medical needs for certain hospitals. In this case, in addition to the application for an import licence, the pharmaceutical company is required to have confirmation from the concerned hospitals about their unmet medical needs and their request for the specific drug. After granting the import licence, drugs used for special treatment demands are only allowed to be used in the specific hospitals concerned.

**Requirements**

The special case of imported drugs discussed above must satisfy the following minimum conditions:

- The drugs are permitted to be circulated in the manufacturing country by a competent state management agency of that country.
- The drug-manufacturing establishments possess a "Good Manufacturing Practice" certificate granted by a competent state management agency of the manufacturing country.
- Drugs without registration numbers which are new drugs and not entitled to exemption from clinical trials or some stages of clinical trials, but are needed for medical treatment, may be considered for import after clinical trials are completed and all regulations of the Ministry of Health on clinical trials are complied with.

LICENSING

3. WHAT IS THE PROCEDURAL STRUCTURE REGARDING LICENSING A DRUG FOR DISTRIBUTION?

**Structure**

The procedure for registering a drug with the Drug Administration of Vietnam (DAV) consists of four primary steps:

- **Submission of the application dossier.** The application dossier is required to comply with the ASEAN Common Technical Dossier (ACTD) requirements for the registration of pharmaceuticals for human use. In particular, an application dossier for a new drug or biological product registration should include the following parts:

- Part I. Administrative data and product information dossier;
- Part II. Quality dossier;
- Part III. Preclinical dossier; and
- Part IV. Clinical dossier.

However, an application dossier for generic drug registration only needs to include Part I and Part II.

- **Validation and assessment of the application dossier.** An application dossier for drug registration will be examined and evaluated by the Drug Evaluation Council of the DAV, which consists of many technical subcommittees of specialists in several professional aspects relevant to pharmaceutical products. In practice, it may take six to eight months for the DAV to assess an application before issuing any response to the applicant.
- **Requirement for amendment and supplementation of the application dossier.** After the validation and assessment process, the DAV usually issues an official letter requesting the applicant to supplement documents or clarify issues regarding the application dossier. The applicant should prepare and supplement documents in accordance with the DAV's requirements. The DAV should then review the supplementation and explanation from the applicant and issue a decision of approval or refusal within three to five months from the date of submission of the supplementation documents.

In practice, it is rarely the case that an application dossier is approved by the DAV after the initial validation and review process without any request for supplementation.

- **Issuance of registration number.** The DAV will grant a marketing authorisation (MA) specifying the unique registration number for such a drug.

### Regulatory authority

The DAV under the Ministry of Health is responsible for the issuance of MA numbers and the licensing procedure in Vietnam.

### 4. IS THERE A SIMPLIFIED LICENCE PROCEEDING, OR RELAXED LICENSING CONDITIONS, FOR DRUGS WHICH HAVE ALREADY BEEN LICENSED FOR DISTRIBUTION IN ANOTHER JURISDICTION?

In general, the Vietnamese regulations give no priority to drugs already licensed for distribution in another jurisdiction. However, a foreign drug is exempted from clinical trials in Vietnam if the drug is:

- A generic drug.
- A drug from a foreign country which has not yet been issued a registration number for circulation in Vietnam but has been lawfully circulated for at least five years in the country of origin (or in a reference country if this is permitted by an international treaty to which Vietnam is a party) and certified by the competent state authority of such country as safe and effective, having the same route of administration, strength, and indication in Vietnam as in such country.

Parallel import is permitted for drugs with the same brand names, active ingredients, contents, and pharmaceutical form as drugs with valid registration numbers for circulation in Vietnam, when the drug is either:

- In insufficient supply for treatment.
- Currently sold in Vietnam at prices higher than the retail price in the country of origin and/or countries with economic conditions similar to Vietnam.

To obtain a parallel import permit, the importer must satisfy conditions on the quality and price of drugs, and the legal requirements for operating in drug trading in Vietnam.

The importer must submit an application for registration of a parallel import permit to the Drug Administration of Vietnam (DAV). The application dossier must include:

- An application form for parallel import (a standard form set out by the Vietnamese Government).
- An order form for parallel import (a standard form set out by the Vietnamese Government).
- Label samples of the drugs.
- A package insert of the drugs (the original and the Vietnamese translation).

Within 15 working days of the receipt of the complete dossier, the DAV will evaluate and approve the permit, unless the application dossier is insufficient. In this case, the DAV will issue an official letter requesting supplementary documents for clarification.

## 5. IS VIRTUAL DRUG DISTRIBUTION POSSIBLE FROM YOUR JURISDICTION?

Virtual drug distribution is not possible from Vietnam. Vietnam has strict regulations on drug trading and distribution that provide various limitations on the distribution of drugs.

## 6. WHAT IS THE PROCEDURE TO APPEAL (LEGAL REMEDY) A LICENSING DECISION?

The applicant has the right to appeal the decisions, provided that the legal remedy is in accordance with the Vietnam Law on Complaints.

The claimant can carry out its complaints in the form of either a petition or a direct complaint. The first complaint can be carried out to the person or agency issuing the administrative decision. The claimant can also file an administrative suit to the court in accordance with the Law of Administrative Litigation. If the claimant does not agree with the first settlement results or the complaint is not settled within the stipulated time, the claimant has the right to complain to the direct supervisor of the competent person for settlement of the first complaint or can file an administrative suit to the court in accordance with the Law of Administrative Litigation.

## 7. WHAT ARE THE COSTS OF OBTAINING LICENSING?

The government fee for an application dossier depends on the type of drug. There are three fee levels for an application dossier:

- Drugs with a data protection requirement: VND6 million (approximately EUR248).
- Drugs requiring a bioequivalence dossier or clinical dossier: VND5.5 million (approximately EUR227).
- Other drugs: VND4.5 million (approximately EUR186).

## DISTRIBUTION TO CONSUMERS

### 8. WHAT ARE THE DIFFERENT CATEGORIES OF DRUGS FOR DISTRIBUTION?

Drugs for distribution in Vietnam are divided into two categories: prescription drugs and non-prescription drugs.

### 9. WHO IS AUTHORISED TO DISTRIBUTE PRESCRIPTION DRUGS AND OVER-THE-COUNTER DRUGS TO CONSUMERS?

The drug retail establishments entitled to distribute prescription drugs and over-the-counter drugs to consumers include:

- Drugstores.
- Dispensaries.
- Drug sale agents of pharmaceutical companies.
- Drug cabinets of health stations.

In order to lawfully distribute prescription drugs to consumers, a drug retail establishment in one of the above categories must obtain a Good Pharmacy Practice (GPP) Certificate from the provincial Department of Health in which the retailing establishment is located. It must satisfy certain conditions on personnel and infrastructure set out by the Ministry of Health (MOH). Specifically, the owner and/or the person in charge of professional matters must have a Pharmaceutical Practice Certificate; while the seller must have professional certificates in the pharmaceutical domain and a training period suitable for the assigned tasks.

The application dossier for a GPP Certificate includes:

- An application form for the examination of conditions on drug retail pursuant to "Good Pharmacy Practice" standards (a standard form set out by the Vietnamese Government).
- A statement of personnel and infrastructure.
- The GPP self-checklist (a standard form set out by the Vietnamese Government).

The Department of Health should establish an inspection team to examine the retailing establishment within 20 working days of the receipt of a complete application dossier. Within five working days, if no re-examination is required, the Department of Health will issue the GPP Certificate which is valid for three years.

Vietnam has not made any commitments to open pharmaceutical distribution under Vietnam's WTO commitments. Therefore, at present, foreign ownership in the distribution of drugs in Vietnam is still prohibited. However, since 1 January 2009, foreign investors have been permitted to establish a wholly foreign-owned company to import or export pharmaceutical products and sell their imported products to licensed local distributors.

### 10. WHAT DRUGS CAN AN ATTENDING PHYSICIAN DISTRIBUTE AND UNDER WHAT CIRCUMSTANCES?

The Law on Medical Examination and Treatment prohibits medical practitioners from selling drugs to patients in any form.

## VIETNAM

### 11. WHO IS AUTHORISED TO PRESCRIBE PRESCRIPTION DRUGS TO CONSUMERS?

A person who prescribes prescription drugs to consumers must meet the following conditions:

- Practises at a legal medical examination and treatment establishment.
- Holds a bachelor's degree issued by a medical university.
- Is assigned by the head of a medical examination and treatment establishment to carry out medical examination and treatment.

### 12. IS DIRECT MAILING/DISTANCE SELLING OF DRUGS PERMITTED IN YOUR JURISDICTION?

Direct mailing/distance selling of drugs is not permitted in Vietnam.

**Conditions**

Not applicable.

**Cross-border sales**

Not applicable.

### 13. WHAT REGULATORY AUTHORITY IS RESPONSIBLE FOR SUPERVISING DISTRIBUTION ACTIVITIES?

The Drug Administration of Vietnam (DAV) under the Ministry of Health (MOH) is the main authority responsible for supervising distribution activities nationally. At the provincial level, the Department of Health, in co-operation with the Market Control Department, is responsible for supervising retail sales activities. Therefore, distribution directly to consumers is under the supervision of three main authorities:

- The pharmaceutical inspection department under the DAV.
- The provincial Department of Health.
- The provincial Market Control Department.

Inspections will be conducted periodically or suddenly if there is any complaint about drug quality.

### 14. WHAT IS THE PROCEDURE TO APPEAL (LEGAL REMEDY) A DISTRIBUTION DECISION?

The violator has the right to appeal the decision, provided that the legal remedy is in accordance with the Vietnam Law on Complaints (*see Question 6*).

### 15. WHAT ARE THE LEGAL CONSEQUENCES OF NON-COMPLIANCE WITH CONSUMER DISTRIBUTION LAWS?

Non-compliance with the law will result in sanctions. Specific sanctions will be applied according to the severity of the violation. These sanctions include:

- Fines for administrative violation with the fine amount ranging from VND200,000 to VND100 million (approximately EUR9 to EUR4,500).

- Suspension of the Pharmaceutical Practice Certificate and Certificate of Eligibility for drug trading for three to six months.

## WHOLESALE DISTRIBUTION

### 16. WHAT IS THE LEGAL REGIME REGARDING WHOLESALE DISTRIBUTION OF DRUGS?

The legal regime regarding the wholesale distribution of drugs includes:

- Vietnam's Commitments to the World Trade Organisation on 11 January 2007 (WTO Commitments).
- Law on Pharmacy No.34/2005/QH11 passed by the National Assembly on 14 June 2005 (Law on Pharmacy).
- Decree No.79/2006/ND-CP of the Government dated 9 August 2006 guiding the implementation of the Law on Pharmacy (Decree 79).
- Circular No.02/2007/TT-BYT of the Ministry of Health dated 24 January 2007 guiding the implementation of a number of articles regarding conditions of drug trading under the Law on Pharmacy and Decree 79 (Circular 02).
- Circular No.10/2013/TT-BYT of the Ministry of Health dated 29 March 2013 amending and supplementing a number of articles of Circular 02.

Foreign-invested companies are prohibited from distributing drugs in Vietnam. Local companies manufacturing or trading in pharmaceuticals may be approved for the wholesale distribution of drugs. To be duly licensed in the wholesale distribution of drugs, local pharmaceutical companies must obtain a Certificate of Eligibility for drug trading in wholesale distribution (CE). The conditions to obtain the CE are:

- The pharmaceutical professional managers must have the appropriate pharmaceutical practice certificates required for the establishment.
- Material and technical foundations and personnel of drug-wholesaling establishments must satisfy the criteria in the Good Distribution Practice standard.

The provincial Department of Health is responsible for granting CEs to drug wholesale establishments.

### 17. WHAT REGULATORY AUTHORITY IS RESPONSIBLE FOR SUPERVISING WHOLESALE DISTRIBUTION ACTIVITIES?

**Regulatory authority**

The pharmaceutical inspection department of the Drug Administration of Vietnam (DAV) is the main authority for supervising wholesale distribution activities.

**Supervision**

Supervision is implemented periodically based on the inspection plan, or irregularly. The inspection decision must be issued to the object of the inspection prior to implementation, with information about the inspected object, content of the inspection, and time and location of the inspection.

### RIGHTS OF APPEAL

See *Question 14*.

### 18. WHAT ARE THE LEGAL CONSEQUENCES OF NON-COMPLIANCE WITH WHOLESALE DISTRIBUTION LAWS?

See *Question 15*.

## MARKETING

### PROMOTION

### 19. WHAT IS THE GENERAL LEGAL REGIME FOR THE MARKETING OF DRUGS?

**Legal regime**

The main laws and regulations governing marketing activities of drugs in Vietnam are as follows:

- Law on Commerce No.36/2005/QH11 passed by the National Assembly on 14 June 2005 (Commercial Law).
- Decree No.37/2006/ND-CP of the government dated 4 April 2006 on trade promotion activities (Decree 37).
- Law on Advertising No.16/2012/QH13 passed by the National Assembly on 21 June 2012 and effective from 1 January 2013 (Law on Advertising).
- Decree No.181/2013/ND-CP of the government dated 14 November 2013 regulating the implementation of a number of articles of the Law on Advertising (Decree 181).
- Law on Pharmacy No.34/2005/QH11 passed by the National Assembly on 14 June 2005 (Law on Pharmacy).
- Decree No.79/2006/ND-CP of the government dated 9 August 2006 guiding the implementation of the Law on Pharmacy (Decree 79).
- Circular No.13/2009/TT-BYT of the Ministry of Health dated 1 September 2009 guiding drug information provision and advertising (Circular 13).

**Limits to marketing activities**

Marketing activities of drugs include:

- Promotion.
- Advertising.
- Drug introduction seminars.
- Dissemination of drug information material to healthcare professionals.
- Trade fairs and exhibitions.

For the promotion of drugs, it is prohibited to promote any drugs used for human treatment (such as giving free samples), except for promotion among drug traders/distributors. The promotion of drugs to end users or health professionals is strictly prohibited.

Drugs can be displayed in a drug introduction seminar, provided that the seminar is approved by the competent health authorities. Drugs which have been issued a marketing authorisation (MA) number by the Ministry of Health (MOH) can be permitted to be displayed at trade fairs and exhibitions, except for addictive drugs, psychotropic drugs, pre-substances used to manufacture drugs, and radioactive drugs. If any entity wishes to display or introduce any drug which has not yet been issued an MA number, such an entity must be issued a licence for the import of drugs by the Drug Administration of Vietnam (DAV) in order to display such drugs at the trade fair or exhibition.

Only over-the-counter drugs granted MA numbers can be advertised to the public. Prescription drugs are prohibited from advertising but can be introduced to healthcare professionals via drug introducers, drug information materials for healthcare professionals, and drug introduction seminars.

## 20. ARE THERE OTHER CODES OF CONDUCT FOR THE MARKETING OF DRUGS (FOR EXAMPLE, BY PROFESSIONAL OR INDUSTRIAL ORGANISATIONS)?

The Foreign Research-Based Pharmaceutical Manufacturers Association in Vietnam, commonly known as the "Pharma Group", is a sector committee under the European Chamber of Commerce in Vietnam. The members of the Pharma Group, representing more than 20 international pharmaceutical companies, are required to adhere to the association's Code of Pharmaceutical Marketing Practices, which includes provisions related to the marketing of drugs in Vietnam. Pharma Group members must comply with regulations in the Code of Pharmaceutical Marketing Practices or those found in the legislation of Vietnam, whichever are stricter.

## MARKETING TO CONSUMERS

## 21. WHAT IS THE LEGAL REGIME FOR MARKETING TO CONSUMERS?

**Legal regime**

The same legal regime as listed in *Question 19* applies to the advertising of drugs to consumers. Consumers are further protected by the Law on Protection of Consumers' Rights and its implementing regulations.

**Products**

Only non-prescription drugs can be advertised to consumers. However, non-prescription drugs whose use should be restricted or subject to the supervision of a doctor, according to the recommendations of the competent state body, cannot be advertised.

It is prohibited to advertise to consumers:

- Drugs without a valid marketing authorisation (MA) number in Vietnam.
- Prescription drugs.
- Vaccines or medical biological products used for disease prevention.

- Non-prescription drugs whose use should be restricted or should be supervised by a doctor, as recommended in writing by the competent state administrative body.

## 22. WHAT KINDS OF MARKETING ACTIVITIES ARE PERMITTED IN RELATION TO CONSUMERS AND THE PRODUCTS WHICH MAY BE ADVERTISED TO THEM?

Drug advertising is the only marketing activity permitted to consumers. The advertising of drugs can be in the following forms:

- Advertisements in books, newspapers, magazines, leaflets, and posters.
- Advertisements on billboards, placards, panels, banners, objects which are illuminated or appear in the air or underwater, means of transportation, and other mobile objects.
- Advertisements on radio and television.
- Advertisements in electronic newspapers, company websites, and websites of advertising service providers.
- Advertisements on other means of advertising as permitted by law.

Over-the-counter drugs can be advertised to consumers.

## 23. IS IT PERMITTED TO PROVIDE CONSUMERS WITH FREE SAMPLES? ARE THERE PARTICULAR RESTRICTIONS ON SPECIAL OFFERS (FOR EXAMPLE, "BUY-ONE-GET-ONE-FREE")?

It is strictly prohibited to use any material or financial benefits in any form to influence doctors or drug users in order to motivate the prescription and use of drugs. Accordingly, providing consumers with free samples or any special offers is prohibited.

## 24. ARE THERE PARTICULAR RULES OF PRACTICE ON THE USE OF THE INTERNET/SOCIAL MEDIA REGARDING DRUGS AND THEIR ADVERTISING?

There are no professional codes of practice regulating the issue. The law is the only means of regulating such activities.

Drug trading establishments are only permitted to advertise drugs that such establishments themselves trade, and they can only advertise on their lawful websites.

Drug trading establishments can authorise another entity to advertise drugs on their website, provided that the entity is an advertising service provider which possesses a licence for internet content provision (ICP) issued by the Ministry of Information and Communications and a business registration certificate for advertising services as stipulated by law.

Advertisements on the website must be conducted in a separate column and not be mixed with other content on the website. The following notice must be clearly stated in such column: "this page is for drug advertising only". This sentence must be in bold and have a larger font size than the font size of the advertisement content, and always appear on the top of the page.

Drug advertisement in this form must be separate, and for the avoidance of doubt, the advertising of many drugs at the same time causing overlapping or intermingling is not permitted. A drug advertisement on a website in the form of a video clip must comply with regulations for the advertising of drugs on radio or television.

## 25. WHAT REGULATORY AUTHORITY IS RESPONSIBLE FOR SUPERVISING MARKETING ACTIVITIES TO CONSUMERS?

**Regulatory authority**

The Drug Administration of Vietnam (DAV) and the Inspectorate of the Ministry of Health (MOH) centrally organise the inspection and monitoring of activities related to the provision of information on and advertising of drugs within the territory of Vietnam. Provincial Departments of Health are responsible for inspecting and monitoring such conduct within the localities they manage.

**Supervision**

There is no specific provision regarding the inspection or supervision of drug advertising.

**Rights of appeal**

Any entity or individual can lodge a complaint or denunciation about the information provision and advertising activities in accordance with the Law on Complaints and the Law on Denunciations.

## 26. WHAT ARE THE LEGAL CONSEQUENCES OF NON-COMPLIANCE WITH CONSUMER MARKETING LAWS?

In general, any entity or individual committing a breach, depending on the severity of the breach, can be subject to:

- An administrative sanction.
- The suspension of advertising.
- The withdrawal of the registration number of the drug in breach.
- An examination for criminal liability in accordance with the law.

Regarding administrative sanctions, the monetary penalty ranges from VND5 million to VND40 million (approximately EUR191 to EUR1,530).

### MARKETING TO PROFESSIONALS

## 27. WHAT KINDS OF MARKETING ACTIVITIES ARE PERMITTED IN RELATION TO PROFESSIONALS?

Drugs can generally be introduced to health officials by medical representatives. They can provide drug information documents or organise drug introduction seminars for health officials, or they can display and introduce drugs at specialised health conferences and seminars.

## 28. ARE THERE ANY RESTRICTIONS ON MARKETING TO PROFESSIONALS?

**Marketing activities**

It is prohibited to use material or financial benefits in any form in order to influence doctors' decisions on the prescription and use of drugs. However, providing reprints, non-interventional studies or educational items to professionals is permitted with the condition that these materials or information are approved by the Drug Administration of Vietnam (DAV).

**Frequency**

Medical representatives can only introduce drugs that have a valid marketing authorisation (MA) number and can only provide drug information strictly in accordance with the content as registered with the DAV. Such persons must wear a drug introducer card during the introduction of drugs and obtain approval from the establishment receiving the drug information before carrying out such an introduction.

Directors of hospitals where medical representatives carry out their work must set out specific internal rules and regulations on the composition, place, and time of the meetings between drug introducers and health officials and organise such meetings in order for the drug introducers to introduce the information to the health officials of such establishments.

**Provision of hospitality**

Medical representatives can meet with groups of professionals at drug introduction seminars for health officials or at health-specialised conferences and seminars.

In order to organise drug introduction seminars for health officials, drug trading establishments and their representative offices must be registered to operate in the pharmaceutical sector in Vietnam and their drugs must have been permitted to be manufactured and circulated in other countries.

Any foreign entity wishing to organise a seminar to introduce drugs in Vietnam is required to co-ordinate with a Vietnamese entity conducting business in drugs or a Vietnamese medical establishment such as a hospital, health-specialised institute, training establishment for health officials, medical professional association, or pharmaceutical professional association. Contents of seminars must comply with applicable requirements and any presenter in a seminar must be a professional who is qualified and experienced with the drugs to be introduced.

In order to display and introduce drugs at a health-specialised conference or seminar, the entity which holds or presides over the health-specialised conference or seminar, prior to holding the seminar, must provide written notice to the local Department of Health at the place where the conference or seminar is to be held. In addition, all advertising activities accompanying the display of drugs at the conferences and seminars must be in accordance with requirements of Circular 13 on advertising of drugs and other relevant laws.

## 29. WHAT INFORMATION IS IT LEGALLY REQUIRED TO INCLUDE IN ADVERTISING TO PROFESSIONALS?

Under Article 14 of Circular 13, the information to be provided to professionals must include the following primary items:

- Drug name, which can be a proprietary or original name.
- Active ingredients.
- Form of preparation.
- Effect and indications.
- Dosage.
- Method of administration.
- Side effects and harmful reactions.
- Contra-indications and precautions.
- Drug interactions.
- Names and addresses of the manufacturer and main distributor.
- New information for reference and documents proving the source of such information.
- A list of extracted documents.

Advertising of a drug in newspapers, magazines, leaflets, on billboards, signs, panels, posters, banners, illuminative objects, aerial or underwater objects, means of transport, and other movable objects must include the following information:

- Name of the drug, which is the name specified in the decision on the drug's registration number of circulation in Vietnam.
- Active ingredients:
  - for Western medicine: using international nomenclature;
  - for a herbal medicament: using the Vietnamese name (except medicinal material whose names in Vietnamese are unavailable. In this case, using the original name of the country of origin together with the Latin name).
- Indications.
- Method of administration.
- Dosage.
- Contra-indications and/or recommendations for special users such as pregnant women, breast-feeding women, children, elderly people, and sufferers of chronic diseases.
- Side effects and harmful reactions.
- Notes on use of drug.
- Name and address of drug manufacturer (name and address of distributor can be added).
- The phrase "Carefully read instructions before use".
- At the end of the first page of the drug advertising document:
  - the number of the slip on receipt of the registration dossier for drug advertising of the DAV in the following form: XXXX/XX/QLD-TT, date/ month/ year;
  - the date of printing the document.

For multiple-page documents, pages must be numbered, with the first page indicating the total number of pages and the number of the page providing detailed information on the drug.

## 30. ARE THERE RULES ON COMPARISONS WITH OTHER PRODUCTS THAT ARE PARTICULARLY APPLICABLE TO DRUGS?

Statements creating an impression on the public such as "this drug is number one and better than others" or "using this drug is the best measure" are strictly prohibited regardless of whether the establishment can prove such a statement or not. Therefore, it is prohibited to make comparisons, with an intention of advertising, that one drug is better than other drugs or goods of other organisations and individuals.

## 31. WHAT OTHER ITEMS, FUNDING OR SERVICES ARE PERMITTED TO BE PROVIDED TO PROFESSIONALS?

**Discounts**

Discounts are permitted only for drug traders but are strictly prohibited for consumers and doctors. Providing any discount to doctors or patients would be regarded as providing a financial benefit that influences their decision to choose the drug, and therefore it is not permitted.

**Free samples**

It is prohibited to use material or financial benefits in any form to influence doctors' decisions in the prescription and use of drugs. Therefore, giving free samples to health professionals is prohibited.

**Sponsorship of professionals**

It is permissible for any entity or individual to provide financial or other material support for organising conferences of health officials on a voluntary, public, and unconditional basis.

The introduction of drugs to health officials by any sponsor at a health-specialised conference must comply with the regulations on provision of information about drugs to health officials.

**Other items, funding or services**

No other indirect incentives are allowed. The sponsoring must be on a voluntary, public, and unconditional basis.

## 32. WHAT REGULATORY AUTHORITY IS RESPONSIBLE FOR SUPERVISING MARKETING ACTIVITIES REGARDING PROFESSIONALS?

**Regulatory authority**

See *Question 25*.

**Supervision**

See *Question 25*.

**Rights of appeal**

See *Question 25*.

### 33. WHAT ARE THE LEGAL CONSEQUENCES IN CASE OF NON-COMPLIANCE WITH PROFESSIONAL MARKETING LAWS?

See *Question 26*.

## ENGAGEMENT WITH PATIENT ORGANISATIONS

### 34. WHAT KINDS OF ACTIVITIES ARE PERMITTED IN RELATION TO ENGAGEMENT WITH PATIENT ORGANISATIONS? WHAT ARE THE RESTRICTIONS THAT ARE IMPOSED ON RELATIONSHIPS WITH PATIENT ORGANISATIONS?

There is no clear regulation on this matter in Vietnamese law.

## REFORM

### 35. ARE THERE ANY PLANS TO REFORM THE LAW ON THE DISTRIBUTION AND PROMOTION OF DRUGS IN YOUR JURISDICTION?

A draft circular of the Ministry of Health on advertising in the healthcare sector is expected to come into force in mid to late 2015 (Q3).

# CONTACT DETAILS

## GENERAL EDITORS

Alison Dennis
Fieldfisher
Riverbank House
2 Swan Lane
London EC4R 3TT
United Kingdom

T: +44 20 7861 4637
F: +44 20 7488 0084
E: alison.dennis@fieldfisher.com
W: www.fieldfisher.com

Markus Schott
Bär & Karrer AG
Brandschenkestrasse 90
Zurich 8032
Switzerland

T: +41 58 261 54 77
F: +41 58 263 54 77
E: markus.schott@baerkarrer.ch
W: www.baerkarrer.ch

## AUSTRALIA

Simone Mitchell, Alexandra Chubb, Jessie Buchan and Matthew Evans
DLA Piper
Level 22 No.1 Martin Place
Sydney NSW 2000
Australia

T: +61 2 9286 8000
F: +61 2 9286 8007
E: simone.mitchell@dlapiper.com
E: alexandra.chubb@dlapiper.com
E: jessie.buchan@dlapiper.com
E: matthew.evans@dlapiper.com

## AUSTRIA

Gabriela Staber, Patricia Kaindl and Egon Engin-Deniz
CMS Reich-Rohrwig Hainz Rechtsanwälte GmbH
Gauermanngasse 2
Vienna 1010
Austria

T: +43 (1) 40443 1550
F: +43 (1) 40443 91550
E: gabriela.staber@cms-rrh.com
E: patricia.kaindl@cms-rrh.com
E: egon.engin-deniz@cms-rrh.com
E: patricia.kaindl@cms-rrh.com
W: www.cms-rrh.com

## BRAZIL

Lívia Figueiredo and João Luis Vianna
Kasznar Leonardos
Rua Teófilo Otoni, 63
5th - 8th floors
RJ 20090-080
Rio de Janeiro
Brazil

T: +55 21 2113 1919
F: +55 21 2113 1920
E: joao.vianna@kasznarleonardos.com
E: elivia.figueiredo@kasznarleonardos.com
W: www.kasznarleonardos.com

## CANADA

Jeffrey S Graham
Borden Ladner Gervais LLP
40 King Street West, Suite 4200
Toronto
Ontario M5H 3Y4
Canada

T: +1 416 367 6174
F: +1 416 361 7377
E: jgraham@blg.com
W: www.blg.com

## CONTACT DETAILS

### CHINA
Jianwen Huang
King & Wood Mallesons
40th Floor, Office Tower A,
Beijing Fortune Plaza
7 Dongsanhuan Zhonglu,
Chaoyang District
Beijing 100020
P. R. China

T: +86 10 5878 5165
F: +86 10 5878 5599
E: huangjianwen@cn.kwm.com
W: www.kwm.com

### DENMARK
Nicolaj Kleist
Bruun & Hjejle
Nørregade 21
Copenhagen DK-1165
Denmark

T: +45 33 34 50 00
F: +45 33 34 50 50
E: nkl@bruunhjejle.dk
W: www.bruunhjejle.com

### EUROPEAN UNION
Alison Dennis
Fieldfisher
Riverbank House
2 Swan Lane
London EC4R 3TT
United Kingdom

T: +44 20 7861 4637
F: +44 20 7488 0084
E: alison.dennis@fieldfisher.com
W: www.fieldfisher.com

### FINLAND
Mikael Segercrantz, Johanna Lilja and Elina Saxlin-Hautamäki
Roschier Attorneys Ltd
Keskuskatu 7 A
Helsinki FI-00100
Finland

T: +358 20 506 6000
F: +358 20 506 6100
E: mikael.segercrantz@roschier.com
E: johanna.lilja@roschier.com
E: elina.saxlin-hautamaki@roschier.com
W: www.roschier.com

### FRANCE
Olivier Lantrès
Fieldfisher
21 boulevard de la Madeleine
Paris 75001
France

T: +33 (0)1 42 96 08 89
F: +33 (0)1 42 96 07 98
E: olivier.lantres@ffw.com
W: www.ffw.com

### GERMANY
Dr Cord Willhöft
Fieldfisher
Campo Sentilo
Gmunder Straße 53
München D-81379
Germany

T: +49 (0) 89 620 6000
F: +49 (0) 89 620 6400
E: cord.willhoeft@ffw.com
W: www.ffw.com

### INDONESIA
Eri Budiarti and Iqsan Sirie
Assegaf Hamzah & Partners
Menara Rajawali 16th Floor
Jalan DR. Ide Anak Agung Gde Agung
Lot no 5.1 Kawasan Mega Kuningan,
Jakarta 12950
Indonesia

T: +62 21 2555 7800
F: +62 21 2555 7899
E: eri.budiarti@ahp.co.id
E: iqsan.sirie@ahp.co.id
W: www.ahp.co.id

### ITALY
Laura Opilio and Maria Letizia Patania
CMS Adonnino Ascoli & Cavasola Scamoni
Via Agostino Depretis, 86
Rome 00184
Italy

T: +39 06 478151
F: +39 06 483755
E: laura.opilio@cms-aacs.com
E: marialetizia.patania@cms-aacs.com
W: www.cms-aacs.com

## CONTACT DETAILS

### JAPAN

Shinya Tago, Atsushi Ueda, Landry Guesdon and Ryohei Kudo

Iwata Godo Law Offices

Marunouchi Building 10th Floor

2-4-1, Marunouchi

Chiyoda-ku

Tokyo 1006310

Japan

T: +81 3 3214 6205
F: +81 3 3214 6209
E: stago@iwatagodo.com
E: aueda@iwatagodo.com
E: lguesdon@iwatagodo.com
E: rkudo@iwatagodo.com
W: www.iwatagodo.com

### THE NETHERLANDS

Willem Hoorneman, Rogier de Vrey, Bart Essink and Anastasia Chistyakova

CMS Derks Star Busmann

Newtonlaan 203

Utrecht 3584 BH

The Netherlands

T: +31 30 2121 111
F: +31 30 2121 157
E: willem.hoorneman@cms-dsb.com
E: rogier.devrey@cms-dsb.com
E: bart.essink@cms-dsb.com
E: anastasia.chistyakova@cms-dsb.com
W: www.cms-dsb.com

### POLAND

Marcin Matczak, Tomasz Kaczyński and Krzysztof Kumala

Domański Zakrzewski Palinka Sp. k.

Rondo ONZ 1,

00-124 Warszawa

Poland

T: +48 22 557 76 00
F: +48 22 557 76 01
E: marcin.matczak@dzp.pl
E: tomasz.kaczynski@dzp.pl
E: krzysztof.kumala@dzp.pl
E: dzp@dzp.pl
W: www.dzp.pl

### PORTUGAL

Fernanda Matoso and Eduardo Maia Cadete

Morais Leitão, Galvão Teles, Soares da Silva & Associados –Sociedade de Advogados, R.L.

Rua Castilho 165

Lisbon 1070-050

Portugal

T: +351 21 381 74 31
F: +351 21 381 74 98
E: fmatoso@mlgts.pt
E: maiacadete@mlgts.pt
W: www.mlgts.pt

### RUSSIA

Vsevolod Tyupa

CMS, Russia

Naberezhnaya Tower, block C

Presnenskaya Naberezhnaya 10

123317 Moscow

Russia

T: +7 495 786 4000
F: +7 495 786 4001
E: vsevolod.tyupa@cmslegal.ru
W: www.cmslegal.ru

### SOUTH AFRICA

Danie Dohmen, Alexis Apostolidis, Jenny Pienaar and Natasha Wright

Adams & Adams

4 Daventry Street,

Lynnwood Manor,

Pretoria 0081

South Africa

T: +27 12 432 6000
F: +27 12 432 6599
E: danie.dohmen@adamsadams.com
E: alexis.apostolidis@adamsadams.com
E: jenny.pienaar@adamsadams.com
E: natasha.wright@adamsadams.com
W: www.adamsadams.com

## CONTACT DETAILS

### SOUTH KOREA

Hyeong Gun Lee and Jin Hwan Chung
Lee & Co
Hanjin Building 63 Namdaemun-ro
Jung-gu
Seoul 04532
Korea

T: +82-2-772-4000
F: +82-2-772-4001/2
E: hyeonggun.lee@leeko.com
E: jinhwan.chung@leeko.com
W: www.leeko.com

### SPAIN

Teresa Paz-Ares and Beatriz Cocina
Uría Menéndez
Príncipe de Vergara, 187
Plaza de Rodrigo Uría
Madrid 28002
Spain

T: +34 915 860 400
F: +34 915 860 403/4
E: teresa.paz-ares@uria.com
E: beatriz.cocina@uria.com
W: www.uria.com

### SWEDEN

Helén Waxberg and Maja Edlund
Mannheimer Swartling Advokatbyrå
Norrlandsgatan 21
Box 1711
Stockholm 111 87
Sweden

T: +46 8 595 064 14
F: +46 8 595 060 01
E: helen.waxberg@msa.se
E: maed@msa.se
W: www.mannheimerswartling.se

### SWITZERLAND

Markus Schott
Bär & Karrer AG
Brandschenkestrasse 90
Zurich 8032
Switzerland

T: +41 58 261 54 77
F: +41 58 263 54 77
E: markus.schott@baerkarrer.ch
W: www.baerkarrer.ch

### THAILAND

Alan Adcock, Siraprapha Rungpry and Areeya Pornwiriyangkura
Tilleke & Gibbins
Supalai Grand Tower, 26th Floor,
1011 Rama 3 Road Chongnonsi, Yannawa
Bangkok 10120
Thailand

T: +66 2653 5555
F: +66 2653 5678
E: alan.a@tilleke.com
E: siraprapha.r@tilleke.com
E: areeya.p@tilleke.com
W: www.tilleke.com

### TURKEY

Özge Atılgan Karakulak and Tuğçe Avcısert Geçgil
Gün & Partners
Kore Sehitleri Cad. No.17
Zincirlikuyu
Istanbul 34394
Turkey

T: +90 212 354 00 00
F: +90 212 274 20 95
E: ozge.atilgan@gun.av.tr
E: tugce.avcisert@gun.av.tr
W: www.gun.av.tr

### UNITED KINGDOM

Alison Dennis
Fieldfisher
Riverbank House
2 Swan Lane
London EC4R 3TT
United Kingdom

T: +44 20 7861 4637
F: +44 20 7488 0084
E: alison.dennis@fieldfisher.com
W: www.fieldfisher.com

## CONTACT DETAILS

### UNITED STATES
Jamie K Wolszon and Andrew J Hull
Hyman, Phelps & McNamara, PC
700 Thirteenth Street, N.W.
Suite 1200
Washington, D.C. 20005
United States

T: +1 202 737 5600
F: +1 202 737 9329
E: jwolszon@hpm.com
E: ahull@hpm.com
W: www.hpm.com

### VIETNAM
Tu Ngoc Trinh and Dzung Nguyen
Tilleke & Gibbins
HAREC Building, 4th Floor
4A Lang Ha, Ba Dinh District
Hanoi
Vietnam

T: +84 4 3772 6688
F: +84 4 3772 5568
E: ngoctu.t@tilleke.com
E: huong.n@tilleke.com
E: vietnam@tilleke.com
W: www.tilleke.com